AutoCAD 2000/2000i

AutoCAD
and its applications
A D V A N C E D

by

Terence M. Shumaker
Chairperson, Drafting Technology
Director, Autodesk Premier Training Center
Clackamas Community College, Oregon City, Oregon

David A. Madsen
Faculty Emeritus
Former Chairperson
Drafting Technology
Autodesk Premier Training Center
Clackamas Community College, Oregon City, Oregon

Former Board of Director
American Design Drafting Association

Publisher
The Goodheart-Willcox Company, Inc.
Tinley Park, Illinois

Library of Congress Catalog Number 99-26501
International Standard Book Number 1-56637-804-4

2 3 4 5 6 7 8 9 10   01   05 04 03 02 01

Library of Congress Cataloging-in-Publication Data

Shumaker, Terence M.
  AutoCAD and its applications : advanced, AutoCAD
2000/2000i / by Terence M. Shumaker, David A. Madsen.

    p. cm.

  Includes index
  ISBN 1-56637-804-4
    1. Computer graphics. 2. AutoCAD I. Madsen, David A.
II. Title

T385.S46126 2000
604.2'0285'5369--dc21   99-26501
                                                     CIP

Introduction

AutoCAD and its Applications—Advanced provides complete instruction in mastering the AutoCAD® 2000 3D modeling commands, Internet access, and various customizing techniques. These topics are covered in an easy-to-understand sequence, and progress in a way that allows you to become comfortable with the commands as your knowledge builds from one chapter to the next. In addition, *AutoCAD and its Applications—Advanced* offers the following features:

- Step-by-step use of AutoCAD commands.
- In-depth explanations of how and why commands function as they do.
- Extensive use of font changes to specify certain meanings. This is fully explained in the next section, *Fonts Used in This Text*.
- Examples and discussions of industrial practices and standards.
- Actual screen captures of AutoCAD and Windows features and functions.
- Professional tips explaining how to use AutoCAD effectively and efficiently.
- Over 75 exercises to reinforce the chapter topics. These exercises also build on previously learned material.
- Chapter tests for review of commands and key AutoCAD concepts.
- A large selection of modeling and customizing problems supplement each chapter. Problems are presented as 3D illustrations, actual plotted drawings, and engineering sketches.

With *AutoCAD and its Applications—Advanced*, you not only learn AutoCAD commands, but you also become acquainted with:

- Constructing models using different 3D coordinate systems.
- 3D object construction and layout techniques.
- User coordinate systems.
- Model space viewports.
- 3D editing and display techniques.
- 3D text and dimensioning.
- Surface modeling and rendering.
- Solid model construction, editing, and display.
- AutoCAD's database connectivity functions.
- Internet access from AutoCAD.
- Customizing the AutoCAD environment.
- Customizing toolbars, pull-down menus, and image tiles.
- Customizing screen, button, and tablet menus.
- The basics of AutoLISP and dialog box (DCL) programming.
- Advanced AutoCAD features such as OLE.

Fonts Used in This Text

Different typefaces are used throughout each chapter to define terms and identify AutoCAD commands. Important terms appear in ***bold-italic face, serif*** type. AutoCAD menus, commands, variables, dialog box names, and tool button names are printed in **bold-face, sans serif** type. File names, directory names, paths, and keyboard-entry items appear in the body of the text in Roman, sans serif type. Keyboard keys are shown inside of square brackets [ ] and appear in Roman, sans serif type. For example, [Enter] means to press the enter (return) key. In addition, commands, menus, and dialog boxes related to Microsoft Windows appear in Roman, sans serif type.

Prompt sequences are set apart from the body text with space above and below, and appear in Roman, sans serif type. Keyboard entry items in prompts appear in **bold-face, sans serif** type. In prompts, the [Enter] key is represented by the ↵ symbol.

Checking the AutoCAD Reference Manuals

For 2000i Users...

The User's Guide in the 2000i help system does not contain chapter numbers. Therefore, the help icons in this book refer to AutoCAD 2000 only.

No other reference should be needed when using this text. However, the authors have referenced relevant topic areas to the *AutoCAD User's Guide* and the *AutoCAD Customization Guide*. An icon in the margin identifies the specific chapter within the reference where additional information can be found. For example, the icon next to this paragraph tells you that you can find more information in Chapter 5 of the *AutoCAD User's Guide*.

The *AutoCAD User's Guide* and *AutoCAD Customization Guide* are part of the help file installed with AutoCAD. To reference these materials, select **AutoCAD Help** from the **Help** pull-down menu.

The AutoCAD help file also includes the *AutoCAD Command Reference*. Commands and variables are presented in alphabetical order in this manual. Refer to it for additional information on specific commands and system variables.

Other Text References

This text focuses on advanced AutoCAD applications. Basic AutoCAD applications are covered in ***AutoCAD and its Applications—Basics***, which is also available from Goodheart-Willcox. ***AutoCAD and its Applications*** texts are also available for AutoCAD Releases 10, 11, 12, 13, and 14.

For your convenience, other Goodheart-Willcox textbooks are referenced, including ***AutoLISP Programming—Principles and Techniques***. These textbooks can be ordered directly from Goodheart-Willcox.

Introducing the AutoCAD Commands

There are several ways to select AutoCAD drawing and editing commands. Selecting commands from a toolbar or pull-down menu is slightly different than entering them from the keyboard. All AutoCAD commands and related options are presented in this text using a variety of command entry methods.

In many examples, command entries are shown as if typed at the keyboard, allowing the text to present the full command name and the prompts that appear on screen. Commands, options, and values you must enter are given in **bold** text, as shown in the following example. Pressing the [Enter] (return) key is indicated with the ↵ symbol.

```
Command: 3DFACE↵
First point: 2,2↵
Second point: 4,2↵
Third point: 4,6↵
Fourth point: 2,6↵
```

General input, such as picking a point or selecting an object, is presented in *italic, serif font*, as shown below.

Command: **3DFACE**↵
First point: *(pick a point)*
Second point: *(pick another point)*
Third point: *(pick a third point)*
Fourth point: *(pick the last point)*

The command line, toolbar button, and pull-down menu entry methods are presented throughout the text. When a command is introduced, these methods are illustrated in the margin next to the text reference. The toolbar in which the button is located is also identified. The example in the margin next to this paragraph illustrates the various methods of initiating the **HIDE** command.

Some commands and functions are handled more efficiently by picking a toolbar button or a menu command. Many of these procedures are described in numbered, step-by-step instructions.

Note for AutoCAD 2000i Users

AutoCAD 2000 and AutoCAD 2000i are very similar programs. This text is designed to be used with either version of AutoCAD. When discussing features that differ between the two versions, a special note is provided for AutoCAD 2000i users. A sample of these notes is shown in the margin next to this paragraph. The note identifies how AutoCAD 2000i is different from AutoCAD 2000 with regards to the specific feature. Features unique to AutoCAD 2000i requiring expanding coverage are detailed in *Appendix G, AutoCAD 2000i Features.*

For 2000i Users...

These notes identify features unique to AutoCAD 2000i. If the feature is discussed in Appendix G, the note includes a reference to the page on which the discussion begins.

Flexibility in Design

Flexibility is the key word when using *AutoCAD and its Applications—Advanced.* This text is an excellent training aid for both individual and classroom instruction. *AutoCAD and its Applications—Advanced* teaches you how to apply AutoCAD to common modeling and customizing tasks. It is also an invaluable resource for any professional using AutoCAD.

When working through the text, you will see a variety of notices. These notices include Professional Tips, Notes, and Cautions that help you develop your AutoCAD skills.

PROFESSIONAL TIP   These ideas and suggestions are aimed at increasing your productivity and enhancing your use of AutoCAD commands and techniques.

NOTE   A note alerts you to important aspects of a command function, menu, or activity that is being discussed. These aspects should be kept in mind while you are working through the text.

CAUTION ⚠ A caution alerts you to potential problems if instructions or commands are used incorrectly, or if an action can corrupt or alter files, folders, or disks. If you are in doubt after reading a caution, always consult your instructor or supervisor.

AutoCAD and its Applications—Advanced provides several ways for you to evaluate your performance. Included are:

- **Exercises.** Each chapter contains in-text Exercises. These Exercises allow you to perform tasks that reinforce the material just presented. You can work through the Exercises at your own pace.
- **Chapter Tests.** Each chapter includes a written test at the end of the chapter. Questions require you to give the proper definition, command, option, or response to perform a certain task.
- **Drawing Problems.** There are a variety of drawing, design, and customizing problems at the end of each chapter. These are presented as real-world CAD drawings, 3D illustrations, and engineering sketches. The problems are designed to make you think, solve problems, use design techniques, research and use proper drawing standards, and correct errors in the drawings or engineering sketches.

Each drawing problem deals with one of six technical disciplines. Although doing all of the problems will enhance your AutoCAD skills, you may be focusing on a particular discipline. The discipline that a problem addresses is indicated by a graphic in the margin next to the problem number. The following graphics represent the disciplines:

 These problems address mechanical drafting and design applications, such as manufactured part designs.

 These problems address architectural and structural drafting and design applications, such as floor plans, furniture, and presentation drawings.

 These problems address civil drafting and design application, such as plot plans, plats, and landscape drawings.

 These problems address graphic design applications, such as text creation, title blocks, and page layout.

 These problems address piping drafting and design applications, such as piping flow diagrams, tank drawings, and pipe layout.

 These problems address a variety of general drafting, design, and customization applications. These problems should be attempted by everyone learning advanced AutoCAD techniques for the first time.

NOTE

Some problems presented in this text are given as engineering sketches. These sketches are intended to represent the kind of materials a drafter is expected to work from in a real-world situation. As such, engineering sketches often contain errors or slight inaccuracies, and are most often not drawn according to proper drafting conventions and applicable standards. Errors in these problems are *intentional* to encourage the user to apply appropriate techniques and standards in order to solve the problem. As in real-world applications, sketches should be considered preliminary layouts. Always question inaccuracies in sketches and designs, and consult the applicable standards or other resources.

Disk Supplements

To help you develop your AutoCAD skills, Goodheart-Willcox offers a disk supplement package to use with *AutoCAD and its Applications—Advanced*. The Autodesk software AutoCAD 2000 is required for Goodheart-Willcox software to operate properly.

The *Student Work Disk* contains a variety of activities. These activities are intended to be used as a supplement to the exercises found in the text. The *Work Disk* activities correspond to Chapter 1 through Chapter 15 of the text. These activities allow you to progress at your own pace.

ABOUT THE AUTHORS

Terence M. Shumaker is Manager of the Autodesk Premier Training Center, and a Drafting Technology instructor at Clackamas Community College. Terence has been teaching at the community college level since 1977. He has commercial experience in surveying, civil drafting, industrial piping, and technical illustration. He is the author of Goodheart-Willcox's *Process Pipe Drafting*, and is coauthor of the *AutoCAD and its Applications AutoCAD 2000* series, *AutoCAD and its Applications* (Release 10, 11, 12, 13, and 14 editions), and *AutoCAD Essentials*.

David A. Madsen is the former Chairperson of Drafting Technology and the Autodesk Premier Training Center at Clackamas Community College. David was an instructor/department chair at Clackamas Community College for nearly 30 years. In addition to community college experience, David was a Drafting Technology instructor at Centennial High School in Gresham, Oregon. David also has extensive experience in mechanical drafting, architectural design and drafting, and construction practices. He is the author or coauthor of several Goodheart-Willcox drafting and design textbooks, including *Geometric Dimensioning and Tolerancing*, the *AutoCAD and its Applications AutoCAD 2000* series, *AutoCAD and its Applications* (Release 10, 11, 12, 13, and 14 editions), and *AutoCAD Essentials*.

ACKNOWLEDGMENTS

The authors and publisher would like to thank the following individuals and companies for their assistance and contributions.

Contributing Authors

The authors wish to acknowledge a number of contributors for their professional expertise in providing in-depth research and testing, technical assistance, reviews, and development of new materials.

Rod Rawls for Chapters 20–25. Rod is an AutoCAD consultant and full-time instructor at the AutoCAD Premier Training Center, Clackamas Community College. He is also the coauthor of *AutoLISP Programming: Principles and Techniques* published by Goodheart-Willcox.

Ron Palma for Chapters 9, 14, and 15. Ron is an architectural applications engineer for Ketiv Technologies, Inc., in Portland, Oregon. Ron provides training, consulting, and technical support for Autodesk software products. Ron was a contributor for *AutoCAD and its Applications—Basics*.

Ethan Collins for Chapters 16, 17, and 19. Ethan is a software specialist for Ketiv Technologies, Inc., and provides technical support for Autodesk software products.

William Murphy for Chapter 18. William is a CAD consultant and adjunct instructor at the AutoCAD Premier Training Center at Clackamas Community College.

Contribution of Materials

Autodesk, Inc.
Bill Fane
CADENCE magazine
EPCM Services Ltd.
Fitzgerald, Hagan, & Hackathorn
Kunz Associates

Trademarks

Autodesk, the Autodesk logo, 3D Studio MAX, 3D Studio VIZ, Advanced Modeling Extension, AME, AutoCAD, Heidi, Inventor, Mechanical Desktop, and *WHIP!* are registered trademarks, and AutoCAD DesignCenter, AutoCAD Learning Assistance, AutoSnap, AutoTrack and Volo View are trademarks of Autodesk, Inc. in the U.S.A and/or other countries.

Microsoft, Windows, Windows NT, Windows 95, Windows 98, Visual Basic, and Microsoft Word are trademarks of Microsoft Corporation.

dBase is a registered trademark of Ashton Tate.

IBM is a registered trademark of International Business Machines.

Pizazz Plus is a registered trademark of Applications Software Corporation.

Contents

PRESENTATION GRAPHICS AND RENDERING

ADVANCED AUTOCAD APPLICATIONS

APPENDICES

The sample drawings provided with AutoCAD 2000 illustrate the complex models and attractive displays that can be created using 3D modeling techniques. (Autodesk, Inc.)

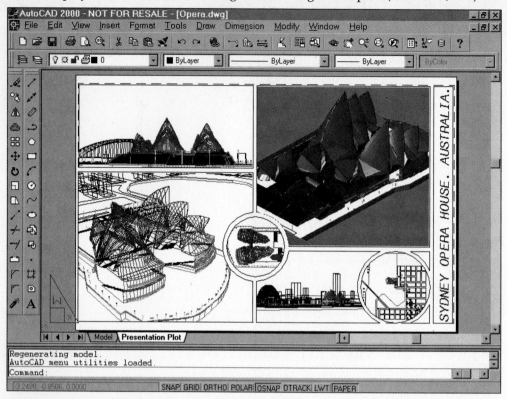

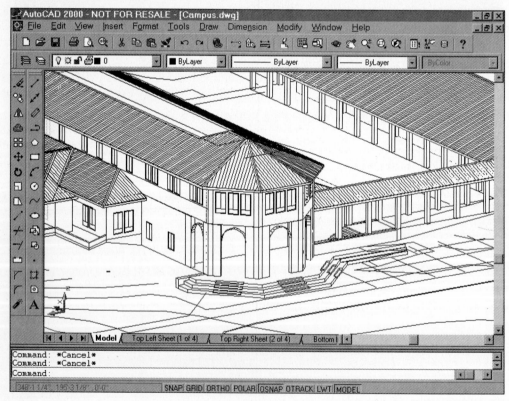

CHAPTER 1

Introduction to Three-Dimensional Drawing

Learning Objectives

After completing this chapter, you will be able to:

- Describe the nature and function of rectangular 3D coordinate systems.
- Describe the "right-hand rule" of 3D visualization.
- Construct extruded and wireframe 3D objects.
- Display 3D objects from any viewpoint.
- Construct 3D face objects using the **3DFACE** command.

The use of three-dimensional (3D) drawing and design as a tool is becoming more prevalent throughout industry. Companies are discovering the benefits of 3D modeling in design, visualization, testing, analysis, manufacturing, assembly, and marketing. Three-dimensional models also form the basis of computer animations and *virtual worlds* used with virtual reality systems. Drafters who can design objects, buildings, and "worlds" in 3D are in demand for a wide variety of positions, both inside and outside the traditional drafting and design disciplines.

The first thirteen chapters of this book present a variety of techniques for drawing and designing 3D wireframes, surfaces, and solids. The skills you will learn will provide you with the ability to construct any object in 3D, and prepare you for entry into an exciting aspect of graphic communication.

To be effective in creating and using 3D objects, you must first have good 3D visualization skills, including the ability to see an object in three dimensions and to visualize it rotating in space. These skills can be obtained by using 3D techniques to construct objects, and by trying to see two-dimensional sketches and drawings as 3D models. This chapter provides an introduction to several aspects of 3D drawing and visualization. Subsequent chapters expand on these aspects and provide a detailed examination of 3D drawing, editing, visualization, and display techniques.

USING RECTANGULAR 3D COORDINATES

AutoCAD User's Guide **17**

In two-dimensional drawing, you see one plane defined by two dimensions. These dimensions are usually located on the X and Y axes. However, in 3D drawing, another plane and coordinate axis is added. The additional plane is defined with a third dimension located along the Z axis. If you are looking at a standard AutoCAD screen, the positive Z axis comes directly out of the screen toward you. AutoCAD can only draw lines in 3D if it knows the X, Y, and Z coordinate values of each point on the object. For 2D drawing, only two of the three coordinates are needed.

Figure 1-1.
A comparison of 2D
and 3D coordinate
systems

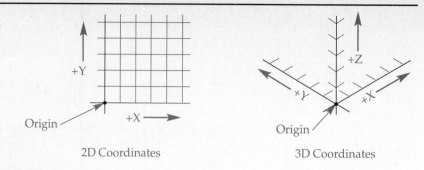

2D Coordinates   3D Coordinates

Compare the 2D and 3D coordinate systems shown in Figure 1-1. Notice that the positive values of Z in the 3D coordinate system come up from the XY plane of a 2D drawing. Consider the surface of your screen as the XY plane. Anything behind the screen is negative Z, and anything in front of the screen is positive Z. The object in Figure 1-2A is a 2D drawing showing the top view of an object. The XY coordinate values of the origin and each point are shown. Think of the object as being drawn directly on the surface of your screen.

To convert this object to its three-dimensional form, Z values are given to each corner point. Figure 1-2B shows the object pictorially with the XYZ values of each point listed. Positive Z coordinates are used. Therefore, the object comes out of your screen. The object can also be drawn using negative Z coordinates. In this case, the object would extend behind, or into, the screen.

Study the nature of the rectangular 3D coordinate system. Be sure you understand Z values before you begin constructing 3D objects. It is especially important that you carefully visualize and plan your design when working with 3D constructions.

Three-dimensional objects can be drawn in AutoCAD using two additional coordinate systems—spherical and cylindrical. These two systems allow you to work with point locations using distances and angles. A complete discussion of spherical and cylindrical coordinate systems is provided in Chapter 2.

**PROFESSIONAL
TIP**  Although the sign of the Z value (positive or negative) makes no difference to AutoCAD, it can be time-consuming to use negative values.

Figure 1-2.
A—The points making up a 2D object require only two coordinates to be drawn.
B—Each point of a 3D object must have an X, Y, and Z value.

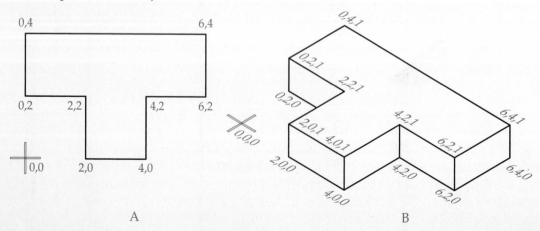

A   B

❏ Study the multiview sketch below.
❏ Freehand sketch the object pictorially using the axes of a 3D coordinate system. Each tick mark represents one unit. Use the correct dimensions as given in the multiview sketch.
❏ When you complete the freehand sketch, draw the object in AutoCAD with the **LINE** command by entering XYZ coordinates for each point.
❏ Save the drawing as EX1-1.

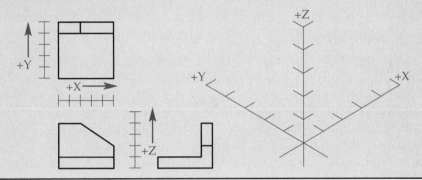

CREATING EXTRUDED 3D SHAPES

Most shapes drawn with AutoCAD are extruded shapes. *Extruded* means that a 2D shape is given a base elevation and a thickness. The object then rises up, or "extrudes" to its given thickness. The **ELEV** command is used to extrude an object. **ELEV** does not draw the object, it merely sets the base elevation and thickness for the next object drawn. To use this command, enter ELEV at the Command: prompt.

NOTE	Keep in mind that the current elevation established by the value set using the **ELEV** command is the level at which the next object is drawn. Therefore, if you set the elevation at 1.0, and then draw the bottom of a machine part, the bottom of that part is now sitting at an elevation of 1.0 units above the zero elevation.
	On the other hand, the setting for the *thickness* is the value that determines the *height* of the next object you draw. Therefore, if you want to draw a part one unit high with the bottom of the part resting on the zero elevation plane, set the elevation to 0.0 and the thickness to 1.0.

To draw the "T"-shaped object shown in Figure 1-3A with sides that are one unit high, first use the **ELEV** command as follows:

Command: **ELEV**↵
Specify new default elevation <0.0000>: ↵
Specify new default thickness <0.0000>: **1**↵

After you have completed this command sequence, nothing happens on screen. However, an elevation of 0 and a thickness of 1 are now the current settings. Now, use the **LINE** command to draw the outline. Although it appears that you are drawing lines, you are actually drawing *planes*. Each plane has a height (thickness) of one unit that you cannot see in this view.

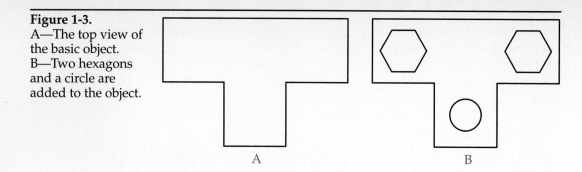

Figure 1-3.
A—The top view of the basic object.
B—Two hexagons and a circle are added to the object.

A

B

Next, use the following instructions to add two hexagons and a circle to the object, as shown in Figure 1-3B. The hexagons should sit on top of the "T" and extend .25 units above. The circle should appear to be a hole through the leg of the "T." Since the circle has the same elevation and thickness as the "T," draw it first. This way you will only need to use the **ELEV** command when drawing the hexagons.

To draw the hexagons, set the base elevation and thickness (height) using the **ELEV** command as follows. The base elevation is set to the top surface of the "T."

> Command: **ELEV**↵
> Specify new default elevation <0.0000>: **1**↵
> Specify new default thickness <1.0000>: **.25**↵

The value of 1 is entered for the elevation because the hexagons sit on top of the "T," which is 1 unit thick. The value of .25 is the thickness, or height, of the hexagons above the base elevation. Now, draw the hexagons. With all of the elements drawn, the object is ready to be viewed in 3D.

PROFESSIONAL TIP

The **ELEV** command can be set to different values in model space and paper space. When an elevation is set in one viewport, it becomes the same in all viewports.

Displaying Quick 3D Views

AutoCAD has several ways to quickly display a 3D view of your drawing. You can select a preset view by picking from the **3D Views** cascading menu in the **View** pull-down menu, picking the appropriate button in the **View** toolbar, or by picking the **Named Views** button in the **Standard** or **View** toolbar and selecting a view in the **View** dialog box, Figure 1-4.

Selecting **Plan View** from the **3D Views** cascading menu and then **Current UCS** displays the current drawing in a plan view of the current user coordinate system. This option is not available in the **View** toolbar. User coordinate systems are discussed in detail in Chapter 3.

To display a 3D view of the object drawn in the previous example, pick the **SW Isometric View** button on the **View** toolbar or select **SW Isometric** from the **3D Views** cascading menu. The display should look like the one shown in Figure 1-5. If you want to return to the previous 2D display, select **Plan View** from the **3D Views** cascading menu and then select **Current UCS**.

Figure 1-4.
A—The **3D Views** cascading menu provides various display options for the current drawing.
B—Display options can also be selected from the **View** toolbar. C—The **Orthographic &
Isometric Views** tab of the **View** dialog box contains the same orthographic and isometric
viewing options provided by the **View** toolbar.

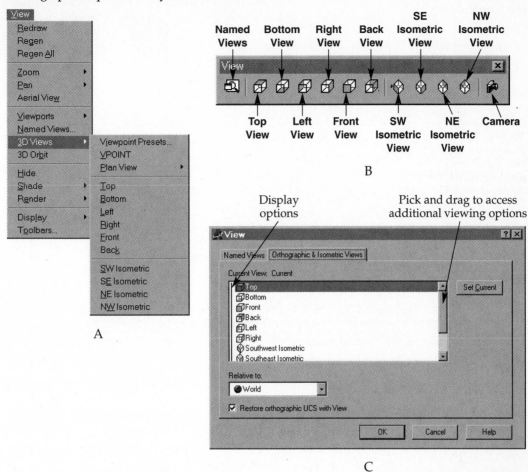

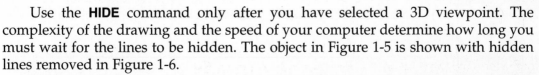

Removing Hidden Lines in 3D Displays

In a wireframe display, every edge of an object can be seen. This type of view can be
confusing, especially if there are several circular features in your drawing. The best way
to mask all lines that would normally be hidden is to use the **HIDE** command. You can
issue the **HIDE** command by picking the **Hide** button on the **Render** toolbar, picking
Hide from the **View** pull-down menu, or entering HI or HIDE at the Command: prompt:

> Command: **HI** *or* **HIDE.**↲
> Regenerating model.

Use the **HIDE** command only after you have selected a 3D viewpoint. The
complexity of the drawing and the speed of your computer determine how long you
must wait for the lines to be hidden. The object in Figure 1-5 is shown with hidden
lines removed in Figure 1-6.

You may think the view in Figure 1-6 does not look quite right. You probably
expected the "T" to appear solid with a circle in the top representing a hole. Think
back to the initial construction of the object. When drawn in the plan view, it
consisted of lines, or planes. It was not drawn with a top or bottom, just sides. Then,
you placed hexagons on top of the "box" with a cylinder inside. However, after doing
so, the object was still made up of only sides. That is why the display with hidden
lines removed appears as it does.

Figure 1-5.
The object shown in Figure 1-3B is viewed here as a 3D drawing by looking at it from the southwest.

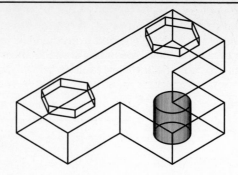

Figure 1-6.
The hidden lines of this object were removed using the **HIDE** command.

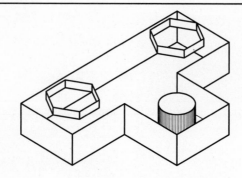

The individual features that make up the object in Figure 1-6 are shown in Figure 1-7. Both wireframe and hidden-line views are given. To redisplay the wireframe view, simply select another viewpoint or enter REGEN and press [Enter]. A regeneration displays all lines of the objects.

Figure 1-7.
The individual features of the object in Figure 1-6 are shown here in wireframe form (A) and with hidden lines removed (B).

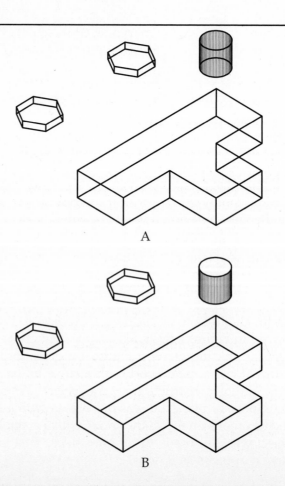

AutoCAD and its Applications—Advanced

Some 3D Drawing Hints

- Erasing a line drawn with the thickness set to a value other than zero erases an entire plane.
- Shapes drawn using the **LINE** and **ELEV** commands are open at the top and bottom. Shapes drawn with the **CIRCLE** and **ELEV** commands are closed at the ends.
- The **PLINE**, **POLYGON**, **RECTANG**, and **TRACE** commands give lines thickness and make them appear as walls in a 3D view. The effects are similar to those obtained with the **LINE** command.

THE RIGHT-HAND RULE OF 3D DRAWING

AutoCAD User's Guide 17

In order to gain a more thorough understanding of how AutoCAD displays 3D objects, it is important for you to become familiar with the method used to present them. The following method is simple and helps you visualize the 3D coordinate system.

The *right-hand rule* is a graphic representation of the positive coordinate values in the three axis directions of a coordinate system. AutoCAD's *UCS (User Coordinate System)* is based on this concept of visualization. To use the right-hand rule, position the thumb, index finger, and middle finger of your right hand as shown in Figure 1-8. Although this may seem a bit unusual to do (especially if you are sitting in a school library or computer lab), it can do wonders for your understanding of the nature of the three axes. It can also help in understanding how the UCS can be rotated about each of the axis lines (fingers).

Imagine that your thumb is the X axis, your index finger is the Y axis, and your middle finger is the Z axis. Hold your hand directly in front of you so that your middle finger is pointing directly at you, as shown in Figure 1-8. This is the plan view. The positive X axis is pointing to the right and the positive Y axis is pointing up. The positive Z axis comes toward you, and the origin of this system is the palm of your hand.

This concept can be visualized even better if you are sitting at a computer and the AutoCAD graphics window is displayed. If the UCS icon is not displayed in the lower-left corner of the screen, turn it on by selecting **Display** from the **View** pull-down menu, and then **UCS Icon** and **On**.

Now orient your right hand as shown in Figure 1-8 and position it next to the UCS icon on the screen. Your index finger and thumb should point in the same directions as the Y and X axes, respectively, on the UCS icon. Your middle finger will be pointing out of the screen directly at you.

There are a number of other ways to practice using the right-hand rule. When you use the **VPOINT** command (discussed in the next section of this chapter), you can display an axes *tripod* on screen. The tripod is composed of three lines representing the X, Y, and Z axes. When you display the tripod, you should be able to see how the right-hand rule works. The relationship between the two viewing techniques is illustrated in Figure 1-9.

Figure 1-8.
Try positioning
your hand like this
to understand the
relationship of the
X, Y, and Z axes.

Figure 1-9.
A comparison between the use of the right-hand rule and the **VPOINT** axes tripod display.

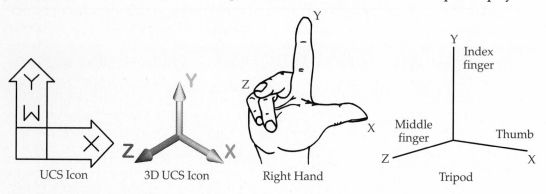

| UCS Icon | 3D UCS Icon | Right Hand | Tripod |

The right-hand rule can be used to eliminate confusion when the UCS is rotated to odd angles. The UCS can be rotated to any position desired. The coordinate system rotates on one of the three axis lines, just like a wheel rotates on an axle. Therefore, if you want to visualize how to rotate the X plane, keep your thumb stationary, and turn your hand. If you wish to rotate the Y plane, keep your index finger stationary and turn your hand to the left or right. When rotating the Z plane, you must keep your middle finger stationary and rotate your entire arm to the right or left.

If your 3D visualization skills are weak or you are having trouble envisioning different orientations of the UCS, don't be afraid to use the right-hand rule. It is a useful technique for improving your 3D visualization skills. The ability to rotate the UCS around one or more of the three axes can become confusing if proper techniques are not used to visualize the rotation angles. A complete discussion of these techniques is provided in Chapter 3.

DISPLAYING 3D DRAWINGS WITH THE **VPOINT** COMMAND

The most basic way to generate a 3D display in AutoCAD is to use the **VPOINT** command. The options used with this command are similar to the pull-down menu and toolbar methods discussed earlier in this chapter. Two other commands, **DVIEW** and **3DORBIT**, are also commonly used to display 3D viewing angles. These commands are more complex and versatile than the **VPOINT** command. They are discussed in detail in Chapter 7.

The **VPOINT** command allows you to display the current drawing at any angle. It may be easier to understand the function of this command as establishing your position relative to the object.

VPOINT
-VP

View
➥ 3D Views
➥ VPOINT

Imagine that you can position yourself at a coordinate location in 3D space in relation to the object. The **VPOINT** command enables you to do this so that the object can be positioned properly. To issue the **VPOINT** command, enter –VP or VPOINT at the Command: prompt:

> Command: **–VP** *or* **VPOINT**↵
> Current view direction: VIEWDIR=0.0000,0.0000,1.0000
> Specify a view point or [Rotate] <display compass and tripod>:

The three numbers in the command sequence above reflect the XYZ coordinates of the current viewpoint. These coordinates are also stored by the **VIEWDIR** system variable. The given values represent the coordinates for the plan view. This means that you see the XY plane. You can enter new coordinates to select a different viewpoint.

It is difficult to visualize a viewpoint as a set of coordinates. A simpler way to obtain a 3D viewing angle is to use the **VPOINT** axes tripod and compass to display a graphic representation of the XYZ axes, and pick the desired viewpoint with your pointing device. To do so, press [Enter] at the **VPOINT** option prompt, or select **VPOINT** from the **3D Views** cascading menu in the **View** pull-down menu. The resulting display is similar to the one shown in Figure 1-10A.

As discussed earlier, the lines making up the tripod represent the three coordinate axes. Next to the tripod are a set of small crosshairs and two concentric circles, which are divided into quarters to represent a compass. As you move your pointing device, notice what happens. The tripod and small crosshairs move. The orientation of the crosshairs represents the viewing angle. When the crosshairs are inside the small circle, you are viewing the object from above. When the crosshairs are located between the two circles, you are viewing the object from below.

In Figure 1-10B, compass directions are added to identify the quadrants of the circles. Notice that the small crosshairs are located in the southwest quadrant. Selecting this display would be similar to using the **SW Isometric** viewpoint. However, it is difficult to create an exact isometric viewpoint using the tripod.

The easiest way to locate the viewpoint is to move the cursor while observing the movement of the tripod. Pick the location where you are satisfied with the appearance of the axes. It may take some practice. Remember that in the top, or plan, view, the X axis is horizontal, the Y axis is vertical, and the Z axis comes out of the screen. As you move the tripod, keep track of where the crosshairs are located inside the compass. Compare their position to that of the tripod. Move the tripod until it is positioned as shown in Figure 1-11. Selecting this display is similar to picking the **SW Isometric View** button in the **View** toolbar.

Figure 1-10.
A—The **VPOINT** tripod and compass display allows you to position yourself in relation to the object. B—Compass directions added to the concentric circles identify the location of the crosshairs and the viewpoint orientation.

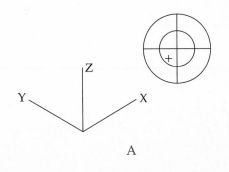

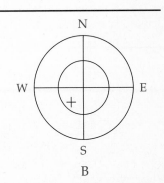

Figure 1-11.
Using the XYZ axes
tripod to display a
southwest isometric
3D view.

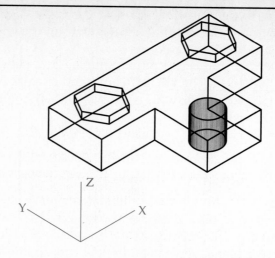

The number of viewpoints you can select is endless. To get an idea of how the axes tripod and compass relate to the viewpoint, see the examples in Figure 1-12.

It can be difficult to distinguish top from bottom in wireframe views. Therefore, the viewpoints shown in Figure 1-12 are all from above the object, and the **HIDE** command has been used to clarify the views. Use the **VPOINT** command to try each of these 3D viewpoints on your drawing.

Figure 1-12.
Examples of different viewpoints in relation to the axes tripod display.

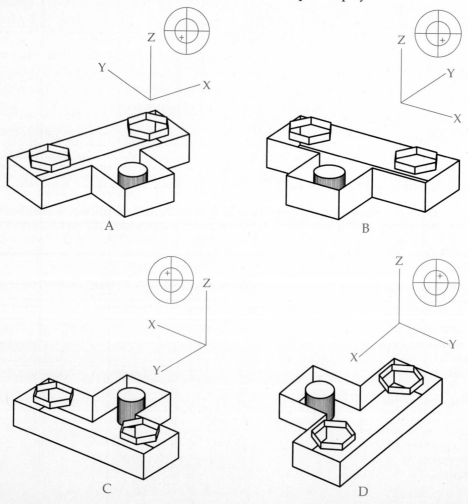

AutoCAD and its Applications—Advanced

When you are ready to return to the plan view, enter PLAN at the Command: prompt and select the default **Current** option, or type the XYZ coordinates for the plan view using the **VPOINT** command:

Command: **–VP** *or* **VPOINT**↵
Current view direction: VIEWDIR=–1.0000,–1.0000,1.0000
Specify a view point or [Rotate] <display compass and tripod>: **0,0,1**↵

This returns your original top view, which fills the screen. You can use the **All** option of the **ZOOM** command to display the drawing limits.

EXERCISE 1-2

❑ Use the **LINE** command to draw Object A below. Do not include dimensions.
❑ Use the **CIRCLE** command to draw Object B below. Do not include dimensions.
❑ Use the **VPOINT** command to display the 3D view of your drawing. Display it from three viewpoints using the axes tripod.
❑ Save the drawing as EX1-2.

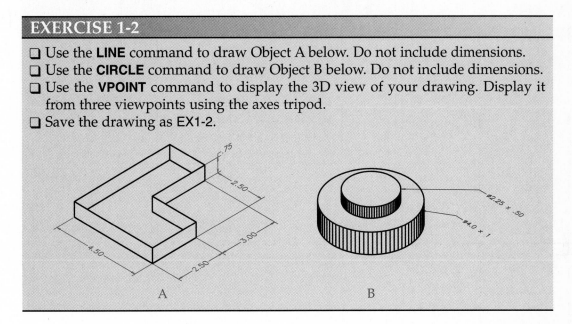

A   B

Creating Extruded 3D Text

Text added on the plan view is displayed in 3D when you use the **VPOINT** command. However, the displayed text does not have thickness, and it always rests on the zero elevation plane. You can give text thickness by accessing the **Properties** window, Figure 1-13. This window can be displayed by picking the **Properties** button in the **Standard** toolbar. After the text has been selected, enter a new value next to Thickness in the **General** category. When you exit the **Properties** window, the text is given the specified thickness. Examples of extruded 3D text before and after using the **HIDE** command are shown in Figure 1-14.

Figure 1-13.
Thickness can be applied to text by selecting the text and changing the Thickness property value in the **Properties** window.

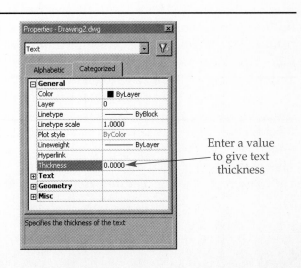

Enter a value to give text thickness

Figure 1-14.
Examples of
applying thickness
to 3D text, before
and after using the
HIDE command.

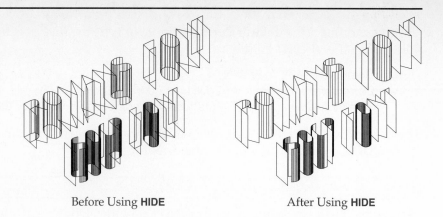

Before Using **HIDE**   After Using **HIDE**

NOTE   Extruded 3D text can only be created with AutoCAD fonts. Text
using TrueType fonts cannot be given thickness. When creating
a text style for extruded text, choose only from the fonts listed
with the AutoCAD calipers icon, not the TrueType icon.

3D CONSTRUCTION TECHNIQUES

Three-dimensional objects can be drawn in three basic forms—as wireframe objects, surface models, and solid models. The following section discusses wireframe construction and the use of 3D faces to apply surfaces to a wireframe. Additional information on wireframe construction is provided in Chapters 2, 3, and 4. A complete discussion of surface modeling is given in Chapter 5. Solid model construction and editing is covered in Chapters 10 through 13.

A *wireframe construction* is an object that looks like it is made of wire. You can see through it. As a result, there are not many practical applications for wireframe models, unless you are an artist designing a new object using coat hangers. A specialized application of 3D wireframe modeling involves single-line piping diagrams for the process piping industry. Wireframe models can be hard to visualize because it is difficult to determine the angle of view and the nature of the surfaces. Compare the two objects in Figure 1-15.

Surface models, on the other hand, are much easier to visualize. A surface model looks more like a real object. Surface models can be used to imitate solid models. Most importantly, color, surface textures, lights, and shadows can be applied for realistic presentations. These "shaded and rendered" models can then be used in any number of presentation formats, including slide shows, black and white or color prints, walk-around or walk-through animations, and animations that are recorded to videotape. A surface model can also be exported from AutoCAD for use in animation and rendering software, such as Autodesk's 3D Studio MAX® or 3D Studio VIZ®.

Surface models are the basis for the construction of composite 3D models, often called *virtual worlds*, which are used in the field of virtual reality. These 3D rendered worlds can then be used with virtual reality. The possibilities are endless. However, remember that the usefulness of surface models is defined by the word *presentation*. This means *seeing* what the model looks like while viewing it from different angles, with different lighting, shading, and surface textures.

Figure 1-15.
A wireframe object may be harder to visualize than a surface model. (Autodesk, Inc.)

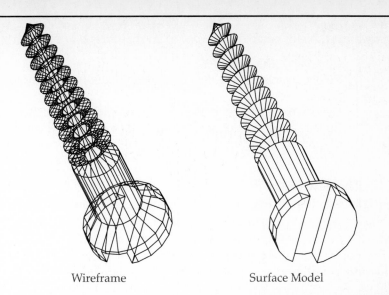

Wireframe   Surface Model

On the other hand, *solid models* more closely represent objects that are designed using the materials they are to be made from. Solid modeling involves using primitive solid shapes such as boxes, cylinders, spheres, and cones to construct an object. These shapes are added and subtracted to create a finished product. The solid model can then be shaded and rendered. More importantly, solid models can be analyzed and tested for mass, volume, moments of inertia, and centroids. Some third-party programs allow you to perform finite element analysis on solid models.

Before constructing a 3D model, you should determine the purpose of your design. What will the model be used for—presentation, analysis, or manufacturing? This helps you determine which tools you should use to construct the model. The discussions and examples that follow in this chapter provide an introduction to the uses of wireframes, 3D faces, and basic surfaced objects in order to create 3D constructions.

CONSTRUCTING WIREFRAMES AND 3D FACES

Wireframes can be constructed using the **LINE**, **PLINE**, **SPLINE**, and **3DPOLY** commands. There are a number of different ways to use these commands to construct wireframes, but one particularly useful method involves filters. A *filter* is an existing point or vector in your drawing file. When using a filter, you instruct AutoCAD to find the coordinate values of a selected point. Then, you specify the next point by supplying the missing X, Y, or Z value, or a combination of values. Filters can be used when working in two-dimensional space, or when using a pictorial projection established with the **VPOINT** command.

Using Filters to Create 3D Wireframe Objects

When using the **LINE** command to draw a wireframe object, you must know the XYZ coordinate values of each corner point on a surface of the object. You can then use filters to complete the object. To draw the object, first decide the easiest and quickest method using the **LINE** command. One technique is to draw the bottom surface first. Then, make a copy of the desired shape at the height of the object using filters. The filters can be used with the **COPY** command, or with grips. Finally, use filters to connect the corners with lines.

For example, first draw the 2D object shown in Figure 1-2A using the **LINE** command. Next, copy the shape up to the height of one unit.

    Command: **CO** *or* **COPY**↵
    Select objects: *(select the shape using a window or crossing box)*
    Select objects: ↵
    Specify base point or displacement, or [Multiple]: *(pick a corner of the shape)*
    Specify second point of displacement or <use first point as displacement>: **.XY**↵
    of *(pick the same corner)*
    of (need Z): **1**↵

The new object is directly above the original object, so there still appears to be a single object on screen. The top surface has the same XY values as the bottom surface. That is why .XY was entered as the second point of displacement. This filter picks up the XY values of the point specified and applies them to the location of the new copy. The copy is completed when the Z value is specified. Check your progress by establishing a different view of the object with the **VPOINT** command. Enter the coordinates given below. Your display should look like that shown in Figure 1-16.

    Command: **–VP** *or* **VPOINT**↵
    Current view direction: VIEWDIR=0.0000,0.0000,1.0000
    Specify a view point or [Rotate] <display compass and tripod>: **1,–1,0.75**↵

Return the drawing to the plan view and finish the object using the **LINE** command and point filters. The eight remaining lines are vertical and one unit long. You can draw these lines by using the **Intersection** object snap, or by using filters as follows:

    Command: **L** *or* **LINE**↵
    Specify first point: *(pick the lower-left corner of the object)*
    Specify next point or [Undo]: **.XY**↵
    of *(pick the lower-left corner again)*
    of (need Z): **1**↵
    Specify next point or [Undo]: ↵

In this example, you are instructing AutoCAD to draw a line from the lower-left corner of the object to the same XY position one unit above. The new line connects the top and bottom planes of the object. The same process can be used to draw the other vertical lines. When finished, use the **VPOINT** command to establish a 3D view of the object. Your drawing should look like that shown in Figure 1-17.

Figure 1-16.
A partially
constructed 3D
shape using the
LINE command and
XYZ filters.

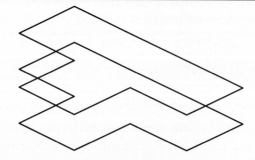

Figure 1-17.
The completed 3D
wireframe object
after connecting the
top and bottom
planes.

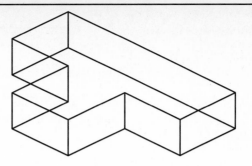

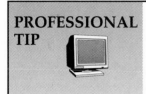

PROFESSIONAL TIP

If the process of drawing Z axis lines in the plan view is difficult to visualize, an easier alternative is to draw them in a pictorial view. After drawing the top and bottom faces of the object, select a viewpoint and zoom in on the object. Next, issue the **LINE** command to construct the vertical lines using object snap modes such as **Endpoint**, **Midpoint**, and **Intersection**. This method allows you to see the lines in 3D as you draw them.

EXERCISE 1-3

❏ Draw the 3D object below to the dimensions indicated. Use the **LINE** and **COPY** commands. Construct the top and bottom planes in the plan view. Connect the vertical lines in a 3D view.
❏ Save the drawing as EX1-3.

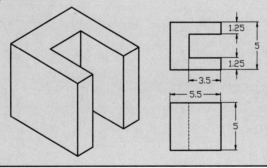

Constructing 3D Faces

Surfaces that appear solid (not as wireframes) are called *3D faces*. They can be drawn with the **3DFACE** command. This command allows you to create three- or four-sided surfaces by picking points in a clockwise or counterclockwise manner. The **3DFACE** command is accessed by picking the **3D Face** button on the **Surfaces** toolbar, selecting **3D Face** from the **Surfaces** cascading menu in the **Draw** pull-down menu, or by entering 3F or 3DFACE at the Command: prompt.

A 3D face drawn in AutoCAD must have at least three corners, but it cannot have any more than four corners. Therefore, to draw the top surface of the "T"-shaped object in Figure 1-17, two 3D faces are required. The resulting shape will look somewhat different from the one drawn as a wireframe. Use the following steps to draw the "T"-shaped object with 3D faces:

1. Set the elevation to zero.
2. Draw the bottom faces.

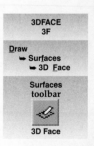

3DFACE
3F

Draw
➥ Surfaces
  ➥ 3D Face

Surfaces
toolbar

3D Face

Figure 1-18.
The bottom surface of the object is composed of two 3D faces.

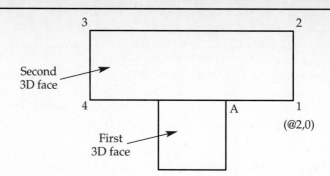

3. Copy the bottom faces up by using a positive Z value (representing the thickness) to create the top faces.
4. Draw 3D faces on all sides of the object.

Using the proper object snap modes, draw the first 3D bottom face. Then draw the adjoining bottom face. Use the following command sequence and refer to Figure 1-18 as you work:

Command: **3F** *or* **3DFACE**↵
Specify first point or [Invisible]: *(pick point 1)*
Specify second point or [Invisible]: *(pick point 2)*
Specify third point or [Invisible] <exit>: *(pick point 3)*
Specify fourth point or [Invisible] <create three-sided face>: *(pick point 4)*
Specify third point or [Invisible] <exit>: ↵

The 3D faces can be copied using the same steps that were taken to copy the wireframe line surface in the previous example.

Finally, draw the vertical sides of the shape. First, establish a 3D viewpoint:

Command: **–VP** *or* **VPOINT**↵
Current view direction: VIEWDIR=0.0000,0.0000,1.0000
Specify a view point or [Rotate] <display compass and tripod>: **1,–1,.75**↵

The drawing should look like the one shown in Figure 1-19. Zoom in if the view is too small. To complete the object, enter the **3DFACE** command and pick points 1 through 4 on the right side. You can construct a series of connected faces without exiting the command. After you have picked the fourth point of the first face, a prompt for the third point reappears. This is because AutoCAD is using the third and fourth points picked for the first face as the first two points of the next face. Continue picking points 3 and 4 around the object until each face has been completed. Press [Enter] to exit the command.

Figure 1-19.
After the top and bottom faces are created, the sides must be added. The numbers indicate the points to pick when using the **3DFACE** command.

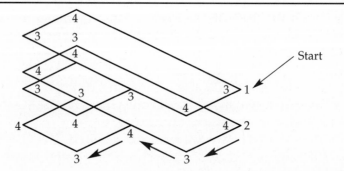

AutoCAD and its Applications—Advanced

Command: **3F** *or* **3DFACE**↵
Specify first point or [Invisible]: *(pick point 1)*
Specify second point or [Invisible]: *(pick point 2)*
Specify third point or [Invisible] <exit>: *(pick point 3)*
Specify fourth point or [Invisible] <create three–sided face>: *(pick point 4)*
Specify third point or [Invisible] <exit>: *(pick point 3)*
Specify fourth point or [Invisible] <create three–sided face>: *(pick point 4)*
Specify third point or [Invisible] <exit>: *(continue picking points 3 and 4 to complete the object)*

The finished object should appear similar to that shown in Figure 1-20A.

Notice in Figure 1-20B that an intersection line is visible between the two faces on the top surface. This surface, and similar arrangements of attached 3D faces, can be drawn so that all intersecting edges are invisible. The procedure requires some planning and is discussed in Chapter 2.

How does a 3D face object differ from objects drawn using the **ELEV** and **LINE** commands? For comparison, Figure 1-21 shows boxes drawn using the **ELEV**, **LINE**, and **3DFACE** commands, with hidden lines removed by the **HIDE** command.

Figure 1-20.
A—The completed object appears to be a wireframe construction before using the **HIDE** command. B—The object after using **HIDE**.

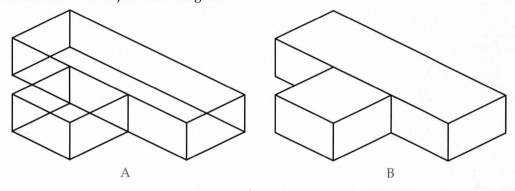

A

B

Figure 1-21.
A comparison of boxes drawn with the **ELEV**, **LINE**, and **3DFACE** commands, with hidden lines removed.

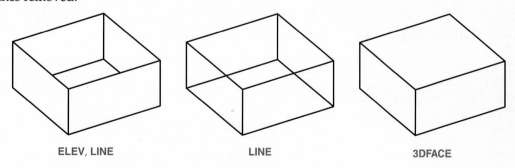

ELEV, LINE

LINE

3DFACE

When moving or copying objects in 3D space, it can simplify matters to use the displacement option to specify positioning data. This allows you to specify the X, Y, and Z coordinate movement simultaneously. For example, to copy a 3D face to a position three units above the original on the Z axis, use the following command sequence:

Command: **CO** *or* **COPY**↵
Select objects: *(pick the 3D face)*
Select objects: ↵
Specify base point or displacement, or [Multiple]: **0,0,3**↵
Specify second point of displacement or <use first point as displacement>: ↵

Because [Enter] was pressed at the prompt for the second point of displacement, the XYZ values entered are used as a relative displacement instead of a base point.

EXERCISE 1-4

❏ Use the **3DFACE** command to construct the object shown below to the dimensions given. The front surface should be drawn with two faces, shown below as A and B.
❏ Use the **HIDE** command when you complete the object.
❏ Save the drawing as EX1-4.

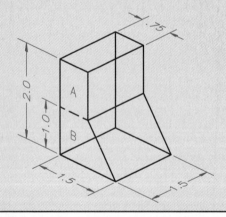

CONSTRUCTING 3D SURFACE-MODELED OBJECTS

Several predrawn 3D surface-modeled objects are provided by AutoCAD for design purposes. These objects can be quickly placed in your drawing by specifying a location and basic dimensions. They can be selected by picking the appropriate button in the **Surfaces** toolbar or by using the **3D Objects** dialog box, Figure 1-22. To access this dialog box, pick **3D Surfaces...** from the **Surfaces** cascading menu in the **Draw** pull-down menu.

Notice the list box to the left of the images in the **3D Objects** dialog box. It contains the names of all the objects shown. An object can be selected by picking either the name or the image. Pick **OK** to draw the highlighted object.

After a selection is made, you are prompted for a location point for the object. The remaining prompts request dimensions, such as the length, width, height, diameter,

Figure 1-22.
A—The **3D Objects** dialog box displays a group of 3D surface-modeled objects that can be quickly drawn by providing a location point and basic dimensions. B—The same objects can be selected from the **Surfaces** toolbar.

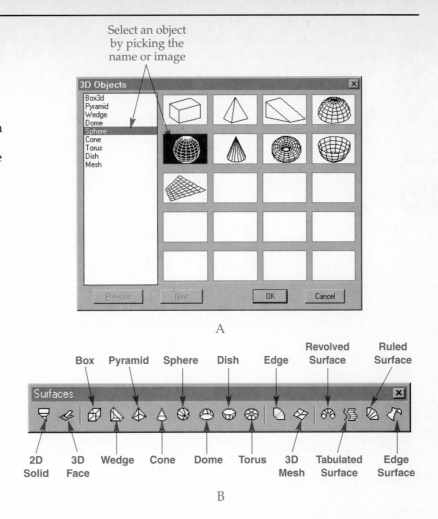

Select an object by picking the name or image

A

B

and radius. Depending on the object selected, other specifications are required, such as the number of longitudinal and latitudinal segments. For example, select **Dome** in the **3D Objects** dialog box. The following prompts appear:

Specify center point of dome: *(pick a point)*
Specify radius of dome or [Diameter]: *(enter a radius or pick a point on screen)*
Enter number of longitudinal segments for surface of dome <16>: ↵
Enter number of latitudinal segments for surface of dome <8>: ↵

The object is drawn in the plan view, as shown in Figure 1-23A. Use the **VPOINT** command to produce a 3D view of the object, and use **HIDE** to remove hidden lines.

In Figure 1-23B, the longitudinal and latitudinal segments of the dome are illustrated. *Longitudinal* refers to an east-west measurement, and *latitudinal* means north-south.

Figure 1-23.
A—The plan view of a dome. B—A 3D view of the dome. Longitudinal segments are measured east-west, and latitudinal segments are measured north-south.

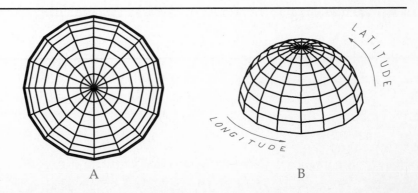

A   B

Remember that if you draw 3D objects in the plan view, you must use the **VPOINT** command to establish a 3D view. The illustrations in Figure 1-24 show the dimensions required to construct the predrawn 3D objects provided by AutoCAD.

Figure 1-24.
The dimensions shown are required to draw AutoCAD's 3D surface-modeled objects.

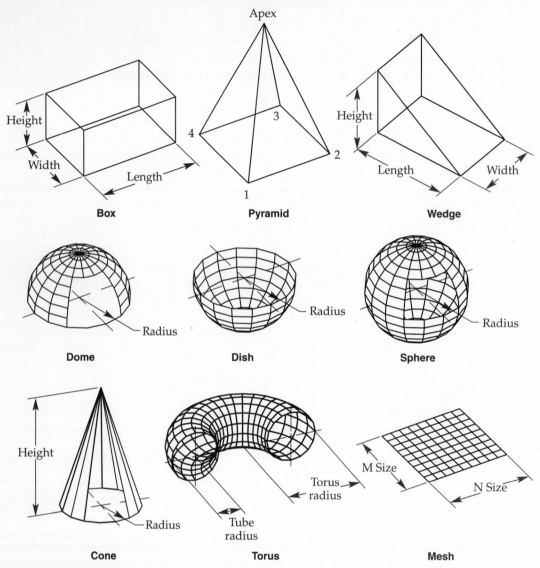

Chapter Test

Answer the following questions on a separate sheet of paper.

1. When looking at a standard AutoCAD screen in plan view, in which direction does the Z coordinate project?
2. Which command allows you to give objects thickness?
3. If you draw a line after setting a thickness, what have you actually drawn?
4. What is the purpose of the right-hand rule?
5. According to the right-hand rule, name the coordinate axes represented by the following fingers:
   A. Thumb.
   B. Middle finger.
   C. Index finger.

6. What is the purpose of the **VPOINT** command?
7. How are you viewing an object when the small crosshairs are inside the small circle in the **VPOINT** command display?
8. How are you viewing an object when the small crosshairs are between the small circle and the large circle in the **VPOINT** command display?
9. How do you create extruded 3D text?
10. What is the function of the **HIDE** command?
11. Define *point filters*.
12. Which command allows you to create three- or four-sided surfaces by picking points in a clockwise or counterclockwise manner?
13. How can you select one of AutoCAD's predrawn 3D surface-modeled objects?

Drawing Problems

For Problems 1–12, draw the objects shown as extruded 3D objects using the **ELEV** *command. Where possible, draw additional 3D faces to enclose the object. Do not include dimensions. Display the drawings in two different 3D views. Use the* **HIDE** *command in one view. Use your own dimensions for objects shown without dimensions. Save the drawings as P1-(problem number).*

1.

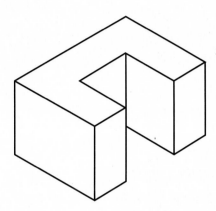

2.

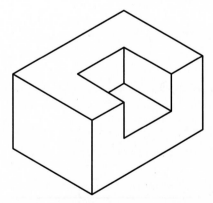

3.

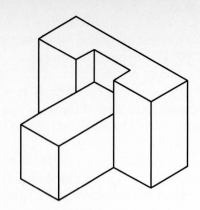

 4.

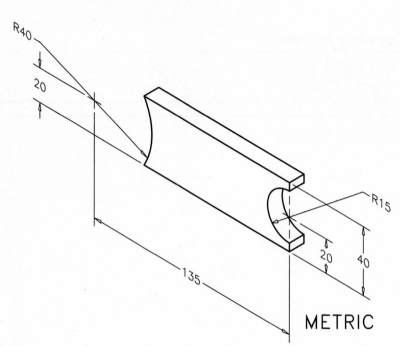

R40

20

R15

20

40

135

METRIC

 5.

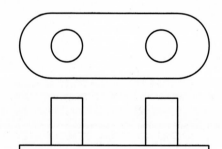

 6.

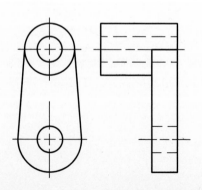

7.

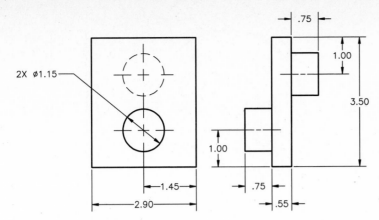

8.

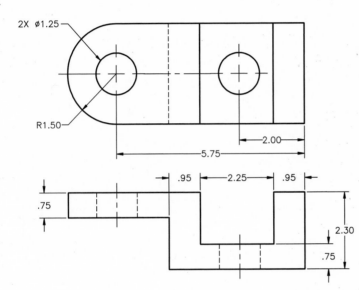

9.

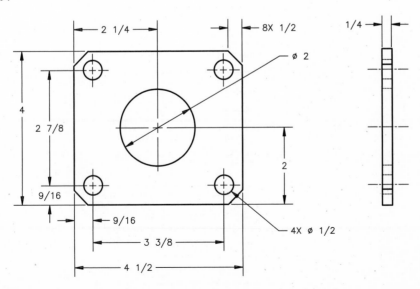

10.

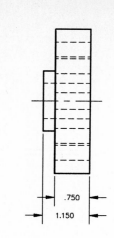

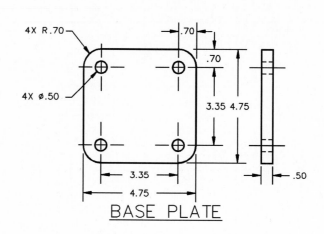

FLANGE

11.

BASE PLATE

12.

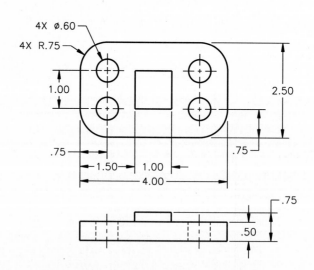

For Problems 13–16, draw the objects shown in 3D form. Use the **3DFACE** *command and the given dimensions. Display the drawings from three different viewpoints. Use the* **HIDE** *command for one of the views. Save the drawings as* P1-*(problem number).*

13.

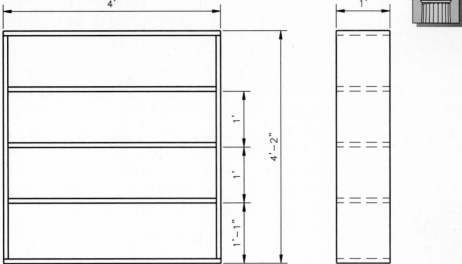

14.

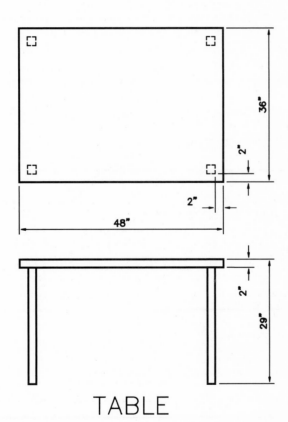

TABLE

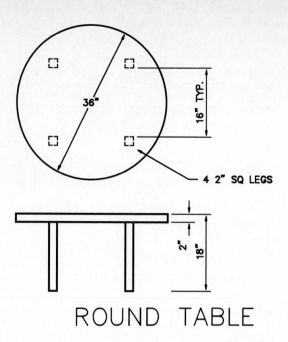

16" TYP.

36"

4 2" SQ LEGS

2"
18"

ROUND TABLE

16.

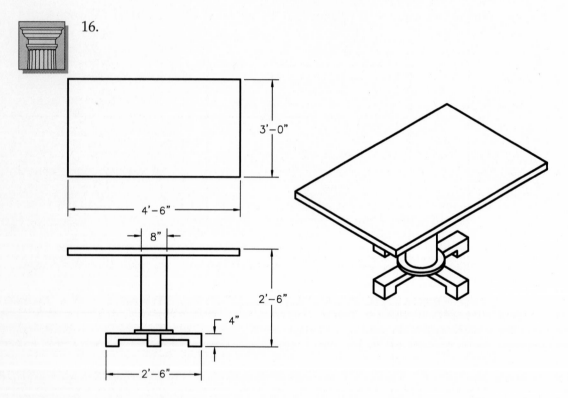

3'-0"

4'-6"

8"

2'-6"

4"

2'-6"

CHAPTER 2

Three-Dimensional Coordinates and Constructions

Learning Objectives

After completing this chapter, you will be able to:
- Describe the functions of rectangular, spherical, and cylindrical 3D coordinate systems.
- Draw 3D surface-modeled objects.
- Use 3D construction methods to create arrays, polylines, and 3D face objects.

The ability to display 3D models at any viewpoint in AutoCAD gives you unlimited possibilities. However, the display and presentation of your models should always be accurate and realistic. Therefore, it is important to be familiar with a variety of coordinate entry methods that can be used to draw different geometric shapes. This chapter covers the three principal forms of coordinate entry and related 3D construction methods. Drawing and display examples are provided throughout the chapter to illustrate each coordinate system.

3D COORDINATE SYSTEMS

You can enter 3D coordinates in three different formats. The rectangular coordinate system is the most commonly used form of 3D coordinate entry. This system was discussed in Chapter 1. The two other 3D coordinate systems involve the use of spherical coordinates and cylindrical coordinates. These two systems are similar and are discussed in the following sections.

Introduction to the Spherical Coordinate System

The method of point entry in the *spherical coordinate system* is similar to locating a point on the earth using longitudinal and latitudinal values, with the center of the earth representing the origin. The origin can be that of the default WCS (World Coordinate System) or the current UCS (User Coordinate System). In this system, lines of longitude connect the north and south poles. These lines provide an east-west measurement on the earth's surface. Lines of latitude extend horizontally around the earth and provide a north-south measurement. See Figure 2-1A.

When entering spherical coordinates, the longitude measurement is expressed as the angle *in* the XY plane, and the latitude measurement is expressed as the angle *from* the XY plane. See Figure 2-1B. A distance from the origin is also provided. The coordinates represent a measurement from the equator toward either the north pole or the south pole on the earth's surface. Spherical coordinate entry is similar to polar coordinate entry. However, an additional angular value is provided, as shown below and in Figure 2-1B:

7.5<35<55

The coordinate given represents an absolute spherical coordinate. Spherical coordinates can also be used as relative coordinates. For example, a point drawn with the relative spherical coordinate @2<35<45 means that the point is located 2 units from the last point, at an angle of 35° *in* the XY plane, and at a 45° angle *from* the XY plane.

Figure 2-1.
A—Lines of longitude, representing the highlighted latitudinal segments in the illustration below, run from north to south. Lines of latitude, representing the highlighted longitudinal segments below, run from east to west. B—Spherical coordinates require a distance, an angle *in* the XY plane, and an angle *from* the XY plane.

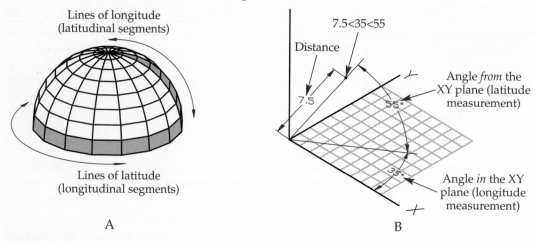

A

B

PROFESSIONAL TIP

Spherical coordinates are useful for locating features on a spherical surface or model. For example, they can be used to specify the location of a hole drilled into a sphere, or a feature located from a specific point on a sphere. If you are working on such a spherical object, you might consider locating a UCS at the center of the sphere, then creating several different user coordinate systems rotated at different angles on the surface of the sphere. Any time a location is required, spherical coordinates can be used.

Using spherical coordinates

Spherical coordinates are well suited for locating points on the surface of a sphere. The following example shows how to draw a sphere and then locate a new object on its surface.

First, a sphere is drawn in the plan view. Then, a preset 3D viewpoint is selected. To draw a second sphere on the surface of the first, locate a point at the center of the sphere using the **POINT** command. Be sure to use a suitable point style so the point is visible on screen. The point style can be changed in the **Point Style** dialog box, which is accessed by selecting **Point Style...** from the **Format** pull-down menu. The point style setting is also stored by the **PDMODE** system variable.

To draw the first sphere, pick **3D Surfaces...** from the **Surfaces** cascading menu in the **Draw** pull-down menu to display the **3D Objects** dialog box. Then, select the **Sphere** image and pick **OK**. You can also pick the **Sphere** button on the **Surfaces** toolbar. The sequence is as follows:

Command: *(pick* **Sphere** *from the* **3D Objects** *dialog box or the* **Surfaces** *toolbar)*
Specify center point of sphere: **7,5**↵
Specify radius of sphere or [Diameter]: **1.5**↵
Enter number of longitudinal segments for surface of sphere <16>: ↵
Enter number of latitudinal segments for surface of sphere <16>: ↵
Command:

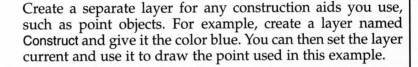

NOTE Create a separate layer for any construction aids you use, such as point objects. For example, create a layer named Construct and give it the color blue. You can then set the layer current and use it to draw the point used in this example.

Now, use the **POINT** command to draw a point at the center of the sphere. When finished, pick **SE Isometric** from the **3D Views** cascading menu in the **View** pull-down menu. You can also pick the **SE Isometric View** button on the **View** toolbar. This displays the object in 3D. Your drawing should look like Figure 2-2A. Center the object on screen, and then pick **Sphere** again to draw the second sphere. Continue as follows:

Specify center point of sphere: **FROM**↵
Base point: **NODE**↵
of *(pick the point at the center of the sphere)*
<Offset>: **@1.5<30<60**↵ *(1.5 is the radius of the first sphere)*
Specify radius of sphere or [Diameter]: **.4**↵
Enter number of longitudinal segments for surface of sphere <16>: ↵
Enter number of latitudinal segments for surface of sphere <16>: ↵
Command:

The objects should now appear as shown in Figure 2-2B. The center of the new sphere is located on the surface of the original sphere. This is clear after using the **HIDE** command, Figure 2-2C. If you want the surfaces to be tangent, add the radius values of each sphere (1.5 + .4) and enter the resulting value when prompted for the offset from the center of the first sphere:

<Offset>: **@1.9<30<60**

Notice in Figure 2-2C that the polar axis lines of the two spheres are parallel. This is because both objects were drawn with the same UCS. This can be misleading unless you

Figure 2-2.
A—A 3-unit diameter sphere shown from the southeast isometric viewpoint.
B—A .8-unit diameter sphere with its center located on the surface of the original object.
C—The objects after using the **HIDE** command.

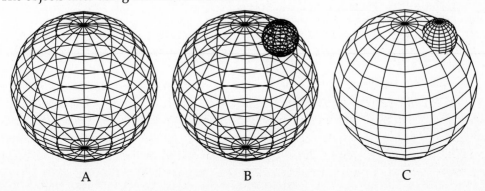

A   B   C

are aware of how objects are constructed based on the current UCS. Test this by locating a cone on the surface of the large sphere, just below the small sphere. First, redisplay the original wireframe view of the objects by typing REGEN at the Command: prompt. Then, pick **Cone** from the **3D Objects** dialog box or the **Surfaces** toolbar. Continue with the process as follows, using object snaps to assist in accurate location:

```
Specify center point for base of cone: FROM⏎
Base point: NODE⏎
of (pick the point at the center of the sphere)
<Offset>: @1.5<30<30⏎
Specify radius for base of cone or [Diameter]: .25⏎
Specify radius for top of cone or [Diameter] <0>: ⏎
Specify height of cone: 1⏎
Enter number of segments for surface of cone <16>: ⏎
Command:
```

The results of this construction, after using the **HIDE** command, are shown in Figure 2-3.

Figure 2-3.
The axis lines of objects drawn in the same coordinate system are parallel. Notice that the cone does not project from the center of the large sphere.

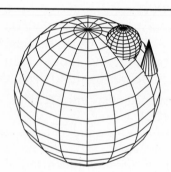

> **NOTE**
>
> The **REGEN** command used in the previous example will not restore hidden lines if the **SHADEMODE** command is set to an option other than **2D wireframe**. If necessary, enter this option and then use the **REGEN** command to redisplay the wireframe view.

Changing the UCS

The axis of the cone in the previous example is a line from the center of the base to the tip of the cone. In Figure 2-3, the axis is tangent to the sphere, and is not pointing to the center. This is because the Z planes of the large sphere and the cone both coincide with the World Coordinate System (WCS). This is the default coordinate system of AutoCAD. In order for the axis of the cone to project from the sphere's center point, the UCS must be changed. This process is discussed in Chapter 3. However, the following is a quick overview.

Study Figure 2-4 and the steps listed below. This sequence illustrates how the UCS can be rotated in order to draw a cone that projects from the center of the sphere. First, move the UCS icon to the center of the sphere:

```
Command: UCS⏎
Current ucs name: *WORLD*
Enter an option [New/Move/orthoGraphic/Prev/Restore/Save/Del/Apply/?/World]
<World>: M⏎
Specify new origin point or [Zdepth]: <0,0,0>: NODE⏎
of (pick the point at the center of the sphere)
```

Figure 2-4.
A—The default World Coordinate System must be rotated to create a new UCS. B—The new UCS is rotated 30° in the XY plane on the Z axis. C—A line rotated up 30° from the XY plane represents the axis of the cone. D—The UCS is rotated 60° about the Y axis. The centerline of the cone coincides with the Z axis.

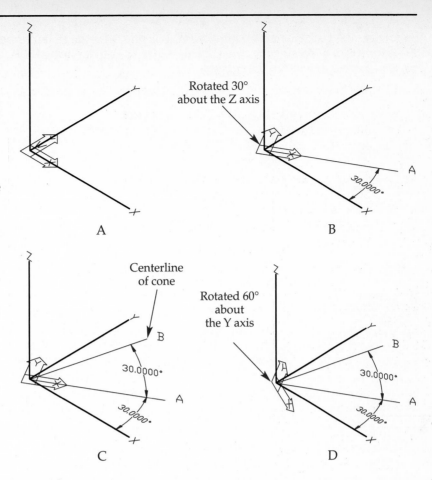

Now, continue as follows. Keep in mind that the point you are locating is 30° from the X axis and 30° from the XY plane.

```
Command: UCS↵
Current ucs name: *NO NAME*
Enter an option [New/Move/orthoGraphic/Prev/Restore/Save/Del/Apply/?/World]
<World>: N↵
Specify origin of new UCS or [ZAxis/3point/OBject/Face/View/X/Y/Z] <0,0,0>: Z↵
Specify rotation angle about Z axis <90>: 30↵
Command: (press [Enter] or the space bar to reissue the UCS command)
Current ucs name: *NO NAME*
Enter an option [New/Move/orthoGraphic/Prev/Restore/Save/Del/Apply/?/World]
<World>: N↵
Specify origin of new UCS or [ZAxis/3point/OBject/Face/View/X/Y/Z] <0,0,0>: Y↵
Specify rotation angle about Y axis <90>: 60↵
```

This new UCS can be used to construct a cone with its axis projecting from the center of the sphere. Figure 2-5A shows the new UCS located at the center of the sphere. Now, pick **Cone** from the **3D Objects** dialog box or the **Surfaces** toolbar. With the UCS rotated, rectangular coordinates can be used to locate the cone:

```
Specify center point for base of cone: 0,0,1.5↵
Specify radius for base of cone or [Diameter]: .25↵
Specify radius for top of cone or [Diameter] <0>: ↵
Specify height of cone: 1↵
Enter number of segments for surface of cone <16>: ↵
Command:
```

The completed cone is shown in Figure 2-5B. You can see that the axis projects from the center of the sphere. Figure 2-5C shows the objects after using the **HIDE** command.

Figure 2-5.
A—A new UCS is created with the Z axis projecting from the center of the sphere.
B—A cone is drawn using the new UCS. C—The objects after using **HIDE**. The axis of the cone
projects from the center of the sphere.

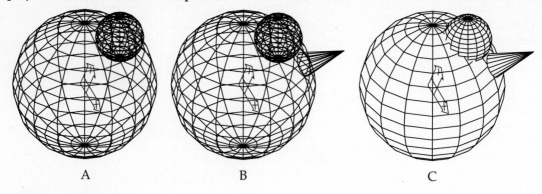

A   B   C

PROFESSIONAL TIP

You can quickly change the UCS by entering one of the axis rotation options at the **UCS** option line without first using the **New** option. Simply type X, Y, or Z after entering the **UCS** command and then specify a rotation angle. See Chapter 3 for a complete discussion of this procedure.

Constructing accurate intersections

When an object is located on a curved surface, there may be a small gap between the curved surface and the object. See Figure 2-6A. In order for the model to display properly when rendered or animated, you need to "make up" for this gap.

For example, refer to the cone and sphere in Figure 2-5. First, lay out an orthographic view of the radius of the sphere. Then, draw a radial centerline for the intersecting cone. Draw a line tangent to the curve with a length equal to the diameter of the cone's base. Refer to Figure 2-6A. Project a new line perpendicular from one end of the tangent line through the curve. Then, move the baseline of the cone to the intersection of the projection line and the curve. This is the new base. See Figure 2-6B.

Figure 2-6.
A—A small gap is created when the base of the cone is located tangent to the sphere's curved surface. B—The base of the cone is moved so that its edge meets the intersection of the projection line and the surface of the sphere. C—The distance from the center of the sphere to the base of the cone is determined. D—The new cone intersects the surface of the sphere with no gap.

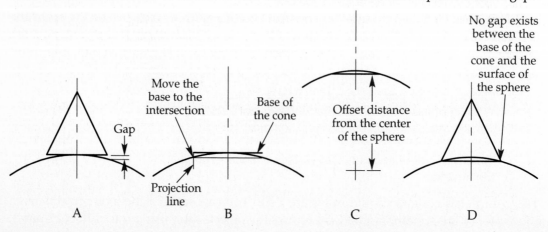

Next, measure the distance from the center of the sphere perpendicular to the new base. See Figure 2-6C. Use this distance when locating the new cone. See Figure 2-6D.

The original and relocated cones after using the **HIDE** and **SHADE** commands are shown in Figure 2-7. Notice in Figures 2-7A and 2-7B that the base edge of the original cone can be seen as a line. This is because the cone is sitting above the surface of the sphere. In Figures 2-7C and 2-7D, the base edge of the relocated cone cannot be seen because it is *inside* the sphere. Therefore, after rendering, the objects appear correct.

Figure 2-7.
A—A cone with the center of its base located on the surface of the sphere. B—When rendered, the edge of the base is visible. C—A cone with the edge of its base intersecting the surface of the sphere. D—When rendered, the edge of the base is not visible.

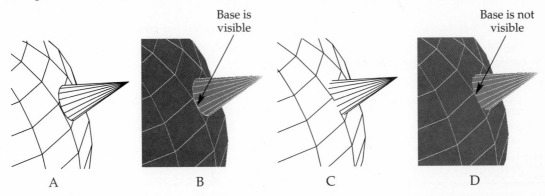

Base is visible

Base is not visible

A   B   C   D

> **NOTE**
>
> You may have expected a line to define the intersection of the cone and the sphere in Figures 2-7C and 2-7D. This is not the case when objects created with surface-modeling techniques intersect. AutoCAD retains the definitions of two separate objects and does not automatically create a line at intersections. If you want a line to be placed at the intersection of two shapes, it may be necessary to draw them as solids and then join them in a union. Solid model construction and editing is covered in Chapters 10, 11, 12, and 13.

EXERCISE 2-1

❏ Start a new drawing for this exercise.
❏ Change the **PDMODE** system variable setting to 3. Set the color to blue and draw a point using the coordinates 6,4.
❏ Set the color to white and draw a 4″ diameter sphere centered on the point.
❏ Set the color to red and draw two .75″ diameter spheres. Center both on the surface of the 4″ diameter sphere. For the first sphere, use angular coordinates of 15° *in* the XY plane and 50° *from* the XY plane. For the second sphere, use angular coordinates of –15° *in* the XY plane and 50° *from* the XY plane.
❏ Set the color to green and draw a cone with a .5″ diameter base. Center the cone on the surface of the 4″ diameter sphere using angular coordinates of 0° *in* the XY plane and 30° *from* the XY plane. Specify a height of one unit for the cone. Create a new UCS and construct another cone with a centerline projecting from the center of the sphere.
❏ Display the objects from a southeast isometric viewpoint and use the **HIDE** command.
❏ Save the drawing as EX2-1.

Displaying drawings using spherical coordinates

When using the **VPOINT** command to display a 3D view of a drawing, you can enter spherical coordinates to change the viewpoint. AutoCAD only needs the two angular values based on the XY plane. This is because the viewpoint does not set a spherical distance from a "center" point, or origin. You can enter spherical coordinates for a viewpoint using the **Rotate** option of the **VPOINT** command as follows:

```
Command: –VP or VPOINT↵
Current view direction: VIEWDIR=0.0000,0.0000,1.0000
Specify a view point or [Rotate] <display compass and tripod>: R↵
Enter angle in XY plane from X axis <current>: 45↵
Enter angle from XY plane <current>: 45↵
Regenerating model.
Command:
```

In Figure 2-8, the viewpoint is rotated 45° counterclockwise from the X axis and 45° from the XY plane. Notice in the command sequence above that no "distance" value is entered for the spherical coordinates.

Figure 2-8.
This view was created using the **Rotate** option of the **VPOINT** command. The rotation angles used are 45° *in the* XY plane and 45° *from* the XY plane.

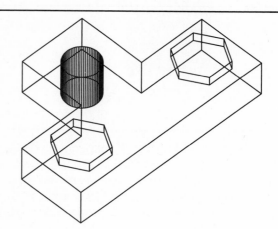

Introduction to the Cylindrical Coordinate System

The *cylindrical coordinate system* provides a method of point entry that specifies coordinate locations based on a cylindrical shape. Cylindrical coordinates are entered using three values. The first value represents the horizontal distance from the origin. The second value represents the angle in the XY plane. The third value represents a vertical, or Z, dimension, measured up from the polar coordinate in the XY plane. See Figure 2-9. An absolute cylindrical coordinate is entered as follows:

7.5<35,6

Like spherical coordinates, cylindrical coordinates can also be used as relative coordinates. For example, a point drawn with the relative spherical coordinate @1.5<30,4 means that the point is located 1.5 units from the last point, at an angle of 30° in the XY plane, and at a distance of 4 units up from the XY plane.

Using cylindrical coordinates

Cylindrical coordinates work well for attaching new objects to a cylindrical shape. An example of this is specifying coordinates for a pipe that must be attached to another pipe, or to a tank or vessel. In Figure 2-10, a pipe must be attached to a 12′ diameter tank at a 30° angle from horizontal and 2′-6″ above the floor.

Figure 2-9.
Cylindrical coordinates require a horizontal distance from the origin, an angle in the XY plane, and a Z dimension.

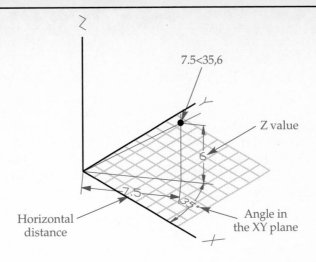

An attachment point can be easily created to begin the pipe run. To do so, move the UCS to the center of the tank. Then, set an appropriate point style and use the **POINT** command to locate the point with cylindrical coordinates. Begin as follows:

```
Command: UCS↵
Current ucs name: *WORLD*
Enter an option [New/Move/orthoGraphic/Prev/Restore/Save/Del/Apply/?/World]
<World>: M↵
Specify new origin point or [Zdepth] <0,0,0>: (pick the center point of the tank)
```

Placing the UCS origin at the center of the tank makes it easier to enter the exact coordinates of the pipe attachment location. Next, change the **PDMODE** system variable setting to 3, and proceed as follows:

```
Command: POINT↵
Current point modes: PDMODE=3 PDSIZE=0.0000
Specify a point: 6'<30,2'6↵
Command:
```

Look at Figure 2-10B. Notice that the attachment point is drawn using the current UCS, which is parallel to the bottom of the tank. A new UCS can be established so that the pipe can be attached at the UCS origin. See Figure 2-10C.

Figure 2-10.
A—A plan view of a tank shows the angle of the pipe attachment. B—A 3D view from the southeast quadrant shows the pipe attachment point located with cylindrical coordinates. C—The pipe is located on the tank using a new UCS.

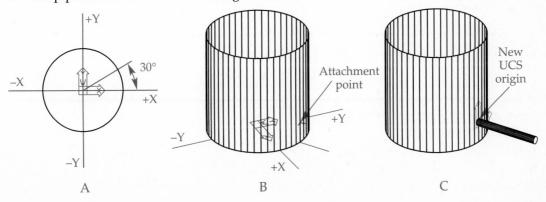

❑ Start a new drawing. Set the current elevation to 0 and the thickness to 3.
❑ Draw a 1.5″ diameter circle.
❑ Display a 3D view of the drawing using the **SW Isometric View** button on the **View** toolbar.
❑ Set a point style of your choice and use the **POINT** command to locate the following points on the surface of the extruded circle:
    ❑ Point 1 = <25,1.5
    ❑ Point 2 = <295,1.5
❑ Draw separate lines from Points 1 and 2 that project from the center of the circle, and extend 2″ from the surface of the extruded circle.
❑ Project new lines from each of the previous lines at 90° angles so that they intersect, as shown in the plan view below.
❑ Save the drawing as EX2-2.

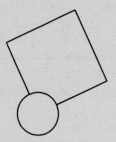

3D SURFACE MODELS

    In Chapter 1, you were introduced to the predrawn 3D surface-modeled objects supplied in AutoCAD. These objects can be accessed using the **Surfaces** toolbar or the **3D Objects** dialog box. The **Surfaces** toolbar displays buttons for all of the 3D objects, Figure 2-11. Picking **3D Surfaces...** from the **Surfaces** cascading menu in the **Draw** pull-down menu displays the **3D Objects** dialog box, Figure 2-12.

    The 3D objects you can select include a box, wedge, pyramid, cone, dome, dish, sphere, torus, and mesh. After making a selection, you only need to specify basic dimensions and an insertion location. The result is a surfaced 3D object. The **HIDE** command makes the object appear solid. Therefore, the design can be used in presentation and animation programs, such as Autodesk's 3D Studio MAX®. The next sections discuss AutoCAD's predefined 3D objects.

    Each of these objects is created as a 3D mesh and treated as a single object. If you wish to edit any part of the object, first use the **EXPLODE** command. After exploding, each object is made up of 3D faces.

Figure 2-11.
AutoCAD's predrawn 3D surface-modeled objects can be selected from the **Surfaces** toolbar.

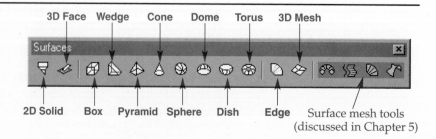

Figure 2-12.
The **3D Objects**
dialog box.

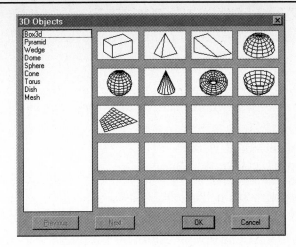

PROFESSIONAL TIP

If you prefer to work from the Command: prompt, you can use the **3D** command to select any of the 3D objects available in the **Surfaces** toolbar and **3D Objects** dialog box.

NOTE

AutoCAD creates two types of 3D shapes—solid primitives and surfaced wireframes. They are listed below:

Solid Primitives	Surfaced Wireframes
Box	Box
Cone	Cone
Cylinder	Dish
Sphere	Dome
Torus	Mesh
Wedge	Pyramid
	Sphere
	Torus
	Wedge

If you enter the name of one of the solid primitives listed above at the Command: prompt, the solid model version of that shape is created. If you want to use the surfaced wireframe version, access the **Surfaces** toolbar or the **3D Objects** dialog box, or enter 3D at the Command: prompt. You can also enter AI before the object name. For example, the following entry can be used to draw a surfaced wireframe version of a cone:

Command: **AI_CONE**↵

In this instance, "AI" refers to an "Autodesk Incorporated" AutoLISP command definition that is found in the 3d.lsp file. When you select a 3D object from the **Surfaces** toolbar, you will notice this entry on the command line. The underscore character (_) is used in the acad.mnu file to enable commands to be automatically translated in foreign language versions of AutoCAD.

Box

You can construct a surface-modeled box by picking the **Box** button on the **Surfaces** toolbar or highlighting the **Box** image in the **3D Objects** dialog box. You can also enter AI_BOX at the Command: prompt. You must provide the location of one corner, the box dimensions, and the rotation angle about the Z axis (with the first corner as the base). Enter the values using the keyboard or pick them with your pointing device.

```
Command: AI_BOX↵
Specify corner point of box: 3,3↵
Specify length of box: 1↵
Specify width of box or [Cube]: C↵
Specify rotation angle of box about the Z axis or [Reference]: 0↵
```

If you enter the **Cube** option, AutoCAD applies the value entered for the length to the width and height. If you enter a value for the width, you are prompted for the height. See Figure 2-13.

Figure 2-13.
A surface-modeled box requires a location for the first corner point, and values for the length, width, height, and rotation angle.

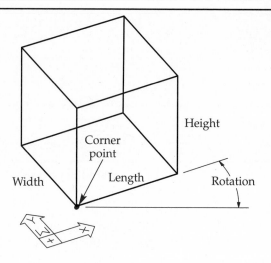

NOTE

The **BOX** command draws a solid 3D model of a box. This is different than the surface-modeled box discussed in this chapter. Solid models are discussed in Chapter 10.

Wedge

You can quickly create a right-angle, surface-modeled wedge by picking the **Wedge** button on the **Surfaces** toolbar, selecting the **Wedge** image in the **3D Objects** dialog box, or entering AI_WEDGE at the Command: prompt. You are then prompted for a corner of the wedge, followed by the length, width, height, and rotation angle. A wedge and its basic dimensions are shown in Figure 2-14.

```
Command: AI_WEDGE↵
Specify corner point of wedge: 6,3↵
Specify length of wedge: 3↵
Specify width of wedge: 2↵
Specify height of wedge: 2↵
Specify rotation angle of wedge about the Z axis: 15↵
Command:
```

Figure 2-14.
A surface-modeled
wedge requires a
corner point
location, length,
width, height, and
rotation angle.

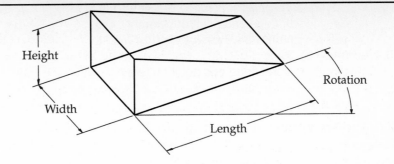

NOTE	The **WEDGE** command draws a solid 3D model of a wedge. This is different than the surface-modeled wedge discussed in this chapter. Solid models are discussed in Chapter 10.

Pyramid

Five varieties of surface-modeled pyramids are available in AutoCAD. You can draw three types of four-sided pyramids, Figure 2-15. You can also draw two types of three-sided pyramids called *tetrahedrons*.

To draw a pyramid, pick the **Pyramid** button on the **Surfaces** toolbar, select the **Pyramid** image in the **3D Objects** dialog box, or enter AI_PYRAMID at the Command: prompt. First, you must draw the base of the pyramid. When you have located the third point, you can draw a tetrahedron or enter the fourth point of the base. If you draw the fourth point on the base, you can then specify an apex point by default, or select from the two other four-sided options (**Ridge** and **Top**). When drawing the apex, use XYZ filters or enter an XYZ coordinate. The following example shows how to draw a four-sided pyramid with an apex:

```
Command: AI_PYRAMID↵
Specify first corner point for base of pyramid: 2,6↵
Specify second corner point for base of pyramid: @2,0↵
Specify third corner point for base of pyramid: @0,2↵
Specify fourth corner point for base of pyramid or [Tetrahedron]: @–2,0↵
Specify apex point of pyramid or [Ridge/Top]: .XY↵
of 3,7↵
(need Z): 3↵
Command:
```

The **Ridge** option requires two points to define the ridge at the top of the pyramid. When you enter this option after drawing the fourth point on the base, the last line drawn on the base is highlighted. This indicates that the first point of the ridge will begin perpendicular to the highlighted line. However, the first point does not need to touch the highlighted line.

Figure 2-15.
Three drawing
options are
available for
pyramids with four-
sided bases.

Pyramid Drawn
with an Apex

Ridge
Option

Top
Option

Specify apex point of pyramid or [Ridge/Top]: **R**↵
Specify first ridge end point of pyramid: **.XY**↵
of (*pick a point inside the highlighted line*)
(need Z): **3**↵
Specify second ridge end point of pyramid: **.XY**↵
of (*pick a point inside the second highlighted line*)
(need Z): **3**↵

The **Top** option creates a *truncated* (flattened) top. This option is similar to the **Ridge** option. However, a "rubber band" line is attached from the first corner of the pyramid base to the screen cursor. You are then prompted for the first corner point of the top of the pyramid. Use filters or XYZ coordinates to locate the top points. After the first top point is located, the rubber band line is attached to the second base point, and so on. When the fourth top point is located, the pyramid is complete.

PROFESSIONAL TIP
Try constructing pyramids in the plan view, using XYZ coordinates or filters. Your constructions will be more accurate, and you can easily see the symmetry or asymmetry required.

As mentioned earlier, a pyramid can also be drawn with a three-sided base. The resulting shape, called a tetrahedron, can have an apex or a flattened top. The following example illustrates how to construct a tetrahedron. Refer to Figure 2-16 as you proceed:

Command: **AI_PYRAMID**↵
Specify first corner point for base of pyramid: **2,2**↵
Specify second corner point for base of pyramid: **@3,0**↵
Specify third corner point for base of pyramid: **@0,3**↵
Specify fourth corner point for base of pyramid or [Tetrahedron]: **T**↵
Specify apex point of tetrahedron or [Top]: **.XY**↵
of (*pick the point projecting to Point P1 in the middle of the triangular base*)
(need Z): **3**↵

A truncated (flattened) top can be given to a tetrahedron by entering the **Top** option. Refer to Figure 2-16B.

Specify fourth corner point for base of pyramid or [Tetrahedron]: **T**↵
Specify apex point of tetrahedron or [Top]: **T**↵
Specify first corner point for top of tetrahedron: (*use filters to pick the first top point*)
Specify second corner point for top of tetrahedron: (*use filters to pick the second top point*)
Specify third corner point for top of tetrahedron: (*use filters to pick the third top point*)
Command:

Figure 2-16.
A—A tetrahedron is a pyramid with a three-sided base.
B—A truncated tetrahedron requires three pick points for the top surface.

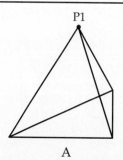

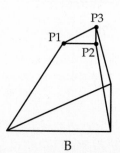

A   B

Cone

Pointed and truncated cones can be easily created in AutoCAD. Three dimensions are required for a cone—the base diameter, the top diameter, and the height. A pointed cone has a top diameter value of zero. A truncated cone has a top diameter value other than zero.

To draw a surface-modeled cone, pick the **Cone** button from the **Surfaces** toolbar, select the **Cone** image in the **3D Objects** dialog box, or enter AI_CONE at the Command: prompt:

Command: **AI_CONE**↵
Specify center point for base of cone: **3,3**↵
Specify radius for base of cone or [Diameter]: **1**↵
Specify radius for top of cone or [Diameter] <0>: **.15**↵
Specify height of cone: **2**↵
Enter number of segments for surface of cone <16>: ↵
Command:

If you want a pointed cone, simply press [Enter] when prompted for the top radius value. The two types of cones are shown in Figure 2-17.

Figure 2-17.
Surface-modeled cones can be truncated or pointed.

Truncated Cone   Pointed Cone

NOTE   The **CONE** command draws a solid 3D model of a cone. This is different than the surface-modeled cone discussed in this chapter. Solid models are discussed in Chapter 10.

Dome and Dish

A dome or a dish can be thought of as a hemisphere, or half of a sphere. If a dome is placed on top of a dish, a sphere is formed. When constructed, the top of the dome represents the north pole. The bottom of the dish represents the south pole. As discussed earlier in this chapter, a spherical object has longitudinal segments that run east and west around the circumference. Latitudinal segments run north and south. Refer to Figure 2-1A.

To draw a dome or dish, pick the **Dome** or **Dish** button from the **Surfaces** toolbar or select the **Dome** or **Dish** image in the **3D Objects** dialog box. You can also enter the following at the Command: prompt:

Command: **AI_DOME**↵ *(or **AI_DISH** to draw a dish)*
Specify center point of dome: *(pick a point)*
Specify radius of dome or [Diameter]: **2**↵
Enter number of longitudinal segments for surface of dome <16>: *(enter a value or press [Enter])*
Enter number of latitudinal segments for surface of dome <8>: *(enter a value or press [Enter])*
Command:

> **NOTE**
> The more segments you use for an object, the smoother the curved surface, but the longer the drawing regeneration time. Use as few segments as possible.

Sphere

AI_SPHERE

Surfaces toolbar

Sphere

A sphere requires the same basic dimensions specified for a dome or dish. Since the sphere is a complete globe, the default values for the number of latitudinal and longitudinal segments are the same.

To draw a surface-modeled sphere, pick the **Sphere** button on the **Surfaces** toolbar or the **Sphere** image in the **3D Objects** dialog box, or enter AI_SPHERE at the Command: prompt:

> Command: **AI_SPHERE**↵
> Specify center point of sphere: *(pick a center point)*
> Specify radius of sphere or [Diameter]: *(pick or enter a radius, or type D to provide a diameter)*
> Enter number of longitudinal segments for surface of sphere <16>: *(enter the number of segments and press [Enter])*
> Enter number of latitudinal segments for surface of sphere <16>: *(enter the number of segments and press [Enter])*
> Command:

Figure 2-18 shows three spheres composed of 8, 16, and 32 segments.

Figure 2-18.
Examples of surface-modeled spheres. The more segments in a sphere, the smoother it appears, but the longer it takes to regenerate.

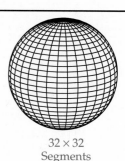

8×8
Segments

16×16
Segments

32×32
Segments

Torus

AI_TORUS

Surfaces toolbar

Torus

A *torus* resembles an inflated inner tube. See Figure 2-19. To draw a torus, you must enter values for the diameter (or radius) of the torus and the tube. The other dimensions required are the number of segments around the torus circumference and around the tube circumference. A torus can be drawn by picking the **Torus** button from the **Surfaces** toolbar, selecting the **Torus** image in the **3D Objects** dialog box, or entering AI_TORUS at the Command: prompt:

> Command: **AI_TORUS**↵
> Specify center point of torus: *(pick the center point)*
> Specify radius of torus or [Diameter]: **2**↵
> Specify radius of tube or [Diameter]: **.5**↵
> Enter number of segments around tube circumference <16>: ↵
> Enter number of segments around torus circumference <16>: ↵
> Command:

Figure 2-19.
To draw a torus, you must specify the radius (or diameter) values of the torus and the tube. You must also specify the number of segments around each.

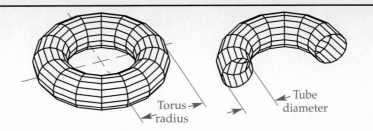

Torus → radius

Tube → diameter

3D CONSTRUCTIONS

There are several different types of construction methods used for 3D objects. These include 3D arrays, 3D polylines, and 3D faces. These constructions are covered in the next sections.

3D Object Arrays

The **3DARRAY** command allows you to array an object in 3D space. This command is very similar to the **ARRAY** command, but a third dimension is used. In a 3D array, as with a regular array, you must enter the number of rows and columns. However, you must also specify the number of *levels*, which represents the third (Z) dimension. There are two types of 3D arrays—rectangular and polar. The command sequence is similar to that used with the 2D array command, with two added prompts.

To create a 3D array, select **3D Array** from the **3D Operation** cascading menu in the **Modify** pull-down menu, or enter 3A or 3DARRAY at the Command: prompt. The following example creates a rectangular 3D array of a pyramid. See Figure 2-20.

3DARRAY
3A

Modify
➥ 3D Operation
➥ 3D Array

> Command: **3A** *or* **3DARRAY**⏎
> Select objects: *(pick the pyramid)*
> Select objects: ⏎
> Enter the type of array [Rectangular/Polar] <R>: ⏎
> Enter the number of rows (–––) <1>: **2**⏎
> Enter the number of columns (|||) <1>: **3**⏎
> Enter the number of levels (…) <1>: **3**⏎
> Specify the distance between rows (–––): **1.5**⏎
> Specify the distance between columns (|||): **1.5**⏎
> Specify the distance between levels (…): **1.5**⏎
> Command:

Figure 2-20.
A rectangular 3D array is made up of rows, columns, and levels.

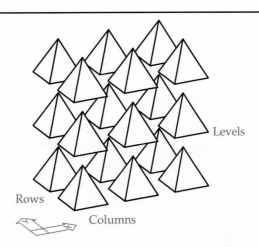

Levels

Rows

Columns

When creating a 3D polar array, you must enter an axis of rotation for the arrayed objects. The axis does not need to be a line in the XY plane. Any axis line can be used. The polar array of pyramids in Figure 2-21 can be created using the following command sequence:

```
Command: 3A or 3DARRAY↵
Select objects: (pick the pyramid)
Select objects: ↵
Enter the type of array [Rectangular/Polar] <R>: P↵
Enter the number of items in the array: 5↵
Specify the angle to fill (+=ccw, −=cw) <360>: −180↵
Rotate arrayed objects? [Yes/No] <Y>: N↵
Specify center point of array: (pick Point P1)
Specify second point on axis of rotation: (pick Point P2 in the XY plane)
Command:
```

In Figure 2-21, the 3D array is tilted 90° to the current UCS. This is because the axis of rotation defined for the 3D array is parallel to the XY plane of the current UCS.

Figure 2-21.
The axis of rotation in a 3D polar array can be defined as any line.

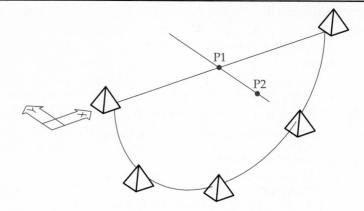

PROFESSIONAL TIP

Toolbar buttons defined for **3D Rectangular Array** and **3D Polar Array** can be used in a custom toolbar or added to an existing toolbar. Refer to Chapter 20 for information on customizing toolbars.

❑ Draw the following 3D objects using the dimensions indicated. Space them evenly in your drawing.

❑ Box	2 × 3 × 1.5h
❑ Wedge	3 × 1 × 1.25h
❑ Pyramid (with apex)	2 × 2 × 2.5h
❑ Pyramid (with ridged top)	2 × 2 × 2.5h
❑ Pyramid (truncated)	2 × 2 × 2.25h
❑ Tetrahedron (with apex)	2 × 2 × 1.5h
❑ Tetrahedron (truncated)	2 × 2 × 1.5h
❑ Cone (with apex)	Ø2 × 1.5h
❑ Cone (truncated)	Ø2 × 1.5h
❑ Dome	Ø2
❑ Dish	Ø2
❑ Sphere	Ø2.5
❑ Torus	Ø3 torus, Ø.5 tube

❑ Display the completed objects in three different 3D viewpoints. Use the **HIDE** command for each display.

❑ Save the drawing as EX2-3.

3D Polylines

The **3DPOLY** command is used to draw *3D polylines*. To access this command, pick **3D Polyline** from the **Draw** pull-down menu, or enter 3P or 3DPOLY at the Command: prompt. A 3D polyline is the same type of object as a regular polyline, with an added third (Z) dimension. Any form of coordinate entry is valid for drawing 3D polylines.

3DPOLY	
3P	
Draw	
➥ 3D Polyline	

> Command: **3P** *or* **3DPOLY**↵
> Specify start point of polyline: **4,3,6**↵
> Specify endpoint of line or [Undo]: **@2,0,1**↵
> Specify endpoint of line or [Undo]: **@0,2,1**↵
> Specify endpoint of line or [Close/Undo]: ↵
> Command:

The **Close** option is used to draw the final segment and create a closed shape. The **Undo** option removes the last segment without canceling the command.

The **PEDIT** command can be used to edit 3D polylines. The **PEDIT Spline curve** option is used to fit a B-spline curve to the 3D polyline. A regular 3D polyline and the same polyline fit with a B-spline curve are shown in Figure 2-22. The **SPLFRAME** system variable controls the display of the original polyline frame, and is either turned on (1) or off (0).

Figure 2-22.
A regular 3D polyline and the B-spline curve version after using the **PEDIT** command.

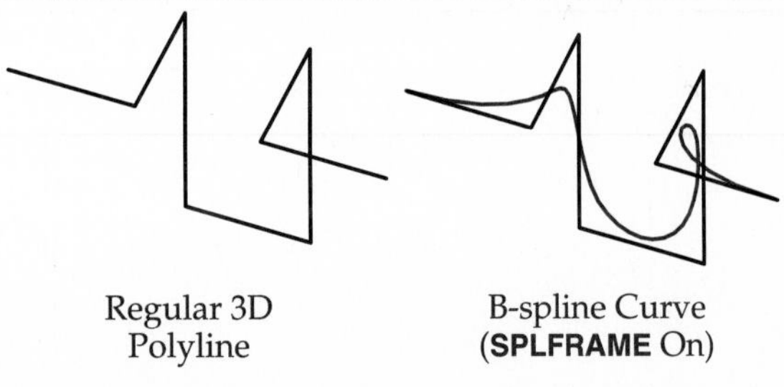

Regular 3D
Polyline

B-spline Curve
(**SPLFRAME** On)

3D Faces

Surfaces that appear solid and not as wireframes are called *3D faces*. These are created using the **3DFACE** command. This command was introduced in Chapter 1.

You may recall that a 3D face can only have three or four straight edges. In Chapter 1, you created a "T"-shaped box using 3D faces. When the **HIDE** command was used, the intersecting edge between the two faces was visible. This line can be made invisible. The next section briefly describes the procedure.

Creating invisible 3D face edges

The **3DFACE** command allows you to remove, or hide, edges that should not appear as lines on a surface. This is done with the **Invisible** option. Before picking the first point of the invisible edge, enter I for the **Invisible** option. The following example illustrates how to do this (refer to Figure 2-23):

```
Command: 3F or 3DFACE↵
Specify first point or [Invisible]: (pick Point P1)
Specify second point or [Invisible]: (pick Point P2)
Specify third point or [Invisible] <exit>: I↵
Specify third point or [Invisible] <exit>: (pick Point P3)
Specify fourth point or [Invisible] <create three-sided face>: (pick Point P4)
Specify third point or [Invisible] <exit>: I↵
Specify third point or [Invisible] <exit>: (pick Point P5)
Specify fourth point or [Invisible] <create three-sided face>: (pick Point P6)
Specify third point or [Invisible] <exit>: (pick Point P7)
Specify fourth point or [Invisible] <create three-sided face>: (pick Point P8)
Specify third point or [Invisible] <exit>: ↵
Command:
```

Figure 2-23.
The **Invisible** option of the **3DFACE** command hides edges that are normally visible.

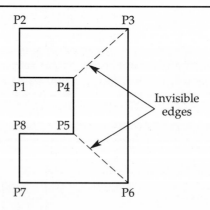

If the **SPLFRAME** system variable is set to its default value of 0, invisible edges are *not* shown. If **SPLFRAME** is set to 1, invisible edges *are* shown. When AutoCAD's screen menus are configured to display, the **SPLFRAME** system variable can be set using the **ShowEdge** and **HideEdge** options that appear in the **3Dface:** menu, Figure 2-24. The functions of these options are as follows:

- **ShowEdge. SPLFRAME** is set to 1 and hidden edges are shown. Selecting this option displays the following message:

    Invisible edges will be shown after next Regeneration.

- **HideEdge. SPLFRAME** is set to 0 and edges drawn with the **Invisible** option are *not* shown. Selecting this option displays the following message:

    Invisible edges will be HIDDEN after next Regeneration.

Figure 2-24.
When AutoCAD is configured to display screen menus, the **ShowEdge** and **HideEdge** options can be used to control the visibility of invisible edges.

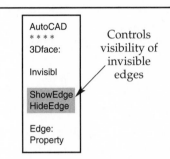

PROFESSIONAL TIP

The following procedure is an easy and time-saving way to create 3D faces. Using it, you do not need to use the **Invisible** option and the **SPLFRAME** system variable.

- Construct your 3D wireframe model using any of the AutoCAD drawing and editing commands.
- Create a separate layer for 3D face objects and assign it a rarely used color. You might name the layer Faces.
- With the Faces layer set current, draw all required 3D faces on your wireframe model. Do not be concerned with any visible edges. Set the appropriate running object snap modes.
- Once your model is completely faced, turn off the Faces layer. Then, use the **HIDE** command.

A layer that is turned off is still evaluated when using the **HIDE** command. Your resulting model will display correctly with all hidden lines removed. In addition, since the Faces layer is not turned on, none of the unwanted 3D face edges are shown.

GUIDELINES FOR WORKING WITH 3D DRAWINGS

Working in 3D, like working with 2D drawings, requires careful planning to produce the desired results efficiently. The following guidelines can be used when working in 3D.

Planning

✓ Determine the type of final drawing you need. Then, choose the method of 3D construction that best suits your needs.

✓ When drawing objects requiring only one pictorial view, draw in isometric mode. This is the quickest and most versatile method. Ellipses and arcs are easy to work with in isometric drawings.

✓ It is best to use AutoCAD's 3D commands to construct objects and layouts that need to be viewed from different angles for design purposes.

✓ Construct only the details needed for the function of the drawing. This saves space and time, and makes visualization much easier.

✓ Use the **Midpoint**, **Endpoint**, and **Intersection** object snap modes with the **LINE** and **3DFACE** commands.

✓ Keep in mind that when grid mode is enabled, the resulting pattern on screen appears at the current elevation and on the XY plane of the current UCS.

✓ Create layers having different colors for different drawing objects. Turn them on and off as needed, or freeze those not being used.

Editing

✓ Use the **Properties** window to change the color, layer, linetype, or thickness of 3D objects.

✓ Use grips or the **STRETCH** or **LENGTHEN** commands in a 3D view to change only one dimension of an object (see Chapter 6). Use the **SCALE** command in the 3D view to change the size of the entire object proportionally.

✓ Do as much editing as possible from a 3D viewpoint. It is quicker and the results are seen immediately.

Displaying

✓ Use the **HIDE** command to help in visualizing complex drawings.

✓ To change views quickly, use the preset views in the **View** toolbar, the **View** dialog box, or the **3D Views** cascading menu in the **View** pull-down menu.

✓ Use the **VIEW** command to create and save 3D views for quicker pictorial displays. This allows you to avoid having to use the **VPOINT**, **3DORBIT**, or **DVIEW** commands.

✓ Freeze unwanted layers before displaying objects in 3D, and especially before using **HIDE**. Also, remember that AutoCAD still regenerates layers that are turned off.

✓ Before using **HIDE**, zoom in on the part of a drawing to display. This saves time in regenerating the view because only the objects that are visible are regenerated.

✓ You may have to slightly move objects that touch or intersect if the display removes a line you need to see or plot.

Chapter Test

Answer the following questions on a separate sheet of paper.

1. Explain the differences between spherical and cylindrical coordinates.
2. A new point is to be drawn 4.5″ from the last point. It is to be located at a 63° angle *in* the XY plane, and at a 35° angle *from* the XY plane. Write the proper spherical coordinate notation.
3. Write the proper cylindrical coordinate notation for a point located 4.5″ in the horizontal direction from the origin, 3.6″ along the Z axis, and at a 63° angle in the XY plane.

4. How do you select one of AutoCAD's predrawn 3D surface-modeled shapes? What shapes are available?
5. When using the **3DFACE** command, how do you indicate that an edge is to be invisible?
6. How many different types of pyramids can you draw with the **AI_PYRAMID** command (*not* including the tetrahedrons)?
7. How does the **SPLFRAME** system variable affect the **3DFACE** command?
8. Define *longitudinal segments* in relation to drawing a dome or dish.
9. What command can you enter at the keyboard to draw a surface-modeled cone?
10. Which command is used to draw a surface-modeled tetrahedron?
11. What two measurements are required to draw a torus?
12. Name the system variable and values that are used to control the following visibility options used with the **3DFACE** command.
    A. **ShowEdge**
    B. **HideEdge**
13. Name the command that is used to draw 3D polylines.

Drawing Problems

For Problems 1–4, draw each object as a wireframe. Then, use the **3DFACE** *command to place surfaces on all sides of the objects. Measure the objects directly to obtain the necessary dimensions. Plot the drawings at a 3:1 scale with hidden lines removed. Save the drawings as P2-(problem number).*

1.

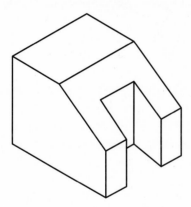

2.

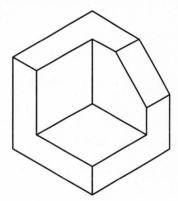

3.

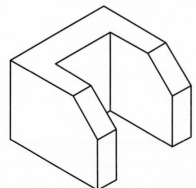

4.

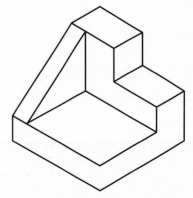

For Problems 5–9, draw each object using the dimensions given. Use 3D objects to create the models. Use grips and editing commands to aid in construction, and remove hidden lines. Do not dimension the objects. Save the drawings as P2-(problem number).

5.

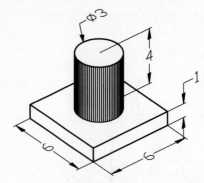

Pedestal #1

6.

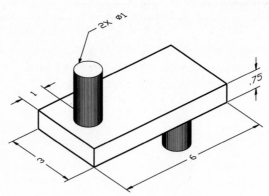

Pivot Bracket

7.

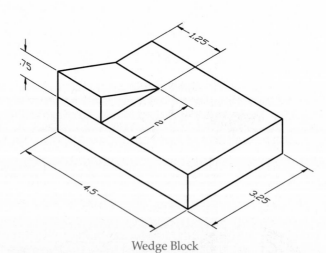

Wedge Block

8.

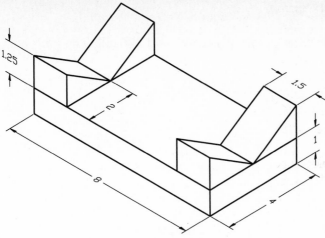

V-Block Guide

9.

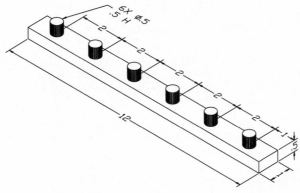

Pin Bar

10. Draw the Ø8" pedestal shown .5" thick. Four Ø.75" feet are centered on a 7" diameter circle and are .5" high. Use elevation and thickness to assist in creating this model. Save the drawing as P2-10.

Pedestal #2

11. Four wedges, each 3" long, 1" wide, and 1" high, support this Ø10" globe. Each wedge sits .8" away from the center of the Ø12" circular base. The base is .5" thick. Save the drawing as P2-11.

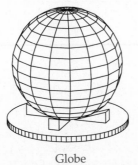

Globe

*For Problems 12–17, construct 3D models of each of the objects shown. Use only the 3D surface-modeled objects provided on the **Surfaces** toolbar. Construct each object using the specific instructions given. Save the drawings as P2-(problem number).*

12. The table legs (A) are 2″ square and 17″ tall. The table top (B) is 24″ × 36″ × 1″.

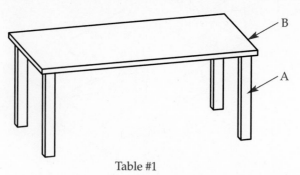

Table #1

13. The table legs (A) for the large table are ⌀2″ and 17″ tall. The table top (B) is 24″ × 36″ × 1″. The table legs (C) for the small table are ⌀2″ and 11″ tall. The table top (D) is 24″ × 14″ × 1″.

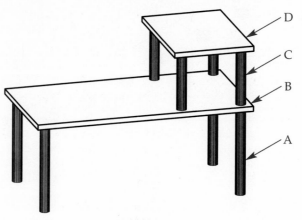

Table #2

14. The spherical objects (A) are ⌀4″. Object B is 6″ long and ⌀1.5″.

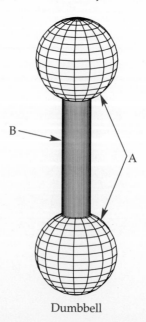

Dumbbell

15. Object A is Ø8" at the base, Ø7" at the top, and is 1" tall. Object B is Ø5" and 7" tall. Object C is Ø2" and 6" tall. Object D is .5" × 8" × .125", and there are four pieces. Object E is Ø18" at the base, Ø6" at the top, and is 12" tall.

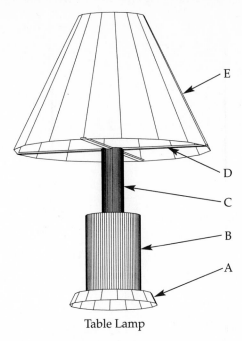

Table Lamp

16. Objects A and B are 5' high brick walls. The walls are two courses of brick thick. Research the dimensions of standard brick and draw accordingly. Wall B is 7' long and Wall A is 5' long. Lamps are placed at each end of the walls. Object C is Ø2" and 8" tall. Object D is Ø10".

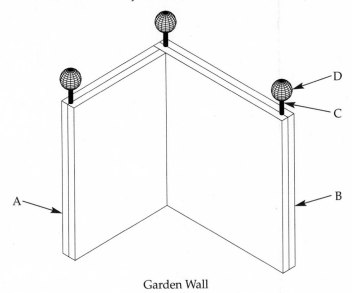

Garden Wall

17. Object A is ∅18″ and 1″ tall. Object B is ∅1.5″ and 6′ tall. Object C is ∅6″ and .5″ tall. Object D is a ∅10″ sphere. Object E is an L-shaped bracket to support the shade to Object C. There are four items. Draw these an appropriate size. Object F has a ∅22″ base and is 12″ tall.

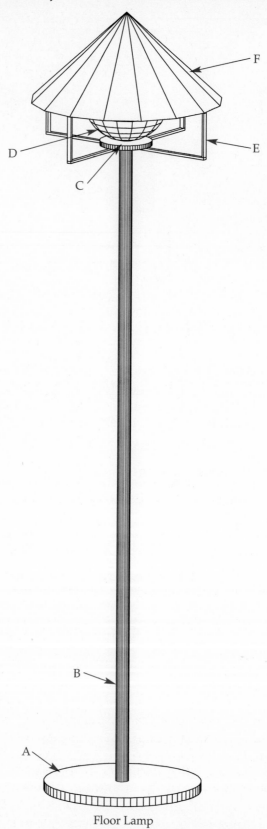

Floor Lamp

CHAPTER 3

Understanding User Coordinate Systems

Learning Objectives

After completing this chapter, you will be able to:

- Describe the function of the world and user coordinate systems.
- Move the coordinate system to any surface.
- Rotate the coordinate system to any angle.
- Change the coordinate system to match the plane of a geometric object.
- Save and manage named user coordinate systems.
- Restore and use named user coordinate systems.
- Change and manage user coordinate systems in various viewports.
- Control user coordinate system icon visibility in viewports using settings and variables.

Part of the flexibility of 3D construction with AutoCAD is the ability to create and use different 3D coordinate systems. All drawing and editing commands can be used in any coordinate system you create. Objects that are drawn will always be parallel to the plane, or coordinate system, you are working in. Therefore, you must be able to change your point of view so it is perpendicular to the plane you want to draw on. Your view is then said to be "plan" to that plane. This chapter provides you with detailed instructions in constructing and working with coordinate systems. This will allow you to draw any type of 3D shape that you need.

INTRODUCTION TO USER COORDINATE SYSTEMS

AutoCAD User's Guide 5

All points in a drawing or on an object are defined with XYZ coordinate values measured from the 0,0,0 origin. Since this system of coordinates is fixed and universal, AutoCAD refers to it as the *world coordinate system (WCS)*. The *user coordinate system (UCS)*, on the other hand, can be defined at any orientation desired. The **UCS** command is used to change the origin, position, and rotation of the coordinate system to match the surfaces and features of an object under construction.

Changes in the UCS are reflected in the orientation and placement of the UCS icon symbol at the lower-left corner of the graphics window. The available options for creating, managing, and displaying a UCS, as well as the UCS icon symbol, are found in the **Tools** pull-down menu and related cascading menus, Figure 3-1A. In addition, UCS options can be selected from the **UCS** flyout in the **Standard** toolbar, and from the **UCS** and **UCSII** toolbars. See Figure 3-1B.

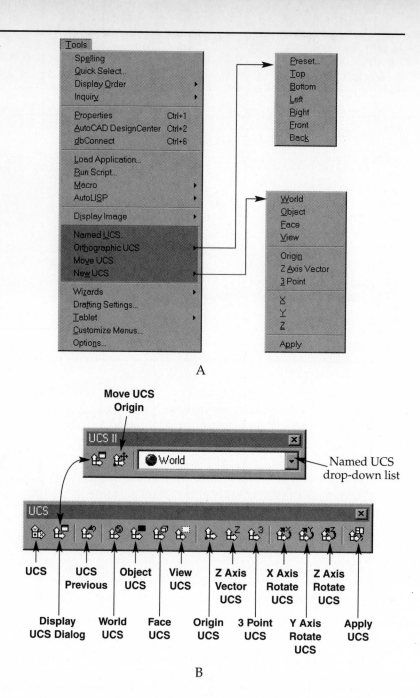

Figure 3-1.
UCS options can be accessed in several ways. A—The UCS selections in the **Tools** pull-down menu. B—The **UCS** toolbars. Most of these buttons are also contained in the **UCS** flyout in the **Standard** toolbar.

Four UCS selections in the **Tools** pull-down menu provide access to all UCS options. Each of these selections is introduced here and discussed in detail later in this chapter.

- **Named UCS.** This item displays the **UCS** dialog box, where the three tabs described below allow you to work with a variety of UCS options and settings.
  - **Named UCSs.** This tab allows you to create, rename, set current, and delete named UCSs. You can also pick the WCS and previous UCS. See Figure 3-2A.
  - **Orthographic UCSs.** This tab allows you to select one of six preset UCSs and adjust its depth. See Figure 3-2B.
  - **Settings.** This tab allows you to adjust UCS and UCS icon settings. See Figure 3-2C.

Figure 3-2.
A—The **Named UCSs** tab allows you to create, rename, set current, and delete a named UCS.
B—In the **Orthographic UCSs** tab you can select one of six preset UCSs, and adjust its depth.
C—The **Settings** tab allows you to adjust UCS and UCS icon settings.

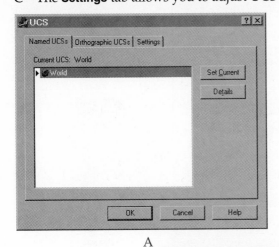

A

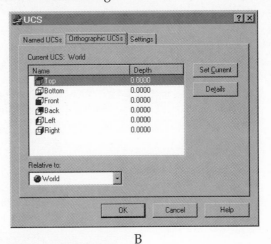

B

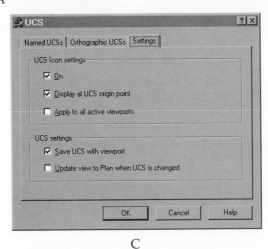

C

- **Orthographic UCS.** This menu item displays a cascading menu with a list of the six preset UCSs. The **Preset...** option in the cascading menu displays the **UCS** dialog box with the **Orthographic UCSs** tab on top.
- **Move UCS.** Selecting this menu item allows you to specify a new UCS origin point or adjust the Z depth of the UCS.
- **New UCS.** This menu item displays many of the UCS options found in the **UCS** toolbar and the **UCS** flyout. See Figure 3-3.

Standard Orthographic UCS Options

The standard UCS orthographic options match the six basic drafting orthographic views. With the current UCS as the top view (plan), all other views are arranged as shown in Figure 3-4. In addition, the **Orthographic UCSs** tab of the **UCS** dialog box also displays the standard faces.

For 2000i Users...

In AutoCAD 2000i, the UCS symbol on the UCS buttons is different from the symbol used in AutoCAD 2000. AutoCAD 2000 uses the 2D UCS symbol, while AutoCAD 2000i uses the 3D UCS symbol. However, the function of the buttons is identical in both versions.

Figure 3-3.
The **New UCS** cascading menu in the **Tools** pull-down menu contains many of the UCS options found in the **UCS** toolbar and the **UCS** flyout.

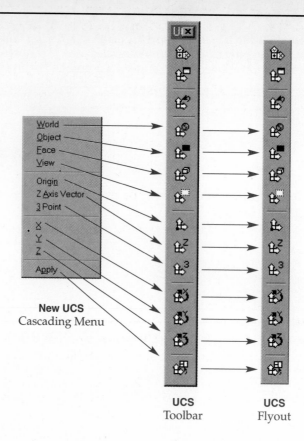

New UCS Cascading Menu

UCS
Toolbar

UCS
Flyout

Figure 3-4.
The standard UCS orthographic options coincide with the six basic orthographic views. Note: The UCS icon has been moved for illustration purposes.

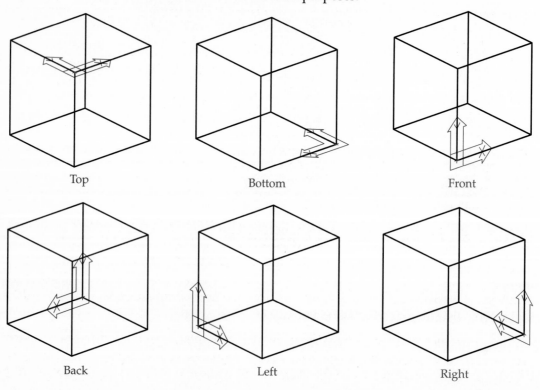

Top

Bottom

Front

Back

Left

Right

AutoCAD and its Applications—Advanced

The UCS icon will not automatically move to a point on the model, as shown in Figure 3-4, when an orthographic UCS is selected. After picking a standard orthographic UCS, you must use the **Origin UCS** button in the **Standard** toolbar, or the **UCS Move** option to relocate the origin of the current UCS.

WORKING WITH UCS BASICS

Once you understand a few of the basic options of user coordinate systems, creating 3D models becomes an easy and quick process. The following sections show how to display the UCS icon, change the UCS in order to work on different surfaces of a model, and name and save a UCS.

Displaying the UCS Icon

The symbol that identifies the orientation of the coordinate system is called the *UCS icon*. It is usually located in the lower-left corner of the viewport. The display of this symbol is controlled by the **UCSICON** command. If your drawing does not require viewports and altered coordinate systems, you may want to turn the icon off.

For 2000i Users...

The appearance of the UCS icon can be modified in AutoCAD 2000i. For a complete discussion, refer to *Modifying the UCS Icon*, beginning on page 629.

```
Command: UCSICON↵
Enter an option [ON/OFF/All/Noorigin/ORigin] <current>: OFF↵
Command:
```

The icon disappears until you turn it on again using the **UCSICON** command. You can also turn the icon on or off and change the icon origin using the options under **UCS Icon** in the **Display** cascading menu in the **View** pull-down menu. Refer to Figure 3-5.

Figure 3-5.
The UCS icon can be turned on/off and set to the origin in the **UCS Icon** cascading menu.

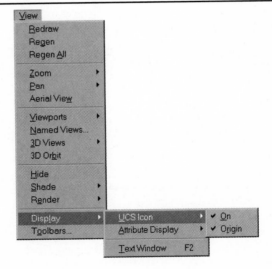

Changing the Coordinate System

To construct a three-dimensional object, you must visualize shapes at many angles. Different planes are needed to draw features on angled surfaces. It is easy to rotate the UCS and UCS icon to match any surface on an object. The following example illustrates this process.

The object in Figure 3-6 has a cylinder on the angled surface. The base of the object is five units long and four units wide. The height is five units, and the cut horizontal

---

Figure 3-6.
This object can be constructed by changing the orientation of the coordinate system. You will construct this object in this chapter.

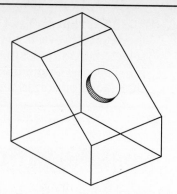

and vertical surfaces are each two units long. The cylinder is 1.5 units in diameter with a height of .35 units.

The first step in creating this model is to draw the base in the plan view. Use the world coordinate system. See Figure 3-7A. Now, display the object in the SE isometric view.

With the base of the object constructed, draw the vertical lines. You can draw the vertical lines using XYZ filters. However, it is easier to rotate the UCS so that the vertical lines can be drawn as if in the front view. Rotate the UCS so that the Y axis is pointing up from the bottom surface of the object and the X axis is pointing to the right side. When this happens, the Z axis is pointing out of the screen to the left.

Rotate the UCS on the X axis by picking the **X Axis Rotate UCS** button from the **UCS** toolbar, selecting **X** from the **New UCS** cascading menu in the **Tools** pull-down menu, or using the **X** option of the **UCS** command as follows:

Tools
↦ New UCS
X

UCS
toolbar

X Axis Rotate UCS

> Command: **UCS**↵
> Current ucs name: *current*
> Enter an option [New/Move/orthoGraphic/Prev/Restore/Save/Del/Apply/?/World]
>   <World>: **X**↵
> Specify rotation angle about X axis <90>: **90**↵
> Command:

The UCS icon changes to reflect the new UCS. See Figure 3-7B. Notice that X (or Y or Z) can be entered even though this is not listed as an option on the command line. This allows you to specify a rotation without having to first specify **New**. Also notice that the UCS icon no longer has the letter *W* in it. This is an indication that the coordinate system is a user coordinate system and not the world coordinate system.

Figure 3-7.
A—The base of the object is constructed on the plan view of the WCS.
B—The UCS icon is rotated 90° around the X axis to draw the sides. Notice how the UCS icon has changed.

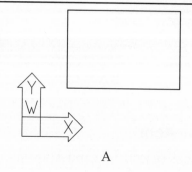

A

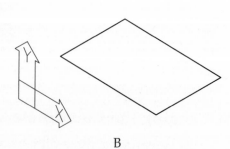

B

The next step is to draw the front face of the object, Figure 3-8A. Use the **LINE** command and your choice of tools and methods (snap and grid, direct distance entry, coordinate entry, object snaps) to complete the side.

The lines just drawn represent the front face of the object. First, copy them to the back edge. Since the back edge is behind the current drawing plane, you must use object snap, AutoTracking, or coordinate entry to specify the location where the lines are copied. Lines connecting the two surfaces can then be drawn. You may want to draw one line and then copy it to the other locations. See Figure 3-8B and Figure 3-8C.

Figure 3-8.
A—The front surface of the wedge is added using the **LINE** command. B—The front surface is copied on the Z axis to create the back surface. C—The object is completed by connecting the front and back surfaces with lines.

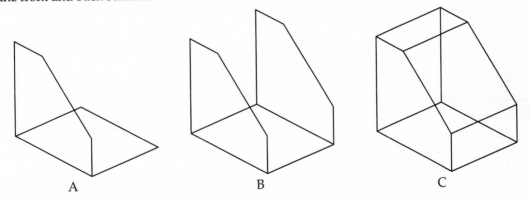

A   B   C

Saving a Named UCS

Once you have created a new UCS that can be used to construct a model, it is best to save it for future use. You can save a UCS in the **UCS** dialog box. First pick **Named UCS...** from the **Tools** pull-down menu. Then, right-click on the entry Unnamed. See Figure 3-9. Pick the **Rename** option in the shortcut menu, then type the new name and press [Enter]. Use this method to save a new UCS or to rename an existing one. A UCS can also be saved using the **Save** option of the **UCS** command:

> Command: **UCS**↵
> Current ucs name: *current*
> Enter an option [New/Move/orthoGraphic/Prev/Restore/Save/Del/Apply/?/World]
>   <World>: **S**↵
> Enter name to save current UCS or [?]: *(enter a name for the UCS, such as* FRONT*)*
> Command:

Now the coordinate system is saved and can be easily recalled for future use.

Figure 3-9.
Create a new UCS
by right-clicking to
rename the Unnamed
UCS.

Right-click
on a UCS name
to display the
shortcut menu

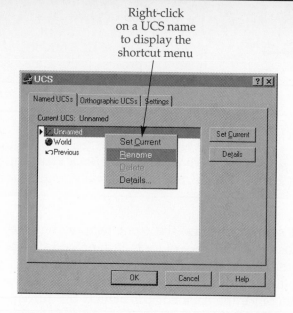

Aligning the UCS with an Angled Surface

The cylinder in Figure 3-6 needs to be drawn on the angled surface. In 2D drafting, an angled surface is seen in its true shape and size only when projected to an auxiliary view. An auxiliary view places your line of sight perpendicular to the angled surface. This means that you see the angled surface as a plan view.

AutoCAD draws objects aligned with the plan view of the current UCS. For the construction in Figure 3-8A, the plan view of the UCS looks like Figure 3-10. A plan view is always perpendicular to your line of sight.

Notice that the UCS icon has exactly the same orientation as the vertical and horizontal lines of the object. The UCS and the front surface are parallel, and your line of sight is perpendicular to those planes. Therefore, if you draw the cylinder with this UCS, it will be perpendicular to this view. You must align the UCS with the angled surface of the object to correctly draw the cylinder.

The **3point** option of the **UCS** command can be used to change the UCS to any angled surface. This option requires that you locate a new origin, a point on the positive X axis, and a point on the positive Y axis. To use this option, pick the **3 Point UCS** button in the **UCS** toolbar, select **New UCS**, then **3 Point** from the **Tools** pull-down menu, or use the **3point** option of the **UCS** command. Refer to Figure 3-11 for pick points as you use the following command sequence. Use the **Endpoint** or **Intersection** object snap to select points that are not on the current XY plane.

Tools
➡ New UCS
   ➡ 3 Point

UCS
toolbar

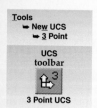

3 Point UCS

Figure 3-10.
Planes
perpendicular to the
XY plane appear as
lines in the plan
view.

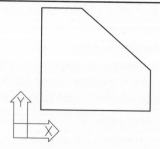

Figure 3-11.
A new UCS can be established by picking three points. P1 is the origin, P2 is the positive X axis, and P3 is the positive Y axis.

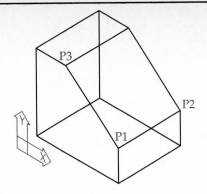

Command: **UCS.**↵
Current ucs name: *current*
Enter an option [New/Move/orthoGraphic/Prev/Restore/Save/Del/Apply/?/World] <World>: **3.**↵
Specify new origin point: <0,0,0>: *(pick P1)*
Specify point on positive portion of X–axis <10.0000,0.0000,–2.0000>: *(pick P2)*
Specify point on positive–Y portion of the UCS XY plane <9.0000,1.0000,–2.0000>: *(pick P3)*
Command:

NOTE Notice that 3 can be entered even though this is not listed as an option on the command line. This allows you to specify a location without having to first specify **New**.

After you pick P3, the UCS icon changes its orientation to align with the angled surface of the wedge. Any coordinate locations you enter will be relative to the new origin. The UCS icon may still appear at the lower-left corner of the view, depending on the current setting for **UCSICON**. To move the icon to the origin of the new UCS, use the **Origin** option of the **UCSICON** command or check **Origin** after picking **UCS Icon** in the **Display** cascading menu of the **View** pull-down menu. The icon is now located on the origin of the user coordinate system.

The cylinder can be drawn in the isometric (3D) view or plan to the current UCS. For this example, the current 3D view is used. First set the thickness. Then, draw the cylinder using the **CIRCLE** command. In this example, AutoCAD's AutoTracking feature is used to locate the center of the face. First set **Midpoint** as a running object snap and turn object snap tracking on.

Command: **ELEV.**↵
Specify new default elevation <0.0000>: ↵
Specify new default thickness <0.0000>: **.35.**↵
Command: **C** or **CIRCLE.**↵
Specify center point for circle or [3P/2P/Ttr (tan tan radius)]: *(acquire the midpoint of a line on the side of the face)*
(acquire the midpoint of the line at the bottom of the face)
Specify radius of circle or [Diameter] <current>: **.75.**↵
Command: ↵

The circle appears in its correct orientation on the angled surface. All edges and features can be seen, Figure 3-12A. The cylinder appears solid when **HIDE** is used, Figure 3-12B.

Figure 3-12.
A—The completed wireframe wedge shows the properly placed cylinder.
B—When **HIDE** is used, the cylinder is solid while the rest of the object is a wireframe.

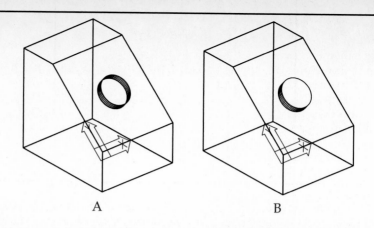

A   B

❑ Construct the 3D object shown using the techniques discussed in this section. Do not include dimensions. Rotate the UCS as needed.
❑ Save the drawing as EX3-1.

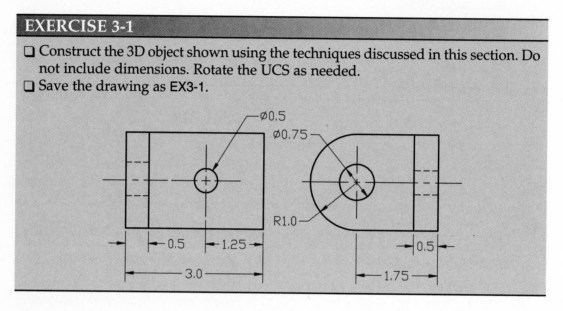

Drawing Wireframe "Holes"

Wireframe holes can be created by drawing a circle and copying it to a new location. To add a hole to the lower surface of the object in Figure 3-12, first move the UCS. Use the **3point** option of the **UCS** command. Place the new UCS on the lower-right vertical surface of the object using the pick points shown in Figure 3-13A.

Set the elevation and thickness to zero before you draw any objects. Then, draw the first circle using AutoTracking as follows.

> Command: **CIRCLE**⏎
> Specify center point for circle or [3P/2P/Ttr (tan tan radius)]: *(acquire the midpoint of a line on the side of the face)*
> *(acquire the midpoint of the line at the bottom of the face)*
> Specify radius of circle or [Diameter] <current>: **.5**⏎
> Command:

Figure 3-13B shows the new circle. Since the UCS is aligned with the lower-right vertical surface, the circle can be copied using a negative Z value. This produces the appearance of a wireframe "hole." You can copy the circle using the **COPY** command with coordinate entry or filters, or by using grips. To use grips, first pick the circle to display the grips. Select one of the grips to make it hot, then copy the circle as described on the next page.

```
**STRETCH**
Specify stretch point or [Base point/Copy/Undo/eXit]: C↵
**STRETCH (multiple) **
Specify stretch point or [Base point/Copy/Undo/eXit]: @0,0,–1↵
**STRETCH (multiple) **
Specify stretch point or [Base point/Copy/Undo/eXit]: ↵
Command:
```

The wireframe hole is shown in Figure 3-13C.

Figure 3-13.
A—Use the **3point** option to set the UCS parallel to the lower-right vertical surface.
B—The first circle representing the hole is drawn. C—The completed wireframe hole.

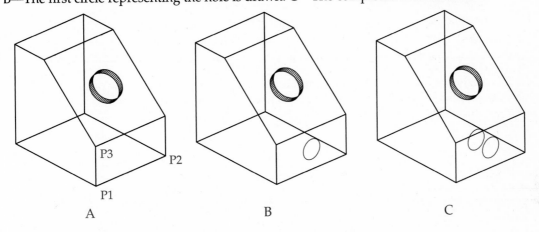

ADDITIONAL WAYS TO CHANGE THE UCS

There are other ways to change the UCS. These options include selecting a new Z axis, picking a new origin for the UCS, rotating the Y and Z axes, and setting the UCS to an existing object.

Selecting a New Z Axis

The **ZAxis** option of the **UCS** command allows you to select the origin point and a point on the positive Z axis. Once the new Z axis is defined, AutoCAD sets the new X and Y axes. Figure 3-14A shows the current UCS on the model from Figure 3-13. You must use an object snap mode to select points P1 and P2 because they are not in the XY plane. Pick **New UCS** and then **Z Axis Vector** from the **Tools** pull-down menu, or pick **Z Axis Vector UCS** from the **UCS** toolbar or the **UCS** flyout. You can also enter the **UCS** command as follows. Notice that ZA for **ZAxis** can be entered directly without first entering N for **New**.

```
Command: UCS↵
Current ucs name: current
Enter an option [New/Move/orthoGraphic/Prev/Restore/Save/Del/Apply/?/World]
<World>: ZA↵
Specify new origin point <0,0,0>: (use an object snap mode to pick P1)
Specify point on positive portion of Z–axis <current>: (use an object snap mode to
    pick P2)
Command:
```

The UCS icon now appears as shown in Figure 3-14B. Notice that the UCS icon is at the origin. If the **Noorigin** option of the **UCSICON** command is used, the icon appears in the lower-left corner of the drawing area.

The same option can be used to quickly move the UCS to the front plane of the wedge, Figure 3-14C. Select point P2 as the origin and press [Enter] to accept the default coordinates of the second prompt. The default coordinates are used because the Z axis does not change. The XY plane is simply moved along the Z axis.

Command: **UCS**↵
Current ucs name: *current*
Enter an option [New/Move/orthoGraphic/Prev/Restore/Save/Del/Apply/?/World]
    <World>: **ZA**↵
Specify new origin point <0,0,0>: *(use an object snap mode to pick P2)*
Specify point on positive portion of Z–axis <*current*>: ↵
Command:

Figure 3-14.
A—The **ZAxis** option of the **UCS** command requires that you select the new origin (P1) and a point on the positive Z axis (P2). B—The UCS icon is located at the new origin. C—The same process can be used to set the front plane as the new UCS.

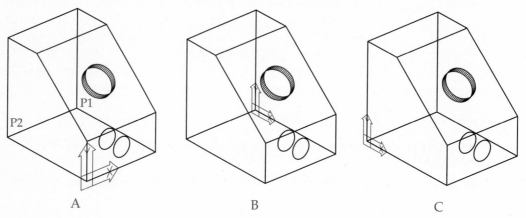

A   B   C

Selecting a New Origin

Tools
↳ **New UCS**
 ↳ **Origin**

**UCS
toolbar**

Origin UCS

Tools
↳ **Move UCS**

**UCS II
toolbar**

Move UCS

The **Origin** option and the **Move** option of the **UCS** command set a new origin point. The **Origin** option can also be accessed by picking the **Origin UCS** button from the **UCS** toolbar or by selecting **New UCS** and then **Origin** from the **Tools** pull-down menu. The **Move** option can also be accessed by picking **Move UCS** from the **Tools** pull-down menu or by picking the **Move UCS Origin** button in the **UCS II** toolbar.

Command: **UCS**↵
Current ucs name: *current*
Enter an option [New/Move/orthoGraphic/Prev/Restore/Save/Del/Apply/?/World]
    <World>: **O**↵
Specify new origin point <0,0,0>: *(pick the new origin)*
Command:

The origin of the UCS moves to the specified point. The XY plane remains parallel to that of the current UCS. Figure 3-15 shows the UCS moved to three different origin points using the **Origin** option. Notice how all of the new locations remain parallel to the current UCS. All coordinate measurements begin at the new UCS origin.

Figure 3-15.
The UCS icon
remains parallel to
the current UCS
when you move the
origin using the
Origin option.

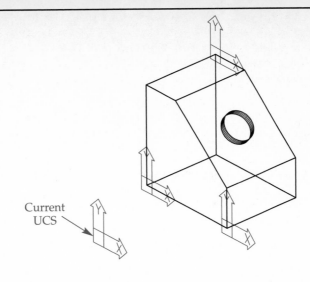

Current
UCS

Rotating the X, Y, and Z Axes

Earlier, you rotated the current UCS about the X axis. This same technique is used to rotate the Y or Z axis. Rotating a single axis is useful when you need to rotate the UCS to match the angle of a surface on a part. Figure 3-16 shows the direction of rotation around each axis when a 90° angle is specified. You can also enter negative angles. The following sequence rotates the Z axis 90°. If you are having trouble visualizing the X, Y, and Z axis rotations, try using the right-hand rule. The right-hand rule is covered in Chapter 1.

```
Command: UCS↵
Current ucs name: current
Enter an option [New/Move/orthoGraphic/Prev/Restore/Save/Del/Apply/?/World]
    <World>: N↵
Specify origin of new UCS or [ZAxis/3point/OBject/Face/View/X/Y/Z] <0,0,0>: Z↵
Specify rotation angle about Z axis <90>: 90↵
Command:
```

**PROFESSIONAL
TIP**

You do not need to enter N for **New** when using the **UCS** command. The options **ZAxis**, **3point**, **OBject**, **View**, **X**, **Y**, and **Z** can all be entered at the first prompt. The **Face** option, however, cannot.

Figure 3-16.
The UCS icon can be rotated around the X, Y, and Z axes by entering an angle. The angle can be positive or negative, as appropriate.

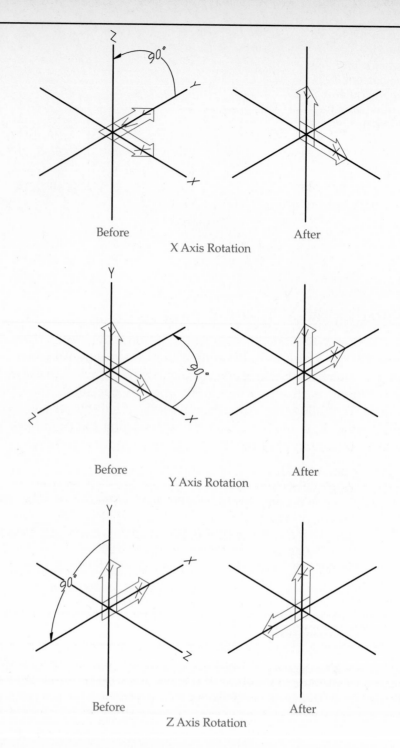

Before — After
X Axis Rotation

Before — After
Y Axis Rotation

Before — After
Z Axis Rotation

Setting the UCS to an Existing Object

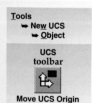

Tools
↳ New UCS
  ↳ Object

UCS
toolbar

Move UCS Origin

The **OBject** option of the **UCS** command can be used to define a new UCS on any object, except a 3D solid, 3D polyline, 3D mesh, spline, multiline, region, or ellipse. This option can also be accessed by picking the **Object UCS** button on the **UCS** toolbar or by selecting **New UCS** and then **Object** in the **Tools** pull-down menu.

There are certain rules that control the orientation of the UCS. For example, if you select a circle, the center point becomes the origin of the new UCS. The pick point on the circle determines the direction of the X axis. The Y axis is relative to X, and the UCS Z axis is the same as the Z axis of the object selected. In the following example, the cylinder in Figure 3-15 is selected for the new UCS.

Command: **UCS**↵
Current ucs name: *current*
Enter an option [New/Move/orthoGraphic/Prev/Restore/Save/Del/Apply/?/World]
　　<World>: **OB**↵
Select object to align UCS: *(pick the top edge of the cylinder)*
Command:

The UCS icon probably looks like the one shown in Figure 3-17A. This may not be what you expected. The X axis is determined by the pick point on the circle. In this case, the pick point was in the lower-left quadrant of the cylinder. To rotate the UCS in the current plane so the X and Y axes are parallel with the sides of the object, use the **ZAxis** option. Refer to Figure 3-17B.

Command: **UCS**↵
Current ucs name: *current*
Enter an option [New/Move/orthoGraphic/Prev/Restore/Save/Del/Apply/?/World]
　　<World>: **ZA**↵
Specify new origin point <0,0,0>: **CEN**↵
of *(pick the cylinder)*
Specify point on positive portion of Z–axis <0.0000,0.0000,1.3500>: ↵
Command:

Figure 3-17.
A—The X axis of the UCS icon is placed in relation to the pick point of the circle.
B—The UCS is rotated parallel to the object with the **ZAxis** option.

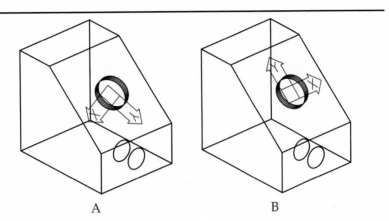

A　　　　　　　　　　B

Setting the UCS to the Face of a 3D Solid

The **Face** option of the **UCS** command allows you to orient the UCS to any face on a 3D solid object. This option works on solids only, not on wireframes or surfaced objects. Access this option by picking the **Face UCS** button in the **UCS** toolbar, by selecting **New UCS** and then **Face** in the **Tools** pull-down menu, or by entering the **UCS** command, then the **New** option, and then the **Face** option.

Tools
↳ New UCS
　↳ Face

UCS toolbar

Face UCS

After you have selected a face on a 3D solid, you have the options of moving the UCS to the adjacent face or flipping the UCS 180° on either the X or Y, or both, axes. Once you achieve the UCS orientation you want, press [Enter] to accept. Notice in Figure 3-18 how many different UCS orientations can be selected for a single face.

Command: **UCS**↵
Current ucs name: *current*
Enter an option [New/Move/orthoGraphic/Prev/Restore/Save/Del/Apply/?/World]
　　<World>: **N**↵
Specify origin of new UCS or [ZAxis/3point/OBject/Face/View/X/Y/Z] <0,0,0>: **F**↵
Select face of solid object: *(pick a face on the object)*
Enter an option [Next/Xflip/Yflip] <accept>: ↵
Command:

Figure 3-18.
Several different UCSs can be selected using the **Face** option of the **UCS** command. This option can only be used on solids.

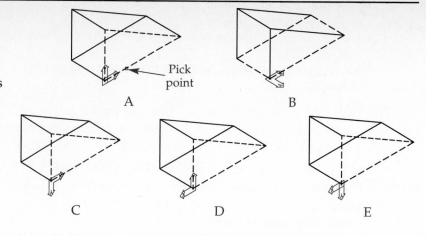

Pick point

A   B

C   D   E

Setting the UCS Perpendicular to the Current View

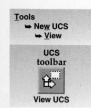

Tools
→ Ne**w** UCS
  → **V**iew

UCS
toolbar

View UCS

You may need to add notes or labels that appear horizontal in the current view to a 3D drawing, such as that shown in Figure 3-19. This is easy to do using the **View** option of the **UCS** command. This option can also be accessed by picking the **View UCS** button in the **UCS** toolbar or selecting **New UCS** and then **View** in the **Tools** pull-down menu.

> Command: **UCS**↵
> Current ucs name: *current*
> Enter an option [New/Move/orthoGraphic/Prev/Restore/Save/Del/Apply/?/World]
> <World>: **V**↵
> Command:

The UCS rotates to a position so that the new XY plane is perpendicular to the current view. Now, anything added to the drawing appears horizontal in the current view.

Figure 3-19.
The **View** option allows you to place text horizontally in the current view.

WIREFRAME OBJECT

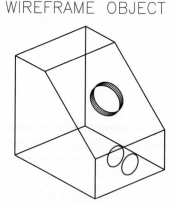

Applying the Current UCS to a Viewport

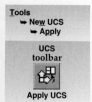

Tools
→ Ne**w** UCS
  → **A**pply

UCS
toolbar

Apply UCS

The **Apply** option of the **UCS** command allows you to apply the UCS in the current viewport to any or all model space or paper space viewports. This is different from the **View** option in that the **View** option applies the UCS to the current viewport only. Using the **Apply** option, you can have a different UCS displayed in every viewport, or you can apply one UCS to all viewports.

Access the **Apply** option by picking the **Apply UCS** button in the **UCS** toolbar, by selecting **New UCS** and then **A**pply in the **Tools** pull-down menu, or by entering the **UCS** command.

Command: **UCS**↵
Current ucs name: *current*
Enter an option [New/Move/orthoGraphic/Prev/Restore/Save/Del/Apply/?/World]
   <World>: **A**↵
Pick viewport to apply current UCS or [All] <current>: *(pick a viewport or type* **A**
   for **All***)*
Command:

Preset UCS Orientations

DDUCSP
UCP

Tools
→ **Orthographic
   UCS**
→ **Preset...**

AutoCAD has six preset orientations that can be selected from the **Orthographic UCSs** tab of the **UCS** dialog box. To use one of these, select **Preset...** from the **Orthographic UCS** cascading menu in the **Tools** pull-down menu, or enter UCP or DDUCSP at the Command: prompt. See Figure 3-20.

Six preset UCS orientations are listed in the **Orthographic UCSs** tab. These are **Top** (or plan), **Bottom**, **Front**, **Back**, **Left**, and **Right**. The selection made in the **Relative to:** drop-down list at the bottom of the tab specifies whether the orthographic UCS is relative to a named UCS or absolute to the WCS. For example, suppose you have a saved UCS named Tilt that is rotated 30° about the X axis of the WCS. If you set the **Front** UCS current relative to the named UCS Tilt, the new UCS is also tilted from the WCS. If **Front** is set current relative to the WCS, the new UCS is not tilted from the WCS. See Figure 3-21.

The Z value, or depth, of a preset UCS can be changed in the **Orthographic UCSs** tab of the **UCS** dialog box. First, pick the UCS you wish to change. Then, right-click on the name and pick **Depth** from the shortcut menu, Figure 3-22A. This displays the **Orthographic UCS depth** dialog box. See Figure 3-22B. You can either enter a new depth value or specify the new location on screen by picking the **Select new origin** button. Once the new depth has been selected, it is reflected in the preset UCS list.

Figure 3-20.
The **Orthographic UCSs** tab of the **UCS** dialog box has six preset UCS configurations.

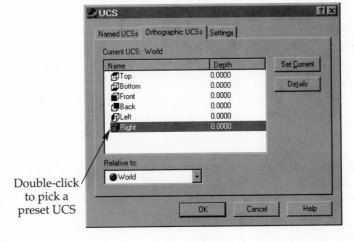

Double-click to pick a preset UCS

Figure 3-21.
The **Relative to:** drop-down list entry in the **Orthographic UCSs** tab determines whether the orthographic UCS is based on a named UCS or the WCS. A—Relative to the WCS. B—Relative to a selected named UCS.

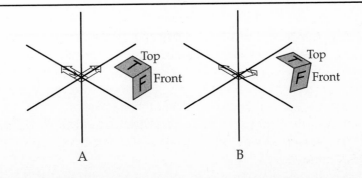

Figure 3-22.
A—The Z value, or depth, of a preset UCS can be changed by right-clicking on the name of a UCS and selecting **Depth**.
B—In the **Orthographic UCS depth** dialog box, enter a new depth value or pick the **Select new origin** button to pick the new location on the screen.

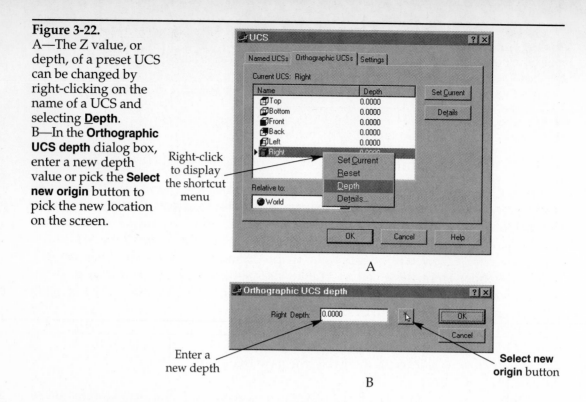

Right-click to display the shortcut menu

A

Enter a new depth

Select new origin button

B

Working with Named User Coordinate Systems

Tools
➥ Named UCS...

UCS toolbar

Display UCS Dialog

User coordinate systems can be created, renamed, selected, and deleted using the **Named UCSs** tab of the **UCS** dialog box, Figure 3-23. This tab is accessed by picking **Named UCS...** from the **Tools** pull-down menu, picking the **Display UCS Dialog** button in the **UCS** toolbar, or entering UC, UCSMAN (UCS manager), or DDUCS (dynamic dialog UCS) at the Command: prompt.

The **Named UCSs** tab contains the **Current UCS:** list box. This list box contains names of all saved coordinate systems plus **World**. If other coordinate systems have been used in the current drawing session, **Previous** appears in the list. **Unnamed** appears if the current coordinate system has not been named. To make any of the listed coordinate systems active, highlight the name and pick the **Set Current** button.

A list of coordinate and axis values of the highlighted UCS can be displayed by picking the **Details** button. This displays the **UCS Details** dialog box shown in Figure 3-24.

Figure 3-23.
The **UCS** dialog box allows you to rename, list, delete, and set current an existing UCS.

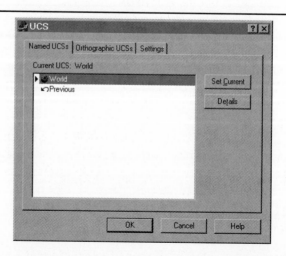

Figure 3-24.
The **UCS Details** dialog box displays the coordinate values of the current UCS. Here, the WCS is the current coordinate system.

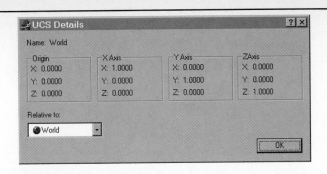

EXERCISE 3-2

❑ Construct the 3D object shown below. Do not include dimensions or labels.
❑ Rotate and relocate the UCS as needed.
❑ Create and save named user coordinate systems as follows.

Label	UCS name
A	Front
B	Right

❑ Save the drawing as EX3-2.

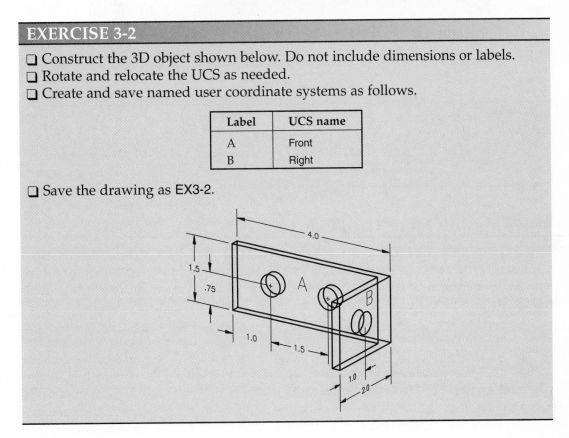

Setting an Automatic Plan Display

After changing the UCS, a plan view is often needed to give you a better feel for the XYZ directions. This makes it easier to decide the best viewpoint orientation to pick. AutoCAD can be set to automatically make your view of the drawing plan to the current UCS. This is especially useful if you will be changing UCSs often but want to work in a plan view.

The **UCSFOLLOW** system variable is used to automatically display a plan view of the current UCS. When it is set to 1, a plan view is automatically created in the current viewport when the UCS is changed. Viewports are discussed in Chapter 4. The default setting of **UCSFOLLOW** is 0 (off). The **UCSFOLLOW** variable can be set for each viewport individually. The following example sets **UCSFOLLOW** to 1 for the current viewport so that a plan view is automatically generated.

    Command: **UCSFOLLOW**↵
    Enter new value for UCSFOLLOW <0>: **1**↵
    Command:

Notice that the view did not change to a plan view. The **UCSFOLLOW** variable generates the plan view only after the UCS is changed.

Figure 3-25.
The **Settings** tab of
the **UCS** dialog box
allows you to
control the UCS
icon settings.

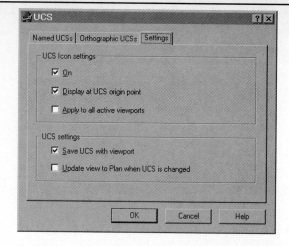

PROFESSIONAL TIP

To get the plan view displayed without changing the UCS, type PLAN at the Command: prompt. The **PLAN** command is discussed in Chapter 7.

Working with More Than One UCS

You can create and use as many user coordinate systems as needed to construct your model or drawing. AutoCAD allows you to name coordinate systems for future use. Several options of the **UCS** command allow you to work with multiple coordinate systems. These are explained below.

- **?.** This option switches the display to the text window and lists all of the named coordinate systems. The display includes the coordinate values of the XYZ axes of each UCS relative to the current UCS. The name of the current UCS is given first. If the current UCS does not have a name and is different than the WCS, *NO NAME* appears.
- **Prev.** This option allows you to display previously used coordinate systems. AutoCAD remembers ten previous systems in both model space and paper space, for a total of twenty. You can step back through them in the same way that **ZOOM Previous** displays previous zooms.
- **Restore.** Entering this option requires the name of the UCS you wish to restore. If you forget the names, enter a question mark (?) to list saved coordinate systems. Only the orientation of the UCS will change; the views remain the same.
- **Save.** Save a UCS by entering a name having 255 characters or less. Numbers, letters, blank spaces, dollar signs ($), hyphens (–), and underscores (_) are valid.
- **Del.** Enter the name of the UCS to be deleted. You can use wild card characters and a question mark (?), or delete a list by separating the names with commas.
- **World.** This option resets the world coordinate system (WCS) as the current UCS.

UCS Settings and Variables

As mentioned earlier in this chapter, the **UCSFOLLOW** system variable allows you to change how an object is displayed in relation to the UCS. There are also system variables that display a variety of information about the current UCS. These variables include the following.

- **UCSFOLLOW.** Has a value of 0 or 1. When set to 1, it displays a plan view when the UCS is changed. This feature is discussed in Chapter 4.
- **UCSNAME.** (Read only) Displays the name of the current UCS.
- **UCSORG.** (Read only) Displays the XYZ origin value of the current UCS.
- **UCSXDIR.** (Read only) Displays the XYZ value of the X axis direction of the current UCS.
- **UCSYDIR.** (Read only) Displays the XYZ value of the Y axis direction of the current UCS.

UCS options and variables can also be managed by using the **Settings** tab of the **UCS** dialog box. See Figure 3-25. The two areas of this tab and their settings are explained below.

- **UCS icon settings**.
  - **On.** If checked, the UCS icon is displayed in the current viewport. The **UCSICON** command is set to a value of 1. If unchecked, **UCSICON** is set to 0.
  - **Display at UCS origin point.** If checked, the UCS icon is displayed at the origin of the current UCS in the current viewport. If this option is not checked, the UCS icon is displayed at the lower-left corner of the viewport. The **Origin** option of the **UCSICON** command also turns this feature on. The **Noorigin** option of **UCSICON** turns it off.
  - **Apply to all active viewports.** When this option is activated, the UCS icon settings above are applied to all active viewports in the drawing.
- **UCS settings**.
  - **Save UCS with viewport.** If checked, the current UCS settings are saved with the viewport, and the **UCSVP** system variable is set to 1. This setting can be either on or off in each viewport in the drawing. Viewports in which this setting is turned off, or unchecked, will always display the UCS settings of the current active viewport.
  - **Update view to Plan when UCS is changed.** If checked, the view in the current viewport is changed to a plan view whenever the UCS is changed in any viewport. This setting controls the **UCSFOLLOW** variable.

Chapter Test

Answer the following questions on a separate sheet of paper.

1. Define the meaning of WCS.
2. What is a user coordinate system (UCS)?
3. What command controls the display of the user coordinate system icon?
4. What is the function of the **3point** option of the **UCS** command?
5. How do you create a display perpendicular to the current UCS?
6. How is the UCS icon moved to the origin of the current coordinate system?
7. When you use the **Object** option of the **UCS** command, how does AutoCAD determine the X axis if you pick a circle for the new UCS?
8. How do you move the UCS along the current Z axis?
9. What is the function of the **Object** option of the **UCS** command?
10. The **Face** option of the **UCS** command can be used on what types of objects?
11. When is the **View** option of the **UCS** command used?
12. What is the function of the **Apply** option of the **UCS** command?
13. How can you make sure that a view will always be plan to the current UCS?
14. How do you access the **Orthographic UCSs** tab of the **UCS** dialog box?
15. What command displays the **UCS** dialog box?
16. What appears in the **Named UCSs** tab of the **UCS** dialog box if the current UCS has not been named?

Drawing Problems

Problems 1–3. These problems are engineering design sketches. They are the types of sketches a drafter is expected to work from in a real-world situation. Therefore, they may contain dimensioning errors and some information may be incomplete. It is up to you to supply appropriate information as needed.

1. This is a concept sketch of a desk organizer. Create a 3D drawing, either wireframe or surfaced, using the dimensions given. Create new UCSs as needed. Length dimensions of the compartments are up to you. Plot your drawing to scale on a B-size sheet of paper. Save the drawing as P3-1.

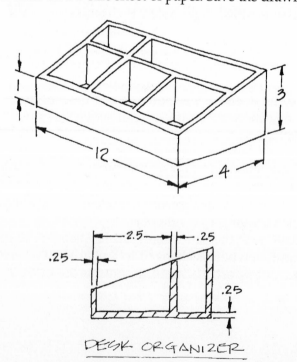

DESK ORGANIZER

AutoCAD and its Applications—Advanced

2. This is a concept sketch of a desk pencil holder. Create a 3D wireframe drawing using the dimensions given. Create new UCSs as needed. Plot your drawing to scale on a B-size sheet of paper. Save the drawing as P3-2.

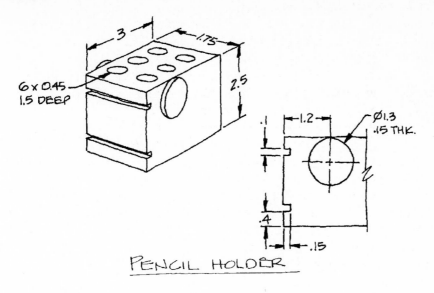

PENCIL HOLDER

3. This is an engineering sketch of a window blind mounting bracket. Create a 3D drawing using the dimensions given. Create new UCSs as needed. Plot two views of your drawing to scale on a C-size sheet of paper. Save the drawing as P3-3.

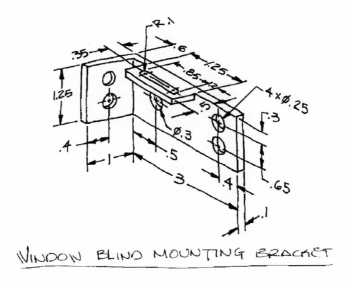

WINDOW BLIND MOUNTING BRACKET

4. This is a two-view orthographic drawing of a window valance mounting bracket. Convert it to a 3D wireframe drawing. Use the dimensions given. Similar holes have the same offset dimensions. Create new UCSs as needed. Plot two views of your drawing to scale on a C-size sheet of paper. Save the drawing as **P3-4**.

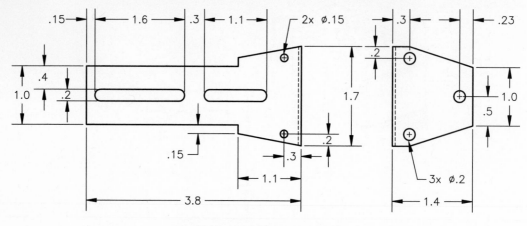

MATERIAL THICKNESS = .125"

5. This is an orthographic drawing of a light fixture bracket. Convert it to a 3D wireframe drawing. Use the dimensions given. Similar holes have the same offset dimensions. Create new UCSs as needed. Plot two views of your drawing to scale on a C-size sheet of paper. Save the drawing as **P3-5**.

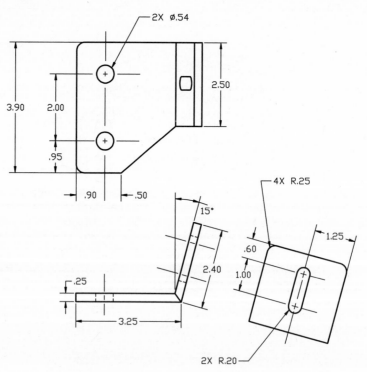

Problems 6–8. These problems are mechanical parts. Create a 3D wireframe drawing of each part. Do not dimension the model. Plot the finished drawings on B-size paper.

6.

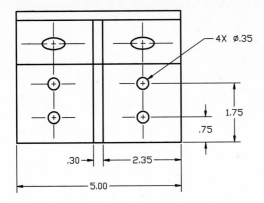

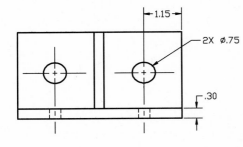 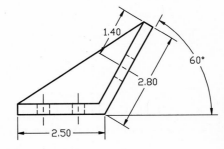

Angle Bracket

7.

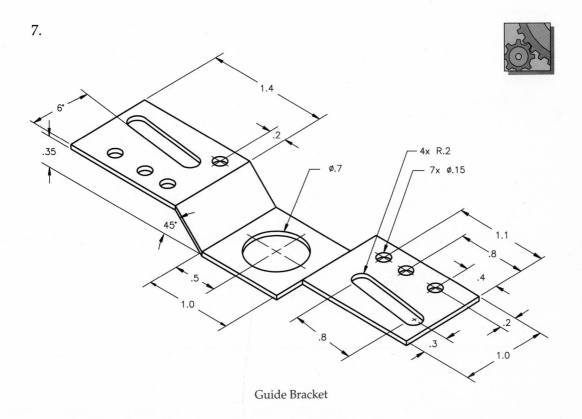

Guide Bracket

8.

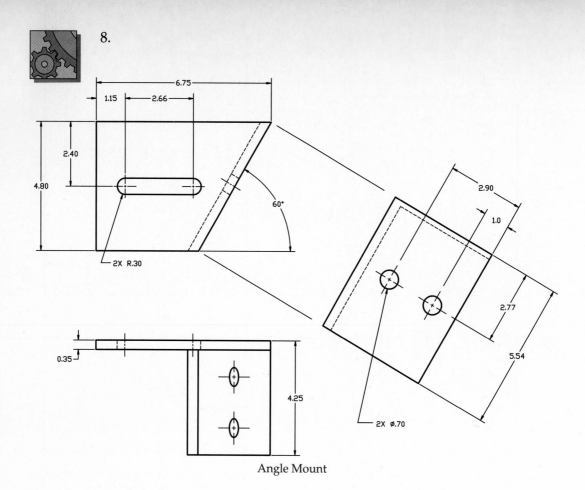

Angle Mount

Using Model Space Viewports

Learning Objectives

After completing this chapter, you will be able to:

- Describe the function of model space viewports.
- Create and save a variety of viewport configurations.
- Alter the current viewport configuration.
- Construct a drawing using multiple viewports.

A variety of views can be displayed in a drawing at one time using model space viewports. This is useful when constructing 3D models. Using the **VPORTS** command, you can divide the drawing area into two or more smaller segmented areas. These areas are called *viewports.* Each viewport can be configured to display a different 2D or 3D view of the model.

The *active viewport* is the viewport where the model is constructed. Any viewport can be made active, but only one can be active at a time. As objects are added or edited, the results are shown in all viewports. A variety of viewport configurations can be saved and recalled as needed. This chapter discusses the use of viewports and shows how they can be used for 3D constructions.

UNDERSTANDING VIEWPORTS

The AutoCAD drawing area can be divided into a maximum of 64 viewports. However, this is impractical due to the small size of each viewport. Four viewports is usually the maximum number practical to display at one time. The number of viewports you need depends on the model you are drawing. Each viewport can show a different view of an object. This makes it easier to construct 3D objects.

NOTE	The **MAXACTVP** (maximum active viewports) system variable sets the number of viewports that can be used at one time. The initial value is 64.

There are two types of viewports used in AutoCAD. The type of viewport created depends on whether it is defined in model space or paper space. *Model space* is the drawing space, or mode, where the drawing is constructed. *Paper space* is the space where a drawing is laid out to be plotted. Viewports created in model space are called *tiled viewports*. Viewports created in paper space are called *floating viewports*.

Model space is active by default when you enter AutoCAD. Model space viewports are created with the **VPORTS** command. These viewports cannot be plotted because they are for display purposes only. Tiled viewports are not AutoCAD objects. They are referred to as *tiled* because the edges of each viewport are placed side to side, as with floor tile, and they cannot overlap.

Floating viewports are used to lay out the views of a drawing before plotting. They are described as *floating* because they can be moved around and overlapped. Paper space viewports are defined objects, and they can be edited. These viewports can be thought of as "windows" cut into a sheet of paper to "see into" model space. You can then insert, or *reference*, different scaled drawings (views) into these windows. For example, architectural details or sections and details of complex mechanical parts may be referenced. Detailed discussions of paper space viewports are provided in Chapters 9, 10, and 24 of *AutoCAD and its Applications—Basics*.

The **VPORTS** command is used to create viewports in a paper space layout. You can also use the **MVIEW** command. The process using the **VPORTS** command is very similar to that used to create model space viewports, which is discussed next.

CREATING VIEWPORTS

Creating model space viewports is similar to working with a multiview layout in manual drafting. In a manual multiview layout, several views are drawn on the same sheet. You can switch from one view to another simply by moving your pencil. With model space viewports, you simply pick with your pointing device in the viewport you wish to work in. The picked viewport becomes active. Using viewports is a good way to construct 3D models because all views are updated as you draw. However, viewports are also good for creating 2D drawings.

The project you are working on determines the number of viewports needed. Keep in mind that the more viewports you display on your screen, the smaller the viewports. Small viewports may not be useful to you. Four different viewport configurations are shown in Figure 4-1. As you can see, when 16 viewports are displayed, the viewports become very small. Normally, two to four viewports are used.

VPORTS

View
→ Viewports
→ New
Viewports...

Standard
toolbar

Viewports
toolbar

Layouts
toolbar

Display Viewports
Dialog

A layout of one to four viewports can be quickly created by using the **Viewports** dialog box, or by selecting from the options in the **Viewports** cascading menu of the **View** pull-down menu. See Figure 4-2. The **Viewports** dialog box is accessed by entering VPORTS at the Command: prompt. A list of preset viewport configurations is provided in the **New Viewports** tab, Figure 4-3. You can access this tab automatically by picking the **Display Viewports Dialog** button from the **Standard**, **Viewports**, or **Layouts** toolbar. You can also select **New Viewports...** from the **Viewports** cascading menu.

There are twelve preset viewport configurations from which to choose, including six different options for three viewports. See Figure 4-4. When you pick the name of a configuration in the **Standard viewports:** list, the viewport arrangement is displayed in the **Preview** area. After you have made a selection, you can save the configuration by entering a descriptive name in the **New name:** text box, and then picking **OK**. When the **Viewports** dialog box closes, the configuration is displayed on screen.

Figure 4-1.
A—A configuration of two vertical viewports. B—Two horizontal viewports. C—AutoCAD's default arrangement of three viewports, with the largest viewport positioned at right. D—Sixteen viewports.

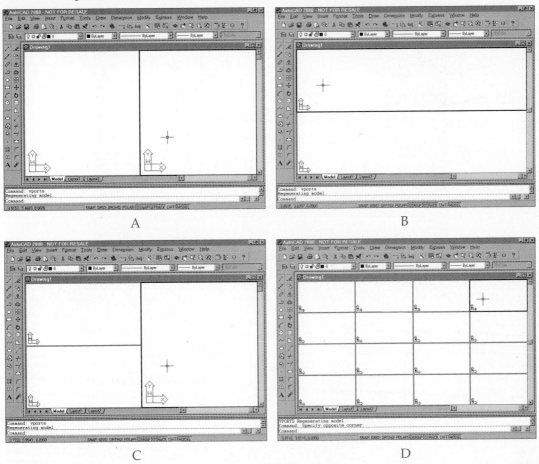

A

B

C

D

Figure 4-2.
Viewport configuration options can be selected from the **Viewports** cascading menu in the **View** pull-down menu.

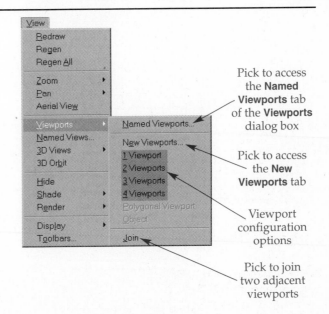

Pick to access the **Named Viewports** tab of the **Viewports** dialog box

Pick to access the **New Viewports** tab

Viewport configuration options

Pick to join two adjacent viewports

Figure 4-3.
Viewports are created using the **New Viewports** tab of the **Viewports** dialog box.

Enter a name to save a configuration

Preset viewport configuration options

Image preview of selected configuration

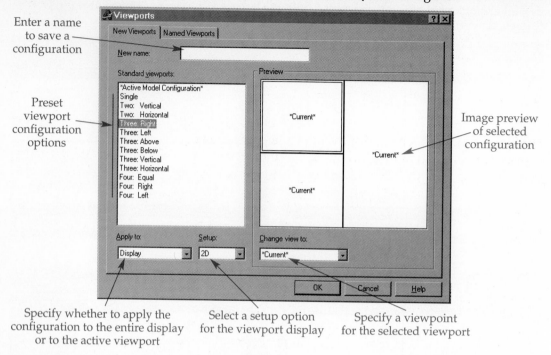

Specify whether to apply the configuration to the entire display or to the active viewport

Select a setup option for the viewport display

Specify a viewpoint for the selected viewport

Figure 4-4.
Twelve preset tiled viewport configurations are provided in the **Viewports** dialog box.

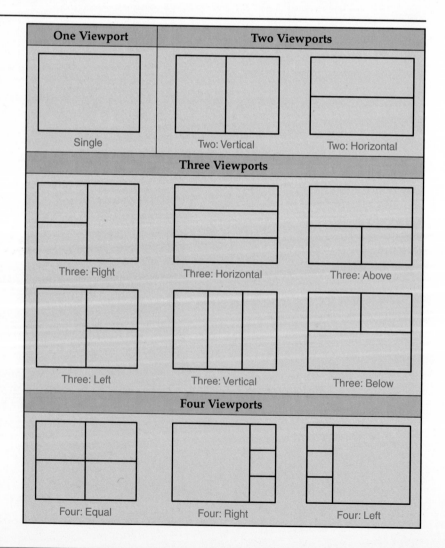

AutoCAD and its Applications—Advanced

Making a Viewport Active

Only one viewport can be active at one time in a drawing. After a viewport configuration has been created, a thick line surrounds the active viewport. When the screen cursor is moved inside the active viewport, it appears as a set of crosshairs. When moved into an inactive viewport, the screen cursor becomes an arrow.

Any viewport can be made active by moving the cursor arrow to the desired viewport and pressing the pick button. You can also press the [Ctrl]+[R] key combination to switch viewports, or use the **CVPORT** (current viewport) system variable:

Command: **CVPORT**↵
Enter new value for CVPORT <*current*>: **3**↵
Command:

The current value given is the ID number of the active viewport. The ID number is automatically assigned by AutoCAD. It is discussed later in this chapter. To change viewports with the **CVPORT** system variable, simply enter a different ID number. Using the **CVPORT** system variable is also a good way to determine the ID number of a viewport. The number 1 is not a valid viewport ID number.

Managing Defined Viewports

If you are working with several different viewport configurations, it is easy to restore, rename, or delete existing viewports. You can do so using the **Viewports** dialog box. To access a list of named viewports, open the dialog box and select the **Named Viewports** tab. See Figure 4-5. This tab can be displayed automatically by picking **Named Viewports...** from the **Viewports** cascading menu in the **View** pull-down menu. To

Figure 4-5.
The **Named Viewports** tab of the **Viewports** dialog box lists all named viewports and displays the selected configuration in the **Preview** area.

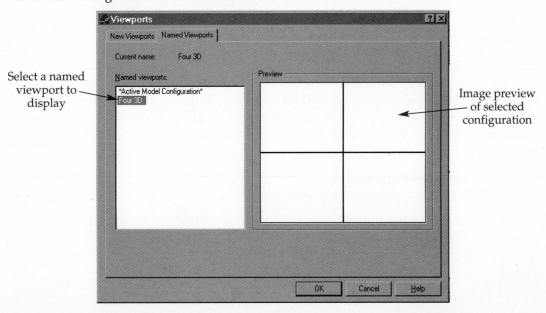

Select a named viewport to display

Image preview of selected configuration

display a viewport configuration, highlight any of the names in the **Named viewports:** list and then pick **OK**.

Assume you have defined a viewport configuration named Four 3D, as shown in Figure 4-5. You want to work in a specific viewport, but do not need other viewports displayed on screen. First, pick the viewport you wish to work in to make it active. Open the **Viewports** dialog box, pick the **New Viewports** tab, and then pick **Single**. The **Preview** area displays the single viewport. Pick **OK** to exit. The active viewport you selected is displayed on screen. To restore the original viewport configuration, redisplay the **Viewports** dialog box, pick the **Named Viewports** tab, and then select the name of the viewport you wish to redisplay. The **Preview** area displays the selected viewport. Pick **OK** to exit.

Viewports can also be renamed and deleted using the **Named Viewports** tab of the **Viewports** dialog box. To rename a viewport, right-click on the viewport name and pick **Rename** from the shortcut menu. When the name becomes highlighted, type the new name and press [Enter]. To delete a viewport configuration, right-click on the viewport name and pick **Delete** from the shortcut menu. Press **OK** to exit the dialog box.

Using the Viewports toolbar

The **Viewports** toolbar, shown in Figure 4-6, is used with both model space and paper space viewports. As discussed earlier, the **Display Viewports Dialog** button displays the **Viewports** dialog box. The **Single Viewport** button allows you to create a single viewport configuration. The remaining three buttons and the drop-down list apply to paper space viewports in a layout. Complete discussions of paper space viewports are given in Chapters 9, 10, and 24 of *AutoCAD and its Applications—Basics*.

Figure 4-6.
The **Viewports** toolbar.

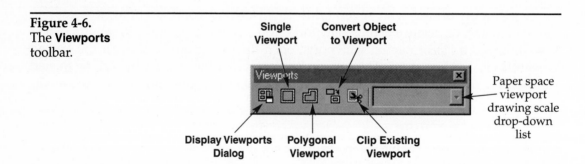

Saving, Restoring, and Deleting Viewports Using the –VPORTS Command

Viewport configurations can be created, saved, restored, and deleted at the Command: prompt using the **–VPORTS** command. When you enter this command, configuration options are presented on the command line. These options are similar to those used in the **Viewports** dialog box and the **Viewports** cascading menu in the **View** pull-down menu. The command sequence appears as follows:

    Command: **–VPORTS**↵
    Enter an option [Save/Restore/Delete/Join/SIngle/?/2/3/4] <3>: ↵

Notice that **3** is the default option. This option creates a configuration of three viewports. If you enter an option for the number of viewports you want to create, you are then prompted to enter the configuration. For the default of three viewports, the prompt is as follows:

    Enter a configuration option [Horizontal/Vertical/Above/Below/Left/Right] <Right>: ↵

The default **Right** option places two viewports on the left side of the screen and a large viewport on the right.

The **Save** option of the **–VPORTS** command allows you to name and save a viewport configuration. The **Restore** option can be used to redisplay a saved configuration. To list the names of all saved configurations in the **AutoCAD Text Window,** enter a question mark and then press [Enter] after entering the **Restore** option:

```
Command: –VPORTS↵
Enter an option [Save/Restore/Delete/Join/SIngle/?/2/3/4] <3>: R↵
Enter name of viewport configuration to restore or [?]: ?
Enter name(s) of viewport configuration(s) to list <*>: ↵

Configuration "*Active":
   0.0000,0.0000 1.0000,1.0000

Configuration "FIRST":
   0.0000,0.5000 0.5000,1.0000
   0.0000,0.0000 0.5000,0.5000
   0.5000,0.0000 1.0000,1.0000

Enter name of viewport configuration to restore or [?]: FIRST↵
Command:
```

The values given above represent the coordinate locations of each viewport. As discussed earlier in this chapter, all viewports are automatically given an ID number by AutoCAD. This number is independent of any name you might give the viewport configuration. Each viewport is also given a coordinate location with 0.0000,0.0000 as the lower-left corner of the drawing area and 1.0000,1.0000 as the upper-right corner. Figure 4-7 shows the coordinate values and ID numbers of the viewport configuration named FIRST.

Unwanted viewport configurations can be removed using the **Delete** option of the **–VPORTS** command. After entering this option, you are prompted to specify the name of the configuration to delete.

Figure 4-7.
The viewport coordinate values of the configuration named FIRST. The ID numbers are also identified.

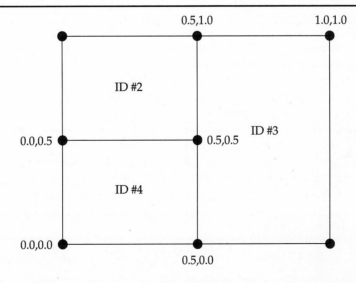

Altering the Current Viewport Configuration

You can join two adjacent viewports in an existing configuration to form a single viewport. This process is quicker than creating an entirely new configuration. However, the two viewports must form a rectangle when joined, Figure 4-8. You can join viewports by selecting **Join** from the **Viewports** cascading menu in the **View** pull-down menu, or by using the **Join** option of the **–VPORTS** command.

When you enter the **Join** option, AutoCAD first prompts you for the *dominant viewport*. All aspects of the dominant viewport are used in the new viewport. These aspects include the limits, grid, UCS, and snap settings. The command sequence for using the **Join** option is as follows:

> Command: **–VPORTS**↵
> Enter an option [Save/Restore/Delete/Join/SIngle/?/2/3/4] <3>: **J**↵
> Select dominant viewport <*current viewport*>: *(select the viewport or press* [Enter]*)*
> Select viewport to join: *(select the other viewport)*
> Regenerating model.
> Command:

The two viewports selected are joined into a single viewport. If you select two viewports that do not form a rectangle, AutoCAD returns this message:

> The selected viewports do not form a rectangle.

The drawing display can also be restored to a single viewport. To do so, access the **New Viewports** tab of the **Viewports** dialog box and pick **Single**, or enter the **SIngle** option of the **–VPORTS** command.

Figure 4-8.
Two viewports can be joined if they will form a rectangle. If the two viewports will not form a rectangle, they cannot be joined.

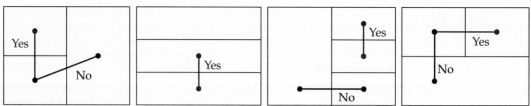

❏ Use the **Viewports** dialog box to create the following viewport configurations. Save each configuration with the name indicated:

Number of Viewports	Configuration	Name
1		ONE
2	Vertical	TWO
3	Above	THREE-A
3	Left	THREE-L
3	Right	THREE-R
4	Equal	FOUR

❏ List the viewports to be sure all were saved.
❏ Restore each named configuration.
❏ Restore configuration THREE-A and join the two small viewports. Save the new configuration under the name TWO. Confirm you want to save when asked if you wish to replace the existing configuration named TWO.
❏ Delete configuration THREE-A.
❏ Restore configuration THREE-L. Set the grid and snap spacing in each viewport to different values. Save the configuration as THREE-L.
❏ Change the display to a single viewport.
❏ Restore configuration THREE-L. Check the drawing aids in each viewport to be sure they have the same values previously set.
❏ Save the drawing as EX4-1.

Applying Viewports to Existing Configurations and Displaying Different Views

You have total control over what is displayed in model space viewports. In addition to displaying various viewport configurations, you can divide an existing viewport into additional viewports and assign a different viewpoint to each viewport. The options for these functions are provided in the **New Viewports** tab of the **Viewports** dialog box. Referring to Figure 4-3, look at the options located along the bottom of the dialog box. These features are described as follows:

- **Apply to.** When a preset viewport configuration is selected from the **Standard viewports:** list, it can be applied to either the entire display or the current viewport. The previous examples have shown how to create viewports that replace the entire display. Applying a configuration to the active viewport rather than the entire display can be useful when you need to display additional viewports. For example, first create a configuration of three viewports using the **Right** configuration option. With the right viewport active, open the **Viewports** dialog box again. Notice that the drop-down list under **Apply to:** is grayed-out. Now pick one of the standard configurations. This activates the **Apply to:** drop-down list. The default option is **Display**, which means the selected viewport configuration will replace the current display. Pick the drop-down list arrow to reveal the second option, **Current Viewport**. Pick this option and then pick **OK**. Notice that the selected viewport configuration has been applied to the active (right) viewport. See Figure 4-9.

- **Setup.** Viewports can be set up to display views in 2D or 3D. The **2D** and **3D** viewport setup options are provided in the **Setup:** drop-down list. Displaying different views while working on a drawing allows you to see the results of your work on each view, since changes are reflected in each viewport as you draw. The viewport setup option controls the types of views available in the **Change view to:** drop-down list, which is discussed below.

Figure 4-9.
The selected viewport configuration has been applied to the active viewport within the original configuration.

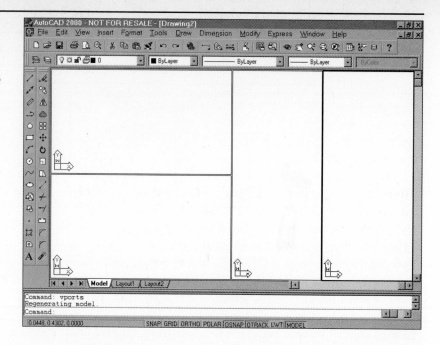

- **Change view to.** The views that can be displayed in a selected viewport are listed in the **Change view to:** drop-down list. If a viewport has been created with a 2D setup, the views available to be displayed are limited to the current view and named views. If a 3D setup is active, the options include all of the standard orthographic and isometric views, along with named views. When an orthographic or isometric view is selected for a viewport, the resulting orientation is shown in the **Preview** area. To assign a different viewpoint to a viewport, simply click within a viewport in the **Preview** area to make it active, and then pick a viewpoint from the **Change view to:** drop-down list.

EXERCISE 4-2

❏ Open the drawing named Truck model in the Acad2000\Sample folder.
❏ Pick the **3D Orbit** button from the **Standard** toolbar. Right-click in the drawing area and pick **Projection** from the shortcut menu, and then pick **Parallel**. Press [Enter] or the [Esc] key to exit the command.
❏ Zoom in on the front end of the truck and use the **VIEW** command to create a new view named Front. Zoom in on the rear end of the truck and create a new view named Rear.
❏ Use the **Viewports** dialog box to create an arrangement of three viewports, with the largest on the right. Pick **OK** to see the viewport configuration on screen. Pick inside the large viewport to make it current.
❏ Open the **Viewports** dialog box again and select an arrangement of two horizontal viewports. In the **Apply to:** drop-down list, pick **Current Viewport**. Pick **OK** to exit the dialog box and view the results.
❏ In the **Viewports** dialog box, pick **3D** from the **Setup:** drop-down list. Then use the **Change view to:** drop-down list to set the following views in the four viewports:

Viewport	View
Upper-left	Top
Lower-left	SW Isometric
Upper-right	Named view Front
Lower-right	Named view Rear

❏ Pick **OK** to view the results. Close the drawing without saving.

DRAWING IN MULTIPLE VIEWPORTS

When used with 2D drawings, viewports allow you to display a view of the entire drawing, plus views showing portions of the drawing. This display method is similar to using the **VIEW** command, except you can have several views on screen at once. You can also adjust the zoom magnification to suit different areas of the drawing in each viewport. Save a viewport configuration if you plan to continue working with it during other drawing sessions. You can create an unlimited number of viewport configurations.

Viewports are also a powerful aid when constructing 3D models. You can specify different viewpoints in each port and see the model take shape as you draw. A model can be quickly constructed because you can switch from one viewport to another while drawing and editing the object. For example, you can draw an object such as a line from a point in one viewport to a point in another simply by changing viewports while inside the **LINE** command. The results are then shown in each viewport.

The following example gives the steps necessary to construct a simple 3D part using two viewports. First, create a vertical configuration of two viewports, and make the right viewport active. Then, create the objects using the following command sequence:

    Command: **L** *or* **LINE**↵
    Specify first point: **3,2**↵
    Specify next point or [Undo]: **@7,0**↵
    Specify next point or [Undo]: **@0,5**↵
    Specify next point or [Close/Undo]: **@–7,0**↵
    Specify next point or [Close/Undo]: **C**↵
    Command: **C** *or* **CIRCLE**↵
    Specify center point for circle or [3P/2P/Ttr (tan tan radius)]: **@3.5,–2.5**↵
    Specify radius of circle or [Diameter] <*current*>: **1**↵
    Command: **–VP** *or* **VPOINT**↵
    Current view direction: VIEWDIR=0.0000,0.0000,1.0000
    Specify a view point or [Rotate] <display compass and tripod>: **–1,–1,1**↵

Use the **PAN** command and its shortcut menu options to center and enlarge the object in the left viewport.

The screen now displays two viewports. The left viewport contains a top view of the part and the right viewport displays the part in a 3D viewpoint, Figure 4-10.

The next step is to copy the shape in the left viewport up 2 units along the Z axis. This can be done using the **COPY** command and XY filters, or grips. For this example, grips are used. Select the entire object in the left viewport so that all grips on the rectangle and circle are displayed. Pick any one of the grips to make it hot.

    ** STRETCH **
    Specify stretch point or [Base point/Copy/Undo/eXit]: ↵
    ** MOVE **
    Specify move point or [Base point/Copy/Undo/eXit]: **C**↵
    ** MOVE (multiple) **
    Specify move point or [Base point/Copy/Undo/eXit]: **@0,0,2**↵
    ** MOVE (multiple) **
    Specify move point or [Base point/Copy/Undo/eXit]: ↵
    Command:

The drawing should now appear as shown in Figure 4-11. The right viewport shows the result of the copy.

Figure 4-10.
The screen is divided into two viewports. The top view of the object appears in the left viewport, and a 3D view appears in the right viewport.

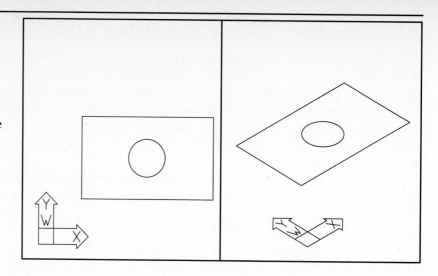

Figure 4-11.
The copied shapes appear automatically in the 3D (right) viewport.

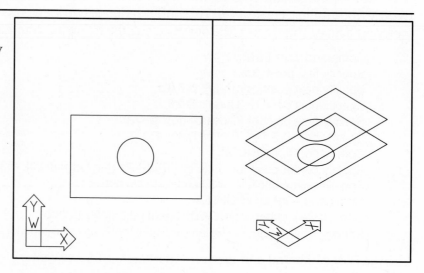

The final step is to connect the corners of the object with vertical lines. Draw the lines in the right viewport. Set the **Endpoint** running object snap and use the **LINE** command. You can draw one line and copy it to the other locations, or use the **MULTIPLE** command as follows:

Command: **MULTIPLE**↵
Enter command name to repeat: **L** *or* **LINE**↵
Specify first point: *(pick a corner on the upper shape)*
Specify next point or [Undo]: *(pick the adjacent corner on the lower shape)*
Specify next point or [Undo]: ↵
LINE Specify first point: *(continue joining the corners)*

Press the [Esc] key to cancel the command when all corners have been joined. The completed object appears in Figure 4-12.

PROFESSIONAL TIP

Displaying saved viewport configurations can be automated by using custom menus. Custom menus are easy to create. If a standard naming convention is used, these named viewports can be saved with template drawings. This creates a consistent platform all students or employees can use.

AutoCAD and its Applications—Advanced

Figure 4-12.
The corners of the upper and lower planes are connected with lines in the right viewport to complete the object.

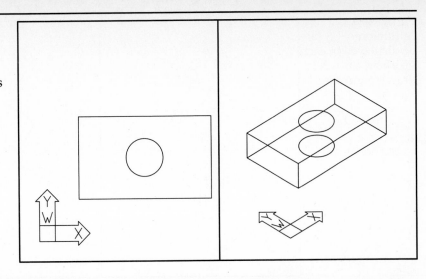

EXERCISE 4-3

❑ Create a viewport configuration with two viewports arranged horizontally. Save it as TWO.
❑ Construct the object shown below. Draw a top view in the upper viewport. Display a 3D viewpoint in the lower viewport. Connect the corners of the object in the lower viewport.
❑ Save the drawing as EX4-3.

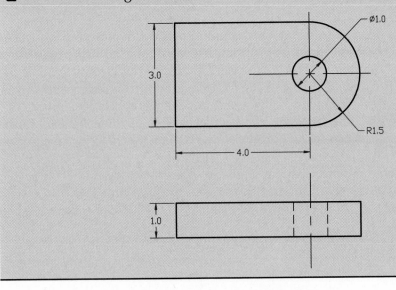

Working with the UCS in Viewports

When an object is displayed in a multiple viewport configuration, the UCS is initially the same in all viewports. You can then change to a different UCS in each viewport as you work. The UCS orientation in one viewport is not affected by a change to the UCS in another viewport. If a viewport arrangement is saved with several different UCS configurations, every named UCS will remain intact and display when the viewport configuration is restored. A multiview drawing with a different UCS configuration in each viewport is shown in Figure 4-13.

Figure 4-13.
A different UCS can be displayed in each viewport for drawing purposes.

UCS icon

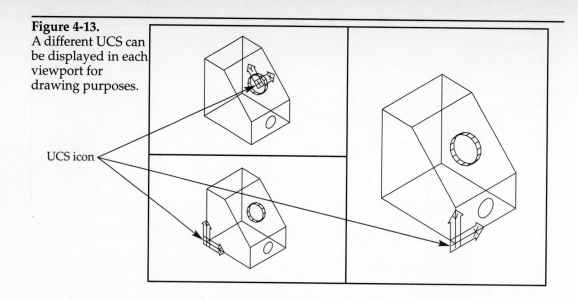

NOTE

The UCS configuration in each viewport is controlled by the **UCSVP** system variable. When **UCSVP** is set to 1 in a viewport, the UCS remains fixed and is independent of any changes to the UCS in the current viewport. If **UCSVP** is set to 0 in a viewport, its UCS will change to reflect any changes to the UCS in the current viewport.

When working on a surface, it may help if the viewpoint is plan to the surface. Simply use the **PLAN** command in the appropriate viewport to establish a plan view. In Figure 4-14, the view in the upper-left viewport is plan to the current UCS. If the UCS in this viewport is changed to one of the UCSs in either of the other viewports, a *broken pencil* icon appears in the lower-left corner of the viewport. See Figure 4-15. The broken pencil icon indicates that the view is perpendicular (or nearly so) to the current UCS. If you draw objects in a viewport with a broken pencil icon, unexpected results may occur.

You can set up any viewport so that it is always plan to the current UCS. If you change the UCS, the viewport automatically changes to the plan view of the new coordinate system. This function is controlled by the **UCSFOLLOW** system variable.

Figure 4-14.
The **PLAN** command is used in the upper-left viewport so that the view is plan to the UCS.

Plan view

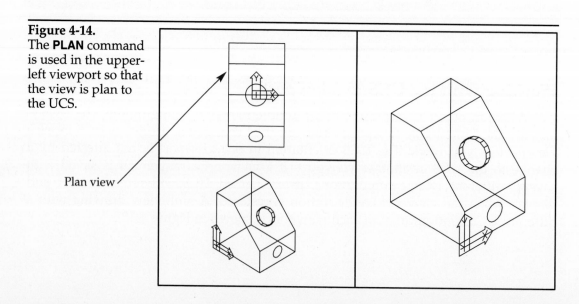

Figure 4-15.
The broken pencil icon indicates that the view is perpendicular to the current UCS.

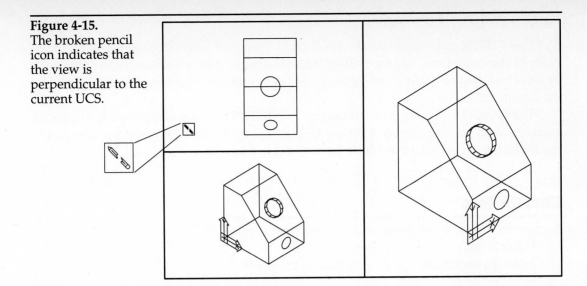

To enable AutoCAD to generate a plan view in a viewport any time the UCS is changed, set the **UCSFOLLOW** system variable to 1 in the viewport. Figure 4-16 shows the results of changing the UCS in the upper-left viewport with **UCSFOLLOW** set to 1. Keep in mind that if you change the **UCSFOLLOW** system variable in a viewport, the display will not change to a plan view until the UCS is changed.

Figure 4-16.
When the **UCSFOLLOW** system variable is activated in a viewport, any change to the UCS will display a view that is plan to the current UCS.

Viewport automatically shows plan view when UCS is changed (**UCSFOLLOW** set to 1)

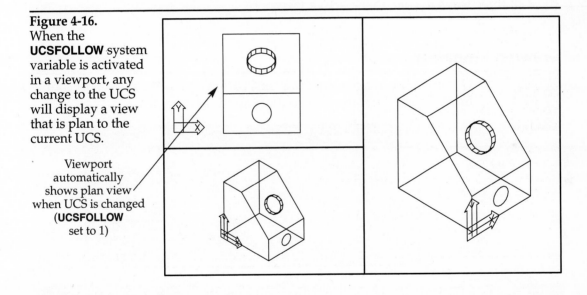

PROFESSIONAL TIP    The **UCSFOLLOW** system variable can be a very useful tool. This feature can be even more useful if the origin of the UCS is the lower-left corner (or some other meaningful reference point) of the plan surface.

Regenerating Viewports

The **REGEN** command affects the current viewport only. To regenerate all viewports at the same time, use the **REGENALL** command. This command can be entered by selecting **Regen All** from the **View** pull-down menu, or by entering REGENALL at the Command: prompt.

The Quick Text mode is controlled by the **REGEN** command. Therefore, if you are working with text displayed with the Quick Text mode in viewports, be sure to use the **REGENALL** command in order for the text to be regenerated in all viewports.

Chapter Test

Answer the following questions on a separate sheet of paper.
1. What is the purpose of viewports?
2. How do you name a configuration of viewports?
3. What is the purpose of saving a configuration of viewports?
4. Explain the difference between *tiled* and *floating* viewports.
5. Name the system variable that specifies the number of viewports that can be used at one time.
6. How can a named viewport configuration be redisplayed on screen?
7. How can a list of named viewport configurations be displayed?
8. What relationship must two viewports have before they can be joined?
9. What is the significance of the dominant viewport when two viewports are joined?
10. List three ways to change the active viewport.

Drawing Problems

1. Construct seven template drawings, each with a preset viewport configuration. Use the following configurations and names:

Number of Viewports	Configuration	Name
2	Horizontal	TWO-H
2	Vertical	TWO-V
3	Right	THREE-R
3	Left	THREE-L
3	Above	THREE-A
3	Below	THREE-B
3	Vertical	THREE-V

2. Construct one of the problems from Chapter 3 using viewports. Use one of your template drawings from Problem 1. Save the drawing as P4-2.

CHAPTER 5

Three-Dimensional Surface Modeling Techniques

Learning Objectives

After completing this chapter, you will be able to:

■ Construct a 3D surface mesh.
■ Create a variety of surface-modeled objects using the **EDGESURF**, **TABSURF**, **RULESURF**, and **REVSURF** commands.
■ Construct a detailed surface model using multiple viewports.

There are several ways to construct surface models using AutoCAD. The method you use will depend on the object you are creating. A surface mesh, or "patch," can be created using either the **3DMESH** or **PFACE** command. The **EDGESURF** command creates a surface mesh using four edges joined at the endpoints. The **RULESURF** command creates a mesh of ruled surfaces between two curves. The **TABSURF** command creates a tabulated surface mesh using a curve and a specified direction to extend the surface. The **REVSURF** command creates a surface of revolution. A surface of revolution is a profile rotated around an axis.

3D MESH TECHNIQUES

AutoCAD User's Guide **18**

Three-dimensional face meshes are used to create surface models that cannot be constructed using surfacing commands. There are four types of 3D face meshes: planar mesh, 3D mesh, pface mesh, and surface patch.

A *planar mesh* is made up of four sides. The corners can have different Z values. However, the mesh lies in a single plane. In other words, a mesh is "flat." A planar mesh is created with the **Mesh** option of the **3D** command.

A *3D mesh* is a polygon mesh composed of 3D faces. This type of mesh is not restricted to a single plane. The **3DMESH** command is used to create a 3D mesh.

A *pface mesh*, or *polyface mesh*, is a general polygon mesh of 3D faces. Each face can have an infinite number of vertices and can occupy a different plane. The **PFACE** command is used to create a polyface mesh.

The fourth type of mesh is a *surface patch*. This is created with the **EDGESURF** command. The **EDGESURF** command is discussed later in this chapter.

Constructing a 3D Mesh

The **3DMESH** command creates a 3D mesh. The mesh is defined in rows and columns. The *N value* defines the number of rows. An N value of three produces two

Figure 5-1.
A 3D polygon mesh
is similar to a grid
of XY coordinates.
M values define
columns and N
values define rows.
This example has an
M value of 4 and an
N value of 3.

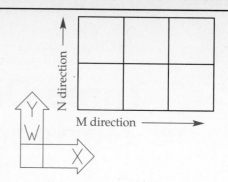

rows. The *M value* defines the number of columns. An M value of four produces three columns. See Figure 5-1.

When using the **3DMESH** command, each vertex in the mesh must be given an XYZ coordinate location. The vertices of the mesh are its definition points. A mesh must have between 2 and 256 vertices in both directions.

When prompting for coordinates, the M and N location of the current vertex is indicated. See the command sequence below. The values for each vertex of the first M column must be entered. Then, values for the second, third, and remaining M columns must be entered.

3DMESH

Draw
→ Surfaces
→ 3D Mesh

Surfaces
toolbar

3D Mesh

To draw a 3D mesh, select **3D Mesh** from the **Surfaces** cascading menu in the **Draw** pull-down menu, pick the **3D Mesh** button from the **Surfaces** toolbar, or type 3DMESH at the Command: prompt. Use the following command sequence to get the feel for the **3DMESH** command. When complete, use **VPOINT** to view the mesh from different angles. The mesh should look like the one shown in Figure 5-2 after using **VPOINT**.

```
Command: 3DMESH↵
Enter size of mesh in M direction: 4↵
Enter size of mesh in N direction: 3↵
Specify location for vertex (0,0): 3,2,1↵
Specify location for vertex (0,1): 3,3,1.5↵
Specify location for vertex (0,2): 3,4,1↵
Specify location for vertex (1,0): 4,2,.5↵
Specify location for vertex (1,1): 4,3,1↵
Specify location for vertex (1,2): 4,4,.5↵
Specify location for vertex (2,0): 5,2,1.5↵
Specify location for vertex (2,1): 5,3,1↵
Specify location for vertex (2,2): 5,4,1.5↵
Specify location for vertex (3,0): 6,2,2.5↵
Specify location for vertex (3,1): 6,3,2↵
Specify location for vertex (3,2): 6,4,2.5↵
Command:
```

Figure 5-2.
A 3D polygon mesh.
The M value is 4 and
the N value is 3.

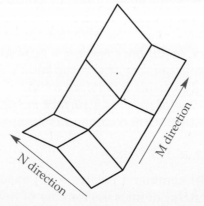

Constructing a Single-Plane Mesh

A *planar mesh* is a 3D mesh that lies in a single plane. It has between 2 and 256 vertices in both M and N directions. To draw a planar mesh, pick **3D Surfaces...** from the **Surfaces** cascading menu in the **Draw** pull-down menu. This displays the **3D Objects** dialog box. Pick **Mesh** from the list or pick the **Mesh** icon. You can select the **Mesh** option of the **3D** command or enter AI_MESH at the Command: prompt:

Command: **AI_MESH**↵

or

Command: **3D**↵
Enter an option
[Box/Cone/DIsh/DOme/Mesh/Pyramid/Sphere/Torus/Wedge]: **M**↵

You are then asked for the four corners of the mesh and the number of vertices.

Specify first corner point of mesh: **4,3**↵
Specify second corner point of mesh: **9,3**↵
Specify third corner point of mesh: **9,8**↵
Specify fourth corner point of mesh: **4,8**↵
Enter mesh size in the M direction: **10**↵
Enter mesh size in the N direction: **8**↵
Command:

The resulting mesh is shown in Figure 5-3.

Figure 5-3.
A planar mesh has between 2 and 256 vertices in both directions.

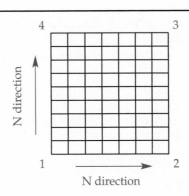

Constructing a 3D Polyface Mesh

A general polygon mesh can be constructed using the **PFACE** command. This creates a mesh similar to the **3DFACE** command. However, you do not need to pick vertices that join another face twice. You can also create faces that have an infinite number of vertices, rather than the maximum of four specified by the **3DFACE** command. You can use the **PFACE** command to construct surfaces that cannot be "faced" using any of the standard surfacing commands. However, using this command is time-consuming, and is best suited for AutoLISP, ObjectARX, or other programming applications.

PFACE

To create a pface mesh, first define all the vertices for the mesh. Then, assign those vertices to a face. The face is then given a number and is composed of the vertices you assign to that face. While creating a pface, you can change the layer or color by entering the **LAYER** or **COLOR** commands when [Color/Layer] appears in the prompt. The following example creates a pface mesh consisting of two faces. See Figure 5-4A. The first portion of the command defines all the vertices of the two faces.

```
Command: PFACE↵
Specify location for vertex 1: 3,3↵
Specify location for vertex 2 or <define faces>: 7,3↵
Specify location for vertex 3 or <define faces>: 7,6↵
Specify location for vertex 4 or <define faces>: 3,6↵
Specify location for vertex 5 or <define faces>: 2,7,3↵
Specify location for vertex 6 or <define faces>: 2,2,3↵
Specify location for vertex 7 or <define faces>: 3,3↵
Specify location for vertex 8 or <define faces>: ↵
```

The next sequence assigns vertices to face number 1.

```
Face 1, vertex 1:
Enter a vertex number or [Color/Layer]: 1↵
Face 1, vertex 2:
Enter a vertex number or [Color/Layer] <next face>: 2↵
Face 1, vertex 3:
Enter a vertex number or [Color/Layer] <next face>: 3↵
Face 1, vertex 4:
Enter a vertex number or [Color/Layer] <next face>: 4↵
Face 1, vertex 5: ↵
```

Now you can change the color of the second face without exiting the command.

```
Enter a vertex number or [Color/Layer] <next face>: COLOR↵
Enter a color number or standard color name <BYLAYER>: GREEN↵
```

The last sequence assigns vertices to face number 2.

```
Face 2, vertex 1:
Enter a vertex number or [Color/Layer]: 4↵
Face 2, vertex 2:
Enter a vertex number or [Color/Layer] <next face>: 5↵
Face 2, vertex 3:
Enter a vertex number or [Color/Layer] <next face>: 6↵
Face 2, vertex 4:
Enter a vertex number or [Color/Layer] <next face>: 1↵
Face 2, vertex 5:
Enter a vertex number or [Color/Layer] <next face>: ↵
Face 3, vertex 1:
Enter a vertex number or [Color/Layer]: ↵
Command:
```

Now use the **VPOINT** and **HIDE** commands to view the faces.

```
Command: –VP or VPOINT↵
Current view direction:  VIEWDIR=0.0000,0.0000,1.0000
Specify a view point or [Rotate] <display compass and tripod>: –1,–1,.75↵
Regenerating model.
Command: HIDE↵
Regenerating model.
Command:
```

Figure 5-4.
A—Creating a pface mesh with two faces. B—When you use **HIDE**, you can see that each face is a surface. Notice that Face 2 partially blocks the view of Face 1.

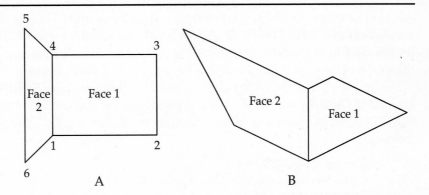

The pface mesh first appears as a wireframe. However, after using the **HIDE** command, the 3D faces can be clearly seen. See Figure 5-4B. Notice that the second face partially blocks the view of the first face after **HIDE** is used.

Polygon Mesh Variations

A polygon mesh created with **3DMESH** can be smoothed using the **PEDIT** command. The smoothness of the surface depends on the value set in the **SURFTYPE** system variable:

SURFTYPE setting	Surface type
5	Quadratic B-spline
6	Cubic B-spline (default)
8	Bézier surface

Before smoothing a polygon mesh, set the **SURFU** (M direction) and **SURFV** (N direction) system variables larger than the M and N values. If you do not change these values, the resulting surface may have less 3D faces than the original. Figure 5-5 illustrates the different types of surfaces that can be created using **SURFTYPE** and **PEDIT** smoothing.

Figure 5-5.
A—The **SPLFRAME** variable set to 1. B—A quadratic B-spline (**SURFTYPE** = 5). C—A cubic B-spline (**SURFTYPE** = 6). D—A Bézier surface (**SURFTYPE** = 8).

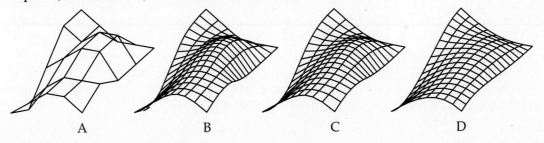

<table>
<tr><td>**NOTE** </td><td>A 3D mesh must have at least three vertices in each direction in order to smooth the surface.</td></tr>
</table>

Constructing Enclosed Surfaces with EDGESURF

The **EDGESURF** command allows you to construct a 3D mesh between four edges. The edges can be lines, polylines, splines, or arcs. The endpoints of the objects must meet precisely. However, a closed polyline *cannot* be used. The four objects can be selected in any order. The resulting surface is a smooth mesh, similar to a planar mesh. The *AutoCAD User's Guide* calls this type of surface mesh a *Coons surface patch*.

The number of faces are determined by the variables **SURFTAB1** (M direction) and **SURFTAB2** (N direction). The default value for each of these variables is 6. Higher **SURFTAB** values increase the smoothness of the mesh. Change these values as follows:

Command: **SURFTAB1**↵
Enter new value for SURFTAB1 <current>: **12**↵
Command: **SURFTAB2**↵
Enter new value for SURFTAB2 <current>: **12**↵

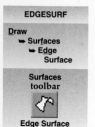

EDGESURF

Draw
  ↳ Surfaces
    ↳ Edge
      Surface

Surfaces
toolbar

Edge Surface

The current **SURFTAB** values will always be displayed on the Command: line when one of the surfacing commands is executed, as shown in the example below.

To draw an edge surface, pick **Edge Surface** from the **Surfaces** cascading menu in the **Draw** pull-down menu, pick the **Edge Surface** button in the **Surfaces** toolbar, or enter EDGESURF at the Command: prompt:

Command: **EDGESURF**↵
Current wire frame density: SURFTAB1=*current* SURFTAB2=*current*
Select object 1 for surface edge: (*pick edge 1*)
Select object 2 for surface edge: (*pick edge 2*)
Select object 3 for surface edge: (*pick edge 3*)
Select object 4 for surface edge: (*pick edge 4*)

A completed surface patch with the **SURFTAB** variables set to 12 is shown in Figure 5-6.

Figure 5-6.
A completed surface patch with both **SURFTAB** variables set to 12.

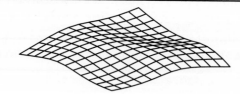

Creating a Surface Mesh with RULESURF

A surface mesh can be constructed between two objects using the **RULESURF** command. This mesh is called a *ruled surface*. The two objects can be points, lines, arcs, circles, polylines, splines, enclosed objects, or a single plane. The two objects must both be either open or closed. A variety of constructions are shown in Figure 5-7. A point can be used with any object to create constructions such as those shown in Figure 5-8. A ruled surface is useful for surfacing holes in parts, exterior fillets (rounds), interior fillets, or flat surfaces of various shapes.

AutoCAD and its Applications—Advanced

Figure 5-7.
Many different
objects can be used
to create a ruled
surface.

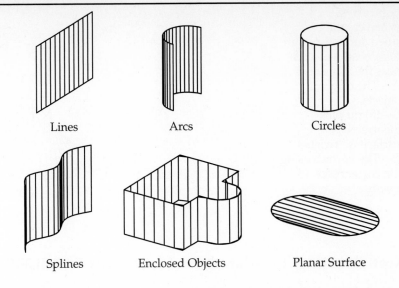

Lines   Arcs   Circles

Splines   Enclosed Objects   Planar Surface

Figure 5-8.
A point can be used
with another object
to create a ruled
surface.

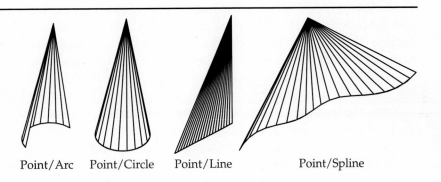

Point/Arc   Point/Circle   Point/Line   Point/Spline

PROFESSIONAL TIP

When constructing holes in surface-modeled objects, always draw the original circles on a separate construction layer. After the hole has been surfaced with the **RULESURF** command, turn off or freeze the construction layer. If you do not turn off the construction layer, the inside of the hole will not be displayed when **HIDE** is used or the object is rendered.

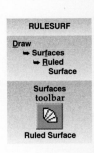

RULESURF

Draw
→ Surfaces
→ Ruled
Surface

Surfaces
toolbar

Ruled Surface

Select the **RULESURF** command by picking **Ruled Surface** from the **Surfaces** cascading menu in the **Draw** pull-down menu, picking the **Ruled Surface** button in the **Surfaces** toolbar, or entering RULESURF at the Command: prompt:

> Command: **RULESURF**↵
> Current wire frame density: SURFTAB1=*current*
> Select first defining curve: *(pick first object)*
> Select second defining curve: *(pick second object)*
> Command:

When using **RULESURF** to create a surface between two objects such as those shown in Figure 5-9A, it is important to select both objects near the same end. If you pick near opposite ends of each object, the resulting figure may not be what you want, Figure 5-9B. The correctly surfaced object is shown in Figure 5-9C.

The number of elements that compose the ruled surface is determined by the **SURFTAB1** system variable. The greater the number of elements, the smoother the surface appears.

Figure 5-9.
When creating a ruled surface, be sure to select the objects near the same end.
A—The original objects.
B—If you pick incorrectly, the surface is "twisted."
C—The surface using the correct pick points.

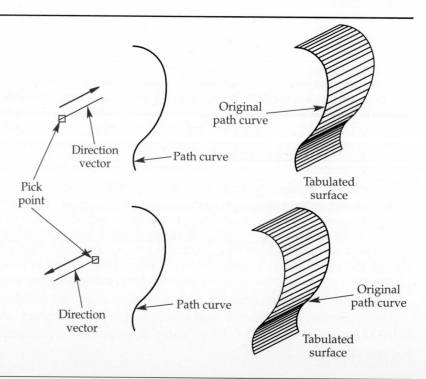

Constructing Tabulated Surfaces with TABSURF

A *tabulated surface* is similar to a ruled surface. However, only one entity is needed. This entity is called the *path curve*. Lines, arcs, circles, ellipses, 2D polylines, and 3D polylines can all be used as the path curve. A line called the *direction vector* is also required. This line indicates the direction and length of the tabulated surface. AutoCAD finds the endpoint of the direction vector closest to your pick point. It sets the direction toward the opposite end of the vector line. The tabulated surface follows the direction and length of the direction vector. The **SURFTAB1** system variable controls the number of "steps" that are constructed. Figure 5-10 shows the difference the pick point makes when assigning the direction.

To create a tabulated surface, select **Tabulated Surface** from the **Surfaces** cascading menu of the **Draw** pull-down menu, pick the **Tabulated Surface** button in the **Surfaces** toolbar, or enter TABSURF at the Command: prompt:

TABSURF

Draw
➥ Surfaces
  ➥ Tabulated
    Surface

Surfaces
toolbar

Tabulated Surface

> Command: **TABSURF**↵
> Select object for path curve: *(pick the curve)*
> Select object for direction vector: *(pick correct end of vector)*
> Command:

Figure 5-10.
The point you pick on the direction vector determines the direction of extrusion for the tabulated surface.

Constructing Revolved Surfaces with REVSURF

With the **REVSURF** command, you can draw a profile and then rotate that profile around an axis to create a symmetrical object. This is a powerful tool and will greatly assist anyone who needs to draw a symmetrical three-dimensional shape. The profile, or *path curve*, can be drawn using lines, arcs, circles, ellipses, elliptical arcs, polylines, spheres, or donuts. The rotation axis can be a line or an open polyline. Notice the initial layout of the revolved surface in Figure 5-11.

Begin the command by selecting **Revolved Surface** from the **Surfaces** cascading menu of the **Draw** pull-down menu, picking the **Revolved Surface** button in the **Surfaces** toolbar, or typing REVSURF at the Command: prompt:

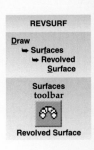

REVSURF

Draw
➥ Surfaces
  ➥ Revolved
     Surface

Surfaces
toolbar

Revolved Surface

> Command: **REVSURF**↵
> Current wire frame density: SURFTAB1=*current* SURFTAB2=*current*
> Select object to revolve: *(pick the profile)*
> Select object that defines the axis of revolution: *(pick an axis line)*
> Specify start angle <0>: ↵
> Specify included angle (+ = ccw, – = cw) <360>: ↵
> Command:

The Specify start angle: prompt allows you to specify an offset angle at which to start the surface revolution. The Specify included angle: prompt lets you draw the object through 360° of rotation or just a portion of that. Figure 5-12 shows the rotated Figure 5-11 profile displayed with hidden lines removed.

The **SURFTAB1** and **SURFTAB2** system variables control the mesh of a revolved surface. The **SURFTAB1** value determines the number of segments in the direction of rotation around the axis. The **SURFTAB2** value divides the path curve into segments of equal size.

The **REVSURF** command is powerful because it can create a symmetrical surface using any profile. Figure 5-13 illustrates additional examples of **REVSURF** constructions.

Figure 5-11.
A path curve
(profile) and an axis
are needed to create
a revolved surface.

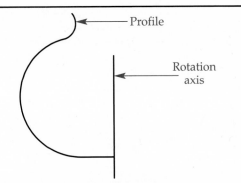

Profile

Rotation
axis

Figure 5-12.
The revolved
surface created with
the profile and axis
in Figure 5-11.

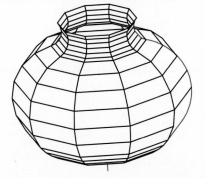

Figure 5-13.
Revolved surfaces created with a variety of profiles.

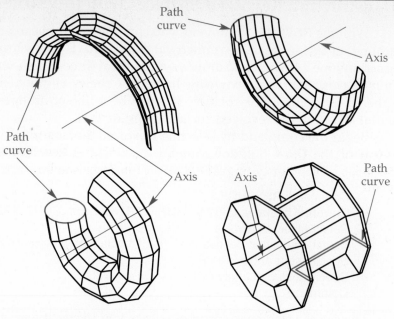

EXERCISE 5-1

❏ Draw the objects shown below and display them in a 3D viewport.
❏ Set the **SURFTAB1** and **SURFTAB2** variables to values of your choice.
❏ Create the surface model constructions as indicated.
❏ Save your drawing as EX5-1.

RULESURF

TABSURF

REVSURF

AutoCAD and its Applications—Advanced

SURFACING AROUND HOLES

AutoCAD cannot automatically create surfacing around a hole. A series of steps is required to do this. A common method is to use the **RULESURF** and **3DFACE** commands to create the required surfaces.

For example, the object in Figure 5-14A must be surfaced. This object has a hole through it. To surface the hole, first construct two 180° arcs where the hole is. Use a construction layer. Next, use **RULESURF** to create the surface connecting the large arc and the hole. Use **RULESURF** again to create the surface connecting the arc and the left end of the object. The two remaining surfaces can be created using **3DFACE**. The result is shown in Figure 5-14B.

Another example is surfacing the space between two holes, as shown in Figure 5-15A. Again, create arcs where the circles are. Then, use **RULESURF** to create the surface connecting the two inside arcs. Also use **RULESURF** to create the surface between the outer arcs and the outside edges. Use **3DFACE** to surface the remaining faces. The surfaced object is shown in Figure 5-15B.

Figure 5-14.
AutoCAD cannot automatically surface a hole. To do so, you must use a combination of ruled surfaces and 3D faces.

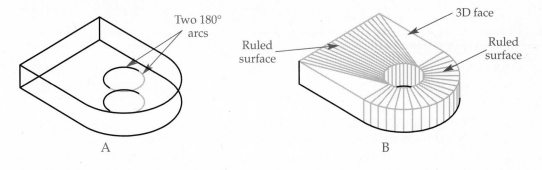

Figure 5-15.
Surfacing an object with two holes.

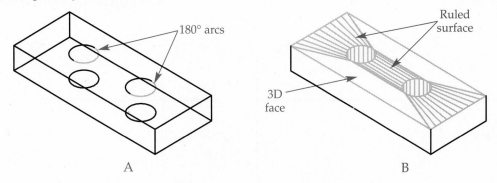

CONSTRUCTING A SURFACE MODEL

The following tutorial shows how surface modeling can be used to create an object composed of several different shapes. A twelve-button digitizer puck will be constructed. See Figure 5-16. If possible, enter the commands on your workstation as you go through this example. It is not necessary to complete this tutorial in one drawing session. Complete what you can, save your work, and return when you have available time.

Figure 5-16.
A 3D surface model
of a twelve-button
puck.

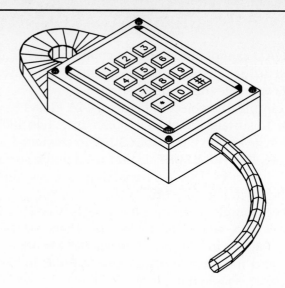

> **NOTE**   Follow the instructions in this tutorial exactly. Once you are experienced with these commands, experiment on your own with different ways of using them.

Drawing Setup

You should plan your work carefully before beginning any 3D drawing. Draw the least amount of elements that can be used to complete the project. Also, use the following guidelines:

✓ Let the computer do as much work as possible.
✓ Use predrawn shapes and create blocks when possible.
✓ Save display configurations, such as views, viewports, and UCSs.
✓ As an optional step, make slides of each step of your work for later reference. Slides are covered in Chapter 28 of *AutoCAD and its Applications—Basics.*

Begin your drawing by setting units as decimal and limits to 18,12. Set the grid spacing to .5 and snap spacing to .25. Then, create the following layers with the color indicated.

Layer Name	Color
Body	red
Body-cap	white
Buttons	magenta
Button1	magenta
Button2	blue
Cable	green
Constr	blue
Edgesurf	green
Eyepiece	yellow
Eyesurf	yellow
Face1	green
Face2	cyan
Numbers	cyan
Screws	red

Using 3D Shapes

The individual parts of the digitizer puck are shown in Figure 5-17. The first step is to create a one-unit cube as a basic 3D building block. This block can then be used for at least three of the puck parts. Rather than drawing the box as a wireframe and adding 3D faces to it, you can use the 3D surface-modeled box from the **3D Objects** dialog box or the **Box** button in the **Surfaces** toolbar. Draw it on Layer 0.

> Command: **AI_BOX**↵
> Specify corner point of box: **0,0**↵
> Specify length of box: **1**↵
> Specify width of box or [Cube]: **C**↵
> Specify rotation angle of box about the Z axis or [Reference]: **0**↵

The box appears to be a wireframe, but it is actually a single entity composed of 3D faces.

Next, use the **BLOCK** command to make a block of the cube. Name it BOX. You can do this in the 3D display. Pick one of the corners as an insertion point using the **Endpoint** object snap, Figure 5-18. Pick the **Delete** radio button in the **Block Definition** dialog box to remove the box from the drawing.

Figure 5-17.
The components needed to make the puck.

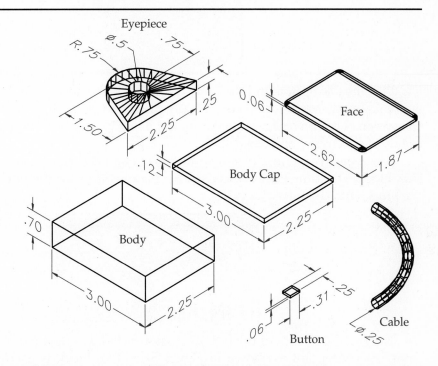

Figure 5-18.
A basic, one-unit cube building block. Select the block insertion point in a logical place, such as the corner.

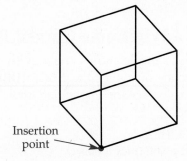

Inserting a 3D Block

The block can now be inserted into the drawing to create the body of the puck. Change the current layer to Body. Change the display to show the plan view. Use the **DDINSERT** or **INSERT** command to insert the BOX block. In the **Insert** dialog box, select BOX from the drop-down list and enter the following values. You may need to uncheck the **Specify On-screen** check box to get access to the text boxes.

Setting	Value
Insertion point	0,0,0
X scale factor	2.25
Y scale factor	3
Z scale factor	.7
Rotation angle	0

Pick the OK button and the body of the puck is placed with the required dimensions. As an alternative, you can visually place and size a 3D block using the **Specify On-screen** check boxes in the **Insert** dialog box. You might try it again for practice to see what specifying on-screen is like.

Select the SW isometric viewpoint. Make Layer 0 current and insert a copy of the BOX block. This time the cube is used to create a block for the puck's buttons. Insert the block with the following values:

Setting	Value
Insertion point	Pick a point
X scale factor	.31
Y scale factor	.25
Z scale factor	.06
Rotation angle	0

Now, make a block of the box you just inserted. Name it BUTTON and give it the same insertion point as shown in Figure 5-18. This block is used later to create an array of buttons. The next section shows how to construct a more detailed button having a curved surface.

Constructing a Wireframe Curved Button (Optional Step)

The following example shows one way to create a wireframe model that you can place surface patches on using the **EDGESURF** command. A *surface patch* is a 3D mesh that creates a surface for a specified area. Begin construction of the button using the **LINE** command.

```
Command: LINE↵
Specify first point: (pick a point)
Specify next point or [Undo]: @.31,0↵
Specify next point or [Undo]: @0,.25↵
Specify next point or [Close/Undo]: @-.31,0↵
Specify next point or [Close/Undo]: C↵
```

AutoCAD and its Applications—Advanced

This creates the base of the button. Zoom in on the object so that it nearly fills the screen. This makes it easier to draw the vertical lines of the corners. Figure 5-19A shows these lines, which can be drawn using the **LINE** command as follows.

> Command: **LINE**↵
> Specify first point: **END**↵
> of *(pick point P1)*
> Specify next point or [Undo]: **@0,0,.03**↵
> Specify next point or [Undo]: ↵
> Command: ↵
> LINE Specify first point: **END**↵
> of *(pick point P2)*
> Specify next point or [Undo]: **@0,0,.06**↵
> Specify next point or [Undo]: ↵
> Command:

The next step is to construct an arc connecting the tops of the two vertical lines. This arc represents the curved shape of the button surface. However, the UCS must be changed from the current WCS so that the X axis is the same direction as the line between P1 and P2. This places the new UCS in the same plane where the arc will be drawn. See Figure 5-19B.

> Command: **UCS**↵
> Current ucs name: *WORLD*
> Enter an option [New/Move/orthoGraphic/Prev/Restore/Save/Del/Apply/?/World]
> <World>: **ZA**↵
> Specify new origin point <0,0,0>: **END**↵
> of *(pick point P2)*
> Specify point on positive portion of Z–axis <*defaults*>: **@–1,0,0**↵

If the UCS icon does not move to the new origin, use the **Origin** option of the **UCSICON** command to move the icon. The UCS icon is a good reminder of the location of the origin of the current UCS.

With the UCS changed, the arc can be drawn. Refer to Figure 5-19C for the pick points of the arc. Use the **ARC** command as follows.

> Command: **ARC**↵
> Specify start point of arc or [CEnter]: **END**↵
> of *(pick point P3)*
> Specify second point of arc or [CEnter/ENd]: **E**↵
> Specify end point of arc: **END**↵
> of *(pick point P4)*
> Specify center point of arc or [Angle/Direction/Radius]: **A**↵
> Specify included angle: **20**↵
> Command:

The final steps in creating the wireframe are to copy the two vertical lines and the arc to the opposite end of the button, and to connect the top edges of the button with straight lines. The completed drawing should look like Figure 5-19D.

Figure 5-19.
Creating a wireframe of a curved button.

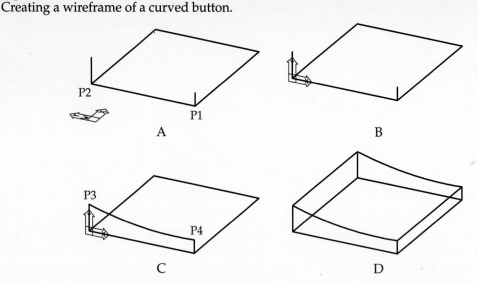

A

B

C

D

Creating Edge Defined Surfaces

Curved surfaces having four sides can be created using the **EDGESURF** command. This command is discussed earlier in this chapter. An *edge surface* is actually a matrix of 3D faces. The number of rows and columns of faces is controlled by the **SURFTAB1** and **SURFTAB2** system variables. Keep in mind that the greater the number of faces you have, the longer the regeneration time is, and the longer it takes to remove hidden lines using the **HIDE** command. Keep the **SURFTAB** values low for small objects.

PROFESSIONAL TIP

When working with 3D surfaces, determine the purpose of your drawing. How will you be viewing it? What other programs will you use to shade, render, or animate the object? If you will not be looking at certain sides of an object, do not apply surfacing to those sides. Also, avoid using large values for the **SURFTAB** variables.

First, set the **SURFTAB** variables. Then, set the current layer to Button1 and create the first surface patch. Refer to Figure 5-20A.

> Command: **SURFTAB1**↵
> Enter new value for SURFTAB1 <*current*>: **6**↵
> Command: **SURFTAB2**↵
> Enter new value for SURFTAB2 <*current*>: **2**↵
> Command: **EDGESURF**↵
> Current wire frame density: SURFTAB1=6 SURFTAB2=2
> Select object 1 for surface edge: (*pick edge 1*)
> Select object 2 for surface edge: (*pick edge 2*)
> Select object 3 for surface edge: (*pick edge 3*)
> Select object 4 for surface edge: (*pick edge 4*)

The first line you pick is divided into six segments (**SURFTAB1**). The second edge is divided into two segments (**SURFTAB2**). See Figure 5-20B.

AutoCAD and its Applications—Advanced

Figure 5-20.
Surfacing the curved button.

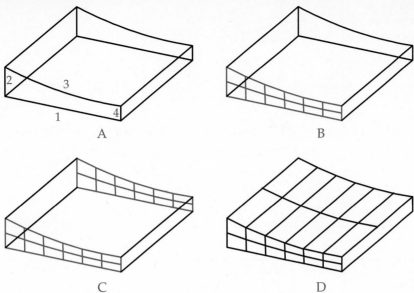

Next, copy the surface patch to the opposite end of the button. Your object should look like Figure 5-20C. Now, turn off layer Button1 and make layer Button2 current. This allows you to select the edges without the surface patch getting in the way. If you select the surface patch while defining a new surface patch, the message Object not usable to define surface patch appears on the command line.

Now, use **EDGESURF** to create the curved top surface of the button. Pick one of the ends that is already surfaced as the first edge. When the curved surface is completed, turn on layer Button1. Finally, use the **3DFACE** command on the two remaining sides. There is no need to use the **3DFACE** command on the bottom because it will sit on another surface. After using the **HIDE** command, the button looks like Figure 5-20D.

This surfaced shape can now be saved as a block or wblocked as a file. Before doing so, place all the surfaces on the same layer, such as Button1. You will use the blocks you have created to complete the digitizer puck later. It is also a good idea to save your drawing at this point.

Using Viewports to Help Create the Puck

Viewports can be a great help in drawing 3D objects. Viewports will be used to help create the puck. To set the viewports, first zoom out so that the entire body shape is displayed. Then, use the **UCS** command to return to the world coordinate system.

Use the **VPORTS** or **VIEWPORTS** command to open the **Viewports** dialog box. Then, select the Three: Right standard viewport configuration in the **New Viewports** tab and pick the **OK** button to close the dialog box. This displays three views of the part, Figure 5-21. Next, create a pictorial view in the right and lower-left viewports. Do this by first picking in the right viewport to make it active. Then, select the SW isometric view. Make the lower-left viewport active and select the NW isometric viewpoint. Use the **ZOOM** command to magnify these views. Use **PAN** if necessary to center the objects in the viewports.

Next, pick the upper-left viewport to make it active and use the **PLAN** command to create a plan view. Use **ZOOM** and **PAN** to adjust all of the views as needed. The final arrangement of the viewports should be similar to Figure 5-22.

Figure 5-21.
Create a three-viewport display to help you draw the puck. The viewpoint for this display is –2,–1,1.

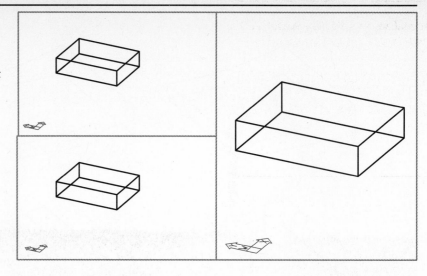

Figure 5-22.
Change the views so that each viewport shows a different aspect of the puck.

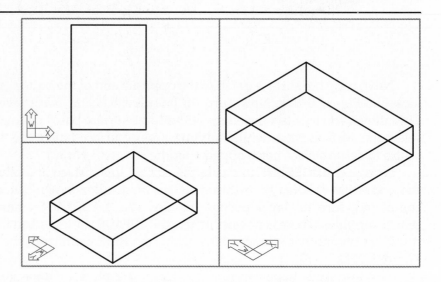

After you have adjusted all three viewports, study the orientation of the views in relation to the UCS icon. The ability to visualize the XYZ axes as they relate to the object is the key to understanding 3D construction and multiple view layouts.

An important tool when working with viewports is the ability to store a configuration. If you need the configuration again, it can simply be recalled instead of recreated from scratch. Saving a viewport configuration is done in the **New Viewports** tab of the **Viewports** dialog box. See Figure 5-23.

To save a configuration, first use the **Viewports** dialog box to configure the viewports as neded. Then, open the **Viewports** dialog box and select *Active Model Configuration* from the list in the **New Viewports** tab. Finally, type a name in the **New name:** text box, such as Three, and pick the **OK** button to close the dialog box. This viewport configuration is now saved and can be recalled at any time. The next time the **Viewports** command is used, the name you gave for the configuration appears in the list in the **Named Viewports** tab.

For example, use the **Viewports** dialog box and return to one viewport. Then, use **Viewports** dialog box again and select the saved configuration, Three, in the **Named Viewports** tab. Pick the **OK** button to close the dialog box and the saved configuration is restored.

Figure 5-23.
Viewport configurations can be saved using the **New Viewports** tab in the **Viewports** dialog box.

Type a name for the configuration

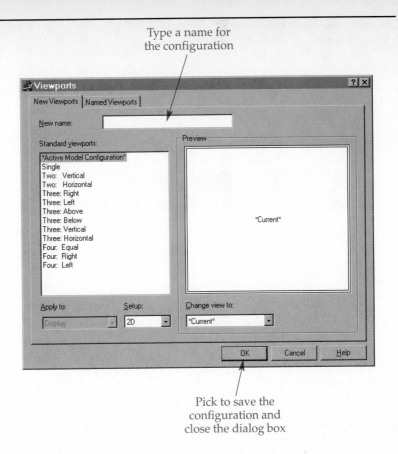

Pick to save the configuration and close the dialog box

Continuing with the Puck Model

Next, you need to add a "cap" to the puck body. First, set the current layer to Body-cap. Then, make the large viewport active. Insert the BOX block and attach it to the body at the insertion point shown in Figure 5-24A. Remember, the box is a one unit cube so you can enter the dimensions of the cap as scale factors. Use the following values for the block insert:

Setting	Value
Insertion point	pick the insertion point shown in Figure 5-24A
X scale factor	2.25
Y scale factor	3
Z scale factor	.12
Rotation angle	0

The inserted body cap is shown in Figure 5-24B.

Figure 5-24.
Inserting the BOX block to create the cap.

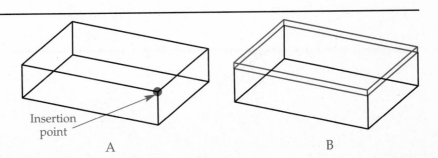

Insertion point

A

B

Using Polylines in 3D

Next, you need to construct the face of the puck. Notice in Figure 5-17 that the face has filleted corners. You must construct it using a combination of polylines, ruled surfaces, and 3D faces. Since the face is placed on top of the body cap, create a UCS on that surface. Also, save the UCS for future use. Be sure the large viewport is active and use the following command sequence.

Command: **UCS.⏎**
Current ucs name: *WORLD*
Enter an option [New/Move/orthoGraphic/Prev/Restore/Save/Del/Apply/?/World]
    <World>: **O.⏎**
Specify origin of new UCS or [ZAxis/3point/OBject/Face/View/X/Y/Z] <0,0,0>:
    (pick the top corner of the body cap above the insertion point)
Command: **UCSICON.⏎**
Enter an option [ON/OFF/All/Noorigin/ORigin] <ON>: **A.⏎** *(this applies the next option to all viewports)*
Enter an option [ON/OFF/Noorigin/ORigin] <ON>: **OR.⏎**
Command: **UCS.⏎**
Current ucs name: *NO NAME*
Enter an option [New/Move/orthoGraphic/Prev/Restore/Save/Del/Apply/?/World]
    <World>: **S.⏎**
Enter name to save current UCS or [?]: **FACE.⏎**

Notice that the UCS icon is at the new origin in the large viewport *only*. See Figure 5-25. To get the new UCS in all viewports, use the **Apply** option of the **UCS** command. Now that the UCS is saved, it can be recalled at any time with the **Restore** option of the **UCS** command.

Begin drawing the puck face by making the upper-left viewport active. Change to the layer Face1. If you return to a single viewport, the object will be larger. This may make it easier to work on. Since you have saved the current viewport configuration, you can always go back to it later. Next, turn off any running object snaps. Then, use the **PLINE** command to draw the face. Be sure to use the **Close** option to complete the shape.

Command: **PLINE.⏎**
Specify start point: **.19,.19.⏎**
Current line-width is 0.0000
Specify next point or [Arc/Close/Halfwidth/Length/Undo/Width]: **@1.87,0.⏎**
Specify next point or [Arc/Close/Halfwidth/Length/Undo/Width]: **@0,2.62.⏎**
Specify next point or [Arc/Close/Halfwidth/Length/Undo/Width]: **@1.87<180.⏎**
Specify next point or [Arc/Close/Halfwidth/Length/Undo/Width]: **C.⏎**

Figure 5-25.
Placing the UCS icon at the origin helps you visualize coordinates better. This also shows that the new UCS needs to be applied to all viewports.

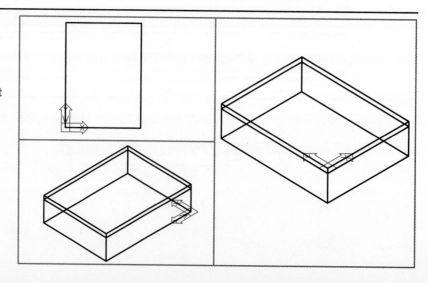

If you returned to a single viewport, restore the three-viewport configuration. Your drawing should now look like Figure 5-26.

Next, place a .125 radius fillet on the corners of the polyline. Then, copy the filleted polyline on the Z axis using the following command sequence. Use the viewport that will allow you to draw most efficiently.

Command: **CO** or **COPY**↵
Select objects: *(select polyline)*
1 found
Select objects: ↵
Specify base point or displacement, or [Multiple]: **@**↵
Specify second point of displacement or <use first point as displacement>:
    @0,0,.06↵

The result is shown in Figure 5-27.

Figure 5-26.
Creating a wireframe of the face starts with drawing a closed polyline "on top" of the cap.

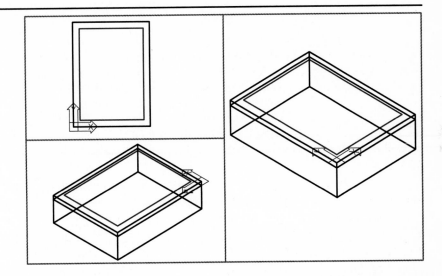

Figure 5-27.
The face wireframe is completed by filleting the polyline and copying it on the Z axis.

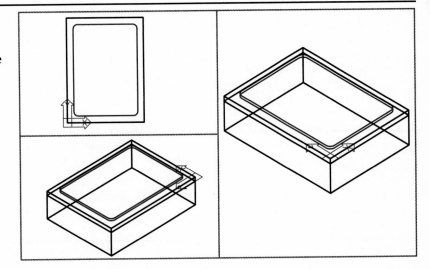

Using RULESURF to Surface Fillets

The **RULESURF** command is used to surface the round corners of the face and the top surface of the face at the corners. To do this efficiently, make a single view of the large viewport. Save this viewport configuration as ONE. Next, zoom in so that the object fills the screen. Use the **VIEW** command to save the current display as ALL. Now, zoom in on the front corner (insertion point) of the face and body cap. Save this display with the name CORNER.

PROFESSIONAL TIP

Do not confuse viewports with views. Model space *viewports* are actually several separate screens displayed on your monitor. Viewports are created using the **VPORTS** command. A *view* is a specific window or "snapshot" of the drawing. Any named view can be displayed in any viewport. This makes using viewports with saved views very versatile.

When you open a drawing that has saved views, you can select the view that is first displayed. Use the **OPEN** command and pick the drawing name. Then, pick the **Select Initial View** check box and pick **Open**. The **Select Initial View** dialog box appears. Select the view you want displayed when the drawing is open and pick **OK**. Each time you open the drawing, you can select a different view.

Next, you need to place a point at the center of a fillet radius on the top of the face. This point is needed to construct the ruled surface. Change to the Constr layer, set an appropriate value for **PDMODE**, and set **PDSIZE** to .04. In this example, a **PDMODE** value of 3 is used so that the point appears as an "X." Then, use the **POINT** command to place a point at the center of the arc, Figure 5-28A. The **Center** object snap can be quickly accessed from the shortcut menu to locate the center of the arc.

Use the **EXPLODE** command to break apart the two polylines that represent the face. This lets you select the corner arcs with the **RULESURF** command, Figure 5-28B. Change to the Face2 layer, set **SURFTAB1** to 6, and select the **RULESURF** command.

```
Command: RULESURF↵
Current wire frame density:  SURFTAB1=6
Select first defining curve: (pick curve 1 in Figure 5-28B)
Select second defining curve: (pick curve 2 in Figure 5-28B)
```

The corner is now surfaced with six segments. See Figure 5-28C. If you want more or fewer segments, erase the ruled surface and redraw it with a different **SURFTAB1** setting.

Next, a ruled surface must be applied to the top of the face. This will connect the corner arc to the point at the center of the arc. You must pick the arc as the first defining curve, not the ruled surface. If you pick the ruled surface, the message Object not usable to define ruled surface appears on the command line. To avoid picking the ruled surface, zoom in on the arc and the point, Figure 5-28D. Notice that the ruled surface on the corner is composed of straight segments and the corner arc is smooth. Use the **RULESURF** command to pick the top curve and the center point. After the top is surfaced, you can either erase the point or turn off the Constr layer. The corner should look like Figure 5-28E. Save your work before continuing.

Figure 5-28.
Surfacing the corners of the face. A—Place a point at the center of the fillet. B—Create a ruled surface using the corner arcs. C—The ruled surface on the edge of the corner. D—Zoom in to make sure you pick the arc, not the first ruled surface, to create an edge surface on the top of the corner. E—The surfaced corner.

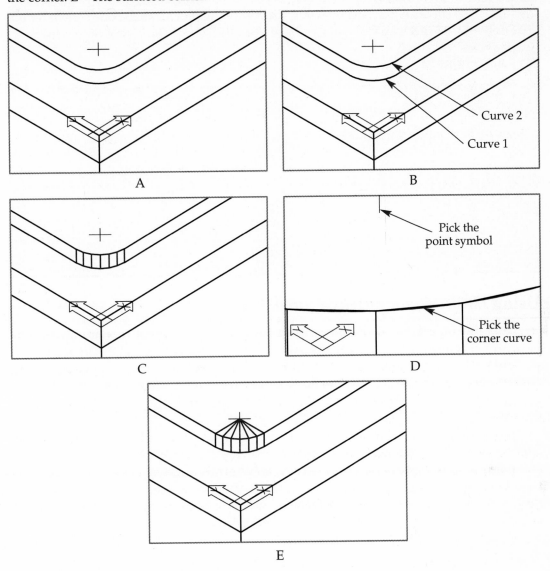

❏ Draw a circle 2″ (50mm) in diameter.
❏ Copy the circle up four units on the Z axis.
❏ Use the **VPOINT** command to get an isometric view (–1,–1,1) of the circles.
❏ Make two copies of the circles so that your drawing looks like the one shown here.
❏ Set the **SURFTAB1** variable to 4 and use the **RULESURF** command on the first set of circles.
❏ Set the **SURFTAB1** variable to 8 and use the **RULESURF** command on the second set of circles.
❏ Set the **SURFTAB1** variable to 16 and use the **RULESURF** command on the third set of circles.
❏ Save your drawing as EX5-2.

A   B   C

Using **MIRROR** and **3DFACE** on 3D Objects

You can repeat the above procedure for each of the three remaining corners. However, it is much faster to let AutoCAD do this for you with the **MIRROR** command. Be sure you have a single viewport and restore the ALL view. For this example, turn Ortho mode on and reflect the surfaces along the X axis. Then reflect *both* corners along the Y axis. Use the **Midpoint** object snap to pick the mirror line. Do not delete the old objects.

Now, there are two 3D faces that must be constructed. Use the **VIEW** command to create a view of the upper-left corner. Name this view CORNER2. Next, use the **VPORTS** command to create a two-viewport vertical configuration. Save it as TWO. Restore the CORNER2 view in the left viewport and the CORNER view in the right viewport. You may also want to remake the CORNER view so that it more closely matches CORNER2. To do this, delete the existing **CORNER** view and create another one. Your screen should look like Figure 5-29.

Figure 5-29.
To draw a 3D face on the edge of the puck face, create two viewports. Then, display a different corner in each.

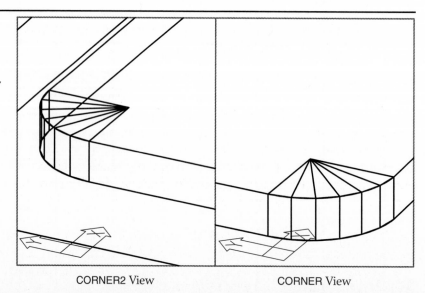

CORNER2 View   CORNER View

Now, you can apply 3D faces to the vertical side of the puck face and the top surface between the rule-surfaced corners. Make sure the Face2 layer is current. Set the **Endpoint** running object snap.

Draw the vertical 3D face using the pick points shown in Figure 5-30A. Then, press [Enter] to end the **3DFACE** command. Remember, to activate a viewport, simply move the cursor to the viewport and pick. Next, draw the top face between the centers of the arcs and the edge of the previous face, Figure 5-30B.

Figure 5-30.
A—Creating a 3D face on the edge of the puck face. B—Creating a 3D face on the top of the puck face. C—The finished 3D faces.

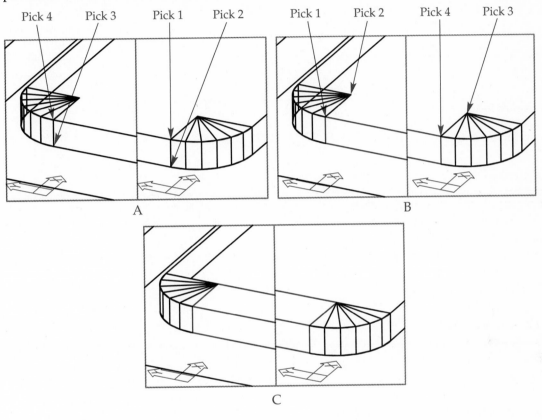

NOTE
You *cannot* switch viewports while using the **PAN** and **VPLAYER** commands.

Restore the ONE viewport and the ALL view. Use the **MIRROR** command to copy the 3D faces and ruled surfaces to the opposite side of the face. See Figure 5-31.

Next, you need to add 3D faces to the narrow vertical ends of the puck face. Then, add one large 3D face to the top of the puck face. It may be easier to change the viewpoint, or even return to a plan view, to draw the 3D face on the top. Use the **3DFACE** command and pick the four corners indicated in Figure 5-32. Use the **Endpoint** object snap to help.

The completed face is shown in Figure 5-33 after using the **HIDE** command. Your screen display may have a line or two missing where the face rests on the body cap. This is because those two surfaces are at the same elevation and AutoCAD "thinks" some lines on the face may be hidden.

Figure 5-31.
Using **MIRROR** to copy the 3D faces. This is quicker than drawing new 3D faces on the other side of the object.

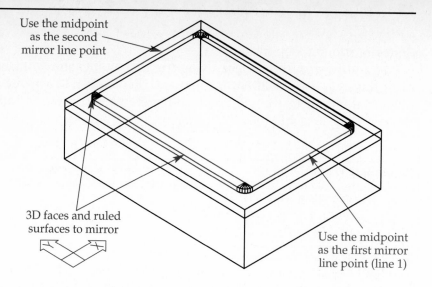

Use the midpoint as the second mirror line point

3D faces and ruled surfaces to mirror

Use the midpoint as the first mirror line point (line 1)

Figure 5-32.
Completing the surfacing of the puck face.

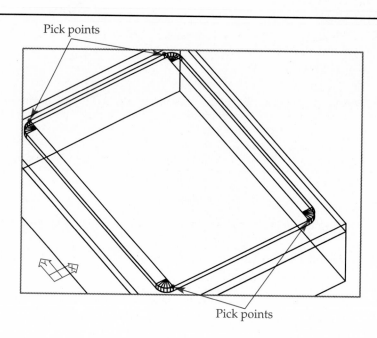

Pick points

Pick points

Figure 5-33.
The surfaced puck face after using **HIDE**.

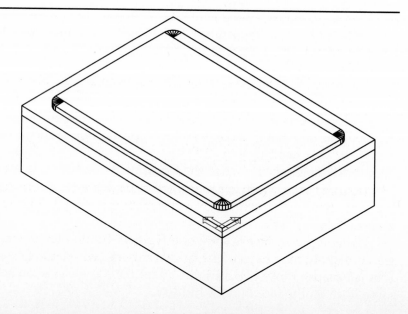

Constructing the Eyepiece with RULESURF

To draw the eyepiece, first set the Eyepiece layer current and restore the viewport configuration THREE. Make the upper-left viewport active and display a plan view showing the upper half of the object. Then, make the large viewport active and use **VPOINT** as follows.

> Command: **–VP** *or* **VPOINT**⏎
> Current view direction: VIEWDIR=1.0000,–1.0000,0.7500
> Specify a view point or [Rotate] <display compass and tripod>: **–2,1.5,1**⏎

Next, pick the lower-left viewport, and continue as follows.

> Command: **–VP** *or* **VPOINT**⏎
> Current view direction: VIEWDIR=–1.0000, 1.0000,1.0000
> Specify a view point or [Rotate] <display compass and tripod>: **–1,–1,1**⏎

Your display should now look like Figure 5-34A.

Now, create a new UCS by moving the origin to where the eyepiece attaches to the body. See Figure 5-34B. Save the new UCS as EYEPIECE and apply it to all viewports. Move the UCS icon to the new origin in all viewports. Save this viewport configuration as THREE. Replace the existing viewport configuration named THREE when prompted. Creating this new UCS allows you to enter the dimensions of the eyepiece from the origin.

To begin drawing the eyepiece, make the upper-left viewport active and return to a single viewport. Use the **CIRCLE** and **LINE** commands to draw the outline as follows. Then, use the **TRIM** command to cut away the unused portion of the circle.

> Command: **C** *or* **CIRCLE**⏎
> Specify center point for circle or [3P/2P/Ttr (tan tan radius)]: **1.125,.75**⏎
> Specify radius of circle or [Diameter]: **D**⏎
> Specify diameter of circle: **.5**⏎
> Command: ⏎
> CIRCLE Specify center point for circle or [3P/2P/Ttr (tan tan radius)]: **@**⏎
> Specify radius of circle or [Diameter]: **.75**⏎
> Command: **L** *or* **LINE**⏎
> Specify first point: **0,0**⏎
> Specify next point or [Undo]: **TAN**⏎
> to (*pick the left side of the large circle*)
> Specify next point or [Undo]: ⏎
> Command: ⏎
> LINE Specify first point: **2.25,0**⏎
> Specify next point or [Undo]: **TAN**⏎
> to (*pick the right side of the large circle*)
> Specify next point or [Undo]: ⏎
> Command: **TR** *or* **TRIM**⏎
> Current settings: Projection=UCS Edge=None
> Select cutting edge(s)…
> Select objects: (*pick the two tangent lines*)
> Select objects: ⏎
> Select object to trim or [Project/Edge/Undo]: (*pick the inside portion of the large circle*)
> Select object to trim or [Project/Edge/Undo]: ⏎

Restore the viewport configuration named THREE. Zoom in closely to the eyepiece in the right-hand viewport. Then, use the **VIEW** command to save the view as EYEPIECE2. Your drawing should look similar to Figure 5-35A.

In the right viewport, copy the eyepiece outline .25" on the +Z axis. Draw a line connecting the two ends of the top surface of the eyepiece. The 3D wireframe of the eyepiece is complete, Figure 5-35B.

Figure 5-34.
A—Change the views to help you draw the eyepiece. B—Place a new UCS at the bottom corner of the puck body to help you locate coordinates better.

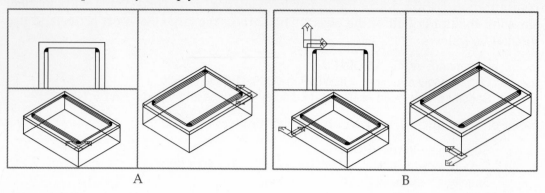

A   B

Figure 5-35.
A—First, draw the bottom of the eyepiece. B—Then, copy the objects on the Z axis to create the top.

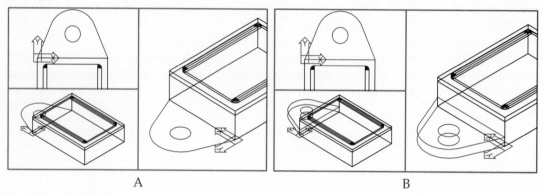

A   B

Before you begin surfacing the eyepiece, however, it is important to determine how to surface the top plane of the eyepiece. Remember that **RULESURF** requires two separate entities, and closed objects, such as circles, cannot be used with an open object. Therefore, you must redraw the circle as arcs on the Constr layer before surfacing.

First, set the Constr layer current. Then, change the UCS origin to the top surface of the eyepiece directly above the current origin. Zoom in on the top circle of the eyepiece. Use the **ARC** command to draw three arcs. Specify the center of each arc as the center of the circle already drawn. Use the **Center** and **Quadrant** object snaps, as indicated in Figure 5-36A. Then, draw a point at the quadrant between arcs two and three. Be sure **PDMODE** is set to 3 and **PDSIZE** is set to .08.

You can now use the **RULESURF** command to surface the entire eyepiece. Change the current layer to Eyesurf. Then, create the following four ruled surfaces:

- The first ruled surface uses the point at the circle quadrant and the adjacent line, Figure 5-37A.
- The second ruled surface uses Arc 2 and the adjacent angled line, Figure 5-37B.
- The third ruled surface uses Arc 1 and the large outside arc, Figure 5-37C.
- The fourth ruled surface uses Arc 3 and the adjacent angled line, Figure 5-37D.

Figure 5-36.
A—Draw three arcs and a point to help you surface the top of the eyepiece. B—The pick points to use when surfacing the eyepiece.

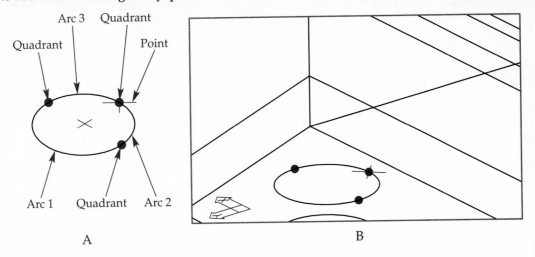

A

B

Figure 5-37.
Use **RULESURF** four times to completely surface the top of the eyepiece.

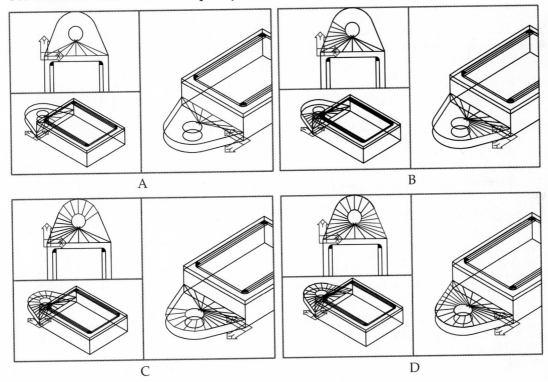

A

B

C

D

Be sure to pick near the same end of both entities when using the **RULESURF** command. If you pick near opposite ends of the two entities, the surfacing segment lines cross over each other. For example, notice in A below that the first pick is located near the far end of the line. Pick number 2 is at the near end of the arc, diagonal to pick 1. This results in crossed segments. In B below, pick points 1 and 2 are near the same ends of the line and arc, or adjacent to each other. This creates a properly ruled surface.

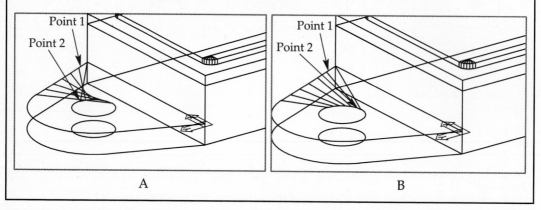

A   B

The hole and the round end of the eyepiece must also be surfaced. These two surfaces are created just like the filleted corners on the puck face. Use zoom so you can pick the original circle and not the ruled surface. Since you cannot mix open and closed paths, remove the arcs from the drawing by turning off the Constr layer. This ensures you will not select an arc and a circle. Use a tight zoom and pick the circles, Figure 5-38. Also, use the **RULESURF** command to surface the curved end of the eyepiece.

Be sure to change **SURFTAB1** if you want more than six segments for the surface of the hole. A **SURFTAB1** setting of 8 is used for the illustration in Figure 5-39. The larger the value, the smoother the circle.

The final step in constructing the eyepiece is to create a 3D face on each vertical side. You can either draw two separate faces, or draw one face and mirror it. When you are finished, use the **HIDE** command to be sure that you have created all of the needed surfaces. See Figure 5-39.

Figure 5-38.
Use zoom to make sure you pick the circles, and not the ruled surface.

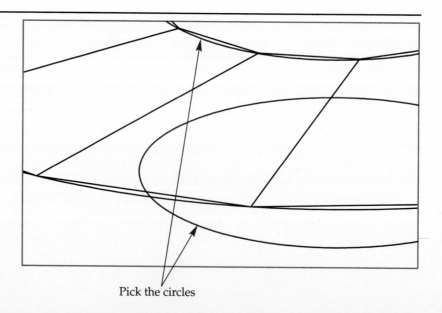

Pick the circles

Figure 5-39.
The completed
eyepiece after using
HIDE.

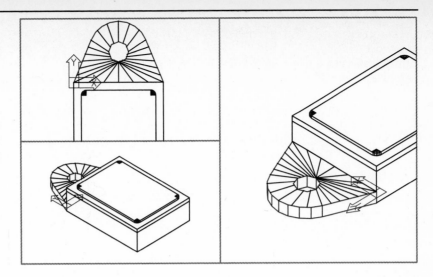

Constructing a Cable with REVSURF

The **REVSURF** (revolved surface) command draws a symmetrical shape revolved around a central axis. To draw a revolved surface, you need a profile and an axis (line). The profile is the shape to be revolved. AutoCAD calls this profile the *path curve*. The *axis* is a line that the shape is revolved around. For the puck cable, the path curve is a circle. A revolved surface can be drawn to fill any angle. A 360° angle creates a full circle. For the puck cable, the circle is revolved 90°.

The **SURFTAB1** variable controls the number of segments on the surface around the axis. The **SURFTAB2** variable controls the number of segments on the path curve. Before using the **REVSURF** command, determine the number of segments needed and set the **SURFTAB** variables. For the puck cable, set **SURFTAB1** to 12 and **SURFTAB2** to 8. This creates eight segments around the circumference of the circle and twelve segments around the axis.

To draw the cable, first make the Cable layer current. Then, use the **VPORTS**, **VPOINT**, **PAN**, and **ZOOM** commands to adjust the viewports so they look like Figure 5-40. For the lower-left viewport, you need to change the UCS. Use the **UCS** command as follows:

```
Command: UCS↵
Current ucs name: current
Enter an option [New/Move/orthoGraphic/Prev/Restore/Save/Del/Apply/?/World]
<World>: X↵
Specify rotation angle about X axis <0>: 90↵
Command: ↵
Current ucs name: current
Enter an option [New/Move/orthoGraphic/Prev/Restore/Save/Del/Apply/?/World]
<World>: Y↵
Specify rotation angle about Y axis <90>: –90↵
Command: ↵
Current ucs name: current
Enter an option [New/Move/orthoGraphic/Prev/Restore/Save/Del/Apply/?/World]
<World>: OR↵
Specify origin of new UCS or [ZAxis/3point/OBject/Face/View/X/Y/Z] <0,0,0>: END↵
of (pick the corner shown in the large viewport of Figure 5-40)
```

Apply this new UCS to all viewports. Then, make the lower-left viewport active. Use the **PLAN** command to make the viewport plan to the current UCS. Once your display looks like Figure 5-40, save the viewport configuration as CABLE.

Figure 5-40.
Create a new viewport configuration to help draw the cable.

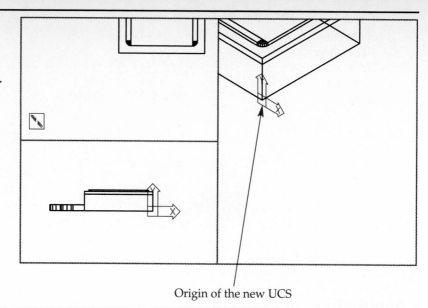

Origin of the new UCS

Now, create a new UCS on the end of the puck. Name this UCS CABLE. Use the **3point** and **Save** options of the **UCS** command. Refer to Figure 5-41. You can now create the profile and the axis. Start in the large viewport and use the **CIRCLE** and **LINE** commands as follows.

```
Command: CIRCLE↵
Specify center point for circle or [3P/2P/Ttr (tan tan radius)]: 1.125,.35↵
Specify radius of circle or [Diameter] <current>: D↵
Specify diameter of circle <current>: .25↵
Command: LINE↵
Specify first point: –1.5,1↵
Specify next point or [Undo]: –1.5,–1↵
Specify next point or [Undo]: ↵
```

Set the two **SURFTAB** variables and then use the **REVSURF** command to complete the cable as follows. If you already have the **SURFTAB** variables set correctly, start with the **REVSURF** command.

Figure 5-41.
Create a new UCS on the end of the puck body. Pick the origin, X axis, and Y axis as shown here.

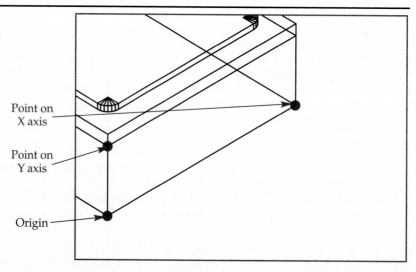

Point on X axis

Point on Y axis

Origin

```
Command: SURFTAB1↵
Enter new value for SURFTAB1 <current>: 12↵
Command: SURFTAB2↵
Enter new value for SURFTAB2 <current>: 8↵
Command: REVSURF↵
Current wire frame density:  SURFTAB1=12  SURFTAB2=8
Select object to revolve: (pick the path curve circle as shown in Figure 5-42A)
Select object that defines the axis of revolution: (pick the axis as shown in Figure 5-42A)
Specify start angle <0>: ↵
Specify included angle (+=ccw, -=cw) <360>: -90↵
Command:
```

You can now erase the axis line. The completed cable is shown in Figure 5-42B after using the **HIDE** command. Save your work before continuing.

Figure 5-42.
A—The path curve on the end of the puck and the axis of revolution. B—The completed cable.

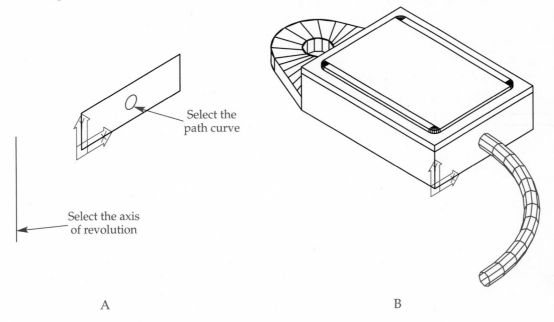

Select the
path curve

Select the axis
of revolution

A

B

NOTE	The -90° rotation for creating the cable is based on picking the lower part of the axis. If you select the upper part of the axis and enter -90°, the cable is rotated the opposite direction.

Creating Screw Heads with the DOME Command

The **3D Objects** dialog box and the **Surfaces** toolbar both contain three different spherical shapes. These are dome, dish, and sphere. The dome and the dish are simply one half of a sphere. For the puck, domes are used to represent screw heads on the face.

To draw the screw heads, first set the Screws layer current. Then, restore the FACE UCS. It may be easiest to switch to a single viewport and zoom in on the origin corner of the puck. Next, draw the screw heads as follows.

```
Command: (pick Dome from the 3D Objects dialog box or Surfaces toolbar)
Command: _ai_dome
Initializing...  3D Objects loaded.
Specify center point of dome: .095,.095↵
Specify radius of dome or [Diameter]: D↵
Specify diameter of dome: .125↵
Enter number of longitudinal segments for surface of dome <16>: 8↵
Enter number of latitudinal segments for surface of dome <8>: 4↵
Command:
```

This places one screw head on the face, Figure 5-43A. Now, use the **ARRAY** command to create the other three screw heads as follows:

```
Command: AR or ARRAY↵
Select objects: L↵
Select objects: ↵
Enter the type of array [Rectangular/Polar] <R>: ↵
Enter the number of rows (– – –) <1>: 2↵
Enter the number of columns (¦¦¦) <1>: 2↵
Enter the distance between rows or specify unit cell (– – –): 2.81↵
Specify the distance between columns (¦¦¦): 2.06↵
Command:
```

Figure 5-43B shows the array of four domes on the digitizer puck from the SW isometric viewpoint after using **HIDE**.

Figure 5-43.
Use domes to represent screw heads on the face of the puck. A—Draw one dome in the lower-left corner. B—Use **ARRAY** to copy the first dome to the other three locations.

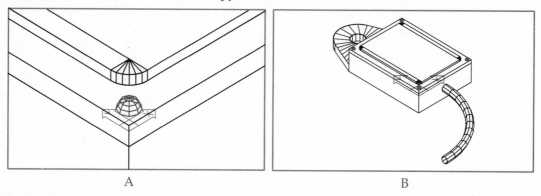

A   B

Inserting the Button 3D Block

The last thing to do is add the buttons. This digitizer has twelve buttons. Earlier, you created a block called BUTTON. If you completed the optional, curved button, you may also have that saved as a block. You must insert the button block on the face of the puck. First, set the Buttons layer current. Then, create and save a new UCS as follows. Be sure that the current UCS is the Face UCS prior to starting the command sequence.

Command: **UCS**↵
Current ucs name: *current*
Enter an option [New/Move/orthoGraphic/Prev/Restore/Save/Del/Apply/?/World]
<World>: **N**↵
Specify origin of new UCS or [ZAxis/3point/OBject/Face/View/X/Y/Z] <0,0,0>:
.19,.19,.06↵
Command: ↵
Current ucs name: *current*
Enter an option [New/Move/orthoGraphic/Prev/Restore/Save/Del/Apply/?/World]
<World>: **S**↵
Enter name to save current UCS or [?]: **BUTTON**↵
Command:

For the insert operation, you need only a single view of the object on the screen. With a single viewport configuration, zoom in on the face of the puck. Then, insert the buttons as follows.

Command: **MINSERT**↵
Enter block name or [?]: **BUTTON**↵
Specify insertion point or [Scale/X/Y/Z/Rotate/PScale/PX/PY/PZ/PRotate]: **.3125,.5**↵
Enter X scale factor, specify opposite corner, or [Corner/XYZ] <1>: ↵
    Enter Y scale factor <use X scale factor>: ↵
    Specify rotation angle <0>: ↵
Enter number of rows (– – –) <1>: **4**↵
Enter number of columns (⁞⁞⁞) <1>: **3**↵
Enter distance between rows or specify unit cell (– – –): **.457**↵
Specify distance between columns (⁞⁞⁞): **.457**↵

The completed puck is shown in Figure 5-44 after using the **HIDE** command.

Figure 5-44.
The completed puck
with buttons.

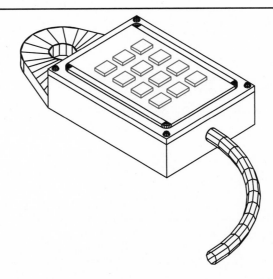

NOTE	Determine the best method for adding numbers to the buttons. If the BUTTON block had been given an attribute, the numbers could be added at insertion. However, the **INSERT** command would need to be used twelve times instead of using **MINSERT** once. If you use **DTEXT**, you can use the **CAL** function to define the center of the button, and then use **DTEXT**. What is the most efficient method?

Chapter Test

Answer the following questions on a separate sheet of paper.
1. Name three commands that allow you to create different types of meshes.
2. What command creates a surface mesh between four edges?
3. How must the four edges be related when using the command in Question 2?
4. What values does AutoCAD need to know for a 3D mesh?
5. AutoCAD's surface meshing commands create what type of entities?
6. Which surface mesh command allows you to rotate a profile about an axis to create a symmetrical object?
7. What object does **TABSURF** create?
8. What do the **SURFTAB1** and **SURFTAB2** variables control?
9. Name three entities that can be connected with the **RULESURF** command.
10. When using **RULESURF**, what happens if the two objects are selected near opposite ends?
11. Why should you avoid using large numbers for the **SURFTAB** settings?

Drawing Problems

Construct 3D surface models of the following problems. For objects without dimensions, measure directly from the text. Problems 1–8 are objects that were drawn as problems in Chapter 1, problems 9–13 are problems from Chapter 3. Save the models as P5-1, P5-2, etc.

1.

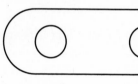

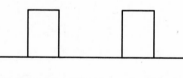

2.

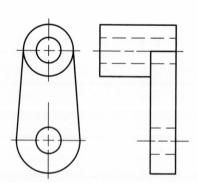

3.

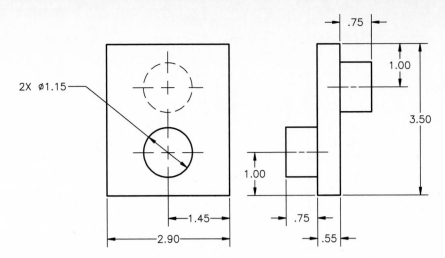

2X ⌀1.15

.75

1.00

3.50

1.00

1.45

2.90

.75

.55

4.

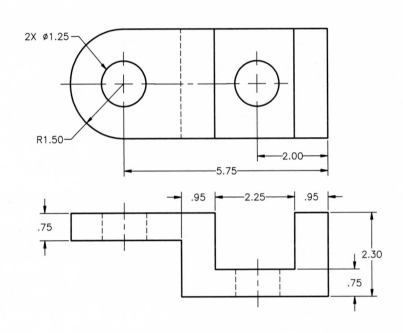

2X ⌀1.25

R1.50

2.00

5.75

.75

.95

2.25

.95

2.30

.75

5.

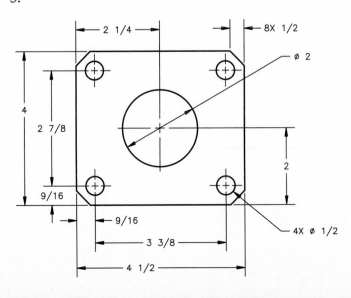

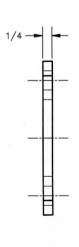

2 1/4

8X 1/2

⌀ 2

1/4

4

2 7/8

2

9/16

9/16

3 3/8

4 1/2

4X ⌀ 1/2

6.

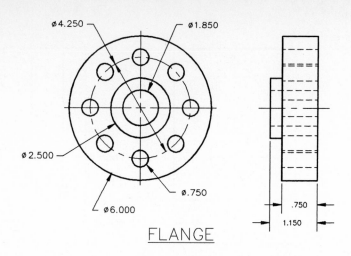

FLANGE

7.

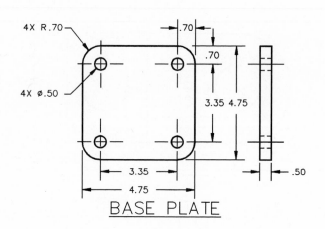

BASE PLATE

8.

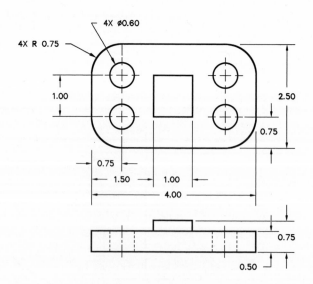

9.

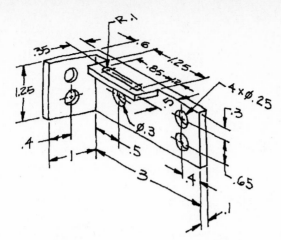

WINDOW BLIND MOUNTING BRACKET

10.

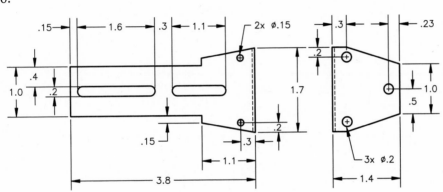

MATERIAL THICKNESS = .125"

11.

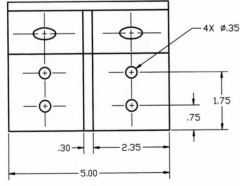

4X Ø.35

1.75
.75

.30
2.35
5.00

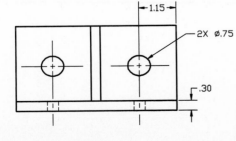

1.15
2X Ø.75

.30

1.40
2.80
60°
2.50

12.

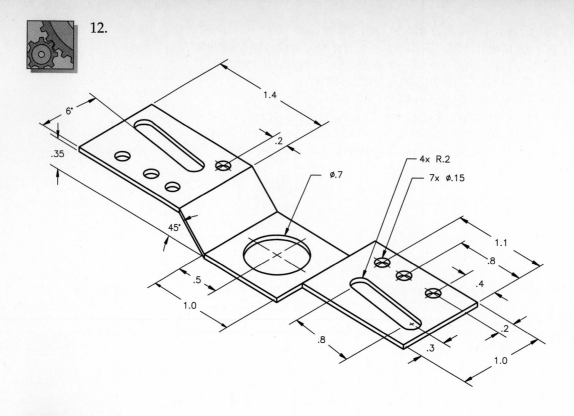

13.

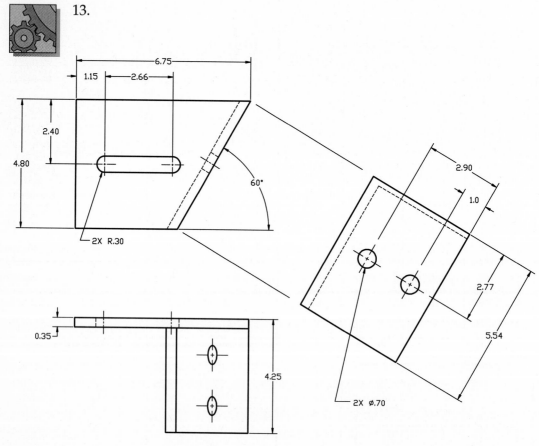

14. Create a surface model of a glass using the profile shown.
    A. Use the **REVSURF** command to construct the glass.
    B. Use the dimensions given for height and radii.
    C. Set the **SURFTAB1** variable to 16.
    D. Set the **SURFTAB2** variable to 8.
    E. Use **HIDE** to remove hidden lines.
    F. Construct the glass a second time using different **SURFTAB** settings.
    G. Plot the drawing on B-size bond both as a wireframe and with hidden lines removed.

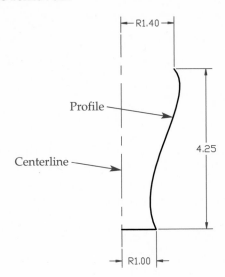

*Problems 15–16. Draw the following objects using the **REVSURF** command. Accept the default values for segments. Display the objects and use **HIDE** on each. Save the drawings as P5-15 and P5-16.*

15.

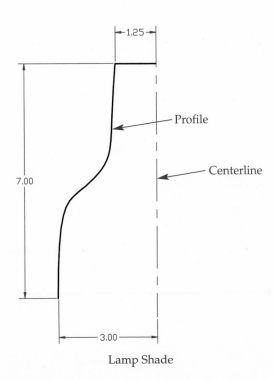

Lamp Shade

16.

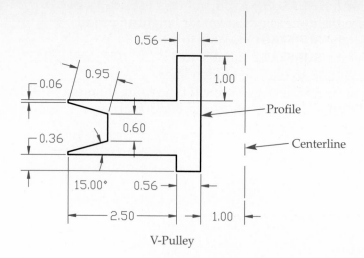

V-Pulley

Problems 17–19. Problems 17 through 19 are plans of two houses and a cabin. Create a 3D model of the house(s) assigned by your instructor. Use all modeling techniques covered in this chapter.

    A. Establish multiple viewports.

    B. Create named user coordinate systems for the floor plan and the various wall elevations.

    C. Create named viewport configurations (using one viewport) of single floors or walls so you can display the working areas as large as possible on the screen.

    D. Use the dimensions given or alter the room sizes and arrangements to suit your own design. Use your own dimensions for anything not specified.

    E. Plot the model on B-size or C-size sheet with hidden lines removed.

 17.

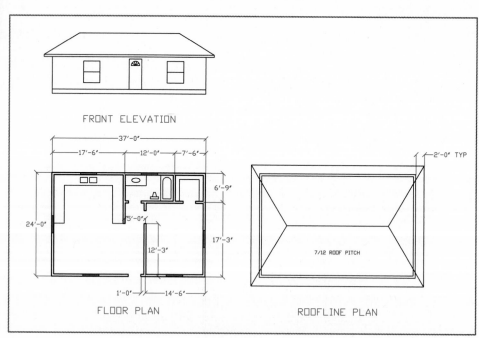

18.

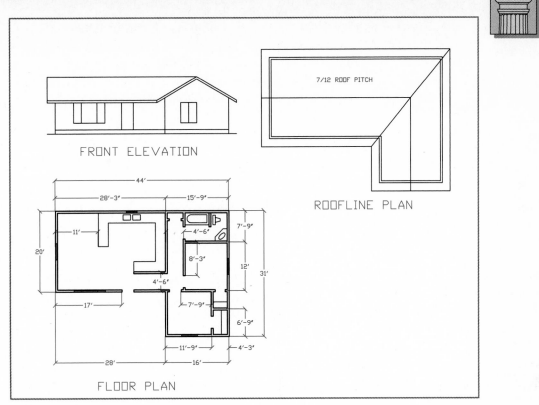

FRONT ELEVATION

7/12 ROOF PITCH

ROOFLINE PLAN

FLOOR PLAN

19.

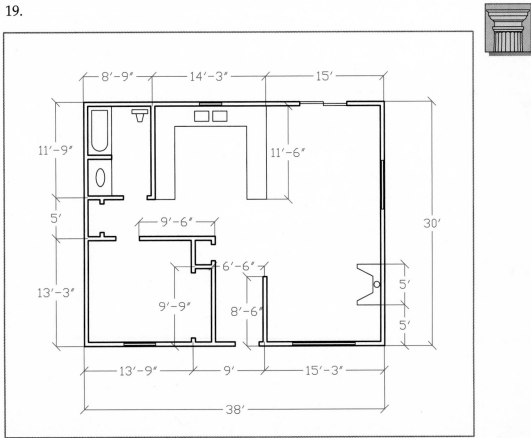

20. Complete the digitizer puck that was demonstrated in the tutorial.
    A. Add numbers to the buttons.
    B. Redraw as many 3D faces as possible using the **Invisible** option of the **3DFACE** command.
    C. Delete the square buttons and insert the curved buttons.
    D. Generate laser prints or pen plots on A-size or B-size paper showing the view in each of the four compass quadrants.

AutoCAD and its Applications—Advanced

CHAPTER 6

Editing Three-Dimensional Objects

Learning Objectives

After completing this chapter, you will be able to:

- Use grips to edit 3D objects.
- Align, rotate, and mirror 3D objects.
- Trim and extend 3D objects.
- Create fillets and rounds.
- Edit polygon meshes.

It is always important to use proper editing techniques and commands. This is especially true when using a variety of user coordinate systems and 3D objects. This chapter covers the correct procedures for editing 3D objects.

CHANGING PROPERTIES

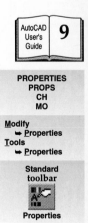

AutoCAD User's Guide **9**

PROPERTIES
PROPS
CH
MO

Modify
➥ Properties
Tools
➥ Properties

Standard
toolbar

Properties

Properties of 3D objects can be modified using the **Properties** window. This window is accessed by picking the **Properties** button in the **Standard** toolbar, picking **Properties** from the **Modify** or **Tools** pull-down menus, or by typing CH, MO, PROPS, PROPERTIES, DDMODIFY, or DDCHPROP at the Command: prompt.

The **Properties** window lists the properties of the currently selected object. For example, Figure 6-1 lists the properties of the selected polygon mesh. The **Categorized** tab lists the properties by category (**General**, **Geometry**, **Mesh**, and **Misc** for a polygon mesh). The **Alphabetic** tab lists properties alphabetically.

To modify an object property, select the property and then enter a new value in the right column. The drawing is updated to reflect the changes.

NOTE	The **Properties** window is discussed more thoroughly in *AutoCAD and its Applications—Basics*.

For 2000i Users...

In AutoCAD 2000i, double-click on an object to select the object and open the **Properties** window.

The **CHANGE** command can also be used to change the base point and some properties of 3D objects from the Command: prompt. However, it has some limitations when an object is not perpendicular to the Z axis of the current UCS. The **CHPROP** command is similar to **CHANGE** command, but can only be used to modify a few object properties.

Figure 6-1.
The **Properties** window can be used to change the properties of an object, from its color to its location.

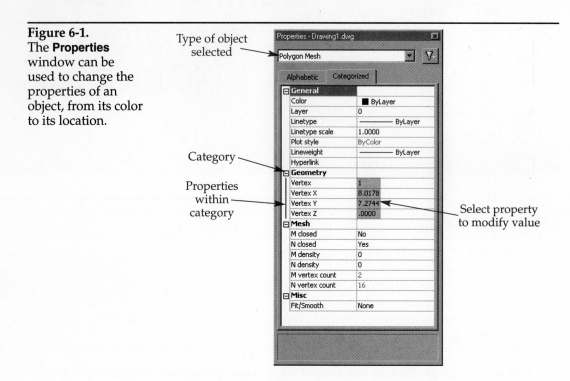

USING GRIPS TO EDIT 3D OBJECTS

Using grips is an efficient way to edit 3D objects. For an in-depth discussion on using grips, refer to Chapter 12 of *AutoCAD and its Applications—Basics*. Editing should be done in a 3D view where you can see the change dynamically. For example, to change the height of a cone using grips, first change to a 3D view, such as the SW isometric view. Next, pick anywhere on the cone and the grips appear, Figure 6-2A. Then, pick the grip at the apex of the cone so it becomes hot, Figure 6-2B. A hot grip is a red square that is filled solid. The **STRETCH** operation can be completed as follows.

STRETCH
Specify stretch point or [Base point/Copy/Undo/eXit]: **.XY**↵
of *(pick the grip at the cone apex again)*
(need Z): **5**↵
Command:

Notice that you can move a hot grip around the screen with your pointing device. It appears that the grip is moving in all three (XYZ) directions. However, this is misleading. You are actually moving the grip in the XY plane. If you pick a point, the Z value of the grip is changed to 0. In other words, you have placed the grip on the current XY plane. Therefore, use XYZ filters or enter relative coordinates to edit 3D objects.

Figure 6-2.
Using grips to edit a 3D object. A—First, pick on the object to make the grips warm. Then, pick the grip to edit so that it becomes hot. B—Next, enter coordinates at the keyboard for the new location of the grip. C—The edited object.

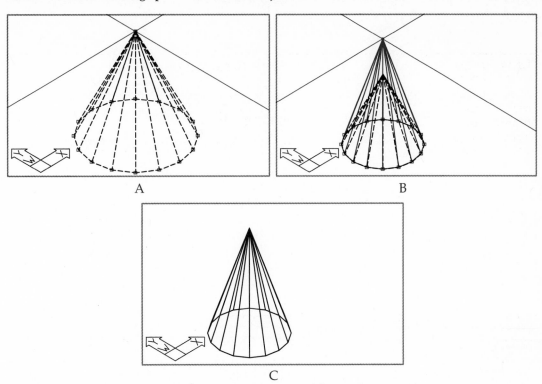

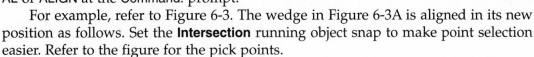

ALIGNING 3D OBJECTS

AutoCAD User's Guide 9

The **ALIGN** command allows you to correct errors of 3D construction and quickly manipulate 3D shapes. **ALIGN** requires existing points (source), and the new location of those existing points (destination). The **ALIGN** command can be selected by picking **Align** from the **3D Operation** cascading menu of the **Modify** pull-down menu, or entering AL or ALIGN at the Command: prompt.

For example, refer to Figure 6-3. The wedge in Figure 6-3A is aligned in its new position as follows. Set the **Intersection** running object snap to make point selection easier. Refer to the figure for the pick points.

> Command: **AL** *or* **ALIGN**↵
> Select objects: *(pick the wedge)*
> Select objects: ↵
> Specify first source point: *(pick P1)*
> Specify first destination point: *(pick P2)*
> Specify second source point: *(pick P3)*
> Specify second destination point: *(pick P4)*
> Specify third source point or <continue>: *(pick P5)*
> Specify third destination point: *(pick P1 again)*
> Command:

The aligned object should look like Figure 6-3B.

Figure 6-3.
The **ALIGN** command can be used to properly orient 3D objects.

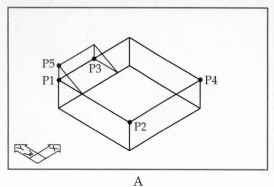
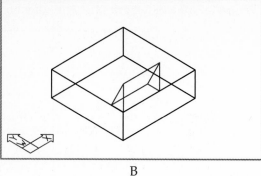

A   B

EXERCISE 6-1

❑ Begin a new drawing.
❑ Draw a box and a wedge arranged like those shown in Figure 6-3A.
❑ Use the **ALIGN** command to create the arrangement shown below.
❑ Save the drawing as EX6-1.

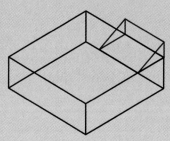

AutoCAD User's Guide **18**

3D ROTATING

The **ROTATE3D** command can rotate objects on any axis, regardless of the current UCS. This is an extremely powerful editing and design feature. When using the default option, you must pick two points to define an axis of rotation and specify a rotation angle. The rotation angle is defined by looking down the axis from the second pick point and specifying an angle. A positive angle rotates the object counterclockwise.

To use the **ROTATE3D** command, select **Rotate 3D** from the **3D Operation** cascading menu in the **Modify** pull-down menu, or enter ROTATE3D at the Command: prompt. The following example rotates the wedge in Figure 6-3 –90° on a selected axis. See Figure 6-4A for the pick points.

Command: **ROTATE3D.**↵
Current positive angle: ANGDIR=*(current)* ANGBASE=*(current)*
Select objects: *(pick the wedge)*
1 found
Select objects: ↵
Specify first point on axis or define axis by
[Object/Last/View/Xaxis/Yaxis/Zaxis/2points]: *(pick P1)*
Specify second point on axis: *(pick P2)*
Specify rotation angle or [Reference]: **–90.**↵
Command:

The rotated object is shown in Figure 6-4B.

There are several different ways to define an axis of rotation with the **ROTATE3D** command. These are explained as follows.

- **Object.** Objects such as lines, arcs, circles, and polylines can define the axis. A line becomes the axis. The axis of a circle or arc passes through its center, perpendicular to the plane of the circle. For a polyline, the selected segment (line or arc) is used to determine the axis.
- **Last.** Uses the last axis of rotation defined.
- **View.** The viewing direction of the current viewport is aligned with a selected point to define the axis.
- **Xaxis/Yaxis/Zaxis.** Aligns the axis of rotation with the X, Y, or Z axis and a selected point.
- **2points.** Allows you to pick two points to define the axis.

Figure 6-4.
The **ROTATE3D** command is used to rotate objects about an axis in 3D space, regardless of the current UCS.

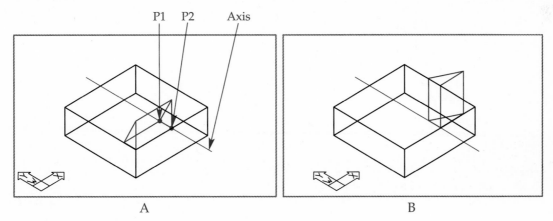

P1   P2   Axis

A   B

PROFESSIONAL TIP The **Rotate 3D** button can be used in a custom toolbar or added to an existing toolbar. Refer to Chapter 20 for information on customizing toolbars.

❏ Open the drawing created in the last exercise (EX6-1).
❏ Use the **ROTATE3D** command to rotate the wedge to the position shown below.
❏ Save the drawing as EX6-2.

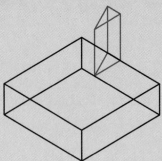

3D MIRRORING

The **MIRROR3D** command allows you to mirror objects about any plane, regardless of the current UCS. The default option is to define a mirror plane by picking three points on that plane, Figure 6-5A. Object snap modes should be used to accurately define the mirror plane.

To use the **MIRROR3D** command, select **Mirror 3D** from the **3D Operation** cascading menu in the **Modify** pull-down menu, or type MIRROR3D at the Command: prompt. To mirror the wedge in Figure 6-4B, set the **Midpoint** running object snap and use the following command sequence.

MIRROR3D

Modify
➥ **3D Operation**
  ➥ **Mirror 3D**

    Command: **MIRROR3D**↵
    Select objects: *(pick the wedge)*
    1 found
    Select objects: ↵
    Specify first point of mirror plane (3 points) or
       [Object/Last/Zaxis/View/XY/YZ/ZX/3points] <3points>: *(pick P1)*
    Specify second point on mirror plane: *(pick P2)*
    Specify third point on mirror plane: *(pick P3)*
    Delete source objects? [Yes/No] <N>: ↵
    Command:

The drawing should now look like Figure 6-5B.

Figure 6-5.
The **MIRROR3D** command allows you to mirror objects about any plane, regardless of the current UCS. A—The mirror plane defined by the three pick points is shown here in color. B—A copy of the original object is mirrored.

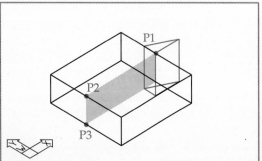

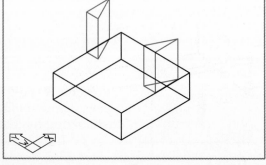

A   B

There are several different ways to define a mirror plane with the **MIRROR3D** command. These are explained as follows.

- **Object.** The plane of selected circle, arc, or 2D polyline segment is used as the mirror plane.
- **Last.** Uses the last mirror plane defined.
- **Zaxis.** Defines the plane with a pick point on the plane and a point on the Z axis of the mirror plane.
- **View.** The viewing direction of the current viewpoint is aligned with a selected point to define the axis.
- **XY/YZ/XZ.** The mirror plane is placed in one of the three basic planes, and passes through a selected point.
- **3points.** Allows you to pick three points to define the mirror plane.

PROFESSIONAL TIP

The **Mirror 3D** button can be used in a custom toolbar or added to an existing toolbar. Refer to Chapter 20 for information on customizing toolbars.

EXERCISE 6-3

❑ Open the drawing created in the last exercise (EX6-2).
❑ Use the **MIRROR3D** command to mirror the wedge to the position drawn below.
❑ Save the drawing as EX6-3.

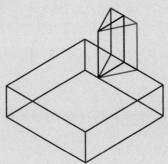

CREATING 3D ARRAYS

AutoCAD User's Guide 18

Creating an array of 3D objects in 3D space is discussed and illustrated in Chapter 2. However, this type of construction is sometimes considered editing. Therefore, a brief discussion also appears here.

Rectangular 3D Arrays

An example of where a rectangular 3D array may be created is the layout of structural steel columns on multiple floors of a commercial building. To use the **3DARRAY** command, select **3D Array** from the **3D Operation** cascading menu in the **Modify** pull-down menu, or enter 3A or 3DARRAY at the Command: prompt. Then, specify the **Rectangular** option when prompted.

3DARRAY
3A

Modify
➥ 3D Operation
➥ 3D Array

In Figure 6-6A, you can see two concrete floor slabs of a building and a single steel column. It is now a simple matter of arraying the steel column in rows, columns, and levels. Use the following procedure.

```
Command: 3A or 3DARRAY↵
Select objects: (pick the object)
1 found
Select objects: ↵
Enter the type of array [Rectangular/Polar] <R>: R↵
Enter the  number of rows (---) <1>: 3↵
Enter the number of columns (¦¦¦) <1>: 5↵
Enter the number of levels (...) <1>: 2↵
Specify the distance between rows (---): 10'↵
Specify the distance between columns (¦¦¦): 10'↵
Specify the distance between levels (...): 12'8↵
```

The result is shown in Figure 6-6B. Constructions like this can be quickly assembled for multiple levels using the **3DARRAY** command only once.

Figure 6-6.
A—Two floors and one steel column are drawn. B—A rectangular 3D array is used to place all the required steel columns on both floors at the same time.

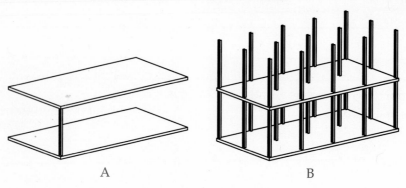

A   B

Polar 3D Arrays

A polar 3D array is similar to a polar 2D array. However, you must also select a center-line axis of rotation. You can array an object in a UCS different from the current one. Unlike a rectangular 3D array, a polar 3D array does not allow you to create levels of the object. The object is arrayed in a plane defined by the object and the selected centerline (Z) axis.

3DARRAY
3A

Modify
↳ **3D Operation**
  ↳ **3D Array**

To use the **3DARRAY** command, select **3D Array** from the **3D Operation** cascading menu in the **Modify** pull-down menu, or enter 3A or 3DARRAY at the Command: prompt. Then, specify the **Polar** option when prompted.

For example, the tank nozzle in Figure 6-7A must be placed at the four quadrant points around the tank at the same elevation. Before using **3DARRAY**, an axis line must be drawn through the center of the tank. Then, continue as follows.

```
Command: 3A or 3DARRAY↵
Select objects: (select the object)
1 found
Select objects: ↵
Enter the type of array [Rectangular/Polar] <R>: P↵
Enter the number of items in the array: 4↵
Specify the angle to fill (+=ccw, -=cw) <360>: ↵
Rotate arrayed objects? [Yes/No] <Y>: ↵
Specify center point of array: (pick center of tank base)
Specify second point on axis of rotation: (pick top end of axis line)
Command:
```

The completed 3D polar array is shown in Figure 6-7B. If additional levels of a polar array are needed, they can be created by copying the array just created.

Figure 6-7.
A—The tank and one inlet are drawn.
B—A polar 3D array is used to create the three other inlets.

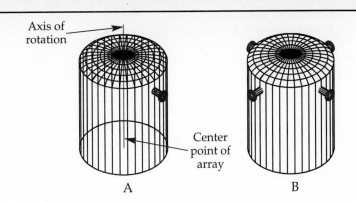

Axis of rotation

Center point of array

A   B

PROFESSIONAL TIP

3D Rectangular Array and **3D Polar Array** buttons can be used in a custom toolbar or added to an existing toolbar. Refer to Chapter 20 for information on customizing toolbars.

TRIMMING AND EXTENDING 3D OBJECTS

AutoCAD User's Guide 18

Using the **TRIM** and **EXTEND** commands on 3D objects may be confusing at first. However, both of these commands can be powerful tools when working in 3D. This section covers using these commands on 3D objects. The discussion centers on the **TRIM** command, but also applies to the **EXTEND** command.

Figure 6-8 shows three wireframe objects. The left viewport is a plan view of the objects. The right viewport is a 3D view. The circle is three inches directly above the ellipse on the Z axis. The bottom edge of the rectangle sits on the same plane as the ellipse. The rectangle passes through the circle at an angle. The right edge of the rectangle in the left viewport is used as the cutting edge in the following example. Use **TRIM** as follows.

For 2000i Users...

In AutoCAD 2000i, you can access the **EXTEND** command while using the **TRIM** command. After selecting the cutting edge, hold the [Shift] key while selecting an object to extend the object to the cutting edge. You can also access the **TRIM** command while using the **EXTEND** command. After selecting the boundary edge, hold the [Shift] key while selecting an object to trim the object at the boundary edge.

Figure 6-8.
Three wireframe objects in 3D space that will be trimmed. The left view is a plan view. The right view is a 3D view.

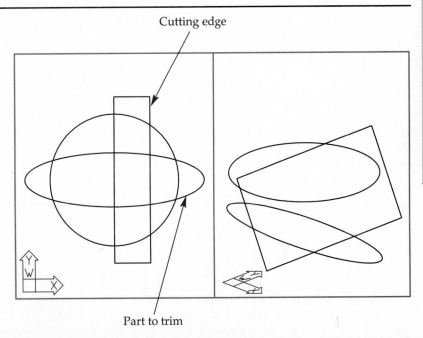

Cutting edge

Part to trim

```
Command: TRIM↵
Current settings: Projection=(current) Edge=(current)
Select cutting edges...
Select objects: (pick the bottom-right edge of the rectangle)
1 found
Select objects: ↵
Select object to trim or [Project/Edge/Undo]: P↵
Enter a projection option [None/Ucs/View] <Ucs>: N↵
Select object to trim or [Project/Edge/Undo]: (pick the right side of the ellipse)
Select object to trim or [Project/Edge/Undo]: ↵
Command:
```

Figure 6-9 shows the results.

The **TRIM** command has two options—**Project** and **Edge**. The **Project** option establishes the projection method for objects to be trimmed in 3D space. This option is also controlled by the **PROJMODE** system variable. The **Project** option displays the following suboptions:

Enter a projection option [None/Ucs/View] <Ucs>:

- **None.** (**PROJMODE** = 0) No projection method is used. Objects to be trimmed in 3D space must form an actual intersection with the cutting edge. In Figure 6-9, you can see that the edge of the rectangle and the ellipse actually intersect.
- **Ucs.** (**PROJMODE** = 1) Cutting edges and edges to be trimmed are all projected onto the XY plane of the current UCS, regardless of the current view. Objects are trimmed even if they do not intersect in 3D space. See Figure 6-10.
- **View.** (**PROJMODE** = 2) Objects are projected along the current view direction and onto the current viewing plane, regardless of the current UCS. Objects are trimmed even if they do not intersect in 3D space. See Figure 6-11.

The **Edge** option of the **TRIM** command determines if an object is to be trimmed at an implied edge or at the actual intersection of an object in 3D space. This option applies specifically to the projection of an edge and *not* a plane. The **Edge** option is selected as follows.

Select object to trim or [Project/Edge/Undo]: E↵
Enter an implied edge extension mode [Extend/No extend] <No extend>:

- **Extend.** The cutting edge is extended into 3D space to intersect objects to be trimmed. The objects must intersect exactly when the cutting edge is extended.
- **No extend.** The cutting edge is not extended, and the object to be trimmed must intersect the cutting edge in 3D space.

Figure 6-9.
With the **None** suboption of the **TRIM** command **Project** option, the ellipse is trimmed where it actually intersects the rectangle.

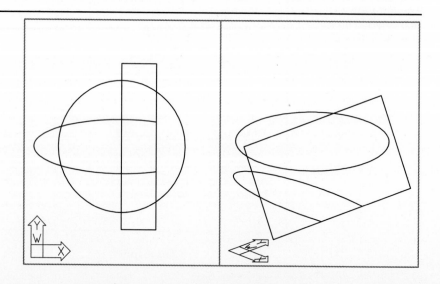

Figure 6-10.
With the **Ucs** suboption of the **TRIM** command **Project** option, the circle is trimmed where it intersects the cutting edge as the edge is projected to the current UCS.

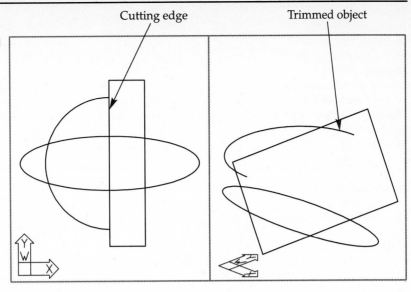

Cutting edge   Trimmed object

Figure 6-11.
With the **View** suboption of the **TRIM** command **Project** option, the rectangle is trimmed where it intersects the cutting edge and the edge is projected along the current viewing angle to the XY plane. If the same pick points are used in the right viewport, more of the rectangle is trimmed. This portion is shown in color.

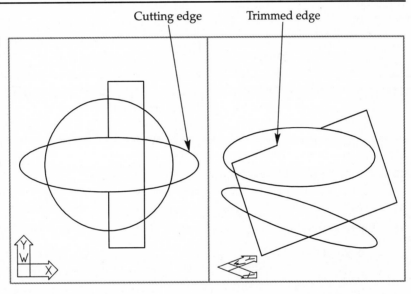

Cutting edge   Trimmed edge

CREATING FILLETS AND ROUNDS

Fillets are rounded inside corners. *Rounds* are rounded outside corners. Both of these are easily created with the surfacing commands **RULESURF** and **TABSURF**. Choose the one you prefer. Notice in Figure 6-12A that arcs have been drawn on the inside and outside corners of a wireframe object in order to create a fillet and round. The arcs are copied to the opposite side and lines are drawn connecting the tangent points of the arcs.

If you use **TABSURF**, you then only need to give direction vectors. If **RULESURF** is used, the lines connecting the arcs are not needed. Select one arc as the first defining curve and the opposite arc as the second defining curve. The result of either process is shown in Figure 6-12B.

The face of the arcs on both sides of the object must be surfaced with **RULESURF**. First, put points at the center of the arc on the round and at the intersection of the two inside edges of the part. See Figure 6-12C. Then, pick the point and the arc as the two defining curves. Now, the **3DFACE** command can be used to construct faces on the object. Three 3D faces must be drawn on the left side of the object. The completed object is shown in Figure 6-12D.

Figure 6-12.
A—To construct fillets and rounds, arcs are drawn first to serve as path curves. The direction vectors are needed if **TABSURF** is used, but not for **RULESURF**.
B—The "edges" of the fillet and round. Now, the "faces" must be drawn.
C—Use construction points and **RULESURF** to surface the "faces" of the fillet and round.
D—Use the **3DFACE** command to complete the surfacing of the entire side of the object.

Hiding 3D Face Edges with the EDGE Command

Notice in Figure 6-12D that the 3D face edges are visible on the left side of the object. These edges can be created as hidden edges by using the **Invisible** option of the **3DFACE** command while drawing them. However, you can quickly hide an existing edge with the **EDGE** command.

To use this command, pick **Edge** from the **Surfaces** cascading menu in the **Draw** pull-down menu, pick the **Edge** button in the **Surfaces** toolbar, or enter EDGE at the Command: prompt:

> Command: **EDGE**↵
> Specify edge of 3dface to toggle visibility or [Display]: *(pick the edge to hide)*
> Specify edge of 3dface to toggle visibility or [Display]: ↵
> Command:

The edge is hidden and the object appears as shown in Figure 6-13. Note that the **Midpoint** object snap mode is automatically activated when using the **EDGE** command. This allows you to select edges that are located outside the current UCS.

Invisible edges can be made visible using the **Display** option of the **EDGE** command as follows.

> Command: **EDGE**↵
> Specify edge of 3dface to toggle visibility or [Display]: **D**↵
> Enter selection method for display of hidden edges [Select/All] <All>:

Use the **Select** option if you want to view the hidden edges of only selected 3D faces. If you wish to view all hidden edges, use the **All** option. Hidden edges are shown as dashed lines. Once the hidden edges are displayed, you can pick the edges to make them visible.

Figure 6-13.
In Figure 6-12D, the edges of the 3D faces can be seen in the middle of the object. The **EDGE** command can be used to make these edges invisible, as shown here.

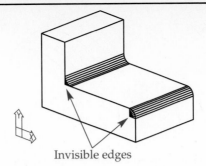

Invisible edges

NOTE The **EDGE** command automatically activates the **Midpoint** object snap mode. Even if you change the object snap mode for a selection, **Midpoint** is automatically reactivated for the next pick.

Using **SPLFRAME** to Control Visibility

The **SPLFRAME** system variable can also be used to control the visibility of 3D face edges. To set this variable, type SPLFRAME at the Command: prompt. A value of 0 does not display any 3D face edges set to invisible. A value of 1 displays all 3D face edges regardless of whether they are set to invisible or not.

EDITING POLYGON MESHES

AutoCAD User's Guide **9**

The **PEDIT** command is used to edit polygon meshes. The entire mesh can be smoothed, individual vertices can be moved, or the mesh can be closed. Enter the command by picking **Polyline** from the **Modify** pull-down menu or by typing PEDIT or PE at the Command: prompt. The following options are displayed when a polygon mesh is selected.

Command: **PEDIT**↵
Select polyline: *(pick a polygon mesh)*
Enter an option [Edit vertex/Smooth surface/Desmooth/Mclose/Nclose/Undo]:

Note: **Mclose** may be **Mopen** and **Nclose** may be **Nopen**, depending on the mesh selected. The **Edit vertex** option is used to alter individual vertices. This option is explained in detail later. The following options are also available.

PEDIT
PE

Modify
➡ Polyline

• **Smooth surface.** Applies a smooth surface to the mesh based on the value of the **SURFTYPE** variable. These types of surfaces are also discussed in Chapter 5.

SURFTYPE Setting	Surface Type
5	Quadratic B-spline
6	Cubic B-spline
8	Bézier surface

• **Desmooth.** Removes smoothing and returns the mesh to its original vertices.
• **Mclose.** The polylines in the M direction are closed if the M direction mesh is open.
• **Mopen.** Opens the polylines in the M direction if they are closed.
• **Nclose.** The polylines in the N direction are closed if the N direction mesh is open.
• **Nopen.** Opens the polylines in the N direction if they are closed.

Figure 6-14A shows a polygon mesh. Figure 6-14B shows the results of using the **Nclose** option on the mesh.

Figure 6-14.
A—A polygon mesh
with a smoothed
surface.
B—The mesh after
using the **Nclose**
option of **PEDIT**.

A

B

The **Edit vertex** option of the **PEDIT** command allows you to move individual vertices of the polygon mesh. When you select the **Edit vertex** option, you get several suboptions:

Enter an option [Edit vertex/Smooth surface/Desmooth/Mopen/Nclose/Undo]: **E**↵
Current vertex *(current)*.
Enter an option [Next/Previous/Left/Right/Up/Down/Move/REgen/eXit] <N>:

Notice in Figure 6-15A that an X marker appears at the first vertex. This X can be moved to the vertex you want to edit. The **Edit vertex** suboptions are explained as follows. Refer to Figure 6-15B.

- **Next.** The X moves to the next vertex in the order drawn. When the end of a line is reached, the X jumps to the start of the next line.
- **Previous.** The X moves to the previous vertex in the order drawn.
- **Left.** The X moves to the previous vertex in the N direction.
- **Right.** The X moves to the next vertex in the N direction.
- **Up.** The X moves to the next vertex in the M direction.
- **Down.** The X moves to the previous vertex in the M direction.
- **Move.** The vertex where the X is can be moved to a new location.

You may notice in Figure 6-15B that the **Right** option is actually moving the vertex to the left of the screen. This is because the right/left and up/down directions are determined by the order in which the vertices were drawn.

When the **Move** option is selected, the crosshairs are attached to the vertex with a rubber band line and the following prompt appears.

Specify new location for marked vertex:

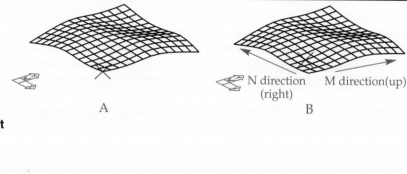

Figure 6-15.
A—An X marker,
shown here in color,
appears at the first
vertex of a polygon
mesh selected using
PEDIT. B—Move the
X marker in the N
direction with the **Left**
and **Right** options.
Move the X in the M
direction with the **Up**
and **Down** options.

A

N direction
(right)

M direction(up)

B

If a new point is picked, the mesh may appear to be altered properly, Figure 6-16A. However, when the viewpoint is changed, as in Figure 6-16B, it is clear that the new point does not have the intended Z value. This is because the Z value will always be zero on the current XY plane. Therefore, do not pick a new polygon mesh location with the pointing device. Instead, enter the coordinates or use XYZ filters.

Specify new location for marked vertex: **@0,0,.6**↵

The new location in Figure 6-17A appears similar to Figure 6-16A. However, when viewed from another direction, it is clear that entering coordinates produced the correct results, Figure 6-17B.

Figure 6-16.
A—A new point picked with the cursor appears correct. B—When the viewpoint is changed, you can see that using the pointing device produces inaccurate results.

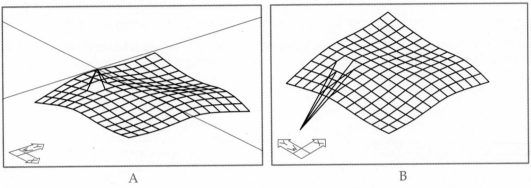

A   B

Figure 6-17.
A—When coordinates are entered at the keyboard, the results at first appear the same as when using the pointing device. B—When the viewpoint is changed, you can see that entering coordinates produces correct results.

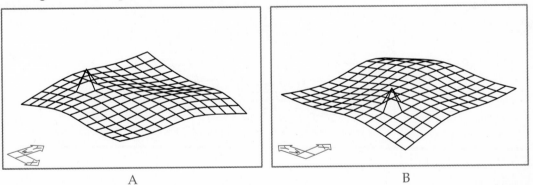

A   B

Editing Polygon Meshes with Grips

When a polygon mesh is selected, all of its grips are displayed. See Figure 6-18A. Individual vertices can be edited by picking the grip you wish to move and entering the new coordinates at the keyboard, Figure 6-18B.

If **EXPLODE** is used on a polygon mesh, the mesh is broken into individual 3D faces. Pick any edge on the mesh and four grips that define the corners of the 3D face appear. See Figure 6-19A. The vertices of each face can be edited using grips. See Figure 6-19B. If you edit a vertex of a 3D face created by exploding a polygon mesh, the vertex will no longer be attached to the original mesh. See Figure 6-19C.

Figure 6-18.
A—When a polygon mesh is selected, the grips become warm. B—Select a single grip to make it hot. This grip can then be moved.

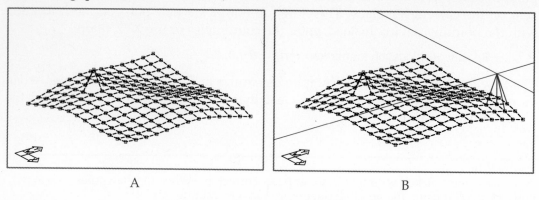

A

B

Figure 6-19.
A—When you select an edge of an exploded polygon mesh, you can see that it is made up of 3D faces. B—A single vertex on a 3D face can be edited using grips. C—The edited 3D face vertex is detached from the original mesh.

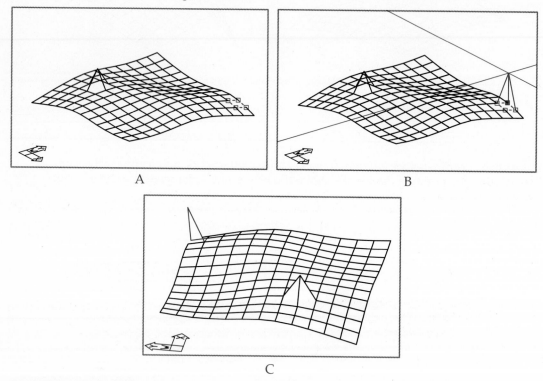

A

B

C

PROFESSIONAL TIP

With careful planning, you can minimize the number of faces you construct. Draw only the number needed and use editing commands to create the rest. As shown in Figure 6-19, a 3D face is easily edited using grips. Use all of the grip editing functions—move, rotate, scale, and mirror—to quickly manipulate 3D faces.

Chapter Test

Answer the following questions on a separate sheet of paper.

1. What command allows you to both move and rotate a 3D object?
2. What feature do you define when using the **ROTATE3D** command?
3. What option of the **ROTATE3D** command allows you to use the center axis of a circle as the feature about which to rotate?
4. What is the default method of picking a mirror plane when using the **MIRROR3D** command?
5. What are the three dimensions of a rectangular 3D array?
6. For each of the following **PROJMODE** values, name the equivalent suboption of the **Project** option of the **TRIM** command. Also, define the function of each suboption.
   A. **PROJMODE** = 0
   B. **PROJMODE** = 1
   C. **PROJMODE** = 2
7. What is the function of the **Edge** option of the **TRIM** command?
8. Which surfacing commands are good for creating fillets and rounds?
9. What is the function of the **EDGE** command?
10. How can invisible 3D face edges be displayed?
11. How can the angular ("flat") faces of a polygon mesh be rounded?
12. Name the three types of smooth curves that can be applied to a polygon mesh, and give their **SURFTYPE** values.
13. What command, option, and suboption are used to relocate a single vertex of a polygon mesh?
14. What is the most accurate way to move a polygon mesh vertex when using the grip method?
15. When a polygon mesh is exploded, what type of objects are created?

Drawing Problems

1. Open Problem 2 from Chapter 1. If you have not done this problem, draw it as a 3D wireframe using your own measurements. Then, do the following.
   A. Construct a box the exact width and depth of the slot in the object, but twice as high as the opening in the object. Draw the box sitting outside the object.
   B. Use the **ALIGN** command to place the box inside the slot.
   C. Edit the object so that the slot is moved half the distance to the left edge of the object. Move the box along with the slot.
   D. Save the drawing as P6-1.

2. Open Problem 1 from Chapter 1. If you have not done this problem, draw it in 3D wireframe using your own measurements. Then, do the following.
   A. Use **ROTATE3D** to rotate the object 90°.
   B. Use **MIRROR3D** to place a second copy at a 180° rotation using the **YZ** option.
   C. Use the **XZ** option of **MIRROR3D** to create a copy of the last operation. The final drawing should look like the one shown below.
   D. Save the drawing as P6-2.

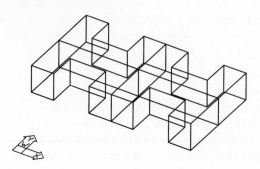

3. Open Problem 3 from Chapter 1. If you have not done this problem, draw it in 3D wireframe using your own measurements. Then, do the following.
   A. Use **ALIGN** to rotate the block that is inserted into the slot of the main body. The block should be rotated 90° so its tall side is aligned with the tall dimension of the body.
   B. Mirror and copy the body 180° so that the copy and the original fully enclose the block.
   C. Save the drawing as P6-3.

4. Draw Problem 5 from Chapter 1 as a 3D surface model using your own measurements. Use the following guidelines.
   A. Construct fillets where the two cylinders join the base.
   B. Construct chamfers at the top of each cylinder.
   C. Apply a fillet around the top edge of the base.
   D. Save the drawing as P6-4.

5. Draw Problem 8 from Chapter 1 as a 3D surface model using the dimensions given. Use the following guidelines.
   A. Construct a .25 radius fillet on all three inside corners.
   B. Construct a .125″ × 45° chamfer at the top of each hole.
   C. Save the drawing as P6-5.

6. Draw Problem 9 from Chapter 1 as a 3D surface model using the dimensions given. Use the following guidelines.
   A. Create a .125″ × 45° chamfer on the top edge of the large hole.
   B. Construct the small holes using **RULESURF**.
   C. Use **3DARRAY** to create a polar array of the four small holes.
   D. Save the drawing as P6-6.

7. Draw Problem 11 from Chapter 1 as a 3D surface model using the dimensions given. Use the following guidelines.
   A. Create a .25″ radius fillet around the top edge of the base plate.
   B. Construct the small holes using **RULESURF**.
   C. Use **ARRAY** to create a rectangular array of the four small holes.
   D. Save the drawing as P6-7.

8. Draw Problem 9 from Chapter 2 as a 3D surface model using the dimensions given. Use the following guidelines.
   A. Draw a bar of the same dimensions to fit over the pin bar in Problem 2-9. Construct it alongside the pin bar.
   B. Use **RULESURF** to construct the holes in the new bar, and be sure to erase the original circles used to construct the holes.
   C. Use **ALIGN** to place the new bar over the pin bar.
   D. Rotate the entire assembly 90°.
   E. Save the drawing as P6-8.

9. Draw Problem 11 from Chapter 2 as a 3D surface model using the dimensions given. Use the following guidelines.
   A. Explode the sphere mesh. Remove 20 3D faces—12 above the equator and 8 below.
   B. Draw a new sphere in the exact center of the existing one, and 1/2 its diameter.
   C. Draw a small diameter tube protruding at a 45° angle from the center of the new sphere into the northern hemisphere. It should extend out through the large sphere.
   D. Create a 3D polar array of six tubes.
   E. Save the drawing as P6-9.

10. Draw Problem 1 from Chapter 3 as a 3D surface model. Use the following guidelines.
    A. Place a .25" radius fillet on all inside vertical corners.
    B. Place a .125" radius round on all outside vertical corners.
    C. Save the drawing as P6-10.

11. Draw Problem 3 from Chapter 3 as a 3D surface model using the dimensions given. Use the following guidelines.
    A. Give the object a .25" radius bend at the "L."
    B. Save the drawing as P6-11.

12. Draw Problem 8 from Chapter 3 as a 3D surface model using the dimensions given. Use the following guidelines.
    A. Draw the 4.80 side at a 15° angle from vertical.
    B. Give the object a .25" inside radius at the bend.
    C. Save the drawing as P6-12.

A wireframe (top) may appear as nothing more than a mess of lines. However, when the **HIDE** command is used on the surface model, you can see that it is a '57 Chevy. (Autodesk, Inc.)

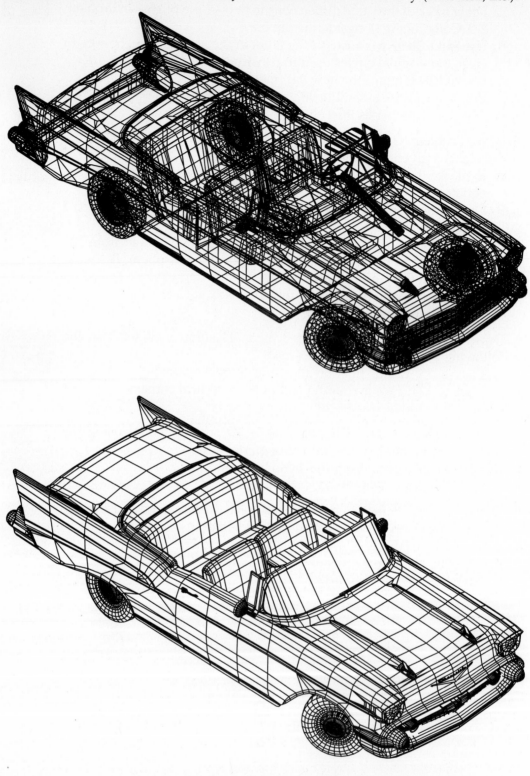

CHAPTER 7

Viewing and Displaying Three-Dimensional Models

Learning Objectives

After completing this chapter, you will be able to:
- Use all options of the **VPOINT** command to display 3D models.
- Describe how to hide lines in a variety of situations.
- Use the 3D orbit view to dynamically rotate and display a 3D model.
- Use the **DVIEW** command to view 3D models.
- Use the **SHADEMODE** command options to create shading variations.
- Use the **RENDER** command to produce quick renderings.

There are three different ways to select a viewpoint for 3D models. These are the **VPOINT**, **3DORBIT**, and **DVIEW** commands. The **VPOINT** command, which was discussed in Chapter 1, is a "static" method. The viewpoint is established first, then the object is displayed. The **DVIEW** command is a "semidynamic" viewing method. You can select a viewpoint while the model is being moved. Once a viewpoint has been selected, you can enhance the display in several ways, such as panning and zooming.

AutoCAD 2000 offers a dynamic new capability for viewing 3D models. The **3DORBIT** command enables you to rotate, pan, and zoom a 3D model while it is fully rendered. This provides a powerful design tool for those working with 3D. In addition, you can display a continuously rotating model, set in motion by just the movement of the mouse. This is ideal for design, demonstrations, and training.

You can use the **HIDE** command to temporarily remove hidden lines. This command has been used in previous chapters. You can also use the **SHADEMODE** command to create a simple rendering. A more advanced rendering can be created with the **RENDER** command. This command creates the most realistic display. The **RENDER** command is introduced in this chapter, but is discussed in detail in Chapter 9 and Chapter 15.

USING THE VPOINT COMMAND

The **VPOINT** command can be used to set the direction from which a 3D object is viewed. The command can be accessed in three different ways. It can be selected from the **View** pull-down menu by picking **3D Views** and then **VPOINT**. This is covered in Chapter 1. Viewpoint angles can also be established using the **Viewpoint Presets** dialog box, the **Viewpoint** flyout in the **Standard** toolbar, or the **View** toolbar. For an overview of the **VPOINT** command and the "right-hand rule," refer to Chapter 1.

3D Display Options Using a Pull-Down Menu

The **View** pull-down menu provides several options of viewpoint selection. Pick the **View** pull-down menu, then select **3D Views**. A cascading menu displays viewpoint options. See Figure 7-1. The selection of preset viewpoints allows you to display six orthographic and four isometric views of the current drawing. Figure 7-2 shows how these different selections affect the drawing display. The appropriate **View** toolbar button also appears next to each view.

Figure 7-1.
The **3D Views** cascading menu has several options for setting a 3D viewing angle.

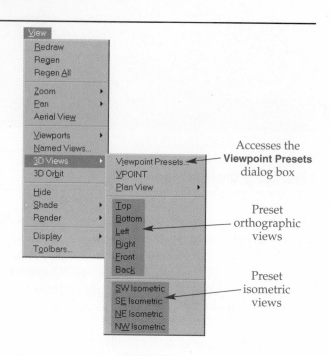

Accesses the **Viewpoint Presets** dialog box

Preset orthographic views

Preset isometric views

Using the **Viewpoint Presets** Dialog Box

You can set the viewpoint by entering two angles. The angles are similar to spherical coordinates, but do not include a distance from the center point. Spherical coordinates can locate any point on, inside, or outside a sphere.

Figure 7-3 shows an example of a point located with spherical coordinates. Notice that the 90° angle is the angle *in* the XY plane from the X axis. The 45° angle is the angle *from* the XY plane.

DDVPOINT
VP

View
➡ 3D Views
➡ Viewpoint
Presets...

You can establish a 3D viewpoint by specifying an angle *in* the XY plane and an angle *from* the XY plane. These angles can be specified in the **Viewpoint Presets** dialog box. To access this dialog box, pick **Viewpoint Presets...** from the **3D Views** cascading menu in the **View** pull-down menu, or enter VP or DDVPOINT at the Command: prompt.

The **Viewpoint Presets** dialog box has a plan view on the left side and an elevation view on the right side, Figure 7-4. This allows you to graphically position your viewpoint.

The centers of the plan view and elevation view represent the origin on your drawing. If you pick the **Absolute to WCS** radio button at the top of the dialog box, the origin is based on the world coordinate system. If you pick the **Relative to UCS** radio button, the origin is based on the origin of the current user coordinate system. (User coordinate systems are discussed in Chapter 3.) You can change the current view back to a plan view by picking the **Set to Plan View** button.

In Figure 7-4, the line of sight from the X axis (0°) is indicated by the line located at the 135° mark in the plan view. The line of sight from the XY plane is indicated by the line at 30° in the elevation view. Settings of 270° and 90° create a plan view. The

Figure 7-2.
Each of the 3D viewpoint presets applied to a link rod model.

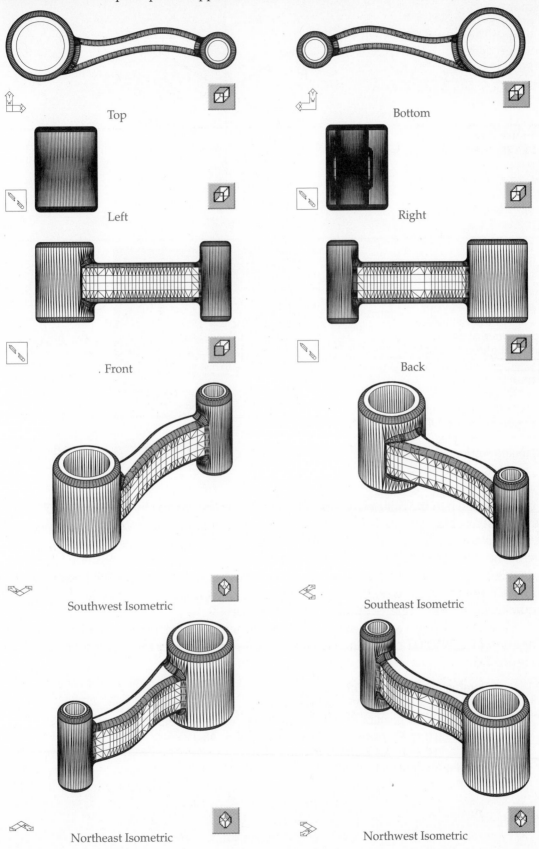

Top

Bottom

Left

Right

. Front

Back

Southwest Isometric

Southeast Isometric

Northeast Isometric

Northwest Isometric

Figure 7-3.
Spherical coordinates are made up of three values. These three values define a point in space.

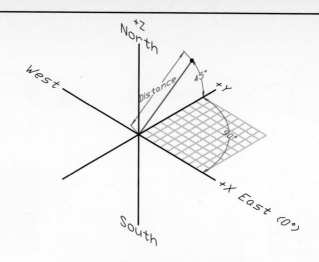

Figure 7-4.
The **Viewpoint Presets** dialog box allows you to graphically set your viewpoint. Pick in the inner region (highlighted here) to select values other than those labeled in the image tile. Picking in the outer region automatically selects the nearest labeled setting.

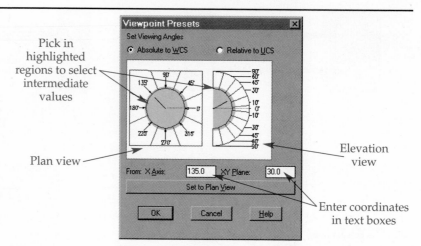

display shown in the right viewport of Figure 7-5 can be created by picking the 45° mark in the plan view and the upper 45° section inside the large arc in the elevation view.

The angle values in the **Viewpoint Presets** dialog box can be set by picking in the graphic or by entering a value in the text boxes. Picking an angle with your pointing device may not be accurate. If you need a specific angle, enter it in the **From: X Axis:** and **XY Plane:** text boxes. If the viewing angle does not need to be exact, it may be quicker to set the angle with the pointing device.

These viewpoint angles can also be set at the Command: prompt using the **Rotate** option of the **VPOINT** command. The following sequence sets the viewpoint shown in Figure 7-5:

```
Command: –VP or VPOINT.↵
Current view direction: VIEWDIR= current
Specify a view point or [Rotate] <display compass and tripod>: R↵
Enter angle in XY plane from X axis <current>: 45↵
Enter angle from XY plane <current>: 45↵
Regenerating model.
Command:
```

Figure 7-5.
The viewpoint in the right viewport was created using the **Viewpoint Presets** dialog box. Both rotation angles are 45°.

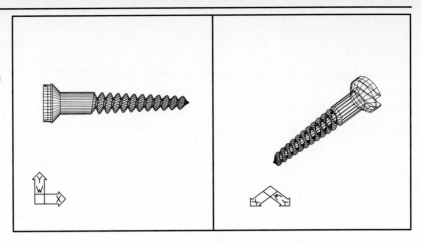

Creating a Plan View

You can quickly create a plan view of any UCS or the WCS using the **PLAN** command. This command can be accessed by picking **Plan View** from the **3D Views** cascading menu in the **View** pull-down menu. Then, select the appropriate option in the menu, Figure 7-6. You can also type PLAN at the Command: prompt. The options are explained below.

- **Current UCS.** This creates a view of the object plan to the current UCS.
- **World UCS.** This creates a view of the object plan to the WCS.
- **Named UCS.** This displays a view plan to a named UCS.

You can also create a plan view by using the **VPOINT** command and typing the XYZ coordinates for the plan view (0,0,1).

Both the **PLAN** and **VPOINT** commands automatically perform a **ZOOM Extents**. This fills the graphics window with the original top view. You can perform a **ZOOM All** to display the original drawing limits, or dynamically zoom to reduce the screen display.

Figure 7-6.
Select the appropriate menu item from the **Plan View** cascading menu to create a plan view.

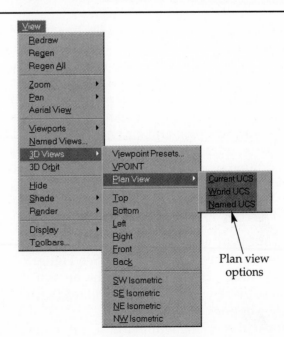

When working in 3D space, using the **CAL** command transparently allows you to set your view perpendicular to any selected object. At the Specify a view point: prompt of the **VPOINT** command, use the calculator and enter the **NOR** function without specifying a vector. This allows you to select a circle, arc, or polyline to set your view perpendicular to.

> Command: **–VP** *or* **VPOINT**⏎
> Current view direction: VIEWDIR= *current*
> Specify a view point or [Rotate] <display compass and tripod>: **'CAL**⏎
> Initializing...>> Expression: **NOR**⏎
> >> Select circle, arc or polyline for NOR function: *(select an object)*

EXERCISE 7-1

❏ Begin a new drawing.
❏ Using the **3D Objects** dialog box or the **Surfaces** toolbar, draw a wedge the size of your choice.
❏ Use the **VPOINT** command to display a 3D view of your drawing. Display it twice using the **Rotate** option.
❏ Display it again using four different views from the **View** toolbar.
❏ Select three different views from the **Viewpoint Presets** dialog box.
❏ Display the object as a plan view.
❏ Quit without saving.

AutoCAD User's Guide **17**

3DORBIT
3DO

View
➥ 3D Orbit

3D Orbit toolbar
Standard toolbar

3D Orbit

VIEWING MODELS DYNAMICALLY

The 3D orbit view replaces most of the functions of the **DVIEW** command (discussed later in the chapter) and is far more powerful and easier to use. If you work with 3D models, it will benefit you to become familiar with this dynamic tool that enables you to rotate a fully rendered 3D object in real time.

The 3D orbit view is accessed through the **3DORBIT** command. To initiate the view, pick the **3D Orbit** button from the **Standard** toolbar or **3D Orbit** toolbar, select **3D Orbit** from the **View** pull-down menu, or type 3DO or 3DORBIT at the Command: prompt.

When the 3D orbit view is active, a variety of options are available from the shortcut menu. In addition, you can select many display options using the **3D Orbit** toolbar. These options are discussed in the following sections. See Figure 7-7.

Basic 3D Orbit Display Controls

Within **3DORBIT** you have the ability to toggle between orbit, pan, and zoom. The shortcut menu displays these options. See Figure 7-7. A check mark appears next to the current setting, with **Orbit** being the default. Use the shortcut menu to switch between these display options. The standard pan and zoom icons are displayed with the respective options.

Panning and zooming within the 3D orbit view are controlled by the **3DPAN** and **3DZOOM** commands. These can be entered at the keyboard, selected from the **3D Orbit** toolbar, or activated by the IntelliMouse.

Figure 7-7.
A—**3DORBIT** command options are easily selected using the 3D orbit view shortcut menu. B—You can select many of the **3DORBIT** display options using the **3D Orbit** toolbar.

The active display control option is identified with a check

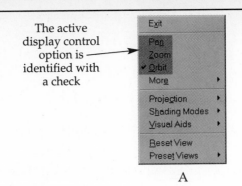

A

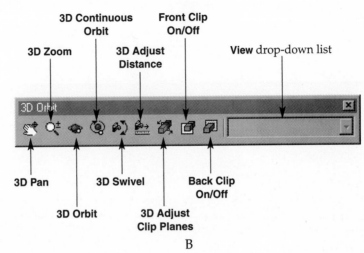

B

The **Zoom Window** and **Zoom Extents** options can also be selected in the shortcut menu by first picking **More**, then the option. See Figure 7-8.

Using the 3D Orbit Cursor Icons

When you enter the 3D orbit view, the following prompt is displayed:

Press ESC or ENTER to exit, or right-click to display shortcut-menu.

If the UCS icon is on, it is changed to a shaded 3D UCS icon. Additionally, a large circle with four smaller circles at its quadrant points is displayed. See Figure 7-9. This is called the *arcball*. As the cursor icon is moved around the arcball, it takes on four different shapes, which provides you with visual cues regarding the type of display available if you pick, hold, and then move the pointer. These cursors are described in the following table.

Figure 7-8.
The **Zoom Window** and **Zoom Extents** options can be selected from the **More** cascading menu in the 3D orbit view shortcut menu.

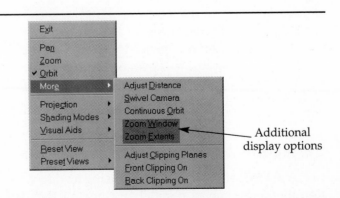

Additional display options

Figure 7-9.
In 3D orbit view, the UCS icon is changed to a shaded 3D UCS icon. Additionally, the arcball is displayed.

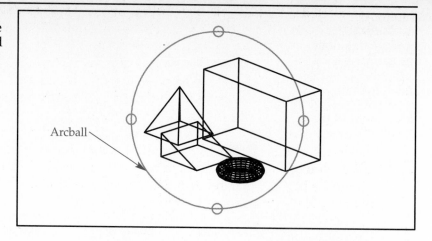

Arcball

For 2000i Users...

In AutoCAD 2000i, the 3D view shortcut menu includes an **Orbit Maintains Z** option. When this option is selected, the Z axis remains fixed as the cursor is moved horizontally within the arcball.

Cursor	Appearance	Description
Two ellipses		This icon appears when you move the cursor inside the arcball. When you pick and drag, the object can be moved in any direction—horizontally, vertically, and diagonally.
Circular arrow		The circular arrow icon appears when the cursor is moved outside the arcball. When you pick and drag, the object is "rolled" around an axis that projects perpendicular from the screen.
Horizontal ellipse		This icon appears when you move the cursor into one of the small circles on the left or right of the arcball. The object can be rotated on the Y axis by picking and dragging. The axis of rotation is vertical through the middle of the arcball.
Vertical ellipse		This icon appears when you move the cursor into one of the small circles on the top or bottom of the arcball. The object can be rotated on the X axis by picking and dragging. The axis of rotation is horizontal through the middle of the arcball.

EXERCISE 7-2

❑ Open the Truck model drawing. It is located in the Acad2000\Sample folder.
❑ Display the **3D Orbit** toolbar.
❑ Use the **3D Pan** and **3D Zoom** commands to adjust the display of the truck.
❑ Select the **3D Orbit** button.
❑ Move the cursor around the outside of the arcball, inside the arcball, and inside each of the small circles at the arcball quadrants. Observe the change in the cursor icon.
❑ Pick and drag outside the arcball to rotate the model clockwise and counterclockwise.
❑ Pick and drag inside one of the small circles on the left or right quadrant of the arcball to rotate the model around the vertical axis (Y axis).
❑ Pick and drag inside one of the small circles on the top or bottom quadrant of the arcball to rotate the model around the horizontal axis (X axis).
❑ Pick and drag inside the arcball to rotate the model in any direction.
❑ This drawing is used in other exercises in this chapter. Leave it open or close the drawing without saving.

Projection, Shading, and Visual Aids

A 3D model can be displayed using a wide variety of options. These include projection methods such as parallel and perspective, smoothness and edge display of the model, and visual aids such as a spherical compass, grid, and shaded UCS icon. These options are selected in the 3D orbit view shortcut menu. The **Projection**, **Shading Modes**, and **Visual Aids** cascading menus are illustrated in Figure 7-10 and described in the following sections.

- **Projection.** Projection of a 3D model can be either parallel or perspective. In parallel projection, sides of objects project parallel to each other. Axonometric views (isometric, dimetric, and trimetric) are all parallel projections. In perspective projection, sides of objects project toward a vanishing point. While in the 3D orbit view, you can pan and zoom the perspective view. However, once you exit the 3D orbit view, you cannot pan or zoom. If you wish to edit the object, you must first switch back to parallel projection. Figure 7-11 shows the difference between a parallel and perspective projection.

- **Shading Modes.** Six shading options are available in this cascading menu. These options are identical to the options of the **SHADEMODE** command, which are also available in the **Shade** cascading menu of the **View** pull-down menu. These options are briefly described later in this chapter and are described in detail in Chapter 9.

- **Visual Aids.** These options assist you in relating the view to the UCS, and to positive and negative values on the Z axis. Figure 7-12 illustrates the following visual aids:

    - **Compass.** A spherical 3D compass, the exact diameter of the arcball, has tick marks and labels indicating the X, Y, and Z axes. The compass can assist you in maintaining a reference for the current UCS. The **COMPASS** system variable controls this display, and is set to 0 if this item is not checked.

Figure 7-10.
The **Projection**, **Shading Modes**, and **Visual Aids** cascading menus in the 3D orbit view shortcut menu.

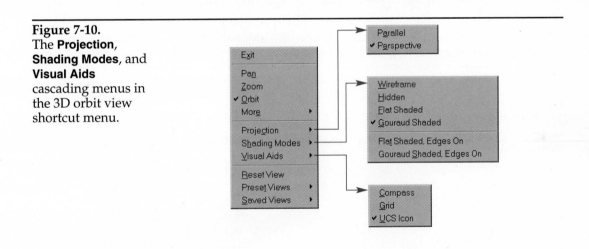

Figure 7-11.
The two types of projection. In parallel projection, parallel lines remain parallel. In perspective projection, parallel lines converge to a vanishing point.

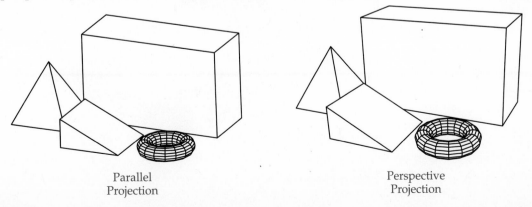

Parallel
Projection

Perspective
Projection

Figure 7-12.
Visual aids can be used to help you visualize the coordinate system. The spherical 3D compass displays tick marks and labels for the X, Y, and Z axes. The compass can assist you in maintaining a reference for the current UCS. The grid matches the drawing limits. The number of grid lines change to maintain a clear display as you zoom in and out.

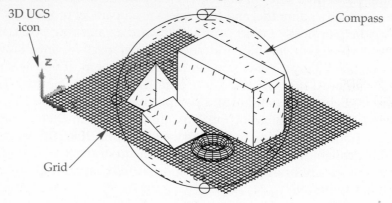

- **Grid.** The grid is displayed within the drawing limits. As you zoom in on a drawing, AutoCAD can display up to ten grid lines between major grid lines. Every tenth line is a *major grid line*, and corresponds to the setting in the **Drafting Settings** dialog box. As you zoom out, grid lines are deleted in order to maintain a clear view of the object.

  The location of the grid is controlled by the value set in the **ELEVATION** system variable. This variable controls the Z value and locates the position of the XY plane on the Z axis. The grid can be used as a plane of reference when you wish to work at a specific elevation. Figure 7-13 shows how the grid moves when the elevation is changed.

Figure 7-13.
The **ELEVATION** system variable changes the Z value of the grid so it can be used as a plane of reference when you wish to work at a specific elevation. A—Elevation set to the bottom of the objects. B—When the elevation is set higher, the grid is shown at that level.

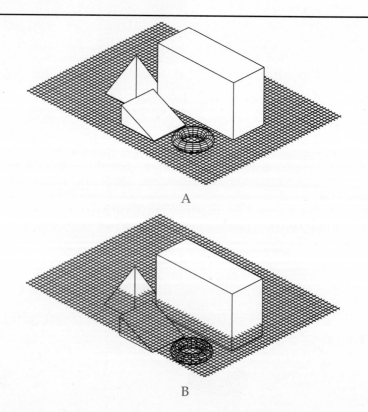

- **UCS icon.** The shaded 3D UCS icon shows the orientation of the UCS. The X axis is red, Y axis is green, and Z axis is blue. The **UCSICON** system variable also controls the visibility of this icon. Once the 3D UCS icon is displayed, you can change it to the 2D version by picking **Shade** and then **2D Wireframe** in the **View** pull-down menu.

EXERCISE 7-3

- ❑ Open the Truck model drawing.
- ❑ Execute the **3DORBIT** command.
- ❑ Use the 3D orbit view shortcut menu to select parallel and perspective projections.
- ❑ Select each of the shading options in the 3D orbit view shortcut menu.
- ❑ Turn the base layer off. Turn on the compass, grid, and UCS icon visual aids.
- ❑ Rotate the model in any direction.
- ❑ Set the **ELEVATION** system variable to 5 and regenerate the view.
- ❑ This drawing is used in other exercises in this chapter. Leave it open or close the drawing without saving.

3D Orbit Viewing Options

The 3D orbit view is extremely versatile because you can use a variety of established views to create a display. In addition, you can use the 3D orbit view to rotate a model for any purpose, and immediately reset it to the view that was displayed prior to using **3DORBIT**. The last three items in the 3D orbit view shortcut menu allow you to set views. See Figure 7-14. The following options are available:

- **Reset View.** Resets the view that was displayed before using **3DORBIT**.
- **Preset Views.** Displays a list of the six orthographic and four isometric preset views. The same views are found in the **3D Views** cascading menu in the **View** pull-down menu. See Figure 7-14.
- **Saved Views.** The named views in the drawing are displayed in this cascading menu. This menu item is not displayed unless the drawing contains named views.

When 3D orbit view is active, the drop-down list in the **3D Orbit** toolbar displays all preset and named views. Simply select a view from this list to display it. See Figure 7-15.

Figure 7-14.
Both saved and preset views can be accessed from the 3D orbit view shortcut menu.

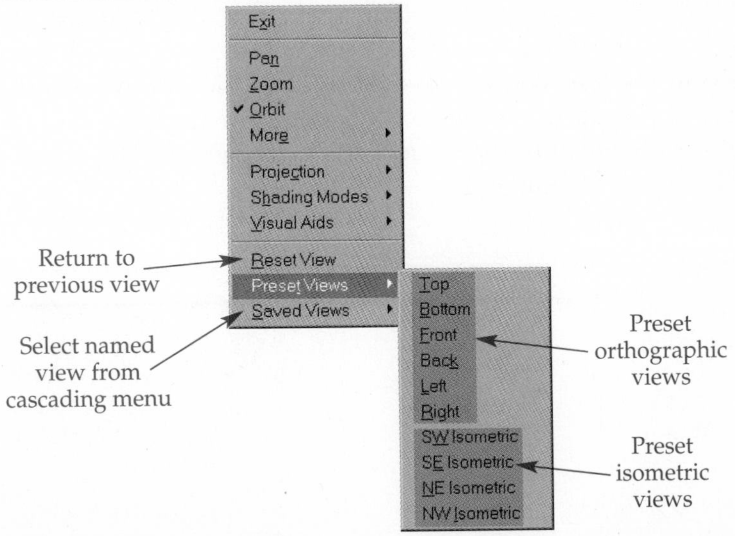

Figure 7-15.
When 3D orbit view is active, the drop-down list in the **3D Orbit** toolbar displays all preset and named views. Simply select a view from this list to display it.

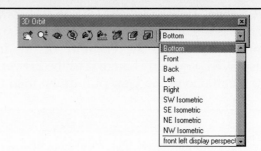

3D Orbit View Camera Settings

Two options in the 3D orbit view enable you to change the display based on functions of a camera. The distance between camera and object can be adjusted, as well as the amount the camera is "swiveled" on a tripod. These options can be selected from the 3D orbit view shortcut menu, the **3D Orbit** toolbar, or typed at the keyboard.

The distance between the viewpoint and the object can be set by adjusting the camera distance. This can be accomplished using the **3DDISTANCE** command. To access this command, pick the **3D Adjust Distance** button from the **3D Orbit** toolbar, select **Adjust Distance** from the **More** cascading menu in the 3D orbit view shortcut menu, or type 3DDISTANCE at the Command: prompt. The cursor changes to an arrow pointing up and an arrow pointing down, Figure 7-16. Hold the pick button and move the cursor up to get closer to the object, or move it down to increase the camera distance from the object.

In addition to adjusting the camera distance, you can also change the view by swiveling the camera. Imagine that the camera is on a tripod. When the camera is turned to the left, you see less of the right side of the object. Conversely, when the camera is turned to the right, you see less of the left side of the object. The same is true for movement of the camera in any direction. The object moves in the opposite direction from the camera.

3DDISTANCE

3D Orbit toolbar

3D Adjust Distance

Figure 7-16.
These cursors appear when you adjust the cameras distance or swivel the camera.

Adjust Camera Distance

Swivel Camera

To swivel the camera, use the **3DSWIVEL** command. To access this command, pick the **3D Swivel** button from the **3D Orbit** toolbar, select **S̲wivel Camera** from the **Mor̲e** cascading menu in the 3D orbit view shortcut menu, or type 3DSWIVEL at the Command: prompt. The cursor changes to a camera icon, Figure 7-16. Hold the pick button and move the cursor to swivel the camera.

3DSWIVEL

3D Orbit
toolbar

3D Swivel

PROFESSIONAL TIP

Try using one of the camera options with any of the pan and zoom options found in the shortcut menu to speed up model display and increase your productivity.

EXERCISE 7-5

❑ Open the Truck model drawing.
❑ Execute the **3DORBIT** command.
❑ Adjust the camera distance to zoom in on the sideview mirror. Adjust the camera distance to fill the screen with the truck model.
❑ Swivel the camera to view only the left rear wheel of the truck. Swivel the camera to view only the front bumper of the truck.
❑ This drawing is used in other exercises. Leave it open or close the drawing without saving.

Using Clipping Planes to Slice Through the Model

An excellent design and visualization feature is the ability to apply front and rear *clipping planes* to the model. These imaginary planes slice through the model, and can be compared to the cutting-plane lines used in drafting to create sections. AutoCAD enables you to adjust these clipping planes and turn them on or off with the **3DCLIP** command. Clipping planes are always parallel to the screen regardless of the current view of the model.

Clipping planes can be set and adjusted in the **Adjust Clipping Planes** window. To access this window, pick the **3D Adjust Clip Planes** button in the **3D Orbit** toolbar, select **Adjust C̲lipping Planes** from the **Mor̲e** cascading menu in the 3D orbit view shortcut menu, or type 3DCLIP at the Command: prompt. See Figure 7-17.

3DCLIP

3D Orbit
toolbar

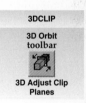
3D Adjust Clip
Planes

Figure 7-17.
Clipping plane options are found in the **Mor̲e** cascading menu in the 3D orbit view shortcut menu.

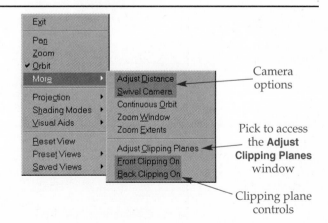

Camera options

Pick to access the **Adjust Clipping Planes** window

Clipping plane controls

The view shown in the **Adjust Clipping Planes** window looks down on the top edges of the clipping planes. The clipping planes are always parallel to the screen (current view). Therefore, if you consider the current view of the model as the front view, the **Adjust Clipping Planes** window shows the top view, hence an edge view of the clipping planes. See Figure 7-18.

Note the buttons at the top of the window. They control the clipping plane options. These options can also be selected from a shortcut menu by right-clicking inside the **Adjust Clipping Planes** window. See Figure 7-19.

- **Adjust Front Clipping.** This option displays the clipping planes icon and activates the front clipping plane for adjustment. The front clipping plane is the line closest to the bottom of the window. Pick and drag to move the clipping plane.
- **Adjust Back Clipping.** Activates the back clipping plane for adjustment. The back clipping plane is the line closest to the top of the window.
- **Create Slice.** Creates a slice through the model, like cutting a slice of bread. When this option is selected, both the front and back clipping planes move as a single unit to create a slice through any part of the model. See Figure 7-20.
- **Front Clipping On/Off.** Toggles the front clipping plane on or off.
- **Back Clipping On/Off.** Toggles the back clipping plane on or off.

Use the following procedure to adjust the clipping planes and view the results.

1. Access the **Adjust Clipping Planes** window using any of the previously mentioned methods.
2. Pick the **Adjust Front Clipping** button. Pick the **Front Clipping On/Off** button to turn it on. Check under **More** in the 3D orbit view shortcut menu to be sure a check mark is next to **Front Clipping On**.

Figure 7-18.
The view shown in the **Adjust Clipping Planes** window looks down on the top edges of the clipping planes.

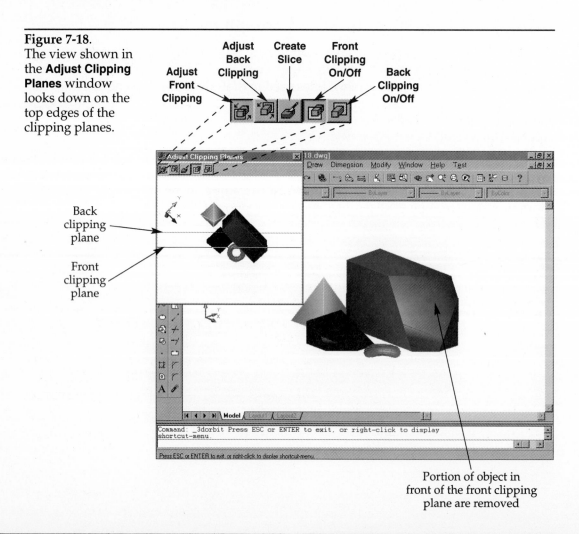

AutoCAD and its Applications—Advanced

Figure 7-19.
The clipping options can be selected by right-clicking inside the **Adjust Clipping Planes** window.

Figure 7-20.
When the **Create Slice** option is selected, both front and back clipping planes are moved as a single unit. Only the portions of the objects between the clipping planes are displayed.

Only the portions of objects between the clipping planes are displayed

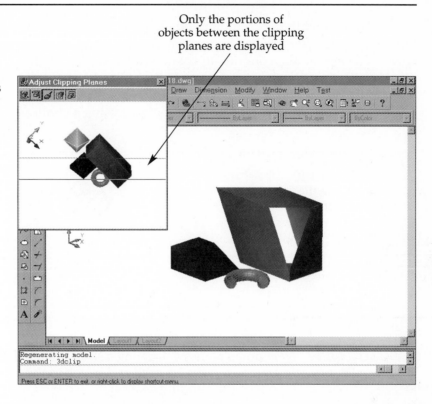

3. Pick and drag the front clipping plane.
4. Pick the **Adjust Back Clipping** button. Pick the **Back Clipping On/Off** button to turn it on.
5. Click and drag the back clipping plane.

You have now adjusted both clipping planes. If you rotate the objects in the 3D orbit view, notice that the clipping planes remain stationary. As an object is rotated, the visible portion of the object varies, based on the location of the clipping planes.

EXERCISE 7-6

❑ Open the Truck model drawing.
❑ In the 3D orbit view, display the preset Front view.
❑ Activate the **Adjust Clipping Planes** window.
❑ Move the front clipping plane to cut through the engine compartment of the truck.
❑ Move the back clipping plane to cut through the airfoil on top of the truck.
❑ Be sure that both front and back clipping planes are turned on.
❑ Create a slice, then move it along the length of the truck.
❑ This drawing is used again. Leave it open or close the drawing without saving.

Creating a Continuous 3D Orbit

The most dynamic aspect of the 3D orbit view is the ability to create a continuous orbit of a model. With the flick of your pointing device, you can set the model in motion in any direction and at any speed (depending on the power of your computer).

To access continuous orbit mode, select **Continuous Orbit** from the **More** cascading menu of the 3D orbit view shortcut menu, pick the **3D Continuous Orbit** button from the **3D Orbit** toolbar, or type 3DCORBIT at the Command: prompt. The continuous orbit cursor icon is displayed. See Figure 7-21.

Pick and hold the left button and move the pointer in the direction you want the model to rotate. Release the button when the pointer is moving at the appropriate speed. The model will continue to rotate until you pick the left mouse button, press [Enter] or [Esc], or right-click and pick **Exit**.

At any time while the model is orbiting, you can left-click and adjust the rotation angle and speed by repeating the process for starting a continuous orbit.

Figure 7-21.
Pick and hold the left button and move the continuous orbit cursor icon in the direction you want the model to rotate.

PROFESSIONAL TIP An impressive display can be achieved by first adjusting the clipping planes or creating a slice through the model. Then activate a continuous orbit and watch as the model rotates in and out of the clipping planes.

USING THE DVIEW COMMAND

AutoCAD User's Guide **17**

The **DVIEW** (dynamic view) command can also be used to establish a viewpoint in 3D space. Many of the **DVIEW** command options can be performed more easily using the 3D orbit view. However, the **DVIEW** command has some options that are not available in the 3D orbit view.

When using the **DVIEW** command, the viewer's eye location is called the *camera*. The focus point is the *target*. These two points form the *line of sight*. The following viewing adjustments can be made with the **DVIEW** command options:
* The camera lens can be specified as telephoto or wide-angle. These lenses allow you to create a close-up or wide field of vision.
* The distance from the camera to the target can be set.
* The line of sight can be adjusted to any angle.
* The entire image can be rotated, or *twisted*, around the center point of the display.
* Front and back cutting planes can be established to "clip" portions of the model you do not wish to view.
* Hidden lines can be removed.

NOTE	Most of the **DVIEW** command's functions have been replaced by **3DORBIT**, which is a much more dynamic and powerful command. **DVIEW** may be useful to some because you can use a small test drawing to establish the display, then return to the current drawing. This requires far less system resources than the **3DORBIT** command.

Test Drawings for DVIEW

The **DVIEW** command may be slow if used on a large drawing. This will depend on how much memory your computer has. Therefore, use a test drawing to create the view needed. Then, display your drawing using the new view settings.

AutoCAD has a test drawing named DVIEWBLOCK. The block is a simple house with a chimney, window, and open door, Figure 7-22. Since there are few objects in the drawing, it can be rotated, zoomed, and panned quickly.

To use the **DVIEW** command, enter DV or DVIEW at the Command: prompt as follows:

    Command: **DV** or **DVIEW**↵
    Select objects or <use DVIEWBLOCK>:

The DVIEWBLOCK drawing is displayed if you press [Enter] at the Select objects: prompt, or you can select objects to be used while establishing the new display. If you press [Enter], the house appears on the screen at the same viewpoint as the current drawing. You may not see the entire house at first, depending on the zoom magnification of the current drawing.

Once you have selected either the DVIEWBLOCK drawing or objects as a sample display while working in the **DVIEW** command, you can select one of the following options:

    Command: **DV** or **DVIEW**↵
    Select objects or <use DVIEWBLOCK>: ↵
    Enter option
    [CAmera/TArget/Distance/POints/PAn/Zoom/TWist/CLip/Hide/Off/Undo]:

Figure 7-22.
The default DVIEWBLOCK drawing is a small house. This can be used to help select a viewing angle.

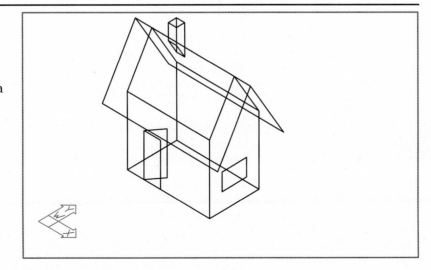

Specifying the Camera Angle

If the initial **DVIEW** display is a plan view, it is best to use the **Camera** option first. This option lets you locate your eye position in two directions relative to object. A vertical movement is the angle *from* the XY plane. A horizontal movement is *in* the XY plane from the X axis. These angular settings are similar to the settings established in the **Viewpoint Presets** dialog box discussed earlier in this chapter.

After selecting the **Camera** option, you can move the pointing device to pick the best display. Placing the cursor at the center of the screen represents an angle of 0° *in* the XY plane and 0° *from* the XY plane. Move the cursor horizontally and the house rotates 180° to the left or right in the XY plane. Experiment moving the cursor first horizontally and then vertically while observing how the view changes. Separating the cursor movement into its two components makes the relationship between the cursor location and the resulting view clear.

Picking a point with the cursor actually selects two angles—the angle *in* the XY plane and the angle *from* the XY plane. These angles can also be entered directly from the keyboard. There is a prompt for each angle.

> [CAmera/TArget/Distance/POints/PAn/Zoom/TWist/CLip/Hide/Off/Undo]: **CA↵**
> Specify camera location, or enter angle from XY plane,
> or [Toggle (angle in)] <90.0000>: **15↵**
> Specify camera location, or enter angle in XY plane from X axis,
> or [Toggle (angle from)] <90.00000>: **–60↵**

While the **Camera** option prompts are on the screen, you can toggle between the horizontal and vertical angle input by using the **Toggle** option. If the prompt reads [Toggle (angle in)], you can switch to this option to input the angle *in* the XY plane by typing T and pressing [Enter]. The prompt changes to [Toggle (angle from)]. This allows you to try several angles while still in the **Camera** option.

You can limit the movement of the camera to one direction by specifying an angle and pressing [Enter]. For example, if you enter 20 for the angle from the XY plane, the object remains stationary at that angle and only moves clockwise or counterclockwise on the X axis. This allows you to view the object at one vertical angle from any horizontal angle in the XY plane.

Selecting the Target Angles

Another way to change your view is with the **Target** option. The *target* is the point where the camera looks. The target can be rotated around the camera to any angle. A 90° vertical rotation angle creates a view of the opposite side of the object, Figure 7-23.

Figure 7-23.
The vertical rotation angle for the target is opposite that of the camera.

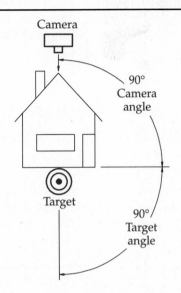

Camera

90° Camera angle

Target

90° Target angle

PROFESSIONAL TIP

Often, it is easier to visualize your viewpoint (camera angle) first, before adjusting the view using other options. This is especially true if the current view is a plan view.

Setting a Distance Between Camera and Target (Perspective)

To this point, you have created views that are parallel projections. A perspective is not a parallel projection. The **Distance** option creates a perspective by moving the camera closer to or farther from the target. This is how your eye actually sees the object. Lines in a perspective view project to vanishing points. Therefore, lines farther from the camera appear to meet. AutoCAD indicates the perspective mode by placing a perspective icon in the lower-left corner of the screen.

A slider bar appears when you select the **Distance** option. See Figure 7-24. When you move the slider bar to the right, the camera moves away from the object. You can pick a distance with the slider bar or enter a distance at the keyboard. You may need to enter a distance greater than the width of your drawing to see all the objects.

The perspective view achieved with the **Distance** option is great for display and plotting purposes, but not practical for working. The **PAN** and **ZOOM** commands do not function in a perspective view, nor can you select points for drawing. Use the **Off** option to turn off the perspective projection and return to parallel projection.

Figure 7-24.
A slider bar appears for many of the **DVIEW** command options.

| 0x | 1x | 4x | 9x | 16x |

Picking Points for the Target and Camera

The **Points** option allows you to pick the target and camera locations using XYZ coordinates, filters, or object snap modes. When entering XYZ coordinates, keep in mind that the coordinates are based on the current UCS. The **Points** option is best used when you have already created a display other than the initial plan view. In addition, the **Points** option works best when objects in the current drawing are selected for display, rather than using the DVIEWBLOCK drawing. As you select the pick points, a rubber band connects the camera and target to help you see the new line of sight.

Figure 7-25 shows target (P1) and camera (P2) pick points and the resulting view. The command sequence for Figure 7-25 follows:

```
Command: DVIEW↵
Select objects or <use DVIEWBLOCK>: (select the objects on the screen)
Enter option
[CAmera/TArget/Distance/POints/PAn/Zoom/TWist/CLip/Hide/Off/Undo]: PO↵
Specify target point <default>: MID↵
of (pick P1)
Specify camera point <default>: END↵
of (pick P2)
```

Notice in Figure 7-25B that the target and camera points are aligned. The camera point at the top of the tripod touches the target point. These two points are the line of sight. A perspective display changes to a parallel projection to allow you to select camera and target points. The display then returns to perspective.

Figure 7-25.
A—The target (P1) and camera (P2) are located using the **Points** option of the **DVIEW** command. B—The resulting pictorial view.

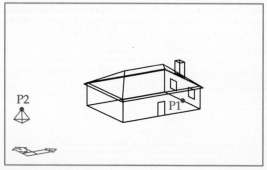

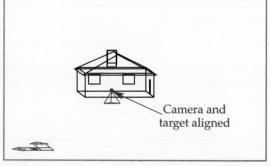

A   B

EXERCISE 7-7

❑ Open one of the 3D models you created in an earlier chapter.
❑ Use the **DVIEW Distance** option to move your viewpoint farther away from the object.
❑ Use the **DVIEW Off** option to turn off the perspective display.
❑ Set the **DVIEW Camera** and **Target** options to both positive and negative angle values. Check each view using the **Hide** option.
❑ Set the **DVIEW Points** option to view the object from two different viewpoints.
❑ Close the drawing without saving.

Changing the Position of the Drawing

The **Pan** option of the **DVIEW** command can be used to specify a pan displacement, similar to picking **Point** from the **Pan** cascading menu in the **View** pull-down menu. Realtime panning is not available in the **DVIEW** command.

Using a Zoom Lens

You can change the lens on the **DVIEW** camera just as you can a real camera. Lens lengths are measured in millimeters. A zoom, or telephoto, lens is greater than 50mm. It allows you to get a close-up view while not changing the camera and target positions. A wide angle lens is less than 50mm. It takes in a wider field of vision as the lens length gets smaller. You can change lenses with the **Zoom** option only if the current display is a perspective as a result of using the **Distance** option.

    [CAmera/TArget/Distance/POints/PAn/Zoom/TWist/CLip/Hide/Off/Undo]: **Z**↵
    Specify lens length <50.000mm>: **28**↵

If your display is not in perspective, **Zoom** requests a scale factor and displays the slider bar.

A 28mm lens is commonly known as a "fish-eye." This lens creates a wide field of vision. However, a fish-eye lens can distort the sides of your drawing and make the model appear farther away, depending on the current distance setting. Two views of the DVIEWBLOCK drawing are shown in Figure 7-26 using a distance of 40 feet.

Figure 7-26.
In perspective view, the UCS icon is replaced by the perspective icon (lower-left corner).
A—A 28mm lens at a distance of 40 feet. B—A 100mm lens at a distance of 40 feet.

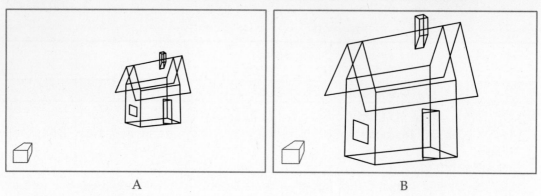

A   B

Rotating the Drawing Around a Point

The **Twist** option allows you to rotate the drawing around the center point of the screen. When the twist, or *tilt angle*, is set with the pointing device, the angle appears in the coordinate display window. A rubber band line connects the center point to the crosshairs. An exact positive or negative angle can be entered at the keyboard.

Rolling the View with Point Specification

You can quickly create a 3D display by simply picking a point on the drawing while the **DVIEW** command is active. The point you pick is a target point about which you drag the object. You can drag the object and pick again to set the display. Or you can enter two angles, separated by a comma, to provide an angle in the XY plane (direction), and an angle from the XY plane (magnitude). Both angles must be between 0 and 360°. When you pick the first point the following prompt appears:

> Enter direction and magnitude angles:

The direction angle rotates in the XY plane, and the magnitude actually "rolls" the object perpendicular to the XY plane.

Clipping Portions of the Drawing

Portions of a drawing can be eliminated from the display by using clipping planes. The planes are always perpendicular to your line of sight. Lines behind the back clipping plane or in front of the front clipping plane are hidden.

The **Clip** option of the **DVIEW** command is used to dynamically place a clipping plane, or enter its distance from the target. The front and back planes are turned on by entering a distance, or turned off by selecting the **Off** option. The camera is the default position of the front plane. The front clipping plane can be returned to the camera position with the **Eye** option.

> [CAmera/TArget/Distance/POints/PAn/Zoom/TWist/CLip/Hide/Off/Undo]: **CL**↵
> Enter clipping option [Back/Front/Off] <Off>: **B**↵
> Specify distance from target or [ON/OFF] <*current*>: (*enter a distance or use the slider bar to pick*)
> [CAmera/TArget/Distance/POints/PAn/Zoom/TWist/CLip/Hide/Off/Undo]: **CL**↵
> Enter clipping option [Back/Front/Off] <Off>: **F**↵
> Specify distance from target or [set to Eye (camera)] <*default*>: **E**↵

When perspective projection is on, the front clipping plane is automatically on. The **On** and **Off** suboptions of the **Front** option are available only if perspective is off.

Undoing DVIEW Options and Exiting

The **Undo** option of the **DVIEW** command undoes the previous operation. This option lets you step back through previous **DVIEW** functions. To exit the **DVIEW** command, press [Enter], [Esc], or the space bar at the **DVIEW** options prompt.

EXERCISE 7-8

❑ Begin a new drawing. Draw a 3D house similar to the DVIEWBLOCK drawing.
❑ Select the **DVIEW** command to select a camera angle. Select the **Zoom** option to see the entire house.
❑ Draw a small box in the center of the house.
❑ Draw another object of your choice outside the house.
❑ Use the **Points** option of the **DVIEW** command to place the camera on the object outside the house. Place the target on a corner of the box inside the house.
❑ Select the **Distance** option to move farther away. Then, move closer to the target.
❑ Zoom to a point on or near the box inside the house.
❑ Select the **Target** option. Pick an angle from the XY plane near zero. Move the pointer to several positions when picking the horizontal rotation. Notice how the house moves around you. Pick a view that allows you to see the object outside the house.
❑ Rotate the view twice by using the point specification method. First, pick two points with the pointing device, then enter two angles for the second display.
❑ Use the **Clip** option to place a back clipping plane that hides the object outside the house.
❑ Save the drawing as EX7-8.

CREATING A STANDARD ENGINEERING LAYOUT

Often, objects created with 3D modeling techniques need to be transferred to 2D paper plots. A *standard engineering layout* is a layout of views of a 3D object including three orthographic views and an isometric view. An experienced print reader can use the views in the standard engineering layout to visualize the 3D object.

A simple 3D model is shown in Figure 7-27. To create the orthographic and isometric views needed to fully describe this object in a two-dimensional plot, you could access a layout tab (paper space) and create several floating viewports. Then, set the correct viewpoint in each viewport and scale the model.

However, this process can be done much more easily using the Create Layout wizard. The following basic procedure is described more thoroughly in the text below.

1. Create the 3D model.
2. Start the Create Layout wizard.
3. Select a title block.
4. Select the standard engineering viewport configuration.

The first step is to create the 3D model. This is done in model space (**Model** tab). When the model is complete, access the Create Layout wizard by selecting **Create Layout...** from the **Wizards** cascading menu in the **Tools** pull-down menu. The wizard requests a name for the layout, the plotter associated with the layout, the paper size, and the paper orientation. The **Title Block** page of the wizard allows you to select a title block to include in the layout. Select the **Std. Engineering Views** option in the **Viewport setup** area of the **Define Viewports** page. See Figure 7-28. This will create the four viewports used in the standard engineering layout.

The four viewports show the Front, Top, Right, and SE Isometric viewpoints. A completed layout, including the ANSI A-size title block, is shown in Figure 7-29.

Figure 7-27.
A simple 3D model
displayed in model
space (**Model** tab).

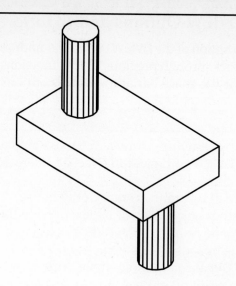

Figure 7-28.
The **Define
Viewports** page of
the Create Layout
wizard.

Pick to create
viewports

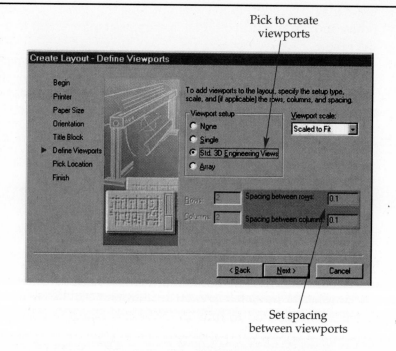

Set spacing
between viewports

Figure 7-29.
A standard engineering layout includes the Front, Top, and Right orthographic views, along with an isometric view. This layout includes the ANSI A-size title block, and hidden lines have been removed in the isometric viewport.

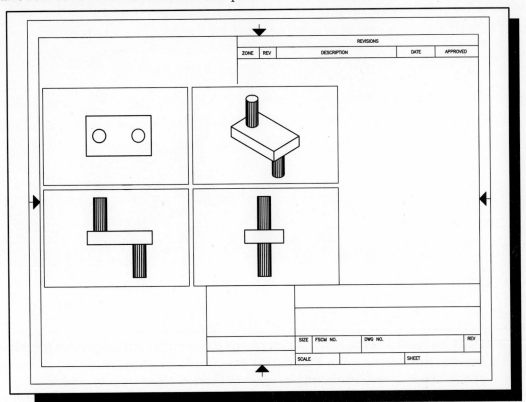

DISPLAYING A 3D MODEL

The *display* of a 3D model is how the model is presented. This does not refer to the viewing angle. The simplest display technique is to remove hidden lines using the **HIDE** command. A simple rendered model can be created with the **SHADEMODE** command. An advanced rendered model can be created with the **RENDER** command. This is the most realistic presentation.

Using the HIDE Command

The **HIDE** command removes hidden lines from the display. The command regenerates the drawing and removes all lines that are behind other objects. Invisible edges of 3D faces are also removed. To use this command, select **Hide** from the **View** pull-down menu, pick the **Hide** button from the **Render** toolbar, or type HI or HIDE at the Command: prompt.

The **HIDE** command affects only the on-screen display—it has no affect on plots. To plot objects with hidden lines removed, use the following guidelines.

- **Plotting from the Model tab.** When plotting from the **Model** tab, all objects were created in model space. To plot with hidden lines removed, select the **Hide objects** check box in the **Plot options** area of the **Plot Settings** tab in the **Plot** dialog box. See Figure 7-30.

HIDE
HI

View
→ Hide

Render
toolbar

Hide

Figure 7-30.
Pick the **Hide objects** check box to have hidden lines removed in a plotted drawing.

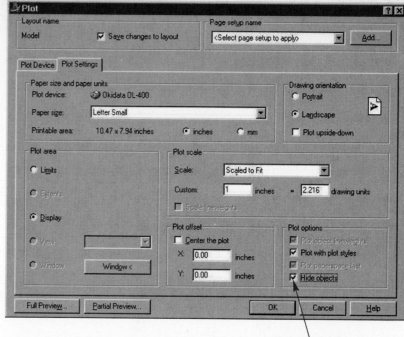

Pick to remove hidden lines

- **Plotting from a layout tab.** When plotting from a layout tab, select the **Hide objects** check box in the **Plot** dialog box to remove hidden lines for paper space objects. However, this setting does not affect model space objects contained in floating viewports. To remove hidden lines within a viewport, use the **Hideplot** option of the **MVIEW** command. Select the viewport to hide as follows:

  Command: **MV** *or* **MVIEW.**↵
  Specify corner of viewport or
  [ON/OFF/Fit/Hideplot/Lock/Object/Polygonal/Restore/2/3/4] <Fit>: **H.**↵
  Hidden line removal for plotting [ON/OFF]: **ON.**↵
  Select objects: *(pick the viewport to hide lines when plotting)*
  Select objects: ↵
  Command:

When you pick the viewport, pick the border of the viewport. Do not pick the objects in the viewport.

CAUTION

Layers that are turned off are still regenerated. Frozen layers are not regenerated. Therefore, objects on layers that are turned off may block your view of objects on visible layers. On the other hand, objects on layers that are frozen will not obscure objects on visible layers.

Using the SHADEMODE Command

The **SHADEMODE** command options can be accessed by selecting the **Shade** cascading menu in the **View** pull-down menu, using the **Shade** toolbar, or typing SHADEMODE at the Command: prompt. See Figure 7-31. If you enter the command at the Command: prompt, the available options are identical to the options in the **Shade** toolbar and the **Shade** cascading menu.

Command: **SHADEMODE**↵
Current mode: 2D wireframe
Enter option [2D wireframe/3D wireframe/Hidden/Flat/Gouraud/fLat+edges/gOuraud+edges] <2D wireframe>:

Figure 7-32 shows the effects of the various shading options. Shading is covered in greater detail in Chapter 9.

Figure 7-31.
Shading options can be selected from the **Shade** cascading menu in the **View** pull-down menu or from the **Shade** toolbar.

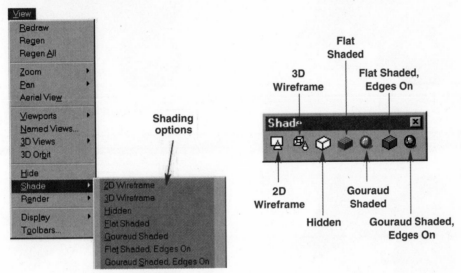

Producing a Quick Rendering

Rendering is covered in detail in Chapter 9 and Chapter 15. The **Render** dialog box is used to specify rendering variables. To access this dialog box, select **Render...** from the **Render** cascading menu in the **View** pull-down menu, pick the **Render** button from the **Render** toolbar, or enter RR or RENDER at the Command: prompt.

Open a model from an earlier chapter and select a 3D viewpoint. Use the defaults shown in the **Render** dialog box and pick the **Render** button (or press [Enter]). A shaded and rendered image is then created, Figure 7-33.

Figure 7-32.
The available shading options produce a variety of displays.

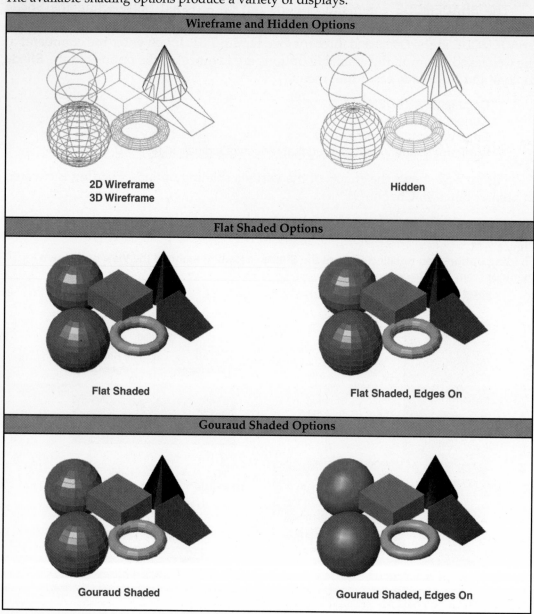

Figure 7-33.
Rendering produces
the most realistic
display.

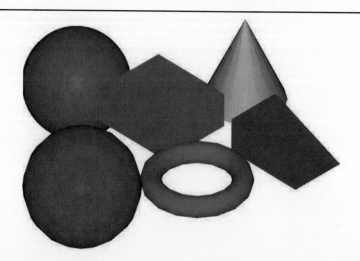

AutoCAD and its Applications—Advanced

Chapter Test

Answer the following questions on a separate sheet of paper.

1. The **Viewpoint Presets** dialog box uses angular measurement identical to which coordinate system?
2. What two angles are needed when using the **Rotate** option of the **VPOINT** command?
3. What command produces a view that is perpendicular to the current UCS?
4. What does the image on the left side of the **Viewpoint Presets** dialog box represent?
5. What is the function of a circular arrow cursor icon in the 3D orbit view?
6. In the 3D orbit view, where must the cursor icon be located in order to rotate the model dynamically in any direction?
7. What type of shade mode produces the smoothest shading?
8. Which system variable controls the location of the grid on the Z axis?
9. How can you select named views while in the 3D orbit view?
10. What is the function of the **3DCLIP** command?
11. What command generates a continuous 3D orbit?
12. What is the function of the DVIEWBLOCK?
13. Which **DVIEW** command option is used to specify a camera angle?
14. What point does the camera look at in the **DVIEW** command?
15. Which option of the **DVIEW** command allows you to create a perspective view?
16. How is a lens length selected in the **DVIEW** command?
17. What portions of an object are removed when clipping planes are set?
18. How do you remove hidden lines when plotting from the **Model** tab?
19. What is the function of the **Hideplot** option of the **MVIEW** command?
20. What command produces the most realistic shaded image?

Drawing Problems

1. Open one of your 3D drawings from a previous chapter and do the following:
   A. Use the **Viewpoint Presets** dialog box to produce a display with a 30° rotation in the XY plane and a 40° rotation from the XY plane.
   B. Shade the object so that faces are shown in object colors and edges are highlighted.
   C. Produce a slide of the image. Refer to Chapter 28 of *AutoCAD and its Applications—Basics* for information on creating slides.

2. Open one of your drawings from a previous chapter, or open the R300-20 drawing from the Acad2000\Sample folder.
   A. Display the drawing using Gouraud shading.
   B. Change the display to perspective and turn on the grid and compass.
   C. Create four named views of different parts on the model. Redisplay these views using the **Saved Views** cascading menu in the 3D orbit view shortcut menu.
   D. Create a slice through the model, then put it into continuous orbit.
   E. Save the drawing as P7-2.

3. Open one of your 3D drawings from a previous chapter and do the following:
   A. Create an arrangement of three floating model space viewports in a paper space layout.
   B. Display the drawing from a different viewpoint in each viewport.
   C. Use a different shading option in each viewport.

4. Open one of your 3D drawings from a previous chapter and perform the following:
   A. Create an arrangement of three floating model space viewports in a paper space layout.
   B. Display the drawing in a different viewpoint in each viewport.
   C. Use options of the **SHADEMODE** command to display a different shading in each viewport.
   D. Create a rendering of the objects in one of the viewports.

5. Open one of your 3D drawings from a previous chapter and perform the following:
   A. Create a standard engineering layout.
   B. Create dimensioning layers for each of the three orthogonal viewports and apply some basic dimensions to each view.
   C. Use the **Hideplot** option of the **MVIEW** command to hide the hidden lines in the 3D viewport.
   D. Plot the drawing from the layout tab using a scale of 1:1.

Three-Dimensional Text and Dimensioning

Learning Objectives

After completing this chapter, you will be able to:

- Create text with a thickness.
- Apply horizontal text and titles to 3D views.
- Rotate 3D text to different planes.
- Describe how 3D objects can hide text.
- Create 3D dimensioning.
- Apply leaders to different UCS planes.

CREATING 3D TEXT WITH THICKNESS

Text does not have a thickness when created. This is true even if thickness is set with the **ELEV** command before drawing text. Text must be given thickness after it is created. This is done using the **Properties** window, which can be accessed by picking the **Properties** button from the **Standard** toolbar, selecting **Properties** from the **Tools** or **Modify** pull-down menus, or typing PROPERTIES at the Command: prompt.

Once a thickness is applied, the hidden lines can be removed using the **HIDE** command. Figure 8-1 shows six different fonts as they appear after being given a thickness with hidden lines removed.

Only text created using the **TEXT** and **DTEXT** commands (text object) can be assigned thickness. Text created with the **MTEXT** command (mtext object) cannot have thickness assigned to it.

Figure 8-1.
Six different fonts with thickness after hidden lines are removed.

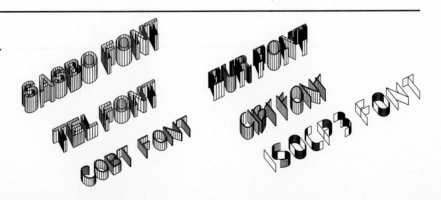

AutoCAD comes with a variety of TrueType fonts, which are listed with a TTF file extension. These fonts *cannot* be given thickness. Standard AutoCAD fonts have an SHX extension. This is a compiled version of the corresponding SHP or *shape*, file. Although none are shipped with AutoCAD 2000, PostScript fonts have a PFB file extension, which is not usable until it is compiled into a PFM file. To compile a SHP or PFB font into a file type that can be used in AutoCAD, type COMPILE at the Command: prompt. The **Select Shape or Font File** dialog box shown below appears. Fonts are contained in the Acad2000\Fonts folder. Pick either *.shp or *.pfb in the **Files of type:** list box. Next, select the font you wish to compile and pick **OK**. The font can now be used in AutoCAD, and the SHX or PFM font can be given thickness.

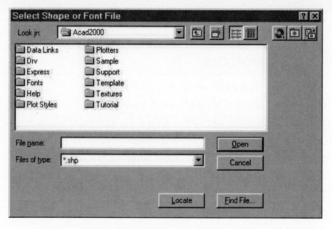

Text and the UCS

Text is parallel to the UCS in which it is drawn. Therefore, if you wish to show text appearing on a specific plane, make that plane the current UCS before placing the text. Figure 8-2 shows several examples of text on different UCS planes.

Figure 8-2.
Text located using three different UCS planes.

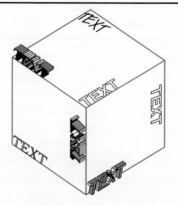

Changing the UCS of a Text Object

If text is placed improperly or on the wrong UCS, it can be edited using grips or 3D editing commands. For example, if the text at the upper-left corner of Figure 8-2 should be "lying" on the top surface, it can be edited as follows:

Command: **ROTATE3D**↵
Current positive angle: ANGDIR=counterclockwise ANGBASE=0
Select objects: *(pick the text object)*
Select objects: ↵
Specify first point on axis or define axis by
    [Object/Last/View/Xaxis/Yaxis/Zaxis/2points]: **X**↵
Specify a point on the X axis <0,0,0>: **END**↵
of *(pick line along the bottom of the text)*
Specify rotation angle or [Reference]: **–90**↵
Command:

This command sequence is based on the UCS in which the text was drawn. The axis of rotation may be different if another UCS is current.

After hidden lines are removed, the object appears as shown in Figure 8-3A. Since this text has a thickness, it appears to be recessed into the surface of the box with its "feet" showing through the side. To place the text on the top surface, use grips to move it the thickness of the text along the appropriate axis. The edited object is shown in Figure 8-3B.

Figure 8-3.
A—Text appears recessed in the box.
B—After being moved using grips.

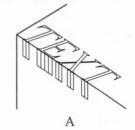
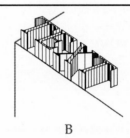

A   B

Using the **UCS** View Option to Create a Title

Text does not always need to be placed in a 3D plane. It can be drawn perpendicular and horizontal to your point of view regardless of the 3D viewpoint displayed. This application is used to insert the title of a 3D view. This is done with the **View** option of the **UCS** command.

To set the UCS to the current viewpoint, pick the **View UCS** button in the **UCS** toolbar, select **View** from the **New UCS** cascading menu in the **Tools** pull-down menu, or enter the following at the Command: prompt:

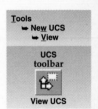

Command: **UCS**↵
Current ucs name: *current*
Enter an option [New/Move/orthoGraphic/Prev/Restore/Save/Del/Apply/?/World]
<World>: **V**↵

A new UCS is created perpendicular to your viewpoint. However, the view remains a 3D view. Name and save the UCS if you will use it again. Since inserted text is placed parallel to the new UCS, it will be horizontal (or vertical) in the current view. See Figure 8-4.

Figure 8-4.
This title (shown in color) has been placed correctly using the **View** option of the **UCS** command.

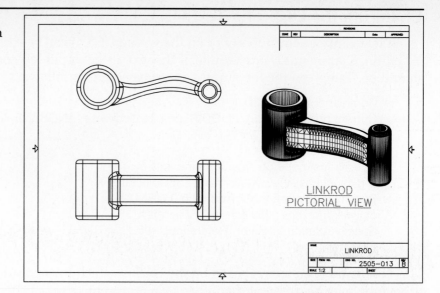

The Limitations of Hiding Text

Text drawn without a thickness will not be properly hidden by the **HIDE** command, even if it is placed behind a 3D object. In order for text behind a 3D object to be hidden, it must be given a thickness. Text that has a thickness will appear correctly when placed inside, outside, or protruding through a 3D object. If you want text to be hidden but not appear to have a thickness, give it a very small thickness, such as .001.

Figure 8-5A shows a variety of text placements in and around a 3D box. The two text objects at the upper left are sitting outside the box. Figure 8-5B shows the display after **HIDE** is used.

Figure 8-5.
A—Text objects placed in and around a 3D box.
B—The display after **HIDE** is used.

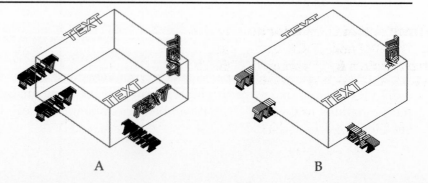

A   B

Dimensioned 3D objects are seldom used for manufacturing, but may be used for assembly. Dimensioned 3D drawings are most often used for some sort of presentation, such as displays, illustrations, parts manuals, or training manuals. Therefore, dimensions shown in 3D must be clear and easy to read. The most important aspect of applying dimensions to a 3D object is planning. That means following a few basic guidelines.

Creating a 3D Dimensioning Template Drawing

If you often create dimensioned 3D drawings, make a template drawing containing a few 3D display settings. These are outlined below:

- Create named dimension styles with appropriate text heights. For more information, see Chapters 18–21 of *AutoCAD and its Applications—Basics* for detailed information on dimensioning and dimension styles.
- Establish several named user coordinate systems that match the planes where dimensions will be placed. See Figure 8-6 for examples of standard named systems.
- Establish several 3D viewpoints that can be used for different objects. These viewpoints will allow you to select the display best for reading dimensions. Name and save these views.

Figure 8-6.
Three named user coordinate systems that can be used for dimensioning.

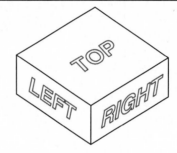

Placing Dimensions in the Proper Plane

To create dimensions that display properly, it may be necessary to create more than one UCS for a single plane. Notice in Figure 8-7A that the left dimension is inverted. Note the orientation of the UCS. A second UCS is created and the dimension is redrawn correctly in Figure 8-7B.

Figure 8-7.
More than one UCS for a given plane may be needed to properly create dimensions.
A—The left-hand dimension is inverted. B—The left-hand dimension drawn correctly using a different UCS.

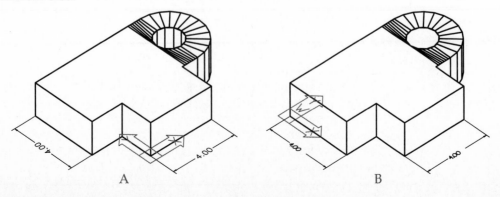

A   B

The location and plane where dimensions are placed is often a matter of choice. For example, Figure 8-8 shows several options for placing a thickness dimension on the object. All of these are correct. However, several of the options can be eliminated when other dimensions are added. This illustrates the importance of planning.

The key to good 3D dimensioning is to avoid overlapping dimension and extension lines in different planes. A freehand sketch can help you plan this. As you lay out the 3D sketch, try to group information items together. Dimensions, notes, and item tags should be grouped so that they are easy to read and understand. This technique is called *information grouping*.

Figure 8-9A shows the object from Figure 8-8 fully dimensioned using the aligned technique. Notice that the location dimension for the hole is placed on the top surface. This avoids dimensioning to hidden points. Figure 8-9B shows the same object dimensioned using the unilateral technique.

Figure 8-8.
The thickness dimension can be located in many different places. All locations shown here are correct.

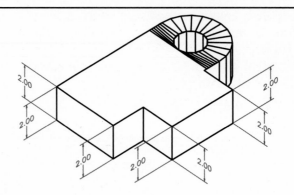

Figure 8-9.
A—An example of a 3D object dimensioned using the aligned technique. B—The object dimensioned with unilateral dimensions.

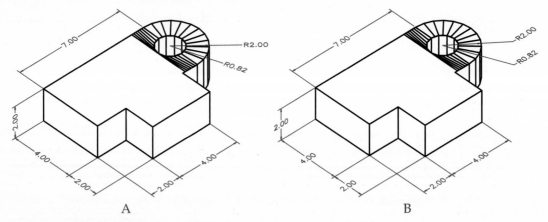

A   B

PROFESSIONAL TIP

Prior to placing dimensions on a 3D drawing, you should determine the purpose of the drawing. What will it be used for? Just as dimensioning a drawing for manufacturing purposes is based on the function of the part, 3D dimensioning is based on the function of the drawing. This determines whether you use chain, datum, arrowless, architectural, or some other style of dimensioning. It also determines how completely the object is dimensioned.

Placing Leaders and Radial Dimensions in 3D

Although standards such as ASME Y14.5M-1994 should be followed, the nature of 3D drawing and the requirements of the project may determine how dimensions and leaders are placed. Remember, the most important aspect of dimensioning a 3D drawing is its presentation. Is it easy to read and interpret?

Leaders and radial dimensions can be placed in, or perpendicular to, the plane of the feature. Figure 8-10A shows the placement of leaders in the plane of the top surface. Figure 8-10B illustrates the placement of leaders and radial dimensions in a UCS that is perpendicular to the top surface of the object.

Remember that text, dimensions, and leaders are always placed in the XY plane of the current UCS. Therefore, to create the layout in Figure 8-10B, you must use more than one UCS. Figure 8-11A and Figure 8-11B show the UCS icon orientations for the two radial dimensions.

Figure 8-10.
A—Leaders placed in the plane of the top surface. B—Leaders placed in a UCS perpendicular to the top surface.

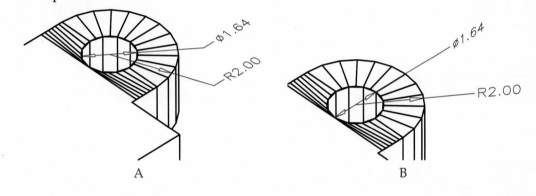

A   B

Figure 8-11.
A—The UCS used to draw the diameter dimension. B—The UCS used to draw the radius dimension.

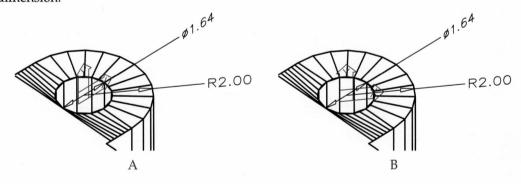

A   B

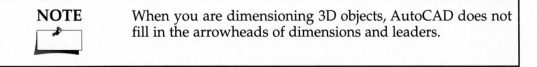

NOTE	When you are dimensioning 3D objects, AutoCAD does not fill in the arrowheads of dimensions and leaders.

Chapter 8   Three-Dimensional Text and Dimensioning

❏ Begin a new drawing and name it EX8-2.
❏ Draw the object shown in Figure 8-9 using the dimensions given. Create as many different user coordinate systems needed to draw and dimension the object.
❏ Place dimensions and leaders to achieve the best presentation.
❏ Save the drawing as EX8-2.

Chapter Test

Answer the following questions on a separate sheet of paper.
1. How does the **ELEV** command affect the thickness of text?
2. How can you create 3D text with thickness?
3. What file extension is used for PostScript font shape files?
4. Can the thickness of text created with TrueType fonts be changed?
5. If text is placed using the wrong UCS, how can it be edited to appear on the correct one?
6. How can text be placed horizontally in your viewpoint if the object is displayed in 3D?
7. How can text be made to appear hidden when it is behind a 3D object and **HIDE** is used?
8. What is the most common use of dimensioned 3D drawings?
9. Name three items that should be a part of a 3D dimensioning template drawing.
10. What is *information grouping*?

Drawing Problems

1. Construct a 4″ cube. Create a named UCS for each of the six sides. Name them FRONT, BACK, RIGHT, LEFT, TOP, and BOTTOM. Place a text label with a .75″ thickness centered on each face of the cube. Save the drawing as P8-1.

Problems 2–10. Create a fully dimensioned 3D drawing of the following problems. Save the drawings as P8-2, P8-3, etc.

2.   Chapter 2, Problem 1.

3.   Chapter 2, Problem 2.

4.   Chapter 2, Problem 3.

5.   Chapter 2, Problem 4.

6.   Chapter 2, Problem 6.

7. Chapter 2, Problem 7.

8. Chapter 2, Problem 8.

9. Chapter 2, Problem 9.

10. Chapter 2, Problem 12.

Problems 11–18. Create a fully dimensioned 3D drawing of the following problems. Place a text label below each drawing. The text should be horizontal in the current viewpoint. Use a label such as **3D VIEW**, *or the name of the object, such as* **GUIDE BRACKET**. *Save the drawings as* **P8-11**, **P8-12**, *etc.*

11. Chapter 3, Problem 1.

12. Chapter 3, Problem 2.

13. Chapter 3, Problem 3.

14. Chapter 3, Problem 4.

15. Chapter 3, Problem 5.

16. Chapter 3, Problem 6.

17. Chapter 3, Problem 7.

18. Chapter 3, Problem 8.

AutoCAD provides many options for displaying 3D models.

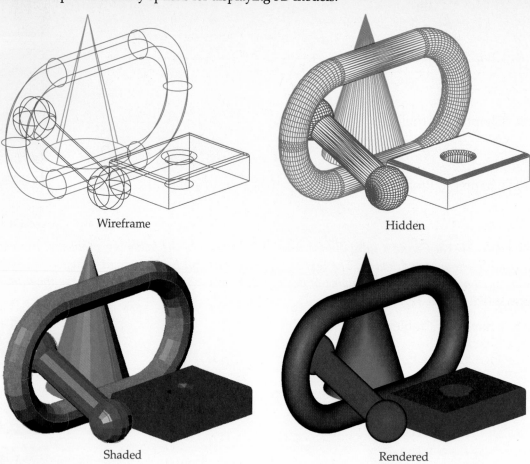

Wireframe

Hidden

Shaded

Rendered

CHAPTER 9

Introduction to Shading and Rendering

Learning Objectives

After completing this chapter, you will be able to:

- Shade a 3D model.
- Display a model using the **SHADEMODE** command.
- Display a model using the **SHADE** command.
- Display a model using the **SHADEDGE** system variable.
- Render a 3D model.
- Render selected parts of a 3D model.

In previous chapters, you used the **HIDE** command to make it easier to visualize a 3D model. The **SHADEMODE** command options display a model more realistically than the **HIDE** command. Shaded images can also be created using the **SHADE** and **–SHADE** commands, with the **SHADEDGE** system variable determining the type of shading. The **RENDER** command produces the most realistic image with highlights, shading, and materials, if applied. Figure 9-1 shows a 3D model of a cast iron plumbing cleanout after using **HIDE**, **SHADE**, and **RENDER**. Notice how different the three displays are.

SHADING A MODEL

The **SHADEMODE** command displays a shaded view of your model. There are several options that allow varying degrees of displayed quality. The color of the shaded image is controlled by the color of the model. A single light source located behind and to the left of the viewer points at the object.

An object can be shaded from any viewpoint. A shaded model can be edited while still keeping the object shaded. This can make it easier to see how the model is developing without having to reshade the drawing. However, when editing a shaded object, it may also be more difficult to select features.

Shaded images cannot be plotted. However, the [Print Screen] button on the keyboard can be used to copy a shaded image to the Windows Clipboard. The image can then be "pasted" into Windows Paint or other image editing software where it can be edited, printed, and saved in different file formats. See Chapter 14 and Chapter 18 for more detailed information on working with images using the Clipboard.

❑ The 3D model created in this exercise is used in the remainder of the chapter. You can use this model or substitute one of your own surfaced or solid models.

❑ Begin a new drawing.

❑ Create the following layers and colors.

Layer Name	Color
Box	red
Cone	yellow
Cylinder	magenta
Torus	blue
Surfaces	white

❑ Make the Surfaces layer current. Use the **3DFACE** command to draw a square floor surface with the coordinates (0,0), (8,0), (8,8), and (0,8). Draw a surface with the coordinates (0,8), (8,8), (8,8,8), and (0,8,8) as a backdrop.

❑ Set a viewpoint of (–3,–2,2).

❑ Use the solid primitives found in the **Solids** toolbar to draw the following objects.
 ❑ Make the Box layer current. Draw a 3D primitive box (**Box** button) with the corner at (5.5,6,2). Select the **Cube** option with a length of 2.
 ❑ Make the Cone layer current. Draw a 3D primitive cone (**Cone** button) with the center at (4,4), a diameter of 3 and a height of 6.
 ❑ Make the Torus layer current. Draw a 3D primitive torus (**Torus** button) with the center at (7,1,2), a diameter of 3 and a tube radius of 1.
 ❑ Make the Cylinder layer current. Draw a 3D primitive cylinder (**Cylinder** button) with the center at (1,7), a diameter of 1.5 and a height of 6.

❑ Save the drawing as EX9-1. Leave AutoCAD open. Your drawing should look like the one shown below.

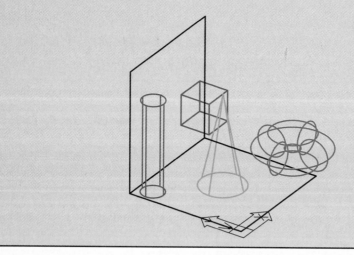

Shading Options

Shading options can be selected from the **Shade** cascading menu in the **View** pull-down menu. This cascading menu contains the **SHADEMODE** command options. To perform a quick shading, select **Fla̱t Shaded, Edges On** from the cascading menu. The objects created in Exercise 9-1 produce the image shown in Figure 9-2A. Notice the difference between the **HIDE** image in Figure 9-2B and the shaded version. The model is shaded using the colors of the objects.

Figure 9-1.
A—Hidden lines removed. B—Shaded. C—Rendered with materials and lights.

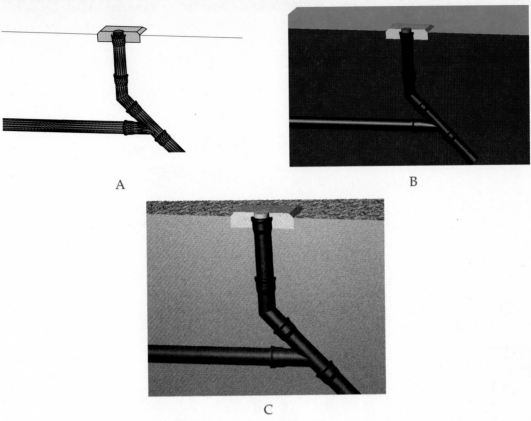

A

B

C

Figure 9-2.
A—The objects created in Exercise 9-1 are shaded. B—Hidden lines removed from the objects using **HIDE**.

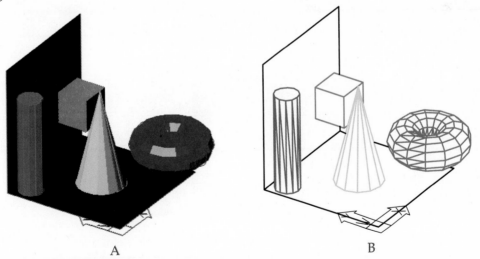

A

B

The **SHADEMODE** command allows control over how the model appears when shaded. Though not as realistic as a rendering, **SHADEMODE** can provide a good quality preview of a rendered object. There are seven options to **SHADEMODE**. Refer to Figure 9-3.

Figure 9-3.
There are seven different **SHADEMODE** options. A—**2D Wireframe**. B—**3D Wireframe**. C—**Hidden**. D—**Flat Shaded**. E—**Gouraud Shaded**. F—**Flat Shaded, Edges On**. G—**Gouraud Shaded, Edges On**.

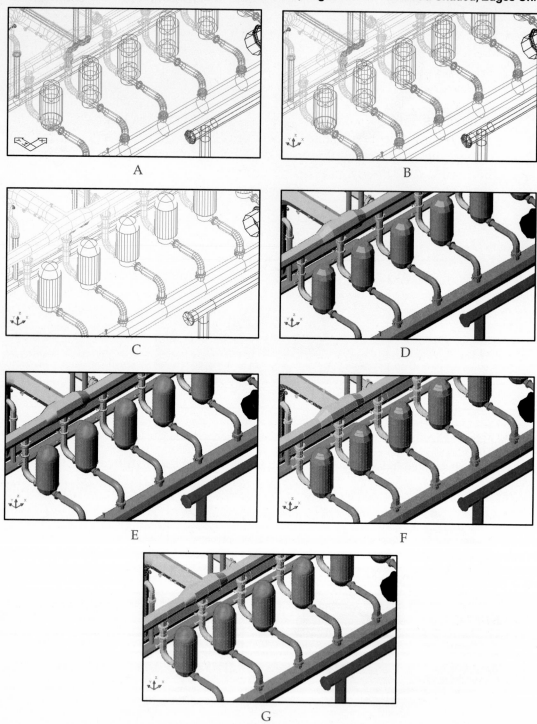

- **2D Wireframe.** This option displays normal wireframe view. Lines and curves are used to represent the edges of 3D objects. Raster images, OLE objects, linetypes, and line weights are visible when this option is used.
- **3D Wireframe.** This option displays the same type of wireframe view as the **2D Wireframe** option. However, raster images, OLE objects, linetypes, and line weights are *not* visible. The UCS icon changes to the 3D UCS icon when this option is used.

AutoCAD and its Applications—Advanced

- **Hidden.** This option is the same as using the **HIDE** command on a 3D wireframe display. The lines representing backfaces are hidden. Unlike using **HIDE** on a 2D wireframe display, tessellation lines are not used to represent the object.
- **Flat Shaded.** This option applies shading to the faces of objects. The edges of the faces are not shown. Smoothing is not applied to the objects. Therefore, curved surfaces appear flat and faceted. Highlights are applied to objects. Raster images, OLE objects, linetypes, and line weights are not visible when this option is used.
- **Gouraud Shaded.** This option applies smoothing to the edges between the faces on an object and shades the faces. This produces a smooth, realistic appearance. Highlights are applied to objects. Raster images, OLE objects, linetypes, and line weights are not visible.
- **Flat Shaded, Edges On.** This option is the same as the **Flat Shaded** option, except wireframe edges are displayed.
- **Gouraud Shaded, Edges On.** This option is the same as the **Gouraud Shaded** option, except wireframe edges are displayed.

The **SHADEMODE** command and its options are accessed by picking the appropriate button in the **Shade** toolbar, Figure 9-4, by selecting the option from the **Shade** cascading menu in the **View** pull-down menu, Figure 9-5, or by typing SHADEMODE at the Command: prompt.

Command: **SHADEMODE**
Current mode: Flat+Edges
Enter option [2D wireframe/3D
    wireframe/Hidden/Flat/Gouraud/fLat+edges/gOuraud+edges] <Flat+Edges>:

Figure 9-4.
The **Shade** toolbar contains all the **SHADEMODE** options.

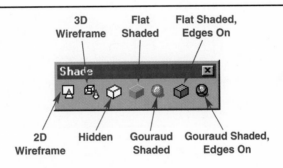

3D Wireframe | Flat Shaded | Flat Shaded, Edges On

2D Wireframe | Hidden | Gouraud Shaded | Gouraud Shaded, Edges On

Figure 9-5.
The **SHADEMODE** options can be selected from the **Shade** cascading menu of the **View** pull-down menu.

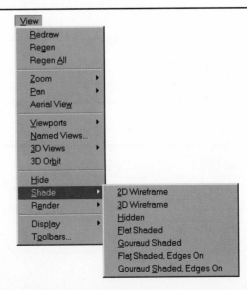

After using **SHADEMODE** to shade your model, **REGEN** will not restore a wireframe view. You must use the **2D Wireframe** option of the **SHADEMODE** command.

PROFESSIONAL TIP

SHADEMODE is a good command to set up an alias for, such as **SM**. See Chapter 28 in *AutoCAD and its Applications—Basics* for instruction on customizing aliases.

Other Shading Commands

In addition to the **SHADEMODE** command, shading can also be accomplished using the **SHADE** and **–SHADE** commands. The type of shading produced by these commands is determined by the setting of the **SHADEDGE** system variable. The four options of the **SHADE** command are identical to four **SHADEMODE** options. The **–SHADE** command produces slightly different images.

The **SHADEDGE** system variable controls how edges are displayed and faces are shaded when you use the **SHADE** and **–SHADE** commands. The four **SHADEDGE** options can be set at the Command: prompt. When you set the variables for **SHADEDGE**, the settings stay in effect for the **SHADE** command until they are changed. The **SHADEDGE** options are explained below. The equivalent **SHADEMODE** command option is also given. Refer to Figure 9-3 for examples of each setting.

SHADEDGE Setting	Description	SHADEMODE Option
0	Faces are shaded and edges are not highlighted.	Gouraud Shaded
1	Faces are shaded and edges are drawn in the background color.	Gouraud Shaded, Edges On
2	Faces are not shaded but are displayed in the background color, and edges are drawn in the object color.	Hidden
3	*(default)* Faces are shaded in the object color, and edges are drawn in the background color.	Flat Shaded, Edges On

---

NOTE

The **SHADE** and **–SHADE** commands produce different results with the same **SHADEDGE** settings.

EXERCISE 9-2

❑ Open the drawing named EX9-1 if it is not displayed on your screen.
❑ Type SHADEDGE and enter the value 0. Use the **SHADE** command to shade the model.
❑ Set **SHADEDGE** to 1. Shade the model.
❑ Set **SHADEDGE** to 2. Shade the model.
❑ Set **SHADEDGE** to 3. Shade the model.
❑ How did each display differ?
❑ Do not save the drawing.

AutoCAD and its Applications—Advanced

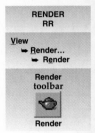

The **RENDER** command creates a realistic image of a model. However, rendering an image takes longer than shading an image. There are a variety of settings that you can change with the **RENDER** command to allow you to fine-tune renderings. These include scenes, lights, materials, backgrounds, fog, and preferences.

The default render settings display an image that is rendered in only the current viewport using a single light source located behind the viewer. The light intensity is set to 1 and the objects are rendered with a matte material the same color as the object display color. The render settings are discussed in detail in Chapter 14.

To produce a simple rendering of your model, select **Render...** from the **Render** cascading menu in the **View** pull-down menu. You can also pick the **Render** button in the **Render** toolbar or type RR or RENDER at the Command: prompt. The **Render** dialog box appears, Figure 9-6. Make sure that Viewport is selected in the **Destination** drop-down list. Then, accept the default options by picking the **Render** button. The rendered model is displayed in the drawing area of the current viewport.

RENDER
RR

View
➡ **Render...**
  ➡ **Render**

**Render
toolbar**

Render

Figure 9-6.
Basic rendering options are set in the **Render** dialog box.

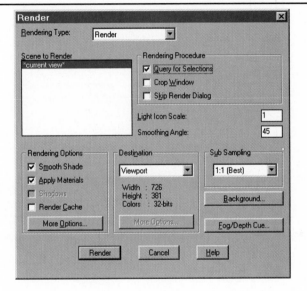

A Smooth Shaded Rendering

Notice in Figure 9-6 that the **Smooth Shade** check box in the **Rendering Options** area is active. This type of rendering applies smoothing to the polygon faces of an object, as happens with **Gouraud** shading. However, this is a more complicated process and takes longer to display. Figure 9-7 shows the effect of smooth shading.

To get back to a wireframe view of the model, use the **REGEN** command. If you used any of the **SHADEMODE** options before rendering, the **REGEN** command will not restore the wireframe display. In this case, use the **2D Wireframe** option of the **SHADEMODE** command to restore the wireframe.

Figure 9-7.
A—A rendering without smooth shading. B—A rendering with smooth shading applied.

A   B

EXERCISE 9-3

❑ Open the drawing named EX9-1 if it is not displayed on your screen.
❑ Change the viewpoint to SW isometric.
❑ Render the drawing.
❑ The image should look like the one shown below.

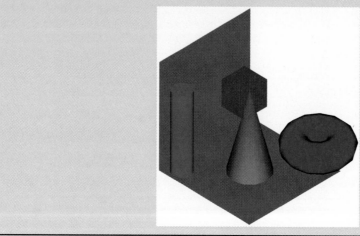

Rendering Specific Areas

There are two time-saving options found in the **Render** dialog box. These are **Crop Window** and **Query for Selections**. Check boxes for both of these options are in the **Rendering Procedure** area of the **Render** dialog box.

Checking the **Crop Window** check box allows you to draw a window around a portion of the drawing area. Only the area inside the window is rendered. When this check box is active, the following prompt appears on the Command: line after you pick the **Render** button in the **Render** dialog box.

Pick crop window to render:

Use the cursor to draw a box around the area you want to render. Once the second point defining the box is picked, the area is rendered. This option can only be used when rendering to the viewport. A small area of the model from Exercise 9-1 is rendered in Figure 9-8.

Figure 9-8.
A portion of the model from Exercise 9-1 rendered using the **Crop Window** check box.

When the **Query for Selections** check box is active, the following prompt appears on the Command: line after you pick the **Render** button to close the **Render** dialog box.

Select objects:

Use the cursor to pick the objects you want to render. You can use all of AutoCAD's normal selection methods. When you are done selecting objects, press [Enter] or the space bar. The rendering is then completed. Only the selected objects are rendered. All other objects are ignored. If an object selected for rendering is behind another object that is not selected for rendering, the object behind is rendered complete as if the object in front had been deleted.

NOTE

You can use both the **Crop Window** and the **Query for Selections** check boxes for the same rendering. You are first prompted to specify the window, then to pick the objects.

EXERCISE 9-4

❏ Open the drawing named EX9-1 if it is not displayed on your screen.
❏ Set the viewpoint to (3.5,–2.7,1.3).
❏ Create a rendered display of only the cylinder.
❏ Change the color of the torus. Render only the torus.
❏ Do not save the drawing.

Chapter Test

Answer the following questions on a separate sheet of paper.
1. What is the difference between the **HIDE** and **SHADEMODE** commands?
2. What determines the color of shaded objects?
3. What is the purpose of the **SHADEDGE** system variable?
4. What does a **SHADEDGE** value of 2 do?
5. After using the **Gouraud Shaded** option of the **SHADEMODE** command, how do you return the display to a wireframe display?
6. What is the default value for **SHADEDGE** and what is the equivalent **SHADEMODE** option?
7. Where is the light source located when shading objects?
8. What is the function of the **RENDER** command?
9. When rendering, what are the benefits of checking the **Crop Window** check box?
10. When active, what does the **Query for Selections** check box in the **Render** dialog box allow?

Drawing Problems

1. Open a 3D drawing from a previous chapter. Set **SHADEDGE** to 1. Shade the drawing using **–SHADE**. Type REGEN. Shade the drawing using **SHADE**. Return the display to wireframe. How are the two different?

2. Open one of your 3D drawings from a previous chapter.
   A. Create a four-viewport configuration.
   B. Use the **Flat Shaded** option of the **SHADEMODE** command in the upper-left viewport.
   C. Use the **Gouraud Shaded** option of the **SHADEMODE** command in the upper-right viewport.
   D. Use the **Hidden** option of the **SHADEMODE** command on the lower-left viewport.
   E. Use the **Flat Shaded, Edges On** option of the **SHADEMODE** command in the lower-right viewport.

3. Open a 3D drawing from the last chapter. Use the **RENDER** command on the current view. Use the same drawing to render two different windowed areas.

4. Begin a new drawing named P9-4.
   A. Make a Box layer and set the color to yellow. Make a Cone layer and set the color to blue. Make a Torus layer and set the color to green. Make the Torus layer current.
   B. Create a torus with a center point at (3,3,3), a diameter of 5, and a tube diameter of 1.
   C. Make the Cone layer current. Create a 3D solid cone. Place the center of the cone at (7,9,1) with a diameter of 2 and height of 7.
   D. Make the Box layer current. Create a solid box. Place the first corner at (1,6,8) and make the box a 2-unit cube.
   E. Make two vertical viewports. In the left viewport, set your viewpoint to the SW isometric. In the right viewport, set the viewpoint to the SE isometric.
   F. Shade the right viewport. Render the left viewport.
   G. Experiment with different shading settings in the right viewport.

CHAPTER 10

Introduction to Solid Modeling

Learning Objectives

After completing this chapter, you will be able to:

- Create regions that can be analyzed.
- Construct 3D solid primitives.
- Create complex solids using the **UNION** command.
- Remove portions of a solid using the **SUBTRACT** command.
- Create a new solid from the common intersection of two or more solids.
- Verify for interference between two solids and create a new solid from the interference volume.

WORKING WITH REGIONS

AutoCAD User's Guide **6**

A *region* is a closed two-dimensional solid. It can be extruded into a 3D solid object. A region can also be analyzed for its mass properties. Therefore, regions are useful for 2D applications where area and boundary calculations must be quickly obtained from a drawing. In addition, a 2D section view can be converted to a region, then extruded into a 3D solid model.

Constructing a 2D Region Model

The **REGION** command allows you to convert closed two-dimensional entities into regions. A region has all the 3D solid model properties except for thickness (Z value). When regions are added to, subtracted from, or intersected with other regions, a *composite region* is created. A composite region is also called a *region model*. A region can be given a thickness, or *extruded*, quickly and easily. This means that you can convert a 2D shape into a 3D solid model in just a few steps.

The following example creates a base for a support bracket. First, set your limits to 18,12 and perform a **ZOOM All**. Next, create the profile geometry in Figure 10-1. The corners of the rectangle are located at (3,3) and (11,11). The .75 diameter circles have centers located one unit from the sides of the rectangle.

Figure 10-1.
These 2D objects can be made into a region. The region can then be made into a 3D solid.

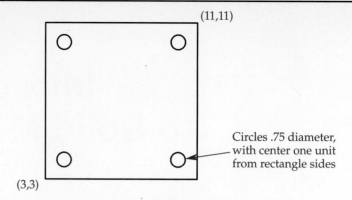

(11,11)

Circles .75 diameter, with center one unit from rectangle sides

(3,3)

REGION
REG

Draw
➥ Region

Draw
toolbar

Region

This creates AutoCAD entities that can now be converted into regions. Convert the rectangle and circles to regions using the **REGION** command. You can select this command by picking the **Region** button in the **Draw** toolbar, selecting **Region** in the **Draw** pull-down menu, or typing REG or REGION at the Command: prompt:

Command: **REG** *or* **REGION.**⏎
Select objects: *(pick the rectangle and circles)*
Select objects: ⏎
5 loops extracted.
5 Regions created.
Command:

SUBTRACT
SU

Modify
➥ Solids Editing
➥ Subtract

Solids Editing
toolbar

Subtract

The rectangle is now a region and each circle is a region. In order to create the surface of the rectangle, the circles must be subtracted from it. Use the **SUBTRACT** command by picking the **Subtract** button in the **Solids Editing** toolbar, selecting **Subtract** from the **Solids Editing** cascading menu in the **Modify** pull-down menu, or entering SU or SUBTRACT at the Command: prompt:

Command: **SU** *or* **SUBTRACT.**⏎
Select solids and regions to subtract from…
Select objects: *(pick the rectangle)*
Select objects: ⏎
Select solids and regions to subtract…
Select objects: *(pick the four circles)*
Select objects: ⏎
Command:

Now if you select the rectangle or any of the circles, you can see that all five objects have been changed into one region.

Using the BOUNDARY Command to Create a Region

BOUNDARY
BO

Draw
➥ Boundary...

The **BOUNDARY** command is often used to create a polyline for hatching or an inquiry. In addition, this command can be used to create a region. To do so, pick **Boundary...** from the **Draw** pull-down menu or type BO or BOUNDARY at the Command: prompt. The **Boundary Creation** dialog box is displayed. See Figure 10-2.

To create a region, pick the **Object Type** drop-down list, then pick **Region**. Next, select the **Pick Points** button. You are returned to the graphics display and prompted to select an internal point. Pick a point inside the object you wish to convert to a region. Press [Enter] when you are finished and the region is created. You can always check to see if an object is a polyline or region by using the **LIST** command and selecting the object.

You can further refine the boundary selection method by picking the type of island detection method. These two options are found at the bottom of the **Boundary Creation** dialog box.

Figure 10-2.
Regions can be
created using the
Boundary Creation
dialog box.

Select a point
inside the region

Select type
of object to
be created

Include
islands

Ignore
islands

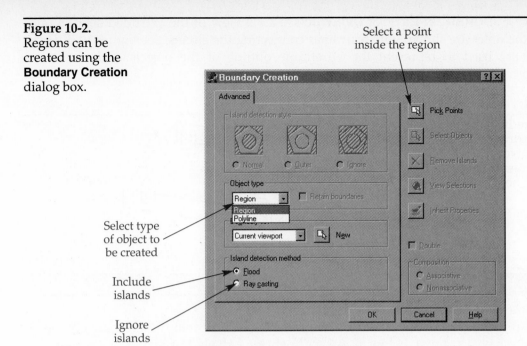

- **Flood.** When you select an internal point on an object, AutoCAD includes any islands that reside inside the object as part of the new region.
- **Ray casting.** When you select an internal point on an object, AutoCAD projects a ray to the nearest object and follows it counterclockwise to create the region. Therefore, islands are not included in the new boundary object.

PROFESSIONAL TIP
A **Boundary** button can be added to a custom toolbar or an existing toolbar. Refer to Chapter 20 for information on customizing toolbars.

Extruding a 2D Region into a 3D Solid

The final step in creating a 3D solid model from a 2D region is to apply a thickness to the region. The **EXTRUDE** command is used for this. A 2D region can be extruded in either a positive or negative Z direction. To use this command, pick the **Extrude** button in the **Solids** toolbar, select **Extrude** from the **Solids** cascading menu in the **Draw** pull-down menu, or enter EXT or EXTRUDE at the Command: prompt:

Command: **EXT** *or* **EXTRUDE**↵
Current wire frame density: ISOLINES=4
Select objects: *(pick anywhere on the region)*
Select objects: ↵
Specify height of extrusion or [Path]: **1**↵

At the next prompt, you can enter an angle value. A positive angle tapers the extruded solid. Press [Enter] to accept the default of 0 for no taper.

Specify angle of taper for extrusion <0>: ↵

The base is now a 3D solid object. A 3D solid object is called a ***primitive.***

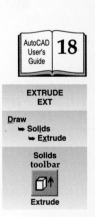

AutoCAD
User's
Guide **18**

**EXTRUDE
EXT**

D̲raw
➡ **Solids**
➡ **Ex̲trude**

**Solids
toolbar**

Extrude

Use **3DORBIT**, **VPOINT**, or **DVIEW** to see a 3D view of the extruded solid. Notice that the holes are shown with four lines connecting the circles. See Figure 10-3. These lines are used to represent the wireframe outline of the objects. This feature is discussed in Chapter 13.

Figure 10-3.
The extruded 3D solid. Notice the wireframe display of the holes.

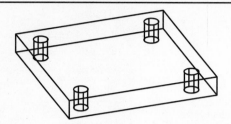

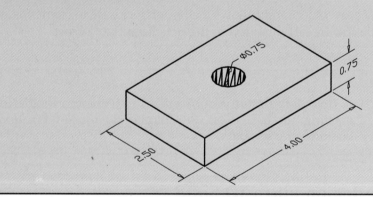

EXERCISE 10-1

❏ Start a new drawing named EX10-1.
❏ Using the **RECTANG** and **CIRCLE** commands, draw a two-dimensional top view of the object shown below. Use the dimensions given, but do not dimension the object.
❏ Using the appropriate commands, create a 2D composite region.
❏ Extrude the region model into a 3D solid with the given thickness.
❏ Save the model as EX10-1.

Calculating the Area of a Region

A region is not a polyline. It is an enclosed area called a *loop*. Certain values of the region, such as area, are stored as a value of the region primitive. The **AREA** command can be used to determine the length of all sides and the area of the loop. This can be a useful advantage of using a region.

For example, suppose a parking lot is being repaved. You need to calculate the surface area of the parking lot to determine the amount of material needed. This total surface area excludes the space taken up by planting dividers, sidewalks, and light posts, because you will not be paving under these items. If the parking lot and all objects inside it are drawn as a region, the **AREA** command can give you this figure in one step. If a polyline is used to draw the parking lot, all internal features must be subtracted each time the **AREA** command is used.

Regions can prove valuable when working with many items:

- Roof areas excluding chimneys, vents, and fans.
- Bodies of water, such as lakes, excluding islands.
- Lawns and areas of grass, excluding flower beds, trees, and shrubs.
- Landscaping areas excluding lawns, sidewalks, and parking lots.
- Concrete surfaces, such as sidewalks, excluding openings for landscaping, drains, and utility covers.

You can find many other applications for regions that can help in your daily tasks.

CONSTRUCTING SOLID PRIMITIVES

AutoCAD User's Guide **18**

Solid primitives are basic 3D geometric shapes such as boxes, spheres, cylinders, cones, wedges, and tori. Unlike 3D surfaced objects, they have the mass properties of a solid. Solid primitives can also be used as building blocks for complex solid models. To create a solid primitive, pick the appropriate button in the **Solids** toolbar, select the object from the **Solids** cascading menu in the **Draw** pull-down menu, or type the primitive command name at the Command: prompt. The pull-down menu and toolbar are shown in Figure 10-4.

Figure 10-4.
A—The **Solids** cascading menu. B—The **Solids** toolbar.

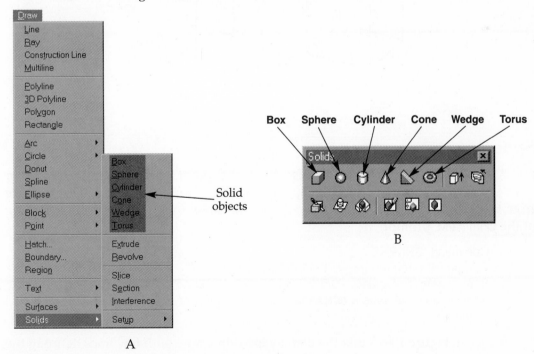

BOX

Draw
➡ Solids
➡ Box

Solids toolbar

Box

Box

A box can be constructed from an initial corner or the center. These options are available by picking the **Box** button from the **Solids** toolbar, selecting **Box** from the **Solids** cascading menu in the **Draw** pull-down menu, or entering BOX at the Command: prompt. Refer to Figure 10-5 as you read the following command sequence:

Command: **BOX**↵
Specify corner of box or [CEnter] <0,0,0>: *(pick a corner or type C for the **Center** option)*
Specify corner or [Cube/Length]: *(pick the diagonal corner of the base, or type L and press [Enter] to provide a length)*
Specify height: **2**↵

If the **Cube** option is selected, the length value is applied to all dimensions.

Figure 10-5.
A—A box created using the **Cube** option. B—A box created by selecting the center point.

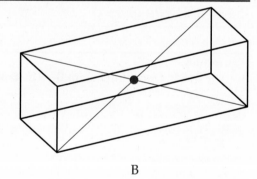

A   B

SPHERE

Draw
➡ Solids
➡ Sphere

Solids toolbar

Sphere

Sphere

A sphere is drawn by first picking its center point, then entering a radius or diameter. To draw a sphere, pick the **Sphere** button in the **Solids** toolbar, select **Sphere** from the **Solids** cascading menu in the **Draw** pull-down menu, or enter the following at the Command: prompt:

Command: **SPHERE**↵
Current wire frame density: ISOLINES=4
Specify center of sphere <0,0,0>: *(pick a point or enter coordinates)*
Specify radius of sphere or [Diameter]: *(pick a point or enter a value)*
Command:

Notice in Figure 10-6A that the display is a wireframe with few lines defining the shape. The lines that form the wireframe of a solid are called *isolines*. Isolines are controlled by the **ISOLINES** system variable, which is discussed in Chapter 13.

Also, notice in Figure 10-6A that there is no outline or silhouette. The **DISPSILH** system variable controls the display of wireframe silhouettes. This variable is set to 0

Figure 10-6.
A—The basic wireframe display of spheres. B—The **DISPSILH** system variable is set to 1.
C—The **DISPSILH** system variable is set to 1 and the **HIDE** command used. D—Spheres
displayed after using **HIDE** with the **DISPSILH** system variable set to 0.

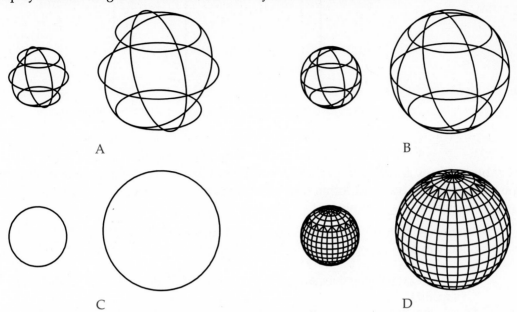

A   B

C   D

by default. When **DISPSILH** is set to 1, the silhouette shown in Figure 10-6B is displayed.
When hidden lines are removed, only the silhouette appears, Figure 10-6C. The sphere
is shown with hidden lines removed and **DISPSILH** set to a value of 0 in Figure 10-6D.
System variables that affect display are discussed in detail in Chapter 13.

NOTE

If **DISPSILH** is set to a value of 1 when **HIDE** is used, the display
will not show *tessellation lines*. These are lines that define
the curved shape of the object. The object will just appear as
a solid with hidden lines removed.

Cylinder

A cylinder can be drawn circular or elliptical. To draw a solid cylinder, pick the
Cylinder button in the **Solids** toolbar, select **Cylinder** from the **Solids** cascading menu
in the **Draw** pull-down menu, or enter CYLINDER at the Command: prompt:

CYLINDER

Draw
→ Solids
→ Cylinder

Solids
toolbar

Cylinder

     Command: **CYLINDER.**↵
     Current wire frame density: ISOLINES=4
     Specify center point for base of cylinder or [Elliptical] <0,0,0>: *(pick a center point)*
     Specify radius for base of cylinder or [Diameter]: **1**↵
     Specify height of cylinder or [Center of other end]: **3**↵

The cylinder shown in Figure 10-7A is displayed.

Figure 10-7.
A—A circular
cylinder.
B—An elliptical
cylinder.

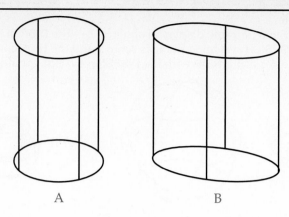

A   B

You can draw an elliptical cylinder two different ways. The default method prompts you to specify the two endpoints of the first axis and the second axis distance. This prompt sequence is as follows:

```
Specify center point for base of cylinder or [Elliptical] <0,0,0>: E↵
Specify axis endpoint of ellipse for base of cylinder or [Center]: (pick the first axis
    endpoint)
Specify second axis endpoint of ellipse for base of cylinder: (pick the second axis
    endpoint)
Specify length of other axis for base of cylinder: (pick the other axis distance)
Specify height of cylinder or [Center of other end]: 3↵
```

The cylinder in Figure 10-7B is created. The second option allows you to select the center point.

```
Specify center point for base of cylinder or [Elliptical] <0,0,0>: E↵
Specify axis endpoint of ellipse for base of cylinder or [Center]: C↵
Specify center point of ellipse for base of cylinder <0,0,0>: (pick the center of the
    ellipse)
Specify axis endpoint of ellipse for base of cylinder: (pick the axis endpoint)
Specify length of other axis for base of cylinder: (pick the other axis distance)
Specify height of cylinder or [Center of other end]: 3↵
```

To set the height, pick two points with the cursor or enter a value at the keyboard. When setting the height, you have the option of picking the center point of the opposite end of the cylinder. This is useful if you are placing a cylinder inside another object to create a hole. The cylinder can then be subtracted from the other object to create a hole. Refer to Figure 10-8 as you go through the following sequence:

```
Specify height of cylinder or [Center of other end]: C↵
Specify center of other end of cylinder: CEN↵
of (pick the top end of the cylinder)
Command:
```

Figure 10-8.
A—A cylinder is drawn inside another cylinder using the **Center of other end** option. B—The large cylinder appears to have a hole after **SUBTRACT** is used.

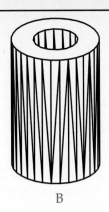

A B

CONE

Draw
➥ Solids
➥ Cone

Solids toolbar

Cone

Cone

The cone can also be drawn circular or elliptical. To draw a cone, pick the **Cone** button in the **Solids** toolbar, select **Cone** from the **Solids** cascading menu in the **Draw** pull-down menu, or enter CONE at the Command: prompt:

> Command: **CONE**↵
> Current wire frame density: ISOLINES=4
> Specify center point for base of cone or [Elliptical] <0,0,0>: *(pick the center point)*
> Specify radius for base of cone or [Diameter]: **1**↵
> Specify height of cone or [Apex]: **3**↵

The cone in Figure 10-9A is displayed. An elliptical cone can be created as follows:

> Specify center point for base of cone or [Elliptical] <0,0,0>: **E**↵
> Specify axis endpoint of ellipse for base of cone or [Center]: *(pick the axis endpoint)*
> Specify second axis endpoint of ellipse for base of cone: *(pick the other axis endpoint)*
> Specify length of other axis for base of cone: *(pick the other axis distance)*
> Specify height of cone or [Apex]: **3**↵
> Command:

The cone shown in Figure 10-9B is displayed. Just as with a cylinder, you can select the center of the cone at the following prompt:

> Specify axis endpoint of ellipse for base of cone or [Center]:

Figure 10-9.
A—A circular cone.
B—An elliptical cone.

A B

The **Apex** option is similar to the **Center of other end** option for drawing a cylinder. This option allows you to orient the cone at any angle, regardless of the current UCS. For example, to place a tapered cutout in the end of a block, locate the cone base and give a coordinate location of the apex. Refer to Figure 10-10. Use object snap tracking and the **Midpoint** running object snap to locate the center of the cone's base as follows:

Command: **CONE**↵
Current wire frame density: ISOLINES=4
Specify center point for base of cone or [Elliptical] <0,0,0>: *(acquire midpoint at P1, then acquire midpoint at P2, then pick intersection of alignment paths as center point)*
Specify radius for base of cone or [Diameter]: **1**↵
Specify height of cone or [Apex]: **A**↵
Specify apex point: **@2,0,0**↵

Figure 10-10 illustrates the construction of the cone and its appearance after being subtracted from the box.

Figure 10-10.
A—Cones can be positioned relative to other objects using the **Apex** option. Use tracking to help locate the base. B—The cone is subtracted from the box.

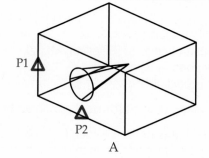
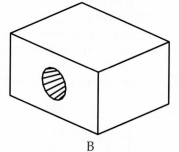

A   B

Wedge

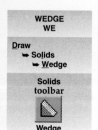

WEDGE
WE

Draw
↪ Solids
   ↪ Wedge

Solids
toolbar

Wedge

A wedge can be constructed by picking corners or by picking the center point. The center point of a wedge is the middle of the angled surface. To draw a wedge, pick the **Wedge** button from the **Solids** toolbar, select **Wedge** from the **Solids** cascading menu in the **Draw** pull-down menu, or enter WE or WEDGE at the Command: prompt:

Command: **WE** *or* **WEDGE**↵
Specify first corner of wedge or [CEnter] <0,0,0>: *(pick a corner location)*
Specify corner or [Cube/Length]: *(pick the diagonal corner location)*
Specify height: **2**↵

See Figure 10-11A. You can also specify the length, width, and height instead of picking the diagonal corner.

Specify corner or [Cube/Length]: **L**↵
Specify length: **3**↵
Specify width: **2**↵
Specify height: **2**↵

The **Center** option is used as follows. Refer to Figure 10-11B.

Specify first corner of wedge or [CEnter] <0,0,0>: **C**↵
Specify center of wedge <0,0,0>: *(pick the center point)*
Specify opposite corner or [Cube/Length]:

You can pick a corner of the wedge or use the **Length** option to specify length, width, and height. The **Cube** option uses the length value for all three sides.

Figure 10-11.
A—A wedge drawn using the **Corner** option. B—A wedge drawn using the **Center** option. Notice the location of the center.

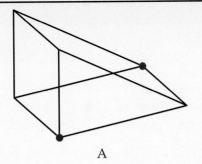

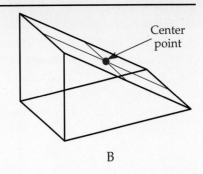

A

B

Torus

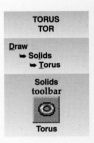

A torus can be drawn in three different ways. Refer to Figure 10-12. To draw a torus, pick the **Torus** button in the **Solids** toolbar, select **Torus** from the **Solids** cascading menu in the **Draw** pull-down menu, or enter TOR or TORUS at the Command: prompt:

> Command: **TOR** *or* **TORUS**↵
> Current wire frame density: ISOLINES=4
> Specify center of torus <0,0,0>: *(pick the center point)*
> Specify radius of torus or [Diameter]: **1**↵
> Specify radius of tube or [Diameter]: **.4**↵

The basic torus shown in Figure 10-12A is drawn. Notice that you can enter either a diameter or a radius.

A torus with a tube diameter that touches itself has no center hole. This type of torus is called *self-intersecting*. See Figure 10-12B. To create a self-intersecting torus, the tube radius must be greater than the torus radius.

The third type of torus looks like a football. It is drawn by entering a negative torus radius and a positive tube diameter of greater value. See Figure 10-12C.

Figure 10-12.
The three types of tori are shown as wireframes and with hidden lines removed.

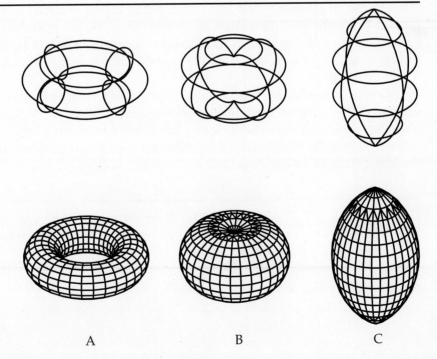

A

B

C

❑ Begin a new drawing named EX10-2.
❑ Construct the following solid primitives:
  ❑ A sphere 1.5″ in diameter.
  ❑ A box 3″ × 2″ × 1″.
  ❑ A cone 2.5″ high with a base diameter of 1.5″.
  ❑ An elliptical cone 3″ high with a major base diameter of 2″ and a minor base diameter of 1″.
  ❑ A wedge 4″ long, 3″ wide, and 2″ high.
  ❑ A cylinder 1.5″ in diameter and 2.5″ high.
  ❑ An elliptical cylinder with a major axis of 2″, a minor axis of 1″, and 3″ high.
  ❑ A basic torus with a radius of 2″ and a tube diameter of .75″.
  ❑ A self-intersecting torus.
  ❑ A football-shaped torus.
❑ Save your drawing as EX10-2.

PROFESSIONAL TIP

When you are working with surface-modeled boxes, wedges, pyramids, and cones, you can select corners using the **Intersection** object snap. However, when working with solid models, you must use the **Endpoint** object snap to select corners.

AutoCAD
User's
Guide **18**

CREATING COMPOSITE SOLIDS

A *composite solid* is a solid model constructed of two or more solid primitives. Primitives can be subtracted from each other, joined to form a new solid, or overlapped to create an intersection or interference. When primitives are joined, it is called a *union*. The commands used to create composite solids are found in the **Solids Editing** cascading menu in the **Modify** pull-down menu and within the **Solids Editing** toolbar. See Figure 10-13.

These commands perform *Boolean operations*. George Boole (1815–1864) was an English mathematician who developed a system of mathematical logic where all variables have the value of either one or zero. Boole's two-value logic, or *binary algebra*, is the basis for the mathematical calculations used by computers, and specifically for those required in the construction of composite solids.

NOTE

AutoCAD 2000 allows you to perform a variety of solids editing functions. The full extent of this capability is discussed in Chapter 12.

Figure 10-13.
Boolean commands can be selected from the pull-down menu or the **Solids Editing** toolbar.

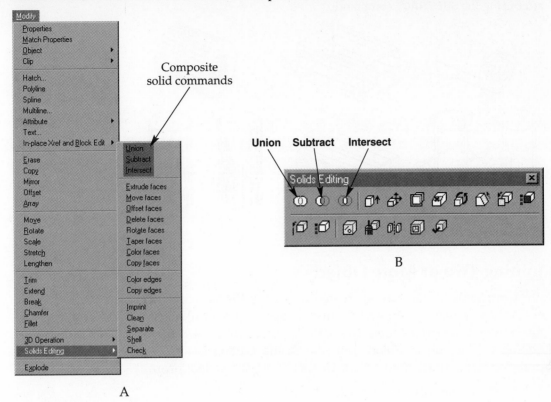

A

B

Subtracting Solids

The **SUBTRACT** command allows you to remove the volume of one or more solids from another solid. The first object selected is the object to be subtracted *from*. The next object is the object to be subtracted from the first. You can subtract solids by picking the **Subtract** button in the **Solids Editing** toolbar, selecting **Subtract** from the **Solids Editing** cascading menu in the **Modify** pull-down menu, or entering SU or SUBTRACT at the Command: prompt:

> Command: **SU** or **SUBTRACT**↵
> Select solids and regions to subtract from...
> Select objects: *(pick the object)*
> Select objects: ↵
> Select solids and regions to subtract...
> Select objects: *(pick the objects to subtract)*
> Select objects: ↵
> Command:

Several examples are shown in Figure 10-14.

SUBTRACT
SU

Modify
↪ Solids Editing
↪ Subtract

Solids Editing
toolbar

Subtract

Figure 10-14.
A—Solid primitives shown here have areas of intersection and overlap. B—Composite solids after using the **SUBTRACT** command.

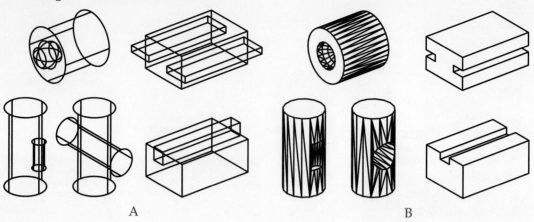

Joining Two or More Objects

Composite solids can be created using the **UNION** command. The primitives do not need to touch or intersect to form a union. Therefore, locate the primitives accurately when drawing them. To create a union, pick the **Union** button in the **Solids Editing** toolbar, select **Union** from the **Solids Editing** cascading menu in the **Modify** pull-down menu, or enter UNI or UNION at the Command: prompt:

Command: **UNI** *or* **UNION**↵
Select objects: *(select all primitives to be joined)*
Select objects: ↵
Command: ↵

In the examples shown in Figure 10-15B, notice that lines, or edges, are shown at the new intersection points of the joined objects.

Figure 10-15.
A—Solid primitives shown here have areas of intersection and overlap. B—Composite solids after using the **UNION** command.

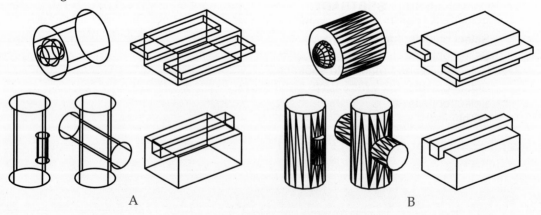

Creating Solids from the Intersection of Primitives

When solid primitives intersect, they form a common volume. This is an area in space that both primitives share. This shared space is called an *intersection*. An intersection can be made into a composite solid using the **INTERSECT** command. To do so, pick the **Intersect** button in the **Solids Editing** toolbar, select **Intersect** from the **Solids Editing** cascading menu in the **Modify** pull-down menu, or enter IN or INTERSECT at the Command: prompt:

> Command: **IN** *or* **INTERSECT**↵
> Select objects: *(select the objects that form the intersection)*
> Select objects: ↵
> Command:

Figure 10-16 shows several examples.

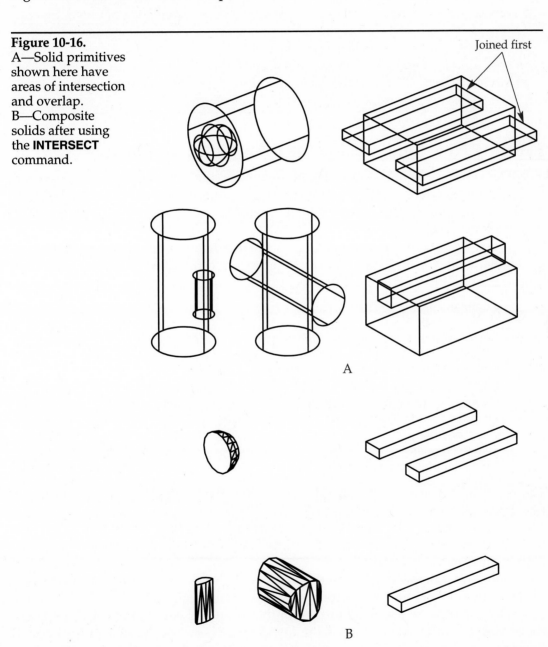

Figure 10-16.
A—Solid primitives shown here have areas of intersection and overlap.
B—Composite solids after using the **INTERSECT** command.

Joined first

A

B

PROFESSIONAL TIP

The **INTERSECT** command is also useful in 2D drawing. For example, if you need to create a complex shape that must later be used for inquiry calculations or hatching, draw the main object first. Then, draw all intersecting or overlapping objects. Next, create regions of the shapes. Finally, use **INTERSECT** to create the final shape. The shape now has solid properties and can be used as a region.

EXERCISE 10-3

❏ Begin a new drawing named EX10-3.
❏ Construct objects similar to those shown in Figure 10-14A using your own dimensions. Be sure the objects intersect and overlap. Make two copies of all objects.
❏ Perform subtractions on all the objects and observe the results.
❏ Perform unions on the copies of the objects and observe the results.
❏ Use the **INTERSECT** command on all the objects and observe the results.
❏ Save your drawing as EX10-3.

INTERFERE
INF

Draw
↪ Solids
  ↪ Interference

Solids
toolbar

Interfere

Creating New Solids Using the INTERFERE Command

When you use the **SUBTRACT**, **UNION**, and **INTERSECT** commands, the original solid primitives are deleted. They are replaced by the new composite solid. The **INTERFERE** command does not do this. A new solid is created from the interference, but the original objects remain.

To use the **INTERFERE** command, pick the **Interfere** button in the **Solids** toolbar, select **Interference** from the **Solids** cascading menu in the **Draw** pull-down menu, or enter INF or INTERFERE at the Command: prompt:

```
Command: INF or INTERFERE↵
Select first set of solids:
Select objects: (select the first solid)
Select objects: ↵
Select second set of solids: (select the second solid)
Select objects: ↵
Comparing 1 solid against 1 solid.
Interfering solids (first set):  1
    (second set):                1
Interfering pairs:               1
Create interference solids? <N>: Y↵
```

The result is shown in Figure 10-17B. Notice that the original solids are intact, but new lines indicate the new solid.

The new solid is a separate object. It can be moved, copied, and manipulated just like any other object. Figure 10-17C shows the new object after it has been moved and lines have been hidden.

AutoCAD compares the first set of solids with the second set. Any solids that are selected for both the first and second sets are automatically included as part of the first selection set, and are eliminated from the second. If you do not select a second set of objects, AutoCAD calculates the interference between the objects in the first selection set. You can do this by pressing [Enter] instead of picking the second set.

Figure 10-17.
A—Two solids form
an area of intersection.
B—After using
INTERFERE, a new
solid is defined and
the original solids
remain. C—The new
solid can be moved
or copied.

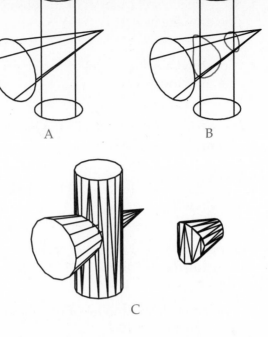

A

B

C

Chapter Test

Answer the following questions on a separate sheet of paper.

1. What is a region?
2. How can a 2D section view be converted to a 3D solid model?
3. What is created when regions are added to or subtracted from one another?
4. What command allows you to remove the area of one region from another
   region?
5. What two types of objects can be created with the **BOUNDARY** command?
6. What is a solid primitive?
7. How is a solid cube created?
8. Name two system variables that control the display of lines in the wireframe
   view of a solid.
9. How is an elliptical cylinder created?
10. Where is the center of a wedge located?
11. What is a composite solid?
12. What type of mathematical calculations are used in the construction of solid
    models?
13. How are two or more solids combined to make a composite solid?
14. What is the function of the **INTERSECT** command?
15. How does the **INTERFERE** command differ from **INTERSECT** and **UNION**?

Drawing Problems

1. Construct a solid model of the object in Problem 1 of Chapter 1. Save the drawing as P10-1.

2. Construct a solid model of the object in Problem 2 of Chapter 1. Save the drawing as P10-2.

3. Construct a solid model of the object in Problem 3 of Chapter 1. Save the drawing as P10-3.

4. Construct a solid model of the object in Problem 4 of Chapter 1. Save the drawing as P10-4.

5. Construct a solid model of the object in Problem 5 of Chapter 1. Save the drawing as P10-5.

6. Construct a solid model of the object in Problem 6 of Chapter 1. Save the drawing as P10-6.

7. Construct a solid model of the object in Problem 7 of Chapter 1. Save the drawing as P10-7.

8. Construct a solid model of the object in Problem 8 of Chapter 1. Save the drawing as P10-8.

9. Construct a solid model of the object in Problem 1 of Chapter 3. Save the drawing as P10-9.

10. Construct a solid model of the object in Problem 2 of Chapter 3. Save the drawing as P10-10.

11. Construct a solid model of the object in Problem 3 of Chapter 3. Save the drawing as P10-11.

12. Construct a solid model of the object in Problem 4 of Chapter 3. Save the drawing as P10-12.

13. Construct a solid model of the object in Problem 5 of Chapter 3. Save the drawing as P10-13.

14. Construct a solid model of the object in Problem 6 of Chapter 3. Save the drawing as P10-14.

CHAPTER 11

Solid Model Construction and Features

Learning Objectives

After completing this chapter, you will be able to:

- Create solid objects by extruding closed 2D profiles.
- Revolve closed 2D profiles to create symmetrical 3D solids.
- Apply fillets to solid objects.
- Apply chamfers to solid objects.
- Construct a variety of detailed solid shapes and features.

Complex shapes can be created by applying a thickness to a two-dimensional profile. This is called *extruding* the shape. Two or more profiles can be extruded to intersect. The resulting union can form a new shape. Symmetrical objects can be created by revolving a 2D profile about an axis to create a new solid. Rounded and angular corners can be constructed using the **FILLET** and **CHAMFER** commands.

CREATING SOLID EXTRUSIONS

An *extrusion* is a closed two-dimensional shape that has been given thickness. The **EXTRUDE** command allows you to create extruded solids using closed objects such as polylines, polygons, splines, regions, circles, ellipses, and donuts. Objects in a block cannot be extruded. Extrusions can be created along a straight line or along a path curve. A taper angle can also be applied as you extrude an object.

Create an extruded solid by picking the **Extrude** button in the **Solids** toolbar, selecting **Extrude** from the **Solids** cascading menu in the **Draw** pull-down menu, or typing EXT or EXTRUDE at the Command: prompt:

> Command: **EXT** *or* **EXTRUDE**↵
> Current wire frame density: ISOLINES=4
> Select objects: *(pick object to extrude)*
> Select objects: ↵
> Specify height of extrusion or [Path]: **.35**↵
> Specify angle of taper for extrusion <0>: ↵
> Command:

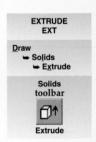

EXTRUDE
EXT

Draw
➥ Solids
    ➥ Extrude

Solids
toolbar

Extrude

Figure 11-1 illustrates a polygon extruded into a solid.

The taper angle can be any value between +90° and –90°. A positive angle tapers to the inside of the object from the base. A negative angle tapers to the outside of the object from the base. See Figure 11-2.

Figure 11-1.
The **EXTRUDE** command creates a solid by adding thickness to a closed 2D profile. A—The initial 2D profile. B—The extruded solid object shown with hidden lines removed.

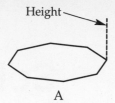
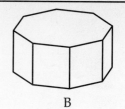

Height

A

B

Figure 11-2.
A—A positive angle tapers to the inside of the object from the base. B—A negative angle tapers to the outside of the object.

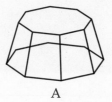
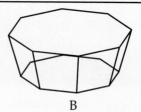

A

B

NOTE The height of extrusion is always applied in the Z direction. A positive value extrudes above the XY plane. A negative height value extrudes below the XY plane.

Extrusions Along a Path

A closed 2D shape can be extruded along a path to create a 3D solid. The path can be a line, circle, arc, ellipse, polyline, or spline. Line segments and other objects can be joined to form a polyline path. The corners of angled segments are mitered, while curved segments are smooth. See Figure 11-3.

Objects can also be extruded along a line at an angle to the base object, Figure 11-4. Notice that the plane at the end of the extruded object is perpendicular to the path. Also notice that the length of the extrusion is the same as that of the path.

```
Command: EXT or EXTRUDE↵
Current wire frame density: ISOLINES=4
Select objects: (pick object to extrude)
Select objects: ↵
Specify height of extrusion or [Path]: P↵
Select extrusion path: (pick the path)
```

Figure 11-3.
A—Angled segments are mitered when extruded. B—Curves are smoothed when extruded.

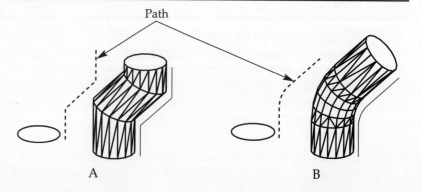

Path

A

B

Figure 11-4.
A—An object extruded along a path.
B—The end of an object extruded along an angled path is perpendicular to the path.

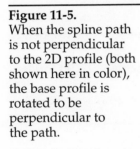

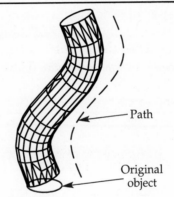

The path does not need to be perpendicular to the object. However, if the path is a spline, the new solid is created so its base is perpendicular to the path. Also, one of the endpoints of the path should be on the plane of the object to be extruded. If it is not, the path is temporarily moved to the center of the profile. The following prompts may appear after the path is selected:

Select path: (pick the path)
Path was moved to the center of the profile.
Profile was oriented to be perpendicular to the path.
Command:

An example of a spline path extrusion is shown in Figure 11-5.

Figure 11-5.
When the spline path is not perpendicular to the 2D profile (both shown here in color), the base profile is rotated to be perpendicular to the path.

Creating Features with EXTRUDE

You can create a wide variety of features with the **EXTRUDE** command. With some planning, you can use regions and **SUBTRACT** to construct solids. Study the shapes shown in Figure 11-6. These detailed solid objects were created by drawing a profile and then using the **EXTRUDE** command. The objects in Figure 11-6C and Figure 11-6D must first be constructed as regions before they are extruded. For example, the five holes in Figure 11-6D must be removed from the base object using the **SUBTRACT** command.

Figure 11-6.
Detailed solids can
be created by
extruding the
profile of an object.
The profiles are
shown here in color.

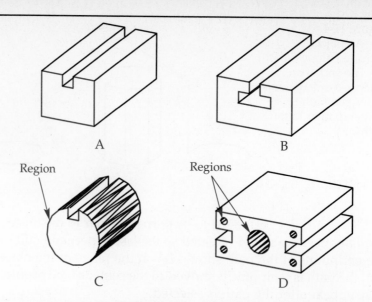

A

B

Region

Regions

C

D

EXERCISE 11-1

❏ Begin a new drawing.
❏ Construct a hex head bolt (excluding threads). Make the bolt body 5/16″ diameter and 2″ long. Make the hex head 1/2″ across the flats and 3/16″ thick.
❏ Construct the bolt oriented vertically with the head at the top.
❏ Construct a second bolt oriented vertically with the head at the bottom.
❏ Construct a flat-head wood screw (excluding threads). Make the body 3/16″ diameter at the base of the head, 7/8″ long, and taper to a point. Make the head 3/8″ in diameter, taper to the 3/16″ diameter body, and 1/8″ thick.
❏ Construct the wood screw so the head faces to the left of the screen at a 90° angle to the bolts.
❏ Save the drawing as EX11-1.

AutoCAD
User's
Guide **18**

REVOLVE
REV

Draw
➥ Solids
➥ Revolve

Solids
toolbar

Revolve

CREATING REVOLVED SOLIDS

The **REVOLVE** command allows you to create solids by revolving closed shapes such as circles, ellipses, polylines, closed splines, regions, and donuts. The selected object can be revolved at any angle up to 360°. To create a solid by revolving, pick the **Revolve** button in the **Solids** toolbar, select **Revolve** from the **Solids** cascading menu in the **Draw** pull-down menu, or enter REV or REVOLVE at the Command: prompt. The default option is to pick the two endpoints of an axis of revolution. This is shown in Figure 11-7.

Figure 11-7.
Points P1 and P2 are
selected as the axis
of revolution.

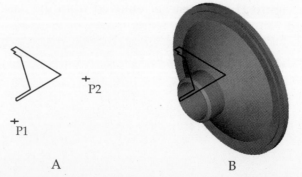

+
P2

+
P1

A

B

Command: **REV** *or* **REVOLVE**⏎
Current wire frame density: ISOLINES=4
Select objects: *(pick the objects to revolve)*
Select objects: ⏎
Specify start point for axis of revolution or
define axis by [Object/X (axis)/Y (axis)]: *(pick P1)*
Specify endpoint of axis: *(pick P2)*
Specify angle of revolution <360>:⏎
Command:

Revolving About an Axis Line Object

You can select an object, such as a line, as the axis of revolution. Figure 11-8 shows a solid created using the **Object** option of the **REVOLVE** command. Both a full circle (360°) revolution and a 270° revolution are shown.

Specify start point for axis of revolution or
define axis by [Object/X (axis)/Y (axis)]: **O**⏎
Select an object: *(pick the axis line)*
Specify angle of revolution <360>: ⏎
Command:

Figure 11-8.
An axis of revolution can be selected using the **Object** option of the **REVOLVE** command. Here, the line is selected as the axis.

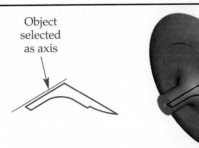

Object selected as axis

Full Circle

270°

Revolving About the X Axis

The X axis of the current UCS can be used as the axis of revolution by selecting the **X** option of the **REVOLVE** command. The origin of the current UCS is used as one end of the X axis line. Notice in Figure 11-9 that two different shapes can be created by changing the UCS origin point of the same 2D profile. No hole appears in the object in Figure 11-9B because the profile was revolved about an edge that coincides with the X axis.

Figure 11-9.
A—A solid is created using the X axis as the axis of revolution. B—A different object is created with the same profile by changing the UCS origin.

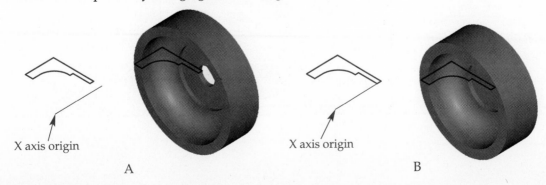

X axis origin

X axis origin

A

B

```
Specify start point for axis of revolution or
define axis by [Object/X (axis)/Y (axis)]: X↵
Specify angle of revolution <360>: ↵
Command:
```

Revolving About the Y Axis

The Y axis of the current UCS can be used as the axis of revolution by selecting the **Y** option of the **REVOLVE** command. The UCS origin determines the shape of the final object. See Figure 11-10. Notice the different shapes created by revolving the same profile with different UCS origins.

```
Specify start point for axis of revolution or
define axis by [Object/X (axis)/Y (axis)]: Y↵
Specify angle of revolution <360>: ↵
Command:
```

Figure 11-10.
A—A solid is created using the Y axis as the axis of revolution. B—A different object is created by changing the UCS origin.

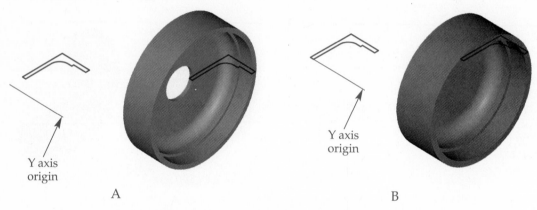

Y axis
origin

A

Y axis
origin

B

EXERCISE 11-2

❏ Begin a new drawing.
❏ Examine the objects shown below. Determine the shape of the closed profiles revolved to create the solids. The dimensions of the objects are not important.
❏ Draw the profiles and revolve them to create a solid.
❏ Use the **RENDER** command to see if your objects match those shown.
❏ Save the drawing as EX11-2.

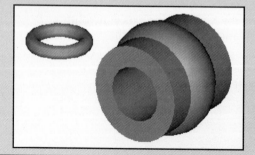

AutoCAD and its Applications—Advanced

FILLETING SOLID OBJECTS

A fillet rounds the edges of an object. Before a fillet is created, solid objects that intersect need to be joined using the **UNION** command. Then, use the **FILLET** command. See Figure 11-11. Since the object being filleted is actually a single solid and not two objects, only one edge is selected. In the following sequence, first the fillet radius is set at .25, then the fillet is created:

For 2000i Users...

When setting a fillet radius in AutoCAD 2000i, you can select the edge to be filleted immediately after entering the radius. In AutoCAD 2000, you must reissue the **FILLET** command after setting the fillet radius.

> Command: **F** *or* **FILLET**↵
> Current settings: Mode = TRIM, Radius = *current*
> Select first object or [Polyline/Radius/Trim]: **R**↵
> Specify fillet radius <*current*>: **.25**↵
> Command: ↵
> FILLET
>   Current settings: Mode = TRIM, Radius = *current*
> Select first object or [Polyline/Radius/Trim]: *(pick edge to be filleted)*
> Enter fillet radius <.025>: ↵
> Select an edge or [Chain/Radius]: ↵ *(this fillets the selected edge, but you can also select other edges at this point)*
> 1 edge(s) selected for fillet.
> Command:

Examples of fillets and rounds are shown in Figure 11-12.

Figure 11-11.
A—Pick the edge where two unioned solids intersect to create a fillet.
B—The fillet after rendering.

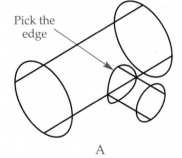
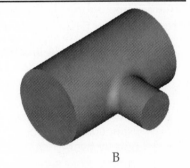

A   B

Figure 11-12.
Examples of fillets and rounds.

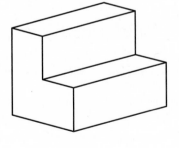

A

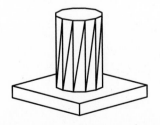

B

AutoCAD User's Guide 18

CHAMFERING SOLID OBJECTS

For 2000i Users...

When setting chamfer distances in AutoCAD 2000i, you can select the edge to be chamfered immediately after entering the second chamfer distance. In AutoCAD 2000, you must reissue the **CHAMFER** command after setting the chamfer distances.

To create a chamfer on a 3D solid, use the **CHAMFER** command. Just as when chamfering a 2D line, there are two chamfer distances. Therefore, you must specify which surfaces correspond to the first and second distances. If you are chamfering a hole, the two objects must first be subtracted. If you are chamfering an intersection, the two objects must first be unioned.

After you enter the command, you must pick the edge you want to chamfer. The edge is actually the intersection of two surfaces. One of the two surfaces is highlighted when you select the edge. The highlighted surface is associated with the first chamfer distance. This surface is called the *base surface*. If the highlighted surface is not the one you want as the base surface, enter N at the [Next/OK] prompt and press [Enter]. This highlights the next surface. When the proper base surface is highlighted, press [Enter] for **OK**. Chamfering a hole is shown in Figure 11-13A.

```
Command: CHA or CHAMFER↵
(TRIM mode) Current chamfer Dist1 = current, Dist2 = current
Select first line or [Polyline/Distance/Angle/Trim/Method]: (pick Edge 1)
Base surface selection...
Enter surface selection option [Next/OK (current)] <OK>: N↵
Enter surface selection option [Next/OK (current)] <OK>: ↵
Specify base surface chamfer distance <current>: .125↵
Specify other surface chamfer distance <current>: .125↵
Select an edge or [Loop]: (pick Edge 2, the edge of the hole)
Select an edge or [Loop]: ↵
Command:
```

The end of the cylinder in Figure 11-13B is chamfered by first picking one of the vertical isolines, then picking the top edge.

Figure 11-13.
A—A hole is chamfered by picking the top surface, then the edge of the hole. B—The end of a cylinder is chamfered by first picking the side, then the end. Both ends can be chamfered at the same time, as shown here.

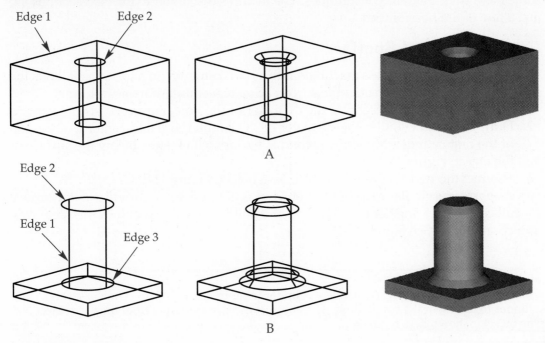

A

B

PROFESSIONAL TIP

Solids cannot be edited to change their shape using the **Properties** window, grips, or standard editing commands. Only properties such as color, layer, and linetype can be changed on a solid. Therefore, if you create a solid that is incorrect or edit it improperly using **FILLET** or **CHAMFER**, it is best to undo or erase and try again.

Faces and edges can be edited using the **SOLIDEDIT** command, which is discussed in Chapter 12.

EXERCISE 11-3

❑ Begin a new drawing.
❑ Draw the locking pin shown below using the appropriate solid modeling and editing commands.
❑ The pin is 3" long and .5" diameter.
❑ The two cotter pin holes are .2" diameter and .35" from each end.
❑ The chamfer on each end is .1" and the fillet on each hole has a .02" radius.
❑ When you complete the object, use **HIDE** and then **RENDER**.
❑ Save the drawing as EX11-3.

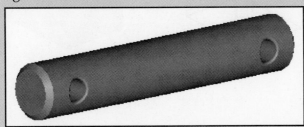

A variety of machining, structural, and architectural details can be created using some basic solid modeling techniques. The features discussed in the next sections are just a few of the possibilities.

Counterbore and Spotface

A *counterbore* is a recess machined into a part, centered on a hole, that allows the head of a fastener to rest below the surface. Create a counterbore as follows:

1. Draw a cylinder representing the diameter of the hole, Figure 11-14A.
2. Draw a second cylinder the diameter of the counterbore and center it at the top of the first cylinder. Move the second cylinder so it extends below the surface of the object, Figure 11-14B.
3. Subtract the two cylinders from the base object, Figure 11-14C.

A *spotface* is similar to a counterbore, but is not as deep. It provides a flat surface for full contact of a washer or underside of a bolt head. Construct it in the same way as a counterbore. See Figure 11-15.

Figure 11-14.
Constructing a counterbore. A—Draw a cylinder to represent a hole. B—Draw a second cylinder to represent the counterbore. C—Subtract the two cylinders from the base object. The object is shown here rendered.

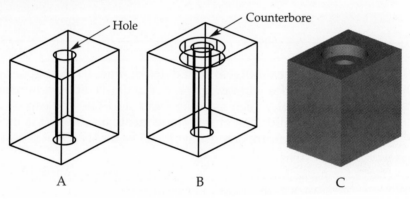

Figure 11-15.
Constructing a spotface. A—The bottom of the second cylinder should be located at the exact depth of the spotface. However, the height may extend above the surface of the cube. Then, subtract the two cylinders from the base. B—The finished solid after rendering.

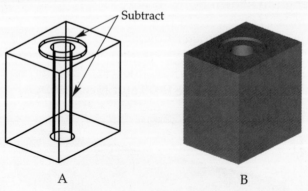

Countersink

A *countersink* is like a counterbore with angled sides. The sides allow a flat head machine screw or wood screw to sit below the surface of an object. A countersink can be drawn in one of two ways. You can draw an inverted cone centered on a hole, or you can chamfer the top edge of a hole. The chamfering technique is the quickest.

1. Draw a cylinder representing the diameter of the hole, Figure 11-16A.
2. Subtract the cylinder from the base object.
3. Select the **CHAMFER** command and enter the chamfer distance(s).
4. Select **CHAMFER** again and pick the top edge of the base object, then pick the top edge of the hole.

Figure 11-16.
Constructing a countersink. A—Subtract the cylinder from the base. B—Chamfer the top of the hole to create a countersink. The object is shown here rendered.

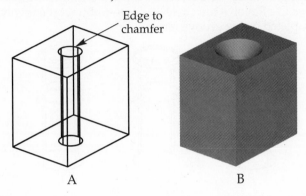

Boss

A *boss* does the same thing as a spotface, but has an area raised above the surface of an object. Draw a boss as follows:

1. Draw a cylinder representing the diameter of the hole. Extend it above the base object higher than the boss is to be, Figure 11-17A.
2. Draw a second cylinder the diameter of the boss. Place the base of the cylinder above the top surface a distance equal to the height of the boss. Give the cylinder a negative height value so that it extends inside the base object, Figure 11-17B.
3. Union the base object and the second cylinder. Subtract the hole from the new unioned object, Figure 11-17C.
4. Fillet the intersection of the boss with the base object, Figure 11-17D.

Figure 11-17.
Constructing a boss. A—Draw a cylinder for the hole extending above the surface of the object. B—Draw a cylinder the height of the boss on the top surface of the object. C—Union the large cylinder to the base. Then, subtract the small cylinder (hole) from the unioned objects. D—Fillet the edge to form the boss. The final object is shown here rendered.

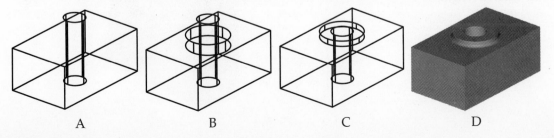

O-Ring Groove

An *o-ring* is a circular seal that resembles a torus. It sits inside a groove so that at least half the o-ring is above the surface. The groove can be constructed by placing the center of a circle on the outside surface of a cylinder. Then, revolve the circle around the cylinder. Finally, subtract the revolved solid from the cylinder.

1. Construct the cylinder to the required dimensions, Figure 11-18A.
2. Rotate the UCS on the X axis.
3. Draw a circle with a center point on the surface of the cylinder, Figure 11-18B.
4. Revolve the circle 360°, Figure 11-18C.
5. Subtract the revolved object from the cylinder, Figure 11-18D.

The object is shown after using **RENDER** in Figure 11-18E.

Figure 11-18.
Constructing an o-ring groove. A—Construct a cylinder. B—Draw a circle centered on the surface of the cylinder. C—Revolve the circle 360°. D—Subtract the revolved object from the cylinder. E—The completed o-ring groove rendered.

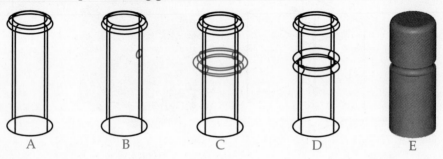

Architectural Molding

Architectural details that contain molding can be quickly constructed using extrusions. The procedure is as follows:

1. Construct the profile of the molding as a closed shape, Figure 11-19A.
2. Extrude the profile the desired length, Figure 11-19B.

Molding intersections at corners can be quickly created by extruding the same shape in two different directions, then joining the two objects.

1. Copy and rotate the molding profile to orient the Z axis in the direction desired for the second extrusion, Figure 11-20A.
2. Extrude the profiles to the desired lengths, Figure 11-20B.
3. Union the two extrusions to create the new mitered corner molding, Figure 11-20C.

A quick rendering of this corner molding clearly displays the features, Figure 11-20D.

Figure 11-19.
A—The molding profile. B—The profile extruded to the desired length and rendered.

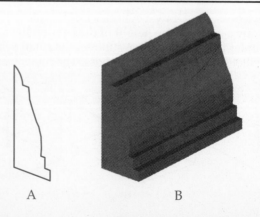

A   B

Figure 11-20.
Constructing corner molding. A—Copy and rotate the molding profile. B—Extrude the profiles to the desired lengths. C—Union the two extrusions to create the mitered corner. D—A rendered view of the molding.

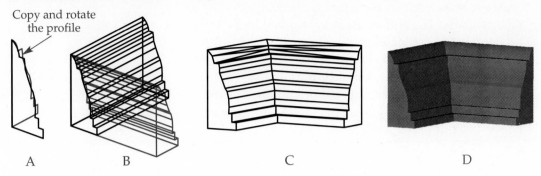

Copy and rotate the profile

A   B   C   D

Multiple Intersecting Extrusions

Many solid objects have complex curves and profiles. These can often be constructed using two or more extrusions joined by intersection. The resulting solid is a combination of only the intersecting volume of the extrusions. The following example shows the construction of a coat hook.

1. Construct the first profile, Figure 11-21A.
2. Construct the second profile located on a common point with the first, Figure 11-21B.
3. Construct the third profile located on the common point, Figure 11-21C.
4. Extrude each profile the required dimension into the same area. Be careful to specify positive or negative heights for each extrusion, Figure 11-21D and Figure 11-21E.
5. Use **INTERSECT** to join the extrusions into a composite solid, Figure 11-21F.

Figure 11-21.
Constructing a coat hook. A—Draw the first profile. B—Draw the second profile. C—Draw the third profile. All three profiles should have a common origin. D—Extrude each profile so that the extruded objects intersect. E—The extruded objects with hidden lines removed. F—Use **INTERSECT** to create the composite solid. The final solid is shown here with hidden lines removed.

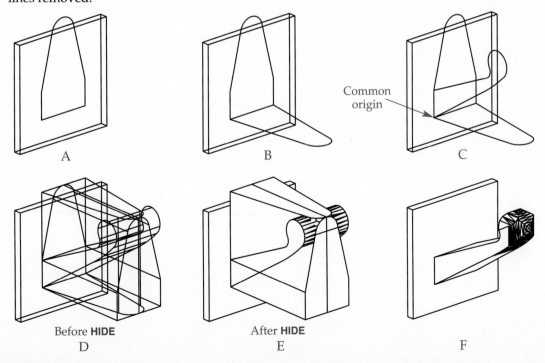

Common origin

A   B   C

Before **HIDE**   After **HIDE**

D   E   F

❑ Begin a new drawing using architectural units.
❑ Construct a closed profile of a piece of corner molding that is 2″ wide by 1.5″ deep. Create your own design with arcs and corners.
❑ Copy the profile and rotate it 90°.
❑ Extrude the first molding profile to a length of 12″.
❑ Extrude the rotated molding profile to a length of 8″.
❑ Union the two pieces of molding.
❑ Alter your viewpoint to get different views of the molding.
❑ Use the **RENDER** command to create a quick rendering of the molding.
❑ Save your drawing as EX11-4.

Chapter Test

Answer the following questions on a separate sheet of paper.

1. What is an extrusion?
2. How can an extrusion be constructed to extend below the current UCS?
3. What is the range in which a taper angle can vary?
4. How can a curved extrusion be constructed?
5. If an extrusion is created as indicated in Question 4, how is the base of the extruded object oriented?
6. What are the four different options for selecting the axis of revolution for a revolved solid?
7. How can a profile be revolved twice (or more) about the same axis and create different shaped solids?
8. Why must only one edge of a solid be selected when using the **FILLET** command?
9. When you are chamfering a solid, how can you select the proper surface if the wrong surface is highlighted when you select an edge?
10. What is the difference between a spotface and a boss?

Drawing Problems

1. Construct an 8″ diameter tee pipe fitting using the dimensions shown below. Hint: Extrude and union two solid cylinders before subtracting the cylinders for the inside diameters.
   A. Use **EXTRUDE** to create two sections of pipe at 90° to each other, then **UNION** the two pieces together.
   B. Use **FILLET** and **CHAMFER** to finish the object. The chamfer distance is .25″.
   C. The outside diameter of all three openings is 8.63″ and the pipe wall thickness is .322″.
   D. Save the drawing as P11-1.

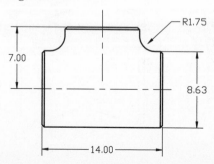

2. Construct an 8″ diameter 90° elbow pipe fitting using the dimensions shown below.

   A. Use **EXTRUDE** to create the elbow.
   B. Use **CHAMFER** to finish the object. The chamfer distance is .25″.
   C. The outside diameter is 8.63″ and the pipe wall thickness is .322″.
   D. Save the drawing as P11-2.

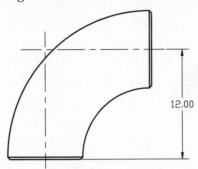

12.00

3. Construct a 12′ long section of wide flange structural steel with the cross section shown below. Use the dimensions given. Save the drawing as P11-3.

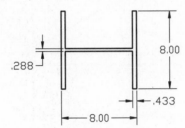

.288

8.00

.433

8.00

Problems 4–13. These problems require you to use a variety of solid modeling functions to construct the objects. Use **EXTRUDE**, **REVOLVE**, **FILLET**, *and* **CHAMFER** *to assist in construction.*

4.

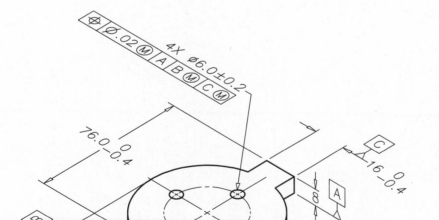

$\phi \, | \, \varnothing .02 \, (M) \, | A \, | B \, (M) \, | C \, (M)$

4X ⌀6.0±0.2

$76.0\,{-0.4}^{\,0}$

C

$16\,{-0.4}^{\,0}$

A

B

$\varnothing 66\,{-0.4}^{\,0}$

⌀36

Spring Clip

5.

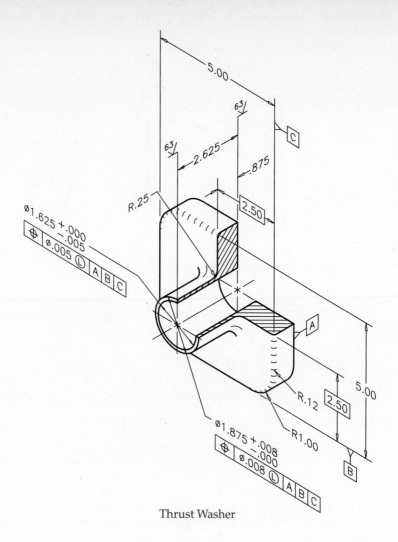

Thrust Washer

6.

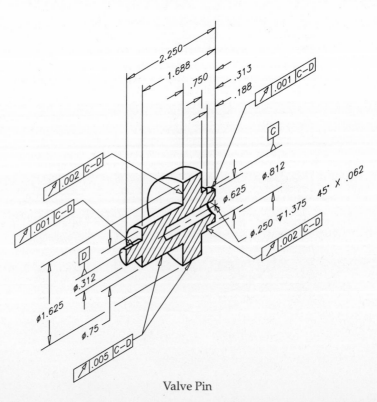

Valve Pin

7.

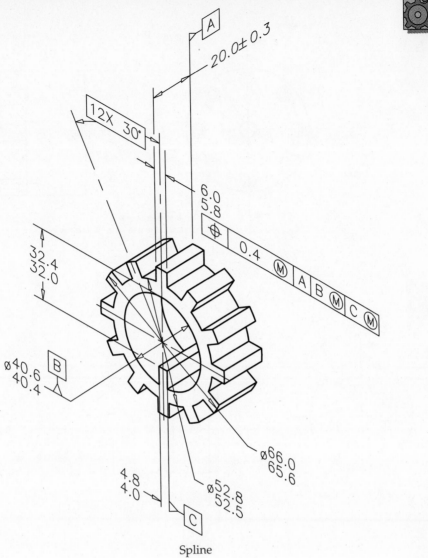

20.0± 0.3

12X 30°

6.0
5.8

| ⌖ | 0.4 Ⓜ | A | B Ⓜ | C Ⓜ |

32.4
32.0

Ø40.6
40.4 B

Ø66.0
65.6

4.8
4.0

Ø52.8
52.5

C

Spline

8.

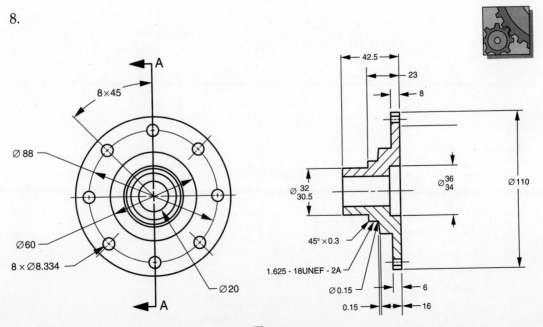

A

8×45

Ø88

Ø60

8 × Ø8.334

Ø20

A

42.5

23

8

32
30.5

36
34

Ø110

45° ×0.3

1.625 - 18UNEF - 2A

Ø0.15

6

0.15

16

Flange

9.

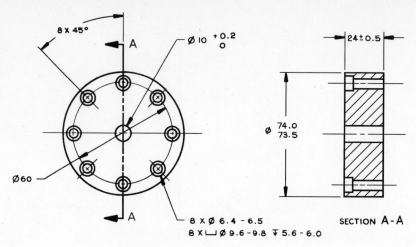

8 × 45°

Ø 10 $^{+0.2}_{0}$

Ø 60

8 × Ø 6.4 - 6.5
8 × ⌴ Ø 9.6 - 9.8 ▽ 5.6 - 6.0

24±0.5

Ø 74.0
73.5

SECTION A-A

Collar

10.

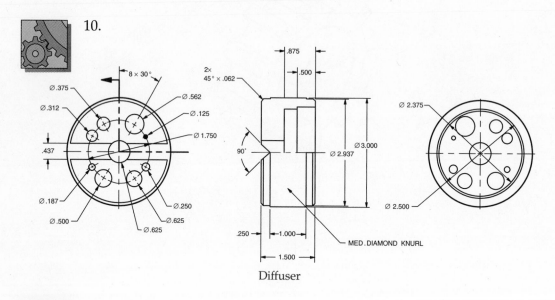

8 × 30°

Ø .375
Ø .312
Ø .562
Ø .125
Ø 1.750
.437
Ø .500
Ø .187
Ø .250
Ø .625
Ø .625

2×
45° × .062

.875
.500

90°

Ø 3.000
Ø 2.937

.250
1.000
1.500

MED. DIAMOND KNURL

Ø 2.375
Ø 2.500

Diffuser

11.

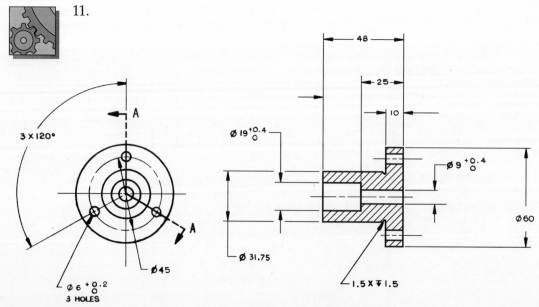

3 × 120°

A

Ø 45

Ø 6 $^{+0.2}_{0}$
3 HOLES

48

25

10

Ø 19 $^{+0.4}_{0}$

Ø 9 $^{+0.4}_{0}$

Ø 60

Ø 31.75

1.5 × ▽ 1.5

SECTION A-A

Bushing

12.

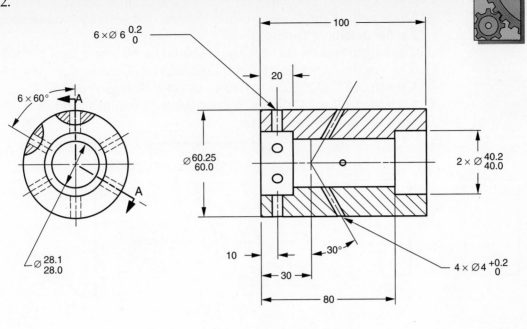

6 × ⌀ 6 $\begin{smallmatrix}0.2\\0\end{smallmatrix}$

6 × 60°

⌀ $\begin{smallmatrix}28.1\\28.0\end{smallmatrix}$

100

20

⌀ $\begin{smallmatrix}60.25\\60.0\end{smallmatrix}$

2 × ⌀ $\begin{smallmatrix}40.2\\40.0\end{smallmatrix}$

10

30°

30

80

4 × ⌀ 4 $\begin{smallmatrix}+0.2\\0\end{smallmatrix}$

SECTION A-A

Nozzle

13.

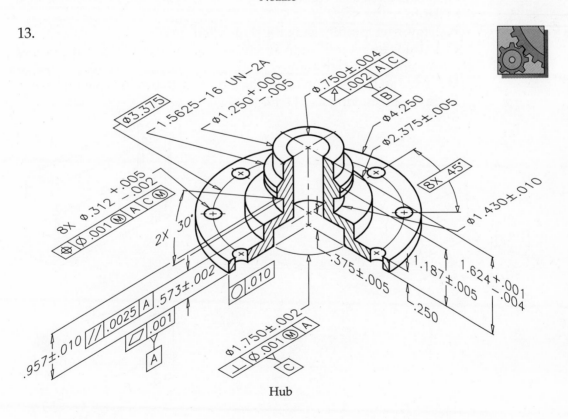

Hub

14. Construct picture frame moldings using the profiles shown below.
    A. Draw each of the closed profiles shown. Use your own dimensions for the details of the moldings.
    B. The length and width of A and B should be no larger than 1.5″ × 1″.
    C. The length and width of C and D should be no larger than 3″ × 1.5″.
    D. Construct 8″ × 12″ picture frames using moldings A and B.
    E. Construct 12″ × 24″ picture frames using moldings C and D.
    F. Save the drawing as P11-14.

A

B

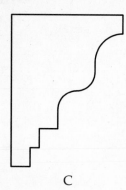

C

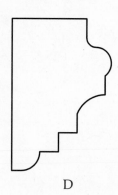

D

15. Construct a solid model of the faucet handle shown below.
    A. Create three user coordinate systems. Use a common origin for each UCS.
    B. Draw each profile using the dimensions given.
    C. Extrude each profile into a common space. Be sure to use the proper Z value when extruding.
    D. Create an intersection of the three profiles to produce the final solid.
    E. Save the drawing as P11-15.

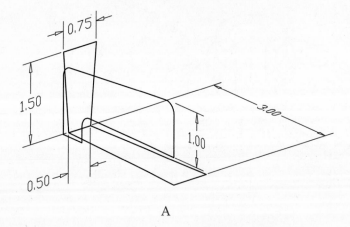

A

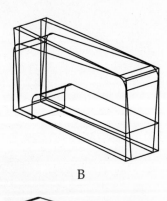

B

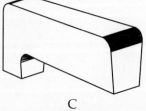

C

CHAPTER 12

Solid Model Editing

Learning Objectives

After completing this chapter, you will be able to:
- Change the shape and configuration of solid object faces.
- Copy and change the color of solid object edges and faces.
- Separate a composite solid having physically separate entities.
- Use the **SOLIDEDIT** command to construct and edit a solid model.

AutoCAD 2000 provides expanded capabilities for editing solid models. A single new command, **SOLIDEDIT**, enables the user to edit faces, edges, or the entire body of the solid. These features are accessed by typing SOLIDEDIT at the Command: prompt, picking an option from the **Solids Editing** cascading menu in the **Modify** pull-down menu, or using the **Solids Editing** toolbar. See Figure 12-1.

OVERVIEW OF SOLID MODEL EDITING

For editing purposes, a solid model has three components: the entire solid body, individual faces, and edges. You should first decide which component of the solid you wish to alter. Most editing will be done to faces and the body, because edge editing involves only copying or coloring.

If the **SOLIDEDIT** command is entered at the Command: prompt, you are first asked to select the portion of the solid with which you wish to work. After selecting either **Face**, **Edge,** or **Body**, the editing options are then displayed. In the following example, the **Face** option is selected:

> Command: **SOLIDEDIT**↵
> Solids editing automatic checking: SOLIDCHECK=1
> Enter a solids editing option [Face/Edge/Body/Undo/eXit] <eXit>: **F**↵
> Enter a face editing option
> [Extrude/Move/Rotate/Offset/Taper/Delete/Copy/coLor/Undo/eXit] <eXit>:

The next step is to enter the option desired and follow the instructions for removing or adding faces to the selection set. This is an important step, and is the same for all face editing options.

Figure 12-1.
The **SOLIDEDIT** command options are found in the **Solids Editing** cascading menu in the **Modify** pull-down menu (A) and the **Solids Editing** toolbar (B).

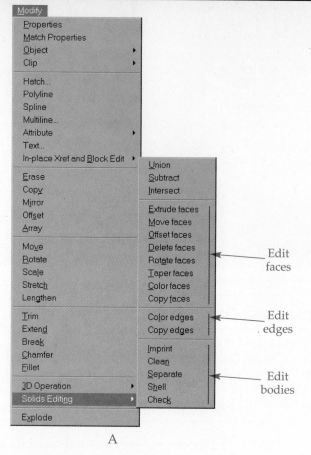

A

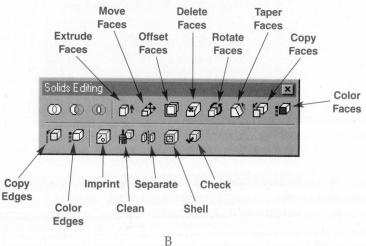

B

Enter a face editing option
[Extrude/Move/Rotate/Offset/Taper/Delete/Copy/coLor/Undo/eXit] <eXit>: **E**↵
Select faces or [Undo/Remove]: *(select an edge)* 2 faces found.
Select faces or [Undo/Remove/ALL]: **R**↵
Remove faces or [Undo/Add/ALL]:

NOTE Selecting either **Face, Edge,** or **Body** is not required if you pick **SOLIDEDIT** command options from the **Solids Editing** toolbar or the **Solids Editing** cascading menu.

Remember the following three steps when using any of the face editing options:

1. First, select a face to edit. If you pick an edge, AutoCAD selects the two faces that share that edge. If this happens, use the **Remove** option to deselect the unwanted face. A more intuitive approach is to select the open space of the face as if you were touching the side of a part. AutoCAD highlights only that face.

2. Adjust the selected face(s) at the Select faces or [Undo/Remove/ALL]: prompt. The following options are available:
   - **Undo.** Removes the previous selected face(s) from the selection set.
   - **Remove.** Allows you to select faces to remove from the selection set.
   - **ALL.** Adds all faces on the model to the selection set.
   - **Add.** Only available when **Remove** is current. Enables you to add faces to the selection set.

3. Press [Enter] to continue with face editing.

The following sections provide an overview of the solid model editing features of the **SOLIDEDIT** command. Each option is explained and the results of each are shown. A tutorial later in the chapter illustrates how these options can be used to construct a model.

EDITING FACES

The basic components of a solid are its faces, and the greatest number of **SOLIDEDIT** options are for editing these faces. All eight face editing options ask you to select faces. Remember, to select specific faces it is quicker to pick inside the boundary of the face.

NOTE AutoCAD displays a variety of error messages when illegal solid editing operations are attempted. Rather than trying to interpret the obscure wording of these messages, just realize that what you tried to do will not work. Actions that may cause errors include trying to rotate a face into other faces, or extruding and tapering an object at too great an angle. When this happens, just try it again.

Extruding Faces

An *extruded face* is one that is moved, or stretched, in a selected direction. The extrusion can be straight or have a taper. To extrude a face, select **Extrude faces** from the **Solids Editing** cascading menu in the **Modify** pull-down menu or pick the **Extrude Faces** button from the **Solids Editing** toolbar. You can also select the **Face** option of the **SOLIDEDIT** command, and then enter E for the **Extrude** option:

Modify
➥ Solids Editing
➥ Extrude faces

Solids Editing toolbar

Extrude Faces

```
Command: SOLIDEDIT↵
Solids editing automatic checking: SOLIDCHECK=1
Enter a solids editing option [Face/Edge/Body/Undo/eXit] <eXit>: F↵
Enter a face editing option
[Extrude/Move/Rotate/Offset/Taper/Delete/Copy/coLor/Undo/eXit] <eXit>: E↵
Select faces or [Undo/Remove]: (select the face to edit)
```

After a face is selected, notice that a single face is highlighted if you pick in the open area of a face, and two faces are highlighted if you pick an edge. The prompt verifies this. For example, when an edge is selected, the prompt reads 2 faces found. If you wish to extrude a single face, use the **Remove** option to deselect one of the faces. If you pick the same edge that you selected the face with, both faces will be removed, so pick an edge that is not common to both faces.

    Select faces or [Undo/Remove/ALL]: **R↵**
    Remove faces or [Undo/Add/ALL]: *(pick the face to be removed)*
    2 faces found, 1 removed.
    Remove faces or [Undo/Add/ALL]:

Next you need to specify the height of the extrusion. A positive value adds material to the solid, while a negative value subtracts material from the solid. A taper, or draft angle, can be given next. Press [Enter] if no taper angle is required.

    Specify height of extrusion or [Path]: *(enter height)*
    Specify angle of taper for extrusion <0>: *(enter an angle or accept the default)*
    Solid validation started.
    Solid validation completed.
    Enter a face editing option
    [Extrude/Move/Rotate/Offset/Taper/Delete/Copy/coLor/Undo/eXit] <eXit>:

Figure 12-2 shows the original solid object, and the result of extruding the top face with a 0° taper angle and a 30° taper angle.

The extruded face can follow a path. Select the **Path** option at the Specify height of extrusion or [Path]: prompt. The path of extrusion can be a line, circle, arc, ellipse, elliptical arc, polyline, or spline. The new extrusion is created the exact length of object picked as the path. See Figure 12-3.

Figure 12-2.
The original object, and the result of extruding the top face with a 0° taper angle, and the same part with a 30° taper angle.

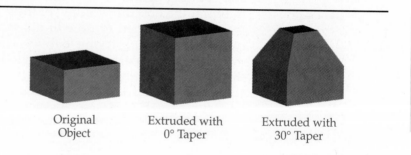

Original
Object

Extruded with
0° Taper

Extruded with
30° Taper

Figure 12-3.
The path of extrusion can be a line, circle, arc, ellipse, elliptical arc, polyline, or spline. The new extrusion is created the exact length of object picked as the path. Here, the paths are shown in color.

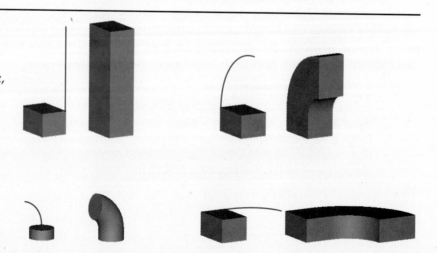

AutoCAD and its Applications—Advanced

❑ Begin a new drawing named EX12-1.

❑ Draw the solid shapes shown below using a color other than black. The dimensions of the shapes are not important.

❑ Copy the shapes and leave the original ones intact. Perform edits on the copies.

❑ Extrude the shapes to resemble the extruded shapes shown below.

❑ Use the **3DORBIT** command and shading to view your work.

❑ Save the drawing as EX12-1. This drawing will be used for other exercises in this chapter.

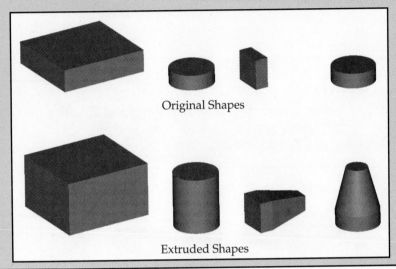

Original Shapes

Extruded Shapes

Moving Faces

The **Move Faces** option moves a face in the specified direction and lengthens the solid object. A solid model feature (such as a hole) that has been subtracted from an object to create a composite solid can be moved with this option. Object snaps may interfere with the operation of this option.

To move a solid face, pick the **Move Faces** button from the **Solids Editing** toolbar or select **Move faces** from the **Solids Editing** cascading menu of the **Modify** pull-down menu. At the Command: prompt, select the **Face** option of the **SOLIDEDIT** command, and then enter the following:

Modify
↳ Solids Editing
↳ Move faces

Solids Editing
toolbar

Move Faces

```
Enter a face editing option
[Extrude/Move/Rotate/Offset/Taper/Delete/Copy/coLor/Undo/eXit] <eXit>:
    MOVE↵
Select faces or [Undo/Remove]: (pick a face to move)
1 face found.
Select faces or [Undo/Remove/ALL]: ↵
Specify a base point or displacement: (pick a base point)
Specify a second point of displacement: (pick a second point or enter coordinates)
Solid validation started.
Solid validation completed.
Enter a face editing option
[Extrude/Move/Rotate/Offset/Taper/Delete/Copy/coLor/Undo/eXit] <eXit>:
```

Faces are moved in a direction perpendicular to the face, so the new position keeps the face parallel to the original. If you are moving a face that is not on the current UCS, you must enter coordinates for the second point of displacement. Faces that are on the current UCS can be moved by picking a new location, or by entering a direct distance. See Figure 12-4.

Figure 12-4.
Faces are moved in a direction perpendicular to the face, so the new position keeps the face parallel to the original.

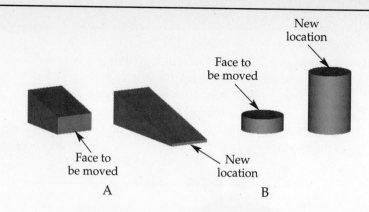

A

B

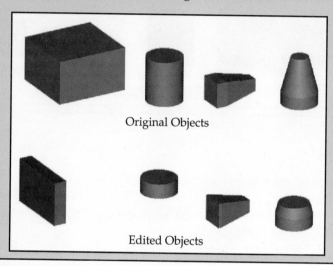
Offsetting Faces

This option may seem the same as the **Extrude** option because it moves faces by a specified distance or through a specified point. Unlike the **OFFSET** command in AutoCAD, this option moves all selected faces a specified distance. It is most useful when you wish to change the size of features such as slots, holes, grooves, and notches in solid parts. A positive offset distance increases the size or volume of the solid, a negative distance decreases the size or volume of the solid. Therefore, if you wish to make the width of a slot wider, provide a negative offset distance to decrease the size of the solid.

To offset a solid face, pick the **Offset Faces** button from the **Solids Editing** toolbar or select **Offset faces** from the **Solids Editing** cascading menu of the **Modify** pull-down menu. At the Command: prompt, select the **Face** option of the **SOLIDEDIT** command, and then select the **Offset** option. See Figure 12-5 for examples of features edited with the **Offset** option.

Modify
➥ Solids Editing
➥ Offset Faces

Solids Editing
toolbar

Offset Faces

Figure 12-5.
A positive offset distance increases the size or volume of the solid. A negative offset distance decreases the size or volume of the solid.

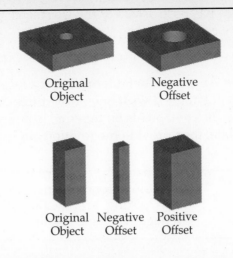

Original
Object

Negative
Offset

Original
Object

Negative
Offset

Positive
Offset

EXERCISE 12-3

❏ Open drawing EX12-2.
❏ Use the **Offset Faces** option to edit the original solid shapes shown below. The dimensions are not important.
❏ The edited objects should resemble the completed shapes shown below.
❏ Shade the drawing to better view your work.
❏ Save the drawing as EX12-3.

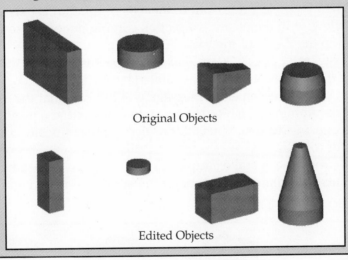

Original Objects

Edited Objects

Deleting Faces

This option deletes a face. This is a quick way to remove features such as chamfers, fillets, holes, and slots. You can avoid the step of removing selected faces from the selection set by picking inside the boundaries of the faces you wish to delete.

To delete a solid face, pick the **Delete Faces** button from the **Solids Editing** toolbar or select **Delete faces** from the **Solids Editing** cascading menu of the **Modify** pull-down menu. At the Command: prompt, select the **Face** option of the **SOLIDEDIT** command, and then select the **Delete** option.

Modify
↳ Solids Editing
↳ Delete faces

**Solids Editing
toolbar**

Delete Faces

Rotating Faces

This option rotates a face about a selected axis. To rotate a solid face, pick the **Rotate Faces** button from the **Solids Editing** toolbar or select **Rotate faces** from the **Solids Editing** cascading menu of the **Modify** pull-down menu. At the Command: prompt, select the **Face** option of the **SOLIDEDIT** command, and then select the **Rotate** option.

Modify
↳ Solids Editing
↳ Rotate faces

**Solids Editing
toolbar**

Rotate Faces

After a face has been selected, the Command: prompt provides several methods by which a face can be rotated.

Specify an axis point or [Axis by object/View/Xaxis/Yaxis/Zaxis] <2points>:

- **2 points.** This is the default option. If a face must be rotated, but the required edge is not aligned with one of the three XYZ axes, use this option to rotate the face. Pick two points on the edge to define the "hinge" about which the face will rotate, then provide the rotation angle.

NOTE A positive rotation angle moves the face in a clockwise direction looking from the first pick point to the second. Conversely, a negative angle rotates the face counterclockwise.

- **Axis by object.** This option allows you to use an existing object to align the axis of rotation. You can select the following objects:
  - **Line.** The selected line becomes the axis of rotation.
  - **Circle, Arc, Ellipse.** The 3D axis of the object becomes the axis of rotation. This 3D axis is a line that passes through the center of the circle, arc, or ellipse and is perpendicular to it.
  - **Polyline, Spline.** A line connecting the polyline or spline's start point and endpoint becomes the axis of rotation.
- **View.** When you select this option, the axis of rotation is perpendicular to the current view, with the positive direction coming out of the screen. This axis is identical to the Z axis of the **View UCS** option.
- **Xaxis/Yaxis/Zaxis.** The X, Y, or Z axis that passes through the selected point becomes the axis of rotation. If the rotated face will intersect or otherwise interfere with other faces, an error message will indicate that the operation failed. In this case, you may wish to try a negative angle if you previously entered a positive one. In addition, you can try selecting the opposite edge of the face at the axis of rotation.

Figure 12-6 provides several examples of rotated faces. Notice how the first and second pick points determine the direction of positive and negative rotation angles.

Figure 12-6.
When rotating faces, the first and second pick points determine the direction of positive and negative rotation angles.

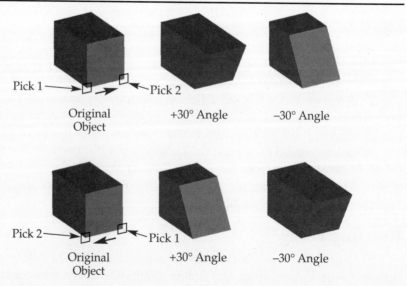

Pick 1 → Pick 2

Original Object   +30° Angle   −30° Angle

Pick 2   Pick 1

Original Object   +30° Angle   −30° Angle

AutoCAD and its Applications—Advanced

❑ Begin a new drawing named EX12-4.
❑ Draw the solid wedge (A) shown below. Dimensions are not important.
❑ Rotate the two side faces at equal angles toward the center of the wedge so the object looks like (B) below.
❑ Shade the drawing.
❑ Save the drawing as EX12-4.

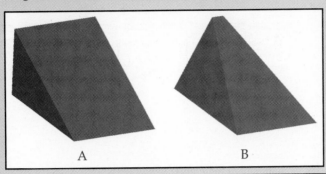

A   B

Tapering Faces

This option tapers an object at the specified angle, from the first pick point to the second, if it is allowable. To taper a solid face, pick the **Taper Faces** button from the **Solids Editing** toolbar or select **Taper faces** from the **Solids Editing** cascading menu of the **Modify** pull-down menu. At the Command: prompt, select the **Face** option of the **SOLIDEDIT** command, and then select the **Taper** option:

Modify
➥ Solids Editing
➥ Taper faces

Solids Editing toolbar

Taper Faces

> [Extrude/Move/Rotate/Offset/Taper/Delete/Copy/coLor/Undo/eXit] <eXit>: **TAPER**↵
> Select faces or [Undo/Remove]: *(pick the object to taper)*
> 1 face found.
> Select faces or [Undo/Remove/ALL]: ↵
> Specify the base point: *(pick the base point)*
> Specify another point along the axis of tapering: *(pick a point along the taper axis)*
> Specify the taper angle: *(enter a taper value)*

Tapers work differently on separate objects and on features inside another object. For example, if a positive taper angle is entered for a solid cylinder, the selected object is tapered in on itself from the base point along the axis of tapering. A negative angle tapers the object out, to increase its size along the axis of tapering. See Figure 12-7.

Figure 12-7.
When entering a positive taper angle for a solid cylinder or bar, the selected object is tapered in on itself from the base point along the axis of tapering. A negative angle tapers the object out, increasing its size along the axis of tapering.

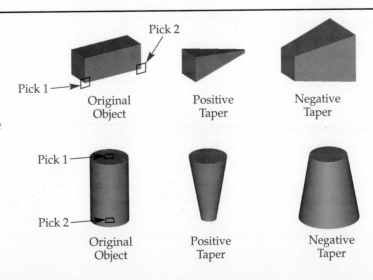

Pick 2

Pick 1 →

Original Object   Positive Taper   Negative Taper

Pick 1 →

Pick 2 →

Original Object   Positive Taper   Negative Taper

On the other hand, if a feature such as a slot or hole inside a solid object is tapered, a positive taper angle increases the size of the feature along the axis of tapering. For example, if an internal feature, such as a hole or slot, is tapered using a positive taper angle, its diameter increases from the base point along the axis of tapering, thus removing material from the solid. Figure 12-8 shows some examples of this function.

Figure 12-8.
If a hole or slot is tapered using a positive taper angle, its diameter increases from the base point along the axis of tapering, thus removing material from the solid. A negative taper angle increases the volume of the solid.

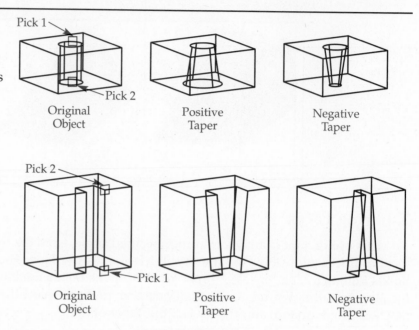

EXERCISE 12-5

❑ Open drawing EX12-1.
❑ Locate a solid cylinder inside the solid box. The cylinder should be the same height as the box.
❑ Subtract the cylinder from the box.
❑ Taper all four sides of the box at a 15° angle. The tapers should angle into the box to create a smaller face on the top.
❑ Taper the hole in the object at an angle that increases the hole diameter from the bottom to the top of the box.
❑ Experiment with tapering the other three objects. Try tapering from one end to the other using both positive and negative angles.
❑ Shade the drawing.
❑ Save the drawing as EX12-5. This drawing will be used in the next exercise.

Copying Faces

This option copies a face to the location or coordinates given. This may be useful when you wish to construct mating parts in an assembly that has the same features on the mating faces, or the same shape outline. This option is quick to use because you can pick a base point on the face, then enter a single direct distance value for the displacement. Be sure an appropriate UCS is set if you wish to use direct distance entry.

To copy a solid face, pick the **Copy Faces** button from the **Solids Editing** toolbar or select **Copy faces** from the **Solids Editing** cascading menu of the **Modify** pull-down menu. At the Command: prompt, select the **Face** option of the **SOLIDEDIT** command, and then select the **Copy** option.

Modify
➥ Solids Editing
➥ Copy faces

Solids Editing toolbar

Copy Faces

AutoCAD and its Applications—Advanced

```
Enter a face editing option
[Extrude/Move/Rotate/Offset/Taper/Delete/Copy/coLor/Undo/eXit] <eXit>: COPY↵
Select faces or [Undo/Remove]: (Select a face)
1 face found.
Select faces or [Undo/Remove/ALL]: ↵
Specify a base point or displacement: (pick a point on the face)
Specify a second point of displacement: (enter or pick a displacement value)
```

See Figure 12-9 for examples of copied faces.

Figure 12-9.
A face can be copied
quickly by picking a
base point on the face
and then entering a
direct distance value
for the displacement.

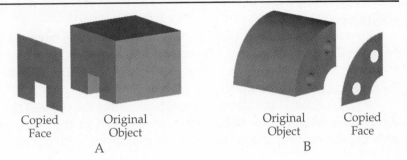

Copied
Face

Original
Object

A

Original
Object

Copied
Face

B

PROFESSIONAL TIP

Copied faces can also be useful for creating additional views. For example, you can copy a face to create a separate plan view with dimensions and notes. A copied face can also be enlarged to show details and to provide additional notation for design or assembly.

Coloring Faces

You can quickly change the selected face to a different color by picking the **Color Faces** button from the **Solids Editing** toolbar or selecting **Color faces** from the **Solids Editing** cascading menu of the **Modify** pull-down menu. You can also select the **Face** option of the **SOLIDEDIT** command, and then select the **Color** option at the Command: prompt.

After accessing the option, simply pick the face, press [Enter], then choose the desired color from the **Select Color** dialog box.

Modify
→ Solids Editing
→ Color faces

Solids Editing
toolbar

Color Faces

EXERCISE 12-6

❏ Open drawing EX12-5.
❏ Use the **Color Faces** option to change the color of the tapered box and the interior of the hole.
❏ Copy the bottom face of the box down and away from the object.
❏ Extrude the copied face to a thickness of your choice.
❏ Save the drawing as EX12-6.

EDGE EDITING

Edges can be edited in only two ways. They can be copied or their color can be changed.

Modify
➥ Solids Editing
➥ Copy edges

Solids Editing toolbar

Copy Edges

To copy a solid edge, pick the **Copy Edges** button from the **Solids Editing** toolbar or select **Copy edges** from the **Solids Editing** cascading menu of the **Modify** pull-down menu. You can also select the **Edge** option of the **SOLIDEDIT** command, and then select the **Copy** option at the Command: prompt.

Copying an edge is similar to copying a face. First, select the edge(s) to copy, then select a base point and a second point. The edge is copied as a line, arc, circle, ellipse, or spline.

Modify
➥ Solids Editing
➥ Color edges

Solids Editing toolbar

Color Edges

To color a solid edge, pick the **Color Edges** button from the **Solids Editing** toolbar or select **Color edges** from the **Solids Editing** cascading menu of the **Modify** pull-down menu. You can also select the **Edge** option of the **SOLIDEDIT** command, and then select the **Color** option at the Command: prompt.

After accessing the **Color Edge** option, select the edge(s) to be modified and press [Enter]. The **Select Color** dialog box appears. Select the new color for the edges and pick the **OK** button. The edges are now displayed with the new color.

BODY EDITING

The body editing options of the **SOLIDEDIT** command perform editing operations on the entire body of the solid model. The more commonly used options are **Imprint**, **Shell**, and **Clean**.

Imprint

Arcs, circles, lines, 2D and 3D polylines, ellipses, splines, regions, bodies, and 3D solids can be imprinted on a solid if the object intersects the solid. The imprint becomes a face regardless of how much overlap exists between the two intersecting objects. Once the imprint has been made, the new face can then be extruded into the solid.

Modify
➥ Solids Editing
➥ Imprint

Solids Editing toolbar

Imprint

To imprint an object on a solid, pick the **Imprint** button from the **Solids Editing** toolbar or select **Imprint** from the **Solids Editing** cascading menu of the **Modify** pull-down menu. You can also select the **Body** option of the **SOLIDEDIT** command, and then select the **Imprint** option at the Command: prompt.

Once the command is activated, you are prompted to select the solid. Then, select the objects to be imprinted. The imprinted face can then be modified using face editing options. Figure 12-10 illustrates objects imprinted and then extruded into a solid model.

Figure 12-10.
Imprinted objects form new faces that can be extruded into the solid. A—Solid box with three objects in the plane of the top face. B—The objects are imprinted, then the faces are extruded through the solid. The solid model is shown with hidden lines removed.

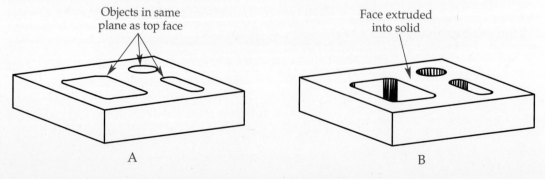

Objects in same plane as top face

Face extruded into solid

A

B

Remember that objects are drawn in the XY plane of the current UCS unless you enter a specific Z value. Therefore, before you draw an object to be imprinted onto a solid model, be sure you have set an appropriate UCS for proper placement of the object.

Separate

This option separates two objects that are both a part of a single solid composite but appear as separate entities. This may be a seldom-used option, but it has a specific purpose. If you select a solid model and an object physically separate from the model is highlighted, the two objects are parts of the same composite solid. If you wish to work with them as individual solids, they must first be separated.

To separate a solid body, pick the **Separate** button from the **Solids Editing** toolbar or select **Separate** from the **Solids Editing** cascading menu of the **Modify** pull-down menu. You can also select the **Body** option of the **SOLIDEDIT** command, and then select the **Separate** option at the Command: prompt.

After picking the **Separate** option, you are prompted to select a 3D solid. After you pick the solid, it is automatically separated and no other actions are required. However, if you select a solid in which the parts are physically joined, AutoCAD indicates this by prompting The selected solid does not have multiple lumps. A "lump" is a physically separate solid entity, and in order to separate a solid, it must be composed of multiple lumps.

Modify
→ Solids Editing
→ Separate

Solids Editing
toolbar

Separate

Shell

A *shell* is a solid that has been "hollowed out" to become only a shell of its former self. The **Shell** option creates a shell of the selected object, using a specified offset distance, or thickness.

To create a shell of a solid body, pick the **Shell** button from the **Solids Editing** toolbar or select **Shell** from the **Solids Editing** cascading menu of the **Modify** pull-down menu. You can also select the **Body** option of the **SOLIDEDIT** command, and then select the **Shell** option at the Command: prompt as follows:

Modify
→ Solids Editing
→ Shell faces

Solids Editing
toolbar

Shell

> Command: **SOLIDEDIT**↵
> Solids editing automatic checking: SOLIDCHECK=1
> Enter a solids editing option [Face/Edge/Body/Undo/eXit] <eXit>: **B**↵
> Enter a body editing option
> [Imprint/seP…arate solids/Shell/cLean/Check/Undo/eXit] <eXit>: **SHELL**↵
> Select a 3D solid: *(select a solid)*
> Remove faces or [Undo/Add/ALL]:

After selecting the solid body, you have the opportunity to remove faces. If you do not remove any faces, the new solid object will appear identical to the old solid object when shaded or rendered. The thickness of the shell will not be visible. If you wish to create a hollow object with an opening, select the face to be removed.

After selecting the object and specifying any faces to be removed, the following prompt appears:

> Enter the shell offset distance: *(enter an offset value)*

A positive shell offset distance creates a shell on the inside of the solid body, whereas a negative shell offset distance creates a shell on the outside of the solid body. See Figure 12-11.

If you shell a solid that contains internal features such as holes, grooves, and slots, a shell of the specified thickness will also be placed around those features. This is shown in Figure 12-12.

Figure 12-11.
Using the **Shell** option.
A—The front, back, and bottom faces (marked here by gray lines) are selected to be removed.
B—The resulting object.

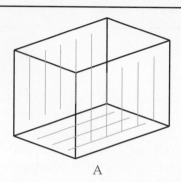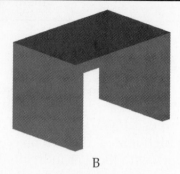

A

B

Figure 12-12.
If you shell a solid that contains internal features such as holes, grooves, and slots, a shell of the specified thickness is also placed around those features. A—Solid object with holes subtracted. B—Wireframe display after shelling. C—Rendering of object.

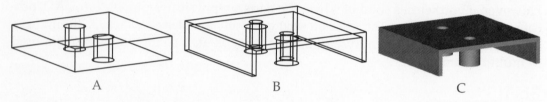

A

B

C

EXERCISE 12-7

- ❑ Create a solid box with the dimensions of 4 × 3 × 2h.
- ❑ Draw a .75″ diameter circle in the center of the top face of the box.
- ❑ Create an imprint of the circle on the top face of the box.
- ❑ Extrude the circle 1.5″ below the top face. Picking the circle edge selects two faces: the face within the circle and the top face of the box. Remove the top face of the box before extruding.
- ❑ Select the **Shell** option and pick the object. Remove the front, back, and bottom faces.
- ❑ Shell the box using a shell offset distance of .25. Your drawing should look like the one shown below.
- ❑ Save the drawing as EX12-7.

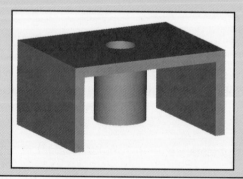

Clean

This option removes all unused objects and shared surfaces. It is accessed by picking the **Clean** button from the **Solids Editing** toolbar or selecting **Clean** from the **Solids Editing** cascading menu of the **Modify** pull-down menu. You can also select the **Body** option of the **SOLIDEDIT** command, and then select the **Clean** option at the Command: prompt. Select the solid to be cleaned and no further input is required. This is useful for removing source objects from imprints.

Check

This option simply determines if the object selected is a valid ACIS solid. If a true 3D solid is selected, AutoCAD displays the prompt This object is a valid ACIS solid. If the object selected is not a 3D solid, the prompt reads A 3D solid must be selected. To access this option, pick the **Check** button from the **Solids Editing** toolbar or select **Check** from the **Solids Editing** cascading menu of the **Modify** pull-down menu. You can also select the **Body** option of the **SOLIDEDIT** command, and then select the **Check** option at the Command: prompt.

CONSTRUCTING A MODEL WITH SOLIDEDIT

This section provides an example of how the **SOLIDEDIT** command can be used to not only edit, but also construct a solid model. As you have noticed, all the solid model editing functions are actually options of the **SOLIDEDIT** command. This makes it easy to design and construct a model without selecting a variety of commands, and also gives you the option of undoing a single editing operation, or an entire editing session, without ever exiting the command.

You can select the **SOLIDEDIT** command options from the **Solids Editing** toolbar, from the **Solids Editing** cascading menu, or by simply typing a single letter of the options while the command is active.

In the following example, **SOLIDEDIT** command options are used to imprint shapes onto the model body, then extrude those shapes into countersunk holes. Then the model size is adjusted, and an angle and taper are applied to one end. Finally, one end of the model is copied to construct a mating part.

NOTE Solid cylindrical and circular shapes are defined by *isolines*. The number of isolines displayed is controlled by the **ISOLINES** system variable. The default setting is four. Increase the value of this variable if you wish to have these shapes displayed with a greater number of defining lines.

Creating Shape Imprints on a Model

The basic shape of the solid model in this tutorial is drawn as a solid box, then shape imprints are added to it. Throughout this exercise, you may wish to change the UCS to assist in the construction of the part.

1. Draw a box using the dimensions shown in Figure 12-13.
2. On the top surface of the box, locate a single .4" diameter circle using the dimensions given, then copy or array the circle to the other three corners as shown.
3. Use the **SOLIDEDIT Imprint** option to imprint the circles on the solid box. Be sure to delete the source objects.

Figure 12-13.

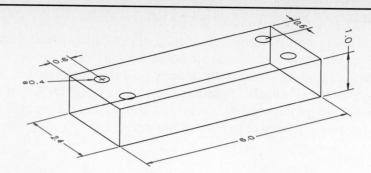

Extruding Imprints to Create Features

Imprinted 2D shapes can now be extruded to create new 3D solid features in the model. Use the **Extrude Faces** option to extrude all four imprinted circles.

1. When you select the first circle, all features on that face will be highlighted, but only the one you picked has actually been selected. Therefore, be sure to pick the remaining three circles.
2. Remove the top face of the box from the selection set.
3. The depth of the extrusion is .16″. Remember to enter −.16 for the extrusion height since the extrusion goes into the solid.
4. The angle of taper for extrusion should be 35°. Your model should look like Figure 12-14.
5. Extrude the small diameter of the four tapered holes so they intersect the bottom of the solid body. If you select the holes by picking either the tapered isolines or the small diameter circles, you can avoid having to remove the top face from the selection set. Your model should now look like Figure 12-15.

Figure 12-14.

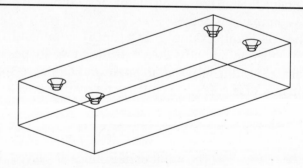

Figure 12-15.

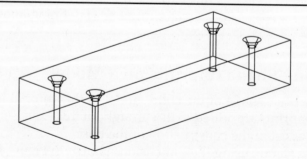

Moving Faces to Change Model Size

The next step is to use the **Move Faces** option to decrease the length and thickness of the solid body.

1. Select either end face and the two holes nearest it. Move the two holes and end face two inches toward the other end, thus changing the length to 4″. See Figure 12-16.
2. Select the bottom face and move it .5″ up toward the top face, thus changing the thickness to .5″. See Figure 12-17A. A rendered version of the object is shown in Figure 12-17B.

Figure 12-16.

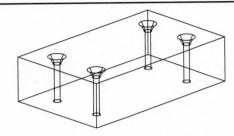

Figure 12-17.

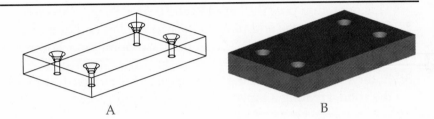

A   B

Offsetting a Feature to Change Its Size

Now we will use the **Offset Faces** option to increase the diameter of the four holes and to adjust a new rectangular slot that will be added to the solid.

1. Using **Offset Faces**, select the four small hole diameters. Be sure to remove the bottom face from the selection set.
2. Enter an offset distance of −.01. This increases the hole diameter and decreases the solid volume.
3. Select the **RECTANG** command and set the fillet radius to .4. Draw a 2″ × 1.6″ rectangle, centered on the top face of the solid. See Figure 12-18.
4. Imprint the new rectangle on the solid. Delete the source object.
5. Extrude the rectangle completely through the solid (.5″). Remember to remove the top face from the selection set when you pick the rectangle. See Figure 12-19.
6. Offset the rectangle using an offset distance of .2″. This decreases the size of the rectangular opening and increases the solid volume. Your drawing should appear as shown in Figure 12-20.

Figure 12-18.

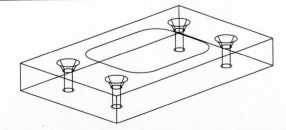

Figure 12-19.

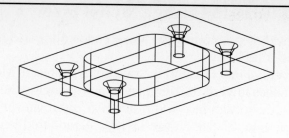

Figure 12-20.

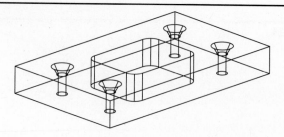

Tapering Faces

This operation uses the **Taper Faces** option to taper the left end of the solid.

1. Select **Taper Faces** and pick the face at the left end of the solid.
2. Pick Point 1 in Figure 12-21 as the base point, and Point 2 as the second point along the axis of tapering.
3. Enter a value of −10 for the taper angle. This moves the upper-left end away from the solid, creating a tapered end. See Figure 12-22.

Figure 12-21.

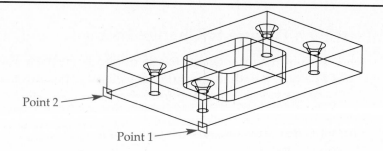

Figure 12-22.

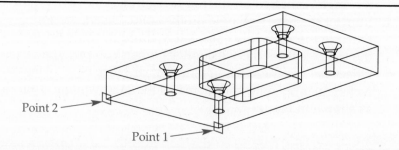

     AutoCAD and its Applications—Advanced

Rotating Faces

Next, use the **Rotate Faces** option to rotate the left end of the solid, which was just tapered. The top edge of the face will be rotated away from the holes, adding volume to the solid.

1. Select **Rotate Faces** and pick the face at the left end of the solid.
2. Pick Point 1 in Figure 12-22 as the first axis point and Point 2 as the second point.
3. Enter a value of –30 for the rotation angle. This rotates the top edge of the left end away from the solid. See Figure 12-23.

Figure 12-23.

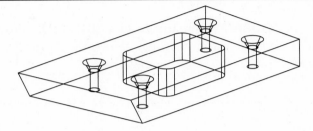

Copying Faces

Faces on a solid model can be copied and used to construct mating parts.

1. Select the **Copy Faces** option and pick the angled face on the left end of the solid.
2. Pick one of the corners as a base point and copy the face 1″ to the left. This face can now be used to create a new solid. See Figure 12-24A.
3. Draw a line 4″ on the negative X axis from the lower-right corner of the copied face. Extrude the copied face 4″ to the left by using the line as the extrusion path. See Figure 12-24B. If you do not use the **Path** option, the extrusion will be projected perpendicular to the face.

> **NOTE** A copied face must first be turned into a solid body using the **EXTRUDE** command, not the **SOLIDEDIT Extrude Faces** option.

Figure 12-24.

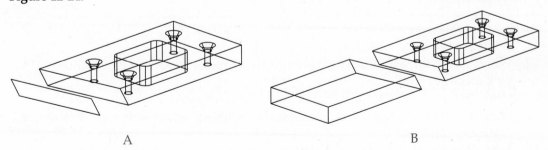

A   B

Creating a Shell

The bottom surface of the solid will be shelled out. Keep in mind that features such as the four holes and the rectangular slot will not be cut off by the shell. Instead, a shell will be placed around these features. This becomes clear when the operation is performed.

1. Select the **Shell** option and pick the solid.
2. At the Remove faces prompt, pick the lower-left and lower-right edges of the solid, shown as Point 1 and Point 2 in Figure 12-25. This removes the two side faces and the bottom face.
3. Enter a shell offset distance of .2. The shell is created and should appear similar to Figure 12-26A.
4. Use the **3DORBIT** command to view the solid from the bottom, and render the model with Gouraud shading. Your model should look like the one shown in Figure 12-26B.

Figure 12-25.

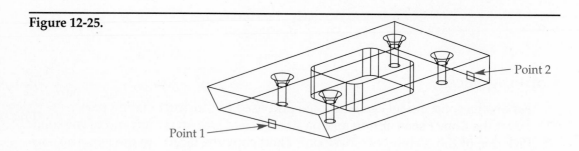

Figure 12-26.

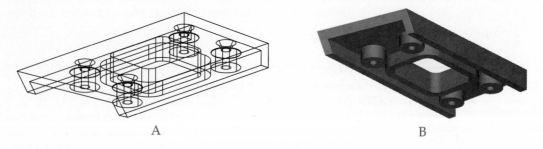

A   B

Chapter Test

Answer the following questions on a separate sheet of paper.

1. What are the three components of a solid model?
2. When using the **SOLIDEDIT** command, how many faces are highlighted if you pick an edge?
3. How do you deselect a face that is part of the selection set?
4. How can you quickly select a single face without additional faces being automatically selected?
5. What two operations can the **Extrude Faces** option perform?
6. How does the shape and length of an object selected as the path of an extrusion affect the final extrusion?
7. What is one of the most useful aspects of the **Offset Faces** option?
8. How do positive and negative offset distance values affect the volume of the solid?
9. How is a single object such as a cylinder affected by entering a positive taper angle when using the **Taper Faces** option?

10. When a shape is imprinted on a solid body, what component of the solid does the imprinted object become, and how can it be used?
11. In what situation would you use the **Separate** option?
12. How does the **Shell** option affect a solid that contains internal features such as holes, grooves, and slots?
13. How can you determine if an object is a valid ACIS solid?

Drawing Problems

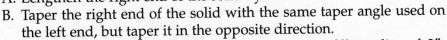

1. Open the tutorial drawing presented in this chapter. If you did not draw this object, draw it now. Perform the following edits to the solid:
   A. Lengthen the right end of the solid by .5″.
   B. Taper the right end of the solid with the same taper angle used on the left end, but taper it in the opposite direction.
   C. Fillet the two long top edges of the solid using a fillet radius of .2″.
   D. Rotate the face at right end of the solid with the same rotation angle used on the left end, but rotate it in the opposite direction.
   E. Save the drawing as P12-1.

2. Construct the solid part shown in Problem 10 of Chapter 1. Use as many **SOLIDEDIT** options as possible to construct the part. After completing the object, make the following modifications:
   A. Lengthen the 2.5″ diameter feature by .125″.
   B. Place a .2″ fillet on the top edge of the 6.0″ diameter flange.
   C. Imprint a 5.80″ diameter circle on the bottom of the flange and extrude it away from the solid .0625″.
   D. Extrude all holes in the solid through the feature added in C above.
   E. Save the drawing as P12-2.

3. Construct the solid part shown in Problem 12 of Chapter 1. Use as many **SOLIDEDIT** options as possible to construct the part. Perform the following edits to the solid:
   A. Lengthen the part on each end by .5″. Move the two holes on each end the same distance.
   B. Change the square feature on the top of the part to 1.25″ square. Add a .80″ square hole through the center of this feature to a depth of .60″.
   C. Add a .15″ chamfer to the top edges of all four holes.
   D. Save the drawing as P12-3.

4. Construct a solid model of the object in Problem 7 of Chapter 3. Use as many **SOLIDEDIT** options as possible to construct the part. Perform the following edits to the solid:
   A. Increase the width of the part to 1.15″.
   B. Change the .7″ diameter hole to .65″.
   C. Change the 45° angle to 50°.
   D. Save the drawing as P12-4.

5. Open the drawing for Problem 5 from Chapter 11. If you have not yet drawn this object, do so now. Use as many **SOLIDEDIT** options as possible to construct the part. Perform the following edits to the solid:
   A. Change the 2.625″ height to 2.325″.
   B. Change the 1.625″ internal diameter to 1.425″.
   C. Taper the outside faces of the .875″ high base at a 5° angle away from the part.
   D. Save the drawing as P12-5.

6. Open drawing Problem 12 from Chapter 11. If you have not yet drawn this object, do so now. Use as many **SOLIDEDIT** options as possible to construct the part. Perform the following edits to the solid:

A. Change the dimensions on the model as follows:

Existing	New
100	106
80	82
φ60	φ94
φ40	φ42
30°	35°

B. Save the drawing as P12-6.

CHAPTER 13

Solid Model Display and Analysis

Learning Objectives

After completing this chapter, you will be able to:
- Control the appearance of solid model displays.
- Construct a 2D section through a solid model.
- Construct a 3D section of a solid model.
- Create a multiview layout of a solid model using **SOLVIEW** and **SOLDRAW**.
- Construct a profile of a solid using **SOLPROF**.
- Perform an analysis of a solid model.
- Export and import solid model files and data.

The appearance of a solid model is controlled by the **ISOLINES**, **DISPSILH**, and **FACETRES** system variables. Internal features of the model can be shown using the **SLICE** and **SECTION** commands. This chapter looks at how these sections can be combined with 2D projections created with the **SOLVIEW** and **SOLDRAW** commands to create a drawing layout for plotting. This chapter also covers how a profile of a solid can be created using the **SOLPROF** command.

CONTROLLING SOLID MODEL DISPLAY

AutoCAD solid models can be displayed as wireframes, with hidden lines removed, shaded, or rendered. A wireframe is the default display and is the quickest to create. The hidden, shaded, and rendered displays require a longer regeneration time.

Isolines

The appearance of a solid model in wireframe form is controlled by the **ISOLINES** system variable. An *isoline* is a line that connects points of equal value. In other words, all points on a horizontal isoline have the same Z value. All points on a vertical isoline have the same X or Y values.

The default **ISOLINES** value is 4. It can have a value from 0 to 2047. All solid objects in the drawing are affected by changes to the **ISOLINES** value.

The setting of the **ISOLINES** system variables can be changed by typing ISOLINES at the Command: prompt and then entering a new value. The **ISOLINES** setting can also be changed in the **Contour lines per surface** text box found in the **Display resolution** area of the **Display** tab in the **Options** dialog box. See Figure 13-1.

Figure 13-2 illustrates the difference between **ISOLINES** settings of 4 and 12.

Figure 13-1.
The **ISOLINES**, **FACETRES**, and **DISPSILH** system variables can be set in the **Options** dialog box.

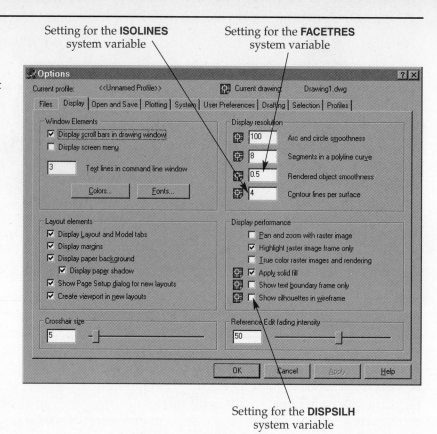

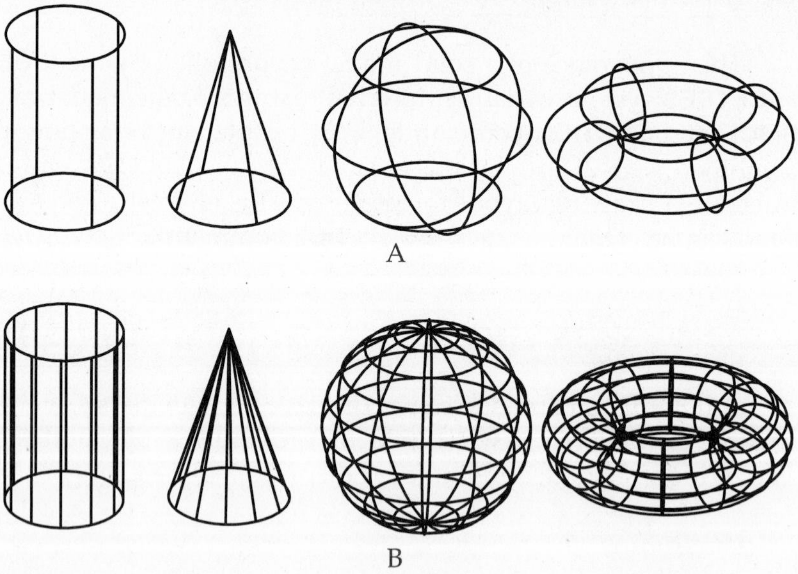

Setting for the **ISOLINES** system variable

Setting for the **FACETRES** system variable

Setting for the **DISPSILH** system variable

Figure 13-2.
Isolines define curved surfaces.
A—**ISOLINES** = 4.
B—**ISOLINES** = 12.

A

B

Creating a Display Silhouette

Solids can appear in two forms when the **HIDE** command is used. The default form shows the model as if it is composed of many individual faces. These faces are defined by tessellation lines. The number of tessellation lines is controlled by the **ISOLINES** system variable for wireframes and by the **FACETRES** system variable in all other displays. The model can also appear smooth, with no tessellation lines on the surface. This is controlled by the **DISPSILH** (display silhouette) system variable.

The **DISPSILH** system variable has two values, 0 (off) and 1 (on). The setting can be changed by typing DISPSILH at the Command: prompt and entering a new value. You can also set the variable using the **Show silhouettes in <u>wireframe</u>** check box in the **Display performance** area of the **Display** tab in the **Options** dialog box (refer to Figure 13-1). Figure 13-3 shows solids with **DISPSILH** set to 1 after using **HIDE**.

NOTE — The **DISPSILH** system variable only affects the display when the **HIDE** command is accessed with the shading mode set to **2D Wireframe**. The **Hidden** option of the **SHADEMODE** command is not affected by **DISPSILH** system variable. If you type HIDE while a **SHADEMODE** option other than **2D Wireframe** is active, you are actually selecting the **Hidden** option of the **SHADEMODE** command.

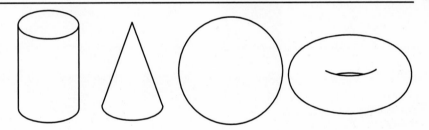

Figure 13-3.
Hidden solids appear as smooth objects with no facets when **DISPSILH** is set to 1 and **SHADEMODE** is set to **2D Wireframe**.

Controlling Surface Smoothness

The smoothness of shaded or rendered images is controlled by the **FACETRES** system variable. This variable determines the number of polygon faces applied to the solid model. The default value is .5. Values can range from 0.01 to 10.0. This system variable can be changed at the Command: prompt or in the **Options** dialog box (refer to Figure 13-1). The illustrations in Figure 13-4 show the effect of two different **FACETRES** settings.

CAUTION — Avoid setting **FACETRES** any higher than necessary. Trying to plot even one solid object with a high **FACETRES** setting can consume system resources and considerable time. Always use the lowest setting that will produce the results that are required by the project for values such as **FACETRES**.

Figure 13-4.
The images in the top row have hidden lines removed, while the bottom row is rendered.
A—The **FACETRES** setting of 0.5 produces these images.
B—The **FACETRES** setting of 5.0 produces smoother surfaces.

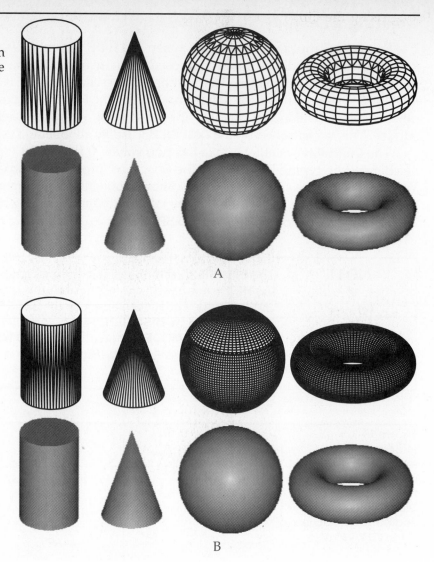

A

B

AutoCAD and its Applications—Advanced

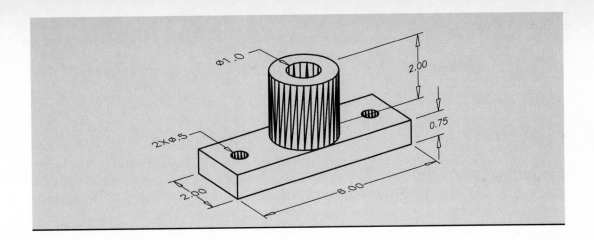

VIEWING 3D MODEL INTERNAL FEATURES

You can "cut" through a 3D solid model to view its internal features and profiles. The **SECTION** command allows you to create a 2D region of the model that is cut. The **SLICE** command allows you to create a 3D cutaway view of the model. These commands can be selected from the **Solids** cascading menu in the **Draw** pull-down menu. See Figure 13-5.

Figure 13-5.
The **SECTION** and **SLICE** commands can be accessed from the **Solids** cascading menu in the **Draw** pull-down menu. The commands are shown here highlighted.

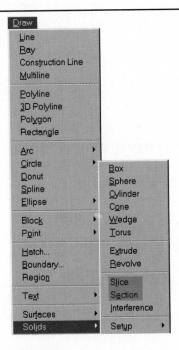

Creating a 3D Solid Model Section

The **SECTION** command places a cutting plane line through your model in the selected location. The default option of **SECTION** is to select three points to define the cutting plane. To access the command, pick **Section** from the **Solids** cascading menu of the **Draw** pull-down menu, pick the **Section** button in the **Solids** toolbar, or type SEC or SECTION at the Command: prompt. The following example selects two quadrant points and one center point on the object in Figure 13-6 to define the cutting plane.

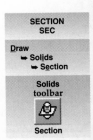

SECTION
SEC

Draw
➡ Solids
  ➡ Section

Solids
toolbar

Section

Command: **SEC** *or* **SECTION**↵
Select objects: *(pick the solid to be sectioned)*
Select objects: ↵
Specify first point on Section plane by [Object/Zaxis/View/XY/YZ/ZX/3points]: *(pick the quadrant at Point 1)*
Specify second point on plane: *(pick the center at Point 2)*
Specify third point on plane: *(pick the quadrant at Point 3)*
Command:

The section created is a 2D region. It has no section lines and is created on the current layer. See Figure 13-6B. If you wish to use the new region as the basis for a 2D hatched section view of the model, do the following:

1. Move or copy the region to a new location. See Figure 13-7A.
2. Explode the region. This creates individual regions if there are two or more separate areas in the section.
3. Explode each separate region again. This breaks the region into objects. These individual objects can be used by AutoCAD to create a boundary for hatching purposes.
4. Use boundary hatching commands to draw section lines inside the areas. See Figure 13-7B. Be sure that the UCS is set to the plane of the area to be hatched. If not, a boundary definition error will appear when an object is selected.
5. Draw any connecting lines required to complete the section view. See Figure 13-7C.

Additional options of the **SECTION** command enable you to specify sectioning planes in a variety of ways. These are explained below.

- **Object.** The section plane is aligned with a selected object, such as a circle, arc, ellipse, 2D spline, or 2D polyline.
- **Zaxis.** Select a point on the new section plane, then pick a point on the positive Z axis of that plane.
- **View.** Select a point on the new section plane and AutoCAD aligns the section perpendicular to the viewpoint in the current viewport.
- **XY.** The new section plane is aligned with the XY plane of the current UCS. The point selected specifies the location of the plane.
- **YZ.** The new section plane is aligned with the YZ plane of the current UCS. The point selected specifies the location of the plane.
- **ZX.** The new section plane is aligned with the ZX plane of the current UCS. The point selected specifies the location of the plane.

Figure 13-6.
A—Three points are picked to define a cutting plane.
B—The section is drawn as a region, without section lines.

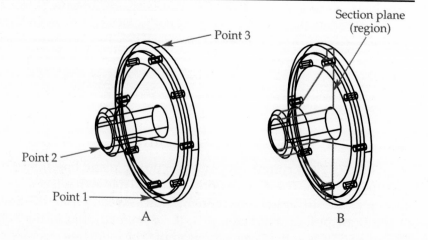

Point 3

Section plane (region)

Point 2

Point 1

A

B

Figure 13-7.
Using a region as a section view. A—First move the region. B—Add section lines.
C—Add any other lines needed to complete the section view.

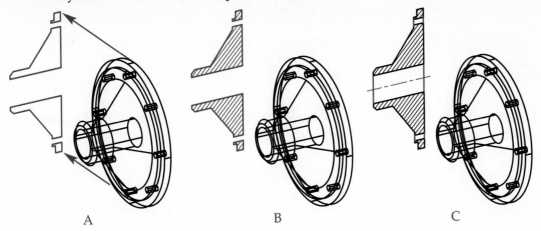

A　　　　　B　　　　　C

Slicing a Solid Model

A true 3D sectioned model is created with the **SLICE** command. You can create a new solid by discarding one side of the cut, or both parts of the sliced object can be retained. **SLICE** does not draw section lines or create regions.

To slice an object, select **Slice** from the **Solids** cascading menu in the **Draw** pulldown menu, pick the **Slice** button from the **Solids** toolbar, or type SL or SLICE at the Command: prompt. The options of the **SLICE** command are the same as those of the **SECTION** command. In the following example, the **YZ** option is used to define the cutting plane. Refer to Figure 13-8.

> Command: **SL** *or* **SLICE**↵
> Select objects: *(pick the solid)*
> Select objects: ↵
> Specify first point on slicing plane by [Object/Zaxis/View/XY/YZ/ZX/3points]
> <3points>: **YZ**↵
> Specify a point on YZ-plane <0,0,0>: ↵
> Specify a point on desired side of the plane or [keep Both sides]: *(pick Point 1 to keep the far side of the object)*

Both sides of the slice can be kept if desired. To do so, select the **keep Both sides** option. The slice plane appears the same as the section plane shown in Figure 13-8B, but the solid is now two separate objects. Test this by picking one side to display grips. Either side can be moved, copied, or rotated. See Figure 13-9.

SLICE SL
Draw ➥ Solids 　➥ Slice
Solids toolbar Slice

Figure 13-8.
A—Specify the cutting plane and pick the side of the object to keep.
B—The completed slice. C—The sliced object after **HIDE**.

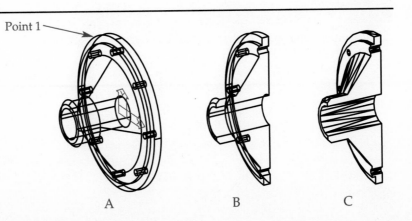

Point 1

A　　　　　B　　　　　C

Figure 13-9.
Keeping both halves of a slice.
A—The slice plane appears as a section.
B—Each part of the sliced object can be moved, copied, or rotated.

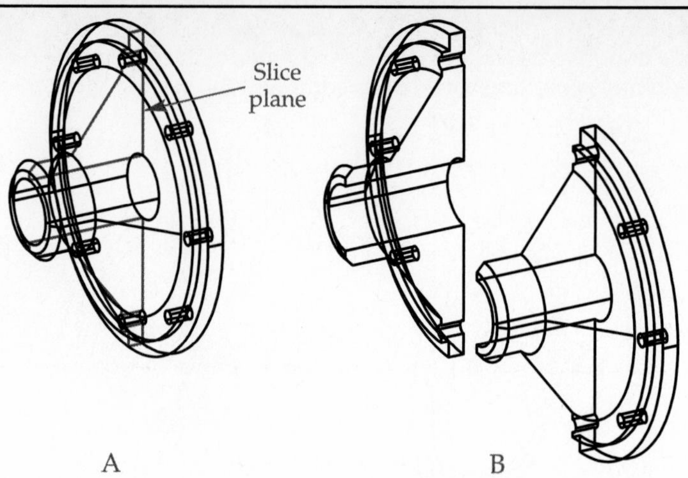

Slice plane

A

B

Creating Special Sections with SLICE

You are not limited to a single slice through an object. For example, you can create a half section of the object in Figure 13-10 by using the **SLICE** command a second time to cut away the top half of the object nearest to you. The example shown in Figure 13-10A shows the use of the **3points** option of **SLICE** to remove one quarter of the original object. The results are shown in Figure 13-10B and Figure 13-10C.

Figure 13-10.
A—A cutting plane is selected to remove one quarter of the original object. B—The cutaway view in wireframe. C—A rendered view of the cutaway.

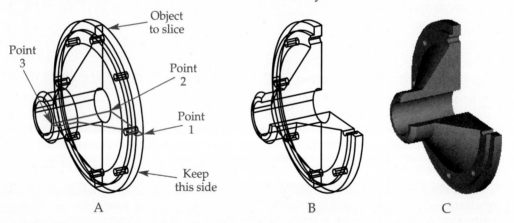

Object to slice

Point 3

Point 2

Point 1

Keep this side

A

B

C

EXERCISE 13-2

❑ Open drawing EX13-1 if it is not on your screen.
❑ Create a full section that cuts through the centers of all three holes.
❑ Move the section region outside the object. Add section lines and connect the section areas with lines to complete the view. The completed section should look like A shown on the following page.
❑ Create a slice through the object on the same plane as the previous section.
❑ Retain both sides of the slice and move both sides apart.
❑ Slice through the large hole on the near side and remove one half of the side. The completed objects should look like B shown on the following page.
❑ Save the drawing as EX13-2.

(Continued)

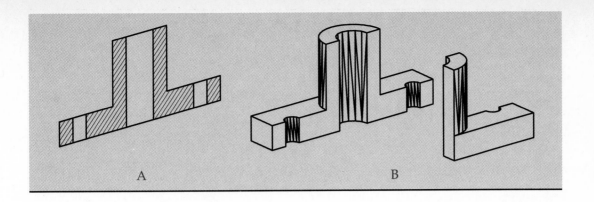

A   B

CREATING AND USING MULTIVIEW LAYOUTS

Once a solid model has been constructed, it is easy to create a multiview layout using the **SOLVIEW** command. This command allows you to create a layout containing orthographic, section, and auxiliary views. The **SOLDRAW** command can then be used to complete profile and section views. **SOLDRAW** must be used after **SOLVIEW**. The **SOLPROF** command can be used to create a profile of the solid in the current view.

Creating Views with SOLVIEW

To use the **SOLVIEW** command, first restore the WCS. This will help avoid any confusion. Then, display a plan view. See Figure 13-11. It helps to have additional user coordinate systems created prior to using **SOLVIEW**. This allows you to construct orthographic views based on a specific named UCS.

Next, create an initial view from which other views can project. This is normally the top or front. In the following example, the top view is constructed first. The top view is created by using the plan view of a UCS named Leftside.

To initiate the **SOLVIEW** command, select **View** from the **Setup** cascading menu after selecting **Solids** from the **Draw** pull-down menu, pick the **Setup View** button from the **Solids** toolbar, or type SOLVIEW at the Command: prompt as follows:

SOLVIEW

Draw
➡ Solids
➡ Setup
➡ View

Solids
toolbar

Setup View

```
Command: SOLVIEW↵
Regenerating layout.
Enter an option [Ucs/Ortho/Auxiliary/Section]: U↵
Enter an option [Named/World/?/Current] <Current>: N↵
Enter name of UCS to restore: LEFTSIDE↵
Specify view scale<1.0000>: .5↵
Specify view center: (pick the center of the view)
Specify view center <specify viewport>: ↵
Specify first corner of viewport: (pick the first corner of a paper space viewport
    outside the object)
Specify opposite corner of viewport: (pick the opposite corner of the viewport)
Enter view name: TOPVIEW↵
UCSVIEW = 1  UCS will be saved with view
Enter an option [Ucs/Ortho/Auxiliary/Section]:
```

You must provide a name for the view in order to continue using **SOLVIEW**. The view shown in Figure 13-12 is displayed.

Figure 13-11.
Before using
SOLVIEW, display
the plan view of
the WCS.

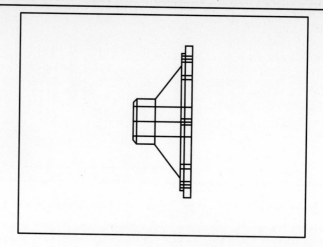

Figure 13-12.
The initial view
named Topview is
created with the **Ucs**
option of **SOLVIEW**.

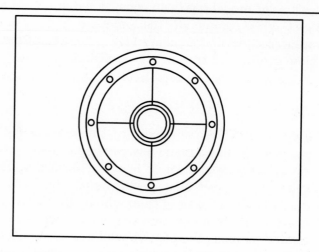

> **NOTE**
>
> When you enter the **SOLVIEW** command while the **Model** tab is active, AutoCAD automatically switches to the **Layout1** tab. The **SOLVIEW** command is used to create new floating viewports and to establish the display within those viewports. You may want to delete the default viewport in the **Layout1** tab before using the **SOLVIEW** command.

The **SOLVIEW** command remains active until you press the [Enter] or [Esc] key. If you exit **SOLVIEW** at this time, you can still return to the drawing and create additional orthographic viewports. Continue and create a section view to the right of the top view as follows:

> Enter an option [Ucs/Ortho/Auxiliary/Section]: **S**↵
> Specify first point of cutting plane: *(pick the quadrant at Point 1 in Figure 13-13)*
> Specify second point of cutting plane: *(pick the quadrant at Point 2)*
> Specify side to view from: *(pick Point 3)*
> Enter view scale <0.5000>: ↵
> Specify view center: *(pick the center of the new section view)*
> Specify view center <specify viewport>: ↵
> Specify first corner of viewport: *(pick one corner of the viewport)*
> Specify opposite corner of viewport: *(pick the opposite corner of the viewport)*
> Enter view name: **SECTION**↵
> Enter an option [Ucs/Ortho/Auxiliary/Section]: ↵

Figure 13-13.
The section view created with **SOLVIEW** (shown on the right) does not show section lines.

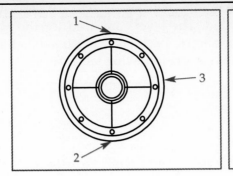

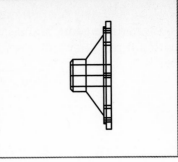

Notice in Figure 13-13 that the new view is shown as a wireframe and not as a section. This is normal. **SOLVIEW** is used to create the views. The **SOLDRAW** command draws the section lines. **SOLDRAW** is discussed later in this chapter.

NOTE	The Specify view center: prompt remains active until [Enter] is pressed. This allows you to adjust the view location if necessary.

A standard orthographic view can be created using the **Ortho** option of **SOLVIEW**. This is illustrated in the following example:

Enter an option [Ucs/Ortho/Auxiliary/Section]: **O**↵
Specify side of viewport to project: *(pick the bottom edge of the left viewport)*
Specify view center: *(pick the center of the new view)*
Specify view center <specify viewport>: ↵
Specify first corner of viewport: *(pick one corner of the viewport)*
Specify opposite corner of viewport: *(pick the opposite corner of the viewport)*
Enter view name: **FRONTVIEW**↵

The new orthographic view is shown in Figure 13-14.

Figure 13-14.
An orthographic front view is created with the **Ortho** option of **SOLVIEW**. This is the view shown at the lower left.

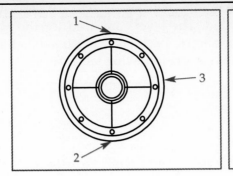

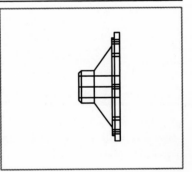

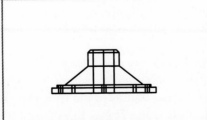

The **SOLVIEW** command creates new layers that are used by **SOLDRAW** when profiles and sections are created. The layers are used for the placement of visible, hidden, dimension, and section lines. Each layer is named as the name of the view with a three letter tag, as shown in the following table:

Layer Name	Object
view name-VIS	Visible lines
view name-HID	Hidden lines
view name-DIM	Dimension lines
view name-HAT	Hatch patterns (sections)

The use of these layers is discussed in the next section.

EXERCISE 13-3

❑ Open drawing EX13-1 if it is not on your screen.
❑ Return the display to a plan view of the WCS.
❑ Use **SOLVIEW** to create a top view of the solid. Locate the view near the top of the screen. Name the view TOP.
❑ Use **SOLVIEW** to create a front section view of the solid located below the top view. Name the view SECTION.
❑ The drawing should look similar to the one shown below.
❑ Save the drawing as EX13-3.

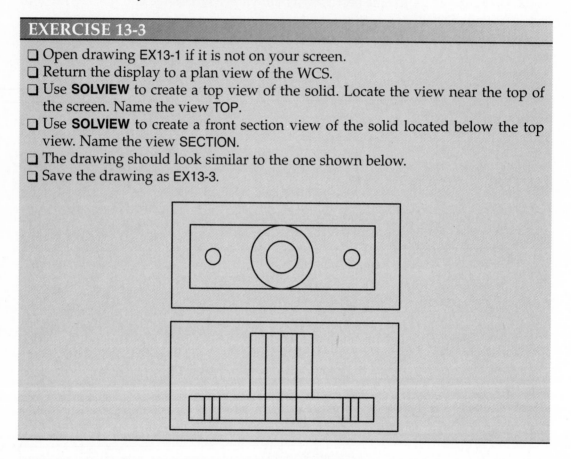

Creating Finished Views with **SOLDRAW**

The **SOLVIEW** command saves information specific to each viewport when a new view is created. This information is used by the **SOLDRAW** command to construct a finished profile or section view. **SOLDRAW** first deletes any information currently on the *view name*-VIS, *view name*-HID, and *view name*-HAT layers for the selected view. Visible, hidden, and section lines are automatically placed on the appropriate layer. Therefore, you should avoid placing objects on any layer other than the *view name*-DIM layer.

The **SOLDRAW** command automatically creates a profile or section in the selected viewport. If you select a viewport that was created using the **Section** option of **SOLVIEW**, the **SOLDRAW** command uses the current values of the **HPNAME**, **HPSCALE**, and **HPANG** system variables to construct the section. These three variables control the angle, boundary, and name of the hatch pattern.

AutoCAD and its Applications—Advanced

If a view is selected that was not created as a section in **SOLVIEW**, the **SOLDRAW** command constructs a profile view. All new visible and hidden lines are placed on the *view name*-VIS or *view name*-HID layer. All existing objects on those layers are deleted.

To initiate the **SOLDRAW** command, select **Drawing** from the **Setup** cascading menu after selecting **Solids** from the **Draw** pull-down menu, pick the **Setup Drawing** button from the **Solids** toolbar, or type SOLDRAW at the Command: prompt as follows:

SOLDRAW
Draw
→ Solids
→ Setup
→ Drawing

Solids
toolbar

Setup Drawing

> Command: **SOLDRAW**⏎
> Select viewports to draw…
> Select objects: *(pick the three viewport outlines)*
> Select objects: ⏎
> One solid selected.

After the profile construction is completed, lines that should be a hidden linetype are still visible (solid). This is because the linetype set for the *view name*-HID layer is Continuous. Change the linetype to Hidden and the drawing should appear as shown in Figure 13-15.

Figure 13-15.
The new front profile view shows hidden lines after the linetype is set to Hidden for the frontview-HID layer.

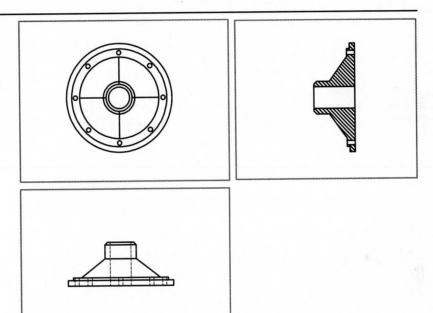

	NOTE	AutoCAD Release 12 drawings used a feature called the Advanced Modeling Extension® (AME®). AutoCAD 2000 uses the ACIS modeling program. In order to use **SOLDRAW** on AutoCAD Release 12 drawings that contain views created with **SOLVIEW,** you must first use **AMECONVERT** to update the solids in the views. Simply enter **AMECONVERT** at the Command: prompt and select the solids to be converted.

Adding a 3D Viewport to the Drawing Layout

If you want to add a viewport that contains a 3D view of the solid, use the **MVIEW** or **VPORTS** command. Create a single viewport by picking the corners. The object will appear in the viewport. Next, use **VPOINT** or **3DORBIT** to achieve the desired 3D view. Pan and zoom as necessary. If you want hidden lines removed on the 3D view when the drawing is plotted, use the **MVIEW Hideplot** option and select the 3D viewport outline. See Figure 13-16.

Remember the following points when working with **SOLVIEW** and **SOLDRAW**:
- Use **SOLVIEW** first and then **SOLDRAW**.
- Do not draw on the *view name*-HID and *view name*-VIS layers.
- Place dimensions for each view on the *view name*-DIM layer for that specific view.
- After using **SOLVIEW**, use **SOLDRAW** on all viewports in order to create hidden lines or section views.
- Change the linetype on the *view name*-HID layer to Hidden.
- Create 3D viewports with the **MVIEW** or **VPORTS** command. Remove hidden lines when plotting with the **MVIEW Hideplot** option.
- Plot the drawing in paper space at the scale of 1:1.

Figure 13-16.
Create a 3D viewport with **MVIEW** and hide the lines with the **MVIEW Hideplot** option. This view is shown at the lower right.

❏ Open drawing EX13-3 if it is not on your screen. If you have not completed any of the exercises in this chapter, complete EX13-1 now and then complete EX13-3.

❏ Use **SOLDRAW** to create profile and section views of the two views on your screen. Adjust layer linetypes so hidden lines show properly.

❏ Add a 3D view to the right of the first two. The drawing should look similar to the one shown below.

❏ Save the drawing as EX13-4.

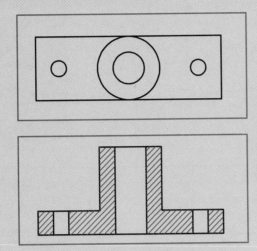
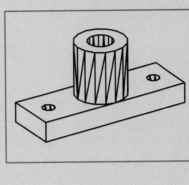

Creating a Profile with SOLPROF

The **SOLPROF** command creates a profile view from a 3D solid model. This is similar to the **Profile** option of the **SOLVIEW** command. **SOLPROF** is limited to creating a profile view of the solid for the current 3D view only.

SOLPROF creates a block of all lines forming the profile of the object. It also creates a block of the hidden lines of the object. The original 3D object is retained. Each of these blocks is placed on a new layer with the name of PH-*view handle* and PV-*view handle*. A *view handle* is a name composed of numbers and letters that is automatically given to a viewport by AutoCAD. For example, if the view handle for the current viewport is 2C9, the **SOLPROF** command creates the layers PH-2C9 and PV-2C9. You must be in a layout tab with a selected floating viewport to use **SOLPROF**.

To initiate the **SOLPROF** command, select **Profile** from the **Setup** cascading menu after selecting **Solids** from the **Draw** pull-down menu, pick the **Setup Profile** button from the **Solids** toolbar, or type SOLPROF at the Command: prompt as follows:

Command: **SOLPROF**↵
Select objects: 1 found
Select objects: ↵
Display hidden profile lines on separate layer? [Yes/No] <Y>: ↵
Project profile lines onto a plane? [Yes/No] <Y>: ↵

If you answer yes to this prompt, the 3D profile lines are projected to a 2D plane and converted to 2D objects. This produces a cleaner profile.

Delete tangential edges? [Yes/No] <Y>: ↵

Answering yes to this prompt produces a proper 2D view by eliminating lines that would normally appear at tangent points of arcs and lines. The original object and the profile created with **SOLPROF** are shown in Figure 13-17.

Figure 13-17.
A—The original
solid. B—A profile
created with
SOLPROF.

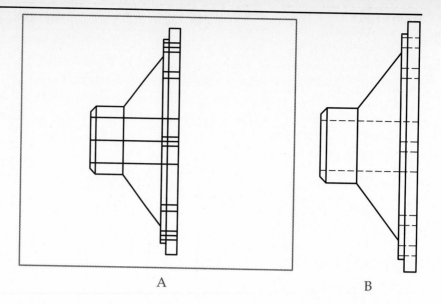

A   B

> **NOTE**
>
>
> When plotting views created with **SOLPROF**, hidden lines may not be displayed unless you freeze the layer that contains the original 3D object.

SOLID MODEL ANALYSIS

The **MASSPROP** command allows you to analyze a solid model for its physical properties. The data obtained from **MASSPROP** can be retained for reference by saving it to a file. The default file name is the drawing name. The file is an ASCII text file with an .mpr extension (mass properties). The analysis can be used for third party applications to produce finite element analysis, material lists, or other testing studies.

Select the **MASSPROP** command by selecting **Inquiry** in the **Tools** pull-down menu and then picking **Mass Properties**, picking the **Mass Properties** button in the **Inquiry** flyout of the **Standard** toolbar (or in the **Inquiry** toolbar), or typing MASSPROP at the Command: prompt:

MASSPROP

Tools
➥ Inquiry
   ➥ Mass
       Properties

**Inquiry
toolbar**

Mass Properties

    Command: **MASSPROP**↵
    Select objects: *(pick the solid model)*
    Select objects: ↵

AutoCAD analyzes the model and displays the results in the **AutoCAD Text Window**. See Figure 13-18. The following properties are listed:

- **Mass.** A measure of the inertia of a solid. In other words, the more mass an object has, the more inertia it has. Note: Mass is *not* a unit of measurement of inertia.
- **Volume.** The amount of 3D space the solid occupies.
- **Bounding box.** A 3D box that fully encloses the solid.
- **Centroid.** A point in 3D space that represents the geometric center of the mass.
- **Moments of inertia.** A solid's resistance when rotating about a given axis.
- **Products of inertia.** A solid's resistance when rotating about two axes at a time.
- **Radii of gyration.** Similar to moments of inertia. Specified as a radius about an axis.
- **Principal moments and X-Y-Z directions about a centroid.** The axes about which the moments of inertia are the highest and lowest.

Figure 13-18.
The **MASSPROP** command displays a list of solid properties in the **AutoCAD Text Window**. These properties are explained in the text.

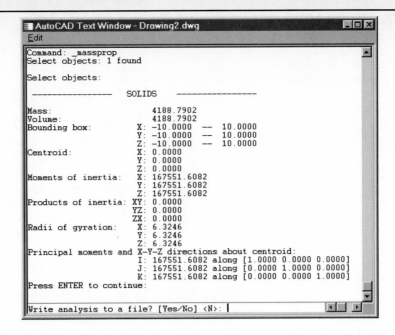

```
 AutoCAD Text Window - Drawing2.dwg                        _ □ ×
 Edit
Command: _massprop
Select objects: 1 found

Select objects:

----------------        SOLIDS       ----------------

Mass:                         4188.7902
Volume:                       4188.7902
Bounding box:         X: -10.0000   --   10.0000
                      Y: -10.0000   --   10.0000
                      Z: -10.0000   --   10.0000
Centroid:             X:  0.0000
                      Y:  0.0000
                      Z:  0.0000
Moments of inertia:   X: 167551.6082
                      Y: 167551.6082
                      Z: 167551.6082
Products of inertia: XY:  0.0000
                     YZ:  0.0000
                     ZX:  0.0000
Radii of gyration:    X:  6.3246
                      Y:  6.3246
                      Z:  6.3246
Principal moments and X-Y-Z directions about centroid:
                      I: 167551.6082 along [1.0000 0.0000 0.0000]
                      J: 167551.6082 along [0.0000 1.0000 0.0000]
                      K: 167551.6082 along [0.0000 0.0000 1.0000]
Press ENTER to continue:

Write analysis to a file? [Yes/No] <N>: |
```

PROFESSIONAL TIP

Advanced applications of solid model design and analysis are possible with Autodesk's Mechanical Desktop® and Inventor® software. These products allow you to create parametric designs and assign a wide variety of materials to the solid model.

SOLID MODEL FILE EXCHANGE

AutoCAD drawing files can be converted to files that can be used for testing and analysis. Use the **ACISOUT** command or **Export Data** dialog box to create a file with an .sat extension. These files can be imported into AutoCAD with the **ACISIN** command or by using the **Select ACIS File** dialog box.

Solids can also be exported for use with stereolithography software. These files have an .stl extension. Use the **STLOUT** command or the **Export Data** dialog box to create STL files.

Importing and Exporting Solid Model Files

A solid model is frequently used with analysis and testing software or in the manufacturing of a part. The **ACISOUT** command allows you to create this type of file. You can type ACISOUT at the Command: prompt. This displays the **Create ACIS File** dialog box.

You can also use the **Export Data** dialog box by picking **Export...** from the **File** pull-down menu or typing EXPORT at the Command: prompt. Pick the **ACIS (*.sat)** selection in the **Save as type:** list box. See Figure 13-19.

An SAT file can be imported into AutoCAD and automatically converted into a drawing file by selecting **ACIS File...** from the **Insert** pull-down menu or entering ACISIN at the Command: prompt. This displays the **Select ACIS File** dialog box.

You can also import a file using the **IMPORT** command. Type IMP or IMPORT at the Command: prompt to display the **Import File** dialog box. Pick the **ACIS (*.sat)** selection in the **Files of type:** list box, Figure 13-20.

For 2000i Users...

The standard file selection dialog box (such as that used for the **Export Data** dialog box and **Import File** dialog box shown in Figure 13-19 and Figure 13-20) has been modified for AutoCAD 2000i. See *AutoCAD and its Applications—Basics* for a complete description of standard file selection dialog box features.

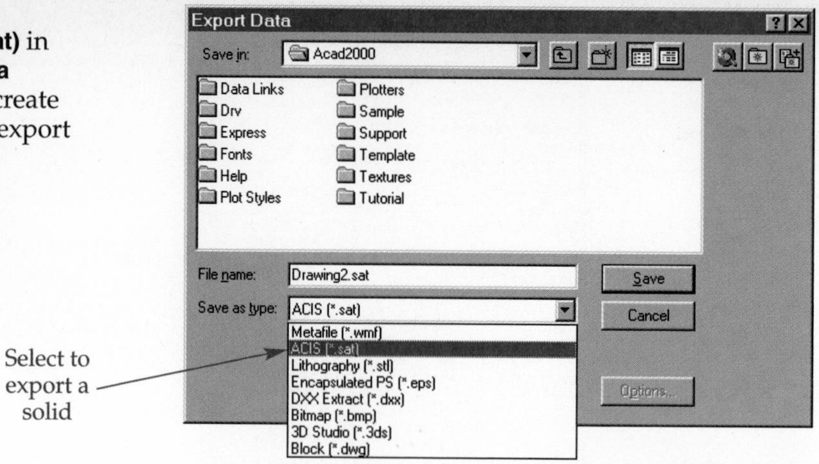

Figure 13-19.
Pick **ACIS (*.sat)** in the **Export Data** dialog box to create a solid model export file.

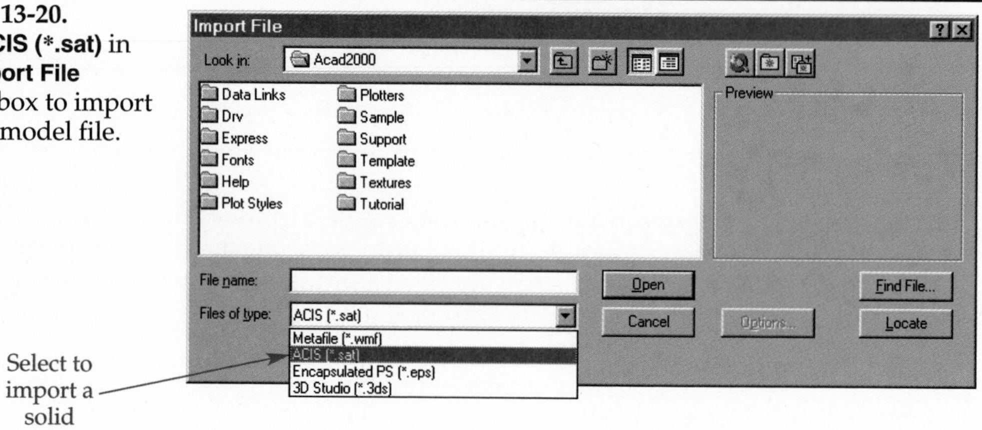

Select to export a solid

Figure 13-20.
Pick **ACIS (*.sat)** in the **Import File** dialog box to import a solid model file.

Select to import a solid

PROFESSIONAL TIP

Solid model drawing files can be saved as SAT files for archive purposes. These files require far less disk space than DWG files and may be a good option when you have limited storage space.

Stereolithography Files

Stereolithography is a technology that creates plastic prototype 3D models using a computer-generated solid model, a laser, and a vat of liquid polymer. This technology is also called *rapid prototyping*. A prototype 3D model can be designed and formed in a short amount of time without using standard manufacturing processes.

Most software used to create a stereolithograph can read STL files. AutoCAD can export a drawing file to the STL format, but *cannot* import STL files. Also, the solid model must be located in the current UCS so the entire object has positive XYZ coordinates.

Use the **Export Data** dialog box to export an STL file, or use the **STLOUT** command at the Command: prompt. You can only select a single object to be exported. You are then asked if you want to create a binary STL file. If you answer no to the prompt, an ASCII file is created. Keep in mind that a binary STL file may be as much as five times smaller than the same file in ASCII format.

After you choose the type of file, the **Create STL File** dialog box is displayed. Type the file name in the **File name:** edit box and pick **OK** or press [Enter].

EXERCISE 13-5

❏ Open drawing EX13-4 if it is not on your screen.
❏ Perform a mass properties analysis of the solid.
   ❏ What is the mass?
   ❏ What is the volume?
   ❏ What is the bounding box?
   ❏ What is the centroid?
❏ Export an SAT file and name it EX13-5.
❏ Begin a new drawing. Import the SAT file named EX13-5.
❏ Export an STL file and name it EX13-5.
❏ Do not save the drawing.

Chapter Test

Answer the following questions on a separate sheet of paper.
1. What is the function of the **ISOLINES** system variable?
2. What variable controls the display of a solid primitive silhouette?
3. What is the function of the **FACETRES** system variable?
4. What command creates a 2D region that represents a cutting plane through the solid?
5. What command can display the true 3D shape of internal features and object profiles?
6. Which command should be used first, **SOLDRAW** or **SOLVIEW**?
7. What command allows you to create a multiview layout from a 3D solid model?
8. Which option of the command in Question 7 is used to create an orthographic view?
9. Name the layer(s) that the command in Question 7 automatically creates.
10. Which layer(s) in Question 9 should you avoid drawing on?
11. What command can automatically complete a section view using the current settings of **HPNAME**, **HPSCALE**, and **HPANG**?
12. When plotting, how are hidden lines removed in a viewport that contains a 3D view?
13. Which command creates a profile view from a 3D model?
14. What is the function of the **MASSPROP** command?
15. What is the extension of the ASCII file that can be created by **MASSPROP**?
16. What is a centroid?
17. What commands export and import solid models?
18. What kind of file has an .stl extension?

Drawing Problems

1. Open one of your solid model problems from a previous chapter and do the following:
   A. Set the **DISPSILH** variable to 1 and use **HIDE**.
   B. Set the **FACETRES** variable to .5 and produce a shaded model. Set **FACETRES** to 1 and shade the model again.
   C. Change the **SHADEMODE** options, set **FACETRES** to 2, and shade the model.
   D. Create a rendering of the model.
   E. Save the drawing as P13-1.

2. Open one of your solid model problems from a previous chapter and do the following:
   A. Construct a section through the model. Cut through as many features as possible.
   B. Move the new section region to a space outside the 3D solid.
   C. Explode the resulting regions as needed and place section lines in the appropriate areas. Add lines to complete the section.
   D. Cut a slice through the original solid in the same location as the previous section.
   E. Retain the piece of the solid that is the same side as the section.
   F. Remove the other side of the slice.
   G. Save the drawing as P13-2.

3. Open one of your solid model problems from a previous chapter and do the following:
   A. Create a multiview layout of the model. One of the views should be a section view. Use a total of three 2D views.
   B. Use **SOLVIEW** and **SOLDRAW** to create the views. Be sure that section lines and hidden lines are displayed properly.
   C. Create a fourth viewport that contains a 3D view of the solid. Label the view PICTORIAL VIEW.
   D. Plot the drawing so the 3D view is displayed with hidden lines removed.
   E. Save the drawing as P13-3.

4. Open one of your solid model problems from a previous chapter and do the following:
   A. Display the model in a plan view.
   B. Use **SOLPROF** to create a profile view. Wblock the profile view to a file named P13-2PLN.
   C. Display the original model in a 3D view.
   D. Use **SECTION** to construct a front-view section of the model. Delete the original 3D solid.
   E. Display the section as a plan view.
   F. Insert the wblock P13-2PLN above the section view. Adjust the views so that they align properly.
   G. Save the drawing as P13-4.

5. Choose five solid model problems from previous chapters and copy them to a new directory on the hard drive. Then, do the following:
   A. Open the first drawing, then export it as an SAT file to the new directory.
   B. Do the same for the remaining four files.
   C. Compare the sizes of the SAT files with the DWG files. Compare the combined sizes of both types of files.
   D. Begin a new drawing and import one of the previous SAT files.

Using Raster and Vector Graphics Files

Learning Objectives

After completing this chapter, you will be able to:

■ Import and export raster files using AutoCAD.
■ Import and export vector files using AutoCAD.
■ Set image commands to manipulate inserted raster files.
■ Import and export PostScript files using AutoCAD.

This chapter introduces using AutoCAD to work with raster and vector graphics files. This includes importing, exporting, and various settings. PostScript files for printing are also covered in this chapter.

The Windows Clipboard can be an important part of creating presentation graphics. In addition, object linking and embedding (OLE) can be used to incorporate AutoCAD graphics into electronic presentations. Both of these topics are covered thoroughly in Chapter 18.

WORKING WITH RASTER FILES

AutoCAD
User's
Guide
20

AutoCAD drawings create what are called vector graphics. A *vector* is an object that is defined by XYZ coordinates. In other words, AutoCAD stores the mathematical definition of an object. *Pixels* (picture elements) are the "dots" or "bits" in the monitor that make up your display screen. When drawing vector objects in AutoCAD, your monitor uses pixels to create a representation of the object on the monitor. However, there is no relationship between the physical pixels in your monitor and a vector object. Pixels simply show the object at the current zoom percentage.

Many illustrations created with drawing, painting, and presentation software are saved as raster files. A *raster file* creates a picture or image file using the location and color of the screen pixels. In other words, a raster file is made up of "dots." Raster files are usually called *bitmaps*. There are several types of raster files used for presentation graphics and desktop publishing. The most common types are covered in the next section.

Common Raster File Types

You can work with raster files using the **Image** dialog box. Some of the most common raster files used in industry today are:

- **GIF (Graphics Interchange Format).** A file format developed by CompuServe to exchange graphic images over an online computer service.

- **PCX (Personal Computer Exchange).** A file format developed by Z-Soft Corporation.
- **TIFF (Tagged Image File Format).** A file format developed by Aldus Corporation and Microsoft Corporation.
- **BMP (Bitmap).** A file format developed by Microsoft Corporation.
- **JPEG (Joint Photographic Experts Group).** Creates a compressed graphics image file of approximately 1/20th the original size.

Other raster file types can also be imported into AutoCAD. If you have a raster image that cannot be imported directly, you will need to first import the file into a paint or draw program. Then, export the image in a format that AutoCAD can read.

Inserting Raster Images

Raster images inserted into AutoCAD drawings using the **IMAGE** command are treated much like externally referenced drawings (xrefs). They are not added to the drawing database, but are attached and referenced by a path name to the raster file's location. Any changes to the image content must be made to the original file. Settings and commands in AutoCAD can, however, control the portion of the image shown and its appearance.

IMAGE
IM

Insert
↪ Raster Image...

Reference
toolbar

Image

Images can be inserted, removed, and modified using commands found in the **Reference** toolbar, Figure 14-1. These functions are discussed in detail in this chapter.

To activate the **IMAGE** command, select **Raster Image...** in the **Insert** pull-down menu, pick the **Image** button in the **Reference** toolbar, or type IM or IMAGE at the Command: prompt. This displays the **Image Manager** dialog box, Figure 14-2. This dialog box lists the images currently attached to a drawing. From this dialog box, you can insert a new image, delete an image from the drawing, and view information about the image.

Just as a raster image is not actually inserted into a drawing, the image details are not stored in the drawing file either. Instead, the directory path to the location of the image file is stored in the drawing file. Then, whenever the drawing is opened, it locates the image file and reloads it into the drawing.

IMAGEATTACH
IAT

Reference
toolbar

Image Attach

The **IMAGEATTACH** command is used to attach an image file to a drawing. To access this command, pick the **Attach...** button in the **Image Manager** dialog box, pick the **Image Attach** button in the **Reference** toolbar, or type IAT or IMAGEATTACH at the Command: prompt. The **Select Image File** dialog box is displayed, Figure 14-3. Pick the **Files of type:** drop-down list to display all the raster file types that can be used. If a folder contains a wide variety of raster files, you can quickly narrow your search by picking one of the file types in this list. Select the raster file and pick **Open**. This displays the **Image** dialog box, Figure 14-4.

Figure 14-1.
The **Reference** toolbar contains buttons for the **Image** family of commands.

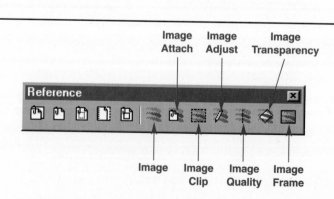

Figure 14-2.
Raster images can
be inserted or
deleted using the
Image Manager
dialog box.

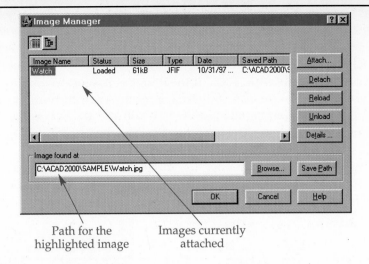

Path for the
highlighted image

Images currently
attached

Figure 14-3.
Select the image file
to be attached to the
drawing in the
Select Image File
dialog box. Pick the
Files of type: drop-
down list to display
the raster file types
that can be used.

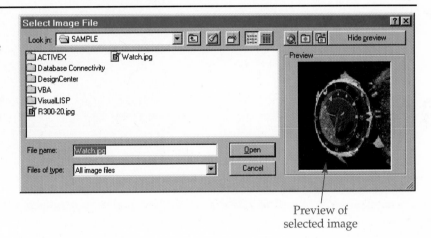

Preview of
selected image

Figure 14-4.
The image name and current path are displayed in the **Image** dialog box. In addition you can
preset image parameters, or choose to specify them on-screen. The dialog box expands to
include the **Image Information** area when the **Details** button is picked.

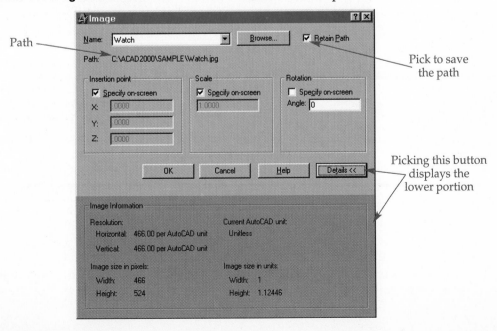

Path

Pick to save
the path

Picking this button
displays the
lower portion

The image name and current path are displayed here. You can preset image parameters, or choose to specify them on-screen. The **Retain Path** box is checked by default. When checked, the path to the image is saved with the drawing file. If this box is not checked, AutoCAD searches through the Support Files Search Path defined in the **Files** tab of the **Options** dialog box. If the image is not located in this path, AutoCAD will not be able to find it. You can view image resolution information in the **Attach Image** dialog box by picking the **Details** button. See Figure 14-4. When the **OK** button is picked and the image placed, it is displayed in the drawing area. See Figure 14-5.

Figure 14-5.
The raster image attached to an AutoCAD drawing.

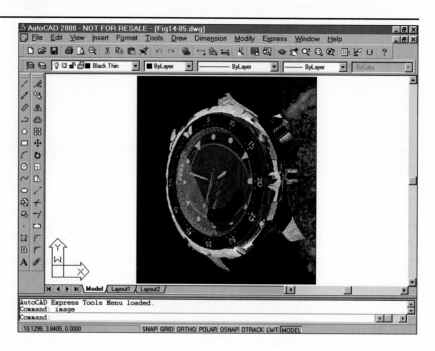

PROFESSIONAL TIP

If you are working on a project that uses xrefs and attached images, adding a "project folder" to the support file search path may be beneficial. This allows all related files for a project stored in a central folder to be "found" by AutoCAD.

Managing Attached Images

The **Image Manager** dialog box is used to control the raster images inserted into the drawing. Refer to Figure 14-2. The dialog box displays the image name, its status (loaded or unloaded), file size, type, date the image was last saved, and the file path. Four options are available to help you manage the images.

- **Attach.** Used to search for and attach image files to the drawing.
- **Detach.** Removes or detaches the selected image file from the drawing.
- **Reload.** Reloads the selected image file. The **Status** column will show Reload if this option is selected. The image is loaded after the dialog box is closed.
- **Unload.** Unloads the selected image, but retains its path information. The **Status** column will show Unload if this option is selected. The image is unloaded after the dialog box is closed. An unloaded image is displayed only as a frame until "reloaded."

PROFESSIONAL TIP	If regeneration time is becoming long, unload attached image files not needed for the current session.

Controlling Image File Displays

Once an image is attached to the current drawing, its display can be adjusted if needed. The commands used to adjust images can be accessed from the **Reference** toolbar, or the **Modify** pull-down menu, Figure 14-6.

Figure 14-6.
Commands used to control image files are found in the **Modify** pull-down menu.

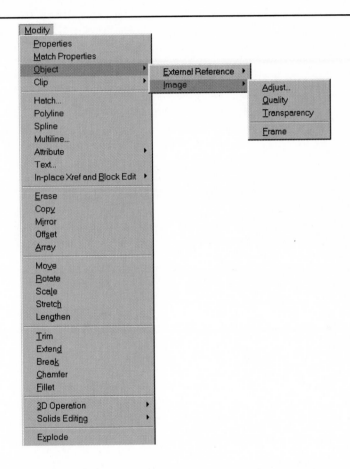

Clipping an image

The **IMAGECLIP** command allows you to trim away a portion of the image that does not need to be seen. The clipping frame can be rectangular or polygonal. To access the **IMAGECLIP** command, select the **Image Clip** button in the **Reference** toolbar, select **Image** from the **Clip** cascading menu in the **Modify** pull-down menu, or type ICL or IMAGECLIP at the Command: prompt.

IMAGECLIP
ICL

Modify
↳ Clip
  ↳ Image

Reference toolbar

Image Clip

Command: **ICL** *or* **IMAGECLIP**↵
Select image to clip: *(pick the image frame)*
Enter image clipping option [ON/OFF/Delete/New boundary] <New>: **N**↵
Enter clipping type [Polygonal/Rectangular] <Rectangular>: **R**↵
Specify first corner point: *(pick the first corner of the clipping boundary)*
Specify opposite corner point: *(pick the second corner)*

Chapter 14   Using Raster and Vector Graphics Files

The **Polygonal** option allows you to construct a clipping frame composed of three or more points as follows.

```
Enter clipping type [Polygonal/Rectangular] <Rectangular>: P↵
Specify first point: (pick first point to be used for the clipping boundary)
Specify next point or [Undo]: (pick second point)
Specify next point or [Undo]: (pick third point)
Specify next point or [Close/Undo]: (pick additional points as needed)
Specify next point or [Close/Undo]: ↵
```

Figure 14-7 shows the results of using the **Rectangular** and **Polygonal** options of the **IMAGECLIP** command on a raster image. Three additional options of **IMAGECLIP** allow you to work with the display of the clipped image.
- **ON.** Turns the clipping frame on to display only the clipped area.
- **OFF.** Turns off the clipping frame to display the entire original image and frame.
- **Delete.** Deletes the clipping frame and displays the entire original image.

Figure 14-7.
A—A rectangular image clip. B—A polygonal image clip (shown here in color for illustration).

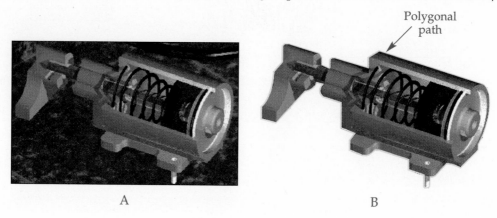

Polygonal path

A   B

> **NOTE** You can pick an unclipped image frame to display the grips for editing. If one grip is stretched it affects the entire image by enlarging or reducing it proportionally. On the other hand, if you select a clipped image for grip editing, stretching the clipping frame does not change the size or shape of the image, but alters the size of the frame and retains the size of the image.

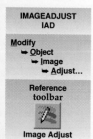

IMAGEADJUST
IAD

Modify
 → Object
  → Image
   → Adjust...

Reference
toolbar

Image Adjust

Adjusting an image

The **IMAGEADJUST** command provides controls over the brightness, contrast, and fade of the image. These adjustments are made in the **Image Adjust** dialog box, Figure 14-8. Access the dialog box by picking the **Image Adjust** button in the **Reference** toolbar; selecting **Object**, **Image**, then **Adjust...** from the **Modify** pull-down menu; or typing IAD or IMAGEADJUST at the Command: prompt. You are first prompted to pick an image. If you want the same settings applied to multiple images, you can pick them all at the same time. When done picking objects, press [Enter] to display the dialog box. Values can be changed by typing in the text boxes or by using the slider bars. The preview tile changes dynamically as the sliders are moved. Pick the **Reset** button to return all values to their defaults.

Figure 14-8.
Brightness, contrast, and fade values can be entered numerically or by using the slider bars in the **Image Adjust** dialog box.

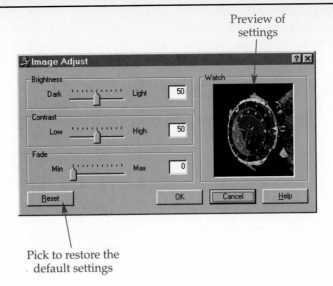

Preview of settings

Pick to restore the default settings

- **Brightness.** Controls pixel whiteness and indirectly affects the contrast. Values can range from 0 to 100, with 50 as the default value. Higher values increase the brightness.
- **Contrast.** Controls the contrast of the image, or how close each pixel is moved toward its primary or secondary color. Values can range from 0 to 100, with 50 as the default value. Higher values increase the contrast.
- **Fade.** Controls the fading of the image, or how close the image is to the background color. Values can range from 0 to 100, with 0 as the default value. Higher values increase the fading.

Image quality

The **IMAGEQUALITY** command provides two options: **High** and **Draft**. The high quality setting produces the best image display, but requires longer to generate. If you are working with several images in a drawing, it is best to set the **Draft** option. The image displayed is lower quality but requires less time to display.

Change the **IMAGEQUALITY** setting by picking the **Image Quality** button from the **Reference** toolbar; selecting **Object**, **Image**, then **Quality** from the **Modify** pull-down menu; or typing IMAGEQUALITY at the Command: prompt. The setting applies to all images in the drawing.

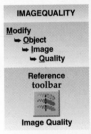

IMAGEQUALITY

Modify
➥ Object
  ➥ Image
    ➥ Quality

Reference toolbar

Image Quality

Transparency

Some raster images have transparent background pixels. The **TRANSPARENCY** command controls the display of these pixels. If **TRANSPARENCY** is on, the drawing will show through the image background. Images are inserted with this feature turned off.

The **TRANSPARENCY** setting can be changed by picking the **Image Transparency** button from the **Reference** toolbar; selecting **Object**, **Image**, then **Transparency** from the **Modify** pull-down menu, or typing TRANSPARENCY at the Command: prompt. The setting applies to individual images. Multiple images can be selected at the same time. Remember, only images that have transparent pixels in them are affected.

TRANSPARENCY

Modify
➥ Object
  ➥ Image
    ➥ Transparency

Reference toolbar

Image Transparency

Image frame

The **IMAGEFRAME** command controls the appearance of frames around all images in the current drawing. When attaching images, AutoCAD will place a frame around the image in the current layer, color, and linetype. There are two settings for the **IMAGEFRAME** command: on and off. When **IMAGEFRAME** is on, a frame appears around the image.

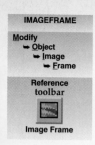
The **IMAGEFRAME** setting can be changed by picking the **Image Frame** button from the **Reference** toolbar; selecting **Object**, **Image**, then **Frame** from the **Modify** pull-down menu; or typing IMAGEFRAME at the Command: prompt. The setting applies to all images in the drawing.

Saving Raster Files

The **SAVEIMG** command is used to save AutoCAD drawings as raster files in three different formats: .bmp, .tga, and .tif. To access the command, pick **Save...** from the **Display Image** cascading menu in the **Tools** pull-down menu or type SAVEIMG at the Command: prompt. This displays the **Save Image** dialog box. Use the dialog box to save the image. This process is discussed in detail in Chapter 15.

Uses of Raster Files in AutoCAD

One use of raster images is sketching or tracing. For example, you may need a line drawing of an image only available as a photo. The photo can be scanned, which produces a raster image. After importing the raster image through the **IMAGE** command, use the appropriate drawing commands to sketch or trace the image. After the object is sketched, the original raster image can be deleted, frozen, or unloaded, leaving the tracing. You can then add other elements to the tracing to create a full drawing. See Figure 14-9.

Figure 14-9.
Using a raster image as a model for a drawing. A—The imported raster image. B—Use AutoCAD commands to trace the image. Then, either delete the image or freeze its layer. C—The completed drawing plotted on a title block.

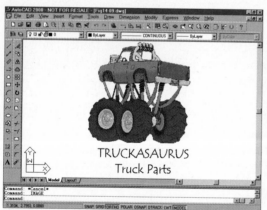

A

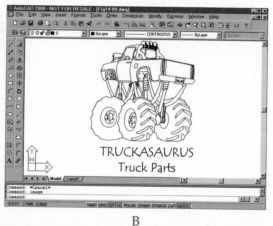

B

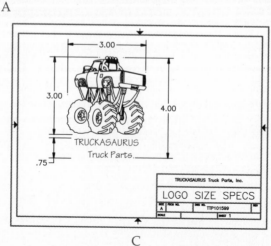

C

Raster files can be combined with AutoCAD drawing and modeling features in many ways to complete or complement the design. For example, company marks or logos can be easily added to title blocks, style sheets, and company drawing standards. Drawings that require designs, labels, and a variety of text fonts can be created using raster files in conjunction with the wide variety of TrueType fonts available with AutoCAD 2000. Archived manual drawings can also be scanned, brought into AutoCAD, and then traced to create a CAD drawing.

You can also add features to complement raster files. For example, you can import a raster file, dimension or annotate it, and even add special shapes to it. Then, export it as the same type of file with a command such as **SAVEIMG**. Now you can use the revised file in the original software in which it was created. As with any creative process, let your imagination and the job requirements determine how you use this capability of AutoCAD. Refer to Chapter 15 for a discussion on the **SAVEIMG** command.

EXERCISE 14-1

❑ Start a new drawing named EX14-1.
❑ Make two new layers. Name one Image and the other Lines. Set the Image layer current.
❑ Find a raster file with a .bmp, .pcx, or .tif extension. It can be a sample file from other software or a file downloaded from the Internet. When downloading files from the Internet, be sure to only use files that are labeled "freely distribute" or "freeware."
❑ Use the **IMAGE** command to import the image into your drawing.
❑ Resize the image using grips, then clip a portion of the image using a rectangular clipping frame. Remove the clipping frame and then use a polygonal clipping frame.
❑ Adjust the brightness, contrast, and fade of the image.
❑ Make the Lines layer current. Use commands such as **LINE, ARC, PLINE**, and **SPLINE** to trace a portion of the image.
❑ Make the Image layer current and freeze the Lines layer. Then, unload all of the images on the Image layer using the **Unload** button in the **Image Manager** dialog box.
❑ Thaw the Lines layer and save the drawing as EX14-1.

WORKING WITH VECTOR FILES

A vector file contains objects defined by XYZ coordinates. AutoCAD's native file format (.dwg) is a vector file. You can also work with other vector file types. These types include DXF, WMF, SAT, EPS, 3DS, STL, and DXX. The two most commonly used types, DXF and WMF, are covered in the next sections.

PROFESSIONAL TIP Though 3D Studio MAX and VIZ can both import .dwg files directly, there can be some problems. It is better to save the AutoCAD drawing as a 3DS file, then import the 3DS file into 3D Studio. The 3DS file type is the native file type for 3D Studio through Release 4.

DXF Files

The DXF file is a generic file type that defines AutoCAD geometry in an ASCII text file. Other programs that recognize the DXF format can then "read" this file. The DXF file format retains the mathematical definitions of AutoCAD objects in vector form. The DXF objects imported into other vector programs, or opened in AutoCAD, can be edited as needed.

Saving DXF files

SAVEAS
DXFOUT

File
➥ Save As...

To save DXF files, select **Save As...** from the **File** pull-down menu or type SAVEAS or DXFOUT at the Command: prompt. This opens the **Save Drawing As** dialog box. See Figure 14-10. Select the DXF file type from the **Save as type:** drop-down list. If you type DXFOUT, the DXF file type is automatically selected. Name the file and specify a location where you want to save it. Notice that you can select different "versions" of DXF. This is to ensure that the file you save is "backward compatible." For example, if you are sharing the file with somebody using AutoCAD R14, save the DXF as that "version" to ensure AutoCAD R14 can read the file.

When a DXF file is saved, all geometry in the drawing is saved, regardless of the current zoom percentage or selected objects. However, the current zoom percentage is saved in the DXF file. As explained later, this differs from the WMF format.

The DXF file format saves any surfaced or solid 3D objects as 3D geometry. When a DXF file with 3D geometry is opened, the surfaced or solid 3D geometry remains intact. In addition, the current **SHADEMODE** setting is saved in the DXF file.

For 2000i Users...

The standard file selection dialog box (such as that used for the **Save Drawing As** dialog box and **Select File** dialog box shown in Figure 14-10 and Figure 14-11) has been modified for AutoCAD 2000i. See *AutoCAD and its Applications—Basics* for a complete description of standard file selection dialog box features.

Figure 14-10.
The **Save Drawing As** dialog box is used to save a DXF file.

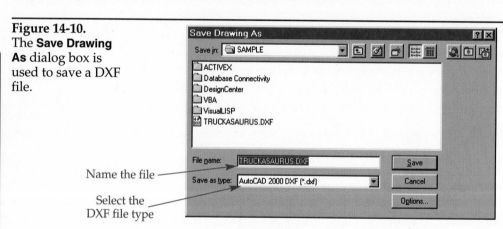

Name the file

Select the DXF file type

> **NOTE**
>
> Not all programs that can import DXF files are capable of correctly "reading" 3D objects or the **SHADEMODE** setting.

Opening DXF files

To open a DXF file, select **Open** from the **File** pull-down menu or type OPEN or DXFIN at the Command: prompt. The **Select File** dialog box appears, Figure 14-11. Select **DXF (*.dxf)** from the **Files of type:** drop-down list. If you type DXFIN, this is automatically selected. Then, select the DXF file you want to open. Notice that there is no preview when the file is selected. AutoCAD does not support previews for the DXF file type. Finally, pick the **Open** button. The DXF file is always opened into a new document window.

Figure 14-11.
When importing a DXF file, the **Select File** dialog box appears after selecting **Open** from the **File** pull-down menu or typing DXFIN.

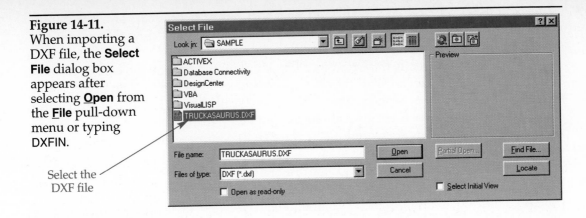

Select the DXF file

To place a DXF file into the current drawing, insert it as a block. If you do not want it inserted as a block, open (**DXFIN**) the file, copy it to the clipboard ([Ctrl]+[C]), and paste ([Ctrl]+[V]) it into the current drawing. The multiple document interface of AutoCAD 2000 makes this easy. Refer to Chapter 12 in *AutoCAD and its Applications—Basics*.

PROFESSIONAL TIP

NOTE

If you open a DXF file, make changes, and then pick the **Save** button (**QSAVE**), the **Save Drawing As** dialog box appears.

Windows Metafiles

The Windows metafile (WMF) file format is often used to exchange data with desktop publishing programs. To create a WMF file from objects drawn in AutoCAD, select **Export...** from the **File** pull-down menu or type EXPORT or WMFOUT at the Command: prompt. This displays the **Export Data** dialog box. Select Metafile (*.wmf) in the **Save as type:** drop-down list. Typing WMFOUT at the Command: prompt displays the **Create WMF File** dialog box. This is the same dialog box with Metafile (*.wmf) file type automatically selected. After specifying the file name and folder location in either dialog box and picking the **Save** button, you must select the objects to place in the file. Press [Enter] when all of the objects are selected and the WMF file is saved.

Only the portions of selected objects visible on-screen are written into the file. If part of a selected object goes off the screen, that part is "clipped." Also, the current view resolution affects the appearance of a Windows metafile. For example, when **VIEWRES** is set low, circles in your AutoCAD drawing may look like polygons. When saved to a Windows metafile, the objects are polygons rather than circles.

| EXPORT |
| WMFOUT |

File
⮡ Export...

NOTE

Windows metafiles are 2D files. Any 3D objects exported as a WMF are translated into 2D projections plan to the current view.

| IMPORT |
| IMP |
| WMFIN |

Insert
⮡ Windows Metafile...

To import a Windows metafile, select **Windows Metafile...** from the **Insert** pull-down menu or type IMP or IMPORT at the Command: prompt. This opens the **Import File** dialog box. Select Metafile (*.wmf) in the **Save as type:** drop-down list, then select a file. You can also type WMFIN at the Command: prompt. This displays the **Import WMF** dialog box. Both of these dialog boxes have a preview window where you can see the image before you import it.

A Windows metafile is imported as a block made up of all the objects in the file. You can explode the block if you need to edit the objects within it. If an object is not filled, it is created as a polyline when brought into AutoCAD. This includes arcs and circles. Objects composed of several closed polylines to represent fills are created from solid fill objects, as if created using the **SOLID** command with the **FILL** system variable off.

There are two settings used to control the appearance of Windows metafiles imported into AutoCAD. Type WMFOPTS at the Command: prompt or pick the **Options...** button in the "import" dialog box. The **WMF In Options** dialog box is displayed. The dialog box contains the following two check boxes.

- **Wire Frame (No Fills).** When checked, filled areas are imported only as outlines. Otherwise, filled areas are imported as filled objects (when **FILL** is on).
- **Wide Lines.** When this option is checked, the relative line widths of lines and borders from the WMF file are maintained. Otherwise, they are imported using a zero width.

WORKING WITH POSTSCRIPT

PostScript is a copyrighted page description language developed by Adobe Systems. PostScript files are widely used in desktop publishing and can be either raster or vector. AutoCAD can import and export PostScript files. This allows you to work with raster or vector files to create presentation-quality graphics and then save the graphics in a format that most desktop publishing software programs can read.

The **PSIN** and **PSOUT** commands are used to import and export Encapsulated PostScript (.eps) files. The **IMPORT** and **EXPORT** commands can also be used. The **PSDRAG** command controls the visibility of the imported image as it is being inserted. A value of 0 will display the PostScript image as an outline, whereas a value of 1 will display the image as you drag it around. The quality, or resolution, of the displayed image is controlled with the **PSQUALITY** command. The pattern that fills the graphic is set with the **PSFILL** command.

Adding Fill Patterns to an Object

Using the **PSFILL** command, you can add PostScript fill patterns to a closed polyline. The types of fill patterns available are shown in Figure 14-12. To access the command, type PSFILL at the Command: prompt. Enter a question mark to see a list of available pattern names. These patterns are defined in the acad.psf file. Type the full name of the pattern you wish to use. AutoCAD does not display the pattern, but includes it in the file when **PSOUT** is used.

Each pattern prompts for different values. For example, the Radialgray fill pattern displays a highlight in the center of the selected polyline, and darkens toward the outer edges. You can control the brightness of the highlight (ForegroundGray), and the darkness of the edges (BackgroundGray).

```
Command: PSFILL↵
Select polyline: (pick the polyline to be filled)
Enter PostScript fill pattern name (. = none) or [?] <.>: RADIALGRAY↵
Enter Levels <256>: ↵
Enter ForegroundGray <0>: ↵
Enter BackgroundGray <100>: ↵
```

AutoCAD User's Guide 24

For 2000i Users...

You can export PostScript files from AutoCAD 2000i, but you cannot import PostScript files. The **PSIN** command is not available, nor is the Encapsulated PostScript (.eps) option in the **Import File** dialog box.

Figure 14-12.
The fill patterns
available with the
PSFILL command.

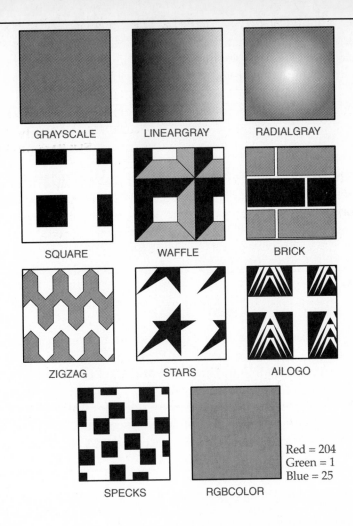

Notice that no change appears on the screen. However, the pattern is included in the file when you use the **PSOUT** command. The appearance of several Radialgray settings are shown in Figure 14-13.

When the **PSOUT** command is used, all **PSFILL** patterns are automatically surrounded by a polyline. This polyline shows on the final print. If you do not want a polyline to surround the fill, place an asterisk (*) in front of the pattern name as shown in the command sequence below. Entering a period in place of a name removes the fill pattern from the selected polyline.

> Enter PostScript fill pattern name (. = none) or [?] <.>: *GRAYSCALE↵

Figure 14-13.
Changing the value of the **Radialgray PSFILL** pattern creates different effects.

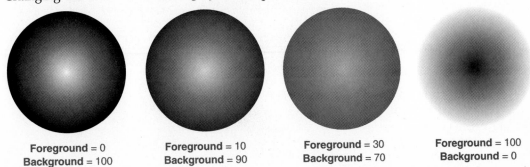

Additional custom fill patterns can be added to the acad.psf file. This is an ASCII text file and can be edited with any text editor. However, the proper PostScript language must be used. See the *AutoCAD Customization Guide* for the correct procedures. The customization guide can be found in the online documentation in the help files.

EXERCISE 14-2

❑ Begin a new drawing named EX14-2.
❑ Draw four rectangles, each measuring 1 × 2 units.
❑ Use the following **PSFILL** patterns to fill the rectangles.
   ❑ Lineargray (use 256 levels and 2 cycles)
   ❑ Radialgray
   ❑ Waffle
   ❑ Stars (BackgroundGray = 20, ForegroundGray = 85)
❑ Save the drawing as EX14-2.

Exporting a PostScript Image

Any drawing created in AutoCAD can be converted to a PostScript file using the **EXPORT** or **PSOUT** commands. A PostScript file is usually created if PostScript fonts or images are added to the drawing, or if the **PSFILL** command is used to add patterns. Remember, an Encapsulated PostScript file can only be printed by a PostScript printer.

If you use the **PSOUT** command, the **Create PostScript File** dialog box is displayed. Enter a name and pick the **OK** button. If you entered EXPORT, the **Export Data** dialog box appears. Pick Encapsulated PS (*.eps) in the **Save as type:** drop-down list, enter a name, and pick **OK**.

A screen preview image can be included with the file. A preview is used by many desktop publishing programs. It allows an artist to see the image. To specify a preview image, select the **Options...** button from the export dialog box. The **PostScript Out Options** dialog box appears. See Figure 14-14.

To create a preview image, select the **EPSI** or **TIFF** radio button in the **Preview** area and then select an image size from the **Pixels** area. The default size of 128 × 128 pixels is small, so it does not slow down the software when the image is imported. Enter appropriate values in the **What to plot**, **Size Units**, **Scale**, and **Paper Size** areas. Pick the **OK** button to return to the **Create PostScript File** dialog box. Pick the **Save** button and the PostScript file is created.

For 2000i Users...

To access the **PostScript Out Options** dialog box in AutoCAD 2000i, select **Options...** from the **Tools** menu in the **Export Data** dialog box.

Figure 14-14.
The **PostScript Out Options** dialog box is used to select settings when exporting a PostScript file.

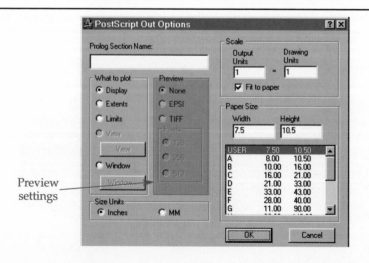

Preview settings

NOTE If you use the **EXPORT** command to export a PostScript file, the **Options...** button is grayed out.

Printing PostScript Files

After the file has been created, it can be printed by a PostScript printer using the DOS prompt. The DOS prompt can be accessed by selecting Programs from the Windows Start menu and then picking MS-DOS Prompt. Then, type the following.

> C:*path to file* > **COPY** *filename.***EPS LPT1:**↵ *(where LPT1 is the parallel port where the system printer is connected)*

or

> C:*path to file* > **PRINT** *filename.***EPS**↵

You cannot use the Windows "drag and drop" capability to print PostScript files. PostScript files must be printed from the DOS prompt.

Importing a PostScript Image

You can use the **IMPORT** or **PSIN** commands to import a PostScript file into AutoCAD. If you use the **IMPORT** command, you must specify Encapsulated PS (*.eps) in the **Save as type:** drop-down list of the **Import File** dialog box. If you use the **PSIN** command, Encapsulated PS (*.eps) is automatically selected in the **Select PostScript File** dialog box. Select the file and pick the **OK** button. It may take a few moments to load the file, depending on its size. Then, the following prompts appear:

> Specify insertion point <0,0,0>: ↵
> Specify scale factor: *(drag the image to fit and pick)*

For 2000i Users...

PostScript files cannot be imported in AutoCAD 2000i. The **PSIN** command is not available, nor is the Encapsulated PostScript (.eps) option in the **Import File** dialog box.

If **PSDRAG** is set to 0, only the outline of the box that represents the image is displayed until you set the scale factor. If you wish to see the image as you drag it, set **PSDRAG** to 1, then use the **PSIN** command to bring in the PostScript.

Now you can place additional entities or text on the drawing. You can then save it again as a PostScript file with the **PSOUT** command or save it as a DWG drawing file.

NOTE Once the **PSIN** or **IMPORT** commands have been used to bring a PostScript file into AutoCAD, then the graphics can be printed through AutoCAD.

PostScript File Quality

The **PSIN** command renders an image according to the value of the **PSQUALITY** system variable. If **PSQUALITY** is set to 0, only a box representing the image is displayed with the file name inside. The default value is 75. This displays the image with 75 pixels per AutoCAD drawing unit. Higher quality values mean longer rendering time. A negative value, such as –75, renders at the same resolution but does not fill PostScript outlines.

NOTE

PostScript fonts are a copyrighted product and must be purchased from authorized dealers. Like all software, the licensing agreement must be followed.

Chapter Test

Answer the following questions on a separate sheet of paper.
1. Name four common formats of raster images that can be imported into AutoCAD.
2. Name the raster file that is the CompuServe image format.
3. What command allows you to attach a raster file to the current AutoCAD drawing?
4. What is the display status of an inserted image that has been unloaded?
5. What two shapes can be used to clip a raster image?
6. What is the function of the **IMAGEADJUST** command?
7. Name two commands that allow you to export bitmap files.
8. Give the name and file type of the vector file that can be exchanged between object-based programs.
9. Name the two sets of commands that allow you to import and export the file type in Question 8.
10. Name the two commands that enable you to import and export PostScript files in AutoCAD.
11. How is an imported DXF inserted into the drawing?
12. What is the three-letter extension given to PostScript files when they are exported?

Drawing Problems

1. Locate some sample raster files with the .jpg, .pcx, or .tif file extensions. These files are often included as samples with software. They can also be downloaded from the Internet, or from computer online services. With the permission of your instructor or supervisor, create a subfolder on your hard disk drive and copy the raster files there.

2. Choose one of your smaller raster files and import it into AutoCAD.
   A. Insert the image so it fills the entire screen.
   B. Undo and insert the image again using a scale factor that fills half the screen with the image.
   C. Stretch the original object using grips, then experiment with different clipping boundaries. Stretch the image after it has been clipped and observe the result.
   D. Create a layer named Raster. Create a second layer named Object. Give each layer the color of your choice. Set the current layer to Raster.
   E. Import the same image next to the previous one at the same scale factor.
   F. Set the current layer to Object and use any AutoCAD drawing commands to trace the outline of the second raster image.

G. Unload the raster image or freeze the Raster layer.

H. Save the drawing as P14-2.

3. For this problem, you will import several raster files into AutoCAD. Then, you will trace the object in each file and save it as a block or wblock to be used on other drawings.

   A. Find as many raster files as you can that contain simple objects, shapes, or figures that you might use in other drawings.

   B. Create a template drawing containing Object and Raster layers.

   C. Import each raster file into AutoCAD on the Raster layer using the appropriate command. Set the Object layer current and trace the shape or objects using AutoCAD drawing commands.

   D. Detach the raster information, keeping only the traced lines of the object.

   E. Save the object as a block or wblock using an appropriate file-naming system.

   F. After all blocks have been created, insert each one into a single drawing and label each with its name. Include a path if necessary.

   G. Save the drawing as P14-3.

   H. Print or plot the final drawing.

4. In this problem, you will create either a style sheet to be used for drawing standards or a presentation sheet for a detail, assembly, or pictorial drawing.

   A. Begin a new drawing and name it P14-4. The drawing should be set up to A-size dimensions and the orientation should be portrait. (A portrait orientation has the long side orientated vertically.)

   B. Create at least two new text styles using TrueType fonts.

   C. Draw one or more closed shapes, such as rectangles. Use the **PSFILL** command to place a pattern of your choice inside the shapes.

   D. Use the various text styles to place title and related text on your drawing. See the example below. Add other graphics or text as desired.

   E. Save the drawing as P14-4. Then, use the **PSOUT** command to save the file as P14-4.EPS.

   F. Start a drawing from scratch. Use the **PSIN** command to import P14-4.EPS into AutoCAD.

   G. Plot the drawing on a plotter or laser printer. If you have a PostScript printer, generate a printed copy of the EPS file through the DOS prompt.

5. Begin a new drawing named P14-5 using P14-4 as the prototype.
   A. Insert the blocks you created in Problem 3 into your style sheet. Arrange them in any order you wish.
   B. Add any notes you need to identify this drawing as a sheet of library shapes. Be sure each shape is identified with its file name and location (path).
   C. Save the drawing with the current name (P14-5). Then, use the **PSOUT** command to create an EPS file using the same name.
   D. Start a drawing from scratch. Use the **PSIN** command to import P14-5.EPS into AutoCAD.
   E. Print or plot the drawing.
   F. If you have a PostScript printer, create a PostScript print of the file.

6. Add a raster image to one of your title block template drawings as a design element or a company logo. Import an existing raster image or create your own using a program such as Windows Paint.

CHAPTER 15

Rendering with AutoCAD

Learning Objectives

After completing this chapter, you will be able to:

- Create shaded and rendered drawings.
- Place light sources.
- Apply surface textures and materials to models.
- Map materials onto AutoCAD objects.
- Create a background for a model.
- Use fog to create the appearance of depth and distance.
- Locate and manipulate landscaping objects.
- Save views, scenes, and image files.
- Render and save bitmaps using Windows Clipboard.

Three-dimensional computer models can provide more information than a set of two-dimensional blueprints. The computer allows you to visualize the model from all sides, including the inside. Surface textures and materials can be added to the model. Rendering "colors" the model with the assigned material. The model can also be placed in a scene with lights, a background, landscaping objects, and fog. Views and scenes can then be created and saved, rendered, and placed in documents or on a Web site.

You can render a model with either the **SHADEMODE** command or the **RENDER** command. The **SHADEMODE** command, which is covered in Chapter 9, provides some control over the type of display and almost no control over lighting. Materials are also not rendered with the **SHADEMODE** command. The **RENDER** command gives you complete control over the lighting and surfaces of your model.

NOTE

You have almost unlimited options and variations when rendering 3D models. Components such as color, light, shadow, sunshine, time of year, location on earth, material, texture, reflections, roughness, viewpoint, and scene (and combinations of all of these) lead to a wide variety of renderings. The purpose of this chapter is to introduce you to the rendering features available in AutoCAD. This chapter does not cover all the possibilities and details surrounding use of the renderer. Use the online help files in AutoCAD for additional information. If you want additional instruction in rendering and animation, sign up for a course at an Autodesk Training Center in your area.

AutoCAD uses four types of lighting. These are ambient, distant, point, and spot. See Figure 15-1. It is important to understand how each type applies light to a model.

Ambient light is like natural light. It is the same intensity everywhere. All faces of the object receive the same amount of light. Ambient light cannot create highlights. The intensity of ambient light can be changed or turned off, but ambient light cannot be concentrated in one area.

A *distant light* is a directed light source with parallel light rays. This acts much like the sun, striking all objects in your model on the same side and with the same intensity. The direction and intensity of a distant light can be changed.

A *point light* is like a lightbulb, shining out in all directions. A point light can create highlights. The intensity of a point light "falls off," or weakens, over distance. Other programs, such as 3D Studio VIZ or MAX, call these lights *omni lights*.

A *spotlight* is like a distant light, but it projects in a cone shape. A spotlight is placed closer to the object than a distant light. Spotlights have a hotspot and a falloff. Both of these features are discussed later in this chapter.

Figure 15-1.
AutoCAD uses ambient, spot, point, and distant light. Ambient light is an overall light and does not have an icon representation. You can see here how the other three lights strike objects.

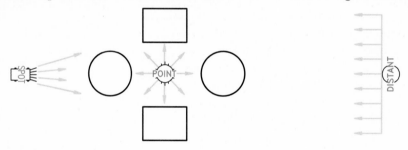

Properties of Lights

There are several properties that affect how a light illuminates an object. These include the angle of incidence, reflectivity of the object's surface, and the distance that the light is from the object.

Angle of incidence

AutoCAD renders the faces of a model based on the angle that light rays strike the faces. This angle is called the *angle of incidence*. See Figure 15-2. A face that is perpendicular to light rays receives the most light. As the angle of incidence decreases, the amount of light striking the face also decreases.

Reflectivity

The angle at which light rays are reflected off a surface is called the *angle of reflection*. The angle of reflection is always equal to the angle of incidence. Refer to Figure 15-2.

The "brightness" of light reflected from an object is actually the number of light rays that reach your eyes. A surface that reflects a bright light, such as a mirror, is reflecting most of the light rays that strike it. The amount of reflection you see is called the *highlight*. The highlight is determined by the angle of the viewpoint relative to the angle of incidence. Refer to Figure 15-2.

The surface of the object affects how light is reflected. A smooth surface has a high *specular factor*. The specular factor indicates the number of light rays that have the same angle of reflection. Surfaces that are not smooth have a low specular factor. These surfaces are called *matte*. Matte surfaces *diffuse*, or "spread out," the light as it strikes the surface. This means that few of the light rays have the same angle of reflection. Figure 15-3 illustrates the difference between matte and high specular finishes. Surfaces can also vary in *roughness*. Roughness is a measure of the polish on a surface. This also affects how diffused the reflected light is.

Figure 15-2.
The amount of reflection, or highlight, you see depends on the angle that you view the object from.

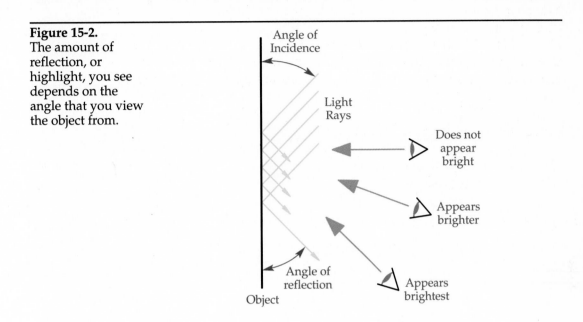

Figure 15-3.
Matte surfaces produce diffuse light. This is also referred to as a low specular factor. Shiny surfaces reflect light evenly, and have a high specular factor.

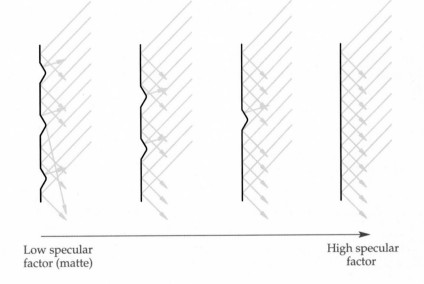

Low specular factor (matte)

High specular factor

Distance
The farther an object is from a point light or spotlight, the less light will reach the object. The intensity of light decreases over distance. This decrease is called *falloff* or *attenuation*. Attenuation only applies to point lights and spotlights. The following attenuation settings are available.
- **None.** Applies the same light intensity regardless of distance. In other words, no falloff is calculated.
- **Inverse Linear.** The illumination of an object decreases in inverse proportion to the distance. For example, if an object is 2 units from the light, it receives 1/2 of the full light. If the object is 4 units away, it receives 1/4 of the full light.

- **Inverse Square.** The illumination of an object decreases in inverse proportion to the square of the distance. For example, if an object is 2 units from the light, it receives $(1/2)^2$, or 1/4, of the full light. If the object is 4 units away, it receives $(1/4)^2$, or 1/16, of the full light. As you can see, falloff is greater for each unit of distance with the **Inverse Square** option than with the **Inverse Linear** option.

NOTE

The layout in Exercise 15-1 is used throughout this chapter to illustrate aspects of rendering. This exercise can be completed in approximately 30 minutes. It combines the use of 3D shapes, user coordinate systems, and viewports.

EXERCISE 15-1

❏ The models created in this exercise are used throughout the rest of this chapter.
❏ Begin a new drawing.
❏ Set units to architectural.
❏ Set limits to 24′,18′. Set the grid to 6″ and snap to 2″. Zoom all.
❏ Create the following layers and assign the colors indicated.

Layer	Color
Floor-Wall	Cyan
Table	Red
Pyramid	Yellow
Cone	Green
Torus	Blue

❏ Make the Floor-Wall layer current.
❏ Using the **3DFACE** command, draw the floor 8′ square starting at (0,0). Draw the wall 8′ long and 6′ high. You may have to change your viewpoint or UCS to draw the wall. This forms the background.
❏ Set a viewpoint of –2.5,–3,1.5. Save the view.
❏ Create a UCS at the lower-front corner of the floor. Save this UCS orientation as FLOOR. Note: Depending on how you drew the floor and wall, this UCS may coincide with the WCS. If it does, you do not need to save the UCS.
❏ Create a 1″ cube surface model on layer 0 by using the **Box** option in the **3D** command or by selecting **Box3d** in the **3D Objects** dialog box. Save the cube as a block named CUBE with an insertion point at one corner.
❏ Set the Table layer current. Use the CUBE block to construct the table. Insert one cube for the first leg and enter the following values:
  ❏ Insertion point: X = 2′10″, Y = 2′
  ❏ Scale factors: X = 4, Y = 4, Z = 16
  ❏ Rotation angle = 0°
❏ Array the first leg using a unit cell distance of 24″ for 2 rows and 2 columns.
❏ Use the CUBE block again for the tabletop as follows.
  ❏ Insertion point: X = 2′10″, Y = 2′, Z = 16″
  ❏ Scale factors: X = 28, Y = 28, Z = 2
  ❏ Rotation angle = 0°
❏ Establish a new UCS on the top surface of the tabletop at the lower-left corner. Save this UCS orientation as Tabletop.
❏ Change the current layer to Pyramid. Select **Pyramid** from the **3D Objects** dialog box or select the **Pyramid** option in the **3D** command. Make sure the Tabletop UCS is current. Then, locate the first base point of the pyramid at X = 12, Y = 10.

Locate the second base point as @0,–8. Locate the third point as @8,0. Locate the fourth point as @0,8. Locate the apex point at 16,6,12. Use the **ROTATE** command or grips to rotate the pyramid 45°. Use the second point of the pyramid (closest to the UCS origin) as the rotation base point.

❑ Set the Cone layer current and draw a surfaced cone centered at X = 8, Y = 20 with an 8″ diameter base, 0″ diameter top, and a 12″ height. Leave the number of segments at 16.

❑ Set the current layer to Torus. Set **ISOLINES** = 12. Draw a solid torus located at X = 14, Y = 14, Z = 22. The torus diameter is 18″ and the tube diameter is 5″.

❑ The drawing should look like the one shown below.

❑ Restore the UCS orientation named FLOOR (or the WCS).

❑ Save the drawing as 3DSHAPES and remain in the drawing editor. These objects will be used throughout this chapter.

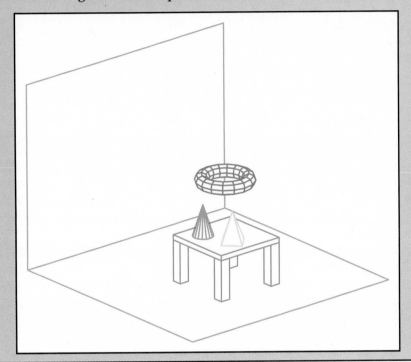

Preparing for Rendering

If you are creating a drawing or model that will be rendered, you must plan to provide enough space around the model to place lights. Creating three viewports using the **VPORTS** command can help. The large view can be used to see a 3D view of the model. The two small viewports can be used for a plan view and a different 3D view, or any other view desired. It is often easier to place lights in the plan view.

An example of this type of layout is shown in Figure 15-4. To create this layout, open the 3DSHAPES drawing created in Exercise 15-1. Next select **Named Viewports...** in the **Viewports** cascading menu in the **View** pull-down menu, pick the **Display Viewports Dialog** button in the **Viewports** toolbar or type VPORTS at the Command: line. This will open the **Viewports** dialog box. In the **New Viewports** tab, select **Three: Right** in the **Standard viewports** area. In the **Apply to:** drop-down list select **Display**. In the **Setup:** drop down list select **3D**. In the **Preview** area pick the top-left viewport to make it active, then select **Top** in the **Change view to:** drop-down list. Pick the lower-left viewport, then select **SE Isometric** in the **Change view to:** drop-down list. Finally, pick the right viewport and select **Current** in the **Change view to:** drop-down list. Press **OK** when done. Pick in the right viewport to make it active, then perform a **Zoom Extents**. This will create an arrangement similar to the one displayed in Figure 15-4.

Figure 15-4.
The final arrangement of viewports for the tutorial in the text.

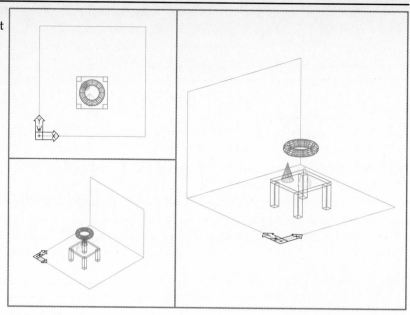

Using the **Lights** Dialog Box

After the objects in your model are constructed, placing lights is the first step in creating a scene for rendering. Consider the properties for each type of light when choosing the lights for the model. Place as many lights as you want. When you create a scene, pick only the lights needed for that scene. You can select a different combination of lights for each scene. A *scene* is like a photograph of your model.

Lights are placed using the **LIGHT** command. Access this command by picking the **Lights** button in the **Render** toolbar, selecting **Light...** from the **Render** cascading menu in the **View** pull-down menu, or typing LIGHT at the Command: prompt. The **Lights** dialog box is then displayed, Figure 15-5. Each light you add into the model (other than ambient) must be named. The name can be up to eight characters long. Uppercase and lowercase letters can be typed, but AutoCAD changes the name to all uppercase. Spaces cannot be used in a light name. All light names must be different.

Figure 15-5.
The **Lights** dialog box.

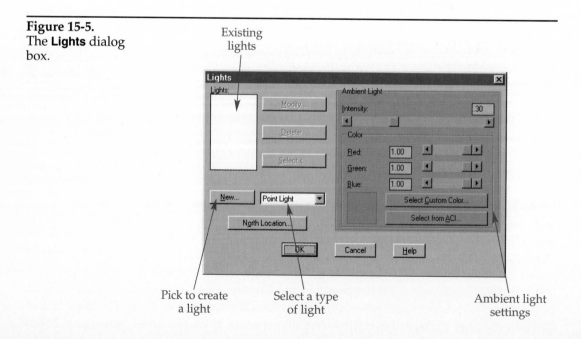

When placing lights in a drawing, use XYZ coordinates or filters to specify a 3D location. Once a light is placed, an icon representing the light appears in the drawing editor. The icons representing point, distant, and spotlights are shown in Figure 15-6.

Ambient light is also set in the **Lights** dialog box. Use the slider bar or type a value in the text box in the **Ambient Light** area to adjust the intensity. You can also change the ambient light color by adjusting the appropriate slider bars. Adjusting light color is discussed later in the chapter.

After lights are created, you can fine-tune them by changing their intensity, location, and color. Lights can also be turned off or deleted if needed. Once a light is selected from the list in the **Lights** dialog box, pick the **Modify...** button to adjust intensity, position, color, and falloff.

Figure 15-6.
Point lights, spotlights, and distant lights appear as icons on the screen.

Placing Point Lights in the Model

A point light radiates light rays outward from a central point, much like a light-bulb. Other programs, such as 3D Studio VIZ or MAX, call point lights *omni lights.* A point light requires a location and a name. Remember, a name can have up to eight characters.

To place a point light in the 3DSHAPES drawing created in Exercise 15-1, first select **Point Light** in the drop-down list at the left of the **Lights** dialog box. Then, pick the **New...** button. This displays the **New Point Light** dialog box shown in Figure 15-7A. Enter the name, such as P-1, in the **Light Name:** text box and pick **OK**. The **Lights** dialog box returns and P-1 is displayed and highlighted in the **Lights:** list box.

Now, pick **Modify...** and the **Modify Point Light** dialog box shown in Figure 15-7B is displayed. Pick the **Modify** button in the **Position** area and you are returned to the graphics window. The prompt on the command line requests a light location. You can pick the location, use filters, or enter coordinates at the keyboard as follows.

        Enter light location <*current*>:**4',3'2",8'**↵

The dialog box then reappears. Pick **OK** in the **Modify Point Light** and **Lights** dialog boxes to complete the command and return to the graphics window. Now, zoom all in the right viewport.

Figure 15-7.
Specifying a point
light. These two dialog
boxes are identical
except for the title bar.
A—The **New Point
Light** dialog box.
B—The **Modify Point
Light** dialog box.

A

B

Setting the Icon Scale

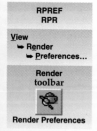

RPREF
RPR

View
↳ Render
  ↳ Preferences...

Render
toolbar

Render Preferences

After you place the point light, you should see the light icon directly above the torus. However, it is too small to be seen clearly. You can change the scale of icons in the **Rendering Preferences** dialog box, Figure 15-8. To access this dialog box, pick the **Render Preferences** button in the **Render** toolbar, select **Preferences...** from the **Render** cascading menu in the **View** pull-down menu, or type RPR or RPREF at the Command: prompt. Pick the **Light Icon Scale:** text box and enter 24. Pick **OK** to return to your model. The icon is now large enough to be seen clearly, Figure 15-9. The light name P-1 appears in the icon.

AutoCAD and its Applications—Advanced

Figure 15-8.
The icon scale is set in the **Rendering Preferences** dialog box.

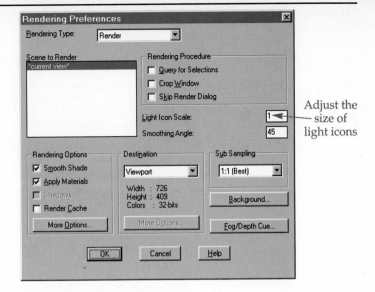

Adjust the size of light icons

Figure 15-9.
After increasing the icon scale, the light icons are larger and can be clearly seen on the screen.

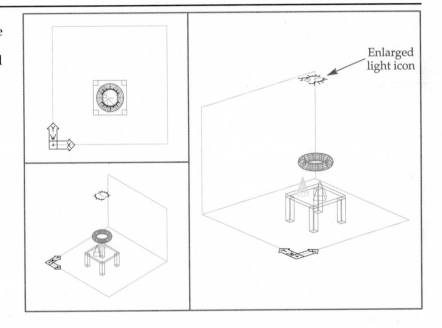

Enlarged light icon

Placing Distant Lights in the Model

The sun's rays are approximately parallel when they reach earth and strike all objects with the same intensity. A distant light is used to simulate the sun's rays in your model. An accurate representation of the sun's angle can be achieved through the use of the sun angle calculator.

Distant lights are placed in the same way as point lights. However, a target location is needed as well as a light location. To place a distant light, first open the **Lights** dialog box. Then, pick **Distant Light** from the lights drop-down list. Pick the **New...** button to display the **New Distant Light** dialog box, Figure 15-10. Notice that this dialog box is different than the **New Point Light** dialog.

Enter a name, such as D-1, in the **Light Name:** text box. The location of the distant light can be entered as XYZ values in the **Light Source Vector** text boxes. Remember, these coordinates are relative to the origin of the current UCS. In addition, you can graphically select the location of the light using the **Azimuth:** and **Altitude:** image tiles. The *azimuth* is the angle *in* the XY plane. This can also be thought of as the angular

Figure 15-10.
The **New Distant Light** dialog box.

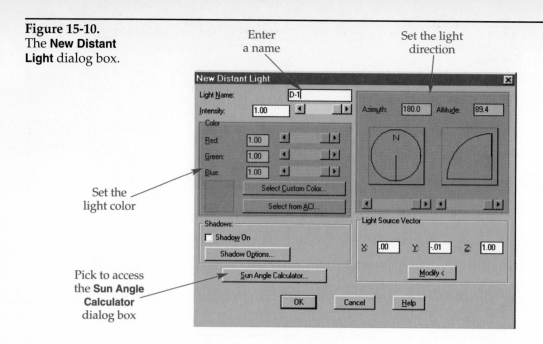

Enter a name

Set the light direction

Set the light color

Pick to access the **Sun Angle Calculator** dialog box

direction of the sun looking south from the North Pole. The *altitude* is the angle *from* the XY plane. This measurement represents the angle of the sun above the horizon. The location can also be set by picking the **Modify** button and entering coordinates at the Command: prompt as follows.

> Enter light direction TO <*current*>: *(pick point P1 in Figure 15-11)*
> Enter light direction FROM <*current*>: **6',–4',30"**⏎

Pick **OK** to return to the **Lights** dialog box. Pick **OK** in that dialog box to return to the graphics window. The distant light is placed in the drawing.

You may need to zoom out in one or more viewports to see the new light icon. Place one more distant light in the model using the following information.

Name	Light direction to	Light direction from
D-2	Point P2 in Figure 15-11	–2',0,30"

The model should look like Figure 15-12 after the second distant light is placed.

PROFESSIONAL TIP

The intensity of the sun's rays do not diminish from one point on earth to another. They are weakened by the angle at which they strike the earth. Therefore, falloff and attenuation are not factors with distant lights. The intensity of a distant light can be changed, but is never greater than 1.0. Similarly, ambient light—which represents the constant background illumination of all objects—can never have an intensity greater than 1.0. Keep ambient light low to avoid "washing out" the image.

Distant lights are especially important in architectural models and any model in which sunlight is a factor. It is good practice to locate as many distant lights in the model as you will need to create scenes at different times of day. Locate distant lights at the extents of the drawing, and always choose only one distant light per scene.

AutoCAD and its Applications—Advanced

Figure 15-11.
The pick points for setting distant light directions in the tutorial.

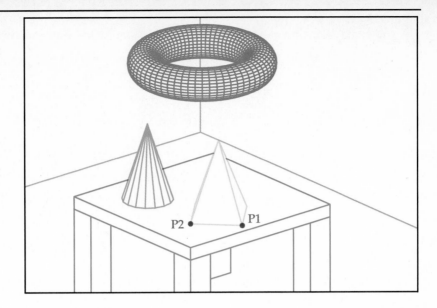

Figure 15-12.
The tutorial model with distant lights placed.

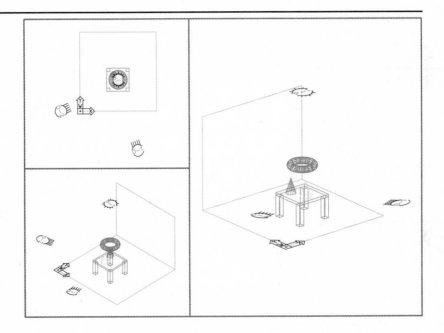

Using the sun angle calculator

AutoCAD has a feature that allows you to quickly set a distant light to replicate the lighting effects of the sun. This feature is called the **Sun Angle Calculator**. To access the **Sun Angle Calculator**, first open either the **Modify Distant Light** or **New Distant Light** dialog box. Both dialog boxes are exactly the same except for the name. Next, pick the **Sun Angle Calculator...** button. This displays the **Sun Angle Calculator** dialog box, Figure 15-13. The sun's angle is adjusted using the values on the left side of this dialog box. The image tiles on the right side graphically represent all the values on the left.

- **Date.** Enter the month and day in the text box, or move the slider bar to set the date desired. One pick on the slider bar arrow changes the date by one day, and one pick in the space to the left or right of the slider bar changes the date by one month. Pick and hold the slider bar and move it left and right. As you do, watch the azimuth and altitude image tiles automatically adjust.
- **Clock Time.** This is a 24-hour clock. One pick on the slider bar arrow changes the time by ten minutes, and one pick in the space to the left or right of the

Figure 15-13.
The sun angle calculator can be used to create a distant light that simulates the sun.

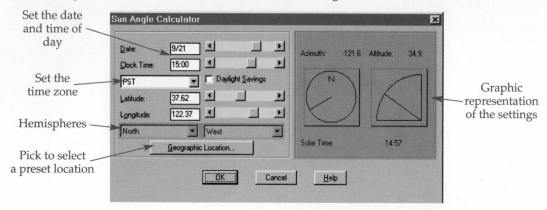

Set the date and time of day

Set the time zone

Hemispheres

Pick to select a preset location

Graphic representation of the settings

slider bar changes the time by one hour. As you move the slider bar, the azimuth and altitude image tiles automatically adjust. Do not forget to select your time zone from the drop-down list, and pick the **Daylight Savings** check box if it applies.

- **Latitude.** This is the angular location of the sun from the equator to the north or south poles. This is an angular measurement from the center of the earth, with the equator being 0° and the north and south poles 90°. This measurement represents the seasonal and daily movements of the sun, and most directly affects the altitude.
- **Longitude.** This represents the east/west location of the sun as the earth rotates. It most directly affects the angle of the sun above the horizon (altitude). This angle determines shadow length.
- **Hemispheres.** Below the **Longitude** text box are two drop-down lists where you can select either the north or south hemisphere, and either the east or west hemisphere. North America is located in the northern and western hemispheres.

If you are unsure of the exact latitude and longitude location of your model, you can select your location by picking the **Geographic Location...** button. This displays the **Geographic Location** dialog box, Figure 15-14. Use the following steps to select your location.

1. Pick the continent (or country) in the drop-down list above the map.
2. Pick the city in the **City:** list on the left of the dialog box. Its latitude and longitude are displayed in the lower left of the dialog box.

Figure 15-14.
Selecting the geographic location of your model automatically sets the latitude and longitude.

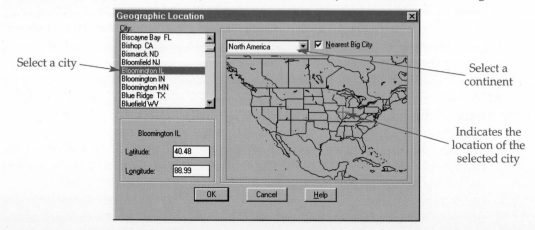

Select a city

Select a continent

Indicates the location of the selected city

If you do not know the nearest city to your location, do the following:
1. Pick the continent (or country) in the drop-down list.
2. Be sure a check mark appears in the **Nearest Big City** check box.
3. Pick your location on the map using your cursor. The nearest big city is located by the blue crosshairs, and its name is highlighted in the **City:** list.

The lower-left area of this dialog box displays the latitude and longitude of the selected city. You can change the latitude and longitude values, but the changes are not graphically updated on the map. When you pick the **OK** button, your changes are displayed in the **Sun Angle Calculator** dialog box.

In order for shadows to be displayed accurately in the model, the north direction must be set properly. By default, AutoCAD locates north in the positive Y direction of the world coordinate system. To change the north direction in your model, pick the **North Location...** button in the **Lights** dialog box. This displays the **North Location** dialog box shown in Figure 15-15.

A new north direction can be assigned by entering an angle in the **Angle:** text box or moving the slider bar. The north line changes in the image tile as the slider bar moves. If you want north to be the X direction in the WCS, enter 90 in the **Angle:** text box. You can also orient north along the Y axis of any named UCS. All named UCSs appear in the list in the **Use UCS:** area at the right of the dialog box. Pick the UCS name from the list and pick **OK**. Before selecting a UCS, be sure that the **X/Y Plane** angle is 0.

Figure 15-15.
The **North Location** dialog box.

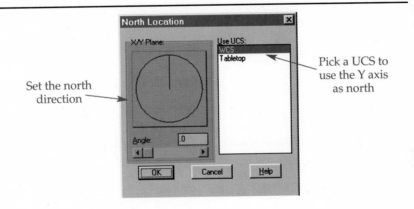

Set the north direction

Pick a UCS to use the Y axis as north

PROFESSIONAL TIP
If it appears shadows are being cast incorrectly for the location and time of day specified, it is possible that the north direction is improperly set. Check the north location to be sure it coincides with the north direction established for the model.

Placing Spotlights in the Model

A spotlight produces a cone of light. The *hotspot* is the central portion of the cone, where the light is brightest. The *falloff* is the outer portion of the cone, where the light begins to blend to shadow. See Figure 15-16A.

Spotlights are located in the same way as distant lights. First, pick **Spotlight** in the **Lights** drop-down list of the **Lights** dialog box. Then, pick the **New...** button. This displays the **New Spotlight** dialog box, Figure 15-17. Name the spotlight S-1.

The angle of the hotspot and the angle of the falloff can be set in the **Hotspot:** and **Falloff:** edit boxes. If you want the hotspot to illuminate a cone of 30° and the falloff

Figure 15-16.
The hotspot of a spotlight is the area that receives the most light. The falloff receives light, but less than the hotspot. A—The smaller cone is the hotspot. The larger cone is the falloff. B—The hotspot and falloff for the example in the text.

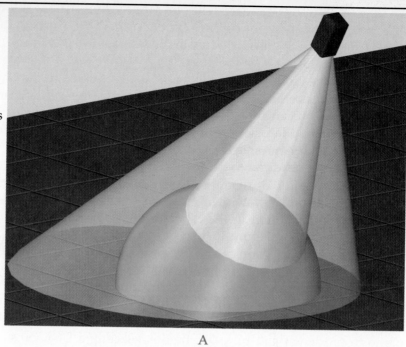

A

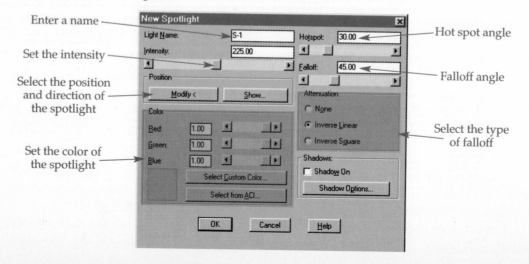

B

Figure 15-17.
The **New Spotlight** dialog box.

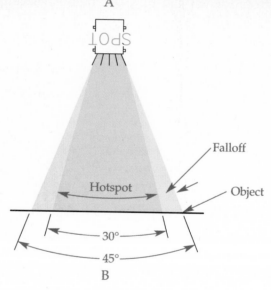

angle to be 45°, enter 30 and 45 in the appropriate text boxes. Figure 15-16B illustrates these values entered in the **New Spotlight** dialog box. The hotspot value must be less than or equal to the falloff value.

Pick the **Modify** button to locate the light in the drawing area. Enter the location at the Command: prompt as follows.

> Enter light target <*current*>: *(pick the apex of the pyramid)*
> Enter light location <*current*>: **@24,–36,48.**⏎

The dialog box returns. Pick **OK** in both dialog boxes to complete the command and return to the graphics window. Your drawing should look like Figure 15-18.

Figure 15-18.
The tutorial model after the spotlight is placed.

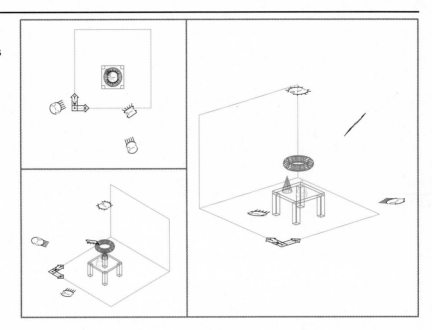

Creating Shadows

Distant, point, and spotlights can all cast shadows. There are two types of shadows that AutoCAD can create. These are raytrace and shadow map.

A *raytrace* shadow is created by beams, or rays, from the light source. These rays trace the path of light as they strike objects to create a shadow. In addition, rays can pass through transparent objects, such as green glass, and project color onto surfaces behind the object. Raytrace shadows have a well-defined edge.

A *shadow map* is a bit map generated by AutoCAD. A shadow map has soft edges that can be adjusted. Raytraced shadows cannot be adjusted to produce a soft edge. A shadow map is the only way to produce a soft-edge shadow. Shadow maps do not transmit object color from transparent objects onto the surfaces behind the object.

The options for creating shadows are the same for all lights, and are selected in the **Shadows:** area of all the light dialog boxes. See Figure 15-19. The **Shadow On** check box must be checked in order for the light to create shadows. Generating shadows in the rendered image is discussed in the next section.

Figure 15-19.
Each type of light has a **Shadows** area in the "light" dialog box.

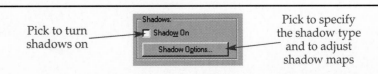

Pick to turn shadows on

Pick to specify the shadow type and to adjust shadow maps

RENDERING THE MODEL

RENDER
RR

View
→ **Render**
  → **Render...**

Render toolbar

Render

You can render your model at any time. If there are no lights in your model, AutoCAD places one behind your viewpoint (behind you). If you have placed lights in your model but have not yet constructed a "scene," AutoCAD uses all the lights and renders the current view in the active viewport. Scenes will be covered later in this chapter.

To render your model, pick the **Render** button from the **Render** toolbar, select **Render...** from the **Render** cascading menu in the **View** pull-down menu, or type RR or RENDER at the Command: prompt. All three methods open the **Render** dialog box. Make sure **Viewport** is selected in the **Destination** drop-down list. Pick the **Render** button in this dialog box. AutoCAD then displays the rendering of your model in the active viewport. See Figure 15-20.

AutoCAD can produce three different types of renderings. These are the default render, photo real, and photo raytrace. These types of rendering are shown in the **Rendering Type:** drop-down list at the top of the **Render** dialog box, Figure 15-21.

Figure 15-20.
The tutorial model rendered after the lights are placed. Note: To obtain a rendering that looks exactly like this one, you may need to adjust the intensity of the lights in your model.

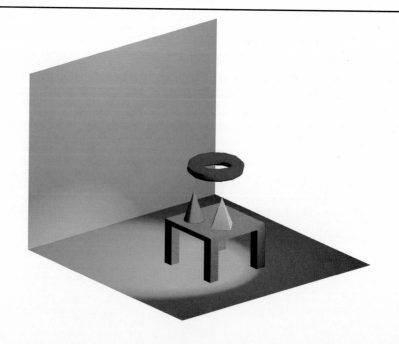

Figure 15-21.
The **Render** dialog box.

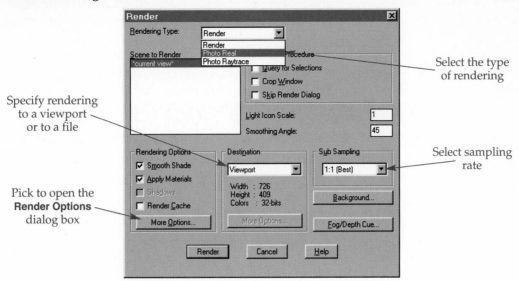

Select the type of rendering

Specify rendering to a viewport or to a file

Pick to open the **Render Options** dialog box

Select sampling rate

Standard Rendering

This is the default option when AutoCAD is first started. Notice that the **Shadows** check box in the **Rendering Options** area is disabled. Shadows are not cast when rendering a model using the **Render** option in the **Rendering Type:** drop-down list. Picking the **More Options...** button displays the **Render Options** dialog box, Figure 15-22. In this dialog box, you can choose the render quality and the 3D face controls.

The type of render quality determines the points where light intensity is calculated. The two options are:
- **Gouraud.** Light intensity is calculated at each vertex with this type of rendering. The intensity of the space between vertices is estimated. This is the lesser realistic of the two options.
- **Phong.** With this type of rendering, light intensity is calculated at each pixel. This creates realistic lighting.

The **Face Controls** area contains two items that determine whether or not hidden faces are calculated. These two items are:
- **Discard back faces.** When checked, AutoCAD does not calculate hidden faces when rendering. This setting can speed the rendering process.
- **Back face normal is negative.** A *normal vector* is perpendicular to a face. A front face has a normal vector that points outward toward the viewer and is positive. A back face normal vector points away from the viewer and is negative. This setting determines which faces on the model are back faces.

Figure 15-22.
The render quality and face control options for the **Render** selection are set in the **Render Options** dialog box.

Select the render quality

Select the face controls

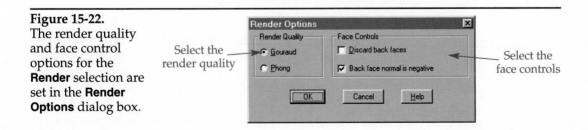

Photo Real Rendering

This type of rendering produces a more realistic image than the default render method. A photo real rendering can cast shadows. To display shadows in the rendering, the **Shadows** check box must be checked. In addition, for shadows to be cast, the lights in the 3D model must be set up to display shadows. You can refine the rendered image by selecting the **More Options...** button to display the **Photo Real Render Options** dialog box. See Figure 15-23. In addition to the face controls discussed previously, you can adjust the antialiasing, depth map shadow controls, and texture map sampling.

Figure 15-23.
This dialog box is used to select settings for a photo real rendering.

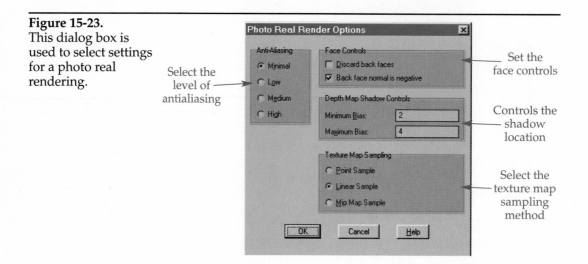

Select the level of antialiasing

Set the face controls

Controls the shadow location

Select the texture map sampling method

Antialiasing

Aliasing is the jagged edges, or "jaggies," that appear on many computer text and graphic images due to low resolution. *Antialiasing* refers to the process of smoothing these jagged edges. A variety of colors and shades per pixel can produce the appearance of a smoother edge. However, an antialiased image may also appear fuzzy or "out of focus." AutoCAD provides four different levels of antialiasing. Each successive option requires a longer time to render the image.

- **Minimal.** This level is the default and uses only horizontal antialiasing. This level of antialiasing requires the least amount of time to render.
- **Low.** This level uses horizontal antialiasing and four shading samples per pixel.
- **Medium.** This level uses horizontal antialiasing and nine shading samples per pixel.
- **High.** This level uses horizontal antialiasing and sixteen shading samples per pixel. This level of antialiasing requires the most rendering time.

Depth map shadow controls

The settings in the **Depth Map Shadow Controls** area control the location of the shadow in relation to the object casting the shadow. This helps prevent detached and misplaced shadows. The higher the settings, the greater distance from the object to the shadow. See Figure 15-24. The following settings are available. You may need to try several different settings to get the best display. For most models, the default settings work fine.

- **Minimum Bias.** The default setting is 2. In general, a value no higher than 20 should be used.
- **Maximum Bias.** The default setting is 4. In general, a value no higher than 20 should be used. This value should also be no more than 10 greater than the minimum bias.

Figure 15-24.
A—Photo real rendered objects with the default minimum bias 2 and maximum bias 4.
B—The same rendering with a minimum bias of 20 and maximum bias of 30.

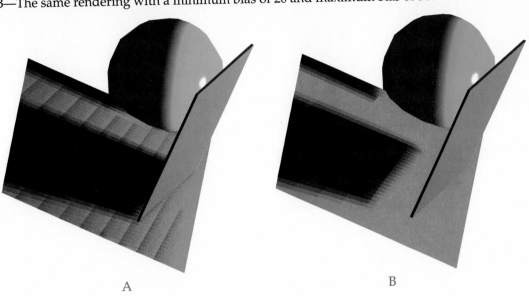

A

B

Texture map sampling

When a bitmap texture is projected onto an object that is smaller than the texture map, a sampling method must be used in order to "map" the texture to the object. There are three sampling methods to choose from. These are described below.

- **Point Sample.** This method uses the pixel nearest to any given pixel in the bitmap for each sample. This method generally requires the shortest rendering time.
- **Linear Sample.** This method averages the four pixels nearest to any given pixel in the bitmap for each sample. This is the default setting.
- **Mip Map Sample.** This method uses a pyramidal average taken from square sample areas. This process is called the *mip* method and generally requires the longest rendering time.

Photo Raytrace Rendering

A photo raytrace rendering provides the most control over the appearance of the scene. The same options available for a photo real rendering are available for a photo raytrace rendering. In addition, there are other options to provide further control of the antialiasing process and control of the depth of rays used in raytracing. Picking the **More Options...** button in the **Render** dialog when **Photo Raytrace** is selected displays the **Photo Raytrace Render Options** dialog box. See Figure 15-25.

Adaptive sampling

When adaptive sampling is turned on, AutoCAD uses a contrast threshold to determine how many samples are needed to produce the level of antialiasing specified. The following items are located in the **Adaptive Sampling** area of the **Photo Raytrace Render Options** dialog box.

- **Enable.** When this box is checked, adaptive sampling is enabled. This option is only available when the antialiasing is set to **Low**, **Medium**, or **High**. If the antialiasing is set to **Minimal**, then this option is grayed out.
- **Contrast Threshold.** The value in this text box determines the number of samples AutoCAD will use to achieve the selected level of antialiasing. A low value means that a greater number of samples will be taken. The greater the number of samples, the longer the rendering time. This value can be between 0.0 and 1.0.

Figure 15-25.
The **Photo Raytrace Render Options** dialog box is used to control photo raytrace renderings.

Pick to turn on adaptive sampling

Set how far a ray "bounces"

Ray tree depth

The ray tree is the path that a light ray takes from the light source. Each path segment is a branch of the tree. See Figure 15-26. The **Ray Tree Depth** area contains two ray tree settings. These settings control the depth of the ray tree used to track rays. In other words, these settings determine how far a ray bounces (reflects).

- **Maximum Depth.** This value represents the maximum length a branch can extend. If a ray does not strike another object before the maximum depth is reached, the tree is "pruned." A value as high as 9999 can be entered. However, a value between 3 (default) and 10 is suggested.
- **Cutoff Threshold.** This value defines a percentage that the next branch must add to last pixel in the branch. A value of .05 means that at least 5% must be contributed to the final pixel value. If the 5% is reached, the ray tree continues. If the 5% is not contributed, the ray tree is pruned.

Figure 15-26.
The ray tree is the path a light ray takes from the light source.

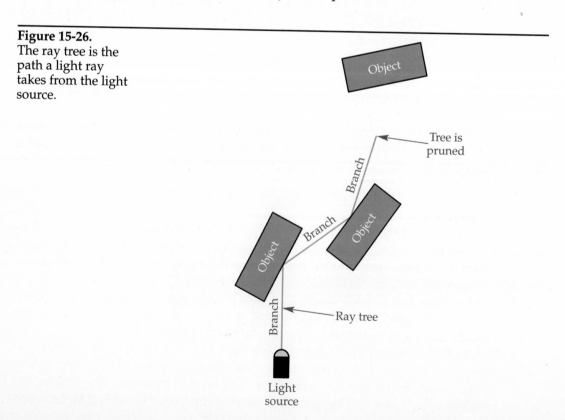

Rendering Destination

The **Desti_n_ation** drop-down list of the **Render** dialog box allows you to specify where a rendered image will be "placed." By default, AutoCAD renders the model in the active viewport. This means that the rendered image is displayed in the current viewport. The image in a rendered viewport cannot be printed or saved. You can also render to an image file or to the **Render** window. Rendering to a **Render** window is discussed in detail later in this chapter.

If you choose **File** in the **Desti_n_ation** drop-down list, the **More Options...** button is enabled. See Figure 5-21. Pick this button to select the file type and adjust the file's options. The **File Output Configuration** dialog box is displayed. See Figure 15-27.

The type of image file to create and the resolution are specified in the **File Type** drop-down lists. The type of file selected determines which options are available in the dialog box. The file types to select from are BMP, PCX, PostScript, TGA, and TIFF. Pick each one of these file types and notice the different options that are available. The following four areas are found in the **File Output Configuration** dialog box.

- **File Type.** In this area, select the type of output file and the file resolution in the drop-down lists. The X and Y values of resolution and the aspect ratio are displayed grayed out at the bottom of this area. These values can be manually set if **User Defined** is picked in the resolution drop-down list.
- **Colors.** This area is where the color depth per pixel is set. The options available in this area depend on the file type.
- **TGA Options.** The options in this area are available for the TGA file type only. You can select a compressed file, specify an image that is scanned from the bottom left, or choose between an interlaced or noninterlaced image. The default **None** produces a noninterlaced image. Pick **2 to 1** or **4 to 1** to create an interlaced file.
- **PostScript Options.** These are available only when the PostScript file type is selected. You can choose between landscape and portrait format, and you can select the method of image sizing. **Auto** instructs AutoCAD to automatically scale the image. **Image Size** uses the exact image size. When **Custom** is selected, you can enter the image size in pixels in the **Image Size** text box.

Figure 15-27.
When rendering to a file, parameters can be set in the **File Output Configuration** dialog box.

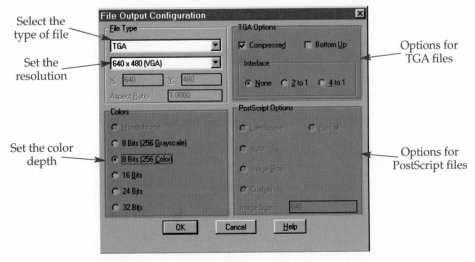

Select the type of file

Set the resolution

Set the color depth

Options for TGA files

Options for PostScript files

Preview Renderings

The **S‍ub Sampling** drop-down list in the **Render** dialog box allows you to specify the sampling rate for the rendering. See Figure 15-21. The amount of rendering time and the image quality is related to the sampling rate. The **1:1** setting produces the best quality image and takes the longest to render. The **8:1** setting provides the lowest quality image, but takes the shortest time to render. Other effects you have selected, such as shadows and materials, are still applied in the rendering. Figure 15-28 shows a model rendered with three different sub sampling settings.

Figure 15-28.
A drawing rendered at various sub sampling settings. Notice the change in image quality.
A—1:1 (Best). B—4:1. C—8:1 (Fastest).

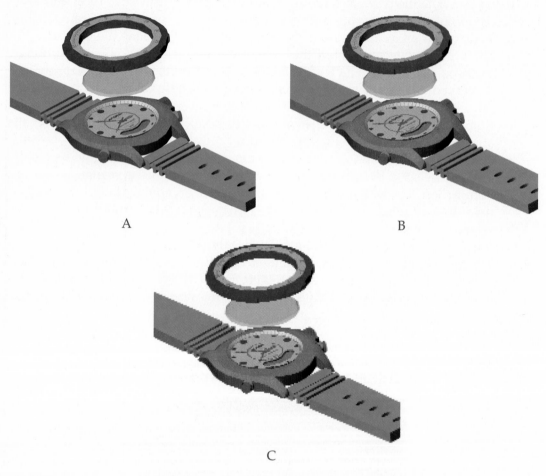

A

B

C

Rendering Procedures

By default, everything visible in the active viewport is rendered. However, there may be times when you want to render only some of the objects or a portion of the viewport. Also, you may want to "skip" the **Render** dialog box and perform the rendering with the current settings. The options listed in the **Rendering Procedure** area of the **Render** dialog box can be used in these situations. See Figure 15-29. These options are described as follows:

- **Q‍uery for Selections.** When checked, this option allows you to select specific objects to be rendered using the cursor.
- **Crop W‍indow.** Check this option to draw a window around a specific area of the model for rendering.

Figure 15-29.
The **Render Procedure**
area of the **Render**
dialog box.

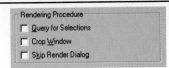

- **Skip Render Dialog.** If this is checked, the **Render** dialog box is not displayed for future uses of the **Render** command. This is a good option if the render settings are used for a series of renderings. You can use the **Rendering Preferences** dialog box to change this setting so that the dialog box appears.

Additional Rendering Options

The **Rendering Options** area of the **Render** dialog box has four options that give you a wide range of control over how the model is rendered. See Figure 15-30. These options not only control the appearance of the rendering, but also affect the rendering speed.

- **Smooth Shade.** When this option is checked, AutoCAD blends colors between faces to produce a smooth surface. When on, the rendering time is increased. The **Smoothing Angle** setting (located just below **Light Icon Scale**) determines at what angle an edge is defined. Angles less than the setting are smoothed. Angles greater than the setting are not smoothed.
- **Apply Materials.** If materials have been assigned to objects in the model, AutoCAD renders them if this box is checked. Rendering materials increases the rendering time. The amount of increase depends on the number and complexity of the textures and materials.
- **Shadows.** Check this box if you want to generate cast shadows. Remember, only those lights set up to cast shadows will do so. Check the lights using the **Modify Light** dialog box if you are unsure.
- **Render Cache.** All of the rendering settings and values are saved to a *cache file* on the hard disk. If you do not change the view or any geometry, AutoCAD can use the cache file for additional renderings. This can save considerable time because tessellation lines, which define 3D surfaces and solids, do not need to be recalculated.

Figure 15-30.
The **Rendering Options** area of the **Render** dialog box.

CREATING VIEWS AND SCENES

A *scene* is like a photograph. It is made up of a view and one or more lights. You can have as many scenes in a model as you want. The current view in the active viewport is used as the "camera" for the scene. Use the **VPOINT**, **DDVPOINT**, **3DORBIT**, or **DVIEW** commands to set the viewpoints you want. Then, use the **VIEW** command to create named (saved) views to recall that particular view in any viewport at any time. For the tutorial model, create the following views using the **DVIEW** command. Be sure the large viewport is active and the current UCS is FLOOR (or the WCS, depending on how you constructed the floor and walls).

Command: **DVIEW**⌐
Select objects or <use DVIEWBLOCK>: *(window the entire model)*
Select objects or <use DVIEWBLOCK>: ⌐
*** Switching to the WCS ***
Enter option
[CAmera/TArget/Distance/POints/PAn/Zoom/TWist/CLip/Hide/Off/Undo]: **POINTS.**⌐
Specify target point <current>: *(pick P2 in Figure 15-11)*
Specify camera point <current>: **@–8'6",–6',4'**⌐
Enter option
[CAmera/TArget/Distance/POints/PAn/Zoom/TWist/CLip/Hide/Off/Undo]: **PAN.**⌐
Specify displacement base point: *(pick a point)*
Specify second point: *(pick a second point to center the drawing)*
Enter option
[CAmera/TArget/Distance/POints/PAn/Zoom/TWist/CLip/Hide/Off/Undo]: ⌐

The view should look like the one shown in Figure 15-31. Now you can use the **VIEW**
command to save the current display as a new view named VIEW1. Next, set up a
second viewpoint with the **DVIEW** command as follows:

Command: **DVIEW.**⌐
Select objects or <use DVIEWBLOCK>: **P.**⌐
Select objects or <use DVIEWBLOCK>: ⌐
*** Switching to the WCS ***
Enter option
[CAmera/TArget/Distance/POints/PAn/Zoom/TWist/CLip/Hide/Off/Undo]: **PO.**⌐
Specify target point <current>: *(pick top of cone)*
Specify camera point <current>: **@–2',–8'6",5'**⌐

Now, turn perspective on by setting a distance.

Enter option
[CAmera/TArget/Distance/POints/PAn/Zoom/TWist/CLip/Hide/Off/Undo]: **D.**⌐
Specify new camera-target distance <current>: **14'**⌐
Enter option
[CAmera/TArget/Distance/POints/PAn/Zoom/TWist/CLip/Hide/Off/Undo]: ⌐
Command:

Your display should look like Figure 15-32. Create a saved view of the current display
named VIEW2.

Figure 15-31.
The large viewport
displays VIEW1.

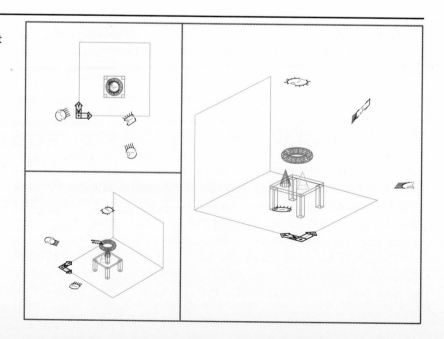

Figure 15-32.
The large viewport
displays VIEW2.

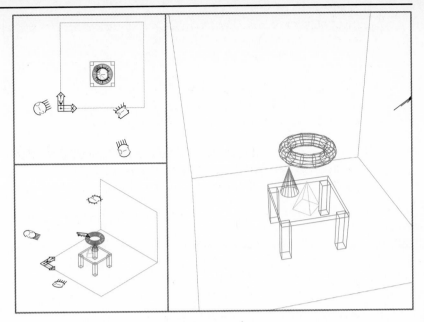

Now that you have two views, make a couple of scenes by picking the **Scenes** button from the **Render** toolbar, selecting **Scene...** from the **Render** cascading menu in the **View** pull-down menu, or typing SCENE at the Command: prompt. This displays the **Scenes** dialog box. See Figure 15-33A. Pick **New...** to display the **New Scene** dialog box, Figure 15-34. This dialog box lists all views and lights in the drawing.

Enter FRONT in the **Scene Name:** text box. Now you need to assign a view and lights to the new scene. Pick VIEW1, then hold the [Ctrl] key and pick lights D-1 and P-1. Pick the **OK** button to save the scene. Pick **New...** again and make another scene named SIDE. Use VIEW2 and lights D-2 and S-1. The **Scenes** dialog box now lists the two scenes, as shown in Figure 15-33B. Pick **OK**.

Render the scene with the **RENDER** command. In the **Render** dialog box, select a scene from the list in the **Scene to Render** list box and pick the **Render** button. The **RENDER** command renders the scene in the current viewport. Therefore, the rendering may not be the same view currently displayed in the active viewport.

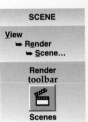

SCENE

View
→ Render
→ Scene...

Render
toolbar

Scenes

Figure 15-33.
A—The **Scenes**
dialog box. B—The
Scenes dialog box
with new scenes
created.

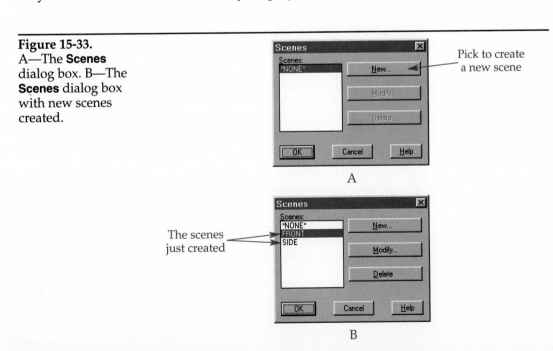

Figure 15-34.
The **New Scene**
dialog box.

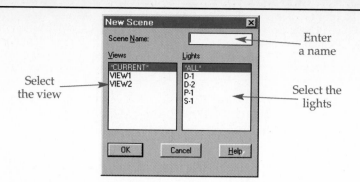

Select
the view

Enter
a name

Select the
lights

Use the **DVIEW** command to establish a new view point using the same target as VIEW1. Make the camera location X = –5′, Y = –8′6″, and Z = 12′. Set the distance in **DVIEW** to 11′6″. Use the **View** command to create a view named **VIEW3**. Create a third scene named SIDE2. Use VIEW3 and lights S-1, P-1, and D-1 for scene SIDE2.

Changing Light Intensities

The full intensity of point lights and spotlights should strike the first object in the model. Full intensity of any light is a value of one. Remember that spotlight falloff (attenuation) is calculated using either the **Inverse Linear** or **Inverse Square** setting.

In the 3DSHAPES model you have been working with, the top of the torus is approximately 55″ from the point light. The spotlight is approximately 43″ from the torus. Use the following calculations for each spotlight setting.

- **Inverse Linear.** If the point light is 55 units above the highest object (torus), that object receives 1/55 of the light. Set intensity to 55 so the light intensity striking the torus has a value of 1. Since the spotlight is 43″ from the nearest object, set its light intensity to 43.
- **Inverse Square.** Set light intensity to 55^2, or 3025, for the point light. Set the intensity to 43^2, or 1849, for the spotlight.

To change the light intensity for your model, open the **Lights** dialog box. First, set the **Ambient Light Intensity** to 0. With ambient light at 0, you can see the effects of changing other lights. Highlight P-1 in the **Lights:** list box, and then pick the **Modify...** button. Enter 55 in the **Intensity:** text box and pick **OK**. Modify S-1 and set the intensity to 43. Be sure the **Inverse Linear** radio button is active for both the point light and the spotlight. Set the intensity of lights D-1 and D-2 to 1. Open the **Render** dialog box. Highlight SIDE2. Pick the **Render** button to see the changes, as shown in Figure 15-35.

You can quickly see the effects of different light combinations. Open the **Lights** dialog box and set each distant light to an intensity of 0. The point light and spotlight are now the only lights that are on. Render the model. The top of the table is bright and the legs have no highlight. See Figure 15-36A. Now, set the ambient light to 1. Render the scene again. Notice the additional even light in the rendered scene. See Figure 15-36B.

Try turning the point light off by setting the intensity to 0. Then, turn on only one of the distant lights at a time. First, set the intensity of light D-2 to .8. Render the current viewport. If you render SCENE2, the light D-2 is not in that scene. The left sides of the objects are illuminated. Now turn off D-2 (intensity 0) and give light D-1 an intensity of 1. Render the current viewport. The front of the objects and the back wall are illuminated. The floor is dark because it is parallel to the light rays. Try additional combinations on your own.

Figure 15-35.
The SIDE2 scene
rendered.

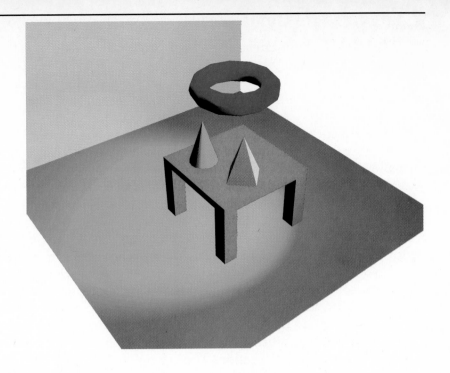

Figure 15-36.
A—The SIDE2 scene rendered with just the point light and spotlight. B—The SIDE2 scene rendered with the point, ambient, and spotlight. Notice how the "outer parts" of the scene now have a small amount of illumination.

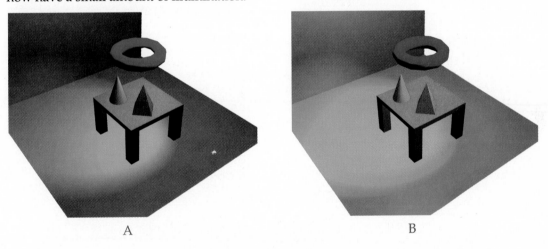

A   B

NOTE	If you render a scene and the image appears black, you may have selected a scene in which all the lights have been turned off (intensity 0).

Changing Light Color

The color of a light can be adjusted if you want the objects in the model to appear tinted differently than they appear in white light. The amount of red, green, or blue (RGB) can be adjusted to produce any color from white to black. White is the presence of all colors. This is a setting of 1.0 for red, green, and blue. Black is the absence of all colors. This is a setting of 0.0 for red, green, and blue.

To set a color for a light, open the **Lights** dialog box. Then, highlight the light you want to adjust and pick the **Modify...** button. In the **Modify Light** dialog box, the **Color** area allows you to adjust the amount of red, green, and blue in the light. In addition, you can select a standard AutoCAD color or choose a custom color.

If you want to select a predefined color, pick the **Select from ACI...** button in the **Color** area. This displays the **Select Color** dialog box shown in Figure 15-37. ACI stands for AutoCAD Color Index. These are the same predefined colors that come with AutoCAD used for objects and layers. You can choose one of the standard colors, one of six gray shades, or select from the full-color palette. Note that the **BYLAYER** and **BYBLOCK** options do not apply to lights and, therefore, those buttons are grayed out.

A third way to adjust the color of a light is to pick the **Select Custom Color...** button. This displays the Windows standard **Color** dialog box shown in Figure 15-38. HLS and RGB color values appear in this dialog box. HLS stands for hue, luminescence (lightness), and saturation. The current color is displayed in the **Color|Solid** image tile.

- **Hue.** A specific color, such as red.
- **Luminescence.** The lightness of the hue. Increasing the luminescence increases the "whiteness" of the color.
- **Saturation.** The amount of the hue in the color. Reducing the saturation increases the "blackness" of the color.

You can create a custom color using several methods.

1. Pick one of the basic colors.
2. Enter new values in the **Hue:**, **Sat:**, and **Lum:** boxes.
3. Enter new values in the **Red:**, **Green:**, and **Blue:** boxes.
4. Pick a location in the large color palette image tile, then adjust the slider arrow along the tall thin color sample to the extreme right of the dialog. This is a visual method to change the numerical values of the color.

When you have created a color that you want to keep, pick the **Add to Custom Colors** button. This places the new color in the **Custom Colors:** palette.

Figure 15-37.
The **Select Color** dialog box.

Current color name

Sample of the current color

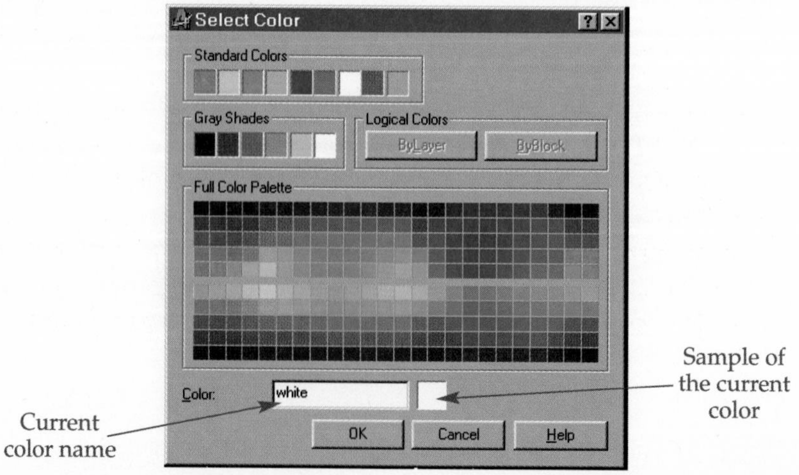

Figure 15-38.
The standard
Windows **Color**
dialog box.

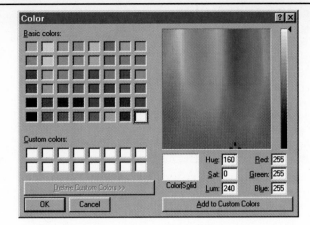

PROFESSIONAL TIP

The best way to see how colored lights affect your model is to experiment. Remember, you can render individual objects in the model. This allows you to see how light intensity and color change each object.

CREATING SURFACE FINISHES WITH MATERIALS

AutoCAD
User's
Guide **19**

A surface finish, or *material*, in AutoCAD can be shiny, dull, or anywhere in-between. You can create a variety of materials by specifying how a surface reflects light. You can also add images to represent textures and bumps. For example, you may add an image to represent wood grain or the grout lines for a tile floor.

To create a material from scratch, first pick the **Materials** button in the **Render** toolbar, select **Materials...** from the **Render** cascading menu in the **View** pull-down menu, or type RMAT at the Command: prompt. This displays the **Materials** dialog box, Figure 15-39A. The **New** drop-down list, to the right of the dialog box, provides four material types: **Standard**, **Marble**, **Granite**, and **Wood**. Select **Standard**, then pick the **New...** button to display the **New Standard Material** dialog box, Figure 15-39B.

RMAT

View
↳ Render
　↳ Materials...

Render
toolbar

Materials

Material attributes are set in the **Attributes** area of the **New Standard Material** dialog box. The following seven attributes are available. These are discussed in detail in the next sections. Also, refer to Figure 15-40.

- **Color/Pattern.** This color is the main color of the object.
- **Ambient.** This is the color of the ambient light reflected from the object.
- **Reflection.** This is the color of the highlight. The highlight is the shiniest spot on the object.
- **Roughness.** This controls the size of the reflection.
- **Transparency.** This controls how transparent the object is.
- **Refraction.** The refraction value specifies how much a light ray is "bent" as it enters a material.
- **Bump Map.** This is used to assign a bitmap image to represent a "bumpy" or embossed surface.

Figure 15-39.
A—The **Materials**
dialog box. Pick the
New... button to
display the **New
Standard Material**
dialog box.
B—The **New
Standard Material**
dialog box.

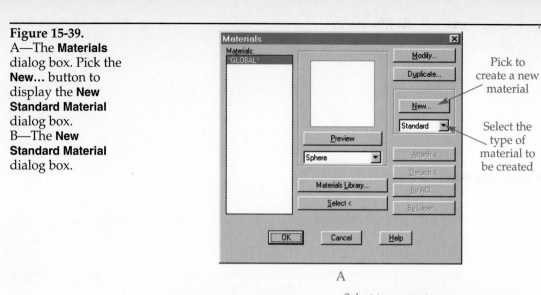

Pick to
create a new
material

Select the
type of
material to
be created

A

Select to generate
a preview

Preview area

Name the
material

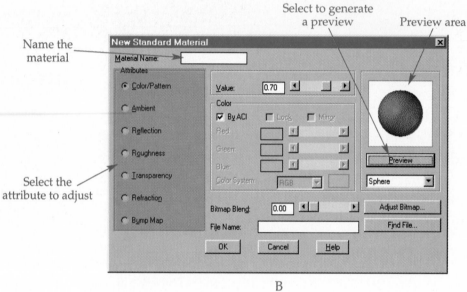

Select the
attribute to adjust

B

Figure 15-40.
Color, ambient, and
reflection all
combine to create
the "color" of a
material.

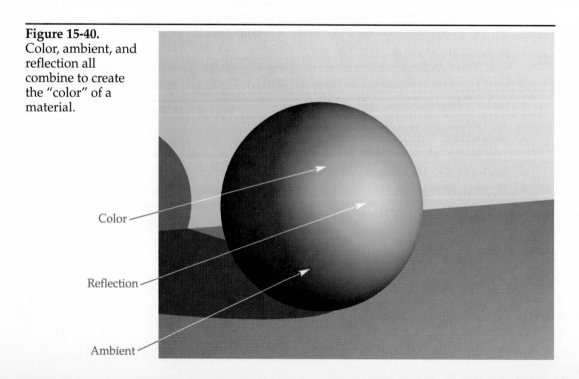

Color

Reflection

Ambient

AutoCAD and its Applications—Advanced

Color/Pattern

When the **C̲olor/Pattern** radio button is active, use the **Color** controls to change the color. By default, the **By̲ ACI** check box is active for color. This means that the main material color is determined by the display color of the object you assign the material to. To make the color independent, uncheck the **By̲ ACI** check box. Then, adjust the color values using the sliders.

Now, pick the **A̲mbient** and then the **R̲eflection** radio button. Notice that the **Lock̲** check box in the **Color** area is active for both. This means that the attribute's color is locked to the main color. This can be changed, as discussed later.

A bitmap image can be used as a pattern and can be blended with the color. For example, in Figure 15-41 the checker.tga bitmap file supplied with AutoCAD has been attached to the floor. Any bitmap file can be used. Either type in the file name and path in the **Fi̲le Name:** text box or pick the **F̲ind File...** button and locate the file. Adjust the **Bitmap Blend:** to show more or less of the material color through the bitmap. A value of 1.00 means that none of the material color will show through the bitmap image. A value of 0.00 means that none of the bitmap image will be shown.

Figure 15-41.
A bitmap, such as the checker pattern, can be attached to an object.

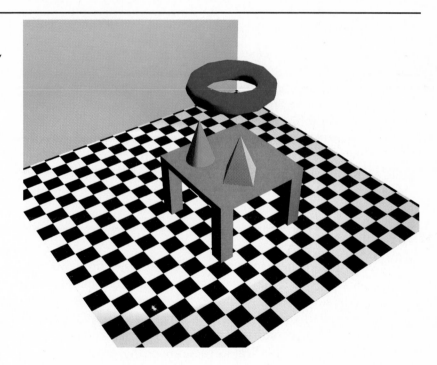

Ambient

The ambient color is the color reflected off the object. The shadows created by the object will have some of the ambient color. By default, ambient color is dependent on the main color. However, to change the ambient color, uncheck the **By̲ ACI** check box. Then, use the sliders in the **Color** area to adjust the ambient color.

Reflection

The reflection is also called the *specular* reflection or highlight. This is the "shiny" part of the material. A very reflective material, such as plastic, often has a reflection that is pure white. By default, the reflection color is dependent on the main color. To change the reflection color, uncheck the **By ACI** check box and use the sliders.

A bitmap can be selected as a *reflection map*. A material like chrome, for example, often has an image attached to simulate a reflection. This makes the material appear shiny enough to reflect other objects, as chrome does. When assigning a reflection map, be sure that the reflection value is high and the roughness value is low. The strength of the reflection bitmap that appears in the object is based on the value set in the **Bitmap Blend:** text box. The higher this value, the clearer the "reflection" is seen.

Roughness

Roughness is a measure of how shiny a material is. The rougher a material is, the less shiny it is. Think of cast iron. That material is very rough. Therefore, there is not much of a "shiny spot" anywhere on a cast iron object. A high roughness value creates a larger highlight area, but the reflected light is not as bright.

Transparency

Transparency is a measure of how "see through" a material is. A glass window is very transparent. However, a white plastic kitchen garbage bag is almost completely opaque. A transparency value of 1.0 makes the material appear completely transparent. Transparency falls off toward the edges of closed objects when photo real and photo raytrace renderings are used.

A bitmap called an *opacity map* can be assigned to control transparency. See Figure 15-42. An opacity map is usually a black and white or grayscale image. The white areas of the bitmap are opaque and the black areas are completely transparent. Colors between black and white have varying degrees of transparency depending on their equivalent grayscale value.

Refraction

The refraction value for a material determines how much a light ray is bent when it enters a transparent material. Refraction is what makes images distort when seen through a glass of water. The higher the refraction value, the more the ray is bent. The refraction value also affects the transparency of a material. If a material has a very high refraction value, you may not be able to see through the material even if the transparency is set high. The refraction setting only applies when creating a photo raytrace rendering.

Bump Map

Bump maps are used to give the illusion of raised or lowered areas to a flat surface. For example, you can specify a brick image as the **Color/Pattern** bitmap. Then, use the same image as the **Bump Map** bitmap using the same scale. Using a bump map gives a 3D appearance to the original pattern. See Figure 15-42. You can increase or decrease this effect by adjusting the bitmap blend value. The higher the blend value, the "deeper" the holes. Bump maps increase the rendering time.

Figure 15-42.
Bitmaps can be used for transparency and "bump" effects. A—The window material is completely transparent and the brick material appears "flat." B—A bitmap has been assigned to the window material as an opacity map. A different bitmap has been assigned to the brick material as a bump map. C—The opacity map used on the window material.

A

B

C

The **V**alue Slider

There is also a **Value:** area in the **New Standard Material** dialog box. This represents the level, or intensity, of the attribute's color. Notice that the default **Value** setting for **Color** is 0.70. When combined with a 0.30 value for **Reflection**, a matte finish is produced. A polished finish is created with a 0.30 setting for **Color** and a 0.70 setting for **Reflection**. The greater the **Ambient** value, the more pale the object appears. The default setting of 0.10 is best here, combined with a setting of 0.30 in the **Lights** dialog box. To have the brightest reflection, keep the **Color** value low and the **Reflection** value at least 0.70.

The **Value** area is also used with **Roughness**. The smaller the value, the smaller the area of highlight. A small specular highlight makes the surface appear shiny. Set a high value for **Roughness** and a low value for **Reflection** if you want the surface to appear rough or dull.

Previewing the Material

Preview the results of your settings by picking the **Preview** button. AutoCAD renders a sample sphere with the material created by the settings. See Figure 15-43. After you preview, you can make any changes necessary and preview again. If the **By ACI** box is checked, AutoCAD creates a preview of the material in a green color. The settings for reflection, roughness, etc., are reflected in the preview, but the actual color is based on an object's display color. If the color sliders have been used to set the material color, that color is reflected in the preview. Picking the drop-down list allows you to choose between a cube and a sphere preview.

Figure 15-43.
A preview of the
TORUS material.

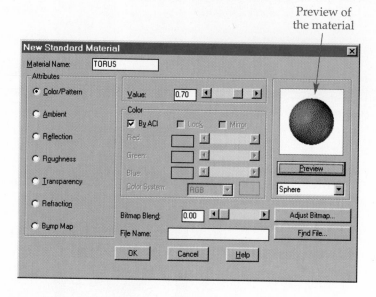

Preview of
the material

Settings for the 3DSHAPES Model

For the tutorial, enter TORUS in the **Material Name:** text box. The maximum length of a material name is 16 characters. Set the **Color** value to 0.70, **Ambient** to 0.10, **Reflection** to 0.30, and **Roughness** to 1.00. Make sure the **By ACI** check box is checked. Pick **OK** to exit the **New Standard Materials** dialog box and return to the **Materials** dialog box. New materials are listed on the left side of the **Materials** dialog box as they are created. Now you must assign the new material to an object. Highlight the TORUS material and pick the **Attach** button. The following prompt appears:

```
Select objects to attach "TORUS" to: (pick the torus)
Select objects: ↵
Updating drawing...done.
```

The dialog box returns. Pick **OK** to exit.

To best see how the light and material changes affect the model, create a close-up view of a single object. Zoom-in close to the torus and create a new view named TORUS. Now create a new scene named TORUS. Use the TORUS view and lights S-1 and D-2. Render the scene and notice the wide area of the reflection. See Figure 15-44A. Now, edit the material TORUS. Enter the **Materials** dialog box, select the TORUS material and pick the **Modify...** button. Change the roughness to 0.10, color to 0.30, and reflection to 0.70. Render the model again. Notice that the area of reflection is much smaller. There is also less diffused light, indicating a smoother surface. See Figure 15-44B.

Figure 15-44.
Adjusting material attributes affects the rendering. A—The TORUS material with high
roughness and color values and low reflection value. B—The TORUS material with low
values for roughness and color and a high reflection value.

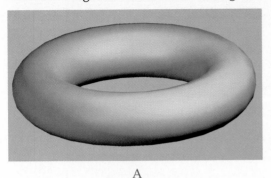

A   B

Other Features of the **Materials** Dialog Box

There are several other features of the **Materials** dialog box that help you work
with materials. These features are explained below.

- **Preview.** Picking this button displays a sphere or cube with the material that
  has been selected in the **Materials:** list. To choose between a cube and a sphere
  preview, select the **Preview** drop-down list and pick the type.
- **Materials Library... button.** Picking this displays the **Materials Library** dialog
  box. This dialog box is discussed later in this chapter.
- **Select.** Picking this button returns to the graphics screen and allows you to
  pick an object. The dialog box returns and the material assigned to the object
  is listed at the bottom of the dialog box.
- **Modify... button.** Picking this button opens the **Modify Material** dialog box. This
  is the same as the **New Materials** dialog box and allows you to adjust material
  attributes for the highlighted material.
- **Duplicate... button.** Picking this button opens the **New Material** dialog box. The
  settings for the material highlight in the **Materials:** list are automatically placed
  in the **New Material** dialog box. The attributes can then be edited to create a
  new, but similar, material.
- **New... button.** Pick this button to create a new material from scratch using the
  New Material dialog box.
- **Attach.** Picking this button returns to the graphics screen. Pick the objects you
  want to have the material highlighted in the **Materials:** list attached to. Press
  [Enter] to return to the dialog box.
- **Detach.** Picking this button returns to the graphics screen. Pick the objects you
  want to have the material highlighted in the **Materials:** list removed from.
  Press [Enter] to return to the dialog box.
- **By ACI... button.** This button opens the **Attach by AutoCAD Color Index** dialog
  box. See Figure 15-45A. The material highlighted is attached to all objects in
  the drawing with the color that you pick from the **Select ACI:** list. You can
  assign the same material to several colors.
- **By Layer... button.** This button opens the **Attach by Layer** dialog box. See
  Figure 15-45B. The material highlighted is attached to all objects on the layer
  you select. You can assign the same material to several layers.

Figure 15-45.
Materials can be attached by color or layer. A—The **Attach by AutoCAD Color Index** dialog box. B—The **Attach by Layer** dialog box.

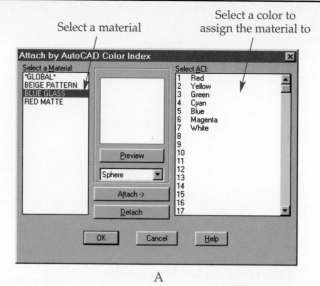

Select a material

Select a color to assign the material to

A

Select a layer to assign the material to

Select a material

B

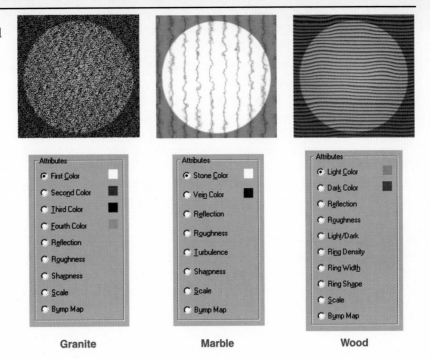

Figure 15-46.
The various material "templates" have different attributes available.

Granite   Marble   Wood

Granite, Marble, and Wood

When creating a material from scratch, you can also select from **Standard**, **Granite**, **Marble**, and **Wood** options. These are found in the **New...** drop-down list in the **Materials** dialog box. Think of these options as "templates" for creating a new material. Creating a new **Standard** material has been discussed to this point. Creating the other materials is basically the same, with some different attributes to set. Select the type of material and pick the **New...** button to open the **New (material) Material** dialog box. Figure 15-46 shows the different attributes for granite, marble, and wood and samples of each.

Granite

To create a granite material, pick **Granite**, then pick the **New...** button. The **New Granite Material** dialog box is displayed. Granite can have up to four colors. If you want only one or two colors, set the colors you do not need to a value of zero. **Sharpness** determines how blurred or distinct the different granite colors are. A value of 1.0 produces distinct colors and a value of 0 creates blurred colors. Colors must be set using the RGB or HLS color system.

Marble

To create a marble material, pick **Marble**, then pick the **New...** button. The **New Marble Material** dialog box is displayed. Marble allows you to choose the stone color and the color of the veins that run through the stone. Colors must be set using the RGB or HLS color system. **Turbulence** refers to how much vein color is present and the amount of swirling the veins display. A higher turbulence value increases swirling and vein color.

Wood

To create a wood material, pick **Wood**, then pick the **New...** button. The **New Wood Material** dialog box is displayed. The **New Wood Material** dialog box provides several attributes that help refine the appearance of the wood color and grain.
- **Light Color.** Controls the color value of light wood. This is usually the "base" color of the wood. The color must be set using the RGB or HLS color system.

- **Dark Color.** Controls the color value of dark wood. This is usually the "ring" color. The color must be set using the RGB or HLS color system.
- **Light/Dark.** This controls the ratio of light to dark rings in the wood. A value of 1.0 creates a material with mostly light color. A value of 0 creates a material with mostly dark color.
- **Ring Density.** This is a scale that sets the number of rings in the wood. Fine, tight rings are achieved with a large value.
- **Ring Width.** This controls the variation in the width of the rings. A variety of ring widths is produced with a value of 1.00. A consistent ring width is achieved with a value of 0.00.
- **Ring Shape.** Irregular-shaped rings are produced with a value of 1.00. Concentric circular rings result from a value of 0.00.

PROFESSIONAL TIP Be creative when testing new materials and try out a variety of attribute settings. You can quickly view the result of new attributes, colors, and values by picking the **Preview** button.

Using Bitmaps

AutoCAD's photorealistic renderer allows you to use bitmap images to enhance the appearance of your model. Bitmap images can be created from an image on a computer screen, a photograph taken with a digital camera, or a paper photo translated by a photo processing service.

A bitmap image can be used in several ways to create and simulate a wide variety of effects. A bitmap must be *mapped* to an object for the image to render correctly. The attributes **Color/Pattern**, **Reflection**, **Transparency**, and **Bump Map** allow you to add a bitmap image by selecting the **Find File...** button or by typing the name and path of the bitmap in the **File Name:** text box. As discussed earlier in this chapter, bitmaps can be used for the following purposes:

- **Texture maps.** These maps are used to define object and surface colors and patterns. Use the **Color/Pattern** attribute setting to specify these maps.
- **Reflection maps.** Also called *environment maps*, these maps simulate a reflection on the surface of a shiny object. Figure 15-47 shows one object rendered before and after applying the reflection map file named sunset.tga. Use the **Reflection** attribute to specify a reflection map.

Figure 15-47.
A reflection map creates the appearance of a reflection on a shiny surface. A—Without reflection map. B—With reflection map.

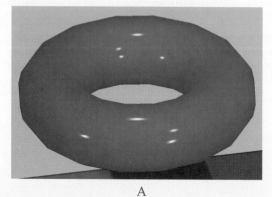
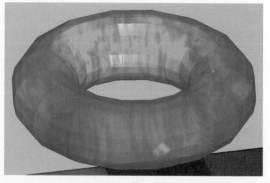

A   B

- **Opacity maps.** These maps specify areas of opacity and transparency. Any black area in the map is transparent when applied to the object. Any area that is white is opaque. For example, if the bitmap image is a black circle in the middle of a white rectangle, the surface appears to have a hole in it where the circle maps onto the object. Use the **Transparency** attribute to specify an opacity map.
- **Bump maps.** These maps create the appearance of raised areas similar to an embossed effect. Use the **Bump Map** attribute to specify a bitmap to use as a bump map.

NOTE Materials, textures, and patterns specified by bitmaps will only display when the photo real or photo raytrace rendering option is used.

If you plan to work with 3D models and apply photorealistic textures and patterns, you should begin collecting a variety of bitmap images to use with those models. For example, architects and interior designers use a variety of carpeting textures, wallpaper designs, flooring tiles, vinyls, and window covering samples. These images can all be easily created using one of the wide variety of digital cameras on the market. Images can also be purchased or downloaded from the Internet. AutoCAD comes with a number of TGA bitmap files that can be used as bitmap images.

Adjusting Material Bitmaps

The "new material" dialog boxes provide similar options. For example, each allows you to select and adjust colors, attributes, and their values. In addition, each dialog box allows you to select bitmap textures and provides a means to adjust and scale the bitmap texture on the object.

Pick the **Adjust Bitmap** button to display the **Adjust Material Bitmap Placement** dialog box. See Figure 15-48. The **Offset** option controls the location of the bitmap on the object(s) and the **Scale** option controls the size of the bitmap. You may see the results of your adjustments easier by selecting the **Cube** option for the **Preview** image. Offset and scale values are shown as **U** and **V**. The **U** value represents a horizontal offset and the **V** value represents the vertical offset.

Figure 15-48.
The **Adjust Material Bitmap Placement** dialog box.

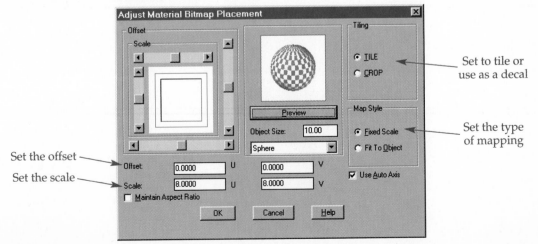

For example, enter .2 in the **Offset U** text box and press [Enter]. Notice that the red box remains in place and the box with the magenta bottom and right side moves to the right in the **Scale** image tile. You have just moved the bitmap texture's origin on the object.

Now pick the **CROP** radio button in the **Tiling** area. To see how this would appear when the object is rendered, pick the **Preview** button. When **CROP** is selected, all areas outside the bitmap are rendered in the material colors. This is also called a *decal map*. See Figure 15-49. If you want the entire object covered with the bitmap after the origin has been adjusted, pick the **TILE** radio button.

The bitmap image can be scaled using the **Scale U** and **V** text boxes or by adjusting slider bars. If you want the **U** and **V** values of the bitmap scale to remain proportional to each other, pick the **Maintain Aspect Ratio** check box. Then, when you change one scale value, the other automatically changes. Set the scale values to .5 and do a preview. Then, set the scale values to 2.0 and do another preview. How is the bitmap affected?

The **Map Style** area of the **Adjust Material Bitmap Placement** dialog box contains two options. The **Fixed Scale** option is only used for "tiled" bitmaps, such as a quarry tile image applied to a counter top. The U and V scale values control at what scale the bitmap will be tiled onto the object being rendered. The **Fit to Object** option is used when placing a single image bitmap onto an object. For example a bitmap image of a

---

Figure 15-49.
A decal map is created by cropping the bitmap. In this example, the bitmap is offset. A—The dialog box settings. B—The rendered image. C—A label on a bottle is an example of when a decal map might be used.

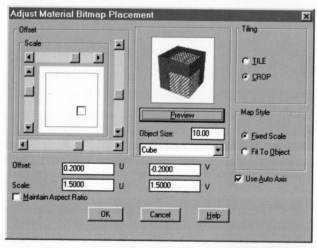

A

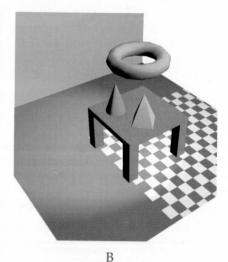

B

C

mountain used in a living room model as a painting would use the **Fit to Object** option. The biggest difference between the two options is that increasing the U/V scale with **Fit to Object** decreases the relative size of the image, while increasing the relative size with the **Fixed Scale** option. Set the scale values to .5 with **Fit to Object** selected and do a preview. Use the same scale with **Fixed Scale** selected and do another preview. How are the two previews different?

When checked, the **Use Auto Axis** check box places the bitmap image on the XY, YZ, and XZ surfaces of the object. If this box is not checked, the bitmap image is only applied to the XY oriented surface of the object. This placement is reflected in the preview when **Cube** is selected.

NOTE The values of **U** and **V** are used for horizontal and vertical adjustments to bitmaps, relative to the object. They are called *mapping axes* and are independent from the WCS and UCS coordinate axes.

EXERCISE 15-3

❏ Open Exercise 15-1 if it is not on your screen.
❏ Display one of the 3D views previously created. If a 3D view does not exist, establish a 3D viewpoint.
❏ Create a new wood material and assign attributes of your choosing. Preview each of the changes you make to the new wood material.
❏ Save the material with the name of TABLEWOOD.
❏ Attach the wood material to the table in the drawing.
❏ Render the drawing using the **Photo Real** option and the scene of your choice.
❏ Save the drawing as EX15-3.

MAPPING TEXTURES TO OBJECTS

If bitmaps are used when creating materials, it is not enough to simply assign the material to an object. In addition, the material must be mapped to the object. *Mapping* is the process of specifying the orientation of a material on the surface of an object. Mapping is important for materials with bitmap images, wood materials, granite materials, and marble materials. When one of these types of materials is selected and attached to an object, it is mapped in a default direction. Mapping allows you to adjust the material's scale, rotation, and which surface the material is being applied to. Once mapping coordinates are set for an object, they are retained until changed, even if the material is removed.

It is always best to preview the material or do a quick rendering to see if it is mapped to your liking. If not, change the offset, scale, and tiling first. If sides of the object are not rendered properly, as in a stretched or "streaked" material, you can use mapping to adjust the texture. Use mapping to rotate the currently assigned texture or to move it to a different plane.

NOTE The adjustments made when mapping a material, such as scale, are cumulative with adjustments made to a bitmap in the **Adjust Bitmap Placement** dialog box.

SETUV

View
↳ Render
  ↳ Mapping...

Render
toolbar

Mapping

The **Mapping** dialog box is accessed by picking the **Mapping** button in the **Render** toolbar, selecting **Mapping...** from the **Render** cascading menu in the **View** pull-down menu, or typing SETUV at the Command: prompt. Mapping applies to individual objects, so when the command is invoked, a Select objects: prompt appears on the Command: line. Pick the object(s) to map and press [Enter]. The **Mapping** dialog box is displayed. See Figure 15-50.

There are four different types of projection that can be used for mapping. These are **Planar**, **Cylindrical**, **Spherical**, and **Solid**. A planar projection places the material flat onto a plane. A cylindrical projection "wraps" the material around an axis. A spherical projection "pushes" the image out from a center point. Pick the type of projection and then pick the **Preview** button to see the results. These options specify how the material is projected onto the selected object. If the mapping appears correct, pick **OK** to exit. If another object in your model has the mapping variables you wish to use, pick the **Acquire From** button, then pick the other object. If you want to give the mapping properties of the current object to another, pick the **Copy To** button and pick the other object(s). The **Adjust Coordinates...** button accesses the **Adjust (projection) Coordinates** dialog box. This dialog box varies slightly for each type of projection.

The **Adjust Planar Coordinates** dialog box is shown in Figure 15-51. The **Parallel Plane** area in the **Adjust Planar Coordinates** dialog allows you to choose which plane the bitmap is projected to. The three preset planes include the world coordinate

Figure 15-50.
The **Mapping** dialog box allows you to pick mapping planes and surfaces on which textures are applied.

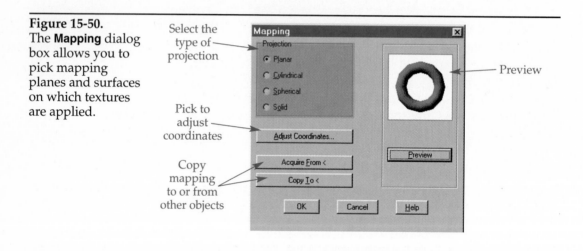

Figure 15-51.
The **Adjust Planar Coordinates** dialog box is used to position a bitmap being used on an object. This dialog box is similar to the dialog boxes used with **Cylindrical** and **Spherical** projections.

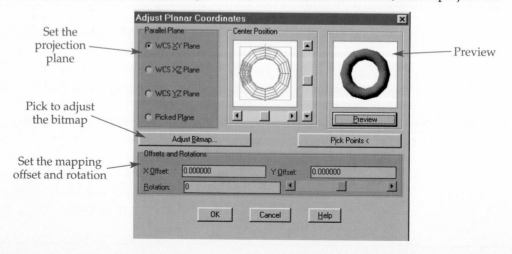

system (WCS) XY plane, the WCS XZ plane, or the WCS YZ plane. In addition, you can pick any plane by selecting the **Picked Plane** option or the **Pick Points** button. Picking either of these returns you to the drawing screen and you are prompted to pick three corners of the plane. Use object snaps for accuracy.

Place the lower left corner of the mapping plane: *(pick lower-left corner)*
Place the lower right corner of the mapping plane: *(pick lower-right corner)*
Place the upper left corner of the mapping plane: *(pick upper-left corner)*

The **Adjust Mapping Coordinates** dialog box is displayed and the **Picked Plane** radio button is checked.

NOTE If the points you pick are the same as one of the WCS axes, AutoCAD saves this as the WCS axis. When the **Adjust Coordinates** dialog box is returned, the button indicates the selected WCS plane, rather than the **Picked Plane**.

The **Center Position** area of the **Adjust *(projection)* Coordinates** dialog box indicates the orientation of the object on the current parallel plane. The object is displayed as red lines. The current projection for the mapped image shows as a blue outline with a small tick mark on the top. The blue outline represents the extent of the object's parallel projection. The left edge of the projection is displayed in green. Use the scroll bars to change the position of the projection axis.

The **Adjust Bitmap...** button in the **Adjust *(projection)* Coordinates** dialog box displays the **Adjust Object Bitmap Placement** dialog box. This is the same dialog discussed for the **RMAT** command, with the addition of the **DEFAULT** radio button in the **Tiling** area. This radio button uses the default tiling set in the material definition. The **TILE** and **CROP** buttons override the tiling set in the material definition.

The **Offsets and Rotations** area in the **Adjust Planar Coordinates** dialog box allows you to offset or rotate the mapping coordinates. The **X Offset:** and **Y Offset:** adjustments shift the mapping similar to how the U/V offset adjustments shifted the bitmap image earlier in this chapter. However, these are XY offsets because they adjust the map plane, not the bitmap image.

If **Cylindrical** projection is selected, the **Adjust Coordinates...** button displays the **Adjust Cylindrical Coordinates** dialog box. This provides the same options as the "planar" dialog, except the cylindrical shape is displayed in the **Central Axis Position** area and the **Pick Points** button is used to set the **Picked Axis** projection.

If **Spherical** projection is selected, the **Adjust Coordinates...** button displays the **Adjust Spherical Coordinates** dialog box. The spherical shape is displayed in the **Polar Axis Position** area, and the red mesh of the object is shown perpendicular to the current axis. A green radius line indicates the wrap line, and the blue circle is the projection axis.

If for any reason you need to detach a map from an object, you must do so using AutoLISP at the Command: prompt as follows:

Command: **(C:SETUV "D" (SSGET))**↵
Select objects: *(pick the object)*
Select objects: ↵

MATLIB

View
➥ Render
　➥ Materials
　　Library...

Render
toolbar

Materials Library

A *materials library* is a saved file with definitions for one or more materials. Any material in this library can be recalled and assigned to an object without having to recreate the material. The standard AutoCAD materials library is a file named render.mli located in the AutoCAD support directory. This file contains a list of materials that are displayed in the **Library List:** area of the **Materials Library** dialog box. This dialog box is used to import/export materials and to perform "housekeeping" functions.

The **Materials Library** dialog box is accessed by picking the **Materials Library** button in the **Render** toolbar, selecting **Materials Library...** from the **Render** cascading menu in the **View** pull-down menu, or typing MATLIB at the Command: prompt. In addition, you can also pick the **Materials Library...** button in the **Materials** dialog box.

Editing the Materials List and Materials Library

The **Current Drawing** area is on the left side of the **Materials Library** dialog box. This list displays all the materials defined in or "loaded into" the current drawing. See Figure 15-52. The **Current Library** area on the right side of the dialog displays all of the materials in the current library file. The name of the current library file appears in the **Current Library:** drop down list. Notice that the file name appears, but not the .mli extension.

You can use a material from the default render.mli library by highlighting the material name in the **Current Library** list and picking the **Import** button. This copies the material from the library list to the **Current Drawing** list, making it available in the current drawing.

You may want to use a different library file than the default render.mli. For example, you may have created unique libraries for different projects or customers. A different library file (.mli) can be used by picking the **Open...** button, which displays the **Library File** dialog box. Change to the folder where the library file is located. Then, highlight the file name and pick **OK**. The materials in that library file are now displayed in the **Current Library** list.

Figure 15-52.
The **Materials Library** dialog box.

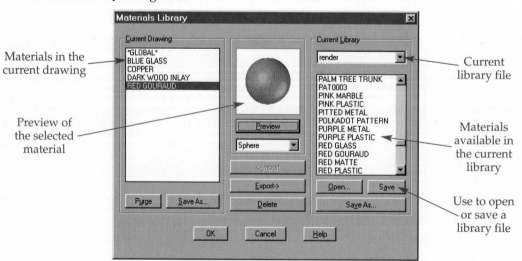

Materials in the current drawing

Preview of the selected material

Current library file

Materials available in the current library

Use to open or save a library file

If you want to use a material that you have created in the current drawing for other applications, you need to export it to the library file. To do so, first highlight the material in the **Current Drawing** list and then pick the **Export** button. The material name appears in the **Current Library** list. Next, pick the **Save...** button and AutoCAD saves the current library file with the new material in it. You can also select the **Save As...** button, which displays the **Library File** dialog box. This allows you to save a copy of the current library file with a new name. The new library file is also set as the current library file when you do this. If you make changes to the library list in the **Materials Library** dialog box and pick **OK** without saving, the **Library Modification** dialog box appears. This gives you the chance to save the changes, discard the changes, or cancel and return to the **Materials Library** dialog box. Pick the appropriate button and continue.

To delete a material, highlight the name and pick the **Delete** button. You can delete materials from the current drawing by picking a name from the **Current Drawing** list. You can also delete a material from the current library file by picking the name from the **Current Library** list. You cannot, however, delete materials that are attached to objects. The **Purge** button deletes *all* materials not attached to objects from the current drawing. The current material library file is unaffected by the **Purge** button.

CREATING BACKGROUNDS FOR MODELS

A background is the backdrop for your 3D model. The background for your scene can be a solid color, a gradient of colors, a bitmap file, or the current AutoCAD drawing background color. Establish a background by picking the **Background** button in the **Render** toolbar, picking **Background...** in the **Render...** cascading menu in the **View** pull-down menu, or typing BACKGROUND at the Command: prompt. The **Background** dialog box is displayed, Figure 15-53. Four radio buttons at the top of the dialog represent the four types of backgrounds. These are **Solid**, **Gradient**, **Image**, and **Merge**. The **Merge** option uses whatever the current AutoCAD drawing background image is as the background. The other three options are discussed in the next sections.

Solid Backgrounds

The default background option is **Solid**, with the AutoCAD background color as the solid color. When the **AutoCAD Background** check box in the **Colors** area is unchecked, you can select a background color using either the RGB or HLS color system. Enter numeric values or use the slider bars to set the **Top** color swatch, which indicates the background color. Pick the **Preview** button to see a larger color sample in the **Preview** area. A color can also be selected from the **Color** dialog box by picking the **Select Custom Color** button.

AutoCAD User's Guide **19**

BACKGROUND

View
→ Render
→ Background...

Render toolbar

Background

Figure 15-53.
A— The **Background** dialog box. B—By creatively using materials and backgrounds, you can produce a variety of scenes, from the average to the fantastic.

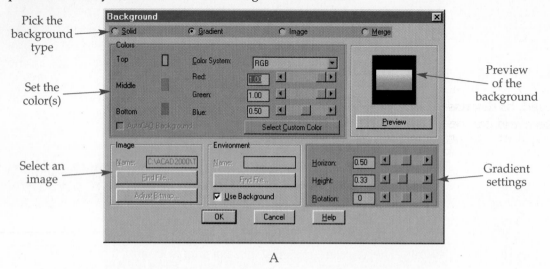

Pick the background type

Set the color(s)

Select an image

Preview of the background

Gradient settings

A

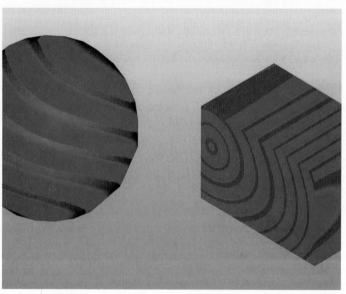

B

Gradient Backgrounds

A **Gradient** background can be composed of two or three colors. These are shown in the **Colors** area of the dialog box as **Top**, **Middle**, and **Bottom**. By selecting one of the color swatches, you are selecting the color to be modified. Use the color slider bars or the **Select Custom Color** button to adjust the color for each swatch. When **Gradient** is picked, the three values in the lower-right corner are activated.

- **Horizon.** This is a percentage value that determines where the center of the gradient is to be placed.
- **Height.** The starting location of the second color in a three-color gradient is determined by this percentage. A two-color gradient is created, composed of the top and bottom colors, if this value is 0.
- **Rotation.** The angle at which the gradient background is rotated.

Pick the **Preview** button to preview how the gradient will appear. Convincing, clear blue skies can be simulated using the **Gradient** option. Initially, set the **Top**, **Middle**, and **Bottom** color values the same. Then, change the lightness in the **Colors** dialog box.

Image Backgrounds

Any bitmap image can be used as a background. This technique can be used to produce realistic or imaginative settings for your models. First, pick the **Image** radio button. This activates the **Image** and **Environment** areas. Use the **Find File...** button in the **Image** area to select the bitmap. Use the **Adjust Bitmap...** button to alter the offset and scale.

An *environment* is a bitmap image mapped onto a sphere that surrounds the scene. This "environment-in-a-sphere" is used by the photo raytrace renderer to project additional images onto objects that have reflective surfaces. This option can provide a realistic "surrounding" environment in your scene. The **Use Background** check box must be inactive in order to use an environment.

LANDSCAPING THE MODEL

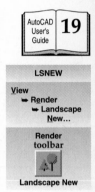

You can easily landscape your model by adding bushes, trees, road signs, and people. Pick the **Landscape New** button in the **Render** toolbar, select **Landscape New...** from the **Render** cascading menu in the **View** pull-down menu, or type LSNEW at the Command: prompt. This displays the **Landscape New** dialog box, Figure 15-54A. The list on the left side shows the object in the current library file. A landscape library file can be modified and saved in a manner similar to managing material libraries. This is discussed later.

Select an object and pick the **Preview** button to view it. Adjust the height by entering a value in the **Height:** text box, or use the slider bar. Changes in the height value are not reflected in the preview. The height is specified in the current drawing units. For example, if architectural units are the current units, then the height of the landscape object is in inches.

Pick the **Position** button and locate the object in your model. Use standard AutoCAD methods, such as zooming and object snaps, to locate the position.

The **Geometry** area allows you to specify the number of faces on the landscape object and how the view is aligned. Pick **Single Face** to display the object as a single plane. If the **View Aligned** box is checked, the object's face is placed perpendicular to the line of sight. A single-face object renders faster than a crossing-face object. The **Crossing Faces** option creates objects with two faces that intersect at a 90° angle. This object creates more realistic images and raytraced shadows. The faces are oriented at a 45° angle to the line of sight if they are view-aligned.

A single-face, view-aligned object is identified by a single triangle with the name of the object at the bottom. This object cannot be rotated. A single-face fixed object (not view-aligned) is displayed as a rectangle, and its name may be right- or wrong-reading. This type of object can be rotated. The objects are drawn to the specified height. A crossing-face object is drawn as two intersecting triangles. If they are view-aligned, they cannot be rotated. Figure 15-54B and Figure 15-54C show the difference between the object symbols and the rendered versions.

Figure 15-54.
A—Landscape objects can be placed and sized using the **Landscape New** dialog box.
B—Single-face and crossing-face object symbols are shown after placement in the model.
C— The same two objects after rendering.

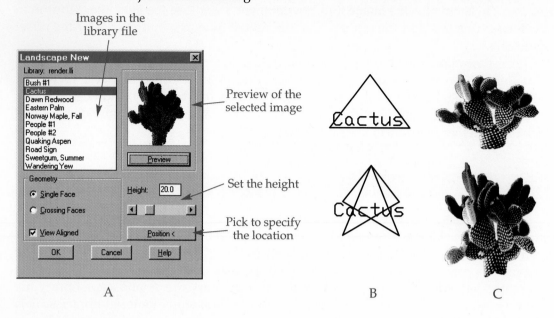

A   B   C

Editing Landscape Objects

LSEDIT

View
➥ Render
➥ Landscape
Edit...

**Render
toolbar**

Landscape Edit

The triangular shapes of landscape objects can be edited using standard AutoCAD methods. The objects have grips at the apex, base, and corners of the triangle. The objects can be moved using the grip at the middle of the base. The size and height of the object is changed using the top and lower corner grips. The size will always remain proportional.

The geometry, position, and height of individual landscape objects can also be edited. Pick the **Landscape Edit** button in the **Render** toolbar, select **Landscape Edit...** from the **Render** cascading menu in the **View** pull-down menu, or type LSEDIT at the Command: prompt. You are first prompted to select a landscape object. After the object is selected, the **Landscape Edit** dialog box is displayed.

The **Landscape Edit** dialog box is the same as the **Landscape New** dialog box, except the landscape objects cannot be selected. If you need to use a different landscape object in place of the one selected, erase the current object and create a new one. Using this dialog box, you can convert between single-face and double-face objects, enter a new value to change the height, or pick the **Position** button to relocate the object.

Remember these points when editing landscape objects:

✓ View-aligned objects cannot be rotated.

✓ Fixed objects (not view-aligned), can be rotated.

✓ The position, height, and width of objects can be quickly changed with grips.

Editing the Landscape Library

LSLIB

View
➥ Render
➥ Landscape
Library...

**Render
toolbar**

Landscape Library

The landscape library files and the individual bitmap files contained in them can be edited. Pick the **Landscape Library** button in the **Render** toolbar, select **Landscape Library...** from the **Render** cascading menu in the **View** pull-down menu, or type LSLIB at the Command: prompt. The **Landscape Library** dialog box is displayed, Figure 15-55. This dialog box contains the following buttons:

- **Modify.** Highlight the landscape object you want to edit, then pick this button. The **Landscape Library Edit** dialog box appears, Figure 15-56. The current name of the object is listed in the **Name:** text box. Each object has an image file and

Figure 15-55.
The landscape library files, and the individual objects contained in them, can be edited using the **Landscape Library** dialog box.

Figure 15-56.
Individual landscape objects can be edited using the **Landscape Library Edit** dialog box.

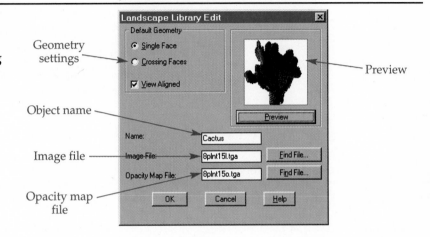

Geometry settings

Preview

Object name

Image file

Opacity map file

an opacity map file. The image file is the image displayed when the object is rendered. The opacity map file is used to outline the object and make it see-through. An opacity map is a file that displays the silhouette of your image in a white color and the area surrounding the image in a black color. You can change the name of this item and replace the current image and opacity files with different ones. You can also change the default geometry settings displayed when inserting a landscape object through the **Landscape New** dialog box.

- **New.** Displays the **Landscape Library New** dialog box, which is exactly the same as the **Landscape Library Edit** dialog box. In this dialog box, name the new landscape object, select the image and opacity map files to define it, and specify the default geometry settings.
- **Delete.** Removes the highlighted object from the library list.
- **Open.** Displays the **Open Landscape Library** dialog box where you can open a different landscape library file (.lli).
- **Save.** Displays the **Save Landscape Library** dialog box used to save the revised landscape library file.

FOGGING UP THE MODEL

Fog is actually a way of using colors to visually represent the distance between the camera and objects in the model. This is similar to looking at an object from a distance and seeing that the object is a little obscured from the haze in the sky. To use fog, pick the **Fog** button in the **Render** toolbar, select **Fog...** from **Render** cascading menu in the **View** pull-down menu, or type FOG at the Command: prompt. This displays the **Fog/Depth Cue** dialog box. See Figure 15-57.

AutoCAD User's Guide **19**

FOG

View
➥ Render
➥ Fog...

Render toolbar

Fog

Figure 15-57.
The **Fog/Depth Cue** dialog box is used to visually portray the distance between the camera and objects in the model.

Check to enable fog

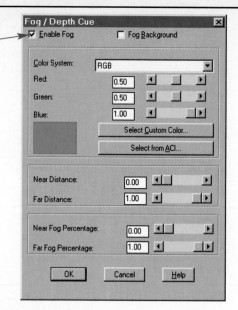

Turn on fog by checking the **Enable Fog** check box. Checking the **Fog Background** check box also applies fog to the background in the model. Fog is composed of three components: color, distance, and percentage.

- **Color.** The color controls are the standard AutoCAD color controls previously discussed. First, select a color system. Then enter values for each color or use the slider bars. You can also select a custom color by picking the **Select Custom Color...** button or select an ACI color.
- **Distance.** The **Near Distance** value is a percentage of the distance from the viewer to the rear of the model, or its back "clipping plane." The viewer has a value of 0 and the back of the model is 1.0, or 100%. Enter values in the text boxes or use the slider bars.
- **Fog percentage.** These values are the percentages of fog at the near distance and far distance. A value of 0 is no fog, and a value of 1.0 is 100% fog. The **Near Fog Percentage** value takes effect at the **Near Distance** value (front of the camera) and increases to the **Far Fog Percentage** value at the back of the model.

PROFESSIONAL TIP

If the **Fog Background** button has been selected, try adjusting the **Far Fog Percentage**. By default this value is set to 1 (100%) which will completely render any background placed using the **BACKGROUND** command with the fog color.

SPECIFYING RENDERING PREFERENCES

The **Rendering Preferences** dialog box is the same as the **Render** dialog box. See Figure 15-58. To access this dialog box, pick the **Render Preferences** button in the **Render** toolbar, select **Preferences...** in the **Render** cascading menu in the **View** pull-down menu, or type RPR or RPREF at the Command: prompt. You can use this dialog box to establish any of the rendering options, and pick the **Skip Render Dialog** check box. Then, when you use the **RENDER** command, the model is immediately rendered without the **Render** dialog box opening.

Figure 15-58.
The **Rendering Preferences** dialog box is used to establish all the rendering options.

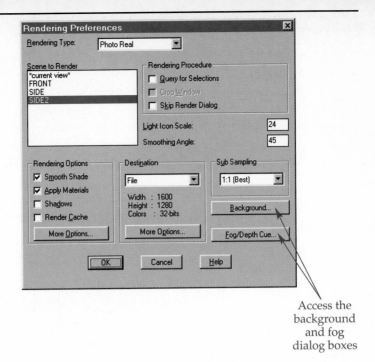

Access the background and fog dialog boxes

All the options in the **Rendering Preferences** dialog box are discussed earlier in this chapter. Note the two buttons at the lower right: **Background** and **Fog/Depth Cue**. These buttons open the background and fog dialog boxes discussed earlier in this chapter.

Rendering Statistics

The **STATS** command provides information about the last rendering performed. Pick the **Statistics** button from the **Render** toolbar, **Statistics...** from the **Render** cascading menu in the **View** pull-down menu, or type STATS at the Command: prompt. See Figure 15-59. The **Statistics** dialog box displays information that cannot be altered, but can be saved to a text file. Place a check in the **Save Statistics to File** check box, type in a name, and use the **Find File** button to specify the location of the saved file.

STATS

View
→ Render
→ Statistics...

Render toolbar

Statistics

Figure 15-59.
Displaying the rendering statistics.

Check to save to a file

Enter a file name

A rendered image can be saved to a file for later use, such as in a desktop publishing program. This is usually done by rendering to a file so that resolution and color depth can be controlled. Refer to the *Rendering Destination* section.

An image rendered to a viewport can also be saved using the **SAVEIMG** command. This command is invoked by picking **Save...** from the **Display Image** cascading menu in the **Tools** pull-down menu or by typing SAVEIMG at the Command: prompt. This displays the **Save Image** dialog box. See Figure 15-60.

SAVEIMG

Tools
➥ Display Image
  ➥ Save...

Figure 15-60.
The **Save Image** dialog box. Notice that only three file types are available.

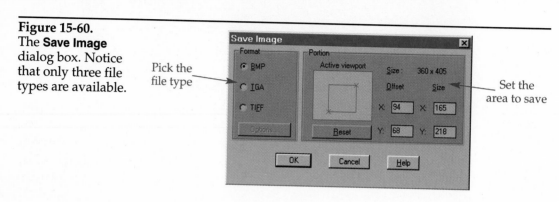

The **SAVEIMG** command does not work with certain viewport configurations. If you encounter this problem, either temporarily switch to a single viewport or render the image to a file.

NOTE

The **SAVEIMG** command saves wireframe and rendered viewports. Shaded views cannot be saved with **SAVEIMG**. Also, there are only three file types available in this dialog box. The TGA and TIF formats can be saved as compressed files. Pick the **Options...** button to open the **TGA Options** or **TIFF Options** dialog box. The compressed form for TGA files is **RLE** (run length encoded). A TIF file can be compressed as **PACK** for Macintosh computers.

The image can be cropped by specifying the XY pixel values. The **Offset X:** and **Y:** text boxes define the lower-left corner of the image. The **Size X:** and **Y:** text boxes define the upper-right corner of the image. You can also use the pointing device and pick the two corners in the **Active viewport** image tile of the dialog box to define the image area. Pick the **Reset** button to return the portion to its default size.

Pick **OK** to close the **Save Image** dialog box. The **Image File** dialog box appears. See Figure 15-61. Enter a file name and location. Then, pick **Save** to save the image.

NOTE

The pixel values shown in the **Save Image** dialog box represent the size in pixels of the current viewport. This will vary depending on screen resolution and whether you are rendering the active viewport, drawing area, or full screen image. Before using **SAVEIMG**, be sure the rendered viewport is current.

Figure 15-61.
In the **Image File**
dialog box, name
the file and specify
the location.

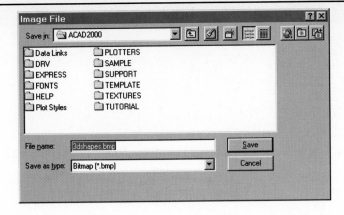

Replaying Image Files

Images saved as TGA, TIF, and BMP files can be displayed in AutoCAD with the
REPLAY command. Access the command by selecting **Display Image** and then **View...**
from the **Tools** pull-down menu or by typing REPLAY at the Command: prompt. This
displays the **Replay** dialog box. Select the folder and file you want to display and pick
the **Open** button. The **Image Specifications** dialog box then appears. See Figure 15-62.
This dialog box allows you to specify the exact portion of the image you want to
display, along with the on-screen location.

REPLAY

Tools
➥ Display Image
➥ View...

The image tile on the left side of the dialog box is titled **IMAGE**. The size of the
image is given in pixels just above the image tile. You can pick two points inside this
tile to crop the image for display. When you do this, notice that the offset location of
the image in the **SCREEN** image tile changes. You can also change the image size by
entering the cropped size of the image in the **Image Offset** and **Image Size** text boxes.
The image offset defines the lower-left corner of the image. The image size defines the
upper-right corner of the image.

In addition to cropping the size of the image, you can determine where it will be
displayed on the screen. Do this visually by picking a point in the **SCREEN** image tile.
This point becomes the center of the image on your screen. You can also specify the
location by entering **Screen Offset** values in the boxes below the tile. Notice that the
Screen Size values cannot be changed. The **Reset** button returns the image and screen
values to their defaults. Pick **OK** when you are ready to display the image.

Figure 15-62.
The **Image
Specifications**
dialog box.

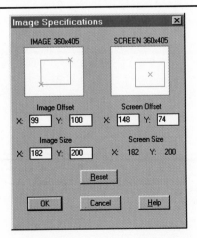

ADVANCED RENDERING

Some of the advanced rendering capabilities of AutoCAD include rendering to a separate window, copying the rendered image to the Windows Clipboard, and advanced printing options. The following sections discuss each of these capabilities.

The Render Window

The **Render** window is the "Render" program that appears in the Windows taskbar once any of AutoCAD's rendering commands are selected. An image rendered to the **Render** window can be saved as a bitmap (.bmp) or printed. The **Render** window can also be used to open and display a bitmap image. Rendering to the **Render** window is done by picking the **Render Window** option in the **Desti̲nation** area of the **Render** dialog box.

The **Render** window is made up of several elements, Figure 15-63. These elements include a menu bar, toolbar, and status area. The menu bar contains the **F̲ile**, **E̲dit**, and **Window** pull-down menus. The toolbar contains five buttons that are shortcuts to the commands in the **F̲ile** and **E̲dit** pull-down menus. The status area contains information about the currently displayed image. The following commands are available:

* **Open.** Opens a bitmap (.bmp). If the **P̲review** check box is checked in the **Open** dialog box, the selected image is previewed before it is displayed in the **Render** window.

Figure 15-63.
The 3dshapes drawing rendered to the **Render** window.

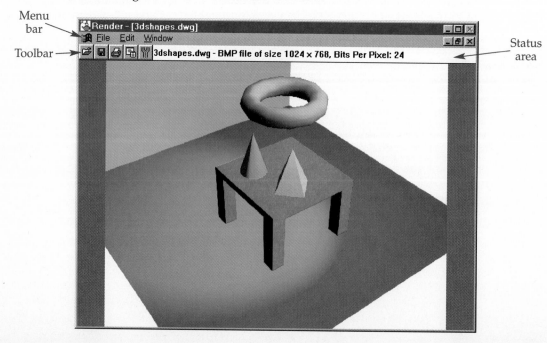

- **Save.** Saves a rendered image to a file using the **Save BMP** dialog box.
- **Print.** Prints the bitmap using the default system printer.
- **Copy.** Copies the image to the Windows Clipboard. This is discussed in the next section, *Copying a rendered image to the Clipboard*.
- **Options.** Displays the **Windows Render Options** dialog box. This dialog box is discussed later in this chapter.

NOTE   The **Render** window can display and save .bmp files *only*.

Copying a rendered image to the Clipboard

Once an image has been rendered, it can be copied to the Windows Clipboard. Once an image is copied to the Clipboard, it can be "pasted" into another Windows application, such as a desktop publishing program. The Clipboard Viewer is used to view the contents of the Clipboard. Refer to Windows documentation for instructions on its use. To copy a rendered image from the **Render** window to the Clipboard, pick the **Copy** button, select **Copy** from the **Edit** pull-down menu, or use the [Ctrl]+[C] key combination.

For example, suppose you want to include your 3dshapes drawing as a rendered image in a memo or letter. First, render the drawing to the **Render** window. Next, copy the image to the Clipboard. Once information is on the Clipboard, start a Windows-compatible word processing program. Finally, paste the contents of the Clipboard into the document. See Figure 15-64. To place the rendered image into AutoCAD, select the **Paste** command from AutoCAD's **Edit** pull down menu, select the **Paste from Clipboard** button, right-click in the drawing area and select **Paste** from the shortcut menu, or use the [Ctrl]+[V] key combination.

Figure 15-64.
Once a rendered image is copied to the Clipboard, it can be pasted into a word processing document.

MEMO

To: Otto Desque
From: Ima Drafter
Date: Thursday, March 14
Subject: AutoCAD Render

Dear Otto,

   Guess what I discovered? I can render an image to a window! Not only that, I can then copy it to the Windows Clipboard. Once it's on the clipboard I can paste it into any document I wish. For example, look how nicely I managed to paste it into this memo. This has the potential to make me more productive, and also more valuable to the design team.

   This is probably grounds for a promotion, wouldn't you think? I anxiously await your reply.

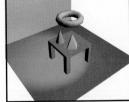

NOTE   For more information regarding bitmaps, metafiles, and Clipboard graphics, see Chapter 14 and Chapter 18 of this text.

❏ Open EX15-4 if it is not already on your screen.
❏ Render a bitmap image to the **Render** window.
❏ Save the bitmap image with the name EX15-5.BMP. Then, copy the image to the Windows Clipboard.
❏ Using a Windows-compatible word processor, begin a new file and paste the contents of the Clipboard into the document.

Render window display options

The **Render** window has options that let you arrange the open display windows. These options are located in the **Window** pull-down menu. These options are explained below:

- **Tile.** Arranges the open display windows so they are adjacent to each other.
- **Cascade.** Arranges the open render windows so they overlap one another
- **Arrange Icons.** Automatically aligns minimized display windows along the bottom of the **Render** window.
- **Reuse Window.** A new rendered image clears the existing image from the active **Render** window and uses the same window.

The Windows Render Options dialog box

You can set the image size and color resolutions for images rendered to the **Render** widow using the **Windows Render Options** dialog box, Figure 15-65. To access this dialog box, pick the **Options** button on the **Render** window toolbar or select **Options...** from the **File** pull-down menu in the **Render** window. Any changes made in this dialog box do not take effect until you render the model again.

Figure 15-65.
The **Windows Render Options** dialog box.

Select the size

Select the color depth

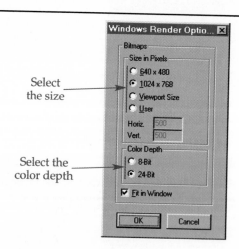

Size

You can specify the image size for rendered images using one of the four radio buttons located in the **Size in Pixels** area of the **Windows Render Options** dialog box. The **640 × 480** and **1024 × 768** radio buttons set the image size to common computer display resolutions. The other radio buttons are explained below:

- **Viewport Size.** This button sets the size of the bitmap to the size of the viewport that you are rendering.
- **User.** This button lets you manually set the size of the image, to a maximum of 4096 × 4096 pixels.
- **Fit in Window check box.** (located at the bottom of the dialog box) Scales the image to the size of the display window and overrides the other options.

Color depth

The color depth is the number of bits used for each pixel. Either 8-bit or 24-bit images can be rendered to the **Render** window. Select one of the radio buttons in the **Color Depth** area of the **Windows Render Options** dialog box. Even when working on a system set up for 8-bit color display (256 colors), you can still render and save a 24-bit (16.7 million colors) image. When the image is displayed on a system set up for 24-bit color, the image displays in true color.

Printing a Rendered Image

You can print a rendered image from the **Render** window. Select **Print...** from the **File** pull-down menu or pick the **Print** button on the toolbar. The **Print** dialog box shown in Figure 15-66 appears. The rendered image is displayed in a border that represents the paper size and orientation of the default Windows system printer. The current system printer is used, regardless of the current printer/plotter in AutoCAD.

In Figure 15-66, the rendered 3dshapes drawing from Exercise 15-1 appears in the dialog box. Notice that the image is located near the top of the outline. Where the image appears in the outline is where it will print on the paper. You can change the position of the printed image by picking and holding anywhere on the image, and dragging the image to a new location.

You can also change the size of the printed image. Notice the solid-filled squares around the boundary of the image. These squares are called *resize handles* and are used to change the size of the image both horizontally and vertically. Handles function much like a hot grip. When you move your cursor over a handle, it changes to a double-headed arrow. Simply hold down the pick button and drag the image to the desired size. If you pick a corner handle, the image is rescaled maintaining the correct aspect ratio.

Once the image is scaled and located as needed, you can set the number of printed copies using the **Copies:** text box. You can also lighten the printed image with the **Lighten** check box. With this box checked, the entire image is printed lighter. Darker colors are lightened more than lighter colors. When you are ready to print, pick the **OK** button.

Figure 15-66.
This **Print** dialog box appears when printing from the **Render** window.

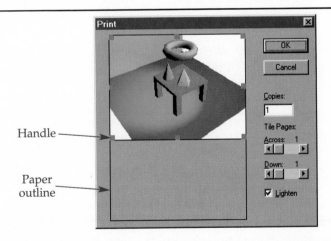

Handle

Paper outline

PROFESSIONAL TIP If you are using a laser or inkjet printer, the **Lighten** feature should be used whenever possible to save toner or ink.

Printing across multiple pages

Tiling is printing an image on more than one sheet of paper to create a larger image, such as a poster-size printout. The sheets are then placed together to form the completed image. The **Tile Pages: Across:** and **Down:** slider bars indicate the number of pages the image will print on. The maximum number of pages that can be tiled depends on the printer you are using. The image can be moved or resized across the tiled pages using the handles.

EXERCISE 15-6

❏ If you are connected to a printer, open EX15-1 if it is not currently displayed on your screen.
❏ Set the rendering preferences to render to a window and render the scene. Without changing any of the printing parameters, print the rendered image.
❏ Turn off **Lighten** in the **Print** dialog box. Print the rendered image again. Compare the two printed images. Which do you prefer?
❏ Return to the **Print** dialog box. Set the slider bars to tile 3 pages across and 3 pages down. Print the multiple-page image. Then, tape the sheets together to complete the image.

Chapter Test

Answer the following questions on a separate sheet of paper.

1. Define the following rendering terms:
   A. Ambient light
   B. Distant light
   C. Point light
   D. Spotlight
   E. Roughness
   F. Diffused light
2. When using the **RENDER** command, what is a scene made up of?
3. Which dialog box allows you to specify the shininess and roughness of a surface?
4. What is the relationship between the numerical value of roughness and the size of the highlight on a shiny surface?
5. What is the meaning of *altitude* and *azimuth* in the sun angle calculator?
6. How must the values of **Hotspot** and **Falloff** relate to each other?
7. What types of renderings can produce cast shadows?
8. What is *antialiasing*?
9. Where do you set the option to send the rendering to a file?
10. What command allows you to crop an image by pixels and save it as a file? What types of files can be saved?
11. What effect does selecting **Smooth Shade** have on the model when rendering?
12. What are the advantages of rendering to a file?
13. To produce a file of a rendering, how should you configure the **Rendering Preferences** dialog box?
14. When working with materials, which attributes allow the use of a bitmap?
15. What is the function of a bump map?
16. List the steps involved in loading a material, customizing the material, and applying it to a surface.
17. What is the difference between point lights and distant lights?
18. What is *attenuation*? Which lights have this attribute?
19. What is *mapping*?
20. How do you remove mapping from an object?

21. Name the different types of backgrounds that can be applied to a model.
22. Name two ways in which landscape objects can be displayed.
23. What aspects of a landscape object can be edited?
24. What is the function of fog?
25. How do you prevent the display of the **Render** dialog box when the **RENDER** command is used?
26. When rendering bitmap images, the **Fit in Window** check box takes precedence over other screen resolution options. (True/False)
27. How can you resize the image area in the **Print** dialog box without losing the correct aspect ratio?
28. When printing across multiple pages, what determines the maximum number of pages that can be tiled?

Drawing Problems

1. In this problem, you will draw some basic 3D shapes, place lights in the drawing, and then render it.
   A. Begin a new drawing and name it P15-1.
   B. Draw the following 3D shapes using the layer names and colors as indicated.

Shape	Layer Name	Color
Box	Box	Red
Pyramid	Pyramid	Yellow
Wedge	Wedge	Green
Cone	Cone	Cyan
Dome	Dome	Blue
Dish	Dish	Magenta
Sphere	Sphere	White

   C. Draw the shapes in a circular layout, as shown below. Each shape should be one unit in size.
   D. Place a point light in the center of the objects, 3 units above them.
   E. Place two distant lights as shown in the drawing, having target points in the center of the objects. Light D-1 should be located at Z = 3 and light D-2 should be located at Z = 2.
   F. Place two spotlights as shown in the figure. Light S-1 has a target of the cone apex and light S-2 has a target of the pyramid apex. Light S-1 should be located at Z = 2.5 and light S-2 should be located at Z = 2.
   G. Render the drawing.
   H. Save the image as a bitmap file named P15-1.
   I. Save the drawing as P15-1.

2. Open drawing P15-1. Generate the following scenes and renderings using the light values given. Adjust the values of the spotlights based on their distance from the objects. See the illustration below for proper view orientations.

View Name	Scene Name	Ambient	Point	D-1	D-2
VIEW1	ONE	.7	2	1	0
VIEW2	TWO	.3	2	0	1
VIEW3	THREE	0	5	1	0

A. Create a material for the sphere with a color of 0.3, reflection of 0.7, and roughness of 0.1. Name it SPHERE1.
B. Create a second material for the sphere named SPHERE2 with a color of 0.7, reflection of 0.3, and roughness of 1.0.
C. Create a third material for the sphere named SPHERE3 with a roughness of 0.7, color of 0.5, and a reflection of 0.5.
D. Set finish SPHERE1 as current and render scene ONE.
E. Set finish SPHERE2 as current and render scene TWO.
F. Set finish SPHERE3 as current and render scene THREE.
G. Save the drawing as P15-2. Create a bitmap and save it as P15-2.

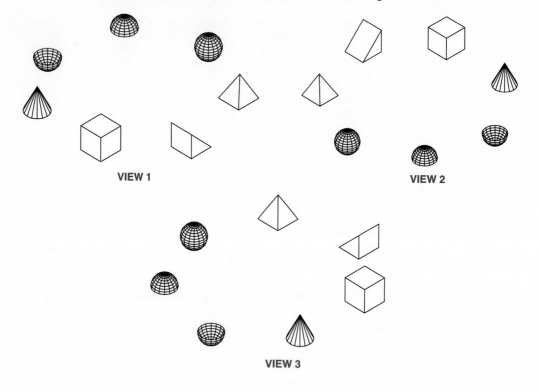

VIEW 1

VIEW 2

VIEW 3

AutoCAD and its Applications—Advanced

3. In this problem, materials and textures are attached to some of the objects in your drawing.
   A. Open the drawing P15-2.
   B. Attach materials to the following objects as indicated.

Object	Material
Box	Wood
Pyramid	Marble
Dome	Granite

   C. Give the wood a dark color with narrow rings of a concentric shape. The marble should have a lot of vein color and swirling. The granite should have a highly polished look. Choose your own colors for the marble and granite.
   D. Create a rendering of these three objects only using each of the three rendering types.
   E. Create a rendering of all objects using shadows. Create a bitmap and save it as P15-3.

4. This problem adds additional light to a drawing. You will then use the Windows Clipboard and place the drawing in a written document.
   A. Open the drawing P15-1.
   B. Place a new point light directly over the cone and a new distant light to one side and slightly below the "ground." Render the drawing.
   C. Place the rendering on the Windows Clipboard.
   D. Minimize AutoCAD.
   E. Open your Windows-compatible word processor.
   F. Type the following sentence:
      This is an example of what AutoCAD can do for documents.
   G. Paste the rendered drawing into the document. Save the document as P15-4.

5. Open a 3D drawing from a previous chapter. Do the following.
   A. Place two point lights around the model.
   B. Place two distant lights around the model.
   C. Place two spotlights around the model.
   D. Create a solid background for the model using a color that complements the model.
   E. Add three appropriate landscape objects in the model. Edit them as needed.
   F. Create three scenes of the model. Choose two different lights for each scene.
   G. Set the ambient light to a value of your choice.
   H. Render each scene once. Change the light attributes to create highlights. Render each scene again.
   I. Render one scene as a TGA file, one as a TIF file, and one as a BMP file.
   J. Replay each image.
   K. Save the drawing as P15-5.

6. Open problem P15-5. Do the following.
   A. Configure AutoCAD to render to a window.
   B. Render each one of the three scenes.
   C. Minimize each of the image tiles.
   D. Open a BMP file from the Windows folder.
   E. Print one of the images centered on a page. Reduce the image size and move it to the upper-right corner. Print it again.
   F. Copy one of the images to the Windows Clipboard.
   G. Paste the Clipboard image into a word processor document.
   H. Print the document.
   I. Save the document as P15-6.

AutoCAD and the Internet

Learning Objectives

After completing this chapter, you will be able to:

- Explain the Internet and its basic operation.
- Launch a Web browser and access Web sites from within AutoCAD.
- Create Drawing Web Format (DWF) files.
- View a DWF file using a Web browser.
- Attach hyperlinks to an AutoCAD drawing.
- Open and insert drawings from the World Wide Web.
- Save drawings to the World Wide Web.
- Download a utility to view a DWF file.
- Create a simple Hypertext Markup Language (HTML) document containing a DWF file.

The Internet started in 1969 as a network consisting of four computers. It now includes millions of computers worldwide, connected to one another through the use of telecommunication lines. The Internet is a powerful and versatile communications medium. One of the most widespread uses of the Internet is for sending and receiving electronic mail. Electronic mail, or *e-mail*, is used to create, send, and receive text messages and other files by telecommunication.

Another widely known application of the Internet is the World Wide Web (WWW). The *World Wide Web*, often called "the Web," uses Hypertext Markup Language (HTML) files to provide a graphic interface to access Internet information. However, it is important to remember that the Web is not the Internet, it *uses* the Internet.

The term *hypertext* refers to an object, such as text or a picture, that is linked to other information. This additional information is displayed when the hypertext is picked. These links are also called *hyperlinks.* A *Web site* is a collection of HTML documents which may include text, graphics, and sound files that others can view on the Internet using a *Web browser.* The *Uniform Resource Locator* (*URL*) refers to the location, or address, of a Web file on the Internet.

AutoCAD 2000 incorporates Internet tools that allow you to communicate AutoCAD drawing information using the Web. A drawing can be saved in a format that can be viewed using a Web browser and placed on a Web site. In this way, drawings can be shared with others who do not have AutoCAD.

Coupling AutoCAD with the Internet opens up whole new worlds of possibilities. With geographic and software restrictions removed, designs can be communicated to anyone, anywhere in the world. This ease of communication lends itself to creating effective virtual workgroups. A *virtual workgroup* is a group of individuals separated by geographic distances who collaborate on a project through the use of telecommunication technologies, such as e-mail and the World Wide Web.

GETTING CONNECTED TO THE INTERNET

The Internet uses telecommunications lines, such as phone lines or cable television lines, to send information between computers. Home Internet users generally use modems and standard phone lines or cable connections to get "online." A *modem* is a device that converts computer data into signals that can be sent through phone or cable services to another computer modem. The other modem receives the signals and converts them back to computer data. In many areas, integrated services digital network (ISDN) or "T-carrier" connections are available. These connections offer much higher speeds than traditional phone lines, but special modems are required. There is usually a higher cost involved with these high-speed connections than with traditional phone lines or cable connections.

An *Internet Service Provider* (*ISP*) is required to use the Internet. An ISP is the company or organization that you "dial up" to get access to the Internet. There are typically several different ISPs in any given region. Online service providers such as CompuServe® and America Online® (AOL) also provide Internet access.

Launching a Web Browser

A Web browser is required to access the World Wide Web. There are several different browsers available. Most have features common to all browsers. It is a matter of personal preference which browser software you use. In order to take advantage of the newest Internet features, your browser should be the most current version available.

BROWSER

Web toolbar

Browse the Web

Selecting the **Browse the Web** button from the **Web** toolbar, Figure 16-1, automatically launches your default Web browser. The **BROWSER** command can also be entered at the Command: prompt by typing BROWSER.

Figure 16-1.
The **Web** toolbar.

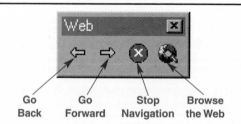

Go Back   Go Forward   Stop Navigation   Browse the Web

PROFESSIONAL TIP

When using both AutoCAD and your Web browser, you can easily move between the two applications by using the taskbar or by using the [Alt]+[Tab] keystroke. To see both windows at once, right-click on the taskbar and select Cascade Windows or one of the Tile Windows options.

When you pick the toolbar button, the **BROWSER** command uses the default URL. The initial default URL is home.htm, which is installed in the AutoCAD 2000 folder. The default URL is stored in the **INETLOCATION** system variable. You can change this value at the Command: prompt as follows:

Command: **INETLOCATION.⏎**
Enter new value for INETLOCATION <"C:\Program Files\ACAD2000\Home.htm">:
    http://www.autodesk.com.⏎
Command:

The default URL should be the location you most frequently access when you start your browser. This may be your own Web site, a client's Web site, or any other site that you frequently access.

When entered at the keyboard, the **BROWSER** command allows you to enter a specific URL or accept the default URL.

Command: **BROWSER.⏎**
Enter Web location (URL) <C:\Program Files\ACAD2000\Home.htm>: *(this path is the default installation location for AutoCAD 2000)*

Figure 16-2 shows the AutoCAD home.htm page as it appears in Microsoft Internet Explorer. This page gives an overview of AutoCAD's Internet features and has some key links to the Autodesk Web site.

Figure 16-2.
The AutoCAD home page is the initial default URL for the **BROWSER** command. (Autodesk, Inc.)

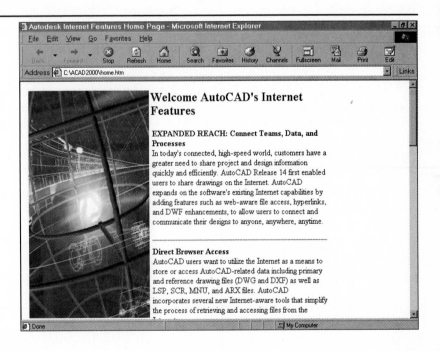

PROFESSIONAL TIP  The Autodesk Web site offers a great deal of information and many valuable resources—product support information, reviews, tips and tricks, white papers, discussion group access—for AutoCAD users of every experience level.

For 2000i Users...

In addition to the Internet features discussed in this chapter, AutoCAD 2000i includes an **eTransmit** feature, which simplifies the process of transferring drawings using e-mail, and a **Meet Now** feature, which allows you to work with AutoCAD in an online meeting setting. For discussion of these features, refer to *Preparing E-Mail Transmittals* on page 637 and *Internet Meetings* on page 640.

AUTOCAD INTERNET UTILITIES

AutoCAD provides powerful tools and options for time data communication with clients, vendors, and colleagues through the Web. It is now possible to get drawings from, or save them to, a Web site using the **Search the Web** button in the **OPEN** and **SAVE** dialog boxes. With Autodesk's *WHIP!*® plug-in for Web browsers, drawing files can be viewed, printed, and saved from the Web.

PROFESSIONAL TIP

When all you need to do is to send a drawing to someone as an e-mail attachment, select **Send...** from the **File** pull-down menu in AutoCAD. This automatically starts your default e-mail tool and supplies the current drawing as an attachment file. If e-mail has not been set up, this option is not available.

Drawing Web Format (DWF) Files

AutoCAD 2000 allows you to create a *Drawing Web Format (DWF)* file from an AutoCAD drawing. A DWF file is a highly compressed vector file that can be viewed in 2D using a Web browser equipped with Autodesk's *WHIP!* plug-in or the Autodesk Volo™ View program. A *plug-in* is an external application used as part of your browser program. *WHIP!* Release 4.0 is installed with AutoCAD 2000. The Volo View program can open a DWG, DWF, or DXF file. Both are free to download from the Autodesk Web site. Getting and setting up the *WHIP!* plug-in and Volo View program are covered later in this chapter.

PROFESSIONAL TIP

For a fast start, the AutoCAD 2000 Learning Assistance has tutorials on working with DWF files. The AutoCAD 2000 Learning Assistance CD comes with AutoCAD 2000.

Creating DWF files

A DWF file is created using the **PLOT** command. The AutoCAD documentation refers to this as the "ePlot" feature. First, open the **Plot** dialog box. In the **Plotter configuration** area of the **Plot Device** tab, the **Name:** drop-down list gives you two choices for creating the DWF file. These are **DWF Classic.pc3** and **DWF ePlot.pc3**, Figure 16-3.

Figure 16-3.
The **Plot** dialog box
is used to create
DWF files.

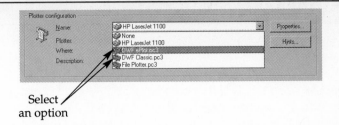

Select
an option

The **DWF Classic.pc3** creates a DWF file with a black background while the **DWF ePlot.pc3** creates a DWF file with a white background.

Once you select a DWF option, specify the **File name:** and the **Location**: in the **Plot to file** area. Use all the other settings in the **Plot Device** and **Plot Settings** tabs just as you would when plotting a hard copy. Refer to Chapter 10 in *AutoCAD and its Applications—Basics* for detailed information on plotting.

The DWF options have property settings that effect the plot output. These settings are accessed by picking the **Properties...** button under the **Plot Device** tab after a DWF plotting option is selected. In the **Plotter Configuration Editor** dialog box, select **Custom Properties** from the **Device and Document Settings** tab, Figure 16-4A. Then, pick the **Custom Properties...** button to display the **DWF Properties** dialog box, Figure 16-4B.

The **Resolution** and **Format** areas in the **DWF Properties** dialog box are primarily used to control the size of the DWF file. Small files make for easy electronic transmission. The **Resolution** setting controls the accuracy of the resulting DWF file. For smaller drawings with little detail, the loss of some drawing accuracy is usually acceptable. A medium resolution is best in most cases. A DWF created with extreme resolution may be too large for practical electronic transmission.

The **Format** area has three options. The **Compressed Binary (recommended)** option is, obviously, the recommended selection. It produces a small, binary file. The **ASCII** option creates an ASCII file.

Figure 16-4.
The **Plotter Configuration Editor** and **DWF Properties** dialog boxes allow you to set up additional parameters used to create the DWF file.

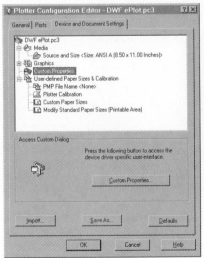

A

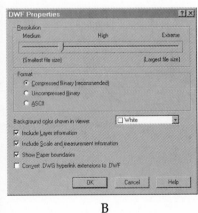

B

NOTE   Commands that control the display of geometry on screen, such as **VIEWRES**, **FACETRES**, and **DISPSILH** are a factor when creating a DWF file.

EXERCISE 16-2

❏ Open an AutoCAD 2000 drawing of your own or one from the AutoCAD "sample" folder.
❏ Type in PLOT at the command line and select the **DWF ePlot.pc3** option for the plot device.
❏ Specify a file name and location to save the file.
❏ Pick the **Full Preview...** button. Make changes in the **Plot Settings** tab as necessary.
❏ Pick the **OK** button to create the DWF file.
❏ Open your Web browser program.
❏ Open the DWF file in the browser.

The **Browse the Web** Button

Browse the Web

Many "open" and "save" dialog boxes in AutoCAD 2000 have the **Browse the Web** button. Picking this button displays a Web browser titled **Browse the Web**–*command*, Figure 16-5. The current AutoCAD command is displayed in the title bar. The default page is set with the **INETLOCATION** variable. Typing the URL of a Web site in the **Look in:** text box will display that site.

Favorites

If you are accessing a URL frequently, you can save the URL so you do not need to type it in every time. Pick the **Favorites** button and select **Add To Favorites...** from the menu. This will allow you to save the URL in the Windows Favorites folder. The contents of this folder are displayed when the **Favorites** button is picked.

Figure 16-5.
The **Browse the Web** dialog box gives you access to files on the Internet.

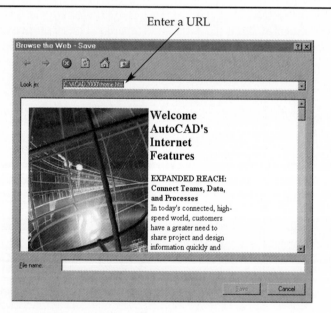

Inserting a Hyperlink

AutoCAD 2000 allows you to hyperlink drawing objects to a file or to a URL. When a DWF is created and then viewed, these links can be picked to display the other files. The hyperlinks can also be accessed directly in AutoCAD. The "link" can be a Web document, a DWF file, or even a word processing document.

For example, an assembly drawing can be created with each part linked to its detail drawing. The individual parts might instead be linked to a Web page that contains part numbers, supplier name, and prices. The assembly drawing could also have a link to a spreadsheet made up for the bill of materials for all the parts in the assembly.

AutoCAD and its Applications—Advanced

To attach a URL to an object, pick the **Insert Hyperlink** button from the **Standard** toolbar, pick **Hyperlink...** from the **Insert** pull-down menu, or type HYPERLINK at the Command: prompt. The key combination [Ctrl]+[K] can also be used. If the drawing has not been saved, a dialog box appears recommending that you save the drawing. A prompt then appears on the Command: line asking you to select objects. Pick the objects that you want to attach a file or URL to and press [Enter]. The **Insert Hyperlink** dialog box is displayed, Figure 16-6.

The **Link to file or URL:** text box is where the path to the document you want to link to is entered. The file to link can be on your local hard drive, any network drive, or a URL. You can either type the path or use the **Browse...** button. Picking the **Browse...** button displays the **Browse the Web–Select Hyperlink** dialog box, Figure 16-7. To link to a URL, pick the **Search the Web** button in this dialog box. Once the path to the link is specified, pick **OK** in the **Insert Hyperlink** dialog box to attach the link.

When the cursor is held over the object with a link, an icon appears next to the crosshairs. See Figure 16-8. To open the hyperlinked file within AutoCAD, first select the object. Next, right-click and select **Hyperlink** then **Open** from the shortcut menu. The path and file name are displayed next to **Open**.

If you have disabled the shortcut menus in AutoCAD, you can open a hyperlink file by selecting the object. Then, click on one of the grips to make it hot and right-click. Select **Go to URL...** from the shortcut menu. This shortcut menu is not disabled.

HYPERLINK
[Ctrl]+[K]

Insert
➥ Hyperlink...

Standard
toolbar

Insert Hyperlink

For 2000i Users...

The **Insert Hyperlink** dialog box has been updated for AutoCAD 2000i. Refer to **Insert Hyperlink** *Dialog Box* on page 630 for a complete discussion.

Figure 16-6.
The **Insert Hyperlink** dialog box allows you to attach a file or URL to objects.

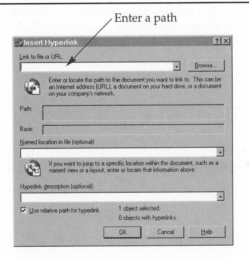

Enter a path

Figure 16-7.
You can browse the Web to insert a hyperlink.

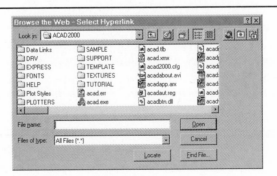

Figure 16-8.
When the cursor is
over an object that
has a hyperlink, the
crosshairs change to
indicate this.

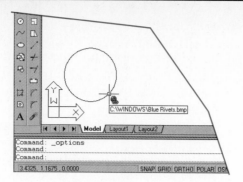

C:\WINDOWS\Blue Rivets.bmp

NOTE

The **Hyperlink/Open** selection opens the link in the associated program, such as Microsoft Paint. If you do not have a program associated with that file type, you will get a "bad argument" message from AutoCAD. The **Go to URL...** selection shows the link in your browser.

EXERCISE 16-3

❑ Start a new drawing session in AutoCAD. Set your limits to 0,0 and 12,9 and then **ZOOM All**.
❑ Draw a rectangle from 3,3 to 10,6.
❑ Save the drawing as EX16-3.dwg.
❑ Select the **Insert Hyperlink** button and then select the rectangle.
❑ Pick the **Browse...** button and choose any type of word processing document or image file, such as a Word, Excel, or JPEG file. Be sure it is an associated file type.
❑ Apply the link.
❑ Select the rectangle, right-click, and select **Open** from the **Hyperlink** cascading menu.
❑ Save the file.

Editing a Hyperlink

HYPERLINK
[Ctrl]+[K]

Insert
➡ Hyperlink...

Standard
toolbar

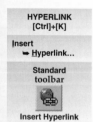

Insert Hyperlink

If the URL or path to a linked file is changed, you will need to open the AutoCAD drawing and edit the hyperlink. Otherwise, AutoCAD will never "find" the link. To edit a hyperlink, select the **Insert Hyperlink** button, pick **Hyperlink...** from the **Insert** pull-down menu, or type HYPERLINK at the Command: prompt. The [Ctrl]+[K] key combination also works. Then, select the hyperlinked object you want to edit.

The **Edit Hyperlink** dialog box that appears is the same as the **Insert Hyperlink** dialog box, with the addition of the **Remove link** button. Use the same methods to edit the hyperlink path as you would when attaching a hyperlink. To delete the hyperlink from the selected object, pick the **Remove link** button at the bottom of the dialog box. You can also remove a link by simply deleting the path in the **Link to file or URL:** text box and picking the **OK** button.

NOTE

Although you can select multiple objects when editing a hyperlink, this may not be wise. Any change made in the **Edit Hyperlink** dialog box is made to *all* selected objects.

Showing the Hyperlinks in a Drawing

AutoCAD's **SHOWURLS** command shows all the hyperlinks in a drawing. This is useful if you cannot remember which objects have hyperlinks, or which hyperlink is attached to which object. Unless the Express menu is installed and loaded, the command must be entered at the Command: prompt as SHOWURLS. With the Express menu loaded, select **Show URLs** from the **Tools** cascading menu in the **Express** pull-down menu.

The **SHOWURLS** dialog box lists the hyperlinks in the drawing, Figure 16-9A. If no hyperlinks are attached to the drawing, the message No URLs found appears on the command line. To find the object that has a hyperlink attached to it, highlight the URL name and then select the **Show URL** button. The dialog box disappears momentarily and a thick magenta bounding box is displayed around the object that has the high-lighted hyperlink, Figure 16-9B. After a few seconds, the dialog box reappears.

SHOWURLS

Express
➥ Tools
➥ Show URLs

For 2000i Users...

The **SHOWURLS** command is an Express Tool. Express Tools are not provided with AutoCAD 2000i but can be downloaded from the Autodesk Point A Web site.

Figure 16-9.
A—The **SHOWURLS** dialog box shows hyperlinks in a drawing file. B—The "pick area" of a link is defined by the object's bounding box.

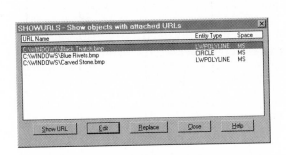

A

B

Line object

Bounding box

PROFESSIONAL TIP

The object that has the hyperlink attached to it does not need to be visible on your screen when you select the **Show URL** button. AutoCAD will adjust the display to show you the object. When the dialog box is closed, the screen is returned to the current zoom.

EXERCISE 16-4

❑ Start a new drawing session in AutoCAD. Set your limits to 0,0 and 12,9 then **ZOOM All**. Using the circle command, create a circle at 6,4.5 with a diameter of 3 units.
❑ Save the file as EX16-4.dwg in its own folder.
❑ Use the **HYPERLINK** command to attach a hyperlink to the circle object.
❑ Use the **SHOWURLS** command to display linked objects.
❑ View the linked object by selecting the **Show URL** button.
❑ Remove the hyperlink from the circle.
❑ Use the **HYPERLINK** command to attach a different hyperlink to the circle object. Name the hyperlink CIRCLE1.HTM. This link will be created in Exercise 16-6.
❑ Create a DWF file named EX16-4.dwf in the same folder as the EX16-4.dwg file.

Opening a Drawing from the Web

The **OPEN** command can be used to open a drawing file on the Web. AutoCAD copies the drawing to a temporary file on your hard disk and loads it into the drawing editor. The drawing can then be edited and saved to the local hard drive.

The **OPEN** command displays the **Select File** dialog box. Pick the **Search the Web** button to open the **Browse the Web–Open** dialog box. Type the URL with the drawing file name in the **File name:** text box and pick the **Open** button. The **Remote Transfer in Progress** dialog box shows the status of the transfer.

PROFESSIONAL TIP

AutoCAD does not check to confirm that an Internet connection exists when you attempt a transfer. If you are not connected to the Internet when attempting to connect to a URL, the **Transfer Status** dialog box will display 0 bytes and 0% complete until you pick **Cancel** or the time out occurs.

Inserting a Drawing from the Web

It is possible to insert a drawing from the Web into the current drawing using the **INSERT** command. The **INSERT** command is accessed by picking the **Insert Block** button from the **Draw** toolbar, picking **Block...** from the **Insert** pull-down menu, or by typing I or INSERT at the Command: prompt.

Selecting the **Browse...** button from the **Insert** dialog box displays the **Select Drawing File** dialog box. Pick the **Search the Web** button to display the **Browse the Web–Open** dialog box. This is the same dialog box discussed in the previous section.

After the drawing is downloaded, you can insert the drawing as a locally defined block. As with other applications of the **INSERT** command, an insertion point, scale factor, and rotation angle must be specified.

Saving a Drawing to the Web

The **SAVE** command allows you to save a drawing directly to the Web. It is accessed by picking **Save As...** from the **File** pull-down menu or by typing SAVE at the Command: prompt. This displays the **Save Drawing As** dialog box. Pick the **Search the Web** button and enter the URL using this syntax.

ftp://*server name/path name/file name*.dwg

Pick the **Save** button to save the drawing. The **Remote Transfer in Progress** dialog box indicates the status of the transfer.

EXERCISE 16-5

❑ Open the drawing EX16-4 in AutoCAD.
❑ With the permission of your system administrator, use the **SAVE** command to save the file to an appropriate location on your Internet server.
❑ Start a new drawing session. Now use **OPEN** to open the drawing that you just saved.
❑ Start a new drawing session again. This time, use **INSERT** to insert the drawing into the current drawing. Save this drawing as EX16-5.

Optional Command Line Hyperlink Utilities

The most common way to insert a hyperlink is to use the **HYPERLINK** command. However, there are three other hyperlink utilities that can be accessed only from the command line. These commands are **ATTACHURL**, **DETACHURL**, and **SELECTURL**.

Using the ATTACHURL command

To use the **ATTACHURL** command, type ATTACHURL at the Command: prompt as follows:

```
Command: ATTACHURL↵
Enter hyperlink insert option [Area/Object] <Object>: ↵
Select objects: (select any number of objects)
Select objects: ↵
Enter hyperlink <current drawing>: http://www.cadnet1.com↵
Command:
```

You can also attach a URL to a rectangular area of the drawing.

```
Command: ATTACHURL↵
Enter hyperlink insert option [Area/Object] <Object>: A↵
First corner: (Pick the first corner)
Other corner: (Pick the other corner)
Enter hyperlink <current drawing>: http://www.cadnet1.com↵
Command:
```

A red rectangle appears in your drawing to show the defined area. The rectangle is on a new layer named URLLAYER. The URLLAYER layer must be visible when you plot the DWF file. The rectangle will not show in the DWF file.

Detaching a URL

The **DETACHURL** command is used to remove a URL attachment from an object or an area in the drawing.

```
Command: DETACHURL↵
Select objects: (pick the first corner of an implied window)
Other corner: (pick the other corner)
6 found
Select objects: ↵
1. C:\WINDOWS\Clouds.bmp ()
2. C:\WINDOWS\Blue Rivets.bmp ()
3. C:\WINDOWS\Carved Stone.bmp ()
4. C:\WINDOWS\Circles.bmp ()
Remove, deleting the Area.
4 hyperlinks deleted.
Command:
```

Objects that do not have a URL are filtered out of the selection set. When an area is removed, the message Remove, deleting the Area appears, as shown above, indicating the area was deleted. Erasing an area also removes the associated URL link.

PROFESSIONAL TIP  After adding, changing, or deleting URL information, you must replot the DWF file for the changes to take effect.

Identifying objects with URLs

The **SELECTURL** command offers a convenient method to edit all URLs in your drawing simultaneously. For example, to remove all URLs from a drawing, use **SELECTURL** followed by **DETACHURL**. Similarly, all URLs can be changed or listed. Only the objects or areas visible in the active viewport are selected. To use the command, type SELECTURL at the Command: prompt. All objects and areas with attached URLs in the current viewport are selected.

GETTING A UTILITY TO VIEW DWF FILES

The *WHIP!* plug-in, the Volo View Express program, or AutoCAD 2000 is required to view DWF files. Both the *WHIP!* plug-in and the Volo View Express program are free and can be downloaded from the Autodesk Web site. Make sure to get the latest version of *WHIP!* that is compatible with AutoCAD 2000. You may be required to electronically "sign" a license agreement before downloading, Figure 16-10. Be certain to review the system requirements and installation instructions.

The *WHIP!* plug-in is about 3.5 Mb in size and can take an hour or more to download. When downloading the *WHIP!* plug-in, you will have the option to install it without exiting your browser. The *WHIP!* plug-in is activated after the installation procedure is complete. The next time you open a Web document that contains a DWF file, the *WHIP!* plug-in is automatically used to view the file.

The Volo View Express program is about 16 Mb in size and can take three hours or more to download. To install Volo View, you will need to exit from your browser and run the downloaded file. Volo View can then be opened using the **Autodesk Volo View Express** icon placed on your desktop during installation.

Figure 16-10.
The *WHIP!* plug-in can be downloaded from Autodesk's Web site.
(Autodesk, Inc.)

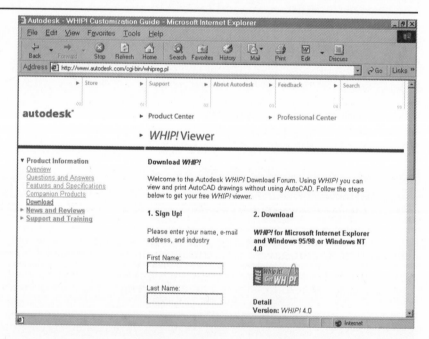

Using the *WHIP!* Plug-In

The cursor changes to a hand with an extended index finger when it is over a link in a DWF file. When viewing a DWF drawing file using the *WHIP!* plug-in and your browser, there are several display options. To display the *WHIP!* menu, right-click while the cursor is within the display area of the DWF drawing. The *WHIP!* menu is shown in Figure 16-11.

Figure 16-11.
The *WHIP!* menu is
displayed by right-
clicking in the
drawing display area.

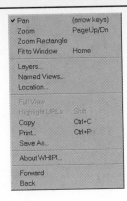

- **Pan.** Works like AutoCAD's realtime pan feature.
- **Zoom.** Works like AutoCAD's realtime zoom.
- **Zoom Rectangle.** Works like AutoCAD's **ZOOM Window** command.
- **Fit to Window.** Fills the browser window with the DWF drawing file.
- **Layers....** Allows you to turn layers that were plotted to the DWF file off and on.
- **Named Views.** Displays the **Named View** dialog box, where any defined view can be restored.
- **Location.** Opens a dialog box that shows the current location of the pointer on the screen in inches.
- **Full View.** Fills the browser window with the DWF drawing file.
- **Highlight URLs.** All URL link areas in the DWF drawing are displayed.
- **Copy.** Copies the DWF file image to the Windows Clipboard.
- **Print.** Sends the current view of the drawing to the system printer.
- **Save As.** Allows the DWF file to be saved to your hard drive. The current view can also be saved as a BMP file. If a DWG file exists in the same location as the DWF file and you have appropriate permissions, you can save as a DWG file.
- **About *WHIP!*.** Provides a dialog box that identifies the version of *WHIP!* you are using. Also provides information about the DWF file you are viewing.
- **Forward.** Works like the Forward button in your browser.
- **Back.** Works like the Back button in your browser.

Using Volo View Express

Once Volo View Express is started, pick the **Open** button and select a DWF, DWG, or DXF file to view it. Volo View Express has a shortcut menu that can be accessed by right-clicking in the display area with a file open, Figure 16-12. The Volo View Express menu options are very similar to the ones in the *WHIP!* menu. Depending on your drawing setup of the open file, some options may not be available.

- **Pan.** Works like AutoCAD's realtime pan feature.
- **Zoom.** Works like AutoCAD's realtime zoom.
- **Zoom Window.** Works like AutoCAD's **ZOOM Window** command.
- **Zoom Extents.** Fills the browser window with the open file.
- **Orbit.** Works like AutoCAD's **3DORBIT** command. Only available when viewing DWG or DXF files.
- **Layers.** Allows you to turn layers included with the file off and on.
- **Named Views.** Displays the **Named View** dialog box where any saved view can be restored.
- **Layouts.** Allows you to switch between saved layouts. Only available when viewing DWG or DXF files.
- **Markup.** This cascading menu contains three options for marking up the drawing. Pick **Sketch** to sketch on the drawing or **Comment** to add a note to the drawing. The **Save...** option allows you to save the drawing with markups as a DWF file.

Figure 16-12.
The Volo View
Express menu is
displayed by right-
clicking in the Volo
View Express drawing
display area.

- **Full View.** Fills the browser window with the DWF drawing file. Only available when Volo View is working as an Internet browser.
- **Show Hyperlinks.** Hyperlinked objects flash. Only available if at least one object has a hyperlink.
- **Copy.** Copies the image to the Windows Clipboard.
- **Print.** Sends the current view of the drawing to the system printer.
- **Save Copy As.** Allows the file to be saved locally. They can be saved as the original format (DWF, DWG, DXF) or as a WMF file.
- **Options.** Displays the **Options** dialog box, where you can set display and print settings.
- **About Volo View.** Displays a dialog box that identifies the version of Volo View you are using. Also shows information about the file you are viewing.

PUBLISHING A DWF FILE ON THE WEB

*For 2000i
Users...*

AutoCAD 2000i
includes the
Publish to Web
wizard, which
automatically
creates a
formatted HTML
Web page using
standard
templates and
DWF or JPEG
files. Refer to
*Publishing to the
Web* on page 632
for a complete
discussion.

Primary benefits of DWF files are small file size and extended viewing capabilities. The small file size allows fast file transfer. The viewing capabilities are extended because the drawing can be viewed or printed from computers that do not have access to AutoCAD. Using a Web browser with the *WHIP!* plug-in or Volo View Express program, anyone can view these drawings.

> **PROFESSIONAL TIP**
>
> When building a Web site, use your browser to check all the files and links while they are still on your local hard drive. This way you can be sure that the files will work properly when uploaded to your Web server.

Creating HTML

In order to make a DWF file easily accessible on the Web, it is best to place it within an HTML document. In the following example, minimal HTML coding is included and a simple text editor is used to create the HTML document. Refer to texts written specifically to teach HTML programming for detailed information.

The following HTML code creates a simple Web page that displays a title and a text heading. Save this as a text file called SAMPLE01.HTM.

```
<html>
<head>
  <title>Title: A Simple HTML Document Example</title>
</head>
<body bgcolor="ffffff">
<h2>This page demonstrates the use of a .dwf file</h2>
</body>
</html>
```

Viewed in the Web browser, this HTML code produces the results shown in Figure 16-13.

Now, a file named example1.dwf that is saved in the same folder as the HTML document is added to the Web page. The complete code is as follows. The existing code is shown in color.

```
<html>
<head>
  <title>Title: A Simple HTML Document Example</title>
</head>
<body bgcolor="ffffff">
<h2>This page demonstrates the use of a .dwf file</h2>
<OBJECT width=420
   height=315
   classid="clsid:B2BE75F3-9197-11CF-ABF4-08000996E931"
   codebase="ftp://ftp.autodesk.com/pub/autocad/plugin/whip.cab#version=2,0,0,0"
>
<PARAM name="Filename"
   value="EXAMPLE1.dwf"
>
<EMBED SRC="EXAMPLE1.dwf"
   PLUGINSPAGE="http://www.autodesk.com/products/autocad/whip/whip.htm"
   WIDTH=420
   HEIGHT=315
   name="EXAMPLE1"
>
</OBJECT>
</body>
</html>
```

Figure 16-13.
A simple HTML document viewed in the Web browser.

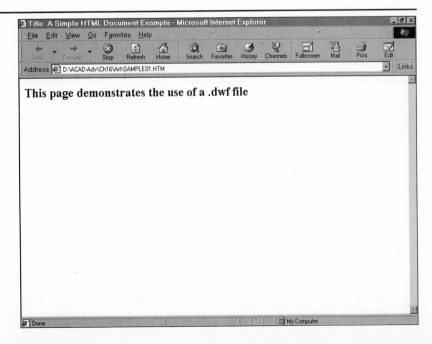

Viewed in the Web browser, this HTML code appears as shown in Figure 16-14. You can use a different drawing by inserting the DWF file name in the three places EXAMPLE1 appears in the code on the previous page.

Figure 16-14.
The DWF file is now displayed in the Web browser.

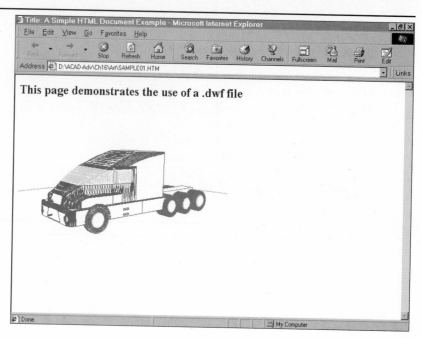

This page demonstrates the use of a .dwf file

NOTE

Do not post any confidential or sensitive information unless your Web site is secure.

EXERCISE 16-6

❑ Open Windows Notepad by typing NOTEPAD at the Command: prompt in AutoCAD. Create a text file that contains the following HTML code.

```
<html>
<head>
  <title>Exercise 16-6</title>
</head>
<body>
<h2>This circle has a diameter of 3.0 units.</h2>
</body>
</html>
```

❑ Save the text file in the same folder where the EX16-4.dwf file was saved. Name the text file CIRCLE1.HTM.
❑ Open Windows Explorer. Find EX16-4.dwf and double-click on it. Your browser should launch and display the DWF.
❑ Point at the circle and you will see by the change in your cursor that the circle contains a hyperlink. Pick the circle to activate the link.
❑ In Exercise 16-4, you attached the URL CIRCLE1.HTM to the circle. After activating the link, the CIRCLE1.HTM file is displayed in the browser window. You can use your browser's Back button to return to the DWF file.

AutoCAD and its Applications—Advanced

Chapter Test

Answer the following questions on a separate sheet of paper.

1. What are the two widely used applications of the Internet?
2. What type of software is used to view documents on the World Wide Web?
3. What does *ISP* stand for?
4. What AutoCAD command can be used to launch your default Web browser software?
5. What does the **INETLOCATION** system variable control?
6. What type of drawing file is created for viewing by a Web browser?
7. How do you create the file type in Question 6?
8. What does *HTML* stand for?
9. What software is used to create an HTML file?
10. In order to view the file type in Question 6, your browser must be equipped with the _____ plug-in, or you need the _____ program.
11. What two "types" of DWF files can be created?
12. On which toolbar is the **Insert Hyperlink** button located?
13. Which command will allow you to attach a hyperlink to an area?
14. What does *URL* stand for and to what does it refer?
15. Which menu must be loaded in order to access the **SHOWURLS** command using a pull-down menu?

Problems

1. Open an existing drawing. Use the **HYPERLINK** command and attach URLs to two objects in the drawing. Select objects that you can write a few lines of text information about. Specify the new URLs to be P16-1A.HTM and P16-1B.HTM. Plot the drawing as a DWF file named P16-1.

2. Create two HTML documents, one for each object in Problem 1. Use Windows Notepad or another text editor and the code below. Save the text files in the same directory as P16-1.DWF as P16-1A.HTM and P16-1B.HTM.

   ```
   <html>
   <head>
       <title>Chapter 16 DWF Links Problem</title>
   </head>
   <body>
   <h2>
   (Write one or two lines of information about the object in this
       section of the document.)
   </h2>
   </body>
   </html>
   ```

3. Use your text editor to create an HTML document named P16.HTM. Refer to the guidelines and examples in this chapter. Write the code so that the DWF file created in Problem 1 is displayed on the Web page. Save the document as P16.HTM. Use your Web browser to open P16.htm. Pick the links to ensure that all links work properly.

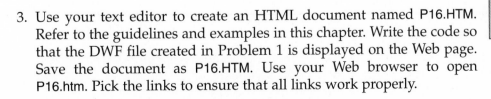

The Autodesk Web site is an exellent source of information for AutoCAD and other Autodesk products. (Autodesk, Inc.)

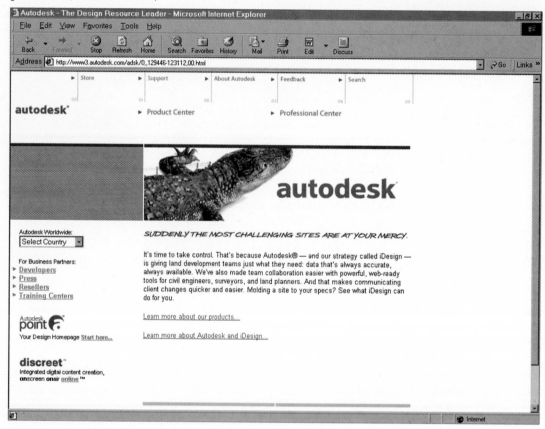

CHAPTER 17

Introduction to dbConnect

Learning Objectives

After completing this chapter, you will be able to:

- Define the term database.
- List the components of a database table.
- Explain SQL.
- Explain dbConnect.
- Describe database and SQL applications.
- Load a database in an AutoCAD drawing.
- Initialize a database to work in an AutoCAD drawing.
- Add and edit database table records using the **dbConnect Manager**.
- Create links between a database and an AutoCAD drawing object.
- Add displayable attributes to the drawing.
- Use SQL queries to ask questions of a database.

When creating an AutoCAD drawing, you are actually creating a very powerful graphic database. This database can be linked to other database software applications to use drawing data in a variety of ways. *Structured Query Language (SQL)* is the industry-standard language used to manage and exchange data between database applications. AutoCAD's *dbConnect* feature is a way to exchange data between AutoCAD drawings and other database applications using SQL. This chapter introduces the dbConnect feature and how to use it to maximize the functionality of your AutoCAD drawings.

NOTE This chapter is intended to be only an *introduction* to the capabilities of dbConnect. It is suggested that you go through the documentation in Chapter 22 of the *AutoCAD User's Guide*, Accessing External Databases. Begin to create your own small database and create a drawing that relates to it. This project should be a subject that is useful for you, and one that you can update and maintain easily. You will begin to see the value of working with a text and graphic relational database.

A *database* is a collection of information with contents that can be easily accessed, managed, and updated. The information stored in many databases represents large collections of data records or files such as inventories, employee records, and customer files. Modern databases are most often stored in computer files. There are many different software programs, called *database management systems* (*DBMS*), used to create, edit, and manage these databases. Most DBMS applications provide capabilities such as quick retrieval of files, report generation, and the ability to exchange information with other software programs.

Microsoft Access, Oracle, and dBASE are a few popular DBMS applications. AutoCAD is itself a very powerful database management system. The examples in this chapter use AutoCAD and a Microsoft Access database. The following external applications can be used with AutoCAD 2000.

- Microsoft Access 97
- dBASE V and III
- Microsoft Excel 97
- Oracle 8.0 and 7.3
- Paradox 7.0
- Microsoft Visual FoxPro 6.0
- SQL Server 7.0 and 6.5

With many DBMS programs, data are created and managed by entering text information in specific locations. These locations are called fields, records, and cells. A *field* is a column within a database. A *record* is a row in a database. The location where a field and a row intersect is called a *cell.* For example, the table in Figure 17-1 represents a portion of an employee record database. Each row represents a single record, and each column represents a field within the record.

An AutoCAD drawing file is a database. It stores a collection of graphic information that makes up the drawing. In the AutoCAD database, each record contains the information needed to define a single object, such as a line, arc, circle, or block. For example, a line object is defined by starting and ending points, as well as other data such as color, layer, and linetype.

Instead of using a table with rows and columns, the interface for creating and editing an AutoCAD database is the drawing editor. Using dbConnect, an AutoCAD database can be linked to an outside database. This establishes an information pool that can be edited and updated by either AutoCAD or the external database application.

Figure 17-1.
Databases are usually shown as tables. Each row is called a record. Each column is called a field.

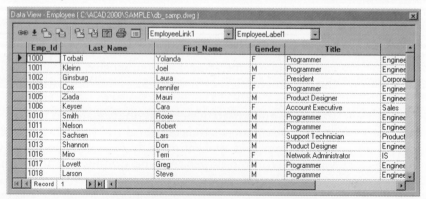

LINKED DATABASE APPLICATIONS

There are many applications for linking drawings to outside databases. One common application in industry is for facilities management. *Facilities management* involves the management of buildings, furnishings, equipment, and resources. An effective facilities management system maintains a record of all physical assets of a company. This record helps the company use existing resources effectively by reducing the number of unnecessary purchases. The records of personnel, physical assets, budgets, and company growth plans can be combined and used to control spending and ensure that the needs of the company are met.

Most companies maintain floor plans in CAD and maintain conventional database records of equipment and furnishings. When the conventional data is linked directly to the graphic data using dbConnect, changes in one database are automatically applied to the other. Therefore, changes to the database are reflected in the drawing, and the database records are updated if the drawing is edited.

The real power of dbConnect is the capability it gives a designer or planner to organize spatial information sources by linking AutoCAD data directly to related text data. This streamlines the process of generating reports and plans regarding space inventory, furniture and equipment inventories, and asset deployment. Equipment and furniture can be tracked when it is moved from one location to another. Any physical asset can be instantly located whenever it is needed.

DATABASE FILE STRUCTURE

The terminology used to describe the components in a database file can be confusing at first. Therefore, read this section carefully. When you understand the nature of a database table, working with dbConnect becomes much easier.

Sample Database Layouts

In the simplest form, a database is a list of items. This list usually appears in a table. A *table* is data arranged in rows and columns. A *row* (record) is a horizontal group of entries. A *column* (field) is a vertical group of entries. A sample Microsoft Access database file—db_samples.mdb—is installed with AutoCAD. A portion of the Employee table from this file is shown in Figure 17-1. In a table, the top row of the table contains the name of each column, such as Last_Name, First_Name, and Title.

Database File Components

A record (row) is shown highlighted in Figure 17-2. The first entry in the row is in the Emp_Id column. Six additional items complete the row. All the fields in a record (row) go together. In this example, all fields in a record are related to the employee identified by the employee number. Each field (column) represents a specific cell within the record. This cell is also called a field. For example, the Last_Name, First_Name, and Department columns define fields within each record. The First_Name column is highlighted in Figure 17-3.

A database table usually has a key. A *key* is assigned to a column in the table and used as a search option to identify different rows in the table. For example, the key for a sales projection table may be the MONTH column. The key can then be used to identify all the sales projections for a certain month, such as February (the FEBRUARY row). If more than one row can have the same value for each column, two or more columns can be specified as keys. This is called a *compound key*. A compound key allows a search to be more selective.

Figure 17-2.

A record is a row in a table. Every cell in the record (row) is related to the "key field." In this example, all cells in a record are related to the employee's ID number.

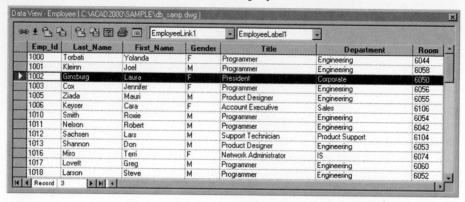

Figure 17-3.

The fields (columns) define specific elements of the record (row). In this example, the employee's first name appears in the highlighted column.

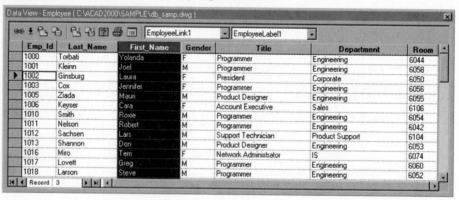

AutoCAD
User's
Guide 22

GETTING STARTED WITH DBCONNECT

Now that you are familiar with the meaning and structure of databases and their files, you can develop an understanding of how the various components of databases and AutoCAD fit together. Figure 17-4 illustrates the relationship of the DBMS tools used in this chapter.

> **NOTE**
>
> Before working through this chapter, make backup copies of the db_samp.dwg and db_sample.mdb files located in AutoCAD's Sample folder. When you want to restore the original files, simply copy them back to the original location.

Figure 17-4.
The relationship of database application software, database files, tables, and queries.

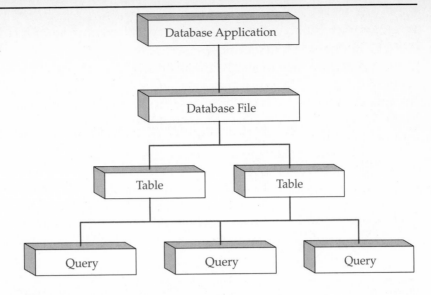

Creating a Database Environment

Before you can get started using a database application with AutoCAD, an ODBC data source needs to be configured within your Windows operating system. ODBC is an interface provided by the Windows operating system that allows application software to access the data in an SQL database. This configuration is necessary to ensure the correct drivers are used by all applications, including AutoCAD, that access the database.

AutoCAD 2000 has a preconfigured setup that allows you to connect to the db_sample Microsoft Access database from AutoCAD. Exercise 17-1 is a step-by-step tutorial on how to configure a new data source within Windows 98.

PROFESSIONAL TIP

When configuring an ODBC data source in Windows, you need to decide if you want the data source to be accessible by other computers. If you create the data source under the User DSN tab, it will only be available to that computer. Use the System DSN tab to configure a data source that can be used by computers that are networked together.

EXERCISE 17-1

- ❑ Note: This exercise is based on Windows 98.
- ❑ Open the Windows Control Panel by picking Start, Settings, and then Control Panel from the Windows taskbar.
- ❑ Double-click on the ODBC (32bit) icon to display the ODBC Data Source Administration dialog box.
- ❑ Select the System DSN tab and then pick the Add... button.
- ❑ Select the Microsoft Access Driver (*.mdb) and then the Finish button. The ODBC Microsoft Access 97 Setup dialog box appears.
- ❑ In the Data Source Name: text box type MyTest.
- ❑ Use the Select... button to select the db_samples.mdb file from AutoCAD's Sample folder.
- ❑ Pick the OK button for all of the ODBC dialog boxes and close the Control Panel.
- ❑ The data source is now configured in Windows.

DBCONNECT
DBC
[Ctrl]+[6]

Tools
→ dbConnect

Standard
toolbar

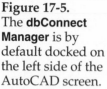

dbConnect

For 2000i Users...

In AutoCAD 2000i, the **dbConnect** button is not available in the **Standard** toolbar.

The **dbConnect Manager** provides the interface that allows you to connect to an external database and then work with the data. To display the **dbConnect Manager**, type DBC or DBCONNECT at the Command: prompt, pick the **dbConnect** button from the **Standard** toolbar, select **dbConnect** from the **Tools** pull-down menu, or use the [Ctrl]+[6] key combination. The **dbConnect Manager** is opened (by default) as a docked window on the left-hand side of the screen, Figure 17-5.

The **dbConnect Manager** window can be docked or floating, and it can be resized. To float the **dbConnect Manager**, double-click over the two horizontal bars at the top of the window or grab the bar and drag it to a different location on the screen. You can close the window by picking the "X" button in the upper-right corner, issuing the **DBCONNECT** command again, or right-clicking in the **dbConnect Manager** window and selecting **Hide** from the shortcut menu.

Figure 17-5.
The **dbConnect Manager** is by default docked on the left side of the AutoCAD screen.

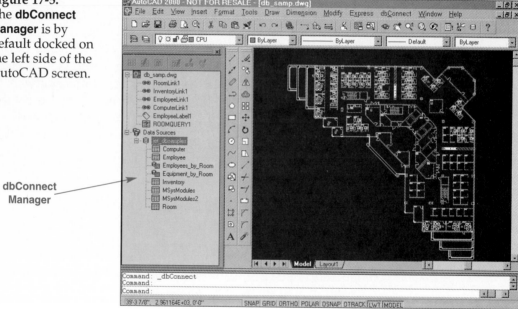

dbConnect Manager

NOTE

To close the **dbConnect Manager**, you cannot issue the **DBCONNECT** command at the Command: prompt. You must issue the command using the pull-down menu, toolbar button, or hot key combination. To close the **dbConnect Manager** using the Command: prompt, type DBCCLOSE.

The **dbConnect Manager** window shows two main things. First, all open drawing files are shown along with any database objects associated with each file. These are called *drawing nodes*. The window also shows all configured data sources and their components. These are shown under the *data sources node*.

When the **dbConnect Manager** is activated, a **dbConnect** pull-down menu is added to the menu bar. The commands used with the **dbConnect Manger** are located in this pull-down menu. The commands can also be accessed in shortcut menus by right-clicking on the components in the **dbConnect Manger** or from the toolbar in the **dbConnect Manager**.

Configuring a Data Source in AutoCAD

Once a data source has been configured in Windows, as shown in Exercise 17-1, you can use it to configure a data source connection in AutoCAD. Simply creating the data source in Windows does not automatically "connect" it to AutoCAD. AutoCAD also comes with a preconfigured data source. The jet_dbsamples data source should appear in the **dbConnect Manager** along with any other configured data sources. A small red "X" to the left of the jet_dbsamples name indicates that the data source is not connected.

To configure a data source in AutoCAD, right-click on **Data Sources** in the **dbConnect Manager**. Then, select **Configure Data Source...** from the shortcut menu. You can also select **Configure...** from the **Data Sources** cascading menu in the **dbConnect** pull-down menu. In the **Data Source Name:** text box, enter a name for the data source. This does not have to be the same name as the data source you will be using. Pick the **OK** button and the **Data Link Properties** dialog box is displayed. See Figure 17-6A.

dbConnect
➥ Data Sources
 ➥ Configure...

Under the **Provider** tab in the **Data Link Properties** dialog box is a list of the OLE DB providers installed on your system. An OLE DB provider allows your drawing data to work with a specific database. Select the correct OLE DB provider for the type of database being connected. Once the provider is selected, pick the **Next** button or the **Connection** tab.

The **Connection** tab settings are used to specify which Windows ODBC data source is going to be used, Figure 17-6B. This is the data source configured using the Windows Control Panel. In the **Specify the source of data:** area, pick the **Use data source name** radio button. Then, pick the Windows-configured data source you want to use from the drop-down list. If the source does not appear in the list but is configured, pick the **Refresh** button. This is necessary if you configure the source in Windows after AutoCAD is launched.

Figure 17-6.
The **Data Link Prpoerties** dialog box is used to configure a data source for AutoCAD.
A—The **Provider** tab is used to specify which type of database will be used.
B—The **Connection** tab is used to connect to a specific ODBC source.

Pick to display configured ODBC sources

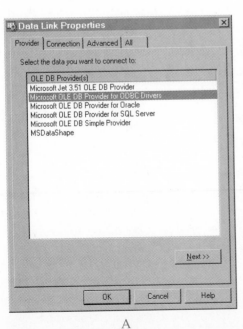

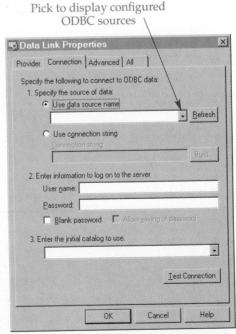

A   B

NOTE Refer to the AutoCAD documentation for information on the **Use connection string** option.

In the **Connections** tab, you can specify a unique user name and password for connecting to the data source. This can provide a level of security for the data source if necessary. This feature is not covered in this text.

At the bottom of the **Connections** tab is the **Test Connection** button. Once a data source is selected, pick this button to see if AutoCAD can connect to the external database. If it can, a message appears indicating the test was successful.

NOTE If the test connection fails, the data source appears in the **dbConnect Manager**, but it cannot be worked within AutoCAD. Make sure the database file has not been moved since it has been configured. Also, make sure the settings are typed in correctly. Spelling errors can cause a failure.

The **Advanced** tab can be used to set a timeout limit and permission rights to the data source. When a value is entered in the **Connect timeout:** text box, an error message is displayed if connecting to the data source takes longer that the specified time. This is very similar to "time out" errors you may have encountered while using the World Wide Web. In the **Access permissions:** area, different read and write permissions can be set. For example, the **Read** option allows a user to "look at" the external database, but not edit it. By default, none of the access options are checked, meaning users have full access.

The first three tabs are similar to a Windows "wizard." They guide you through the configuration process. The **All** tab lists all the current configuration settings. You can change an individual setting by highlighting it in the list and picking the **Edit Value** button. Use the **All** tab once you have become skilled at configuring a data source to streamline the process.

When all settings are correct, pick the **OK** button in the **Data Link Properties** dialog box. The data source name then appears as a data source in the **dbConnect Manager**. A red "X" appears next to the name indicating it is disconnected.

EXERCISE 17-2

❏ Make sure you have completed Exercise 17-1 before starting this exercise.
❏ In AutoCAD, open the **dbConnect Manager**.
❏ Right-click on **Data Sources** and select **Configure Data Source...** from the shortcut menu.
❏ In the **Data Source Name:** text box of the **Configure a Data Source** dialog box, type ACADTest and then pick **OK**.
❏ In the **Provider** tab of the **Data Links Properties** dialog box, select the Microsoft OLE DB Provider for ODBC Drivers.
❏ In the **Connection** tab, make sure the **Use data source name** radio button is selected and select MyTest from the drop-down list. If you do not see MyTest and you have completed Exercise 17-1, pick the **Refresh** button.
❏ Pick the **Test Connection** button to ensure a proper connection has been established.
❏ Pick the **OK** button to close the dialog box. The ACADTest data source should now be listed in the **dbConnect Manager** under the **Data Sources** node.

Connecting a Data Source in AutoCAD

Once a data source is configured in AutoCAD and appears in the **dbConnect Manager**, it must be connected. Once connected, you will be able to view, edit, and link the data from within AutoCAD.

The easiest way to connect a data source is to double-click on its name in the **dbConnect Manager**. You can also highlight it in the **dbConnect Manager**, right-click on it and select **Connect** from the shortcut menu, or select **Connect...** from the **Data Sources** cascading menu in the **dbConnect** pull-down menu. The tables and queries stored in the external database appear below the data source name, Figure 17-7. Notice how this appears similar to the folder structure of Windows Explorer.

dbConnect
➥ **Data Sources**
➥ C**onnect...**

To hide the tables and queries under a data source, pick the minus sign to the left of the data source or double-click on the name. To disconnect a data source, right-click on the name and select **Disconnect** from the shortcut menu. Disconnecting a data source automatically hides the tables and queries. You can change configuration properties for a disconnected data source by right-clicking on it and selecting **Configure...** from the menu.

Links can get broken or become invalid if the source table structure is changed or if the source table is moved to a different location. The **Synchronize** tool detects errors in links. To synchronize a link, right-click on the data source name and select **Synchronize...** from the shortcut menu or select **Synchronize...** from the **dbConnect** pull-down menu. Then, in the **Select a Database Object** dialog box, pick the link template to synchronize. If errors are detected, the **Synchronize** dialog box lists the errors and a description. The **Fix** and **Delete** tools can be used on the error that is currently selected.

dbConnect
➥ **Synchronize...**

Figure 17-7.
The queries and tables stored in a data source appear below the data source name in the **dbConnect Manager** once the data source is connected.

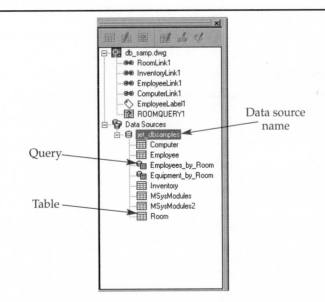

EXERCISE 17-3

❑ Make sure you have completed Exercise 17-1 and Exercise 17-2 before starting this exercise.

❑ The source ACADTest should appear under the **Data Sources** node in the **dbConnect Manager** with a red "X" indicating that it is not connected.

❑ In the **dbConnect Manager**, right-click on ACADTest and select **Connect**.

❑ The red "X" disappears and all tables and queries in the MyTest database are listed below the source name.

Deleting Data Sources

When a data source is configured in AutoCAD, a UDL file with the same name as the data source is placed in the AutoCAD Data Links folder. Any configured data source appears in all sessions of the **dbConnect Manager**. To remove a data source from the **dbConnect Manager**, delete the UDL file from the AutoCAD Data Links folder. AutoCAD can only use the database source files that are in the Data Links folder.

Data Source Path

You can change where AutoCAD saves and looks for database source files by changing the default path. To do this, select **Options...** from the **Tools** pull-down menu or type OP or OPTIONS at the Command: prompt. In the **Files** tab of the **Options** dialog box, select the plus sign next to **Data Sources Location**. This expands the branch and shows the current path for database source files, Figure 17-8. To change the path, highlight it and use the **Browse...** button to specify a different location.

Figure 17-8.
The location of data link files can be specified using the **Options** dialog box.

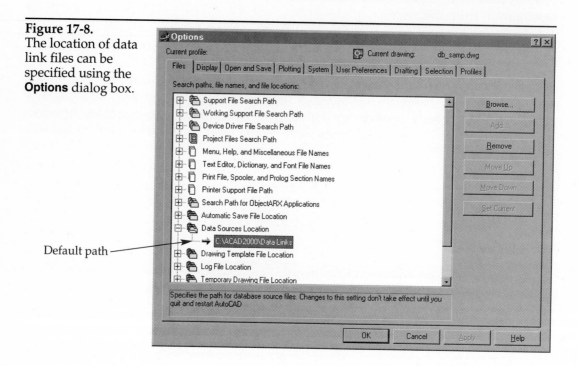

Default path

 NOTE After you change the data source path, the changes will not take effect until AutoCAD is restarted.

AutoCAD and its Applications—Advanced

With a connection established to an external database, AutoCAD can serve as a database viewer and editor. You can link records to objects, add records to the database, and query information from tables. There are many other possibilities as well. This section covers how to work with a connected database.

The Data View Window

The **Data View** window is used to view external database information within AutoCAD. It displays the data in columns and rows. The **Data View** window has its own toolbar and shortcut menus. When the **Data View** window is activated, the **Data View** pull-down menu is added to the AutoCAD menu bar next to the **dbConnect** pull-down menu. When the **Data View** window is closed, the **Data View** pull-down menu is removed.

The **Data View** window can be open while working in an AutoCAD drawing and can be docked or floating. To dock the **Data View** window, right-click on either scroll bar in the **Data View** window and select **Allow Docking** from the shortcut menu. To make it floating once it has been docked, select **Allow Docking** again from the shortcut menu.

To view a table in the **Data View** window, right-click on the table name in the **dbConnect Manager** and select either **View Table** or **Edit Table** from the shortcut menu. Selecting **View Table** allows you to view the data, but not edit it. The data background is shaded to indicate the "view mode." If **Edit Table** is selected, data can be edited, deleted, or added to the database. The data background is the Windows background color to indicate the "edit mode." The **Edit Table** option is only available if you have "write" permissions.

The table in the **Data View** window can be printed by selecting the **Print Data View** button from the **Data View** window toolbar. Then, in the **Print** dialog box, select the printer you want to use and specify any other settings. This is the standard Windows print dialog box, not the AutoCAD **Plot** dialog box.

External tables that are not linked can also be accessed by selecting either **View External Table...** or **Edit External Table...** from the **View Data** cascading menu in the **dbConnect** pull-down menu. Doing so automatically connects the data source.

dbConnect
→ View Data
    → View External Table...

dbConnect
→ View Data
    → Edit External Table...

Working with columns

A properly formatted database has a heading for each column that describes the type of information in the record field. These headings are shown in the **Data View** window. A properly formatted table also has one column that is unique and used as an identifier. In the Computer table, it is the Tag_Number column. This means that a "tag number" will never appear in more than one cell.

You can rearrange the order of the columns by first selecting the column heading to be moved. The entire column is highlighted. Then, drag the column heading to a different location.

NOTE   When rearranging the order of columns, the changes are only effective for that session of **Data View**. To permanently change the order of columns, the changes need to be made to the external database file.

One of the most powerful features of any database is the ability to sort. *Sorting* is arranging the data in a column in a certain order that you specify. A sort can be done by ascending (lowest to highest) or descending (highest to lowest) values.

Right-clicking a column heading displays a shortcut menu with **Sort** and other column tools.

Selecting **Sort** displays the **Sort** dialog box, Figure 17-9. In this dialog box, you can specify the sort settings. You can specify the primary sort column, which is usually the identifier column, such as Tag_Number. You can also further refine the sort by specifying other columns by which to sort. You can also specify whether each sorted column is in ascending or descending order.

Figure 17-9.
Use the **Sort** dialog box to specify sort settings.

Specify primary sort column

Specify order

PROFESSIONAL TIP

Double-clicking a column heading sorts in ascending order by that column's data. Double-clicking the same column heading a second time sorts in the reverse order.

Copying database information

The cells from the **Data View** window can be copied and pasted into another program, such as Microsoft Excel. To copy an individual cell's data, right-click in the cell and select **Copy** from the shortcut menu. To copy a record (row), right-click on the row's header and select **Copy** from the shortcut menu. An entire column can be copied by selecting the column header and using the [Ctrl]+[C] keyboard shortcut. To paste the column into another application, use the [Ctrl]+[V] key combination. To copy multiple columns, drag the mouse pointer over the columns and then use the [Ctrl]+[C] key combination.

LINK TEMPLATES AND LINKING DATA

AutoCAD User's Guide **22**

Before data can be linked to AutoCAD objects, a link template must be created. A link template is used to identify which fields from a database are used for the link. Each table that has data linked to AutoCAD has a link template. More than one link template can be made for a table. The difference between the templates is key value, or identifier, settings. Link templates are saved with the drawing.

Creating a Link Template

dbConnect
→ Templates
→ New Link
Template...

To create a link template, highlight the table name and select **New Link Template...** from the shortcut menu, pick the **New Link Template** button from the **dbConnect Manager** toolbar, or select **New Link Template...** from the **Templates** cascading menu in the **dbConnect** pull-down menu. The **New Link Template** dialog box is displayed, Figure 17-10.

New Link Template

Enter a name in the **New link template name:** text box. A name based on the table name appears in the text box as a suggestion. You do not have to use the suggested name. If a template is already created for the table, it is listed in the **Start with template:** drop-down list. An existing link template can be used as a base for a new one. Picking the **Continue** button displays the **Link Template** dialog box.

The **Link Template** dialog box is where key fields are set. All column headings from the table are shown. At least one column must be selected as a key field. The **OK** button is grayed out until a column is checked. Pick **OK** and the link template appears under the drawing name in the **dbConnect Manager**, Figure 17-11.

Figure 17-10.
The **New Link Template** dialog box is where a name is specified for the new link template.

Enter a template name

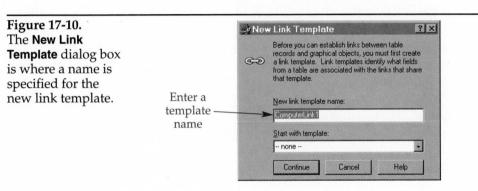

Figure 17-11.
The new link template appears in the **dbConnect Manager**.

New link template

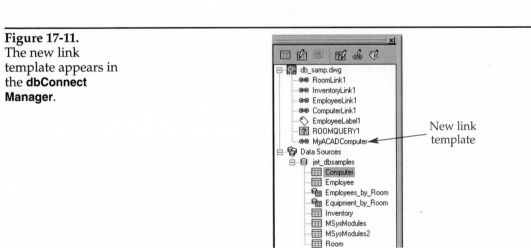

Deleting a Link Template

To delete a link template, right-click on it and select **Delete** from the shortcut menu. If **Delete** is shaded out, there is at least one active link using that link template. All links using a template can be deleted by right-clicking on the template and selecting **Delete links** from the shortcut menu. Then, the link template itself can be deleted.

You can also delete a link template by selecting **Delete Link Template...** from the **Templates** cascading menu in the **dbConnect** pull-down menu. Doing this opens the **Select a Database Object** dialog box. All link templates in the current drawing are listed in this dialog box. You can pick one or multiple link templates to delete. Pick **OK** to close the dialog box and delete the templates.

dbConnect
→ Templates
→ Delete Link
Template...

❑ Start a new drawing and open the **dbConnect Manager**.
❑ Connect the jet_dbsamples data source.
❑ Create a new link template using the Computer table. Name it My ACAD Link and use Tag_Number as a key field.
❑ Save the drawing as EX17-4.

Linking Data to AutoCAD Objects

dbConnect
➥ View Data
   ➥ View Linked
     Table...

View Table

After creating a link template, records (rows) from a table can be linked to AutoCAD objects. To link a record, first select a link template under the current drawing node in the **dbConnect Manager**. Then, right-click and select **View Table** or pick the **View Table** button in the **dbConnect Manager** toolbar. You can also pick **View Linked Table...** from the **View Data** cascading menu in the **dbConnect** pull-down menu and select the table to view from the **Select a Database Object** dialog box. The table is displayed in the **Data View** window, Figure 17-12.

Next, in the **Data View** window, pick the record (row) header to highlight all the fields in the record. If you have more than one link template tied to a particular table, use the **Select a Link Template** drop-down list to choose the link template you want to use.

The setting in the **Link and Label Settings** drop-down list, located on the far left of the **Data View** window toolbar, determines if a link or a label is created. Labels are discussed later in this chapter. The icon for the drop-down list reflects the current setting, Figure 17-13. These same options are available in the **Link and Label Settings** cascading menu of the **Data View** pull-down menu. To create a link, make the setting **Create Links**.

Figure 17-12.
A table displayed in the **Data View** window.

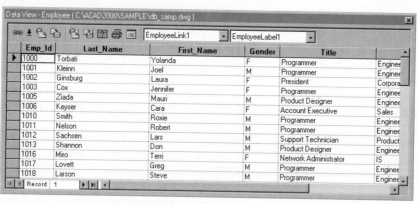

Figure 17-13.
The setting in the **Link and Label Settings** drop-down list specifies the current method of linking records. A—The icon when the **Create Links** setting is selected. B—The icon when the **Create Attached Label** setting is selected. C—The icon when the **Create Freestanding Label** setting is selected.

Link!

Create Attached
Label

Create Freestanding
Label

A

B

C

With the record (row) highlighted, pick the **Link!** button from the **Data View** window toolbar or select **Link!** from the **Data View** pull-down menu. The **Data View** window disappears, if floating, so objects can be selected. Select the object to which the record needs to be linked. Multiple objects can be selected. When done selecting objects, press [Enter] and the **Data View** window reappears.

The external data is now linked to the AutoCAD object. The linked record (row) is highlighted yellow until another record is linked or the **Data View** window is closed. One record can be linked to more than one object. Also, an object can have more than one record linked to it.

Viewing Linked Data and Objects

Using the **Data View** window, you can find out which record is linked to an object or which object is linked to a record. First, view the table in the **Data View** window. Then, select the **View Linked Objects in Drawing** button from the **Data View** window toolbar or pick **View Linked Objects** from the **Data View** pull-down menu. The drawing pans so the linked object is displayed in the center of the drawing screen. The object is also selected. The Command: line indicates how many objects were found and how many records are linked.

Data View
➡ **View Linked Objects**

View Linked Objects in Drawing

Data View
➡ **View Linked Records**

View Linked Records in Data View

To see which record is attached to an object, pick the **View Linked Records in Data View** button, or select **View Linked Records** from the **Data View** pull-down menu. The Command: line prompts you to select objects. Pick the object and press [Enter]. The **Data View** window now displays the record(s) linked to the object that was selected. If more than one object is selected, all the records linked to the objects are displayed. By default, all the records that are not attached to the selected objects disappear. To get all the records back, double-click on the table in the **dbConnect Manager**. However, this puts it in "edit table mode" instead of in "view table mode."

Data View
➡ A<u>u</u>toView
Objects

AutoView Linked
Objects in Drawing

Data View
➡ Au<u>t</u>o View
Linked
Records

AutoView Linked
Records in Drawing

Picking the **AutoView Linked Objects in Drawing** button automatically shows any linked objects when a record is selected. This allows you to quickly select different records and see the linked objects. You can also select **A<u>u</u>toView Linked Objects** from the **D<u>a</u>ta View** pull-down menu to use this option. Picking the **AutoView Linked Records in Drawing** button or selecting **Au<u>t</u>oView Linked Records** from the **D<u>a</u>ta View** pull-down menu automatically shows the records attached to an object when it is selected. To turn off AutoView, pick the button or menu selection again.

Saving a Link

Links can be saved as an external text file. This allows you to create a file of the data for other uses, such as a chart for a Web site, where you do not want to have a link to the database. First, select the linked object. Then, right-click to display the shortcut menu and select **Export link...** from the **Link** cascading menu. In the **Export Links** dialog box, the field (column) headings are shown in the **Include Fields:** area. See Figure 17-14. Select the headings of the fields you want to save. More than one can be selected. In the **Save as type:** text box, select to save the file in a comma-delimited, space-delimited, or native database format. "Delimited" indicates how the information is separated, by commas or spaces. Finally, name the file in the **File <u>n</u>ame:** text box and specify where to save the file.

Figure 17-14.
When exporting a link, you must select which fields to include.

Select fields to include

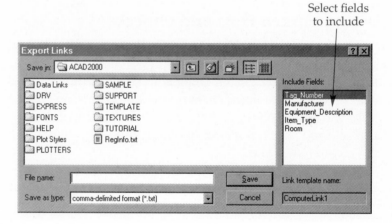

Options for Viewing Data and Object Links

Data View
➡ <u>O</u>ptions...

Data View and
Query Options

To change the settings for viewing linked data and objects, select **<u>O</u>ptions...** from the **D<u>a</u>ta View** pull-down menu or pick the **Data View and Query Options** button in the **D<u>a</u>ta View** window toolbar. This displays the **Data View and Query Options** dialog box, Figure 17-15.

In the **Record Indication Settings** area, selecting **Show all records, <u>s</u>elect indicated records** highlights all linked records when viewing linked data from objects. The highlight color is set from the **Marking Color** drop-down list. The **Show <u>o</u>nly indicated records** radio button hides all unlinked records. This is the default setting.

In the **Accumulate Options** area, if **<u>A</u>ccumulate selection set in drawing** is checked, objects are added to the selection set when viewing additional linked objects. **Accumulate <u>r</u>ecord set in data view** can only be selected if **Show all records, s<u>e</u>lect indicated records** is chosen. If this is checked, records are added to the highlighted "record set" as additional objects are selected.

The **Automatically <u>p</u>an drawing** setting in the **AutoPan and Zoom** area controls whether or not the drawing is panned when viewing linked objects. If **Automatically <u>z</u>oom drawing** is checked, a **Zoom <u>f</u>actor** can be set. AutoCAD then uses that zoom percentage when viewing linked objects instead of the current zoom factor.

Figure 17-15.
There are various
options for viewing
data and objects.

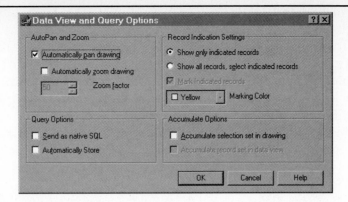

WORKING WITH LABELS

AutoCAD
User's
Guide
22

A *label* is a multiline text object that shows data from a table field. For example, a label might be placed in a floor plan drawing to display the contents of an employee name field. Then, as employees move to different offices or leave the company, the database is updated. The drawing always displays the name of the person who currently has the office.

A label can be linked to an object (attached) or "freestanding." Attached labels have a leader line connecting the label to an object. A freestanding label is simply inserted text from the record. A label template is used to insert a label.

Creating a Label Template

A label template must be created before any labels. A *label template* specifies which fields from the database table are displayed in the label and the formatting of the label text. The **Label Template** editor is used for creating label templates. This is the **Multiline Text Editor** with two additional tabs. These tabs are used for specifying which fields to use and label formatting.

dbConnect
➡ Templates
  ➡ New Label
    Template...

New Label Template

To create a label template, first highlight a table in the **dbConnect Manager**. Then, right-click and select **New Label Template...** from the shortcut menu, pick **New Label Template...** from the **Templates** cascading menu in the **dbConnect** pull-down menu, or pick the **New Label Template** button in the **dbConnect Manager** toolbar. The **New Label Template** dialog box appears.

In the **New label template name:** text box, name the label. A name based on the highlighted table appears as a suggestion, but you do not have to use it. If a label already exists for the table, that name appears in the **Start with template:** drop-down list. Pick the **Continue** button and the **Label Template** editor opens, Figure 17-16.

The **Label Fields** tab is where fields (columns) from the table are specified to be included in the label. In the **Field:** drop-down list, select a column heading. Then, pick the **Add** button. The field is added to the label and appears in the editor. Also notice the table name appears next to the **Field:** drop-down list. A label can contain text as well as column fields. For example, if there are two fields on the same line in the editor, a comma can be added in between them. A label must contain at least one field (column).

The **Start:** setting on the **Label Offset** tab determines the direction the leader line arrowhead points in relation to an imaginary bounding box around the selected object. See Figure 17-17. Use the **Leader offset** settings to make the leader line longer. The **Leader offset** and **Start:** settings only affect attached labels. The **Tip offset** settings represent how far, in drawing units, the arrowhead is offset from the **Start:** position. For example, if an object is a 1×1 box and **Middle Center** is used for the **Start:** setting, the arrowhead points to the middle of the box. If the **Tip offset** settings for **X:** and **Y:** are changed to .5, the arrowhead points to the upper-right corner of the box.

Pick the **OK** button in the **Label Template** dialog box to create the label. The label name appears under the drawing name node in the **dbConnect Manager**, Figure 17-18.

NOTE

The **Character**, **Properties**, and **Find/Replace** tabs are the same as in the **Multiline Text Editor**.

Figure 17-16.
A label is constructed using the **Label Template** dialog box.

Current field

Pick to add the current field

Label Template - ComputerLabel1

Character | Properties | Find/Replace | Label Fields | Label Offset

Field: Tag_Number ▾ | Add | Table : Computer

OK
Cancel
Import Text...
Help

Modify label fields.   Ln 1 Col 1   AutoCAPS

Figure 17-17.
There are nine different justification options in the **Start:** drop-down list. Each has a distinctive icon shown next to the option in the list.

Top Left Middle Left Bottom Left Top Center Middle Center Bottom Center Top Right Middle Right Bottom Right

Figure 17-18.
The new label
template appears in
the **dbConnect**
Manager.

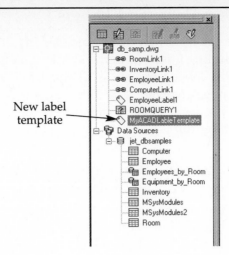

New label
template → MyACADLableTemplate

Inserting an Attached Label

To insert an attached label, first open the table used to create the template using the **Data View** window. For example, if the Computer table is used to create a label template, open the Computer table in the **Data View** window. Next, select **Create Attached Labels** from the **Link and Label Settings** drop-down list in the **Data View** window or select **Create Attached Labels** from the **Link and Label Settings** cascading menu in the **Data View** pull-down menu.

Make sure the label template and the link template you want to use are displayed on the **Data View** toolbar. Next, select a record (row) header. Then, pick the **Create Attached Label** button from the **Data View** window toolbar or select **Link!** from the **Data View** pull-down menu. When prompted to Select objects:, select all the objects the label is to be attached to and then press [Enter]. The record is linked to the label and label to the object. If the object is moved the label moves with it.

If an object already has a record linked to it, a label can be attached by selecting the object and right-clicking. In the shortcut menu, select **Label the Link...** from the **Label** cascading menu.

Data View
↳ Link and Label
Settings
↳ Create
Attached
Labels

Data View
↳ Link!

Create Attached
Label

NOTE   The leader style set in the current dimension style is used for attached labels.

Inserting a Freestanding Label

A freestanding label can be inserted anywhere in the drawing. To insert this type of label, first open the table used to create the label template in the **Data View** window. Then, select **Create Freestanding Labels** from the **Link and Label Settings** drop-down list in the **Data View** window or select **Create Freestanding Labels** from the **Link and Label Settings** cascading menu in the **Data View** pull-down menu. Next, select the record (row) header in the **Data View** window. Then, pick the **Create Freestanding Label** button from the **Data View** window toolbar or select **Link!** from the **Data View** pull-down menu. Finally, pick a point in the drawing where you want the label.

Data View
↳ Link and Label
Settings
↳ Create
Freestand-
ing Labels

Data View
↳ Link!

Create Freestanding
Label

Editing Label Templates and Labels

A label template can be edited by double-clicking on the template name or right-clicking on it and selecting **Edit...** from the shortcut menu. The **Label Template** dialog box used to create the label template is displayed. Different column fields can be added, formatting can be changed, or a different text style can be specified. Changes made in this dialog box are applied to *all* labels in the drawing that are based on this template once the **OK** button is selected.

Label visibility

The visibility of labels can be controlled globally or individually in a drawing. To control them globally, right-click on the drawing name node in the **dbConnect Manager** to display the shortcut menu. **Show Labels** displays all the labels in the drawing, including hidden ones. **Hide Labels** hides all labels. The **Reload** option updates the labels if the database record label template has changed.

Show Labels and **Hide Labels** can be set on individual templates by right-clicking on the template name to display the shortcut menu. In this menu there is also a **Delete Labels** option. This option deletes all the labels in the drawing inserted using that template.

Individual label properties can also be changed. First, select the label in the drawing area and right-click. Then, choose **Label** from the shortcut menu to display the cascading menu. The label editing menus for attached and freestanding labels are shown in Figure 17-19. Both have the following options:

- **Reload.** Resets or updates the label data.
- **Restore Properties.** Restores the formatting settings from the label template.
- **Change Label Template.** Allows you to select a different label template.
- **Show Label.** Displays the label if it is hidden. The object must be selected when using this option.
- **Hide Label.** Hides the label.

The following options are available for attached labels:

- **Detach Label.** Changes the label to a freestanding label. The link to the object is retained.
- **Delete Label (keep link).** Deletes the label, but the link to the object is retained.

Freestanding labels have two different additional options:

- **Attach to an Object.** Allows you to attach the label to an object.
- **Delete Label and Link.** Deletes the label and the link.

Figure 17-19.
A—The shortcut menu for editing a freestanding label.
B—The shortcut menu for editing an attached label.

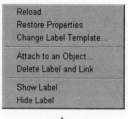

A   B

NOTE

Do not edit labels using the **Multiline Text Editor**. If the labels are reloaded, their values change back to match the label template settings.

❑ Open EX17-5.
❑ Create a new label template based on the Computer table. Name it ACAD Computer. Add the Tag_Number, Item_Type, and Room fields.
❑ Open the Computer table in the **Data View** window.
❑ Create an attached label for the circle using the first record (row) and the ACAD Computer label template.
❑ Create a freestanding label placed inside the rectangle using the second record (row) and the ACAD Computer label.
❑ Zoom all.
❑ Right-click on the ACAD Computer label template in the **dbConnect Manager** and select **Hide Labels** from the shortcut menu. Observe what happens. Then, select **Show Labels** from the shortcut menu.
❑ Save the drawing as EX17-6.

EDITING DATA IN THE DATA VIEW WINDOW

AutoCAD
User's **22**
Guide

An important reason for linking to a database is to ensure there is only one data source. This means that a change in data needs to be entered only once. An external database can be edited in AutoCAD's **Data View** window. Records can be added, deleted, or modified and information in individual fields (cells) can be changed.

To edit an existing record, open the table in **Data View**. Then, double-click inside the field (cell) to be modified. The record header changes to a pencil icon indicating that the cell can be edited, Figure 17-20. After a cell is edited and another record selected, a triangular "delta" icon is displayed in the record header that was modified and at the top of the header column, Figure 17-20. This icon indicates that a record has been modified, but the external database has not been updated.

To update the external database, right-click on the top of the header column and select **Commit** from the shortcut menu. This updates the changes that were made in **Data View** window to the external database. Closing the **Data View** window also commits the changes to the database. If the changes have not yet been committed, they can be undone by right-clicking on the top of the header column and selecting **Restore** from the shortcut menu.

Figure 17-20.
The pencil icon in a record header indicates that the record is in "edit mode." A delta icon appears in the header of any record that has been changed.

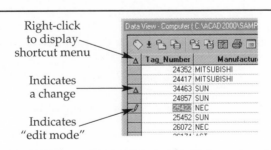

Right-click to display shortcut menu

Indicates a change

Indicates "edit mode"

PROFESSIONAL TIP   You can move from cell to cell in the **Data View** window using the arrow keys on the keyboard.

To add a new record to a table, right-click on any record header and select **Add new record** from the shortcut menu. The new record is inserted at the bottom of the table. Edit each cell by double-clicking in them and typing text. A record can be deleted by right-clicking on the record's header and selecting **Delete record** from the shortcut menu.

If records that have labels in the drawing are modified, the labels need to be updated. To update all labels using a label template, right-click on the label template name in the **dbConnect Manager** and select **Reload** from the shortcut menu. Individual labels can be updated by selecting either the object with the attached label or the label itself and right-clicking. In the shortcut menu, select **Reload** from the **Label** cascading menu.

If a change is made to the key column assigned in a link template, the **Reload** option *cannot* be used to update the label. Instead, select **Link Manager...** from the **Links** cascading menu in the **dbConnect** pull-down menu. When prompted to Select objects:, select the object with the attached label or the label itself. In the **Link Manager** dialog box, the **Key** columns are listed with the **Value** of its cell. Pick inside the "value" cell that needs to be changed and then select the ellipsis (...) button that appears at the far right of the same cell. Select the correct value from the **Column Values** dialog box. Now, the **Reload** option can be used to update the label in the drawing.

NOTE

If you get an error message stating Unable to reload some of labels, the **Link Manager** needs to be used to update the label before **Reload** can be used.

EXERCISE 17-7

❑ Open EX17-6.
❑ Open the Computer table in the **Data View** window. Zoom in on the line in the drawing.
❑ Pick the **View Linked Records in Data View** button from the **Data View** window toolbar and then select the label attached to the line to find the linked record.
❑ Double-click in the Item_Type cell and change it to your name.
❑ Click in a different record to make the "delta" icon appear. Right-click on the top of the record column and select **Commit** from the shortcut menu.
❑ Right-click on the ACAD Computer label template and select **Reload** from the shortcut menu to update the label.
❑ Do a zoom all and save the drawing as EX17-7.

WORKING WITH QUERIES

The ability to use queries is one of the biggest advantages of a database. A *query* is a request for data from a table that meets specified criteria. If you have ever used an Internet search engine, you have used queries. For example, suppose you need to find out how many computers are in room 102. A query could be created from a table with the criteria being "102" in a Room column and "computer" in an Equipment_Type column. The resulting data are displayed just like the table with only the records that meet the specified criteria shown. Queries are very powerful and easy to create once you get the hang of them. AutoCAD provides four ways to create queries. These are quick query, range query, query builder, and SQL query.

AutoCAD and its Applications—Advanced

To create a query, first open the **dbConnect Manager** and highlight the table to be used for the query. Then, right-click and select **New Query...** from the shortcut menu or pick the **New Query** button in the **dbConnect Manager** toolbar. You can also select **New Query on an External Table...** from the **Queries** cascading menu of the **dbConnect** pull-down menu. Then, in the **Select Data Object** dialog box, pick the table for the query. The **New Query** dialog box opens. Enter a name for the query in the **New query name:** text field. If saved queries already exist for the table, one can be selected from the **Existing query names:** drop-down list. The existing query is then used as a base for the new query. Next, pick the **Continue** button to display the **Query Editor**.

dbConnect
➥ Queries
  ➥ New Query
    on an
    External
    Table...

New Query

PROFESSIONAL TIP   New queries can be created and saved in an external database file for use in AutoCAD.

Creating a Quick Query

A quick query is a "template" designed to introduce queries to the beginner. In the **Quick Query** tab, a query can be created based on the data in a single field (column). In the **Field:** area, highlight the name of the field you want to use, Figure 17-21. The **Operator:** drop-down list sets the conditional operator. A conditional operator, like **Equal to** or **Greater than or equal to**, specifies parameters for the values being looked for in the table. The value being looked for in the table is entered in the **Value:** text box. Picking the **Look up values** button shows a list of all the values in the highlighted field. A value can be picked from this list or typed in the **Value:** text box. Checking the **Indicate records in data view** check box returns query matches in the **Data View** window. Checking the **Indicate objects in drawing** check box returns query matches by selecting all objects in the drawing linked to matches. Pick the **Execute** button to complete the query.

Figure 17-21.
A quick query is a simple, fast way to create a query.

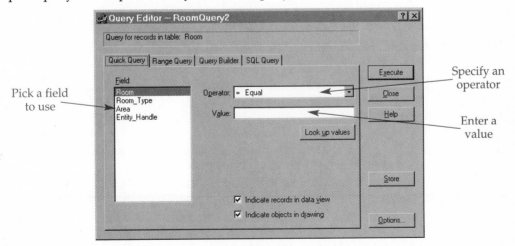

Creating a Range Query

A range query is basically the same as a quick query. However, two values are specified to create a range for the query. To create a range query, pick the **Range Query** tab in the **Query Editor**, Figure 17-22. As with a quick query, you must specify a single field (column) for the query. The **From:** text box is where one range value is specified. The **Through:** text box is where the other range value is specified.

Once executed, the query results show everything matching the **From:** and **Through:** values, and everything that falls in between. For example, if the range values are 4 and 9, and the query is for whole numbers, the numbers 4, 5, 6, 7, 8, and 9 are returned as matches to the query.

Figure 17-22.
A range query is used to find all values between the specified range.

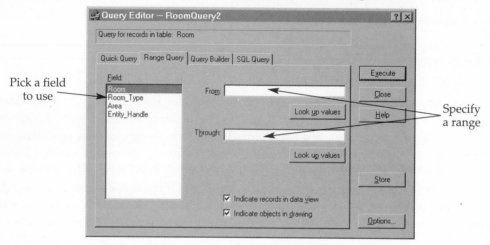

Creating a Query Using the Query Builder

In a query created with query builder, multiple columns can be used for the search. Criteria can be parenthetically grouped, ascending or descending sort values can be assigned, and fields can be specified not to show. For example, you may want to find out which programmers work in the engineering department with the results sorted by last name and some of the fields (columns) hidden. This query should be built like the one shown in Figure 17-23.

To create a query using query builder, first pick the **Query Builder** tab in the **Query Editor**. At the top of this tab are the **Field**, **Operator**, **Value**, and **Logical** columns. Picking inside a cell in any of these columns (except **Logical**) displays a drop-down list button. Pick in a **Field** cell, pick the drop-down list button, and select a field (column) name from the list. Next, pick in an **Operator** cell, pick the drop-down list button, and select an operator from the list. Then, pick in a **Value** cell, pick the ellipsis (...) button, and pick a value from the list. A value can also be typed in the **Value** cell.

In the **Logical** column, an operator can be used to set a relationship between that row and the one below it. Picking in the cell changes from **And** to **Or**. Highlighting the cell and pressing the delete key clears the cell. If **And** is used, the resulting records meet the criteria specified in that row *and* the one below it. If **Or** is used, the resulting records meet the criteria specified in that row *or* the one below it.

The **Fields in table:** area shows a list of all the field (column) headings in the table. To show a column in the query results, highlight the name in the **Fields in table:** area and pick the **Add** button. The name appears in the **Show fields:** area. Only the columns

Figure 17-23.
The query builder allows you to create an advanced query.

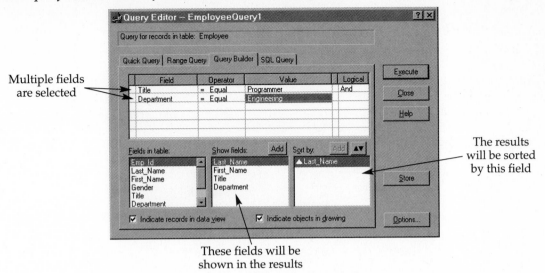

Multiple fields are selected

The results will be sorted by this field

These fields will be shown in the results

listed in the **Show fields:** area are displayed in the query results. If you do not "add" field names, all fields are automatically added when the query is executed. To remove a field name from the **Show fields:** area, right-click on the name and select **Clear field name** from the shortcut menu.

To specify a sort on a field listed in the **Show fields:** area, highlight the name and pick the **Add** button. The name appears in the **Sort by:** area with an "up arrow" next to it. This arrow indicates that the field will be sorted in ascending order. To sort in descending order, select the button with the up and down arrows. More than one field can be sorted, but the first field in the list takes precedence over the others. To remove a field name from the **Sort by:** area, right-click on the name and select **Clear field name** from the shortcut menu.

To complete the query, pick the **Execute** button. The results are displayed in the **Data View** window if the **Indicate records in data view** check box is checked. The matching objects are selected in the drawing if the **Indicate objects in drawing** check box is checked.

Creating an SQL Query

When creating a query using any of the first three tabs in the **Query Editor**, AutoCAD translates your settings into an SQL statement. The SQL statement created for a query can be seen by switching to the **SQL Query** tab after making the settings but before executing the query. Advanced users can create an SQL statement directly in this tab by typing the statement or using the tools in the **SQL Query** tab.

Notice the **Table:** area lists all the tables and queries from the external database, Figure 17-24. When constructing a query from the **SQL Query** tab, multiple tables and queries can be used. Suppose a report needs to be created that shows what type of computer each employee is using. The Computer table contains a column that shows the employee ID number, but not their name. The ID number is also in the Employee table, which has columns for employee names. Therefore, both tables need to be used to create the report.

To add criteria to an SQL statement, highlight a table or query from the **Table:** area and pick the **Add** button. Then, add a field, an operator, and a value by selecting each and picking the **Add** button. Picking the **Check** button tests the SQL statement for valid syntax. When an SQL statement is complete and the syntax valid, pick the **Execute** button to perform the query.

Figure 17-24.
The SQL statement for a query can be written or viewed in the **SQL Query** tab.

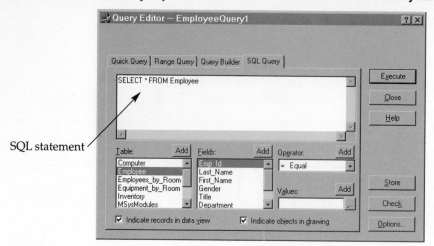

SQL statement

Saving, Executing, and Editing a Query

Before executing a query, it can be saved in the current drawing by picking the **Store** button. Once the **Execute** button is picked, the query settings are lost. When a query is stored, the query name appears in the **dbConnect Manager** under the drawing name node, Figure 17-25.

After a query is stored, it can be executed by double-clicking on the name in the **dbConnect Manager** or right-clicking on the name and selecting **Execute** from the shortcut menu. Also, selecting **Execute Query...** from the **Queries** cascading menu of the **dbConnect** pull-down menu opens the **Select a Database Object** dialog box. Saved queries appear in this dialog. Pick the name of the query to execute from the list and pick the **OK** button. The query is executed.

A saved query can be edited by right-clicking on the name and selecting **Edit...** from the shortcut menu. You can also pick **Edit Query...** from the **Queries** cascading menu in the **dbConnect** pull-down menu. Then, in the **Select a Database Object** dialog box, pick the query you want to edit. To save the changes to an edited query, you must pick the **Store** button after the changes have been made.

Figure 17-25.
The saved query appears in the **dbConnect Manager**.

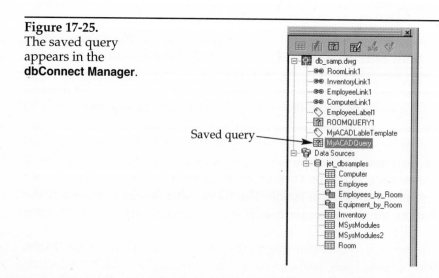

Saved query

NOTE	The **Data View** options can be set to automatically save a query when it is executed.

EXERCISE 17-8

❏ Open the db_samp.dwg file from the AutoCAD Sample folder.
❏ Open the **dbConnect Manager.**
❏ Create a new quick query called QuickQuery using the Employee table. Use Department as the field. Use an operator of Equal. Use a value of Engineering.
❏ Save, then execute the query.
❏ Save the drawing as EX17-8.
❏ Create a new query named QueryBuilder based on the Inventory table using the query builder.
❏ In the first row, use Type as the field, Equal as the operator, and Furniture as the value. In the **Logical** column, enter And.
❏ In the second row, use Price as the field, Greater than or equal as the operator, and 500 as the value.
❏ Save, then execute the query.
❏ Save the drawing.

Creating Selection Sets from Queries

AutoCAD's **Link Select** can be used to construct a selection set of AutoCAD objects. The selection set can then be refined. A selection set can be created by either selecting linked AutoCAD objects or by making a database query. This initial selection set is referred to as set A. To refine set A, another selection set is created. This set is called set B. Relationship operators can then be used on the two selection sets to create one selection set.

To open the **Link Select** dialog box, right-click on a link template and select **Link Select...** from the shortcut menu or select **Link Select...** from the **Links** cascading menu in the **dbConnect** pull-down menu. The **Link Select** dialog is displayed, Figure 17-26. Notice the **Quick Query**, **Range Query**, and **Query Builder** tabs in the middle of the box. These are the same as the ones found in the **Query Edit** dialog box.

dbConnect
↳ Links
 ↳ Link
  Select...

To create a selection set using a query, pick the **Use Query** radio button. Use any of the query methods to create the query. Then, pick the **Execute** button to create the selection set.

To create a selection set by selecting objects in the drawing, pick the **Select in Drawing** radio button. Notice that the "query settings" disappear from the dialog box. Then, pick the **Select** button and pick the objects in the drawing.

The **Do:** drop-down list in the **Link Select** dialog box contains the relationship operators. The following options are available:
- **Select.** Creates an initial selection set.
- **Union.** The results of the new selection set (set B) are added to the first selection set (set A).
- **Intersect.** Displays the records and objects that set A and set B have in common.
- **Subtract A – B.** Subtracts the records and objects from the new selection set (set B) from the first selection set (set A).
- **Subtract B – A.** Subtracts the records and objects from the first selection set (set A) from the new selection set (set B).

Figure 17-26.
The **Link Select** dialog box is used to build a selection set based on linked objects.

Pick a relationship operator

Query tabs

Specify how the selection set is created

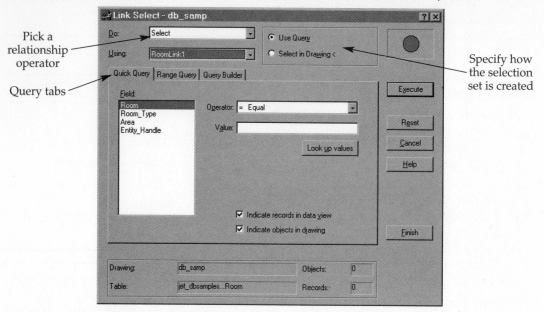

The link template that you want to use can be selected in the **Using:** drop-down list. This drop-down list contains all the link templates in the current drawing. Picking the **Reset** button discards the current settings so a new link selection operation can be defined. Picking the **Finish** button closes the **Link Select** dialog box and displays the selection set of AutoCAD objects and/or the **Data View** window records. The **Indicate records in data view** and **Indicate objects in drawing** check boxes in the **Link Select** dialog box determine how the selection set is displayed.

EXPORTING AND IMPORTING TEMPLATES

Link, label, and query templates are saved in the drawing in which they are created. However, they can also be saved as an external file and used in other drawings. Link and label templates are saved as a "set" in a DBT file. All of the queries in a drawing are also called a "set" and can be saved as a DBQ file.

To save a link and label template set, highlight the name of the drawing node in the **dbConnect Manager**. Then, right-click and select **Export Template Set...** from the shortcut menu or select **Export Template Set...** from the **Templates** cascading menu in the **dbConnect** pull-down menu. In the **Export Template Set** dialog box, specify the file name and the location where you want to save it, Figure 17-27. Then, pick the **Save** button.

dbConnect
➥ Templates
➥ Export
Template
Set...

To import a template set, highlight the drawing name node in the **dbConnect Manager**. Then, right-click and select **Import Template Set...** from the shortcut menu or select **Import Template Set...** from the **Templates** cascading menu in the **dbConnect** pull-down menu. Browse to the DBT file and select it. Pick the **Open** button to import the file.

dbConnect
➥ Templates
➥ Import
Template
Set...

To save a query set, first highlight the drawing name node in the **dbConnect Manager**. Then, right-click and select **Export Query Set...** from the shortcut menu or select **Export Query Set...** from the **Queries** cascading menu in the **dbConnect** pull-down menu. In the **Export Query Set** dialog box, specify the file name and the location where you want to save it. Then, pick the **Save** button.

dbConnect
➥ Queries
➥ Export
Query
Set...

Figure 17-27.
Template and query sets can be saved and used in other drawing files.

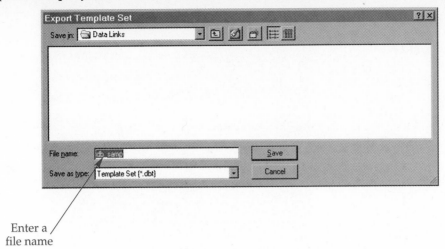

Enter a
file name

To import a query set, highlight the drawing name node in the **dbConnect Manager**. Then, right-click and select **Import Query Set...** from the shortcut menu or select **Import Query Set...** from the **Queries** cascading menu in the **dbConnect** pull-down menu. Browse to the DBQ file and select it. Pick the **Open** button to import the file.

dbConnect
➥ Queries
　➥ Import
　　Query
　　Set...

 NOTE　　An imported template set can only be used if the data source it was created with is configured and connected.

CONVERTING ASE LINKS FROM PREVIOUS VERSIONS OF AUTOCAD

ASE links in previous versions of AutoCAD drawings need to be converted to work in AutoCAD 2000. If a file is opened from a previous version of AutoCAD that has links, AutoCAD 2000 attempts to convert the information automatically. This may not always be successful. To manually convert a link, select **Link Conversion...** from the **dbConnect** pull-down menu. The **Link Conversion** dialog box appears, Figure 17-28. Select the AutoCAD drawing version that needs to be converted using the **Link Format:** radio buttons. In the **Old Link Format** area, enter the settings from the old ASE link. In the **New Link Format** area, enter the new settings. After selecting the **OK** button, you can open the old drawing in AutoCAD 2000 and save it to convert the links.

dbConnect
➥ Link
　Conversion...

Figure 17-28.
Older AutoCAD ASE
links can be converted
to AutoCAD 2000
dbConnect links using
the **Link Conversion**
dialog box.

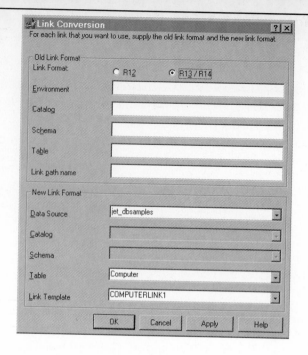

Chapter Test

Answer the following questions on a separate sheet of paper.

1. What is a database?
2. What is a DBMS?
3. What is a field?
4. What does SQL stand for?
5. What is a database table?
6. A row in a table is called a(n) _____.
7. A column in a table is called a(n) _____.
8. A data source needs to be ____ in Windows and then ____ and ____ in AutoCAD.
9. Which AutoCAD 2000 folder are data source files stored in by default?
10. How is the **Data View** window docked?
11. How can a column in **Data View** be sorted quickly?
12. Why does a link template need to be created?
13. Which of the following table components can be linked to AutoCAD objects?
    A) cell
    B) record
    C) field
14. What two types of labels can be created?
15. Which type of label can be inserted without linking to an object?
16. Which shortcut menu option updates a label in the drawing?
17. Which **Data View** shortcut menu option updates the external database when changes have been made?
18. What is a query?
19. Which type of a query retrieves records that fall between two values?
20. Which types of queries allow more than one column to be used?

Drawing Problems

Make a copy of the db_samples.mdb file found in AutoCAD's Sample directory before completing any of these problems. When finished with the problems, restore the original file.

1. Make a copy of the db_samp.dwg drawing in the AutoCAD Sample folder and name it P17-1. Open P17-1 and connect the jet_dbsamples data source.
   A. Add the following records to each table shown below.

EMPLOYEE	
EMP_ID	1064
LAST_NAME	Robinson
FIRST_NAME	Lonnie
GENDER	F
TITLE	Counselor
DEPARTMENT	Human Resources
ROOM	6125

INVENTORY	
INV_ID	1268
TYPE	Laser printer
DESCRIPTION	Personal inventory
MANUFACTURER	Quasar Lasers
MODEL	QLP-600
PRICE	1250
ROOM	6125

   B. View the new records to check for errors and then commit the changes.
   C. Zoom in on the drawing so you can see about four cubicles. Open the Room table.
   D. Use the **View Linked Objects in Drawing** button to find room 6125 in the drawing.
   E. Link the new employee and the new laser printer (added above) to room 6125. Save the drawing as P17-1.

2. Open drawing P17-1 and make the following changes to the indicated tables. Check each table for errors when done.
   A. EMPLOYEE table: Change EMP_ID 1006's last name to Wilson-Jenkins, and change her title to International Sales Mgr.
   B. INVENTORY table: Change the price of INV_ID 1141 to 5300 and change the manufacturer to Tradewinds Computers.
   C. COMPUTER table: For Tab_Number 29733, change the manufacturer to SUN, and the room to 6180.

3. If you have database software, create a new database called Facilities and add a new table called Computers. Columns in the table should be: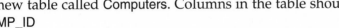
   - COMP_ID
   - CPU
   - HDRIVE
   - INPUT
   - MFR
   - RAM
   - FDRIVE
   - GRAPHICS
   A. Make a list of each computer in your drawing lab. Make note of the above information for each. Enter all of the data into the database.
   B. Make a print out when you have completed the database.

4. Construct a drawing of your computer lab. Create blocks for each workstation.

   A. Set the proper database and table in order to work with the computers in your drawing.

   B. Link each one of the computers in the drawing with the appropriate record in your database table created in Problem 3.

   C. View the links you created to check for accuracy. Edit any links that are not correct.

   D. Create labels for each workstation. The labels should use the COMP_ID and MFR columns.

   E. Place a label in the title block, or as a general note, referring to the database name that is linked to this drawing.

   F. Save the drawing as P17-4 and print or plot a copy of the drawing.

CHAPTER 18

Advanced AutoCAD Features and OLE

Learning Objectives

After completing this chapter, you will be able to:

■ Identify and use advanced Clipboard text and graphics options.
■ Copy and reference AutoCAD drawing data to other Windows applications using Object Linking and Embedding (OLE).
■ Describe the differences between linking and embedding.

ADVANCED CLIPBOARD SUPPORT

Copying, cutting, and pasting are the primary methods for relocating and duplicating data in Windows-based applications. With the help of the Windows Clipboard, AutoCAD allows you to copy objects within a drawing, from one drawing to another, or from one application (software program) to another.

The Windows Clipboard is one of the applications included with Microsoft Windows. Anytime you cut or copy data in a Windows application, it is automatically stored in the Clipboard.

The Windows Clipboard provides a simple means of taking information from one application into another application, or from one drawing into another. Think of the Clipboard as a temporary storage area, or buffer, for text and graphic information. Once an image or text is copied to the Clipboard, it can be pasted as desired into any Windows program file, such as a word processor document, a spreadsheet, or even an AutoCAD drawing. Information copied to the Clipboard remains there until it is replaced by copying new information.

Copying, Cutting, and Pasting

The copy, cut, and paste features are typically found under the **Edit** pull-down menu of the Windows application you are using. Like most other Windows applications, AutoCAD has an **Edit** menu with these Clipboard-based options available. See Figure 18-1A. You can also right-click in the drawing area and access these options from the shortcut menu. See Figure 18-1B.

Figure 18-1.
Selecting Clipboard-based options in AutoCAD.
A—Options in the **Edit** pull-down menu. B—Options in the shortcut menu.

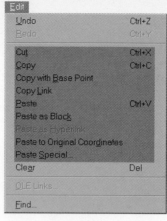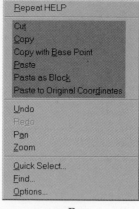

A   B

The primary function of each option is listed here. Detailed information on the use of these features is provided using several examples throughout this chapter.

- **Cut.** Removes the selected text or graphic objects and places them on the Clipboard. In AutoCAD, this activates the **CUTCLIP** command, which can also be accessed using the [Ctrl]+[X] key combination.
- **Copy.** Copies the selected text or graphic objects and places them on the Clipboard. In AutoCAD, this starts the **COPYCLIP** command.
- **Copy with Base Point.** Copies selected objects and allows you to specify a base point. In AutoCAD, this starts the **COPYBASE** command, which can also be accessed using the [Ctrl]+[C] key combination.
- **Copy Link.** Copies objects to the Clipboard in preparation to link the drawing objects to another application. In AutoCAD, this starts the **COPYLINK** command.
- **Paste.** Pastes the contents of the Clipboard into the current drawing. In AutoCAD, this starts the **PASTECLIP** command, which can also be accessed using the [Ctrl]+[V] key combination. Note that pasted objects are not removed from the Clipboard. They can be pasted into multiple locations in your drawing.
- **Paste as Block.** Pastes the contents of the Clipboard as a block. This accesses the **PASTEBLOCK** command.
- **Paste to Original Coordinates.** Pastes objects from the Clipboard to the coordinates from which they were cut or copied. Same as the **PASTEORIG** command.
- **Paste Special.** Opens the **Paste Special** dialog box, where additional parameters can be set for the incoming data. In AutoCAD, this starts the **PASTESPEC** command.
- **Clear.** Starts the **ERASE** command. This option is included for Microsoft Office compliance only, and is in no way different than the standard **ERASE** command in AutoCAD.

These Clipboard-based options can be used in many ways in AutoCAD. They can be used to copy information within a drawing session. Both drawing data and text data can be manipulated this way to help save time and maintain accuracy.

Copying, Cutting, and Pasting in an AutoCAD Drawing Session

Typically, when you need to copy or move drawing objects in AutoCAD, you use the **COPY** and **MOVE** commands. For most drawing requirements, these commands are easier to use than **COPYCLIP**, **CUTCLIP**, and **PASTECLIP**. When using these features, it is important to understand how each of the available commands works.

The **Cut** and **Copy** options place drawing information on the Clipboard in the same manner. The difference is similar to the relationship between the **MOVE** and the **COPY** commands in AutoCAD. **Cut** works like **MOVE**—it removes the drawing information from its original location and places it on the Clipboard. The **Copy** options place the same information on the Clipboard but leave the original objects in place. Deciding which one to use depends on whether or not you require the original objects to remain in place.

There are three different options for copying objects to the Clipboard. The **Copy** option copies the selected objects to the Clipboard. The **Copy Link** option is used when copying AutoCAD objects to be inserted into another application. Finally, the **Copy with Base Point** option allows you to select a base point for the selected objects that are copied to the Clipboard.

The **Paste** option takes the information from the Clipboard and inserts it into the current drawing session identical to the original object or group of objects.

The **Paste as Block** option takes the information from the Clipboard and inserts it into the current drawing session as an *unnamed block* (a block that AutoCAD has named through an automated process). Unnamed blocks typically have names similar to A$C48534010. The pasted objects are assembled into a block, which you need to explode if you wish to edit.

The primary advantages of using the Clipboard for copying and moving objects in a drawing session are speed and convenience. By pressing the [Ctrl]+[C] keystroke or a menu pick, you enter the **COPYCLIP** command and can select objects to be copied. When using this command, there is no need to indicate a base point for the copy operation. To place the objects or copies in the desired location, press [Ctrl]+[V] or pick **Paste**. When the incoming data from the Clipboard is AutoCAD geometry, the **PASTECLIP** command asks for an insertion point. In this situation, the base point is at the lower-left corner of the incoming block.

The following sequence shows the steps followed to copy and paste objects in a drawing:

```
Command: (press [Ctrl]+[C])
Command: _copyclip
Select objects: (select the desired objects)
Select objects: ↵
Command: (press [Ctrl]+[V])
Command: _pasteclip
Specify insertion point: (select the insertion point)
Command:
```

If the **COPYCLIP** command is used when objects are grip-selected and Noun/Verb selection is enabled, the selected objects are copied directly to the Clipboard with no further prompts.

The Clipboard-based features can be very useful when editing dialog box text. Text objects in your drawing are treated like any other drawing object. In an edit box within a dialog session, the text is copied, cut, and pasted as text only. This is true within any edit box in any dialog session, as well as the text-editing area of the **Multiline Text Editor** dialog box.

The following example shows the **Edit Attributes** dialog box while editing attributes in a drawing title block. In this example, the drawing was completed, checked, and approved on the same date. Observe how a quick copy and paste operation can be used to reduce typing requirements.

In Figure 18-2A, the text listed in the **Date drawn** edit box has been highlighted. The entire contents of an edit box can be highlighted by using the [Tab] key to set the keyboard focus, or you can double-click in the target edit box. After highlighting the text to be copied, press [Ctrl]+[C] to copy it to the Clipboard. Now, move your cursor to the edit box that you are copying the text to, as shown in Figure 18-2B. Press [Ctrl]+[V] to paste the copied text to its destination.

Figure 18-2.
Copying and pasting in a dialog box. A—Within the edit box, highlight the text to be copied and then press [Ctrl]+[C]. B—Move the cursor to another edit box and press [Ctrl]+[V]. The copied text is inserted.

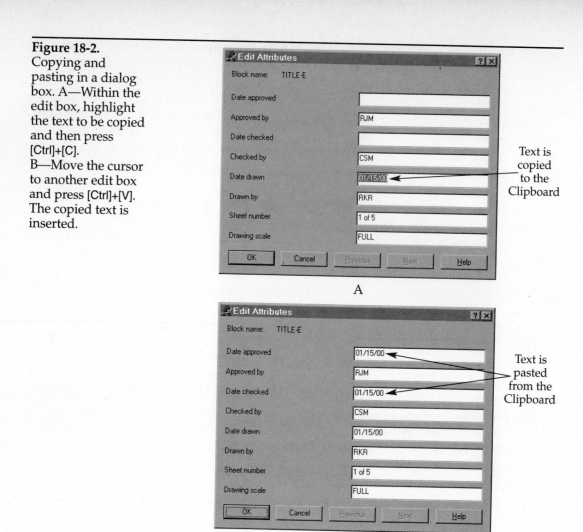

Text is copied to the Clipboard

A

Text is pasted from the Clipboard

B

The previous example shows the entire contents of the edit box being copied, but it could just as well be only a portion of the contents. An example of this more specialized editing technique is demonstrated here using the **Multiline Text Editor** dialog box to copy part of one multiline text object into another. In this example, the customized portion of the text defined for a dimension object is cut and moved to another dimension.

Figure 18-3A shows the **Multiline Text Editor** dialog box after a dimension object has been selected for editing with the **DDEDIT** command. Highlighting the text is done by pointing to the start, pressing and holding the pick button, and then dragging the cursor to the end of the text and releasing the pick button.

In Figure 18-3B, a second dimension object is selected for editing with the **DDEDIT** command. In this illustration, the dimension text is the default value, as specified by the "< >" symbols.

Position the cursor where the Clipboard text is to be pasted. Next, press [Ctrl]+[V] to paste the Clipboard contents, Figure 18-3C.

Figure 18-3.
Copying and pasting text in the **Multiline Text Editor** dialog box. A—Highlight the text being copied and press [Ctrl]+[C]. B—Select a different dimension for editing and position the cursor where the new text is to be located. C—Press [Ctrl]+[V] to paste the text from the Clipboard.

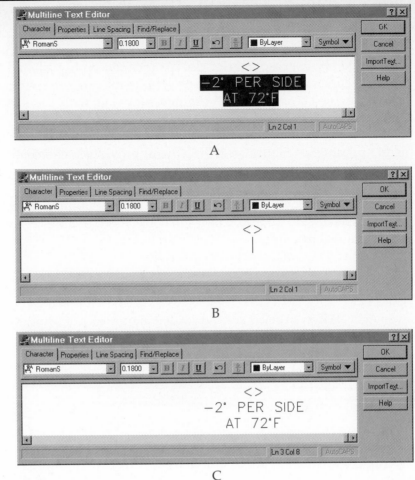

Copying Information Between Drawings

AutoCAD 2000 allows multiple drawings to be opened in a single session at the same time. This provides a powerful means for bringing partial drawing information from one drawing to another.

The following sequence shows an example of how to copy drawing information from one drawing to another using **COPYCLIP** and **PASTECLIP**. First, open both the drawing you wish to copy objects *from* and the drawing you wish to copy objects *to*.

Go to the drawing window that contains the geometry you wish to copy. An easy way to make both drawing windows visible at once is to select the **Tile Vertically** option from the **Window** pull-down menu. Now do the following:

    Command: *(press [Ctrl]+[C])*
    Select objects: *(select the desired objects)*
    Select objects: ↵
    Command:

Next, pick in the drawing area of the drawing you are copying *to*. Enter the **PASTECLIP** command:

    Command: *(press [Ctrl]+[V])*
    Specify insertion point: *(select the insertion point)*
    Command:

Copying Objects Using the Drag-and-Drop Method

To copy objects between drawings using the drag-and-drop method, first select the object. The object's grips are displayed. To copy, place the cursor on any part of the selected object except a grip. Use the pick button to pick and hold, and the drag-and-drop cursor appears. Drag the object into the other drawing and release the pick button. The object is copied to the new drawing with the same properties as the source object.

If you right-click on the object and then drag it into another drawing, a shortcut menu appears. See Figure 18-4. This menu provides a choice of how the object is to be inserted into the other drawing.

- **Copy Here.** Copies the object at the location selected.
- **Paste as Block.** Copies the object as a block at the selected location.
- **Paste to Orig Coords.** Copies the object to the same XYZ coordinates as in the original drawing.
- **Cancel.** Terminates the copy activity.

Figure 18-4.
If you right-click on an object and then drag it into another drawing, this shortcut menu appears.

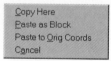

Pasting Objects from Other Applications

When the content of the Clipboard is text from a standard text editor (such as the Windows Notepad), pasting it into AutoCAD brings it in as a multiline text object. AutoCAD places the new object at the upper-left corner of the current drawing display area.

Other object types pasted from the Clipboard, such as Microsoft Word text, are brought in as OLE objects. OLE objects are covered later in this chapter.

Using the Clipboard Viewer

Once a graphic image or an item of text is copied to the Clipboard, it remains there until something new is copied or until you exit Windows. The contents of the Clipboard can be available for use long after you have copied them. The application provided for you to work with the Clipboard contents is called the Clipboard Viewer.

The Clipboard Viewer allows you to examine the current contents of the Clipboard. Additionally, you can clear the Clipboard and save the contents to a file for later use. The program icon for the Clipboard Viewer is located in the **Accessories** group menu in the **Programs** menu, Figure 18-5.

When the viewer is launched, it displays the currently stored data. If you cannot see all the image or text, use the scroll bars. In Figure 18-6, several AutoCAD objects have been copied and are displayed in the Clipboard Viewer window.

The contents of the Clipboard can also be saved to disk for later use. The Clipboard contents are saved as a CLP file, regardless of the type of information. This file can then be opened later using the Clipboard Viewer. To save a CLP file, select **Save As...** from the **File** pull-down menu in the Clipboard Viewer. Specify the folder and file name in the **Save As** dialog box. To open a saved file, select **Open...** from the **File** pull-down menu and specify the file to open in the **Open** dialog box. When a CLP file is opened, the contents of the file are copied to the Clipboard, and are then ready to be pasted into other applications.

Figure 18-5.
The Windows Clipboard Viewer is accessed from the Accessories menu.

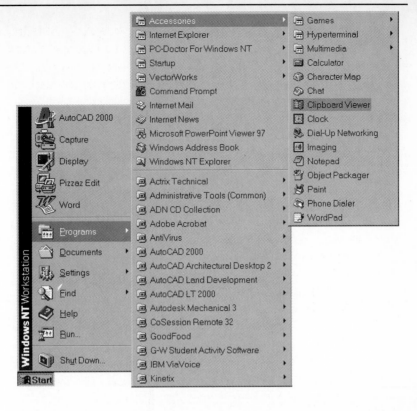

Figure 18-6.
The Windows Clipboard Viewer displays shaded objects that were copied to the Clipboard.

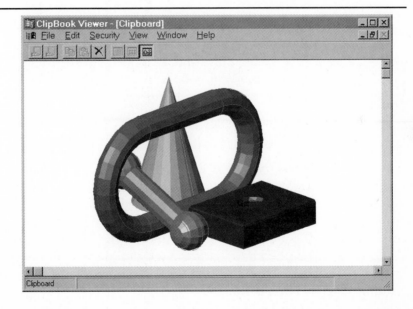

If you have copied a very large image or many pages of text to the Clipboard and no longer need the data, you can clear the contents of the Clipboard. This is useful when you are running low on memory and need to free up resources. To clear the contents of the Clipboard, select Delete from the Edit pull-down menu in the Clipboard Viewer.

Object Linking and Embedding, or *OLE*, is a feature of the Windows operating system that allows data from many different source applications to be combined into a single document. A technical document will often present data in several forms to ensure effective communications. For example, the technical documentation for a product might include formatted text from a word processor, technical drawings from AutoCAD, charts and graphs from a spreadsheet program, and even graphic images from a paint program. Understanding the use of OLE will help you to produce high quality documentation to communicate your ideas effectively.

As implied by the name, there are two distinct aspects to OLE: *linking* and *embedding*. Both linking and embedding allow you to insert data from one application into another, but they differ in the way they store the information. The following terms are used in the OLE process:

- **Object.** A piece of data created by a Windows application that supports OLE server functions. Such data could be text from a word processor, an AutoCAD drawing, or a graphic image.
- **OLE server.** A source application. For example, when using OLE to bring an AutoCAD drawing into your word processor, AutoCAD becomes the OLE server.
- **OLE client.** A destination application. AutoCAD is an OLE client when you use OLE to bring an object into AutoCAD from another application.

NOTE

While working through these examples, you will be switching between applications in Windows. One convenient means of switching applications is using the [Alt]+[Tab] keystroke. Or, you may find it more convenient to have both windows visible at once on your desktop.

Embedding Objects in AutoCAD

The term *embedding* refers to storing a copy of an OLE object in a client document. Embedding differs from importing because an imported object maintains no association with its source application. An embedded object is edited using the source application, or server. For example, if a Corel Photo-Paint picture (PCX file) is embedded in an AutoCAD drawing, double-clicking on the picture starts the Corel Photo-Paint application and loads the selected picture. Using the **Image** command to bring a PCX file into AutoCAD brings in the graphic image, but it has no association with the original application.

To embed an OLE object in an AutoCAD drawing, first copy it to the Clipboard from the source application. Return to AutoCAD and paste the Clipboard contents using **PASTECLIP**. When the content of the Clipboard is not AutoCAD data and contains OLE information, it is embedded in the AutoCAD drawing.

One application for using embedded graphics is placing a Paint picture in a title block for a logo design. In Figure 18-7, the Paint program has been used to design a logo graphic. Selecting the graphic image and pressing [Ctrl]+[C] copies the selected image to the Clipboard.

Once you have copied the image to the Clipboard, return to AutoCAD. Now press [Ctrl]+[V] to paste the Clipboard contents into the AutoCAD drawing. A pasted image appears in the upper-left corner of the graphics screen, along with the **OLE Properties** dialog box. See Figure 18-8.

Figure 18-7.
A graphic image can be designed in the Paint program.

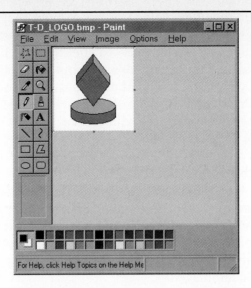

Figure 18-8.
Pasting an object into AutoCAD. A—The pasted image appears in the upper-left corner. B—The **OLE Properties** dialog box appears automatically.

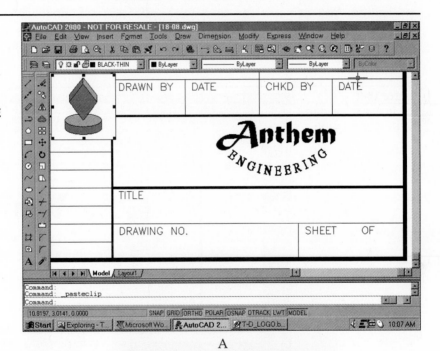

A

Set size of embedded object

Scale embedded object

Maintain height-to-width ratio

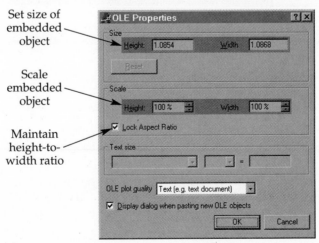

B

The **OLE Properties** dialog box has settings that allow you to change the size and scale of the embedded image. If the embedded object is text, you can specify the text size. This dialog box can be accessed after the object is embedded by right-clicking on the object and selecting **Properties...** from the shortcut menu.

Moving your cursor to point at the pasted image changes your cursor into a four-way arrow. Press and hold the pick button to move the image. Release the pick button when the image is in the desired location.

Once the image is positioned correctly, pick anywhere on the screen that is not on the image and the grips will disappear. Figure 18-9 shows the image in its final position within the title block.

Note that the filled squares surrounding the image can be used to adjust the size and proportions of the image. Pointing to the grips changes the cursor to the appropriate resizing cursor. Press and hold the pick button to move the grip. Release the pick button when you are finished adjusting the image. The illustration in Figure 18-10 shows the function of each of the grip points, as well as the appearance of the cursor when moving an image.

Because the image is embedded, it maintains an association with the original application. You can use the original application whenever you need to edit the image. The application can be initiated by double-clicking on the image. You can also right-click on the object and select options from the shortcut menu. See Figure 18-11.

Figure 18-9.
The image moved to the proper location.

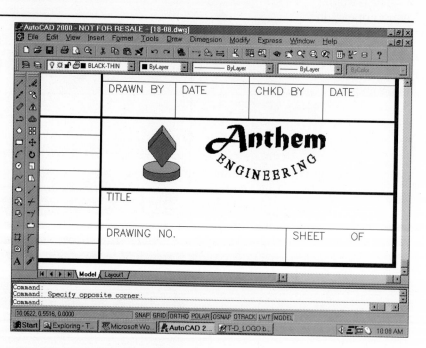

Figure 18-10.
The resize and move cursor shapes for pasted images.

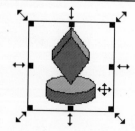

AutoCAD and its Applications—Advanced

Figure 18-11.
Right-clicking on an embedded object displays a shortcut menu with options for modifying the object.

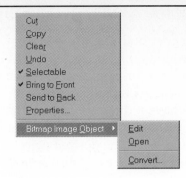

The bottom line on this menu indicates the type of object. In this case, it is a Bitmap Image Object. The menu items function as follows:

- **Cut.** Removes the OLE object and copies it to the Clipboard.
- **Copy.** Copies the object to the Clipboard.
- **Clear.** Removes the object from the drawing without copying it to the Clipboard.
- **Undo.** Reverses the last action performed with this menu. Similar to AutoCAD's **U** command, this can be used repeatedly. Note that this will not undo object updates done by the server application.
- **Selectable.** Controls whether the OLE object can be selected when using AutoCAD's editing commands. When a check mark appears by this option, the object can be selected by pointing at it and picking. Whether an item is selectable or not, right-clicking on it displays the shortcut menu.
- **Bring to Front.** Brings the item to the front, similar to the function of the **DRAWORDER** command.
- **Send to Back.** Sends the item to the back, similar to the function of the **DRAWORDER** command.
- **Properties.** Displays the **OLE Properties** dialog box.
- **Object Type Cascading Menu.** Displays options for editing, opening, and converting the object to other object types. For example, a Bitmap Image Object can be converted into a Picture Object. When converted to a Picture Object, the object has the same properties as an image attached using the **IMAGE** command. It loses its association with the Paint program.

It is possible to embed virtually any OLE object into an AutoCAD drawing. This includes word processing documents, charts, graphs, spreadsheets, audio clips, and video clips. Using these various OLE data types can transform a standard technical drawing into a complete multimedia presentation. As you use these techniques, try to use only objects that have significant communication value, rather than cluttering up a drawing with unnecessary "bells and whistles."

NOTE

The **U** and **UNDO** commands in AutoCAD have no effect on any changes made to an OLE object. Additionally, the **REDO** command does not reverse an undo executed from the shortcut menu accessed from an embedded object.

PROFESSIONAL TIP

OLE objects that are linked or embedded in an AutoCAD drawing only print on printers or plotters that use the Windows System Printer driver. They will still be displayed on screen, but cannot be printed using non-Windows drivers.

Embedding AutoCAD Drawing Objects in Other Documents

AutoCAD provides both client and server OLE functions. This means that in addition to using embedded OLE objects, AutoCAD can provide objects for other applications. A common use for this feature is to combine technical drawings and illustrations with text in a technical document created with a word processing program.

If you already have a drawing created that you need to embed in another document, first open the drawing in AutoCAD. Press [Ctrl]+[C] or select **Copy** from the **Edit** pull-down menu and select the desired objects. This places the selected objects on the Clipboard. For this example, the entire AutoCAD drawing shown in Figure 18-12 is copied to the Clipboard.

Figure 18-12.
To prepare to embed a drawing, copy it to the Clipboard using [Ctrl]+[C] or by picking **Copy** from the **Edit** pull-down menu.

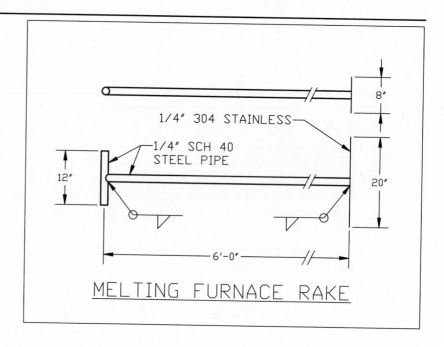

In this example, the Windows WordPad program is used as the client application. In this next step, the destination document is opened in WordPad, Figure 18-13A. After opening the document, select the **E**dit menu and pick the **P**aste option to embed the AutoCAD drawing. Note that the embedded drawing is placed at the current cursor location. You are not prompted for a location or a size. If you need to change either the location or the size, you can do so by picking on the drawing or on the grips at the edges or corners and dragging the image. Figure 18-13B shows the document with the drawing embedded, resized, and moved to the center of the document.

Embedding an OLE object in an application also modifies the menu to display new options when the object is highlighted. The **E**dit menu in the WordPad program appears as shown in Figure 18-14 after highlighting the embedded drawing.

Once the drawing is embedded, it loses all connection with the original drawing file. This means that subsequent editing of this drawing will not affect the original source file. In order to edit the embedded drawing, highlight the image and select Edit Drawing **O**bject from the **E**dit pull-down menu or simply double-click on the drawing. When the AutoCAD window opens, examine the title bar and note the specified file name. The title bar shows the drawing name as Drawing in Document. If you access the **SAVEAS** command, the current file name is set to something similar to A$C37DA7DFF.DWG. This is a temporary name assigned to the drawing while it is being edited, and may change from one editing session to another.

Figure 18-13.
Inserting an AutoCAD drawing object into a WordPad document.
A—The original document.
B—The document after the drawing is embedded.

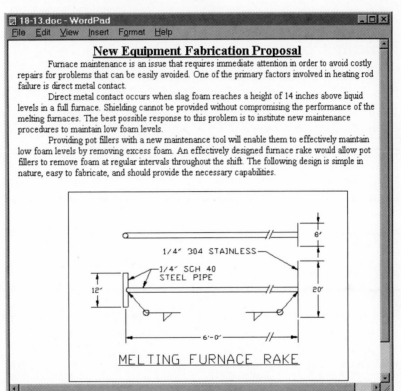

A

B

Figure 18-14.
New choices are displayed on the Edit menu when the embedded drawing is selected.

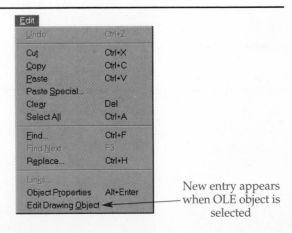

New entry appears when OLE object is selected

Updating refers to recording your changes to the embedded object within the client document. There are two ways to update the file when you have finished editing it. Picking the **File** pull-down menu displays a new option, such as **Update WordPad**. Selecting this option replaces the currently embedded drawing with the revised version. You can also simply close the current drawing or exit AutoCAD. If changes have been made, the dialog box shown in Figure 18-15 is displayed. Selecting the **Yes** button updates the client document.

Figure 18-15.
If there are unsaved changes in your drawing, this dialog box is displayed.

Linking Objects in AutoCAD

Linking is similar to embedding in that objects from one application are brought into another application. With linking, however, a direct link is maintained between the source data and the OLE object in the client application. Linked objects support *Dynamic Data Exchange* (*DDE*). As the source data is modified, the link in the client application is updated.

To link an object within AutoCAD, it must first be copied to the Clipboard. When bringing the object into AutoCAD, select the **Paste Special...** option from the **Edit** pull-down menu. Using this option activates the **Paste Special** dialog box, see Figure 18-16.

Figure 18-16.
The **PASTESPEC** command opens the **Paste Special** dialog box. The Clipboard contains text from a Word document. A—The **Paste** option embeds the object, and several formats are available. B—The **Paste Link** option creates a link to the object, and only a single format can be used.

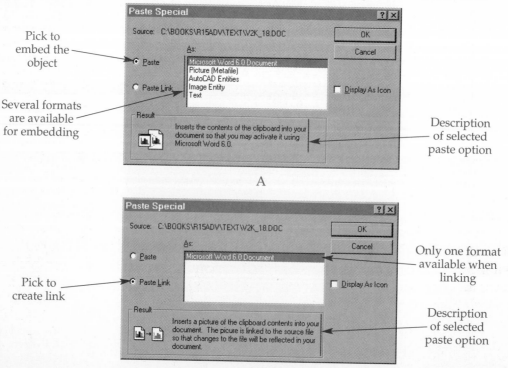

The source of the information currently on the Clipboard is displayed in the upper-left area of the dialog box. Two radio buttons allow you to specify whether or not to copy the information as a link. If **Paste** is active, the object will be embedded. If the **Paste Link** option is active, the object will be brought in as a link. If you are embedding the object, you may have several format options, depending on the type of data being pasted. These formats are shown in the **As:** list box. A linked object comes in as the file type associated with the server application.

PROFESSIONAL TIP

Objects can only be linked through OLE if they exist as a file on disk. If you copy data from an application without first saving it to disk, the **Paste Link** radio button is disabled (grayed out). A link maintains a direct association with the original source file, meaning that editing a linked OLE object changes its source file as well. Pasting an object when the **Paste Link** option is not available creates an embedded OLE object.

INSERTOBJ
IO

Insert
➥ OLE Object...

Insert
toolbar

OLE Object

A linked object can also be inserted using the **INSERTOBJ** command. Select this command by picking the **OLE Object** button from the **Insert** toolbar, selecting **OLE Object...** from the **Insert** pull-down menu, or typing IO or INSERTOBJ at the Command: prompt. The following example uses this command.

First, create a simple image in Paint and save the image as a bitmap (BMP) file. Then in AutoCAD, select **OLE Object...** from the **Insert** pull-down menu. The **Insert Object** dialog box appears, Figure 18-17A.

The **Create New** radio button is selected by default. The **Object Type:** list box shows the registered applications that support OLE functions. This list varies based on the software installed on your system. Read each selection carefully, because some programs can produce varied types of data. For example, if you have Microsoft Word installed, you may see options for producing a picture or a document. The option you select affects how the specified program is started, and the data type it will be sending back to AutoCAD.

To create a new object, highlight the desired program and pick the **OK** button. The appropriate application is called, and you can create the object. When you are finished creating the OLE object, select the Update option from your File menu or just exit the application. If you exit before you save, the application will ask you if you want to update the object before you exit.

If the object is already created and saved, select the **Create from File** radio button. The dialog box appears as shown in Figure 18-17B. Enter the path and file name in the **File:** edit box or pick the **Browse...** button to select the file from a selection dialog box. Activate the **Link** check box to create a link between the object file and the AutoCAD drawing. Pick the **OK** button, and a copy of the selected object appears in the upper-left corner of the graphics screen area. See Figure 18-18.

To edit the linked OLE object, double-click on it. This opens Paint, the server application. See Figure 18-19. Any changes you make to the image are updated in both the OLE object in the drawing and in the source file. The title bar of the Paint program shows that the object's original file is opened for editing.

All linked OLE objects behave in much the same manner as the previous example. In certain applications, the updates may be slower, but they are still automatic. To change the way a link is updated or to adjust current links in a drawing, select **OLE Links...** from the **Edit** menu. This opens the **Links** dialog box, as shown in Figure 18-20. If no links are present in the current drawing, this item is grayed-out in the pull-down menu.

Figure 18-17.
The **Insert Object** dialog box can be used to link an object to an AutoCAD drawing. A—To create a new object, select the type of object and pick **OK**. B—To create a link to the object's file, pick the **Create from File** radio button, select the file name, and pick the **Link** check box.

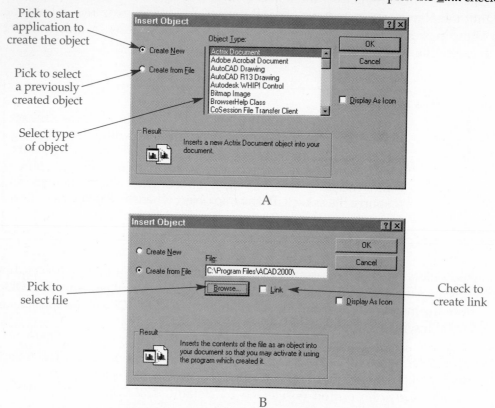

Pick to start application to create the object

Pick to select a previously created object

Select type of object

A

Pick to select file

Check to create link

B

Figure 18-18.
The linked object is inserted in the upper-left corner of the drawing area.

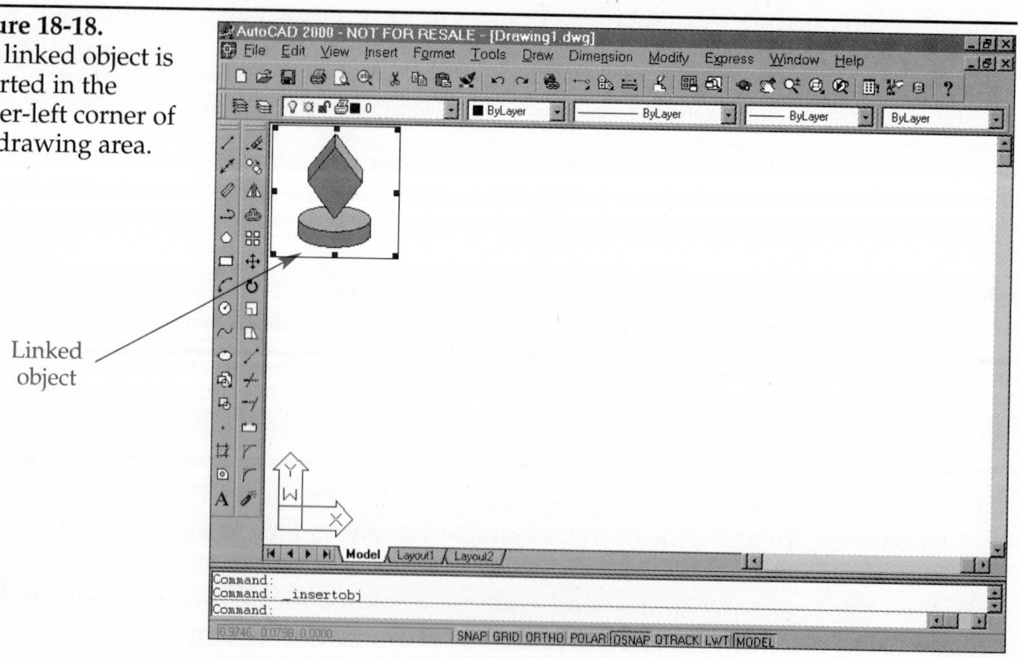

Linked object

Figure 18-19.
Double-clicking on the linked object starts the server application and opens the source file.

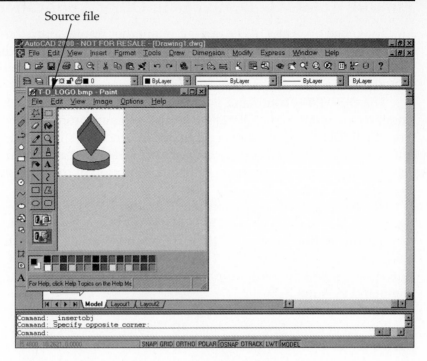

Source file

Figure 18-20.
The **Links** dialog box displays all active links.

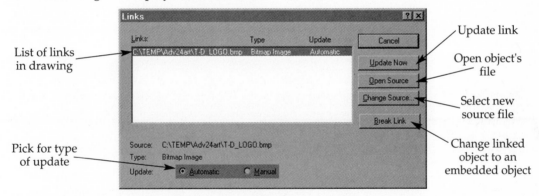

List of links in drawing

Pick for type of update

Update link

Open object's file

Select new source file

Change linked object to an embedded object

The **Links:** list box displays all active links in the current drawing. The file name of the link and the update method are also shown. By default, a link is automatically updated. If you do not want the updates to be automatic, pick the **Manual** radio button. To force an update, select the **Update Now** button. The **Break Link** button removes link information from the OLE object and removes any association with the source file, effectively converting a linked object into an embedded object. Select the **Change Source...** button to change the source file with which the link is associated. Selecting **Open Source** opens the linked file using the originating application.

NOTE
Some types of files (such as sound files, video clips, and animations) offer additional options within the AutoCAD drawing. For example, when you right-click on a linked or embedded video clip, the object type cascading menu shows a **Play** option. In the case of a video clip, the **Play** option is only enabled if an associated application for playing the clip is available.

Linking AutoCAD Drawings in Other Applications

To embed an AutoCAD drawing in another application, the AutoCAD object is copied to the Clipboard using the **COPYCLIP** command and then pasted into the other application. To insert a linked AutoCAD object into another application, the **COPYLINK** command is used.

COPYLINK
Edit
➥ Copy Link

The **COPYLINK** command is accessed by selecting **Copy Link** from the **Edit** pull-down menu or entering COPYLINK at the Command: prompt. Using **COPYLINK** differs from **COPYCLIP** in that there is no selection process. All currently visible objects are automatically selected as they appear on screen. Also similar to **COPYCLIP**, the selected objects are displayed in a client application in the view that was active when the copy was made.

The Paste Special... selection found on the Edit menu of most Windows applications is used to paste a linked OLE object. The Paste Special dialog box displayed by picking this option may vary slightly from one application to the next, but several basic features are standard. See Figure 18-21. You can also select Object from the Insert pull-down menu in most applications. This is similar to using the **INSERTOBJ** command in AutoCAD.

Remember that the Paste Link option is only available if the source drawing has been saved to a file. Selecting AutoCAD Drawing Object as the data type maintains the pasted material as AutoCAD drawing data. Selecting Picture brings the information in as a WMF file and Bitmap converts the incoming data to a BMP file. Using bitmaps ensures that what you see on the screen is exactly what will print, but tends to make the client files very large and uses more memory. Your choice for the incoming data type has no effect on the original file, and the link is still maintained if the data type supports linking.

Figure 18-21.
The Paste Special dialog box is similar in most Windows applications. This is the dialog box in Microsoft Word.

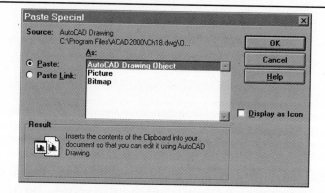

Chapter Test

Answer the following questions on a separate sheet of paper.

1. What Windows application assists in copying objects from one software program to another?
2. How long does information copied to the application in Question 1 remain there?
3. What are the functions of the [Ctrl]+[C] and [Ctrl]+[V] keystrokes?
4. What two commands are used to copy drawing information from one AutoCAD drawing to another?
5. What type of file can be saved from the Clipboard Viewer?
6. What does *OLE* stand for?
7. Define the following terms:
   A. Object
   B. OLE server
   C. OLE client

8. What does *embedding* mean?
9. How can you resize an object that has been pasted into another application?
10. How can you edit an object that has been embedded into an application?
11. What does *linking* mean?
12. How do you insert a new object that has not yet been created into an AutoCAD drawing?

Drawing Problems

1. Begin a new drawing, name it P18-1, and then do the following:
   A. Insert a title block.
   B. Open the Windows Paint program.
   C. Draw a company logo. Copy the design to the Clipboard.
   D. Paste the design into the AutoCAD drawing.
   E. Position the design in the title block.
   F. Save the drawing.

2. Open one of your 3D drawings from a previous chapter, then do the following:
   A. Display the object in a hidden line removed format, or as a rendered image.
   B. Copy the object to the Clipboard.
   C. Open a word processing program and paste the Clipboard contents to create an embedded object.
   D. Create a memo to a coworker or instructor in which you describe the process used to create the document.
   E. Save the document as P18-2 but do not close the application. Return to AutoCAD and close the drawing without saving.
   F. Return to the word processor and double-click on the pasted object.
   G. Edit the object in some way and save the drawing.
   H. Return to the document and save.

3. Open one of your 3D drawings from a previous chapter. Perform the same functions outlined in Problem 2, but this time create a link between the AutoCAD drawing and the word processing document. Edit the drawing in AutoCAD and observe the results in the document file. Save the document as P18-3 and close the word processor.

The appearance of the AutoCAD graphics window can be modified.
A—In this configuration, the number of lines in the command line window has been increased to five, the background and text color in the command line window has been changed, the font type and size have been changed, and the screen menus are displayed.
B—This configuration maximizes the AutoCAD drawing area and is appropriate for a designer who does not use toolbar buttons to initiate commands.

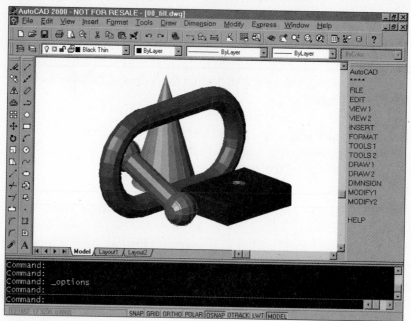

A

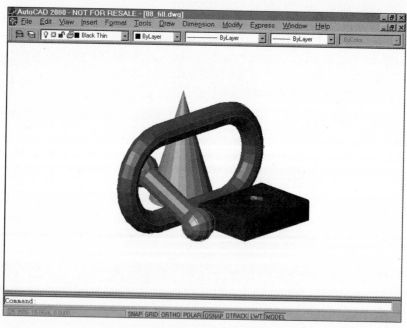

B

CHAPTER 19

Customizing the AutoCAD Environment

Learning Objectives

After completing this chapter, you will be able to:

- Set environment variables.
- Assign colors and fonts to the text and graphics windows.
- Control general AutoCAD system variables.
- Set options that control display quality and AutoCAD performance.
- Control shortcut menus.
- Modify program icon properties.
- Set up AutoCAD for multiple configurations.

AutoCAD provides a variety of options to customize the user interface and working environment. These options permit users to configure the software to suit personal preferences. These options include defining colors for the individual window elements, assigning preferred fonts to the command line window, controlling shortcut menus, and assigning properties to program icons.

The options for customizing the AutoCAD user interface and working environment are found in the **Options** dialog box, Figure 19-1. This dialog box is accessed by selecting **Options...** from the **Tools** pull-down menu, by typing OP or OPTIONS at the Command: prompt, or by right-clicking in the drawing area and selecting **Options...** from the shortcut menu.

OPTIONS
OP

<u>T</u>ools
↳ Opti<u>o</u>ns...

Changes made in the **Options** dialog box do not take effect until either the **Apply** or the **OK** button is picked. If you pick the **Cancel** button, all changes are discarded. Each time you change the options settings, the system registry is updated and the changes are used in subsequent drawing sessions. Settings that are stored within the drawing file have the AutoCAD icon next to them. These settings take effect immediately when the **Apply** or **OK** button is picked. Settings without the icon indicate that the option affects all AutoCAD drawing files.

Figure 19-1.
The **Options** dialog box is used to customize the AutoCAD working environment. Each tab contains a variety of options and settings.

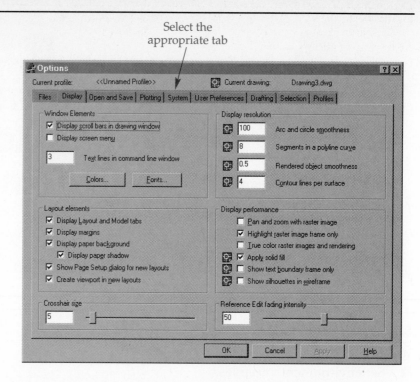

Select the appropriate tab

SETTING AUTOCAD ENVIRONMENT VARIABLES

There are numerous settings that control the manner in which AutoCAD behaves in the Windows environment. These settings are made through the use of environment variables. These variables are used to specify such items as which folders to search for driver and menu files, and the location of your temporary and support files. The default settings created during installation are usually adequate, but changing the settings may result in better performance.

When AutoCAD is used in a network environment, files pertaining to AutoCAD may reside on a network drive so they can be accessed by all workstations. The type of files may include drawings containing blocks, external reference files, and custom menu files. Adding these paths to AutoCAD can make it easier to load these files.

While several different options exist for setting many of the environment variables, the simplest method is to use the **Options** dialog box. The **Files** tab of the **Options** dialog box is used to specify the path AutoCAD searches to find support files and driver files. It also contains the paths where certain types of files are saved, and where AutoCAD looks for specific types of files. Support files include text fonts, menus, AutoLISP files, ADS files, blocks, linetypes, and hatch patterns.

The folder names shown under the Support File Search Path heading in the **Search paths, files names, and file locations:** list are automatically created by the AutoCAD during installation. See Figure 19-2. The Support, Fonts, and Help folders are created in a standard installation. The Express folder is only created if a full installation is performed. You can add the path of any new folders you create that contain support files.

As an example, suppose you store all the blocks you typically use in a separate folder named Blocks. Unless this folder name is placed in the support files search path, AutoCAD will not be able to find your blocks when you attempt to insert them (unless you specify the entire folder path location).

You can add this folder to the existing search path in two ways. The first method is to highlight the Support File Search Path heading and pick the **Add...** button. This places a new, empty listing under the heading. You can now type C:\BLOCKS to complete the entry. Alternatively, instead of typing the path name, you can pick the

Figure 19-2.
Folder paths can be customized in the **Files** tab of the **Options** dialog box

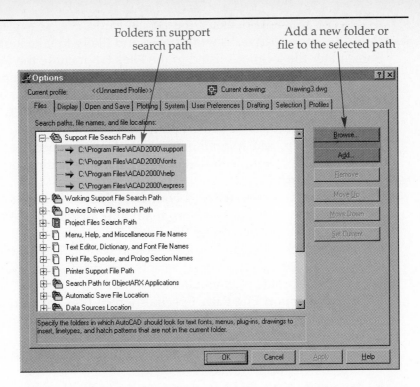

Folders in support search path

Add a new folder or file to the selected path

Browse... button to display the **Browse for Folder** dialog box. You can then use this dialog box to select to the desired folder. The new setting takes effect as soon as you pick **Apply** or the **OK** button and close the **Options** dialog box.

NOTE   The terms *directory*, *subdirectory*, and *folder* are used interchangeably.

Specifying the Help File

The AutoCAD help file is named acad.hlp. During installation, this file is placed in the Acad2000\Help folder. You can use the Help file heading under the Menu, Help, and Miscellaneous File Names entry to specify a different path and file name for the help file. This is particularly handy if you want to locate the help file on a network drive, or if you are using a custom help file.

AutoCAD is able to use any Windows format or platform-independent help file, so custom help files can be generated as needed. This can be a formidable undertaking, and is usually done by third-party developers to supplement their software add-ons. If you are using a third-party application with AutoCAD, you may have an alternate help file.

Other Environment Settings

Another setting that can be specified from the **Files** panel is the location of HDI (Heidi® Device Interface) driver files. The *Heidi Device Interface* is a specification for dealers, manufacturers, and users developing device drivers for peripherals that work with AutoCAD and other Autodesk products.

By default, the drivers supplied with AutoCAD are placed in the Acad2000\Drv folder. If you purchase a third-party driver to use with AutoCAD, be sure to load the driver into this folder. If the third-party driver must reside in a different folder, you should specify that folder using the Device Driver File Search Path. Otherwise, the search for the correct driver is widespread and likely to take longer.

Some other file locations listed in the **Files** tab include the following:

- **Working Support File Search Path.** Lists the active support paths AutoCAD is using. These paths are only for reference, they cannot be added to.
- **Project Files Search Path.** Sets the value for the **PROJECTNAME** system variable and specifies the project path names.
- **Menu, Help, and Miscellaneous File Names.** Specifies which files are used for the base menu, help file, default Internet location, configuration file, and license server.
- **Text Editor, Dictionary, and Font File Names.** Specifies which files are used for the text editor application, main and custom dictionaries, alternate font files, and the font mapping file.
- **Print File, Spooler, and Prolog Section Name.** Sets the file names for the plot file name for legacy plotting scripts, the print spool executable file, and the PostScript prolog section name.
- **Printer Support File Path.** Specifies which files are used for the print spooler file location, printer configuration search path, printer description file search path, and plot style table search path.
- **Search Path for ObjectARX Applications.** Specifies which files to search for ObjectARX applications.
- **Automatic Save File Location.** Sets the path where the autosave (.sv$) file is stored. An autosave file is only created if the **Automatic save** option is checked in the **Open and Save** tab of the **Options** dialog box.
- **Data Sources Location.** Specifies the path for database source files (.udl).
- **Drawing Template File Location.** Specifies the default location for drawing template files.
- **Log File Location.** Specifies the path for the acad.log file. A log file is only created if the **Maintain a log file** option is checked in the **Open and Save** tab of the **Options** dialog box.
- **Temporary Drawing File Location.** Sets the folder where AutoCAD stores temporary drawing files.
- **Temporary External Reference File Location.** Indicates where temporary external reference files are placed.
- **Texture Maps Search Path.** Location of texture map files for rendering.

CUSTOMIZING THE GRAPHICS WINDOW

Numerous options are available to customize the graphics window to your personal liking. Select the **Display** tab in the **Options** dialog box to view the display control options, Figure 19-3.

The **Window Elements** area has settings used to turn the scroll bars and the screen menu on or off, set the number of visible command lines, and select the color and font settings. The **Crosshair size** setting is a percentage of the drawing screen area. The higher the value, the further the crosshairs extend. The **Reference edit fading intensity** value determines the display intensity of the unselected objects in reference edit mode. A higher value means the unselected objects are less visible.

Figure 19-3.
Use the **Display** tab
to set many visual
elements of the
AutoCAD
environment.

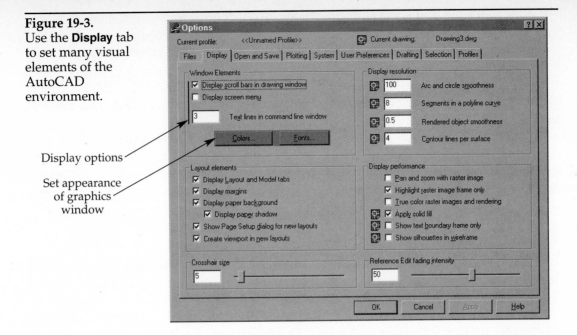

Display options

Set appearance
of graphics
window

Changing Colors

By customizing colors, you can add your personal touch and make AutoCAD stand out among other active Windows applications. AutoCAD 2000 provides this capability with the **Color Options** dialog box, Figure 19-4. This dialog box is accessed by picking the **Colors...** button in the **Window Elements** area of the **Display** tab in the **Options** dialog box.

The **Window Element:** drop-down list allows you to select elements of the graphics and text windows. These elements include the model space background and pointer, the layout space background and pointer, the command line background, and the command line text. To customize colors, do the following:

1. Pick the **Color...** button in the **Options** dialog box. The **Color Options** dialog box appears.
2. Select the feature to have its color changed. You can pick the feature in the **Model tab** or **Layout tabs** window or select the item from the **Window Element:** drop-down list. If you pick in one of the windows, the **Window Element:** drop-down list displays the name of the selected item.

Figure 19-4.
Change AutoCAD
color settings using
the **Color Options**
dialog box.

Pick item to
change its color

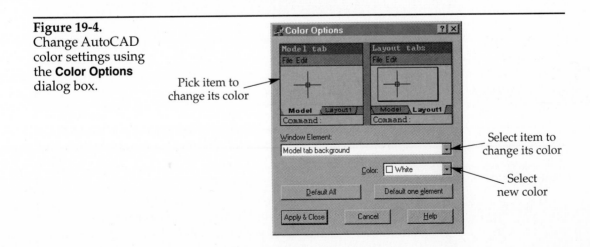

Select item to
change its color

Select
new color

3. Pick the color you want from the **Color:** drop-down list. The color you select is immediately reflected in the sample area. Pick the **More...** option to pick a color from the **Select Color** dialog box. To select a color from the Windows Color dialog box, pick the **Windows...** option.

The **Default All** button changes all colors back to the default AutoCAD settings. To change only the selected element back to its default, pick the **Default one element** button.

Once you have made your color selections, pick the **Apply & Close** button and then pick **OK** in the **Options** dialog box to implement your color changes. The graphics window regenerates and displays the color changes you made. If you modified the colors for the text window as well, you should see the difference in the floating command window.

Changing Fonts

You can also change the fonts used in the command line window. The font you select has no effect on the text in your drawings, nor is the font used in the AutoCAD dialog boxes, pull-down menus, or screen menus.

To change the font used in the command line window, pick the **Fonts...** button in the **Display** tab of the **Options** dialog box. The **Command Line Window Font** dialog box appears, Figure 19-5.

The default font used by AutoCAD for the graphics window is Courier. The font style for Courier is Regular (not bold or italic), and it defaults to a size of 10 points. You can retain this font and just change the style and size. Select a new font from the **Font:** list. This displays the system fonts available for use. The **Sample Command Line Font** area displays a sample of the selected font.

Once you have selected the desired fonts, font styles, and sizes for the command line window, pick the **Apply & Close** button to assign the new fonts.

Figure 19-5.
The command line window font can be changed to suit your preference. The Courier font is used by default.

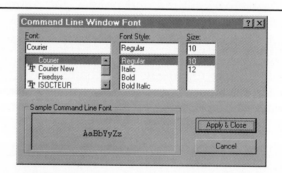

NOTE
The Windows system font controls the font style for the text displayed in the screen menu.

PROFESSIONAL TIP
The **UNDO** command does not affect changes made to your system using the **Options** dialog box. If you have made changes you do not want to save, pick **Cancel** to dismiss the **Options** dialog box. Picking **Cancel** does not dismiss changes that have been applied using the **Apply** button.

EXERCISE 19-1

- ❑ Start AutoCAD.
- ❑ Use the **Options** dialog box to change the color elements and fonts for the command line window to your personal liking.
- ❑ Once you are satisfied with your modifications, pick **OK** to save your changes.

Command Line Window Size

In addition to changing the colors and fonts used in the command line window, the number of command lines can be set. The **Text lines in command line window** setting can be specified in the **Window Elements** area of the **Display** tab.

The default is 3 lines, but this value can be set higher so that more of your commands are visible. Increasing the number of lines displayed here affects the size of your drawing area. Also, you can dynamically change the size of the command line window (whether floating or docked) using the ***resizing*** cursor, Figure 19-6. Changing the size of the command line window in this manner automatically updates the value in the edit box.

Figure 19-6.
This cursor appears when resizing the command line window.

Layout Display Settings

The appearance of a layout tab is different than the appearance of the **Model** tab. The idea of the default layout tab settings is to provide a picture of what the drawing will look like when plotted. You can see if the objects will fit on the paper or if some of the objects are outside the margins. The following options, which are found in the **Layout elements** area of the **Display** tab in the **Options** dialog box, are shown in Figure 19-7:

- **Display Layout and Model tabs.** Displays the **Model** and **Layout** tabs at the bottom of the drawing screen area.
- **Display margins.** The margins are shown as dashed lines on the paper. Any object outside the margins is not plotted.
- **Display paper background.** Displays the paper size specified in the page setup.
- **Display paper shadow.** Displays a shadow to the right and bottom of the paper. This option is only available if **Display paper background** is checked.
- **Show Page Setup dialog box for new layouts.** Determines if the **Page Setup** dialog box is displayed when a new layout is selected or created.
- **Create viewport in new layout.** Determines whether a viewport is created automatically when a new layout is selected or created.

Figure 19-7.
Customizing the display of layouts. A—The options are available in the **Layout elements** area of the **Display** tab in the **Option** dialog box. B—Layout display features.

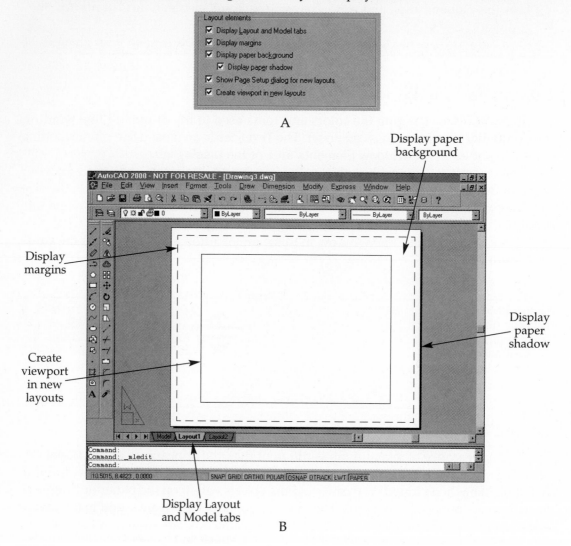

Performance Display Settings

The settings in the **Display resolution** and **Display performance** areas of the **Display** tab in the **Options** dialog box affect the performance of AutoCAD. The settings can affect regeneration time and realtime panning and zooming. The following options are available from the **Display resolution** area:

- **Arc and circle smoothness.** This setting controls the smoothness of circles, arcs, and ellipses. The default value is 100, the range is from 1 to 20,000, and the system variable is **VIEWRES**.
- **Segments in a polyline curve.** This value determines how many line segments will be generated for each polyline curve. The default value is 8, the range is from –32767 to 32767, and the system variable is **SPLINESEGS**.
- **Rendered object smoothness.** This setting controls how smooth curved solids are when hidden, shaded, or rendered. This value is multiplied by the **Arc and circle smoothness** value. The default value is 0.5, the range is from 0.01 to 10, and the system variable is **FACETRES**.
- **Contour lines per surface.** Controls the number of contour lines per surface on solid objects. The default value is 4, the range is from 0 to 2047, and the system variable is **ISOLINES**.

AutoCAD and its Applications—Advanced

The following options are available from the **Display performance** area:

- **Pan and zoom with raster image.** If this is checked, raster images are displayed when panning and zooming. If it is unchecked, only the frame is displayed. The system variable is **RTDISPLAY**.
- **Highlight raster image frame only.** If this is checked, only the frame around a raster image is highlighted when the image is selected. If this option is unchecked, the image displays a diagonal checkered pattern to indicate selection. The system variable is **IMAGEHLT**.
- **True color raster images and rendering.** When checked, this setting allows AutoCAD to display raster images and renderings at the highest display quality set for the Windows system.
- **Apply solid fill.** Controls the display of solid fills in objects. Affected objects include hatches, wide polylines, solids, multilines, and traces. The system variable is **FILLMODE**.
- **Show text boundary frame only.** This setting controls the Quick Text mode. When checked, text is replaced by a rectangular frame.
- **Show silhouettes in wireframe.** Controls whether or not the silhouette curves are displayed for solid objects. The system variable is **DISPSILH**.

NOTE After changing display settings, use the **REGEN** or **REGENALL** command to make the settings take effect on the objects in the drawing.

PROFESSIONAL TIP If you notice performance slowing down, you may want to adjust display settings. For example, if there is a lot of text in the drawing, you can activate Quick Text mode to improve performance. When the drawing is ready for plotting, deactivate Quick Text mode.

FILE SAVING OPTIONS

The settings specified in the **Open and Save** tab of the **Options** dialog box deal with how drawing files are saved, safety precautions, xrefs, the loading of ObjectARX applications, and proxy objects. This tab is shown in Figure 19-8.

Default Settings for Saving Files

The settings in the **File Save** area determine the defaults for saving files. The setting in the **Save as:** drop-down list determines the default file type. You may want to change this setting if you are saving drawing files as a previous release of AutoCAD or saving drawings as DXF files. If the **Save a thumbnail preview image** box is checked, a preview image for the drawing is displayed in the **Select File** dialog box. The **Incremental save percentage** value determines how much of the drawing is saved when a **SAVE** or **QSAVE** is performed. If new data in a drawing file reaches the specified percentage, a full save is performed. To ensure that a full save is performed, set the value to 0.

Figure 19-8.
The **Open and Save** tab settings control default save options, file safety features, xref options, and ObjectARX application options.

Set default values for saving files

Autosave options

Safety options

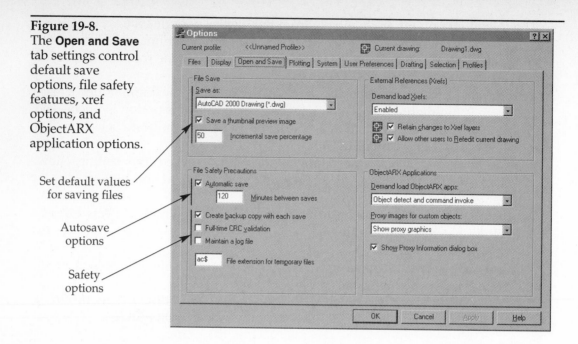

Autosave Settings

When working in AutoCAD, there is always a risk of data loss. This data loss can occur due to a sudden power outage or an unforeseen system error. AutoCAD provides several safety precautions to help minimize data loss when these types of events occur. These settings are found in the **File Safety Precautions** area in the **Open and Save** tab of the **Options** dialog box.

When the **Automatic save** check box is enabled, AutoCAD automatically creates backup files at a specified interval. The **Minutes between saves:** edit box sets this interval (the edit box contains the value of the **SAVETIME** system variable). Removing the check sets **SAVETIME** to 0.

The automatic save feature does not overwrite the source drawing file with its incremental saves. Rather, AutoCAD creates a drawing to save temporary files. The path for autosave files is specified in the **Files** tab in the **Options** dialog box, Figure 19-9. Autosave files have an .sv$ extension with the drawing name and some random numbers generated by AutoCAD.

The autosave file is stored in the location specified until the drawing is closed. When the drawing is closed, the autosave file is deleted. If AutoCAD quits unexpectedly, the autosave file is not deleted and can be renamed with a .dwg extension so it can be opened in AutoCAD.

The interval setting you should use is based on working conditions and file size. It is possible to adversely affect your productivity by setting your **SAVETIME** value too small. For example, in larger drawings (1 Mb and above), a **SAVE** command can take a significant amount of time. If a save takes two minutes and your autosave is set to save every five minutes, you would spend more than fifteen minutes of every hour waiting on AutoCAD to finish saving the file.

Ideally, it is best to set your **SAVETIME** variable to the greatest amount of time you can afford to repeat. While it may be acceptable to redo the last fifteen minutes or less of work, it is unlikely that you would feel the same about having to redo the last hour.

Figure 19-9.
The location of the autosave file is set in the **Files** tab of the **Options** dialog box.

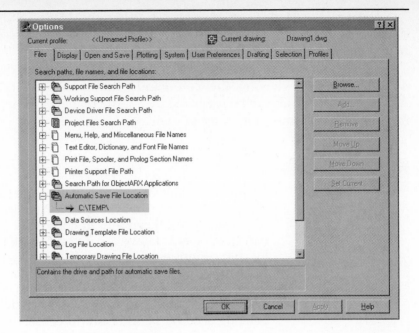

PROFESSIONAL TIP

Setting and resetting the **SAVETIME** variable according to any given situation is often the best approach. The factors that should influence the current setting include not only file size, but also the working conditions. If your computer system is experiencing frequent lock-ups or crashes, your automatic saves should occur often. Weather can also be a factor. Wind or electrical storms should be an immediate cue to reduce the value of the **SAVETIME** variable.

Backup Files

AutoCAD can also create a backup of the current drawing file. The backup file uses the same name as the drawing, but has a .bak file extension. The backup is not overwritten when another drawing is opened or saved. When the **Create backup copy with each save** option is selected, the backup file feature is enabled. If there is no check in this toggle box, the file is not backed up when you save. Unless you prefer to take unnecessary risks, it is usually best to leave this feature enabled.

CRC Validation

Full-time CRC validation is a feature you can use when drawing files are being corrupted and you suspect a hardware or software problem. CRC stands for *cyclic redundancy check*, which verifies that the number of data bits sent is the same as the number received. When using full-time CRC validation, the CRC check is done every time data is read into the drawing. This ensures that all data is received correctly.

Log Files

When the **Maintain a log file** check box is activated, AutoCAD creates a file named acad.log. The name and location of the log file can be specified using the Log File Location listing under the **Files** tab of the **Options** dialog box. When activated, all prompts, messages, and responses that appear in the command line window are saved to this file. Exiting AutoCAD or turning off this check box disables the log file feature.

The log file status can also be set using the **LOGFILEON** and **LOGFILEOFF** commands. Each individual session of AutoCAD contained in a single log file is separated by a line of dashes with a date and time stamp.

The log file can serve a variety of purposes. The source of drawing errors can be determined by reviewing the commands that produced the incorrect results. Additionally, log files can be reviewed by a CAD manager to determine the need for training and customization of the system.

PROFESSIONAL TIP

Toggle the log file open before listing any saved layers, blocks, views, or user coordinate systems. You can then print the log file contents and keep a hard copy at your workstation as a handy reference. However, if you choose to keep it open, the log file continues to grow with each subsequent AutoCAD session. As a result, the increased size of acad.log file consumes valuable hard disk space. AutoCAD does not delete or shorten this file for you. Therefore, make a point of shortening or deleting acad.log periodically to conserve disk resources. Do not be concerned about deleting this file because AutoCAD will create another file the next time you toggle the log file open.

External Reference and ObjectARX Options

The external reference options are important if you are working with xrefs. These options are found in the **External Reference (Xrefs)** area of the **Open and Save** tab in the **Options** dialog box.

The **Demand load Xrefs:** setting can affect performance and the ability for another user to edit a drawing currently referenced into another drawing. This setting is also controlled by the **XLOADCTL** system variable.

If the **Retain changes to Xref layers** option is checked, xref layer settings are saved with the drawing file. The **VISRETAIN** system variable also controls this setting. The **Allow other users to Refedit current drawing** setting controls whether or not the drawing can be edited in-place when it is referenced by another drawing. This setting is also controlled by the **XEDIT** system variable.

The **ObjectARX Applications** area controls the loading of ObjectARX applications and the displaying of proxy objects. The **Demand load ObjectARX apps:** setting specifies if and when AutoCAD loads third-party applications associated with objects in the drawing. The **Proxy images for custom objects:** setting controls how objects created by a third-party application are displayed. When a drawing with proxy objects is opened, the **Proxy Information** dialog box is displayed. To disable the dialog box, uncheck the **Show Proxy Information dialog box** option.

SYSTEM SETTINGS

Options for the pointing device, graphic settings, general system options, and dbConnect can be found in the **System** tab of the **Options** dialog box, Figure 19-10. These settings affect the interaction between AutoCAD and your operating system.

In the **Current 3D Graphics Display** area, you can set the 3D graphics display system using the drop-down list and modify its properties. AutoCAD is configured with the Heidi 3D graphics display system (GSHEIDI10).

Figure 19-10.
General AutoCAD system options and hardware settings can be controlled in the **System** tab.

3D graphics display options

Pointing device used for AutoCAD

Regeneration options available in AutoCAD 2000i only

Options for working with databases

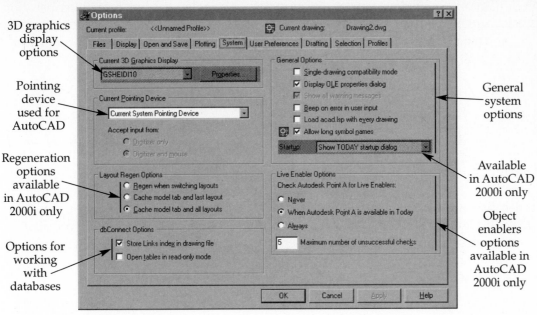

General system options

Available in AutoCAD 2000i only

Object enablers options available in AutoCAD 2000i only

For 2000i Users...

In AutoCAD 2000i, the **System** tab of the **Options** dialog box includes two additional areas: **Layout Regen Options** and **Live Enabler Options**. The **Layout Regen Options** setting determines what is regenerated and when it is regenerated when working with layout tabs. The **Live Enabler Options** specifies when the Autodesk Point A Web site is checked for object enablers.

The **Current Pointing Device** area determines the pointing device used with AutoCAD. The default is the current system pointing device (usually your mouse). If you have a digitizer tablet, you will want to select the Wintab Compatible Digitizer option.

NOTE

You must configure your tablet before it can be used. For detailed instructions on using your tablet as a digitizing device, see Chapter 23 of this text or Appendix M of *AutoCAD and its Applications—Basics*. Refer to the *AutoCAD Installation Guide* for more information about digitizer configuration options.

The settings in the **General Options** area control general system functions. The following options are available:

- **Single drawing compatibility mode.** By default, you can open multiple drawings in a single session of AutoCAD. To allow only one drawing to be open in a session, check this option. This is also controlled by the **SDI** system variable.
- **Show Startup dialog.** This option controls whether the **Startup** dialog box is displayed when you begin an AutoCAD session.
- **Display OLE properties dialog.** When inserting an OLE object, the **OLE Properties** dialog box is displayed if this option is checked.
- **Show all warning messages.** Controls the display of dialog boxes that include a **Don't Display This Warning Again** option.
- **Beep on error in user input.** Specifies whether AutoCAD alerts you of incorrect user input with an audible beep.
- **Load acad.lsp with every drawing.** This setting turns the persistent AutoLISP feature on or off.
- **Allow long symbol names.** Determines if long symbol names can be used in AutoCAD. If this option is checked, up to 255 characters can be used for layers, dimension styles, blocks, linetypes, text styles, layouts, UCS names, views, and viewport configurations. The system variable is **EXTNAMES**.

For 2000i Users...

The **Show Startup dialog** check box in AutoCAD 2000 is replaced with the **Startup** drop-down list in AutoCAD 2000i. This drop-down list controls the behavior when AutoCAD is launched and when a new drawing is created.

The following options are available from the **dbConnect Options** area:

- **Store Links index in drawing file.** When this option is checked, the database index is saved within the drawing file. This makes the link selection operation quicker, but increases the drawing file size.
- **Open tables in read-only mode.** Determines whether tables opened in read-only mode.

USER PREFERENCES

A variety of settings are found in the **User Preferences** tab of the **Options** dialog box. See Figure 19-11. AutoCAD allows users to optimize the way they like to work in AutoCAD by providing options for the accelerator keys and shortcut menu functions. The shortcut menus provide an easy means of accessing common commands, but if you are a keyboard person, you may want to disable the shortcut menus to avoid the extra mouse picks. **AutoCAD DesignCenter** units, hyperlink icon display, coordinate data entry, object sorting methods, and default lineweight setting are also controlled in this tab.

Figure 19-11.
The **User Preferences** tab allows you to set up AutoCAD in a manner that works best for you.

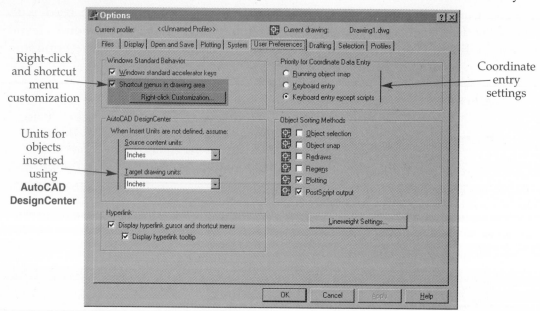

Keystrokes

AutoCAD supports the common keystroke combinations recognized by many other Windows applications. For example, pressing [Ctrl]+[S] activates the **QSAVE** command to save your file. The [Ctrl]+[P] keystroke prints (plots) your file, [Ctrl]+[O] opens a drawing, and [Ctrl]+[N] starts a new drawing.

In AutoCAD releases previous to Release 13, the [Ctrl]+[C] key combination is used as a **CANCEL**. In later releases this combination starts the **COPYCLIP** command. For an experienced user of AutoCAD upgrading to AutoCAD 2000, it may be a significant hurdle to "unlearn" several years of canceling with a [Ctrl]+[C]. For these users, AutoCAD provides a way to switch the new keystroke model with the old keystroke standards. Unchecking **Windows standard accelerator keys** in the **Windows Standard Behavior** area enables the old-style keystroke model.

Shortcut Menus

AutoCAD 2000 has shortcut menus that make common commands easy to access. These shortcut menus are context sensitive, meaning the options available in the shortcut menu are determined by the active command, cursor location, or objects selected.

The shortcut menu settings are located in the **Windows Standard Behavior** area on the **User Preferences** tab of the **Options** dialog box. To disable the shortcut menus, uncheck the **Shortcut menus in drawing area** option.

You can also customize the setting for the right mouse button. Pick the **Right-click Customization...** button to access the **Right-Click Customization** dialog box. See Figure 19-12. Different settings can be used for the three different modes:

- **Default mode.** No objects are selected, and no commands are active. The **Repeat Last Command** option activates the last command issued. This is the right mouse button behavior in previous releases of AutoCAD.
- **Edit mode.** An object is selected, but no command is active.
- **Command mode.** A command is active. The **ENTER** option corresponds to the behavior of previous releases of AutoCAD.

Figure 19-12.
Use this dialog box
to customize the
right mouse button.

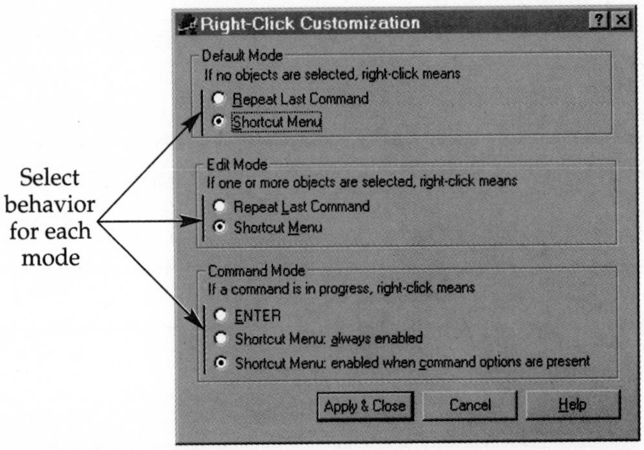

Select
behavior
for each
mode

Other User Preferences Options

In the **AutoCAD DesignCenter** area, unit values can be set for objects when they are inserted into a drawing from the **AutoCAD DesignCenter**. The **Source content units:** specifies the units for objects being inserted into the current drawing. The **Target drawing units:** determines the units in the current drawing. These settings are used when there are no units set with the **INSUNITS** system variable.

Options for the hyperlink display can be set in the **Hyperlink** area. If **Display hyperlink cursor and shortcut menu** is checked, the hyperlink icon appears next to the crosshairs when they are over an object containing a hyperlink. Additional hyperlink options are available from the shortcut menu when an object with a hyperlink is selected. The **Display hyperlink tooltip** option controls whether the text from the **Link to file or URL** text box for the hyperlink target is displayed when the cursor is held over an object with a hyperlink.

The **Priority for Coordinate Data Entry** area controls how AutoCAD responds to input of coordinate data. The system variable for this is **OSNAPCOORD**.

The sort order of objects is controlled in the **Object Sorting Methods** area, or by the **SORTENTS** system variable. When an option is checked, AutoCAD sorts selectable objects from those created first to those created last. If the option is unchecked, AutoCAD sorts selectable objects randomly.

SAVING YOUR CONFIGURATION PROFILES

The AutoCAD environment settings can be saved as a user profile. A *profile* is a set of custom preferences. In cases where multiple users are using the same workstation at different times, each user can save an individual profile and then reload it at every session. Various profiles may also be useful to a single user with different preferences for different projects.

If no one has previously created a custom profile, the only profile listed will be <<Unnamed Profile>>. Unless you have defined a custom profile and set it to be current, AutoCAD saves all your preference changes to <<Unnamed Profile>>.

Pick the **Profiles** tab of the **Options** dialog box to define or load a profile. See Figure 19-13. The available profiles are displayed in the **Available profiles:** list. You can create your own profile by picking the **Add to List...** button. This accesses the **Add Profile** dialog box, shown in Figure 19-14, which is used to name and create a description for a new profile.

Next, set the new profile name to be the current profile by highlighting it and picking the **Set Current** button. Now, all changes to your options are saved in this profile. At any point, you can make a different profile active by highlighting it and picking the **Set Current** button.

It is possible for another user to unknowingly change your preferences if the current profile is not changed before editing options. To ensure maximum safety of a profile, you can save the profile data to a file. Pick the **Export...** button to display the **Export Profile** dialog box. The default file extension is .arg, and you can specify any valid file name. To access the saved settings at a later time, pick the **Import...** button to display the **Import Profile** dialog box. Now you can select any saved profile to import.

Figure 19-13.
Settings can be saved within a profile.

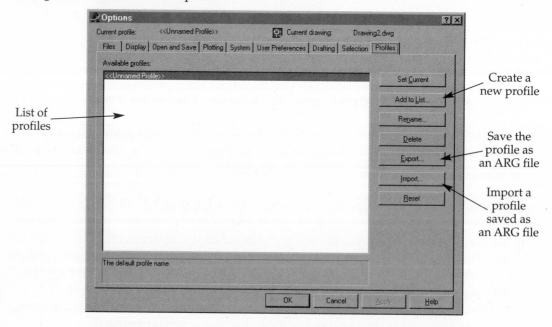

AutoCAD and its Applications—Advanced

Figure 19-14.
The **Add Profile** dialog box is used to create a new profile.

Enter name for new profile ⟶

Enter description for new profile

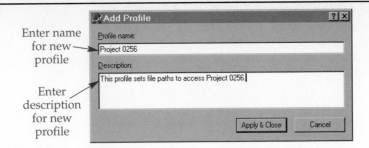

EXERCISE 19-2

- ❑ Open the **Options** dialog box and pick the **Profiles** tab.
- ❑ Pick the **Add to List...** button. In the **Profile name:** text box, type in your name and then pick the **Apply & Close** button.
- ❑ Highlight your new profile and pick the **Set Current** button. Close the **Options** dialog box.
- ❑ Type TOOLBAR at the Command: prompt to display the **Toolbars** dialog box. Add three or four toolbars to the screen (it doesn't matter which ones).
- ❑ Close the **Toolbars** dialog box and reopen the **Options** dialog box.
- ❑ In the **Display** tab, pick the **Colors...** button and change the Model tab background to cyan, and the Command line background to yellow. Pick the **Apply & Close** button.
- ❑ Pick the **Profiles** tab. Highlight the <<Unnamed Profile>> and pick the **Set Current** button.

CHANGING PROGRAM PROPERTIES

When AutoCAD is first installed on your computer, the installation program setup.exe automatically creates the AutoCAD group and several program items, then places a program icon on the Windows desktop. If desired, you can modify the program icon properties. These properties include such things as the file attributes, the folder where AutoCAD is started, and the icon representing AutoCAD for the application shortcut.

To modify the AutoCAD program icon properties, right-click on the AutoCAD 2000 icon on the desktop and then select Properties from the shortcut menu. See Figure 19-15. You can also pick the icon and then use the [Alt]+[Enter] key combination. Either action displays the AutoCAD 2000 Properties dialog box, Figure 19-16.

NOTE

Be sure to check with your instructor or system administrator before modifying the AutoCAD program properties.

There are two main tabs, General and Shortcut. The following items can be specified in this dialog box:

- **Attributes.** These radio buttons on the General tab can be used to set the attributes for the file containing the shortcut information.
- **Target.** This text box contains the name of the executable program and its path. If the folder that contains the AutoCAD executable has changed, this line can be edited so it still links to the correct file. If you are not sure of the exact path name, you can pick the **Find Target** button to locate it.

Figure 19-15.
This shortcut menu
appears when you
right-click on an icon
in the Windows
desktop.

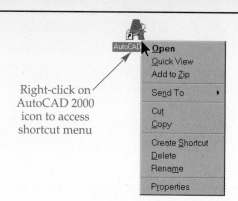

Right-click on
AutoCAD 2000
icon to access
shortcut menu

Figure 19-16.
The AutoCAD 2000 Properties dialog box. A—The General tab. B—The Shortcut tab.

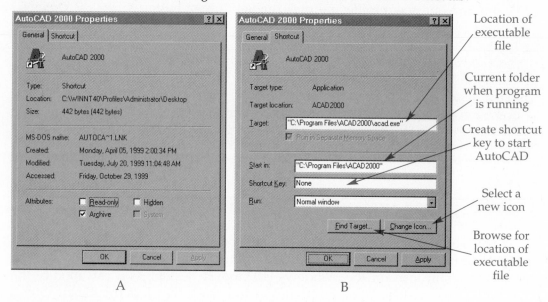

A

B

Location of
executable
file

Current folder
when program
is running

Create shortcut
key to start
AutoCAD

Select a
new icon

Browse for
location of
executable
file

- **Start in.** This text box specifies the name of the folder where the AutoCAD program files are located. The folder specified in this text box becomes the current directory when AutoCAD is running. Any new files are placed here.
- **Shortcut Key.** Microsoft Windows provides a special feature called an *application shortcut key*. This feature permits you to launch AutoCAD with a user-defined key combination. Assigning a shortcut key for AutoCAD is described later in this section.
- **Run.** This listing offers options to run the program in a normal, maximized, or minimized window. It is not recommended to run the program minimized, otherwise AutoCAD appears only as a button on the taskbar when you run it. You can easily restore or maximize it, but when it does not automatically appear on screen, it may be confusing to newer users.

When you are finished making your changes, pick the OK button to exit the AutoCAD 2000 Properties dialog box. Since any changes you make take effect immediately, there is no need to restart Windows.

Changing the AutoCAD Icon

The AutoCAD 2000 Properties dialog box provides the option to change the program icon used by AutoCAD. Use the following procedure to change the icon:

1. Pick the Change Icon... button in the Shortcut tab of the AutoCAD 2000 Properties dialog box. The Change Icon dialog box is then displayed, Figure 19-17A. Observe that there are many icons from which to choose, but none of these icons represent the AutoCAD application.
2. To display icons for AutoCAD, use the Browse... button to find the file named acad.exe in the Acad2000 folder. Pick the Open button to display the AutoCAD icons, as shown in Figure 19-17B. Six icons are shown—the standard icon, a drawing icon, two that closely resemble a text window, one for the aerial view window, and the standard icon for an AutoLISP file.
3. Select the icon you wish to use and pick the OK button to exit the Change Icon dialog box. Your icon selection is now displayed in the AutoCAD 2000 Properties dialog box.

Figure 19-17.
A—A new icon can be selected in the Change Icon dialog box.
B—Icons available in the acad.exe file.

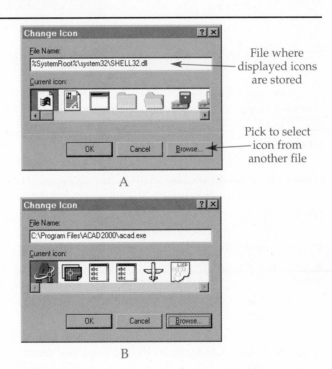

File where displayed icons are stored

Pick to select icon from another file

A

B

Defining a Shortcut Key

Microsoft Windows provides the option of assigning a shortcut key that starts an application. You can use any letter, number, or special character for a shortcut key. Whichever key you choose, Windows automatically adds a [Ctrl]+[Alt] in front of it. To assign a shortcut key for launching AutoCAD, do the following:

1. Return to the desktop and open the AutoCAD 2000 Properties dialog box.
2. Pick within the Shortcut Key: text box. The flashing vertical cursor appears at the end of the word None.
3. Now, press [A] (or whichever key you prefer).
4. The character string Ctrl + Alt + A appears in the text box, Figure 19-18.
5. Pick OK to exit the AutoCAD 2000 Properties dialog box.

Your new shortcut key is immediately active. Now, no matter which Windows-based application is running, you can start AutoCAD with the keyboard combination [Ctrl]+[Alt]+[A]. Refer to the Microsoft Windows *User's Guide* for more information regarding shortcut keys.

Figure 19-18.
Setting the
[Ctrl]+[Alt]+[A] key
combination to
automatically start
AutoCAD.

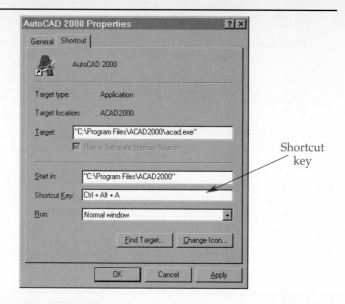

Shortcut
key

CREATING ALTERNATE AUTOCAD CONFIGURATIONS

The information you specify for AutoCAD regarding the pointing and printing devices is recorded in a configuration file. Your pointing and printing devices are specified in the **Options** dialog box, but the information is stored in the current configuration file.

The default configuration file is acad2000.cfg. By default, this file is located in the folder that contains the AutoCAD program files. Each time you specify a new pointing or printing device, the existing acad2000.cfg file is overwritten with the new information.

Under most circumstances, a single configuration file is all that is necessary. Some users, however, may require multiple configurations. As an example, if you use a mouse most of the time but sometimes need a digitizer tablet for your AutoCAD work, you may find it convenient to set up AutoCAD to use multiple configurations. This can save you the time required to reconfigure AutoCAD each time you need to switch your pointing devices.

To save multiple configurations, you must specify a new location for AutoCAD to store the acad2000.cfg so that it does not overwrite the previous version. This way, you actually have more than one configuration file, with each file located in a specific folder.

As you set up your system for multiple AutoCAD configurations, the first step is to create an alternate folder where the new configuration file is located. Do this using Windows Explorer, or any regular file dialog box. It is recommended that these folders be placed under the Acad2000 directory so they are easy to locate. For this example, create a directory named Acad2000\Altcfg. Now, find the acad2000.cfg file in the Acad2000 folder and copy it to the new folder.

In the Windows desktop, press the [Ctrl] key and pick the AutoCAD 2000 icon to create a copy. This creates a new icon for starting the new configuration. Open the AutoCAD 2000 Properties dialog box and go to the Shortcut tab. In the Target: edit box, place a /c after the existing target, followed by the directory path location for the alternate configuration. For example, in Figure 19-19, the configuration directory is entered as:

"C:\Program Files\Acad2000\acad.exe" /c "C:\Program Files\Acad2000\altcfg"

The new path must be placed in quotation marks due to the space in the path name. The /c is not in quotation marks. Command line switches are separated by spaces, and the space is interpreted as the end of the path name.

It is also recommended that you change the title of the shortcut icon on the desktop to match the configuration. For example, one shortcut icon could be called AutoCAD 2000 – Mouse and the other could be called AutoCAD 2000 – Digitizer. Do this by picking the text below the icon once, pausing for a moment, then picking again. Now you can enter the new text.

When you start AutoCAD using the new icon, the alternate configuration file directory is used. This means that any configuration changes you make are stored in the new configuration file and do not affect other configurations.

Figure 19-19.
If multiple configurations are used, the location of the alternate configuration file must be specified in the Target edit box.

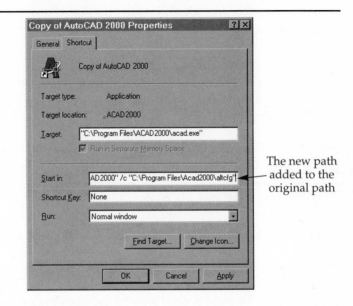

The new path added to the original path

NOTE You can set up unique shortcut keys for each AutoCAD shortcut icon on your desktop.

PROFESSIONAL TIP

A profile can be accessed directly from an AutoCAD icon on the desktop using a /p switch and then the exact profile name. For example, if you created a profile called Project 0256, the Target: text box in the AutoCAD 2000 Properties dialog box would read:

"C:\Program Files\Acad2000\acad.exe" /p "Project 0256"

Chapter Test

Answer the following questions on a separate sheet of paper.

1. List three methods used to access the **Options** dialog box.
2. How do you access the **Color Options** dialog box?
3. What are the advantages of toggling the log file open? The disadvantages?
4. Name the two commands that toggle the log file on and off.
5. AutoCAD resides in the C:\Program Files\Acad2000 folder on your workstation. You have created two folders under \Acad2000 named Projects and Symbols. You want to store your drawings in the Projects folder and your blocks in the Symbols folder. What should you enter in the Support File Search Path area so these folders are added to the search path?
6. How do you select the folder in which the autosave file is saved?
7. How would you set the right mouse button to perform an [Enter], rather than displaying shortcut menus?
8. What is a *profile*?
9. How and why are profiles used?
10. What is the file extension used for a profile when it is exported?
11. Which file must be copied to a separate folder before creating an alternate AutoCAD configuration?

Problems

1. Create an alternate configuration for AutoCAD dedicated to 3D modeling and rendering using the methods described in this chapter. Use the following instructions:
   A. Assign a different program icon for the 3D configuration.
   B. Name the program icon AutoCAD 3D.
   C. Define a shortcut key for the configuration.
   D. Add a directory to the support path that contains 3D shapes.

2. Create an alternate configuration for AutoCAD dedicated to dimensioning. Use the following instructions to complete this problem:
   A. Assign a different program icon for the dimensioning configuration.
   B. Name the program icon AutoCAD Dimensioning.
   C. Define a shortcut key for the configuration.
   D. Add a directory to the support path that contains 3D shapes.

CHAPTER 20

Customizing Toolbars

Learning Objectives

After completing this chapter, you will be able to:
- Position and resize toolbars.
- Display and hide toolbars.
- Modify existing toolbars.
- Create new toolbars.
- Create new toolbar buttons.
- Construct new button images.
- Create and modify flyouts.
- Describe the purpose and function of the AutoCAD menu files.

One of the easiest ways of altering the AutoCAD environment is to customize toolbars. This requires no programming and little use of text editors. Existing toolbars can be modified quickly by removing and adding buttons, or by changing the toolbar shape. New buttons can also be created and assigned to an existing toolbar. The most powerful aspect of customizing toolbars is the ability to quickly create entirely new functions and buttons to help you in your work.

WORKING WITH TOOLBARS

Toolbars provide access to most AutoCAD commands with one or two quick "picks." This graphical interface provides much flexibility. Toolbars can be quickly and easily resized, repositioned, hidden from view, or made visible.

Positioning and Sizing Toolbars

A *docked toolbar* is positioned so that it appears as if it is part of the AutoCAD window. By default, the **Standard** and **Object Properties** toolbars are docked at the top of the screen and the **Draw** and **Modify** toolbars are docked at the left side of the screen. When a visible toolbar is not docked, it is a floating toolbar. A *floating toolbar* appears as a small window with a title bar. When a toolbar is floating, it can be adjusted and repositioned like any other window.

A docked toolbar can be *floated* by pointing to the grab bar and double-clicking; this returns the toolbar to its last floating position. Optionally, you can point to the grab bar and then press and hold the pick button. Next, move the cursor to drag an outline of the toolbar. When you release the pick button, the toolbar appears in the new location.

To reposition a floating toolbar, place the cursor on the title bar, press and hold the pick button, and move the toolbar to the new location. The outline of the toolbar is visible while you are moving it, Figure 20-1A. Release the pick button when the toolbar is where you want it.

Unlike windows, toolbars can only be resized in one direction at a time. Moving the cursor to a vertical border changes the cursor to a horizontal resizing cursor. Again, press and hold the pick button and an outline is displayed. Move the cursor to resize the toolbar. Release the pick button to create the new size. Figure 20-1B and Figure 20-1C show the **Draw** toolbar being resized.

To dock a toolbar, reposition it at any edge of the AutoCAD window. A toolbar can be docked on the right, left, top, or bottom of the window. Figure 20-2 shows the **Draw** toolbar docked on the left side of the screen and the **Modify** toolbar in the process of being docked on the right side. Note that the outline of the toolbar changes shape and is displayed with a thinner line when it is in position to be docked. Releasing the pick button completes the docking operation. Double-click on the title bar of a floating toolbar to quickly dock it in the top area of the AutoCAD program window.

If you need to place a floating toolbar near the edge of the AutoCAD window but you do not want it to dock, simply hold the [Ctrl] key down while you reposition the toolbar. A reminder of this option appears on the status line as you move a toolbar, as shown in Figure 20-2.

Figure 20-1.
A—Repositioning a floating toolbar. B—Resizing a floating toolbar horizontally.
C—Resizing a toolbar vertically.

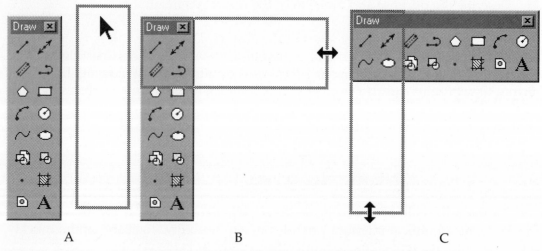

A B C

AutoCAD and its Applications—Advanced

Figure 20-2.
Toolbars can be docked on the edge of the AutoCAD window. Press the [Ctrl] key while moving the toolbar to prevent docking.

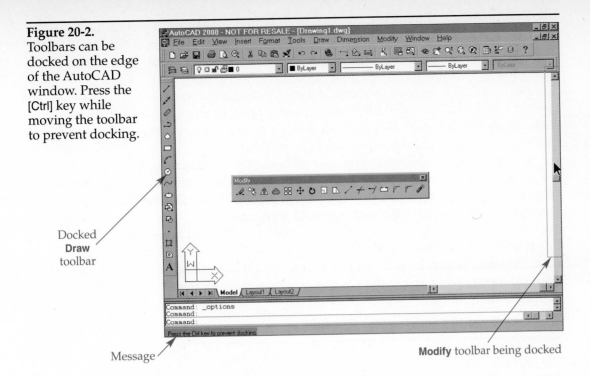

Docked **Draw** toolbar

Message

Modify toolbar being docked

NOTE Toolbar modifications are unaffected by the **UNDO** command. For example, if you hide all your toolbars, you cannot use **UNDO** to make them visible again.

Controlling Toolbar Visibility

You can adjust the AutoCAD screen so that only the toolbars you need are visible. This helps conserve drawing window space. If too many toolbars are visible at one time, the drawing window can become small and crowded. When your drawing area is small, too much of your time is spent making display changes so you can clearly see parts of the drawing. Figure 20-3 shows an example of a small and crowded drawing window.

Figure 20-3.
Too many toolbars visible at once can cut down on the useful drawing area.

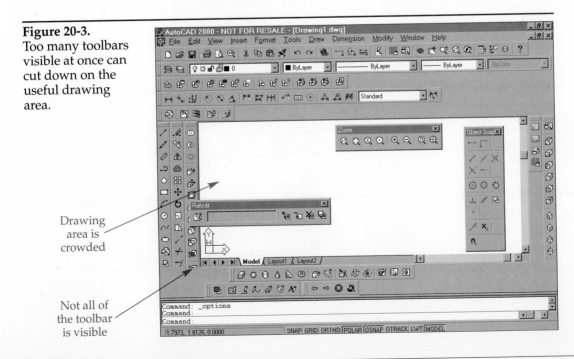

Drawing area is crowded

Not all of the toolbar is visible

Also, look closely at the toolbars docked on the left side of the window. They are partially hidden from view. The length of some of the toolbars is longer than the available space. Remember this when arranging your toolbars. You should have access to all of the buttons.

AutoCAD 2000 provides a shortcut menu for fast and convenient control of toolbar visibility. To access the toolbars shortcut menu, point at any toolbar button and right-click. As shown in Figure 20-4, a check mark is displayed next to the currently visible toolbars. Pick any menu name to toggle its visibility.

Toolbars can also be turned on and off using the **Toolbars** dialog box. Access this dialog box by picking **Customize...** from the toolbars shortcut menu, selecting **Toolbars...** from the **View** pull-down menu, or typing TO or TOOLBAR at the Command: prompt. The **Toolbars** dialog box is shown in Figure 20-5. There are several options available in this dialog box for controlling the visibility and appearance of toolbars.

If there are toolbars defined in more than one menu, select the appropriate menu from the **Menu Group** drop-down list. If you loaded partial menus in addition to your primary menu, you must make the menu group name current to access the toolbars defined in that menu.

TOOLBAR
TO

View
➡ Toolbars...

Figure 20-4.
The toolbars shortcut menu is accessed by right-clicking on any toolbar button.

Check marks identify the currently visible toolbars

Pick to access the **Toolbars** dialog box

For 2000i Users...

The **Toolbars** dialog box in AutoCAD 2000 is replaced by the **Toolbars** tab of the **Customize** dialog box in AutoCAD 2000i. Refer to *Customizing Toolbars* on page 641 for more information.

Figure 20-5.
The **Toolbars** dialog box is used to turn toolbars on and off, create new toolbars, and customize existing toolbars.

An "X" means the toolbar is visible

Toolbars in this menu are listed

Display options

Create a new toolbar

Delete highlighted toolbar

Add or delete toolbar buttons

Pick to change properties

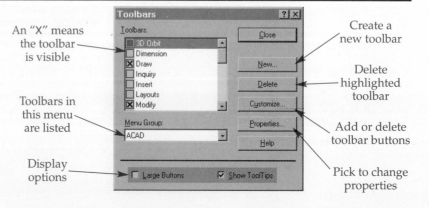

The **Toolbars:** list shows all the toolbars defined in the selected menu group. To make a toolbar visible, place a check in the check box next to the toolbar name by picking the box. To hide a toolbar, remove the check. The results are immediate. When you are finished, pick the **Close** button.

Another way to hide a floating toolbar is to pick its menu control button, Figure 20-6. If you wish to hide a docked toolbar, you can first move it away from the edge to make it a floating toolbar. Then, pick the menu control button. However, if you hide a docked toolbar in this manner, it will appear in the floating position when you make it visible again. When the **Toolbars** dialog box is used to hide a docked toolbar, it will appear in its docked position when reactivated.

The **Toolbars** dialog box displays two check boxes at the bottom. They are toggles for the button features they represent:

- **Large Buttons.** Checking this box increases the size of your toolbar buttons from 16×15 to 24×22 pixels. At very high screen resolutions, such as 1280×1024, the smaller 16×15 buttons can be difficult to see. Setting the buttons to the larger size is easier on the eyes. At lower screen resolutions, the large buttons take up too much of the available space in the AutoCAD window.
- **Show ToolTips.** This allows you to turn off the tooltip feature, which displays the name of the button you are pointing to. Unless you are very familiar with the button interface, it is usually best to leave tooltips on.

For 2000i Users...

In addition to the **Large Buttons** and **Show ToolTip** options, the **Toolbar** tab of the **Customize** dialog box also includes a **Show shortcut keys in ToolTip** option.

Figure 20-6.
Pick the menu control button and the toolbar is hidden.

Menu control button

NOTE

When the **Toolbars** dialog box is displayed, it may cover toolbars located near the center of the screen. Both toolbars and the **Toolbars** dialog box can be freely moved whenever necessary to view the desired features.

Working with Toolbars at the Command Line

Use the **–TOOLBAR** command to work with toolbars at the command line. When using this method, you are prompted for the toolbar name. The complete toolbar name consists of the menu group and toolbar name, separated by a period. For example, the toolbar name for the **Draw** toolbar defined in the acad.mnu menu is ACAD.DRAW. After specifying the toolbar name (or selecting ALL for all toolbars), you can select an option from the following prompt:

```
Command: –TOOLBAR↵
Enter toolbar name or [ALL]: ACAD.DRAW↵
Enter an option [Show/Hide/Left/Right/Top/Bottom/Float] <Show>:
```

The options are used to hide, show, or specify a location for the toolbar. The following options are available:

- **Show.** This option makes the toolbar visible. Selecting this option is identical to activating the check box next to the toolbar name in the **Toolbars** dialog box.
- **Hide.** This option causes the toolbar to disappear. Selecting this option is identical to disabling the check box next to the toolbar name in the **Toolbars** dialog box.

- **Left.** Places the toolbar in a docked position at the left side of the window.
- **Right.** Places the toolbar in a docked position at the right side of the window.
- **Top.** Places the toolbar in a docked position at the top of the window.
- **Bottom.** Places the specified toolbar in a docked position at the bottom of the window.
- **Float.** Places the toolbar as a floating toolbar.

The **Left**, **Right**, **Top**, **Bottom**, and **Float** options show a toolbar (if it is not already visible) and places it in the specified position in the AutoCAD window. To dock the **Zoom** toolbar on the left side of the AutoCAD window, use the following command sequence:

Command: **–TOOLBAR.**↵
Enter toolbar name or [ALL]: **ACAD.ZOOM.**↵
Enter an option [Show/Hide/Left/Right/Top/Bottom/Float] <Show>: **LEFT.**↵
Enter new position (horizontal,vertical) <0,0>: ↵

The last option of the **–TOOLBAR** command is the **Float** option. This places the toolbar in a floating position specified in pixels at the Position <0,0>: prompt. The anchor point of a floating toolbar is the upper-left corner. If you place the toolbar at 400,300, the upper-left corner of the toolbar is at this coordinate location. You are then asked to establish the shape of the new toolbar by specifying the number of rows of buttons for the toolbar. For example, this sequence places the **Solids** toolbar as shown in Figure 20-7:

Command: **–TOOLBAR.**↵
Enter toolbar name or [ALL]: **ACAD.SOLIDS.**↵
Enter an option [Show/Hide/Left/Right/Top/Bottom/Float] <Show>: **F.**↵
Enter new position (screen coordinates) <0,0>: **400,300.**↵
Enter number of rows for toolbar <1>: **2.**↵

Figure 20-7.
Locating a floating toolbar at a 400,300 position using the **–TOOLBAR** command.

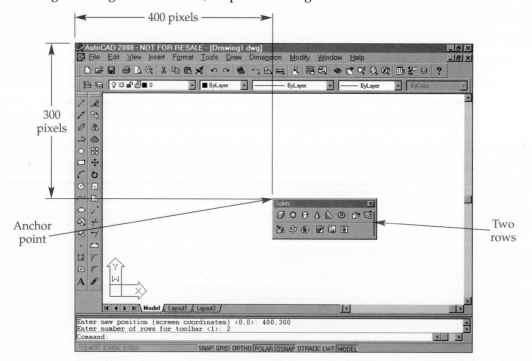

NOTE

When using the **Float** option to relocate a toolbar that is currently docked, the toolbar is located at the upper-left corner of the screen (0,0) regardless of the actual coordinates specified. A toolbar that is currently floating is correctly relocated to the specified screen coordinates.

While using the **–TOOLBAR** command is very accurate for placement, it is also time-consuming. Using the cursor is much quicker, though not as accurate. When using floating toolbars, it is also possible to overlap the toolbars to save screen space. To bring a toolbar to the front, simply pick on it. Be sure to leave part of each toolbar showing.

Another capability of the **–TOOLBAR** command is to show or hide all toolbars at once. When prompted for the toolbar name, enter ALL. The only two options that appear are **Show** and **Hide**. If you use the **Hide** option, no toolbars are displayed. Then, you can use the **Toolbars** dialog box to select the toolbars you need.

NOTE

The **–TOOLBAR** command is most useful when creating menu macros, script files, or AutoLISP functions designed to perform automated toolbar setups.

EXERCISE 20-1

❑ Open AutoCAD and maximize it so that it occupies the entire screen.
❑ Use the appropriate method to display the **Draw, Modify,** and **Dimension** toolbars.
❑ Position the three toolbars in a floating configuration. Move them to several different floating positions around the screen.
❑ Move the **Draw** and **Modify** toolbars to a docked position at the top of the screen.
❑ Move the **Dimension** toolbar to a docked position at the right side of the screen.
❑ Position all three toolbars in a docked position at the right side of the screen.
❑ Position each of the toolbars in two additional docked positions on the screen.
❑ Return the screen to the original configuration.

CUSTOMIZING TOOLBARS

In addition to positioning and sizing toolbars, you can also customize the toolbar interface. You can add new buttons or place existing buttons in new locations for quick access. Infrequently used buttons can be deleted or moved to an "out-of-the-way" location. Entirely new toolbars can be created and filled with redefined buttons, or custom button definitions can be created. Toolbars are customized using the **Toolbars** dialog box.

Adding, Deleting, Moving, and Copying Buttons

The **Toolbars** dialog box allows you to manipulate toolbars and toolbar buttons. One common modification to the toolbars is to place an existing button in a new location. For example, if your current project requires you to modify the properties of existing hatch patterns, you may wish to have access to the **Edit Hatch** button. One approach would be to make the **Modify II** toolbar visible, but if you do not want an extra toolbar on your screen, you can simply move or copy the **Edit Hatch** button to a currently visible toolbar.

The following sequence adds the **Edit Hatch** button to the **Modify** toolbar. First, access the **Toolbars** dialog box. To begin customizing your toolbar, pick the **Customize...** button. This displays the **Customize Toolbars** dialog box, Figure 20-8A. The **Customize Toolbars** dialog box provides access to all of AutoCAD's predefined toolbar buttons.

The **Categories:** drop-down list contains general command classifications. Some of these correspond to toolbar names. Each category displays a different group of buttons. Use this list to select the **Modify** category, where the **Edit Hatch** button is located. The **Customize Toolbars** dialog box changes, as shown in Figure 20-8B.

Pick a button to display its description in the **Description** area. The buttons displayed in the dialog box can be added to an existing toolbar. Point to the button, then press and hold the pick button. Drag the button to the toolbar and release the pick button. Figure 20-9 shows the **Edit Hatch** button being dragged from the **Customize Toolbars** dialog box to the **Modify** toolbar.

Position the button in the toolbar where you would like it to be located. If you position it between two other buttons, it is placed between them. The existing buttons are adjusted to accommodate the new button.

You can continue to customize toolbars while the **Customize Toolbars** dialog box is open. To remove an existing button from a toolbar, first point to the button. Then, press and hold the pick button on your pointing device. Now drag the toolbar button

Figure 20-8.
The **Customize Toolbars** dialog box.
A—First select the proper category for the command.
B—Pick a displayed button to view its description.

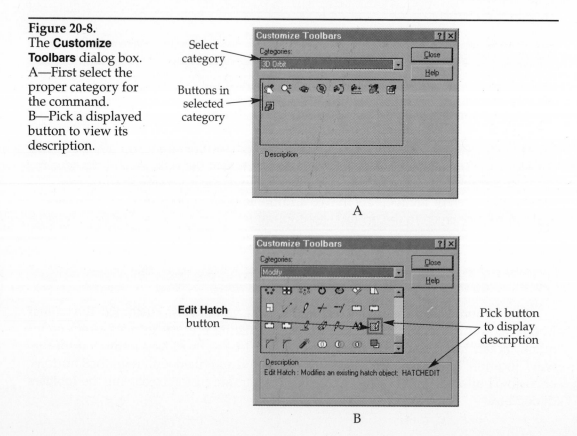

AutoCAD and its Applications—Advanced

out to a clear area of the graphics screen and release the pick button. The toolbar button disappears and is removed from the toolbar.

Moving a button to a new location is accomplished the same way. Simply drag it to the new location. This includes repositioning a button on the same toolbar, or moving it to a new toolbar. By pressing and holding the [Ctrl] key while you move a button, the button is *copied* to the new location rather than being *moved*. A copied button appears in both the new and old locations.

PROFESSIONAL TIP You will notice that many buttons are displayed in the **Customize Toolbars** dialog box. Some of them may be familiar and some may not. Unfortunately, tooltips are not available for the buttons displayed in this dialog. If you are unsure of what a specific button is, pick it and read the description.

Figure 20-9.
Adding the **Edit Hatch** button to the **Modify** toolbar.
A—Dragging the button from the **Customize Toolbars** dialog box.
B—Positioning the button in the toolbar. C—The toolbar with the added button.

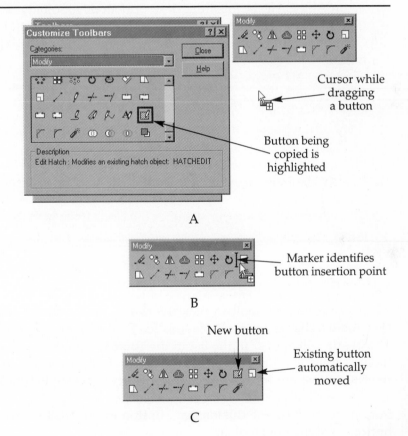

Toolbar Properties

The basic properties of a toolbar include the toolbar name and help string. These properties can be adjusted by picking the **Properties...** button in the **Toolbars** dialog box. This displays the **Toolbar Properties** dialog box for the currently selected toolbar. See Figure 20-10.

The **Toolbar Properties** dialog box lists the name, help string, and alias for the toolbar. The toolbar name appears in the list in the **Toolbars** dialog box and in the title bar of a floating toolbar. The help string appears at the left of the status bar when the cursor is pointing to any area of the toolbar other than a button or the title bar. To

Figure 20-10.
The **Toolbar Properties** dialog box.

Modify entries

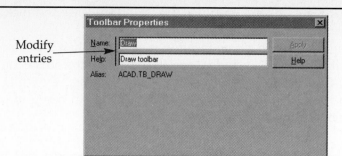

change the name of a toolbar or the associated help string, enter the new text in the appropriate text box. The **Apply** button is grayed-out unless a change has been made. However, changes are not applied until the **Apply** button is picked. To close the dialog box without saving changes, pick the menu control button or press [Esc].

EXERCISE 20-2

❑ Begin AutoCAD. Display the **Draw** and **Modify** toolbars as floating toolbars.
❑ If you have not added the **Edit Hatch** button to the **Modify** toolbar, do so now.
❑ Copy the **Donut** button to the **Draw** toolbar, and place it adjacent to the **Circle** button.
❑ Copy the **3D Polyline** button to the **Draw** toolbar, and place it adjacent to the **Polyline** button.
❑ Move the **Mirror** button to a new position in the **Modify** toolbar.
❑ Remove the **Donut**, **Edit Hatch**, and **3D Polyline** buttons from the **Draw** and **Modify** toolbars.
❑ Modify the title of the **Draw** toolbar to read Draw/Construct.
❑ Modify the help string of the **Draw** toolbar to read Displays the Draw/Construct toolbar.
❑ Change the title and help string of the **Draw** toolbar to the original wording and apply the changes.

Creating New Toolbars

To create a new toolbar, pick the **New...** button in the **Toolbars** dialog box. The **New Toolbar** dialog box is displayed. See Figure 20-11A. Enter a name for the toolbar. This name will appear in the list in the **Toolbars** dialog box and in the title bar of the toolbar when it is floating. Select the menu group in which to store the toolbar. Pick the **OK** button and the new toolbar appears on screen, Figure 20-11B.

The toolbar can now be customized just as any other toolbar. Add predefined buttons by picking the **Customize...** button in the **Toolbars** dialog box and dragging buttons into the new toolbar.

For 2000i Users...

The process used to create new toolbars has been slightly modified for AutoCAD 2000i. Refer to *Creating New Toolbars* on page 643 for details.

Figure 20-11.
A—Creating a toolbar named **Custom Tools** in the **New Toolbar** dialog box. B—The newly created toolbar.

Enter new toolbar name

Select menu group for toolbar

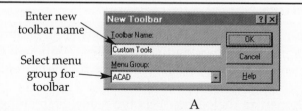

A   B

Creating New Buttons

For 2000i Users...

The process used to create new buttons has been slightly modified for AutoCAD 2000i. Refer to *Creating New Buttons* on page 643 for details.

New buttons can be created and added to toolbars. To create a new button, pick the **Customize...** button from the **Toolbars** dialog box. Using the **Categories:** drop-down list, pick the **Custom** category. This category displays a standard button and a flyout button, Figure 20-12. Notice that both of these buttons are blank. No border is displayed by these buttons unless they are selected.

To begin creating your own custom button, drag a blank button to the new toolbar. Now, point to it and right-click your mouse (or pick using the [Enter] button of a digitizer). The **Button Properties** dialog box is displayed. See Figure 20-13. This dialog box allows you to define a new button.

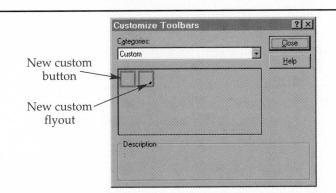

Figure 20-12. The blank buttons available in the **Customize Toolbars** dialog box are shown highlighted here. The first step in creating a customized button is to drag the blank button to a toolbar.

New custom button

New custom flyout

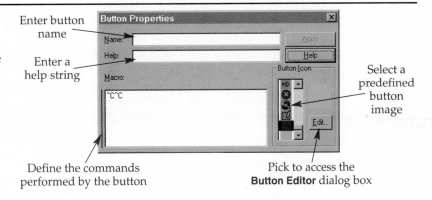

Figure 20-13. Right-click on a blank button in a toolbar to access the **Button Properties** dialog box.

Enter button name

Enter a help string

Define the commands performed by the button

Select a predefined button image

Pick to access the **Button Editor** dialog box

NOTE

When you right-click on a button, the **Toolbars** shortcut menu appears. If you right-click on a button when the **Toolbars** dialog box is currently displayed, the **Button Properties** dialog box for the selected button appears. Therefore, if the **Toolbars** dialog box is not displayed, you need to right-click on a toolbar button, select **Customize...** from the toolbars shortcut menu, and then right-click on the button again to access the **Button Properties** dialog box.

When the **Button Properties** dialog box is accessed for a blank button, the **Name:** and **Help:** text boxes are blank by default. If the button was created in an earlier session but was not defined, the name is temporarily set to No Name. The characters ^C^C appear in the **Macro:** field. These represent two cancel commands. No graphic appears initially. You can fill in all of the fields as desired. For the purpose of this example, a macro will be created that draws an E-size rectangular border (44″ × 34″) using a wide polyline, sets the drawing limits, and finishes with **Zoom Extents**.

First, enter a name in the **Name:** field. All buttons must have a name, or AutoCAD will not accept the button definition. For this example, assign the name **E-Size Setup**. This will appear as the tooltip after you finish defining the button.

The next field is the **Help:** field. This is where you specify the help string that appears on the status line when you point to the button with the cursor. All help strings should provide a clear description of what the associated button actually does. While help strings should be clear, they should also be brief. Set this help string to read Draws an E-size sheet, sets and displays the limits.

Now it is time to define the macro to be performed when the button is picked. Move your cursor to the **Macro:** field. Whenever a command is not required to operate transparently, it is best to begin the macro with two cancel keystrokes (^C^C) to cancel any current command and return to the Command: prompt. Two cancels are required to be sure you begin at the Command: prompt. If you are using a command at the Dim: prompt and issue one cancel, you are returned to the Dim: prompt. Pressing the [Esc] key a second time cancels the Dim: prompt and returns you to the Command: prompt.

NOTE	Some earlier versions of AutoCAD used the [Ctrl]+[C] key combination to issue a cancel. In later releases, this key combination is used to copy objects. In AutoCAD 2000, the [Ctrl]+[C] key combination can also be used to copy text in the AutoCAD's text window. However, when writing a menu macro, the notation of ^C is still used to indicate a cancel.

The macro information must match the requirements of the activated commands perfectly. For example, if the **LINE** command is issued, the subsequent prompt expects a coordinate point to be entered. Any other data is inappropriate and will cause an error in your macro.

It is best to walk through each step in the desired macro manually, writing down each step and the data required by each prompt. The following sequence walks through the creation of the rectangular polyline border with a line width of .015.

```
Command: PLINE↵
Specify start point: 0,0↵
Current line–width is 0.0000
Specify next point or [Arc/Close/Halfwidth/Length/Undo/Width]: W↵
Specify starting width <0.0000>: .015↵
Specify ending width <0.0150>: ↵
Specify next point or [Arc/Close/Halfwidth/Length/Undo/Width]: 44,0↵
Specify next point or [Arc/Close/Halfwidth/Length/Undo/Width]: 44,34↵
Specify next point or [Arc/Close/Halfwidth/Length/Undo/Width]: 0,34↵
Specify next point or [Arc/Close/Halfwidth/Length/Undo/Width]: C↵
Command:
```

Creating the menu macro involves duplicating the above keystrokes, with a couple of differences. Some symbols are used in menu macros to represent keystrokes. For example, the ^C is not entered by pressing the [Ctrl]+[C] button combination. Instead, the [Shift]+[6] key combination is used to access the *caret* symbol, which is used to represent the [Ctrl] key in combination with the subsequent character (a 'C' in this case).

Another keystroke represented by a symbol is the [Enter] key. An [Enter] is shown as a semicolon (;). A space can also be used to designate [Enter]. However, the semicolon is more commonly used because it is very easy to count to make sure that the correct number are supplied. Spaces are not so easy to count.

Keeping these guidelines in mind, the following entry draws the required polyline:

^C^CPLINE;0,0;W;.015;;44,0;44,34;0,34;C;

Compare this with the previous command line entry example to identify each part of the menu macro. The next step is to set the limits and zoom to display the entire border. To do this at the command line would require the following entries:

> Command: **LIMITS**↵
> Reset Model space limits:
> Specify lower left corner or [ON/OFF] <0.0000,0.0000>: **0,0**↵
> Specify upper right corner <12.0000,9.0000>: **44,34**↵
> Command: **ZOOM**↵
> Specify corner of window, enter a scale factor (nX or nXP), or
> [All/Center/Dynamic/Extents/Previous/Scale/Window] <real time>: **E**↵
> Command:

Continue to develop this macro by entering the following sequence immediately after the previous one (shown in italics):

^C^CPLINE;0,0;W;.015;;44,0;44,34;0,34;C;LIMITS;0,0;44,34;ZOOM;E

Note that an automatic carriage return is issued at the end of the macro, so it is not necessary to enter a semicolon at the end. The **Button Properties** dialog box now appears as shown in Figure 20-14.

Next, you should create a graphic image for the button. A button can be selected from the graphic list in the **Button Icon** area of the **Button Properties** dialog box. However, having duplicate images can be a source of confusion. It is best to either modify an existing image or create a brand new image using the **Button Editor**.

Figure 20-14.
The properties for the **E-Size Setup** button.

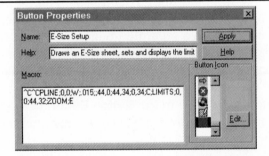

Creating Button Images

It is important to consider the needs of the persons who will be using your custom menu system when you design buttons. All the standard buttons in AutoCAD show a graphic that implies something about the commands the button executes. Buttons you create will be most effective if they use this principle as well.

Simple abstract designs may be recognizable to you because you created them and you know what they do. When someone else uses this menu system, they may not recognize the purpose of the button.

Rather than edit an existing button in this example, an entirely new button will be created. Highlight one of the blank button icons in the **Button Icon** list of the **Button Properties** dialog box. Next, pick the **Edit...** button. The **Button Editor** dialog box is displayed, Figure 20-15.

The **Button Editor** dialog box has basic pixel painting tools and several features to simplify the editing process. The four tools are shown as buttons at the top of the dialog box. The pencil paints individual pixels in the current color. The line tool

For 2000i Users...

When creating a button image for a new button in AutoCAD 2000i, select the blank button from the **Button Properties** tab of the **Customize** dialog box and then pick the **Edit...** button to access the **Button Editor** dialog box.

Figure 20-15.
The **Button Editor**
dialog box.

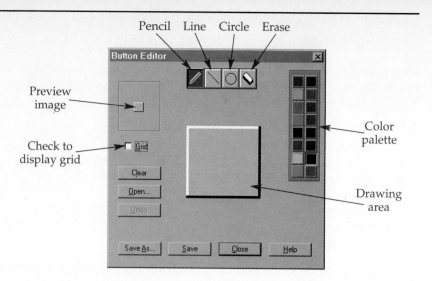

allows you to draw a line between two points. The circle tool allows you to draw center/radius style ellipses and circles. The erase tool clears the color from individual pixels. The current color is selected from the color palette on the right side of the dialog box. Anything you draw appears in the selected color.

Drawing a graphic is usually much easier with the grid turned on. The grid provides outlines for each pixel in the graphic. Each square is representative of one pixel. Picking the **Grid** check box toggles the state of the grid.

The area just above the **Grid** toggle is the button preview area. The preview displays the appearance of the button in its actual size while you draw the image.

When the toolbar buttons are set in their default size, the button editor provides a drawing area 15 pixels high by 16 pixels wide. If **Large Buttons** is turned on in the **Toolbars** dialog box, then this will be a 24×22 pixel image.

Buttons require two separate images, one at 16×15 and one at 24×22. If you only create a 16×15 pixel image, your custom button will be blank when you switch to large buttons because there is no image defined at that size. You must create a second 24×22 pixel image for the large button.

Other tools available in the **Button Editor** include the following:

- **Clear.** If you want to erase everything and start over, pick the **Clear** button to clear the drawing area.
- **Open.** Use this button to open existing bitmap (BMP) files.
- **Undo.** You can undo the last operation by picking this button. An operation that has been undone cannot be redone. Only the last operation can be undone.
- **Save As.** Saves a file using the **Save As** dialog box. Use this when you have opened a file and want to save it as well as keep the original file.
- **Save.** Saves the current bitmap file. If the current image has not yet been saved, then the **Save As** dialog is displayed.
- **Close.** Ends the **Button Editor** session. A message is displayed if you have unsaved changes.
- **Help.** Provides context-sensitive help.

Figure 20-16A shows a 16×15 pixel image created for the **E-Size Setup** button with the **Grid** option activated. After saving your button image, pick the **Close** button to return to the **Button Properties** dialog box. Your newly created image appears above the **Edit...** button, as shown in Figure 20-16B. Pick the **Apply** button to apply the changes. Your button displays the new image, Figure 20-16C.

Figure 20-16.
Creating a new button image.
A—A 16×15 pixel image for the **E-Size Setup** button.
B—The **Button Properties** dialog box displays the new image.
C—The **E-Size Setup** button after applying the new image.

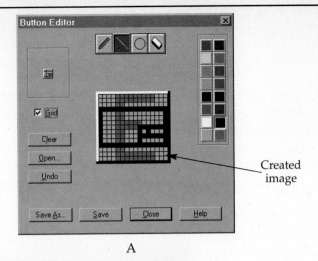

Created image

A

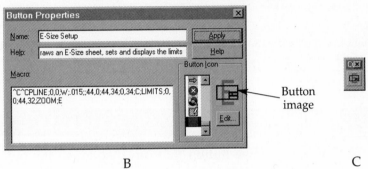

Button image

B

C

PROFESSIONAL TIP

The images defined for your custom buttons must be in a location where AutoCAD will find them. You could simply drop all your bitmap images into one of AutoCAD's support directories, but this may not be the best choice. A better option might be to create a directory just for your bitmap images and add this directory to the support directories specified in the **Files** tab of the **Options** dialog box.

Existing bitmap images can be used for button images. The **Open...** button in the **Button Editor** dialog box allows you to open any BMP file up to 380×380 pixels in size. The image is automatically resized to fit the current button size.

When you have completed your button and applied the changes, pick the menu control button in the upper-right of the **Button Properties** dialog box to close it. Pick the **Close** button in the **Customize Toolbars** dialog box, then pick **Close** in the **Toolbars** dialog box.

The menu file is then recompiled, adding your new changes. More discussion of menu files is found at the end of this chapter and in Chapter 21.

❑ Begin AutoCAD. Access the **Toolbars** dialog box.
❑ If you have not created the **Custom Tools** toolbar and the **E-Size Setup** button as shown in the previous discussion, do so now.
❑ Copy the **Paper Space** button from the **Standard** category into the **Custom Tools** toolbar, and place it to the left of the **E-Size Setup** button.
❑ Create a new button that does the following:
  ❑ Executes the **MVIEW** command.
  ❑ Selects the **4** option of **MVIEW** to construct four viewports.
  ❑ Uses the **Fit** option to fit the four viewports in the current display.
❑ Test these commands at the keyboard before entering the code as a macro.
❑ Name the button **4 PS Viewports**, and enter the following as the help string: Fits four paper space viewports into the current drawing.
❑ Create a button icon of your own design.
❑ Place the button next to the **E-Size Setup** button in the **Custom Tools** toolbar.
❑ Close each dialog box to save the new macro and toolbar configuration.
❑ The arrangement of the three icons allows you to enter paper space, create an E-size layout, then divide it into four paper space viewports.

WORKING WITH FLYOUTS

For 2000i Users...

The process used to create a flyout has been slightly modified for AutoCAD 2000i. Refer to *Creating Flyouts* on page 644 for details.

A flyout is a single button that can display all the buttons from an associated toolbar. A pick on a flyout button activates the command assigned to the currently visible toolbar button. When you point to a flyout and hold the pick button, the buttons from the associated toolbar are displayed. Move the cursor to the desired button and release the pick button. This activates the associated command or macro, and leaves the selected button's image displayed as the image for the flyout.

To create a new flyout button, you should create the associated toolbar first. Then, associate the toolbar with the flyout using the **Flyout Properties** dialog box.

Creating a toolbar with frequently used buttons can help you to save time and increase productivity. However, each displayed toolbar takes up some of the available screen area. If too many toolbars are displayed at once, this can become a problem, especially with low-resolution screens.

You can conserve on-screen space using flyouts. Follow through this discussion to create a customized toolbar flyout for working with 3D projects.

First, access the **Toolbars** dialog box. Then, select the **New...** button and name the new toolbar **3D Tools**. The toolbar appears on the screen, ready to be customized. Pick the **Customize...** button, then pick the **Categories** drop-down list in the **Customize Toolbar** dialog box. Use the predefined buttons found in the **Surfaces**, **Render**, and **View** categories, and set up your new toolbar as shown in Figure 20-17.

After you have set up your **3D Tools** toolbar, use the drop-down list to access the **Custom** category. Drag-and-drop a blank flyout button to your **Modify** toolbar. Right-click on this button to activate the **Flyout Properties** dialog box. Complete the fields for the dialog box as shown in Figure 20-18, and highlight the ACAD.3D Tools line in the **Associated Toolbar:** field.

Picking the **Apply** button activates the changes, and the upper-left button in the **3D Tools** toolbar becomes the current image in the flyout on the **Modify** toolbar. Close the **Flyout Properties** dialog box by picking the menu control button. Pick the **Close** button in the **Customize Toolbars** dialog box. Next, pick the **Close** button in the **Toolbars** dialog box and the menu is recompiled. Now when you pick the flyout, your custom **3D Tools** toolbar is displayed, as shown in Figure 20-19.

Figure 20-17.
The customized **3D Tools** toolbar is created using a combination of buttons in existing toolbars.

Figure 20-18.
The **Flyout Properties** dialog box for the **3D Tools** flyout button.

Flyout name

Toolbar contained in flyout

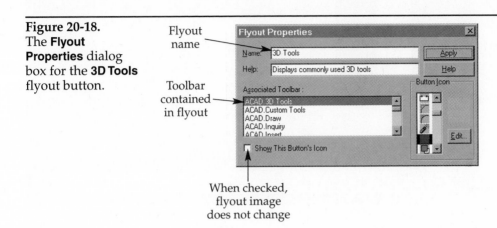

When checked, flyout image does not change

When you point at the flyout button, the name and help string you supplied in the **Flyout Properties** dialog box are not used. This is because the flyout button is defined as having no icon (or image) of its own. It assumes the identity of the most recently used button in its associated toolbar.

By picking the check box for **Show This Button's Icon** in the **Flyout Properties** dialog box, you can define a flyout that has its own identity and properties. If this box is checked, you need to define an icon image using the **Button Editor**.

After this is done, the assigned properties are displayed when the flyout is pointed to, as shown in Figure 20-20. The tooltip now displays the button's name, and the help string also displays the information associated with this flyout.

While both methods of creating a flyout are acceptable, it is most effective to allow the flyout to be "transparent"—or assume the identity of the most recently picked button. Commands are often used several times consecutively in a standard editing session. For example, rarely will you need to draw only a single line. Normally, several lines must be drawn in sequence. This is generally true of many different AutoCAD commands. Therefore, having the last button picked as the default makes it more convenient to select it again. This can increase your efficiency by requiring fewer picks for the same amount of work.

Figure 20-19.
The **3D Tools** flyout button placed on the **Modify** toolbar.

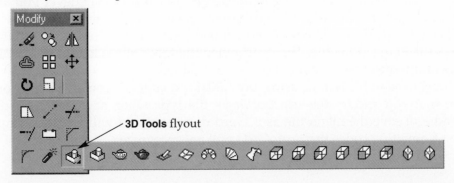

3D Tools flyout

Figure 20-20.
The new flyout
displays its own
tooltip and help
string.

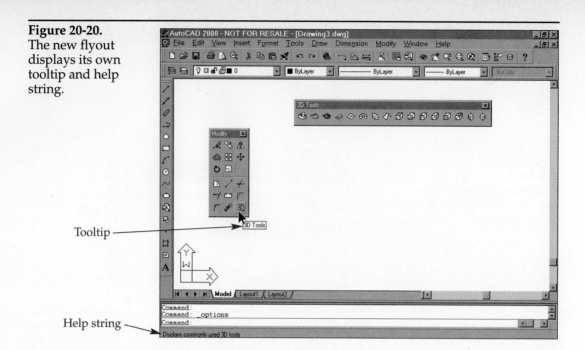

Tooltip

Help string

TOOLBARS AND MENU FILES

As toolbars are adjusted and customized, the changes are stored in files. AutoCAD maintains a record of these changes in one of several files associated with the menu system. Each of these files has the same file name, but different file extensions. The standard menu provided with the AutoCAD software is named acad, and the files associated with this menu are located in the Acad2000\Support folder.

It is important to understand the handling of menu files, otherwise it is very easy for your toolbar customization work to simply disappear. The menu files associated with the acad menu are as follows:

- **ACAD.MNU.** This is the fully documented *template* file. This provides the initial menu setup. If this menu is edited and then loaded using the **MENU** command, it creates a new menu *source* file.
- **ACAD.MNS.** This is the menu *source* file. Most documentation is stripped from the file to reduce its size. All code changes to the toolbar menu are recorded into this file. This is the file that is used in the creation of a *compiled* menu file.
- **ACAD.MNC.** This is a *compiled* menu file. AutoCAD creates this optimized file to handle the menus in your drawing sessions.
- **ACAD.MNR.** This is the menu *resource* file. It stores all bitmap images associated with the menu for quick access.

As noted, the MNS file is the location for code changes to the toolbars. However, when an MNU file is loaded, it overwrites the current MNS file—losing all your changes to the toolbars. A warning to this effect is displayed whenever you attempt to load an MNU file. In order to make your changes permanent, you should open both files with an ASCII text editor and cut and paste the new or changed data from the MNS file to the MNU file. That way, when the MNU file is loaded, it keeps these changes and writes them again to the new MNS file.

Editing a menu file is done using any ASCII text editor. If you are using WordPad, be sure that you specify the Text Document file type when saving. If you do not, WordPad will save the menu file as a Word document and will incorporate printer and text formatting codes that AutoCAD will not recognize.

Once you have opened the file, search the text for ***TOOLBARS—this begins the toolbar data section. You can then find the listings in each file for changed toolbars and update the MNU file using the code in the MNS file. New toolbars can be copied and pasted into the MNU file. More information on editing menu files is found in Chapter 21.

PROFESSIONAL TIP

There are other approaches to making your menu changes permanent. You can rename or delete the MNU file, since it is not necessary to AutoCAD. You can also copy the MNS file directly over the MNU file.

These approaches are used by AutoCAD professionals, but there is a drawback for those who are just learning to work with menus. The MNU file is well-documented and can be a valuable tool for learning your way around the menu file. It may be best to keep this file on hand while you are learning to work with menus.

If you wish to keep the MNU file available, you should make a copy of the MNS file each time you modify the toolbar menus. Keep this file in an alternate directory as a backup in case you accidentally overwrite the original MNS file.

Chapter Test

Answer the following questions on a separate sheet of paper.

1. What four toolbars are shown by default when AutoCAD is loaded?
2. Describe the flexibility inherent in a floating toolbar.
3. How is resizing toolbars different than resizing other windows?
4. How do you prevent a floating toolbar from being docked when repositioning it?
5. Which dialog box provides the means to show or hide toolbars?
6. List three ways to access the dialog box described in Question 5.
7. Explain how to display a toolbar using the dialog box described in Question 5.
8. In which dialog box can you find all predefined buttons divided by category?
9. How do you copy an existing button from a toolbar category to another toolbar?
10. How do you remove an existing button from a toolbar?
11. How can you copy an existing button to a new location?
12. How do you access the **New Toolbar** dialog box in order to create a new toolbar?
13. Once the new empty toolbar is displayed on the screen, how do you place the first blank button inside it?
14. When the new toolbar is displayed on the screen with a blank button inside it, how do you access the **Button Properties** dialog box in order to create a custom macro?
15. How do you create a tooltip for a new button?
16. How do you create a help string for a new button?
17. How should you develop and test a new macro before creating it in a new button?
18. Name two ways to specify an [Enter] in a macro, and indicate which of the two is the safest.
19. What type of file is a button graphic saved as?
20. Name the four tools that are provided in the **Button Editor** dialog box.
21. What is the default size (in pixels) of the button editor drawing area?

22. If **Large Buttons** is turned on in the **Toolbars** dialog box, what is the size (in pixels) of the button editor drawing area?
23. How do you insert a flyout button into a toolbar?
24. How do you access the **Flyout Properties** dialog box in order to supply a tooltip and help string to a new flyout button?
25. Why is it more effective to allow a flyout button to assume the identity of the most recently picked button?
26. What is the name and extension of the AutoCAD menu file in which all code changes to the toolbar are recorded?
27. Which AutoCAD menu file is fully documented and is used to create a new menu source file?

Drawing Problems

Before customizing or creating any menus, check with your instructor or supervisor for specific instructions or guidelines.

1. Create a new toolbar using the following information:
   A. Name the toolbar **Draw/Modify**.
   B. Copy at least three, but no more than six, commonly used drawing buttons into the new toolbar.
   C. Copy at least three, but no more than six, commonly used editing buttons into the new toolbar.
   D. Use only existing buttons, do not create new ones.
   E. Remove the default **Draw** and **Modify** toolbars from the display.
   F. Dock the new **Draw/Modify** toolbar to the upper-left side of the screen.

2. Create a new toolbar using the following information:
   A. Name the toolbar **My 3D Tools**.
   B. Copy the following existing buttons from the **Surfaces** toolbar into the new toolbar:

Dish	**Box**	**Wedge**
Torus	**Pyramid**	**Cone**
Sphere	**Dome**	

   C. Copy the following existing buttons from the **View** toolbar into the new toolbar:

Top View	**Bottom View**	**Left View**
Right View	**Front View**	**Back View**

   D. Copy the following existing buttons from the **UCS** toolbar into the new toolbar:

Display UCS Dialog	**Object UCS**	**World UCS**
Origin UCS	**3 Point UCS**	**UCS Previous**

   E. Use only existing buttons, do not create new ones.
   F. Dock the toolbar in a location of your choice.

AutoCAD and its Applications—Advanced

3. Create a new toolbar using the following information:
   A. Name the toolbar **Paper Space Viewports**.
   B. The toolbar should contain eight buttons that use the **MVIEW** command to create paper space viewports as follows:
      - 1 viewport—allow user to pick location
      - 2 viewports—(horizontal)—allow user to pick location
      - 3 viewports—allow user to pick orientation and location
      - 4 viewports—allow user to pick location
      - 1 viewport—fit
      - 2 viewports—vertical
      - 3 viewports—right
      - 4 viewports—fit
   C. The toolbar should contain two additional buttons that do the following:
      - Switch to floating model space
      - Switch to paper space from floating model space
   D. Construct new button icon graphics for the ten buttons. Save the images in a new directory that has been specified in the AutoCAD support environment.
   E. Dock the toolbar on the right side of the screen.

4. Create a new toolbar that contains eight new buttons for the insertion of a paper space border and title block drawings.
   A. The six buttons should do the following:
      - Insert the ANSI A title block drawing
      - Insert the ANSI B title block drawing
      - Insert the ANSI C title block drawing
      - Insert the ANSI D title block drawing
      - Insert the ANSI E title block drawing
      - Insert the Architectural Title Block drawing
   B. Construct your own button icon images for each of the six new buttons. Save the images in a new directory that has been specified in the AutoCAD support environment.
   C. Dock the toolbar on the left side of the screen.

5. Customize the **Open** button on the **Standard** toolbar to display a flyout menu of the six title blocks you created in Problem 4. Use the following information for this problem:
   A. Use the **OPEN** command for each of the buttons.
   B. The **OPEN** command should always be the default button of the flyout menu and should not be replaced by the most recently used button.
   C. Construct your own button icon images for each of the eight new buttons, or use the same images created in Problem 4. Save the images in a new directory that has been specified in the AutoCAD support environment.

Solid modeling can be used to produce detailed assembly drawings.
(Courtesy of George Argiris, Palomar College)

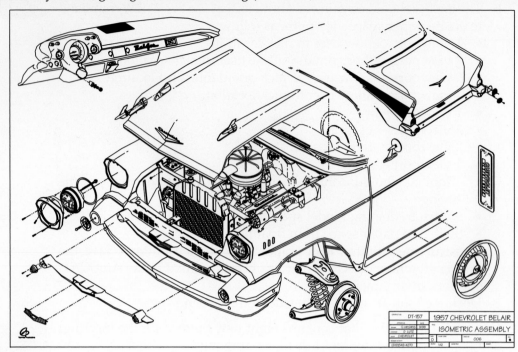

CHAPTER 21

Customizing Screen and Button Menus

Learning Objectives

After completing this chapter, you will be able to:
- Describe the structure of button and screen menus.
- Create new button menus.
- Customize existing screen menus and create new ones.

In Chapter 19, you learned how to customize the AutoCAD working environment to suit your preferences. AutoCAD menus can also be customized to suit specific needs. Users can add special commands to the standard menus or create their own menu system from scratch. As with customized toolbars and toolbar buttons, existing commands can be used in a macro. A *macro* is a function that combines the capabilities of multiple commands and options.

All aspects of the menu system can be changed. This includes the cursor button functions, standard screen menus, pull-down menus, and image file menus. Study this chapter carefully to create your own menus.

AUTOCAD'S MENU STRUCTURE

Before constructing your own menus, look at AutoCAD's standard menu structure to get a feel for the layout. This will give you a better understanding of the tools and techniques you can use to build custom menus. The basic components of a menu are the main sections, submenus, item titles, and command codes.

For Chapters 21–24, it is assumed you are familiar with a programmer's text editor or word processor program. You must be familiar with the commands or keys in your text editor that allow you to scroll or page through a file.

AutoCAD's Menu Files

Several files are used to produce AutoCAD's menu system. As noted in Chapter 20, the file extensions may vary, but the file names are the same. AutoCAD comes with one primary menu file. This file is named acad. Figure 21-1 shows the AutoCAD screen with this menu loaded.

The acad menu files are discussed in this chapter. The primary files are acad.mnu, acad.mns, acad.mnl, acad.mnc, and acad.mnr. The acad.mnl is a menu LISP file that holds the AutoLISP program code. This defines any AutoLISP functions used in the menu. The acad.mnc and acad.mnr files are automatically created and updated by AutoCAD whenever an edited acad.mnu or acad.mns is loaded and compiled. More information on menu files is provided later in this chapter.

You can directly edit both the MNU and MNS files. As mentioned in Chapter 20, the MNU file is more completely documented and is, therefore, a bit easier to navigate through and understand. All work in this chapter requires the MNU file to be edited.

Loading an edited MNU file overwrites the existing MNS file of the same name. Since your interactive toolbar modifications are written to the MNS file, they would be overwritten and lost.

Figure 21-1.
The AutoCAD screen with the acad menu loaded.

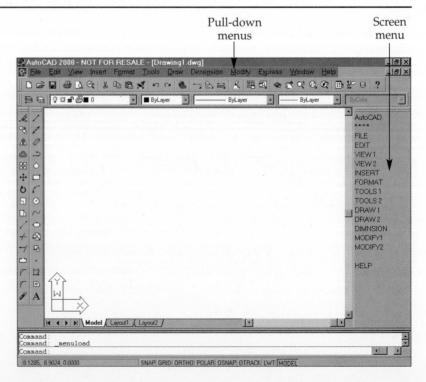

Rather than edit the current menu structure, a copy of the MNU file should be created. This way, any changes you make to the menu will not affect your standard menu. Additionally, since the menu you will be editing will have a different name, previous toolbar changes will not be lost as you work in this chapter.

To give you a clear idea of how the MNU and MNS files differ, look at the excerpts of menu code in Figure 21-2. Note that the acad.mnu file has documentation that explains the purpose of the code.

Figure 21-2.
The acad.mnu file contains helpful documentation not found in the acad.mns file.

ACAD.MNU	ACAD.MNS

`//`
`//   Default AutoCAD NAMESPACE declaration:`
`//`
`***MENUGROUP=ACAD`
 	
`//`
`//   Begin AutoCAD Digitizer Button Menus`
`//`
`***BUTTONS1`
`//   Simple + button`
`//   if a grip is hot bring up the Grips Cursor Menu`
`     (POP 500), else send a carriage return`
`//   If the SHORTCUTMENU sysvar is not 0 the`
`     first item (for button 1) is NOT USED.`
`$M=$(if,$(eq,$(substr,$(getvar,cmdnames),1,5),`
`     GRIP_),$P0=ACAD.GRIPS $P0=*);`
`$P0=SNAP $p0=*`
`^C^C`
`^B`
`^O`
`^G`
`^D`
`^E`
`^T`
	`//`
	`//   AutoCAD menu file - C:\Program Files\`
	`     ACAD2000\support\acad.mnc`
	`//`
	
	`***MENUGROUP=ACAD`
	
	`***BUTTONS1`
	`$M=$(if,$(eq,$(substr,$(getvar,cmdnames),1,5),`
	`     GRIP_),$P0=ACAD.GRIPS $P0=*);`
	`$P0=SNAP $p0=*`
	`^C^C`
	`^B`
	`^O`
	`^G`
	`^D`
	`^E`
	`^T`

PROFESSIONAL TIP

Regardless of your level of experience in working with menu files, it is best to maintain appropriate backup copies of prior revisions. This way, you always have something to refer back to if you encounter problems or data loss.

One approach is to create backup copies of the menu in a separate directory. Another approach is to make a copy of the current menu with a different name for your customization work. For example, make a copy of the acad.mns file named work.mns and do your customization in the new file to protect the original menu. Also, this would give you something to refer back to if you have difficulties getting the new menu to function.

Menu Section Labels

Open the acad.mnu file found in the Acad2000\Support folder using your text editing program. Use your keyboard cursor keys and the [Page Up]/[Page Down] keys to page through the file.

As you look through the menu file, notice the menu section headings. Major menu headings are identified by three asterisks (***) in front of the name. Submenus are listed with two asterisks (**) in front of the name. The following are the major menu headings:

For 2000i Users...

The acad.mnu file for AutoCAD 2000i includes a POP512 section.

```
***MENUGROUP
***BUTTONS1
***BUTTONS2
***BUTTONS3
***BUTTONS4
***AUX1
***AUX2
***AUX3
***AUX4
***POP0 through POP11
***POP500 through POP511
***TOOLBARS
***IMAGE
***SCREEN
***TABLET1
***TABLET2
***TABLET3
***TABLET4
***HELPSTRINGS
***ACCELERATORS
```

In this chapter, you will be working with button and screen menus. Pull-down menus and image tiles are discussed in Chapter 22, and tablet menus are discussed in Chapter 23. The AUX menu headings are used for system pointing devices.

Menu Layout

Before beginning any editing of the acad.mnu file, take a few minutes to peruse it. Load the acad.mnu file into your text editor and locate the line containing ***BUTTONS1. The following portion of the menu should be displayed:

```
***BUTTONS1
// Simple + button
// if a grip is hot bring up the Grips Cursor Menu (POP 500), else send a carriage
    return
// If the SHORTCUTMENU sysvar is not 0 the first item (for button 1) is NOT USED.
$M=$(if,$(eq,$(substr,$(getvar,cmdnames),1,5),GRIP_),$P0=ACAD.GRIPS $P0=*);
$P0=SNAP $p0=*
^C^C
^B
^O
^G
^D
^E
^T

***BUTTONS2
// Shift + button
$P0=SNAP $p0=*

***BUTTONS3
// Control + button

***BUTTONS4
// Control + shift + button
```

This is the first part of the acad.mnu file. The entire file has over 4600 lines. The line ***BUTTONS1 is the beginning of the button menu. The items that follow are specific assignments to the buttons on your pointing device.

Scroll down until you see the ***POP1 heading. This is the first pull-down menu, which appears at the left end of the menu bar near the top of the AutoCAD graphics window. Notice that the first word on each line is preceded with the characters "ID_". This is known as a *name tag*. AutoCAD associates other lines in the menu with these name tags. Name tags are covered later in this chapter. The next item is the label, enclosed in brackets ([ ]). Any word or character string appearing inside these brackets is displayed in the pull-down menu or on the menu bar.

Also note that one of the characters within the brackets is preceded by an ampersand (&). The character preceded by an ampersand in a pull-down menu label defines the keyboard shortcut key used to enable that item. Thus, since the title of the **File** pull-down menu is defined as [&File], it can be accessed by pressing [Alt]+[F].

Once a pull-down menu is displayed, a menu item within it may be selected using a single menu shortcut key. The menu shortcut keys defined for the **New...** and **Open...** items in the **File** pull-down menu appear in the acad.mnu file as &New and &Open. Therefore, these menu items are selected with the [N] and [O] keys, respectively. Do not confuse menu shortcut keys with *accelerator keys*, which are the Windows keystrokes such as [Ctrl]+[N] and [Ctrl]+[O].

Menu Item Titles

Learn to use the "search" function of your text editor. This function is extremely useful for moving around a file. Use the search function or the [Page Down] key to find the **09_DRAW1 menu. Remember, the two asterisks represent a subheading under a major section. The **09_DRAW1 menu is the first page of the **DRAW1** screen menu. In Figure 21-3, the **DRAW1** screen menu as seen in AutoCAD is shown on the left, and the same page is shown on the right as it appears in the acad.mnu file.

Notice that the menu entry is the same as its label inside the brackets ([ ]). As a general rule, a screen menu name can be up to eight characters long. You can have longer names and descriptions inside the brackets. However, the width of the screen menu area is fixed and longer names may be truncated. The number of usable characters varies based on the properties of the current Windows system font.

Figure 21-3.
On the left is the **DRAW1** screen menu as it appears on screen. On the right is the related command lines from the acad.mnu file.

AutoCAD Screen Menu (DRAW1)	ACAD.MNU Menu Code
	**09_DRAW1 3
Line	[Line]^C^C_line
Ray	[Ray]^C^C_ray
Xline	[Xline]^C^C_xline
Mline	[Mline]^C^C_mline
Pline	[Pline]^C^C_pline
3Dpoly	[3Dpoly]^C^C_3dpoly
Polygon	[Polygon]^C^C_polygon
Rectang	[Rectang]^C^C_rectang
Arc	[Arc]^C^C_arc
Circle	[Circle]^C^C_circle
Donut	[Donut]^C^C_donut
Spline	[Spline]^C^C_spline
Ellipse	[Ellipse]^C^C_ellipse

The text to the right of the closing bracket is the menu macro. Figure 21-4 shows the difference between label information and a menu macro.

Figure 21-4.
A—The first eight characters in the label appear as the screen menu selection. Additional comments can be included in the label. B—The menu macro, which follows the closing bracket, is processed by AutoCAD.

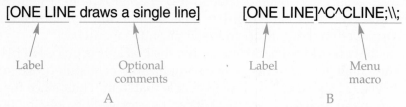

Menu Macro Syntax

When paging through the menu file, you probably noticed several characters and symbols that did not make much sense, such as $S=ACAD.01_FILE and \. These are menu codes, and have explicit functions in the menu. You will be using these codes to create menus.

The characters listed here can be used for button and screen menus. Special characters for pull-down menus are described later. The following is a list of characters and their functions:

Character	Function
***	Major menu sections—Must be placed directly in front of the name of the section, for example: ***SCREEN.
**	Submenu section—Appears in front of the submenu name. The **DRAW1** screen menu shown in the previous section has the name **09_DRAW1.
[ ]	The label, which contains the menu selection, is enclosed in brackets. Only the first eight characters inside the brackets are displayed in the screen menu.
$S=	This indicates that another screen menu is to be displayed and enables AutoCAD to move between submenus. Other similar codes are $B (BUTTONS), $T (TABLET), $I (IMAGE), $P (POP), and $A (AUX).
^C^C	This cancels any current command. If you are in a transparent or Dim: command, two ^Cs are needed to get you out. Placing this in front of your commands ensures that you begin the new command cleanly by canceling any active command.
;	The semicolon represents pressing [Enter].
\	The backslash represents a pause for user input, where information must be typed at the keyboard or entered with the pointing device.
+	The plus symbol is placed at the end of a long menu line and tells AutoCAD that there is more of this sequence on the next line.
=*	The current shortcut, pull-down, or image tile menu is displayed.
(space)	A blank space between items is the same as pressing [Enter] or the space bar.
*^C^C	Creates a repeating command.
si	Specifies immediate action on a single selected item. Placed at the occurrence of a Select objects: prompt during a macro. (For example: Erase;si)

Using Variables and Control Characters

AutoCAD system variables and control characters can be used in screen menus. They can be included to increase the speed and usefulness of your menu commands. Become familiar with these variables so you can make use of them in your menus:

- **^B.** Snap mode toggle
- **^C.** Cancel

- **^D.** Coords mode toggle
- **^E.** Isoplane crosshair toggle
- **^G.** Grid mode toggle
- **^H.** Issues a backspace
- **^M.** Issues a return
- **^O.** Ortho mode toggle
- **^P. MENUECHO** system variable toggle
- **^T.** Tablet toggle
- **^V.** Switches current viewport

CREATING BUTTON MENUS

Button menus control the functions of the pointing device buttons. If you use a stylus or a mouse with only one or two buttons, you will not be using button menus. If you have a pointing device with more than two buttons, you can alter the functions of the buttons to suit your needs. This can add to your drawing productivity and speed the access of commonly used commands.

The BUTTONS*n* (where *n* represents a number from one to four) menu sections are used for pointing devices such as digitizer pucks. The AUX*n* menus are used for a system mouse, such as the mouse you use in Windows. A standard mouse does not provide as much room for customization as a digitizer puck. The pick button on a mouse cannot be changed by editing the menu file. Therefore, a two-button mouse has a single button that can be customized, and a three-button mouse has two customizable buttons. Still, by using the [Shift]+, [Ctrl]+, and [Ctrl]+[Shift]+ combinations described in this section, added functionality is possible even for a standard mouse.

Standard Button Menu Layout

The main button menu is BUTTONS1. It is arranged for a device with nine program-mable buttons. A list of this button menu and its functions is shown in Figure 21-5.

Figure 21-5.
On the left is the ***BUTTONS1 menu and on the right is the meaning of the command lines and the associated buttons. Button #1 is the pick button and cannot be customized in the menu file.

Menu File Listing	Button Number	Function
***BUTTONS1		Menu section name
// Simple + button		Comment
// if a grip is hot bring up the Grips Cursor Menu(POP 500), else send a carriage return		Comment
// If the SHORTCUTMENU sysvar is not 0 the first item (for button 1) is NOT USED.		Comment
$M=$(if,$(eq,$(substr,$(getvar,cmdnames),1,5), GRIP_),$P0=ACAD.GRIPS $P0=*);	2	Return, or display grips shortcut menu
$P0=SNAP $p0=*	3	Displays Object Snap shortcut menu
^C^C	4	Cancel
^B	5	Snap mode toggle
^O	6	Ortho mode toggle
^G	7	Grid mode toggle
^D	8	Coords mode toggle
^E	9	Isoplane crosshair toggle
^T	10	Tablet toggle

Additional Button Menus

If you are using a digitizer puck, you can have instant access to the four button menus, BUTTONS1 through BUTTONS4. Each of these menus can be accessed with a keyboard and puck button combination:

Action	Button Menu
puck button only	BUTTONS1
[Shift]+puck button	BUTTONS2
[Ctrl]+puck button	BUTTONS3
[Ctrl]+[Shift]+puck button	BUTTONS4

Each of these button menus can contain any commands you need. For example, you can place a variety of display commands in the BUTTONS2 menu. To access these commands, simply hold down the [Shift] key on the keyboard and press the appropriate puck button.

Copying the ACAD.MNU File

Before you edit the acad.mnu file, check with your instructor or supervisor to find out what procedures should be used. As discussed previously, you should first copy the acad.mnu file to your own directory folder. Then experiment and make changes to your copy. This protects the original program. It also prevents undue frustration for students or employees who find that the revised menu does not function properly.

To avoid confusing acad.mnu with your customized menu, name the new copy mymenu.mnu. You can also use your first name, such as nancy.mnu. This distinguishes it from all others.

PROFESSIONAL TIP

You must understand how commands work to create AutoCAD menus. Know the command options, when they can be used, and how they are used. Always plan your commands and macros using the following steps:

1. Write out what you want the command or macro to do.
2. Write the macro as it will appear in the menu file using command codes.
3. Check the written macro to be sure it has the proper commands, options, and syntax.
4. Add the macro to the menu file.
5. Test the macro.

Replacing Button Menu Items

The process of replacing button menu items is the same as editing a line in a text file. An example is replacing the existing button commands shown in Figure 21-6 with the new commands given. Place a double cancel before each command. This cancels the current command when the button is picked.

Figure 21-6.
Existing button functions can be easily replaced with new commands.

Button Number	Existing Function	New Command
6	Ortho mode toggle	**LINE**
7	Grid mode toggle	**ERASE**
8	Coords mode toggle	**CIRCLE**
9	Isoplane crosshair toggle	**ARC**

When you have finished editing, the new button menu should look like this:

```
***BUTTONS1
$M=$(if,$(eq,$(substr,$(getvar,cmdnames),1,5),GRIP_),$P0=ACAD.GRIPS $P0=*);
$P0=SNAP $p0=*
^C^C
^B
^C^CLINE
^C^CERASE
^C^CCIRCLE
^C^CARC
^T
```

Before testing the new menu, you must load it into memory with the **MENU** command, otherwise AutoCAD will work with the old copy. The **MENU** command displays the **Select Menu File** dialog box, Figure 21-7. Select the **Files of type:** drop-down list. Note that you can specify either Menu Files (*.mnc,*.mns) or Menu Template (*.mnu) files.

Select the Menu Template (.mnu) option and find your menu file using the directory windows. Then, pick your menu from the file list and select the **OK** button. A warning dialog is displayed:

> Loading of a template menu file (MNU file) overwrites and
> redefines the menu source file (MNS file), which results in the
> loss of any toolbar customization changes that have been made.
>
> Continue loading MNU file?

In this case, you want to load the MNU file, so pick the **OK** button. There is a slight delay as AutoCAD compiles the MNU file into an MNC file. The status bar shows the progress as the menu is compiled. The MNC file is written in a format that makes it usable by AutoCAD. You cannot directly edit the MNC file.

For 2000i Users...

The standard file selection dialog box (such as that used for the **Select Menu File** dialog box shown in Figure 21-7) has been modified for AutoCAD 2000i. See **AutoCAD and its Applications— Basics** for a complete description of standard file selection dialog box features.

Figure 21-7.
The **Select Menu File** dialog box is used to load the new menu file.

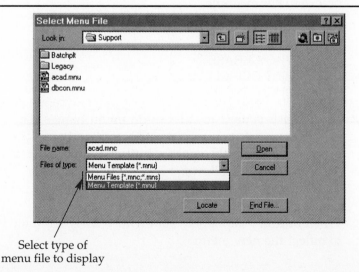

Select type of
menu file to display

Providing for User Input

An important aspect of menu customization is having a good grasp of AutoCAD's commands and options. Most commands require some form of user input—picking a location on the screen or entering values at the keyboard.

The final action of any input is using a button on the pointing device or pressing [Enter] on the keyboard. The symbol used to indicate a pause for user input is the backslash (\). A second important aspect of menu customization is inserting returns, or specifying when the [Enter] key is pressed. This is handled with the semicolon (;).

When a command is listed in a menu file, AutoCAD automatically inserts a space after it, which is interpreted as a return. The following command executes the **LINE** command and prompts Specify first point:

LINE

If the command is followed by a semicolon, backslash, or plus sign, AutoCAD does not insert a space. Therefore, there is no automatic return. If you want to allow for user input, and then provide a return, you should end the line with a semicolon:

LINE;\\;

This executes the **LINE** command, waits for the user to pick the start and end points of a line, and then terminates the command.

The button menus perform additional functions with the user input symbols. If a backslash is provided after the command, the coordinates of the crosshairs on the screen are recorded when the pick button is pressed. Therefore, the following button command accepts the current location of the crosshairs as the Specify first point: for the **LINE** command when the button is pressed, and the Specify next point or [Undo]: prompt is displayed:

LINE;\

This instant input can be used for other applications. For example, object snap modes can be executed transparently using a button menu.

Adding New Button Menus

You are not limited to the four button menus. You can create as many as needed. However, one button should be used to switch menus. Here are a few things to keep in mind when creating new button menus:

✓ There is no screen display of button names. Use brackets in your menu file to contain button labels or numbers. AutoCAD does not act on anything inside brackets. For example:

```
***BUTTONS4
[6]^C^CLINE
[7]^C^CERASE
[8]^C^CCIRCLE
[9]^C^CARC
```

✓ The letter B is used to call button menu names. The code $B= is used to call other button submenus, just as $S= is used to call other screen submenus. For example, you could specify button 9 in the ***BUTTONS1 menu to call submenu **B1 as follows:

[9]$B=B1

When button 9 is pressed, submenu **B1 is activated and the buttons change to reflect the new menu.

✓ A button menu selection can also call a screen menu in the same manner. For example, button 9 could call the **OSNAP** screen menu in addition to changing the button submenu to B1. The entry in the menu file would look like this:

> [9]$B=B1 $S=OSNAP

You will alter the **OSNAP** screen menu for using buttons in one of the chapter problems.

✓ A button menu selection can display a pull-down menu as follows:

> $P11=*

The P11 calls for pull-down menu 11 (the <u>H</u>elp pull-down menu), and the =* displays it on screen.

✓ In the file, a space is not required after a button submenu to separate it from its submenus.

The following example shows revisions to the ***BUTTONS1 menu. It includes a selection for button 10 that switches to the B1 button menu and also displays the **OSNAP** screen menu. The B1 menu provides eight object snap options, and button 10 returns to the BUTTONS1 menu and displays the **S** screen menu.

```
***BUTTONS1
[2]$M=$(if,$(eq,$(substr,$(getvar,cmdnames),1,5),GRIP_),$P0=ACAD.GRIPS
   $P0=*);
[3]$P0=SNAP $p0=*
[4]^C^C
[5]^B
[6]^C^CLINE
[7]^C^CERASE
[8]^C^CCIRCLE
[9]^C^CARC
[10]$B=B1 $S=OSNAP
**B1
[2]ENDpoint
[3]INTersect
[4]MIDpoint
[5]PERpendicular
[6]CENter
[7]TANgent
[8]QUAdrant
[9]NEArest
[10]$B=BUTTONS1 $S=S
```

PROFESSIONAL TIP

When using button submenus, it is a common technique to combine menu calls with the macro in order to automatically reset the previous button menu. For example:

```
**B1
[2]$B=BUTTONS1 ENDpoint
```

EXERCISE 21-1

❑ Copy the acad.mnu file into your folder or onto a floppy disk. Change the name of the file to mymenu.mnu or use your name.
❑ Create a button submenu named **B2.
❑ Include three drawing commands and three editing commands in the submenu.

Once enabled, standard screen menus are located along the right side of the screen. They are created with the same techniques used for button menus. Screen menus are more versatile than button menus because you can see the command titles.

The positions of commands within the screen menu are referred to as *screenboxes*. The number of boxes available depends on the current size of the AutoCAD program window. You can find out how many boxes are available using the **SCREENBOXES** system variable as follows:

Command: **SCREENBOXES**↵
SCREENBOXES = 27 (read only)

Most people rarely use all the commands found in AutoCAD's screen menus. In time, you will find which commands you use most often, and those you seldom use. Begin to develop an idea of what the menu structure should look like. Then start constructing custom menus, even though you may not completely know what to include. Menus are easy to change, and can be revised as many times as needed.

NOTE   If screen menus are not enabled, the **SCREENBOXES** system variable returns a value of 0.

PROFESSIONAL TIP   Develop a plan for your menus, but build them over time. Create one command or macro and then test it. It is much easier to create one macro and test it than to create an entire untested menu. Building menus a small portion at a time is also more efficient. It can be done as you work or study, or when you have a spare minute.

Screen Menu Items

A screen menu item is composed of the item label and menu macro. The label is enclosed in brackets. The menu macro is a combination of commands, options, and characters that instruct AutoCAD to perform a function or series of functions. Take a closer look at the example in Figure 21-8. It is the same one that was introduced in Figure 21-4. The following parts are included in the macro:

- Brackets ([ ]) enclose the item label. The first eight characters within the brackets are displayed on the screen.
- The command name ONE LINE is displayed on the screen. Try to give descriptive names to your commands so they indicate what the command does.
- The double cancel (^C^C) cancels out any command that is active when you pick the menu item.

Figure 21-8.
The components of a screen menu item. The item label is followed by the menu macro.

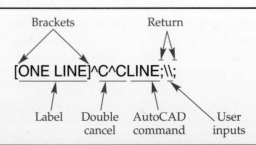

- AutoCAD commands determine what function the macro performs (**LINE**).
- A return (;) represents pressing the [Enter] key after typing LINE at the keyboard.
- The two backslashes (\\) pause for user input to the Specify first point: and Specify next point or [Undo]: prompts. Remember, each backslash indicates a value entered at the keyboard or a selection made with the pointing device.
- A final return (;) represents pressing the [Enter] key to end the **LINE** command.

As you can see, you need to know the commands, prompts, options, and entries required to perform AutoCAD functions before you can modify screen menus. Look at the next menu item and try to determine what it is doing.

[Erase 1]^C^CERASE;si;\

The title should give you a clue. It erases a single object. The **ERASE** command is followed by a return, which is followed by "si" to allow a single selection and then a single backslash to pause for the user selection. This allows a single selection and then automatically executes the **ERASE** command. Here is another one.

[Extend 1]^C^CEXTEND;\;\;

This macro issues the **EXTEND** command, then allows for one user input to pick a boundary edge. Then a return is entered and one additional user input is allowed for the object to extend. After one object is picked, the last return completes the command automatically.

Look at one more menu item that combines two commands. What function do you think this macro performs?

[Line T]^C^CLINE;\\;;MID;\\;

Notice that the first half of the item is exactly the same as the macro shown in Figure 21-8. It draws a single line. The return before MID selects the **LINE** command again. MID specifies an object snap mode at the Specify first point: prompt. At the first backslash, pick the line on which the midpoint is needed. The second backslash is the Specify next point or [Undo]: prompt. The final return ends the command.

PROFESSIONAL TIP

When writing menu commands and macros, write them as if you are entering the commands and options at the keyboard. Use the semicolon (;) for the [Enter] key. Use first letters where appropriate for command options.

Constructing Menu Commands

When you think of a useful command or function to include in a menu, the first step is to write it out in longhand. This gives you a clear picture of the scope of the command. The second step is to list the keyboard steps required to execute the new function. Third, write out the menu item as it will appear in the menu file. The following examples each use this three-step process:

Example 1
1. Make a menu pick called ERASE L to erase the last object drawn.
2. **ERASE⏎**
   LAST⏎
   ⏎
3. [ERASE L]^C^CERASE;L;;

Example 2

1. Make a menu pick called ERASE 1 that erases a single selection and returns to the Command: prompt.
2. **ERASE.⏎**
   (select entity)⏎
3. [ERASE 1]^C^CERASE;si;

Example 3

1. Make a menu pick called ZOOM D that enters the **ZOOM Dynamic** display without the user having to pick the **Dynamic** option.
2. **ZOOM.⏎**
   DYNAMIC.⏎
3. [ZOOM D]^C^CZOOM;D

Example 4

1. Make a menu pick called ZOOM P that zooms to the previous display.
2. **ZOOM.⏎**
   PREVIOUS.⏎
3. [ZOOM P]^C^CZOOM;P

Example 5

1. Make a menu pick that draws as many circles as needed.
2. **MULTIPLE.⏎**
   CIRCLE.⏎
3. [M CIRCLE]^C^CMULTIPLE;CIRCLE or *^C^CCIRCLE

   These examples should give you the feel for the process used when creating menu items. The command items can now be written to a menu file and tested. Before doing this, though, take a look at two more examples that are a little more involved.

Example 6

1. Create a new menu pick called 25FILLET that can set a .25 fillet radius on a polyline without restarting the **FILLET** command.
2. **FILLET.⏎**
   RADIUS.⏎
   .25.⏎
   FILLET.⏎
   POLYLINE.⏎
   (select 2D polyline)
3. [25FILLET]^C^CFILLET;R;.25;;P;\

Example 7

1. Create a new menu pick called DWG AIDS that sets the grid to .5, sets the snap grid to .25, and turns Ortho mode on.
2. **GRID.⏎**
   .5.⏎
   SNAP.⏎
   .25.⏎
   ORTHO.⏎
   ON.⏎
3. [DWG AIDS]^C^CGRID;.5;SNAP;.25;ORTHO;ON

Adding Macros to the Menu File

The next step is to add the new macros to the menu file and then test them. Create a new submenu after the **S menu. Load your copy of the acad.mnu file into your text editor and search to find the following:

```
***SCREEN
**S
```

Listed below **S is AutoCAD's familiar root menu. Find the last sequential command in that menu, which is [LAST]. If you are editing the acad.mnu file, then just below the [LAST] option is the **SNAP_TO menu. It is preceded by three lines of comments. Move your cursor to the beginning of the first comment line and press the [Enter] key twice, then press the up arrow key twice. Your cursor will now be on a blank line separated from the subsequent menu by an additional blank line.

This can be done between the end of any screen submenu and the start of the next. Remember that the first screen menu listed in the ***SCREEN section is displayed when you enter the drawing editor. (If you insert your submenu in front of the **S menu, yours will be the first displayed when AutoCAD enters the drawing editor.)

Name this first submenu TEST. Type the entries in your text editor exactly as they are shown below. Be sure to press [Enter] at the end of each line. Your first entries in this menu should look like the following:

```
**TEST 3 (the "3" begins the menu on the third line from the top of the screen)
[ TEST]
[ MENU]
[Erase L]^C^CERASE;L;;
[Erase 1]^C^CERASE;\;
[Zoom W]^C^CZOOM;W
[Zoom P]^C^CZOOM;P
[M Circle]^C^CMULTIPLE;CIRCLE
[25Fillet]^C^CFILLET;R;.25;;P;\
[Dwg Aids]^C^CGRID;.5;SNAP;.25;ORTHO;ON
```

Long Menu Items

If a menu item occupies more than one line, instruct AutoCAD that there is more to the item. Type a plus symbol (+) at the end of the line. Do not put spaces in before or after the mark. Use the long-line technique to create a command that does the following:

- Perform a **ZOOM All**.
- Set the limits to 0,0 and 20,12.
- Set the snap grid to 0.25.
- Set the grid to 0.50.
- Draw a polyline border from 0.5,0.5. The border should be 17″ × 11″.
- Set the **MIRRTEXT** system variable to zero.
- Set the **APERTURE** system variable to 3.
- Set Ortho mode on.
- Set Grid mode on.
- Perform a **ZOOM Extents**.

The item name and code for this macro is written as follows:

```
[B-11x17]^C^CZOOM;A;LIMITS;;20,12;SNAP;.25;GRID;.5;PLINE;0.5,0.5;+
17.5,.5;17.5,11.5;0.5,11.5;C;MIRRTEXT;0;APERTURE;3;ORTHO;+
ON;GRID;ON;ZOOM;E
```

Place Your Menu in the Root Menu

You have created your first screen menu, but how do you access it from the root menu of AutoCAD? There is nothing in the root menu that calls the **TEST** menu. You need to add that item to the root menu now.

Look again at the **S menu and notice that only 18 lines are occupied with commands inside brackets. You can insert your menu name on the line after [HELP], or any other blank line in this area. Insert the following item:

    [TEST] $S=ACAD.TEST

Do not press [Enter] at the end of the line or you will insert an additional line in the menu. This could push the last menu item off the screen if the AutoCAD window displays only 26 lines in the menu area.

The Menu Stack

The item you entered above calls your submenu TEST. A screen menu call is different from other menu calls because the previous menu is not removed prior to displaying the subsequent menu. Instead, the new menu is overlaid on the existing menu, with the first item being placed on the specified line. This creates a menu stack.

For example, the **TEST menu has a 3 following the menu name. This indicates that the first two lines are to remain unchanged and the menu data placement begins on line 3 of the screen menu display area. The new items are then used to replace existing screen menu selections.

In the **TEST menu, nine items are defined with the menu beginning on the third line. The previous menu, **S, has many additional lines. Since the **TEST menu only redefines lines 3 through 11, lines 12 and on remain unchanged. To clear these lines out when the submenu is displayed, place an appropriate number of blank lines after the code for the submenu. Figure 21-9A shows the **S menu with the addition of the TEST menu item, and Figure 21-9B shows the screen menu after calling the **TEST menu.

The standard approach is to begin submenus on the third line of the menu display area. This results in the first two lines of the **S menu being preserved regardless of which submenu is currently displayed. This is important due to the functions performed by these two items. The first two items of the **S menu are the following:

    AutoCAD
    * * * *

Picking the word **AutoCAD** displays the **S menu (the root menu), and picking the four asterisks displays an object snap menu. This way, no matter where you are in the menu system, it takes only one pick to get to these frequently needed items.

PROFESSIONAL TIP

When creating screen menus, always use the standard convention for menu label appearances. On the AutoCAD screen menu, the label for an item that calls another menu is shown with all UPPERCASE characters. Items that start a command are shown in Title Case, with the first character of each word in uppercase.

Figure 21-9.
A—The screen
menu with the TEST
menu item added
below HELP.
B—Calling the
**TEST submenu
results in this
display.

```
AutoCAD
* * * *
 FILE
 EDIT
 VIEW1
 VIEW2
 INSERT
 FORMAT
 TOOLS1
 TOOLS2
 DRAW1
 DRAW2
 DIMNSION
 MODIFY1
 MODIFY2

 HELP
 TEST
```

A

```
AutoCAD
* * * *
 TEST
 MENU
 Erase L
 Erase 1
 Zoom W
 Zoom P
 M Circle
 25Fillet
 Dwg Aids



 HELP
 TEST
```

B

EXERCISE 21-2

❏ Use the three-step process to write the menu items given below.
  ❏ [SNAPGRID]. Toggle the Snap mode and Grid mode on or off.
  ❏ [MTEXT-S.1]. Set the snap at .1 and select the **MTEXT** command.
  ❏ [MIRROR]. Turn the **MIRRTEXT** system variable off and select the **Window** option of the **MIRROR** command for a single selection. Do not delete the old objects. This command should return the user to Command: prompt.
  ❏ [BREAK @]. Break a line into two parts with a single pick.
  ❏ [CHMFER.5]. Set a chamfer distance of .5 and allow two lines to be picked.

Chapter Test

Answer the following questions on a separate sheet of paper.
1. The name and extension of the file that contains the fully documented standard menus for AutoCAD is _____.
2. List the names of the major sections in AutoCAD's default menu.
3. All interactive toolbar modifications are written to which file?
4. Why should you edit a copy of the acad.mnu file when customizing menus?
5. Can you have more than four button menus?
6. What kind of symbol is used to indicate a screen submenu?
7. Describe the function of each of the following screen menu commands:
  A. ^C^CTRIM;\;\;
  B. ^C^CCOPY;W;\\
  C. ^C^CCHANGE;\;
8. Give the function of the following menu command codes:
  A. Brackets ([ ])
  B. Semicolon (;)
  C. Backslash (\)
  D. Plus sign (+)
  E. Single (si)

---

9. What key combinations are used to access the following button menus:
   A. BUTTONS2
   B. BUTTONS3
   C. BUTTONS4
10. Which system variable lists the number of screen menu items?
11. List the three steps you should use when creating a new menu command.
12. Suppose you add a new menu to the acad.mnu file. How does the new menu get displayed on the screen?
13. Define *menu stack*.
14. Define the use of the following control characters.
    A. ^B
    B. ^G
    C. ^O
    D. ^V

Drawing Problems

1. Begin an entirely new AutoCAD menu composed of a general button section and an object snap button menu. Name the menu P21-1.MNU. Plan your menu items before you begin. The main button menu (***BUTTONS1) should have the following items:

Button Number	Function
2	**DDEDIT** command.
3	**LINE** command.
4	**CIRCLE** command.
5	**ZOOM Dynamic**.
6	Leave blank.
7	Erase one object and end the **ERASE** command.
8	**ZOOM Window**.
9	[Enter].
10	**ZOOM Previous**.

The ***BUTTONS2 menu is an object snap interrupt menu. All object snap items should activate the object snap mode specified and select a point when the button is pressed. The ***BUTTONS2 menu should contain the following items:

Button Number	Function
2	**Endpoint** object snap mode.
3	**Intersection** object snap mode.
4	**Perpendicular** object snap mode.
5	**Midpoint** object snap mode.
6	**Center** object snap mode.
7	**Tangent** object snap mode.
8	**Quadrant** object snap mode.
9	Return to main button and screen menus.
10	**Node** object snap mode.

Write the menus in small segments and be sure to test all items. Generate a printed copy of the menu file.

2. Add the screen menu given below to the P21-1.MNU file you created in Problem 1. The section name should be ***SCREEN. The main menu name should be **S. Plan your menu items before entering them in the text editor. The following items should be included.

Position	Menu Items
1	Menu title [HOME]
2	Cancel and **ARC**.
3	Cancel and **POLYGON**.
4	Cancel and **PLINE**.
5	Cancel and **LIST**.
6	Cancel and **DIST**.
7	Cancel and **SCALE**.
8	Cancel and **OFFSET**.
9	Cancel and **ROTATE**.
10	Cancel and **STRETCH**.
11	Blank.
12	Cancel and **ZOOM**.
13	Blank.
14	Rotate crosshairs axis to user-specified angle. Allow user to set base point and leave Snap mode on.
15	Reset crosshairs axis to zero and turn Snap mode off.
16	Allow user to pick a single object and change it to a new layer.

Test all menu items to ensure that they are working properly before going to the next problem. Generate a printed copy of the menu file.

3. Add the following screen menu to your P21-1.MNU file. This is an editing menu and should be named **EDIT. At position 18 in your main screen menu (see Problem 2), add an item that calls the **EDIT** menu. Place the following items in the **EDIT** menu:

Position	Menu Items	Function
1	[Erase-F]	Erase with **FENCE** option.
2	[Copy-WP]	Copy with **Window Polygon** option.
3	[Move-W]	Move with **Window** option.
4	[Break-F]	Activate **BREAK**, allow user to select object, then pick first and second points without entering F.
5	[Change-1]	Activate **CHANGE**, select object, and stop for user input.
6	[Reword-M]	Allow user to edit a line of text.
7	[0-Fillet]	Select two lines and clean up corners with zero radius fillet. Allow selection of five clean-ups without restarting the command.
8	[0-Break]	Select line or arc and split into two parts.
9	[0-Corner]	Select two intersecting lines at the intersection. Clean up corner using two picks.

Generate a printed copy of the menu file.

4. Add an item to the main button menu at button 6 that calls the **BUTTONS2 menu and a new screen menu called **OSNAP. The line should read:

    [6]$B=BUTTONS2 $S=OSNAP

The new **OSNAP screen menu should contain the following items:

Position	Menu Items	Function
1	[BUTTONS]	Label
2	[2=Endpt]	Show button assignment and activate **Endpoint** object snap mode if picked from the screen.
3	[3=Inter]	Show button assignment and activate **Intersection** object snap mode if picked from the screen.
4	[4=Perp]	Show button assignment and activate **Perpendicular** object snap mode if picked from the screen.
5	[5=Midpt]	Show button assignment and activate **Midpoint** object snap mode if picked from the screen.
6	[6=Center]	Show button assignment and activate **Center** object snap mode if picked from the screen.
7	[7=Tangent]	Show button assignment and activate **Tangent** object snap mode if picked from the screen.
8	[8=Quad]	Show button assignment and activate **Quadrant** object snap mode if picked from the screen.
9	[9=HOME]	Page back to main button and screen.
10	[10=Node]	Show button assignment and activate **Node** object snap mode if picked from the screen.
11	[Nearest]	Activate **Nearest** object snap mode from screen.
12	[Insert]	Activate **Insert** object snap mode from screen.

Generate a printed copy of the menu file.

5. Alter the **OSNAPB menu in your copy of acad.mnu to function with a button menu in the same manner as given in Problem 4. If you have not added a **BUTTONS2 menu to your acad.mnu file (explained earlier in this chapter), do so for this problem.

CHAPTER 22

Customizing Pull-Down Menus and Image Tiles

Learning Objectives

After completing this chapter, you will be able to:

- Understand the structure of pull-down menus.
- Create single- or multiple-page pull-down menus.
- Create user-defined accelerator keys.
- Load pull-down menus from multiple menu groups.
- Describe the purpose and function of image tile menus.
- Describe the purpose and the function of a slide library.
- Create slides for image tile menus.
- Create a slide library for an image tile menu.
- Create an image tile menu file listing.

PULL-DOWN MENUS AND ACCELERATOR KEYS

AutoCAD
Custom
Guide
4

The names of the standard pull-down menus appear in the menu bar at the top of the AutoCAD graphics window. They are selected by placing the cursor arrow over the menu item and picking to select it.

Pull-down menus are referred to as "POP" menus in the menu file, and are given numerical designations such as POP0 and POP1. Pull-down menus are defined in the POP1 through POP499 sections. POP0 is the object snap shortcut menu, which is enabled by simultaneously pressing the [Shift] key and clicking the [Enter] button on your mouse or digitizer tablet puck. By default, this shortcut menu displays each of the object snap modes. Context shortcut menus are defined in the POP500 through POP999 sections. The grips shortcut menu is defined in the POP500 section of the menu file. Right-clicking while a grip is hot displays this menu. Some shortcut menus, such as the zoom and toolbars shortcut menus, are handled by AutoCAD and are not defined in the menu file.

Once you understand how pull-down menus are designed, you can customize existing menus and create your own. Some basic information about pull-down menus follows:

- The titles of POP menus 1 through 16 are shown along the menu bar.
- If no POP1 through POP16 menus are defined, AutoCAD inserts default **File** and **Edit** menus (similar to when AutoCAD is displayed without an open drawing).

- POP menus 17 through 499 are not shown on the menu bar by default. They can be inserted using the proper menu code or the **MENULOAD** command, or they can be used for menu swapping.
- The title of the pull-down menu should be as concise as possible. On low-resolution displays, long menu names may cause the menu bar to be displayed on two lines, which reduces your effective display area.
- Menu item labels can be any length. The menu is as wide as its longest label.
- Each menu can have multiple cascading submenus.
- A pull-down menu can have up to 999 items (including cascading submenus).
- A shortcut menu can have up to 499 items (including cascading submenus).

Pull-Down Menu Structure and Codes

Many of the same codes used for writing screen menus are used for pull-down menus. The primary difference is the sequence of characters, or *syntax*, used for cascading submenus. This syntax also allows for the definition of accelerator and mnemonic shortcut keys used in the pull-down menus.

The pull-down menu syntax is best seen by loading your copy of the acad.mnu file into your text editor. Look for the ***POP3 heading. This is the **View** pull-down menu. The first part of this menu is shown in Figure 22-1.

Compare the appearance of the menu file syntax and the pull-down menu. A few new menu syntax characters are found in this menu. These characters are explained below. They provide a separator line, indicate where cascading submenus begin and end, and define accelerator and mnemonic shortcut keys.

Character	Function
[– –]	Two hyphens are used to insert a separator line across the pull-down menu. The line is automatically drawn the width of the menu.
–>	Indicates that the item has a cascading submenu.
<–	Indicates the last item in the cascading menu.
<–<–	Indicates the last item in the cascading submenu and the last item of the previous menu (parent menu).
&*c*	The ampersand specifies the mnemonic key in a pull-down or shortcut menu label. The "*c*" shown here represents any character.

Figure 22-1.
The first part of the POP3 (**View**) pull-down menu. Note the placement of the ampersand character (&) to define accelerator and mnemonic shortcut keys.

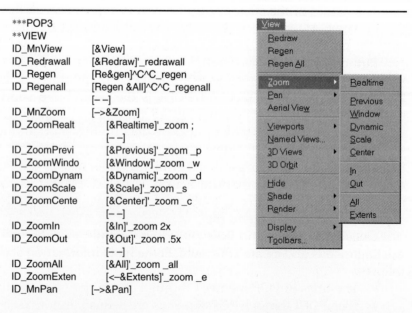

```
***POP3
**VIEW
ID_MnView        [&View]
ID_Redrawall     [&Redraw]'_redrawall
ID_Regen         [Re&gen]^C^C_regen
ID_Regenall      [Regen &All]^C^C_regenall
                 [– –]
ID_MnZoom        [–>&Zoom]
ID_ZoomRealt        [&Realtime]'_zoom ;
                    [– –]
ID_ZoomPrevi        [&Previous]'_zoom _p
ID_ZoomWindo        [&Window]'_zoom _w
ID_ZoomDynam        [&Dynamic]'_zoom _d
ID_ZoomScale        [&Scale]'_zoom _s
ID_ZoomCente        [&Center]'_zoom _c
                    [– –]
ID_ZoomIn           [&In]'_zoom 2x
ID_ZoomOut          [&Out]'_zoom .5x
                    [– –]
ID_ZoomAll          [&All]'_zoom _all
ID_ZoomExten        [<–&Extents]'_zoom _e
ID_MnPan         [–>&Pan]
```

Menu Entry   Resulting Pull-Down Menu

Notice in the POP3 pull-down menu listing in Figure 22-1 that indentation has been used to indicate cascading submenus. Indenting is not necessary to write a valid menu file, but it gives the file an appearance similar to the actual submenus. It also makes the file easier to read and understand.

Marking Menu Items

Menu items can be marked with a check mark (✓) or other character of your choosing. You can also have items "grayed-out." The following characters are used for these purposes:

Character	Function
[~]	The tilde grays out any characters that follow.
!.	The combination of an exclamation point and a period places a check mark (✓) before the menu item.

When these marking characters are used in a menu, they mark an item permanently. This may be desirable for the separator line and for graying out specific items, but a check mark is often related to an item that is toggled on or off. Look at the sample menu file and its pull-down menu in Figure 22-2.

Figure 22-2.
An example of check mark and grayed-out character definitions in a pull-down menu.

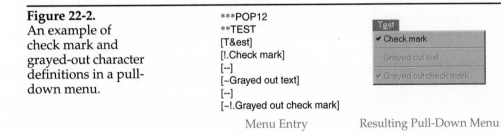

```
***POP12
**TEST
[T&est]
[!.Check mark]
[--]
[~Grayed out text]
[--]
[~!.Grayed out check mark]
```

Menu Entry   Resulting Pull-Down Menu

Creating "Smart" Pull-Down Menu Items

A check mark is often placed by any item to indicate that it has been selected, or that it is on. You can add this capability to your pull-down menus by using a string expression language called DIESEL (Direct Interpretively Evaluated String Expression Language). A *string* is simply a group of characters that can be input from the keyboard or from the value of a system variable. DIESEL uses a string for its input and provides a string for output. In other words, you give DIESEL a value, and it gives something back to you.

Using the check mark is an excellent example of how DIESEL can be used in menu items. For example, you may want to toggle the Ortho mode from a pull-down menu and indicate when it is on with a check mark. Use the following line in your menu:

[$(if,$(getvar,orthomode),!.)&Ortho]^O

The first $ signals the pull-down menu to evaluate a DIESEL macro. This macro gets the value (getvar) of the **ORTHOMODE** system variable, and places the check mark by the item if the value is 1 (on). Notice that the Ortho mode toggle is executed (^O) when the item is picked.

Figure 22-3 shows how two DIESEL additions to the previous **Test** menu look in the menu file and the pull-down menu. The pull-down menu shows that Ortho mode is on and Snap mode is off.

Figure 22-3.
An example of
DIESEL macros
added to a pull-
down menu. Note
that Ortho mode is
on and Snap mode
is off.

```
***POP12
**TEST
[T&est]
[$(if,$(getvar,orthomode),!.)&Ortho]^O
[$(if,$(getvar,snapmode),!.)&Snap]^B
[!.Check mark]
[--]
[~Grayed out text]
[--]
[~!.Grayed out check mark]
```

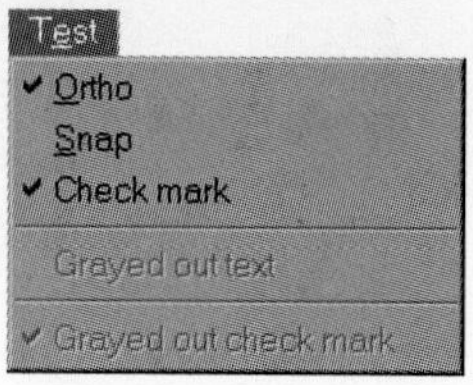

Test
✓ Ortho
Snap
✓ Check mark
Grayed out text
✓ Grayed out check mark

Menu Entry   Resulting Pull-Down Menu

The use of DIESEL expressions in your menus can enhance their power and make them more "intelligent." See Chapter 5 of the *AutoCAD Customization Guide* for a complete discussion of the DIESEL language.

Referencing Other Pull-Down Menus

A pick on one menu can activate, or "reference," another pull-down menu. A menu pick can also gray out or place a marking character by another pull-down menu item. The following character codes are used for these purposes:

Character	Function
pn=	Makes another pull-down menu current, where n is the number of the menu. Alternately, any specified alias for the menu can be referenced. The alias is defined by the **alias* label after the menu section name.
pn=*	Displays the currently active pull-down menu.
pn.1=	References a specific item number on another pull-down menu.

When referencing other pull-down menus, you can combine the marking symbols to add "gray out" or place check marks. Study the following menu item examples. The first example activates POP12 and displays it.

> $p12=*

The next menu item places a check mark on item 4 of POP12.

> $p12.4=!.

Now, study these menu item examples. The first entry grays out item 3 of POP6.

> $p6.3=~

The following menu item places a check mark by item 2 of POP8 and grays it out.

> $p8.2=!.~

The next menu item removes all marks and any "gray out" from item 2 of POP8.

> $p8.2=

The following examples show how these techniques can be combined in a macro.

```
[Insert desk]^C^C-insert;desk;\\\\$p12=*
[Setup .5]^C^Cgrid;.5;snap;.25;$p12.1=!. $p12.2=!.~
[Defaults]^C^Cgrid;off;snap;off;$p12.1= $p12.2=
```

Figure 22-4 shows an example using these techniques, and the appearance of the pull-down menu it defines.

AutoCAD and its Applications—Advanced

Figure 22-4.
A sample of linking
pull-down menu
items.

```
***POP12
**TEST
[T&est]
[$(if,$(getvar,orthomode),!.)&Ortho]^O
[$(if,$(getvar,snapmode),!.)&Snap]^B
[!.Check mark]
[Item 4]
[--]
[~Grayed out text]
[--]
[~!.Grayed out check mark]
[--]
[Check Mark Item 4]$p12.4=!. $p12=*
[Gray Out Item 4]$p12.4=~ $p12=*
[Gray/Check Item 4]$p12.4=~!. $p12=*
[Clear Item 4]$p12.4= $p12=*
```

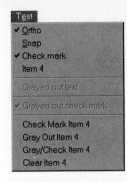

Menu Entry   Resulting Pull-Down Menu

NOTE   Menu item numbering begins with the first line of the pull-down menu below the title and continues to the bottom of the file. Separator lines are also counted when determining line numbers. AutoCAD numbers items consecutively through all submenus, without considering submenu levels.

Creating a New Pull-Down Menu

When adding a new pull-down menu, first scroll through the acad.mnu file until you find the ***POP500 pull-down menu. If you want to add any additional pull-down menus, they should be inserted before the ***POP500 section. Your new pull-down menus will be located in the menu bar after the **Help** menu. Be sure to leave an empty line between pull-down menu definitions.

Test each item of a new menu to make sure it works properly. Remember, when you return to the drawing editor, you must use the **MENU** command to reload the revised MNU file. If you neglect to do this, you will be working with the old version of the menu.

PROFESSIONAL TIP   A pull-down menu item can be as long as needed, but should be as brief as possible for easy reading. The pull-down menu width is automatically created to fit the width of the longest item.

Sample Menu Items

The following examples show how AutoCAD commands and options can be used to create pull-down or screen menu items. They are listed using a three-step process:
- Step 1 is a verbal description of the macro.
- Step 2 lists the keyboard strokes required for the macro.
- Step 3 gives the actual macro as it appears in the menu file.

Example 1
1. This **HEXAGON** command will start the **POLYGON** command and request a six-sided polygon inscribed in a circle.

2. **POLYGON**↵

   6↵

   (select center)

   I↵

3. [&Hexagon]*^C^Cpolygon;6;\l

The asterisk in front of the ^C^C repeats the command continuously until it is canceled. As mentioned earlier, you can indicate a return in a command or macro by using either a space or a semicolon. Notice the following two commands. Both commands perform the same function.

    [Hexagon]*^C^Cpolygon 6 \l
    [Hexagon]*^C^Cpolygon;6;\l

The first example uses spaces and the second example uses semicolons to represent pressing the [Enter] key. The technique you use is a matter of personal preference, but it is recommended that you use semicolons.

PROFESSIONAL TIP

It is generally preferred to use a semicolon for a return to clearly indicate that a return has been inserted. Spaces can be difficult to count, and when using spaces, an extra space can slip into a menu item and go unnoticed until the item is tested.

Example 2

1. This **DOT** command draws a solid dot .1 inch in diameter. Use the **DONUT** command. The inside diameter is 0 (zero) and the outside diameter is .1.
2. **DONUT**↵

   0↵

   .1↵

3. [&Dot]^C^Cdonut;0;.1

Example 3

1. This **X-POINT** command sets the **PDMODE** system variable to 3 and draws an X at the pick point. The command should be repeated.
2. **PDMODE**↵

   3↵

   POINT↵

   (Pick the point)

3. [&X-Point]*^C^Cpdmode;3;point

Example 4

1. This command, named **Notation**, could be used by a drawing checker or instructor. It allows them to circle features on a drawing and then add a leader and text. It first sets the color to red, then draws a circle, snaps a leader to the nearest point that is picked on the circle, and prompts for the text. User input for text is provided, then a cancel returns the Command: prompt and the color is set to Bylayer.
2. **–COLOR**↵

   RED↵

   CIRCLE↵

   (Pick center point)

   (Pick radius)

   DIM↵

LEADER.↵

NEA.↵

(Pick a point on the circle)

(Pick end of leader)

(Press [Enter] *for automatic shoulder)*

(Enter text)↵

(Press [Esc] *to cancel)*

–COLOR.↵

BYLAYER.↵

3. [&Notation]^C^C-color;red;circle;\\dim;leader;nea;\\;\^C-color;bylayer

---

PROFESSIONAL TIP

Some commands, such as the **COLOR** command, display a dialog box. Menu macros can provide input to the command line, but cannot control dialog boxes. To access the command line version of a command, prefix the command name with a hyphen (–).

Example 5

1. A repeating command named **Multisquare**, which draws one-inch squares oriented at a 0° horizontal angle.

2. **RECTANG.↵**

   (Pick lower-left corner)

   @1,1.↵

3. [&Multisquare]*^C^Crectang;\@1,1

EXERCISE 22-1

❏ Copy the acad.mnu file and rename the copy EX22-1.MNU. Use the renamed copy for this exercise.

❏ Use your text editor and put the following three commands in a new ***POP12 menu titled **Custom**.

   ❏ [Copy Two M]—Make multiple copies after two selections.

   ❏ [Rotate45]—Rotate an object 45° counterclockwise.

   ❏ [Fillet .5]—A repeating command that applies a .5 fillet.

❏ All commands should display their mnemonic keys.

❏ Write out the commands before you enter them in the computer.

❏ Save EX22-1.MNU for the next exercise.

Creating Help Strings for Pull-Down Menus

Help strings are the brief descriptions on the status line describing the menu item currently highlighted. These can provide helpful information to those who are using your menu. It becomes very important to create appropriate help strings when you are adding new items to the menu, since these items may be unfamiliar to even experienced AutoCAD users.

To get an idea of the ideal content of a help string for your menu item, carefully review some of AutoCAD's existing help strings. Help string definitions are placed in the ***HELPSTRINGS section in your menu file, but references to a help string can be placed throughout your menu file. For example, if a 0.5" wide polyline option is added to a pull-down menu, the menu code might look like this:

    [0.5 Polyline]^C^Cpline;\w;0.5;0.5;

To create a help string for this selection, open your menu file and find the ***HELPSTRINGS section. The beginning of the ***HELPSTRINGS section looks like this:

```
***HELPSTRINGS
ID_2doptim       [Set viewport to 2D wireframe:  SHADEMODE 2]
ID_3darray       [Creates a three-dimensional array:  3DARRAY]
ID_3dclip        [Starts 3DORBIT and opens the Adjust Clipping Planes
window: 3DCLIP]
ID_3dclipbk      [Toggles the back clipping plane on or off in the 3D Orbit
Adjust Clipping Planes window:  DVIEW ALL CL B]
ID_3dclipfr      [Toggles the front clipping plane on or off in the 3D Orbit
Adjust Clipping Planes window:  DVIEW ALL CL F]
ID_3dcorbit      [Starts the 3DORBIT command with continuous orbit active
in the 3D view: 3DCORBIT]
```

The format for an entry in the ***HELPSTRINGS section is as follows:

ID_*name tag* [*Help message*]

The ID_ *name tag* should be unique. Duplicate name tags can cause unexpected results. Do a text search using your text editor's "find" function to see if the name tag you select is already in use. The help message should be short enough to fit along the bottom of the screen, and as clearly worded as possible. A search of the acad.mnu file reveals that the name tag selected for the wide polyline (ID_Wpline) is not already in use. To prepare the help string for use, find the ***HELPSTRINGS section of your menu file and enter the following line:

ID_Wpline [Draws a 0.5" wide polyline.]

Now that the help string definition has been created, any menu item referencing the ID_Wpline tag will display this help string. To place a reference to this help string, you need to precede the menu item label with the name tag as follows:

ID_Wpline [0.5 Polyline]^C^Cpline;\w;0.5;0.5;

When the **0.5 Polyline** menu item is highlighted, the help string "Draws a 0.5" wide polyline" is displayed on the status line.

PROFESSIONAL TIP

A new help string can be placed anywhere within the help string section. Since this section is rather extensive, it can be helpful to place all of your custom help string definitions together at the bottom. This makes them easy to locate when you need to edit them.

EXERCISE 22-2

❑ Use your text editor and open the menu file EX22-1.MNU from Exercise 22-1.
❑ Using the EX22-1.MNU file, create a help string for each of the three new commands you developed in Exercise 22-1.
❑ Test each command to be sure each help string is displayed properly.
❑ Save the menu file for the next exercise.

Creating and Using Accelerator Keys

AutoCAD supports user-defined accelerator keys. The accelerator keys are the keystrokes available when you specify **Windows standard accelerator keys** in the **Windows Standard Behavior** area of the **User Preferences** tab of the **Options** dialog box. These include [Ctrl]+[C] as **COPYCLIP**, [Ctrl]+[S] as **QSAVE**, and [Ctrl]+[P] as **PLOT**. If you remove the check mark from the **Windows standard accelerator keys** check box, these keystrokes are set to be compatible with older releases of AutoCAD and the Windows standard accelerator keys cannot be used.

The accelerator key definitions are contained in the ***ACCELERATORS section of your menu file:

```
***ACCELERATORS
ID_Hyperlink    [CONTROL+"K"]
[CONTROL+"L"]^O
[CONTROL+"R"]^V
ID_Copyclip     [CONTROL+"C"]
ID_New          [CONTROL+"N"]
ID_Open         [CONTROL+"O"]
ID_Print        [CONTROL+"P"]
ID_Save         [CONTROL+"S"]
ID_Pasteclip    [CONTROL+"V"]
ID_Cutclip      [CONTROL+"X"]
ID_Redo         [CONTROL+"Y"]
ID_U            [CONTROL+"Z"]
ID_Modify       [CONTROL+"1"]
ID_Content      [CONTROL+"2"]
ID_dbConnect    [CONTROL+"6"]
ID_VBARun       [ALT+"F8"]
ID_VBAIDE       [ALT+"F11"]
```

For 2000i Users...

Most of the accelerator keys in the AutoCAD 2000i menu file include a "TOOLBAR+" prefix in the keystroke definition. This restricts the search for the ID name tag to the toolbars section of the menu file.

There are two different ways to specify an accelerator key. The second entry defines the [Ctrl]+[L] keystroke as an Ortho mode toggle. This method allows you to specify the keystroke as a label, followed by any menu code required. For example, to define a [Ctrl]+[I] keystroke to start the **DDINSERT** command, enter the following line into your ***ACCELERATORS section:

```
[CONTROL+"I"]^C^CDDINSERT
```

It is also possible to create macros associated with accelerator keys. Simply enter the menu code just as you would for any other menu area. For example, to create a [Ctrl]+[SHIFT]+[A] accelerator key that automatically sets up A-size drawing limits and draws a 0.15 wide polyline border, enter the following in the ***ACCELERATORS section:

```
[CONTROL+SHIFT+"A"]^C^CLIMITS;;11,8.5;W;0.15;RECTANG;0.5,0.5;10.5,8;ZOOM;A
```

The second accelerator key definition type references an ID_*name tag* for a menu pick as the source code, followed by the keystroke definition. Any item in the menu file that displays a name tag can be used in this manner. For example, under the **Viewports** cascading menu in the **View** pull-down menu, the **4 Viewports** selection includes the label ID_Vports4. Searching through the menu for this item reveals the following code for this menu pick:

```
ID_Vports4 [&4 Viewports]^C^C_–vports _4
```

The ID_Vports4 tag can be referenced in the ***ACCELERATORS section to execute the menu code listed for this item as follows:

```
ID_Vports4 [CONTROL+"4"]
```

Pressing [Ctrl]+[4] now activates the **4 Viewports** menu selection. Basically, it is the same as entering the following under ***ACCELERATORS:

[CONTROL+"4"]^C^C_–vports _4

Either way works equally well, but it is unnecessary to duplicate existing menu code if you reference the name tag.

PROFESSIONAL TIP   Accelerators have some specific limitations. For example, an accelerator cannot pause for user input or use repeating commands.

EXERCISE 22-3

❑ Use your text editor and open the menu file you used in Exercise 22-2.
❑ Create an accelerator key for each of the three new commands you developed in Exercise 22-1.
❑ Test each command to be sure that each accelerator functions properly.

Some Notes about Pull-Down Menus

Here are a few more things to keep in mind when developing pull-down menus:
- Pull-down menus are disabled during the following commands:
  ✓ **DTEXT**, after the rotation angle is entered.
  ✓ **SKETCH**, after the record increment is set.
- Pull-down menus that are longer than the screen display are truncated to fit on the screen.
- The object snap shortcut menu is named POP0. It can contain items that reference other pull-down and screen menus.

AutoCAD Custom Guide **4**

MENU GROUPS AND PARTIAL MENUS

In addition to the **MENU** command, two other menu file handling commands are provided. The **MENU** command initially loads a base menu in its default condition, and provides no menu display options. However, it is possible to load multiple menus at one time and use only the desired elements of each, or modify the way a base menu is displayed by using the **MENULOAD** command.

The purpose of the **MENULOAD** command is to allow loading of partial menus. This allows you to add additional options from a different menu to your base menu (e.g. acad menu). Thus, you can customize your menu so you have access to desired features from two or more different menu files.

AutoCAD menu files are assigned menu group names. For example, near the beginning of the acad.mnu file, you will find the line:

***MENUGROUP=ACAD

This assigns the group name ACAD to this menu. However, if you open the sample menu file acetmain.mnu, which is found in the Acad2000\Express folder, you will find the specification:

***MENUGROUP=EXPRESS

This identifies items in this menu as being in the EXPRESS menu group. This allows you to identify items from different menus easily. For example, when working with screen menus, your calls to submenus were preceded by ACAD. This identified the group containing the desired menu. In Chapter 21, your call to the TEST screen submenu appeared as:

$S=ACAD.TEST

If the acetmain menu was loaded and also had a screen submenu named TEST, your menu call would specify from which group to obtain the definition for the TEST menu.

If you have not changed the group name and you try to load your mymenu menu with **MENULOAD** while the acad menu is already loaded, you will get an error message. This is because these two menus both use the same group name. You can force AutoCAD to replace existing group definitions with newly loaded menu data.

The **MENULOAD** command can be accessed by picking **Customize Menus...** from the **Tools** pull-down menu, or it can be typed directly at the Command: prompt. Entering the **MENULOAD** command displays the **Menu Customization** dialog box, as shown in Figure 22-5. There are several options available:

MENULOAD

Tools
➥ Customize
 Menus...

- **Menu Groups.** This list shows the currently loaded menu groups. Items on this list can be highlighted in preparation for other actions.
- **File Name.** This edit box shows the name of the currently selected menu file.
- **Replace All.** A check in this check box forces newly loaded group names to replace existing duplicate file names.
- **Unload.** This button unloads the definition for the menu group highlighted in the **Menu Groups** list box.
- **Load.** This button loads the menu file specified in the **File Name** edit box and places its associated group name in the **Menu Groups** list box.
- **Browse.** Select this button to specify a new menu file name for loading. It displays the **Select Menu File** dialog box and allows you to select a menu file.

To practice loading an additional menu, use the **Select Menu File** dialog box to find the acetmain.mnu file. Remember that when loading a menu template file, you must first specify *.mnu in the **Files of type:** drop-down list.

After selecting the acetmain.mnu file, you are returned to the **Menu Customization** dialog box. The acetmain.mnu file and path name appear in the **File Name** edit box. Pick the **Load** button to load the menu definition and the new group name is displayed in the **Menu Groups** list box.

Figure 22-5.
The **Menu Groups** tab of the **Menu Customization** dialog box.

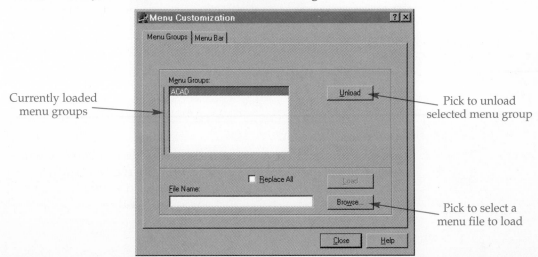

NOTE

The Acad2000\Express folder is only present if a full installation of AutoCAD was performed.

Now that you have loaded an additional menu definition, you can specify which menus to display. First, pick the **Menu Bar** tab, Figure 22-6. The features of this tab are as follows:

- **Menu Group.** This drop-down list provides access to the currently loaded menu group names. The currently selected menu group name is displayed here.
- **Menus.** All pull-down menu names defined in the selected group are displayed here.
- **Menu Bar.** This list shows the pull-down menus that are currently available on the menu bar. The top item of the list takes a position at the far left of the menu bar, and each subsequent menu title is displayed to the right of the previous one.
- **Insert.** Picking this button inserts the currently highlighted menu in the **Menus** list into the highlighted position in the **Menu Bar** list.
- **Remove.** Removes the currently highlighted menu title from the **Menu Bar** list.
- **Remove All.** Removes all menu titles from the **Menu Bar** list.

The EXPRESS menu group displays only one menu name, because that is all that is contained in the menu file. Other menu files may display one or more menu names. By selecting the desired group name and adjusting the various individual menu titles, you can completely customize the menu bar to have only the pull-down menus that are necessary for your current project.

Figure 22-6.
The **Menu Bar** tab of the **Menu Customization** dialog box.

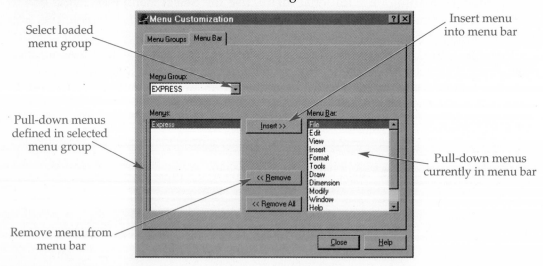

PROFESSIONAL TIP

It is also possible to customize the pull-down menu bar with only one menu group loaded. You can remove unwanted menus as desired, and replace them later if needed.

Image tile menus contain graphic symbols displayed in dialog boxes. They appear in certain dialog boxes, such as the **3D Objects** dialog box, Figure 22-7. This dialog box is accessed by selecting **3D Surfaces...** from the **Surfaces** cascading menu in the **Draw** pull-down menu.

The dialog box shown contains several small boxes. Each box contains a small image. These displays are AutoCAD slides.

The slides are saved in a file created with the **SLIDELIB** program. This DOS-based program creates a file with an SLB extension. The slides can be used in an image tile menu by entering the required data in the menu file. Chapter 28 of *AutoCAD and its Applications—Basics* explains the use of the **SLIDELIB** program.

Image Tile Menu Creation

The addition of image tile menus can enhance the operation of AutoCAD. However, you must create images using certain guidelines:

- ✓ Keep images simple. This saves display time and storage space. The image can be a simplified version of the actual symbol.
- ✓ When making slides, fill the screen with the image to be sure the image tile is filled. Center long items on the screen using **PAN**. This centers them in the image tile.
- ✓ Use image tile menus for symbols only. Do not clutter your program with image tile menus of text information. This slows the system down.
- ✓ AutoCAD does not display solid filled areas in image tiles. If you use fills, such as arrowheads, shade the display prior to making the slide image file.
- ✓ A maximum of 20 slides can be displayed in one image tile menu. The names of the images are automatically displayed in a list box to the left of the image tiles. Image names (up to 19 characters) are displayed in the list box.
- ✓ If you have more than 20 slides in an image tile menu, AutoCAD creates additional "pages," each containing a **Next** and a **Previous** button for changing pages. The **OK** and **Cancel** buttons are automatically provided in the image tile menu.
- ✓ If an item label in an image tile menu has a space before the first character, no image is displayed for that label, but the label name is shown. This can be used to execute other commands or call other image tile menus.

Figure 22-7.
The **3D Objects** dialog box has an image tile menu.

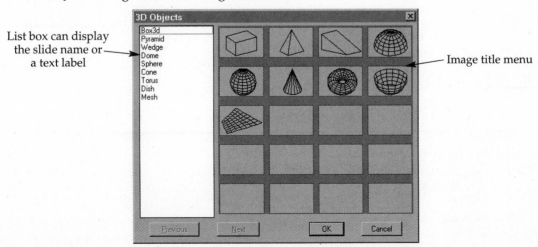

List box can display the slide name or a text label

Image title menu

Making Symbols and Slides for the Image Tile Menu

Image tile menus can be used for a variety of purposes, but they are most commonly used to display images of blocks. Regardless of the types of symbols used, follow these steps when making image tile menus:

1. Draw the symbol or block.
2. Center the drawing on the display screen. When the drawing appears in the image tile menu, it is displayed in a box with a 1.5:1 ratio of width to height. With your drawing on the screen, switch to a layout tab (paper space), and create a 3 × 2 viewport. Now, **ZOOM Extents** and then switch back to model space. The drawing is now at the correct ratio.
3. Make a slide of the symbol using the **MSLIDE** command.
4. Write the **SLIDELIB** file.
5. Write the image tile menu file and test it.

Draw the three shapes shown in Figure 22-8. They represent a table, desk, and chair. Draw them any size you wish. Save each as a wblock, and name them TABLE, DESK, and CHAIR. Do not include text or attributes.

Use the **MSLIDE** command to make a slide of each block, centering the slide as previously discussed. Give the slides the same name as the block. This completes the third step. Now you will use the **SLIDELIB** program to make the slide file.

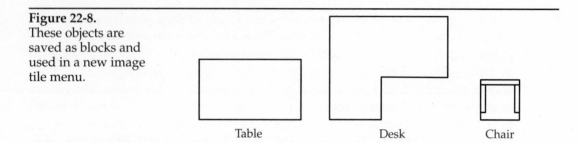

Figure 22-8.
These objects are saved as blocks and used in a new image tile menu.

Table   Desk   Chair

Using the SLIDELIB Program for an Image Tile Menu

The **SLIDELIB** program operates in DOS and allows you to create a list of slide (SLD extension) files. This list of slides can then be used for slide shows and image tile menus.

To use the **SLIDELIB** program, you must launch the MS-DOS Prompt from your Windows taskbar. You can also use the **SHELL** command from within AutoCAD. Either method opens an MS DOS window.

The creation of a slide file called FURNITUR begins as follows:

    Command: **SHELL**↲
    OS Command: ↲

You will now see the following in the MS DOS window:

    Microsoft(R) Windows NT(TM)
    (C) Copyright 1985-1996 Microsoft Corp.
    C:\Program Files\ACAD2000> **SUPPORT\SLIDELIB FURNITUR**↲
    SLIDELIB 1.2 (3/8/89)
    (C) Copyright 1987-1989,1994,1995 Autodesk, Inc.
      All Rights Reserved
    TABLE.↲
    CHAIR.↲
    DESK.↲
    ↲
    ↲

The second [Enter] on a blank line after the last slide name exits the **SLIDELIB** program. Check to see that the slide library file was created by listing all files with an SLB extension.

       C:\Program Files\Acad2000> **DIR *.SLB**⏎

The file should be listed as furnitur.slb. Type EXIT to return to the AutoCAD graphics window.

       C:\Program Files\Acad2000> **EXIT**⏎

A second method of creating a slide library involves using an existing list of slides in a text file. This method is useful if you add slide names to a text file (TXT extension) as the slides are made. The method is discussed in Chapter 28 of *AutoCAD and its Applications—Basics*.

Creating an Image Tile Menu File Listing

Load your copy of the acad.mnu file into the text editor and page through the file until you find the ***image section. You can insert your new image tile menu between any of the existing ones. Be sure to leave a space between the previous and following menus.

Begin a menu called furniture below the last image tile heading, **image_vporti. The first item in the menu is used as the title. If you neglect to put a title here, the first line of the menu will be used as the title. Your new menu should look like the following:

```
**image_furniture
[Select Furniture]
[furnitur(Table)]^C^C–insert;table
[furnitur(Desk)]^C^C–insert;desk
[furnitur(Chair)]^C^C–insert;chair
[ Plants]$I=plants $I=*
```

Notice the space after the left bracket in the last entry, [Plants]. This produces a label without an image tile. This label is used to execute other commands, or as in this case, display other image tile menus.

These are called *branching* image tile menus. In this example, the Plants menu may show images of several types of plants. You can have as many branching image tile menus as needed.

The new image tile menu is still not usable because there is no selection that calls this menu to the screen. The **Draw** pull-down menu is a good place to put the call for this menu. Insert the following line in the pull-down menu:

       [Furniture]$I=image_furniture $I=*

The first part of this entry, $I=image_furniture, calls the new furniture menu. The second part, $I=*, displays the menu and makes the items selectable.

Save the file and use the **MENU** command to reload the menu. Test all the items in the menu and correct any problems. The new image tile menu should look like the one in Figure 22-9.

EXERCISE 22-4

❏ Using your text editor, create an image tile menu named EX22-4 using three blocks that you have on file.
❏ Plan this menu so that you can add to it in the future.
❏ Remember to include an entry in the **Draw** pull-down menu that calls the new icon menu.

Figure 22-9.
This customized image tile menu uses previously created objects.

A block can be selected
with the label or the image

A label with no
image is used to
initiate a command
or access another
menu

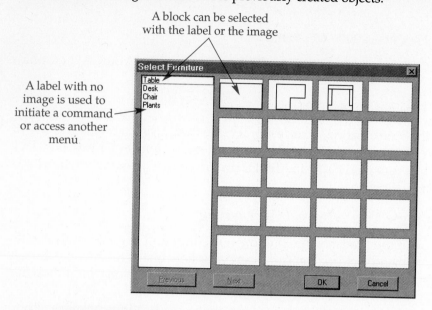

PROFESSIONAL TIP    Your primary goal in developing menus is to eliminate extra steps required to perform a function. The end result is that you can execute a thought or idea with one pick, rather than labor through a series of commands and options.

Chapter Test

Answer the following questions on a separate sheet of paper.

1. How many items can a pull-down menu contain?
2. Define the following pull-down menu characters.
    A. ->
    B. <-
    C. <-<-
    D. &
3. Provide the character(s) required to perform the following functions:
    A. Insert a separator line across the pull-down menu.
    B. "Gray out" characters.
    C. Place a check mark before the menu item.
    D. Specify a menu shortcut key.
4. What code is used to make pull-down menus display and be selectable?
5. Name two ways to represent a return in a menu item.
6. How many pull-down menus can be displayed on one screen?
7. How wide is a pull-down menu?
8. What is the function of the following DIESEL expression?

    [$(if,$(getvar,snapmode),!.)Snap]^B

9. What is the function of the following menu item characters?
    A. $p3=*
    B. $p4.1=~
    C. $p6.7=!.

10. Interpret the following menu item:

    ^C^Crectang;\@1,1

11. Why is it a good idea to make a copy of the acad.mnu file before you begin experimenting or customizing?

12. Write the general syntax for an entry in the ***HELPSTRINGS section of the acad.mnu file.

13. You wish to create a new macro that executes the **PURGE** command, and uses the **Blocks** option. Write the macro as it would appear in the menu file, and the correct notation in the ***HELPSTRINGS section of the acad.mnu file.
    A. Menu file
    B. Help string

14. What is the key combination called that allows you to press the [Ctrl] key and one additional key to execute a command?

15. Write the proper notation to define the type of key mentioned in Question 14 using the [M] key to execute the **MVIEW** command.

16. What is the purpose of the **MENULOAD** command?

17. Which command is used to create the slide file?

18. What is the first line of an image tile menu called?

19. List the steps required to create an image tile menu.

20. Describe the function of the following entry in an image tile menu file.

    [Fittings]$I=fittings $I=*

Drawing Problems

1. Create a dimensioning pull-down menu. Place as many dimensioning commands as you need in the menu. Use cascading submenus if necessary. One or more of the submenus should be dimensioning variables. Include menu shortcut keys.

2. Create a pull-down menu for 3D objects. Add it to your copy of acad.mnu. Include menu shortcut keys. The contents of the menu should include the following items:

   - 3D solid objects
   - 3D surface objects
   - **ELEV** command
   - **3DFACE** command
   - **VPOINT** command
   - **VPORTS** command
   - **HIDE** command

3. Create a new pull-down menu named **Special**. The menu should include the following drawing and editing commands:

   - **LINE**
   - **ARC**
   - **CIRCLE**
   - **POLYLINE**
   - **POLYGON**
   - **RECTANGLE**
   - **DTEXT**
   - **ERASE**
   - **MOVE**
   - **COPY**
   - **STRETCH**
   - **TRIM**
   - **EXTEND**
   - **CHAMFER**
   - **FILLET**

   Use cascading submenus if necessary. Include a separator line between the drawing and editing commands, and specify appropriate menu shortcut keys.

4. Create a single pull-down menu used to insert a variety of blocks or symbols. These symbols can be for any drawing discipline that you use. Use cascading menus and menu shortcut keys if necessary. This menu should have a special group name that will enable it to be loaded with the **MENULOAD** command. This menu can be added to the existing pull-downs in the ACAD menu, or it can replace one of them.

5. Choose one of the previous problems and create help strings for each of the new menu items. Use existing defined help strings whenever possible. When you define new help strings, always do a search of the menu file to see if the string is being used.

6. Refer to Problem 3. Create an accelerator key for each of the drawing and editing commands in that problem. Search the menu file to see if any of the commands are currently tagged with an accelerator key to avoid duplication.

7. Construct an image tile menu of a symbol library that you use in a specific discipline of drafting or design. This menu can be selected from the **Draw** pull-down menu, or from a new pull-down menu of your own creation. Use as many image tiles as needed. You can call additional image tile menus from the initial one. The following are examples of disciplines that could be used:
   - Mechanical
   - Architectural
   - Civil
   - Structural
   - Piping
   - HVAC
   - Electrical
   - Electronics
   - PC board layout
   - Geometric tolerancing
   - 3D construction

8. Modify the existing **3D Objects** dialog box and image tile menu to include additional 3D objects of your own creation. Create additional menus, or "pages," if needed.

9. Create a new image tile menu and dialog box that illustrates a variety of hatch patterns. When an image is selected, it should set a specific hatch pattern, then execute the **HATCH** command so that the user can set the scale and angle for the hatch pattern. Be sure to include the proper name of the hatch pattern in your menu file so that the user does not have to enter it when the **HATCH** command is executed.

10. Create a new image tile menu that provides images of a variety of dimensioning styles. When a specific image is picked, it should automatically set the appropriate dimension variables in order to achieve the appearance of the dimension in the selected image. Test each of these selections carefully before incorporating them into the file. This may be an excellent menu for using branching image tile dialog boxes in order to display variations in different dimension styles.

Customizing Tablet Menus

Learning Objectives

After completing this chapter, you will be able to:
- Configure and use the AutoCAD tablet menu template.
- Customize the AutoCAD tablet menu.
- Create a new tablet menu.

If you have a digitizer, the AutoCAD standard tablet menu is an alternative to keyboard entry or picking commands on screen. The tablet menu template supplied by Autodesk is a thick piece of plastic that measures approximately 11″ × 12″. Printed on it are many of the commands available in AutoCAD. See Figure 23-1. Some commands are accompanied by small symbols, or icons, that indicate the function of the command. The menu template is helpful because it provides a clear display of AutoCAD's various commands.

Like the screen menus, the tablet menu can be customized. Notice the empty space at the top of the template. This space is available for adding commands and symbols. You can have several overlays for this area.

Most people discover that many of the commands in the AutoCAD tablet menu are not used for specific types of drawings, so they construct their own tablet menus. This process is similar to creating custom screen menus and is the focus of this chapter.

USING THE AUTOCAD TABLET MENU

To use a tablet menu, the digitizer and digitizing tablet must first be configured for your specific hardware configuration and the type of menu you will be using. When you initially configure AutoCAD to recognize a digitizer, the entire surface of the digitizing tablet represents the screen pointing area. The **TABLET** command allows you to configure the digitizer to recognize the tablet menu template, or overlay. When using this command, you inform AutoCAD of the exact layout of the menu areas and the size and position of the screen pointing area. Depending on the type of pointing device you are using with Microsoft Windows, there are additional aspects of tablet configuration to be considered.

Using a Digitizer for All Windows Applications

If you are using your digitizer as the sole pointing device for all Windows applications, you will require a driver called WINTAB. The WINTAB driver configures a digitizer to act as a mouse for Windows-based applications, but permits you to use the tablet screen pointing area and menus when running AutoCAD. This is called *absolute mode*.

You must install the WINTAB driver as your system pointing device in Windows before starting AutoCAD. WINTAB drivers are supplied by the digitizing tablet manufacturers, not by Autodesk. If you have access to an online service, you can typically download the current WINTAB driver for your particular digitizing tablet.

Tablet Menu Layout

The AutoCAD tablet menu presents commands in related groups. Referring to Figure 23-1, notice the headings below each menu area. The headings identify the types of commands available. Find the **TABLET** command in the **TOOLS** section of the menu. This command is used to configure, calibrate, and toggle your tablet.

Figure 23-1.
The AutoCAD standard tablet menu template. The large area across the top of the template is used for customization. (Autodesk, Inc.)

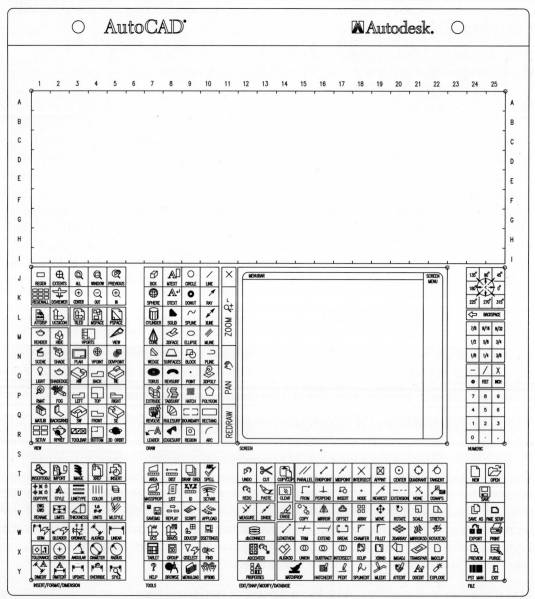

AutoCAD and its Applications—Advanced

The available menu space near the top of the template is called Menu Area 1. As you develop your own customized tablet menu, make a point of taking advantage of this unused space. Suggestions and instructions for customizing Menu Area 1 appear later in this chapter.

Configuring the Tablet Menu

As previously mentioned, the **TABLET** command is used to tell AutoCAD the layout of the tablet menu. It prompts for three corners of each menu area and the number of columns and rows in each area. The screen pointing area is defined by picking two opposite corners. Three corners of each menu area are marked with small donuts. As you read the following example, look at Figure 23-2. It illustrates the configuration of the AutoCAD standard tablet menu and shows the donuts marking the menu area corners.

Command: **TABLET**↵
Enter an option [ON/OFF/CAL/CFG]: **CFG**↵
Enter number of tablet menus desired (0-4): **4**↵

Figure 23-2.
Small donuts mark the corners of the menu areas on the AutoCAD tablet menu template.

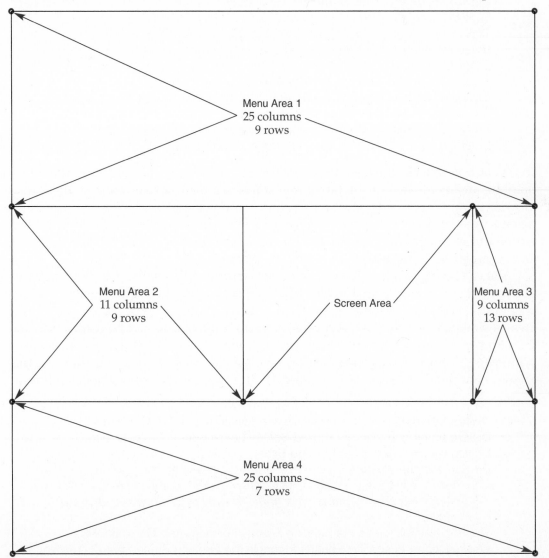

If tablet menus are currently in use and the same number is specified for menu areas, AutoCAD issues the following prompt:

> Do you want to realign tablet menus? [Yes/No] <N>: **Y**↵

Next, you are prompted to select the points that define each menu area with the digitizer pointing device.

> Digitize upper-left corner of menu area 1: *(pick the donut at the upper-left corner)*
> Digitize lower-left corner of menu area 1: *(pick the point)*
> Digitize lower-right corner of menu area 1: *(pick the point)*
> Enter the number of columns for menu area 1: *(n-nnnn)* <25>: ↵
> Enter the number of rows for menu area 1: *(n-nnnn)* <9>: ↵

You have now given AutoCAD the location of Menu Area 1 and specified the number of selection boxes that are available. The command continues with Menu Area 2:

> Digitize upper-left corner of menu area 2: *(pick the point)*
> Digitize lower-left corner of menu area 2: *(pick the point)*
> Digitize lower-right corner of menu area 2: *(pick the point)*
> Enter the number of columns for menu area 2: *(n-nnnn)* <11>: ↵
> Enter the number of rows for menu area 2: *(n-nnnn)* <9>: ↵
> Digitize upper-left corner of menu area 3: *(pick the point)*
> Digitize lower-left corner of menu area 3: *(pick the point)*
> Digitize lower-right corner of menu area 3: *(pick the point)*
> Enter the number of columns for menu area 3: *(n-nnnn)* <9>: ↵
> Enter the number of rows for menu area 3: *(n-nnnn)* <13>: ↵
> Digitize upper-left corner of menu area 4: *(pick the point)*
> Digitize lower-left corner of menu area 4: *(pick the point)*
> Digitize lower-right corner of menu area 4: *(pick the point)*
> Enter the number of columns for menu area 4: *(n-nnnn)* <25>: ↵
> Enter the number of rows for menu area 4: *(n-nnnn)* <7>: ↵

Next, you must locate the opposite corners of the screen pointing area. The screen pointing area is an area of the tablet that translates the digitizer motion into cursor movement on your screen. This mimics mouse movement. The screen pointing area maps to the computer display *absolutely*. This means that when you are pointing within the screen pointing area, the digitizer can be used to access windows, menus, and other applications outside of AutoCAD's drawing area.

You can configure two different screen pointing areas, one fixed and one floating. The *fixed* screen pointing area is the entire tablet by default. You can reconfigure the area of the tablet that is used as the fixed screen pointing area to match the smaller area as shown in Figure 23-2. A *floating* screen pointing area can be configured and then used to access menus and other applications outside the drawing area, such as Windows system menus and dialog boxes. You can then designate a function that toggles between the two areas. The screen pointing areas are configured as follows:

> Do you want to respecify the Fixed Screen Pointing Area? [Yes/No] <N>: **Y**↵
> Digitize lower-left corner of Fixed Screen pointing area: *(pick the point)*
> Digitize upper-right corner of Fixed Screen pointing area: *(pick the point)*
> Do you want to specify the Floating Screen pointing area? [Yes/No] <N>: **Y**↵
> Do you want the Floating Screen Pointing Area to be the same size as the Fixed Screen Pointing Area? [Yes/No] <Y>: *(enter Y or N; if you enter Y, digitize the lower-left and upper-right corners of the floating screen pointing area when prompted.)*
> The F12 Key will toggle the Floating Screen Pointing Area ON and OFF.
> Would you like to specify a button to toggle the Floating Screen Area? [Yes/No] <N>: *(enter Y or N)*

If you choose to use a digitizer puck button as the toggle, the following prompt is issued:

> Press any non-pick button that you wish to designate as the toggle for the Floating Screen Area.

Press the button of your choice. Do not press the pick button.

Use the same configuration process outlined above when configuring the tablet for your custom menus. The tablet configuration is saved in the acad2000.cfg file, which is in your Acad2000 folder. The system reads this file when loading AutoCAD to determine what kind of equipment you are using. It also determines which menu is current.

Configuring the AutoCAD standard tablet menu can be done in more simple fashion by selecting the **Reconfig** option from the **Tablet:** screen menu. First enable the screen menu display by activating the **Display screen menu** check box in the **Display** tab of the **Options** dialog box. Then pick **TOOLS2** from the AutoCAD root menu. Next, pick **Tablet** and then select **Reconfig**. The **Tablet:** screen menu options are shown in Figure 23-3.

When the **Reconfig** option is selected, the configuration prompts appear as shown in the previous example. However, you do not need to enter the number of columns and rows. The **Reconfig** option assumes you are realigning the AutoCAD tablet menu template. Therefore, it only requires the locations of the menu areas and the screen pointing area. Use this screen menu option when you wish to return to the AutoCAD standard tablet menu after using a custom menu.

Figure 23-3.
Selecting **Reconfig** from the **Tablet:** screen menu allows you to quickly configure the AutoCAD standard tablet menu.

```
AutoCAD
****
Tablet:

Calibrat
Config
Reconfig
Re-DfCfg

On
Off
Yes
No

Orthognl
Affine
Projectv
```

NOTE

Shortcut menus are not available during the digitizer configuration process. When you finish configuring the digitizer, shortcut menus are available to both the mouse and the digitizer.

CUSTOMIZING THE TABLET MENU

The empty upper portion of the AutoCAD tablet menu can be used to add custom commands. As mentioned earlier, this portion of the tablet is Menu Area 1. It contains 225 selection boxes that can be programmed for additional commands, macros, scripts, and blocks. It is a good place to locate frequently used symbols and shapes.

An overlay containing block names and drawings can be plotted and slipped under the plastic menu template. Several overlays can be used for different disciplines, and structured to operate in different ways.

Plan the Overlay

Before adding items to the AutoCAD tablet menu, take time to think about what the overlay should include. Ask yourself the following questions:
- ✓ For what kinds of drawings will the overlay be used?
- ✓ What commands or macros should be a part of the overlay?
- ✓ What kind of symbols should be placed in the overlay?
- ✓ Should the symbols be stored as blocks or drawing files?
- ✓ Which symbols and blocks are used most often?
- ✓ If the symbols are blocks, should they be stored in a prototype drawing or a template file?

After answering these questions, you will be able to lay out a quality overlay. The next step is to draw the overlay.

Draw the Overlay

Part of your customization plan should be to draw or sketch the menu area before creating the actual drawing file for the custom menu. The quickest way to make an accurate representation of the menu is to plot Menu Area 1 from the Tablet 2000 drawing file. This drawing is located in the Acad2000\Sample folder. The following steps should be used to create the drawing of Menu Area 1:

1. Open the drawing file named Tablet 2000.dwg.
2. Perform a **ZOOM Window** and zoom into the drawing around Menu Area 1. See Figure 23-4.
3. Freeze all layers except the Borders layer. The drawing should now appear as shown in Figure 23-5A.
4. Make a new layer named Area1, and give it the color cyan.
5. Use the **PLINE** command to trace over the outline of Menu Area 1.
6. Draw a vertical line between two tick marks on the right or left side and array it in 24 columns. Use object snap modes to set the correct spacing. See Figure 23-5B.
7. Draw a horizontal line between two tick marks at the top or bottom and array it in 8 rows. Use object snap modes to set the correct spacing.
8. Erase the remaining lines in the drawing outside Menu Area 1. See Figure 23-5C.
9. Plot the drawing on B-size or larger paper. A plot using a 1.5 = 1 or 2 = 1 scale provides a larger drawing, which is easier to work with for initial menu design purposes.
10. Erase all unnecessary layers.
11. Save the drawing with a new name (such as menu area 1.dwg) for future use.

Make several copies of your drawing. Pencil in the command and symbol names. Try more than one arrangement based on some of the considerations previously discussed. Keep in mind the purpose of the overlay you are making. Symbols that are used frequently should be placed along the outer edges for quick selection.

Figure 23-4.
A representation of Menu Area 1 in the Tablet 2000 drawing. The area contains a grid of 225 selection boxes within its borders.

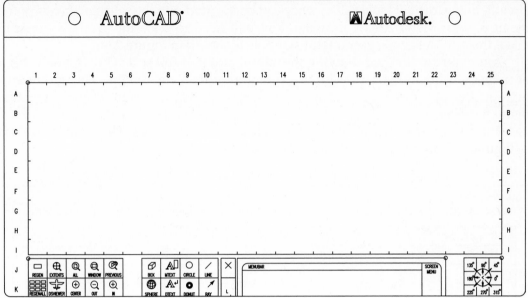

Figure 23-5.
A—The Tablet 2000 drawing in its unedited form, after freezing each layer except the Borders layer.
B—Menu Area 1 after drawing vertical lines.
C—The completed drawing of Menu Area 1.

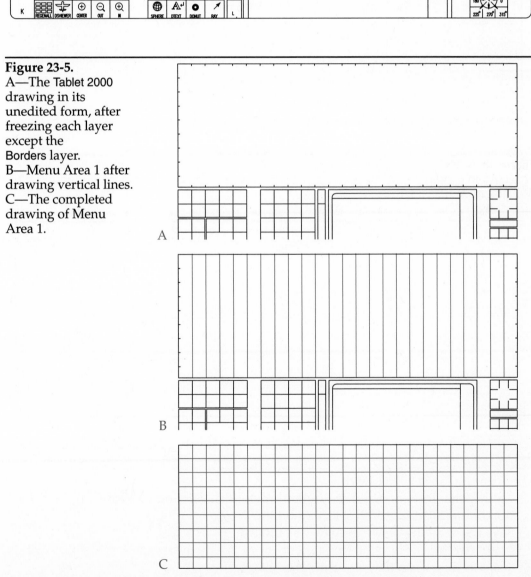

Complete the Menu Drawing

The next step in creating your customized AutoCAD tablet menu is to draw the symbols in the menu. This should be relatively easy if the symbols you are using are already in the form of blocks. If so, they can be inserted into the selection boxes of the menu in your Menu Area 1 drawing. You will need to scale the symbols down to make them fit. A sample menu with symbols is shown in Figure 23-6.

After you are finished drawing the menu, plot it at full scale (1 = 1). Use vellum or polyester film and wet ink. Use black ink rather than colored ink. This produces a high-quality plot that can be clearly seen when slipped under the AutoCAD tablet menu template.

The custom menu area can be modified to suit your needs. The symbols shown in Figure 23-7 are used for isometric process piping drawings.

Figure 23-6.
Symbols saved as blocks are inserted into the boxes of the menu in the Menu Area 1 drawing.

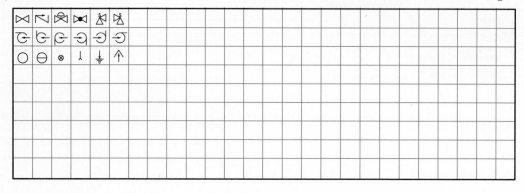

Figure 23-7.
This custom overlay for Menu Area 1 is used for isometric process piping drawings. (Willamette Industries, Inc.)

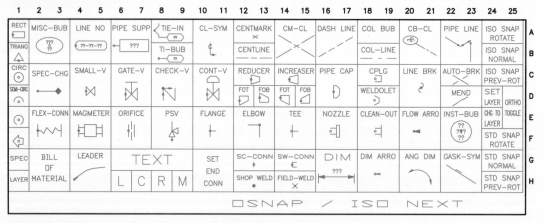

Write the Menu File

The final step in customizing the AutoCAD tablet menu is to write the menu file in the ***TABLET1 section of the acad.mnu file. Load the file into your text editor and find the menu section ***TABLET1. It should look like the following:

```
***TABLET1
**TABLET1STD
[A-1]\
[A-2]\
[A-3]\
[A-4]\
[A-5]\
```

Referring to the tablet menu template in Figure 23-4, notice the column and row numbers and letters along the top and sides of the tablet. These correspond to the numbers in brackets in the acad.mnu file under the ***TABLET heading. Each row contains 25 selection boxes numbered from left to right. There are 225 boxes in all. Therefore, box number 70 would be identified as C-20.

Referring to Figure 23-6, notice that the symbols placed in the menu occupy the first six boxes of each row. The first box of each row is labeled [A-1], [B-1], and [C-1], respectively.

The macros for the tablet menu file can be entered in two ways. They can replace the selection box numbers listed in the menu file, or they can be entered after the box numbers. The latter method is recommended because it leaves you with reference numbers for the selection boxes. There are no screen labels for tablet menus. Thus, anything inside brackets is not displayed, nor is it read by AutoCAD. The notations inside the brackets can be left as helpful reminders.

Before making changes to the acad.mnu file, make a copy of the file. Then load your copy of acad.mnu into the text editor. The following example gives the menu entries for the customized tablet menu shown in Figure 23-6.

```
**TABLET1STD
[A-1]^C^C–insert;gatevalve
[A-2]^C^C–insert;checkvalve
[A-3]^C^C–insert;controlvalve
[A-4]^C^C–insert;globevalve
[A-5]^C^C–insert;safetyvalv-r
[A-6]^C^C–insert;safetyvalv-l

[B-1]^C^C–insert;pumpr-top
[B-2]^C^C–insert;pumpr-up
[B-3]^C^C–insert;pumpr-dn
[B-4]^C^C–insert;pumpl-dn
[B-5]^C^C–insert;pumpl-up
[B-6]^C^C–insert;pumpl-top

[C-1]^C^C–insert;instr-loc
[C-2]^C^C–insert;instr-pan
[C-3]^C^C–insert;trans
[C-4]^C^C–insert;instr-con
[C-5]^C^C–insert;drain
[C-6]^C^C–insert;vent
```

After you edit or create a new menu in this manner, save the menu file and then exit the text editor. Use the **MENU** command to load your copy of the acad.mnu file. Be sure to enter the proper path to the file.

<table>
<tr>
<td>**NOTE**
</td>
<td>When you load an MNU file, any custom toolbar modifications are lost. To avoid losing any custom toolbars you have created or modified, copy any new toolbar data from the MNS file and place it in the MNU file before loading.</td>
</tr>
</table>

<table>
<tr>
<td>**PROFESSIONAL TIP** </td>
<td>If you will be editing your menu often, consider defining a menu pick on the screen that automatically loads the menu file:

[LOADMENU]^C^Cfiledia;0;menu;*file path/menu name*;filedia;1

In this example, the **FILEDIA** system variable is set to 0 and then changed back to its default value of 1 after loading the menu file. The **FILEDIA** system variable controls the display of file selection dialog boxes. Setting the variable to 0 enables entry at the command line after the **MENU** command is issued and suppresses display of the **Select Menu File** dialog box. If you have previously set the **FILEDIA** system variable to 0, simply change the setting after using the menu pick above.</td>
</tr>
</table>

Alternate Ways to Customize the Tablet Menu

The customization method previously discussed uses blocks that have been saved in a prototype drawing file. In order to use the blocks, the file must first be inserted into the current drawing. As an alternative, a new drawing can be started based on a template file containing the blocks.

For example, suppose the piping flow diagram symbols are saved in a template drawing named pipeflow.dwt. You can use the symbols if you specify **Use a Template** in the **Create New Drawing** dialog box, and select the pipeflow template. All the blocks in the pipeflow template can then be picked to draw your new tablet menu.

The method used in the previous discussion inserts blocks located in another drawing. You can insert one drawing into another using the **–INSERT** command. You may consider putting an insertion command in your tablet menu. In the following example, only the named items in the drawing, such as blocks, views, and layers, are inserted.

```
Command: –INSERT↵
Enter block name or [?]: PIPEFLOW↵
Specify insertion point or [Scale/X/Y/Z/Rotate/PScale/PX/PY/PZ/PRotate]:
    (press [Esc] to cancel)
```

Remember to specify the correct path for the drawing file when using this command. Press the [Esc] key to cancel the command when prompted for the insertion point. This allows you to insert all named items into the drawing without inserting the actual drawing on screen. You can insert prototype drawings containing blocks (DWG files), but you cannot insert template drawings (DWT files).

The **Insert Prototype Drawing** pick in your tablet menu file could be written as follows:

```
^C^C–INSERT;PIPEFLOW;^C
```

A third way to customize the menu is to use separate drawing files for the symbols instead of blocks in a prototype drawing. The drawing files can be located on the hard disk or on diskettes. Remember that symbols stored as individual drawing files require more disk storage space. In addition, disk access time is often slower.

PROFESSIONAL TIP

Evaluate your present use of blocks and drawing files when making or modifying tablet menus. Take into account your current method of symbol creation, storage, and usage when developing tablet menus that incorporate symbols. If symbol drawings (prototypes) are working best for your application, develop your tablet menu around these. If individual drawing files are used, the menus should access these. While the **AutoCAD DesignCenter** also provides access to external symbols and drawing data, a menu macro can automatically load all required information with a single pick.

DESIGNING A NEW TABLET MENU

Working with a tablet menu is somewhat inefficient because it requires you to move your eyes away from the screen to find a tablet command. However, there are advantages to using tablet menus over menus on screen.
- Screen menus must be "paged" or "cascaded" when looking for a command. Flipping through pages of screen menus and submenus slows down the drawing process.
- A tablet menu provides immediate access to most commands. If necessary, it can be paged for additional commands and symbols.
- Available tablet commands can be chosen with only one pick of the pointing device.
- Graphic symbols on the tablet menu make it easy to identify commands.
- Numerous commands can be printed on a tablet menu. This encourages users to select commands that they might seldom select if using screen menus only.

Any technique that increases your drawing efficiency and productivity should be investigated and incorporated as part of your operating procedures. You will find that making custom tablet menus is one such procedure. They can be used alone or together with screen menus. A tablet menu pick can display a specialized screen menu or load new tablet menus. After gaining experience and confidence in your menu-creating abilities, you will become aware of the value of tablet menus.

Planning Your New Tablet Menu

Planning custom screen menus was discussed earlier in this text. Planning is also needed when developing new tablet menus. The creation of a tablet menu should not be the first thing you do when customizing AutoCAD. There are several important preliminary steps that should be taken before designing a menu:
- ✓ List the commands that you use most often.
- ✓ Develop macros that automate your CAD work as much as possible.
- ✓ List the different types of symbol overlays you may need.
- ✓ List each group of symbols used in order of most frequently used to least frequently used.

After listing the items outlined on the previous page, begin the process of creating commands, macros, and menus.

1. Develop and test individual macros in a screen menu or tablet menu.
2. Determine major groups of commands and macros based on their frequency of use.
3. Design the tablet menu layout. Draw it larger than actual size, using a pencil. This gives you room for lettering and sketches. You can have up to four menu areas and a screen pointing area. Several sample layouts are shown in Figure 23-8.
4. Draw the basic menu layout with AutoCAD. This should be a preliminary test menu. Do not add text or graphics yet. Pencil in commands on a plotted copy of the menu.
5. Write the macros for the menu and test each function for convenience.
6. Add text and graphics to the menu, then plot it. Revise the menu as needed to make it more efficient.

Figure 23-8.
Some common tablet menu layouts.

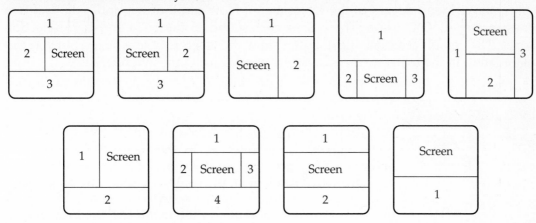

Creating the Tablet Menu

The overlay area at the top of the AutoCAD standard tablet menu template provides limited room and flexibility for customization. For some applications, you may wish to develop an entirely new tablet menu. The process of developing your own menu is similar to customizing the AutoCAD tablet menu. Of course, it takes additional planning because you are creating the entire tablet menu.

It is not required to configure four separate menu areas for your tablet menu. You can refer to the sample menus in Figure 23-8 when creating a layout, or you can design something completely new. When planning your tablet menu, it is a good idea to first sketch out the entire menu area. You can use the Tablet 2000 drawing as a source drawing, or you can create an entirely new drawing based on the size of your digitizer tablet and your custom menu needs. Start with a simple grid and sketch in the details, just as if you were customizing the overlay area of the AutoCAD tablet menu.

Although you are laying out selection boxes on a grid, it is not necessary to make the selection areas square or even completely rectangular. The same menu macro can be entered for any number of selection boxes, and the boxes may be interconnected or placed in separate locations. This means that there may be several boxes on the tablet menu that represent the same function. Look at the **FILE** area of the AutoCAD standard tablet menu and notice the **SAVE** selection box, Figure 23-9. AutoCAD does not designate the **SAVE** selection box as one large box because Menu Area 4 of the tablet is divided into 175 equally sized boxes. The **SAVE** command on the tablet menu is located across two boxes. Therefore, two macro lines in the menu file are required to define the **SAVE** command.

Figure 23-9.
The **SAVE** selection box on the AutoCAD tablet menu is actually composed of two smaller boxes.

Load the acad.mnu file into your text editor and page to the ***TABLET4 section. You should notice several lines with just a backslash (\). These lines specify the blank space above Menu Area 4 of the tablet menu. Now scroll down until you find two lines that read ^C^C_qsave. These lines correspond to the U-24 and U-25 selection boxes. The default acad.mnu file does not show the labels for these boxes, but you can place labels in the tablet menu area where needed for your own reference.

PROFESSIONAL TIP

Always place a backslash on the menu file lines for selection boxes that have no function. In the menu file, AutoCAD automatically places a space at the end of every line that does not end with a semicolon, plus sign (+), space, or backslash. Since a space issues an [Enter] keystroke, if there is no entry on a line for a selection box in the menu file, the previously used command is repeated when the corresponding tablet menu selection box is picked. By placing a backslash on such lines, you specify for AutoCAD to continue to await input and nothing actually happens if the related box is picked.

A Sample Tablet Menu

An example of a custom tablet menu is shown in Figure 23-10. It is similar to the AutoCAD standard tablet menu, but it contains fewer boxes. The template is made up of a grid with numbers along the top and letters down the left side. The selection box locations are identified at the beginning of each macro in the menu file for reference:

```
***TABLET1STD
[A-1]
[A-2]
[A-3]
```

Anything inside brackets in the tablet menu section is not displayed, and does not affect the macro. This notation can be used in the acad.mnu file to indicate each tablet menu section, and the selection box number within the section.

PROFESSIONAL TIP

When creating a tablet or screen menu, provide a reference number in brackets for each menu entry. This immediately tells you the tablet menu selection box, grid location, or screen menu line on which you are working. Numbers used in tablet menus are not displayed on screen. Numbers in screen menu macros must follow the eighth space in the command name. Otherwise, they are displayed on screen.

In Figure 23-10, notice that the most frequently used commands, such as **RETURN, ACADMENU** (a command that loads the AutoCAD menu file), **DIM STYLE**, and **EXIT** (a command that exits from the Dim: mode), are placed inside large boxes. This allows you to pick them quickly.

Look at the menu file in Figure 23-11 and compare the entries to the corresponding selection boxes in Figure 23-10. The grid locations of each menu item are indicated in brackets for quick identification. The button menu is for a 12-button pointing device.

Figure 23-10.
A sample layout of a custom tablet menu.

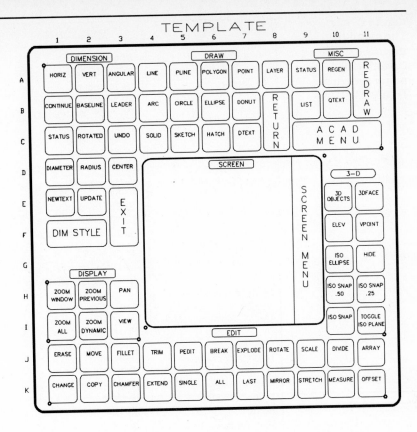

If you plan to try this menu, enter the macros with your text editor. Assign the name MENU1.MNU. The new menu cannot be used until it is loaded into AutoCAD using the **MENU** command. In the following example, the **FILEDIA** system variable is set to 0:

Command: **MENU**↵
Enter menu file name or [. (for none)] <*current*>: **SUPPORT\MENU1**↵

The compiled version of the menu file has an .mnc extension. AutoCAD looks for the latest version of the compiled menu file when you begin a new drawing. If there is no such file, AutoCAD compiles the menu file again.

PROFESSIONAL TIP

The name of the particular menu you use to construct a drawing is saved in the drawing file. If you use different menus, be sure that they are in the same directory as the drawings, or use the proper path when loading the menu. This path is saved with the drawing file. If AutoCAD cannot find a menu, the following message appears if the **FILEDIA** system variable is set to 0:

Menu load failed. File not found: menu1.mnu

At this time, you can reissue the **MENU** command and enter the proper path to the menu, or enter the name of another menu.

After loading your new menu, enter the **TABLET** command and configure the new tablet menu. If you are using the **Tablet:** screen menu, do not pick the **Reconfig** option. This starts the configuration routine for the AutoCAD tablet menu. Instead, use the **Config** option.

Figure 23-11.
The menu file macros for the custom tablet menu shown in Figure 23-10.

MENU1.MNU		
***BUTTONS	[B-9]^C^Clist	***TABLET3
;	[B-10]^C^Cqtext	[D-10]\
'REDRAW	[B-11]'redraw	[D-11]\
^C	[C-1]^C^Cdim;status	[E-10] $i=3dobjects $l=*
^B	[C-2]^C^Cdim;rotated	[E-11]^C^C3dface
^O	[C-3]^C^Cdim;undo	[F-10]^C^Celev
^G	[C-4]^C^Csolid	[F-11]^C^Cvpoint;;
^D	[C-5]^C^Csketch	[G-10]^C^Cellipse;i
^E	[C-6]^C^Chatch	[G-11]^C^Chide
^T	[C-7]^C^Cdtext	[H-10]^C^Csnap;s;i;.5
	[C-8]^C^C;	[H-11]^C^Csnap;s;i;.25
	[C-9]^C^Cmenu;acad	[I-10]^C^Csnap;s;i;;
	[C-10]^C^Cmenu;acad	[I-11]^E
	[C-11]^C^Cmenu;acad	
***TABLET1	***TABLET2	***TABLET4
	[D-1]^C^Cdim;diameter	[J-1]^C^Cerase
	[D-2]^C^Cdim;radius	[J-2]^C^Cmove
[A–1]^C^Cdim;horiz		[J-3]^C^Cfillet
[A-2]^C^Cdim;vert		[J-4]^C^Ctrim
[A-3]^C^Cdim;angular	[D-3]^C^Cdim;center	[J-5]^C^Cpedit
[A-4]^C^Cline	[E-1]^C^Cdim;newtext	[J-6]^C^Cbreak
[A-5]^C^Cpline	[E-2]^C^Cdim;update	[J-7]^C^Cexplode
[A-6]^C^Cpolygon	[E-3]exit	[J-8]^C^Crotate
[A-7]^C^Cpoint	[F-1]^C^Cdim;style	[J-9]^C^Cscale
[A-8]^C^Clayer	[F-2]^C^Cdim;style	[J-10]^C^Cdivide
[A-9]^C^Cstatus	[F-3]exit	[J-11]^C^Carray
[A-10]^C^Cregen	[G-1]\	[K-1]^C^Cchange
[A-11]'redraw	[G-2]\	[K-2]^C^Ccopy
[B-1]^C^Cdim;continue	[G-3]\	[K-3]^C^Cchamfer
[B-2]^C^Cdim;baseline	[H-1]'zoom;w	[K-4]^C^Cextend
[B-3]^C^Cdim;leader	[H-2]'zoom;p	[K-5]single
[B-4]^C^Carc	[H-3]'pan	[K-6]all
[B-5]^C^Ccircle	[I-1]'zoom;a	[K-7]last
[B-6]^C^Cellipse	[I-2]'zoom;d	[K-8]^C^Cmirror
[B-7]^C^Cdonut	[I-3]^C^Cview	[K-9]^C^Cstretch
[B-8]^C^C;		[K-10]^C^Cmeasure
		[K-11]^C^Coffset

The configuration routine prompts for the number of tablet menus. The MENU1 template requires four. You are then asked if you want to realign the tablet menu areas. Enter Y (Yes). Now digitize the upper-left, lower-left, and lower-right corners of each of the four tablet menu areas. When prompted, provide the number of columns and rows in each area. The corners of the MENU1 tablet menu are shown in Figure 23-12. The columns and rows in each area are given in the following chart:

Menu Area	Columns	Rows
1	11	3
2	3	6
3	2	6
4	11	2

The final prompt in the configuration process asks you to specify the lower-left and upper-right corners of the screen pointing area. These are also shown in Figure 23-12.

Test all of the menu items to be sure they function properly. Correct any mistakes you find. You may encounter one shortcoming if you select the **ACAD MENU** item in Menu Area 1. The AutoCAD menu will be loaded, but how do you return to the MENU1 tablet menu? There must be a call, or item in the AutoCAD menu, that loads the MENU1 tablet menu. Load the acad.mnu file into your text editor and add the following line to the **S menu, or to a pull-down menu:

    [MENU1]^C^Cmenu;menu1

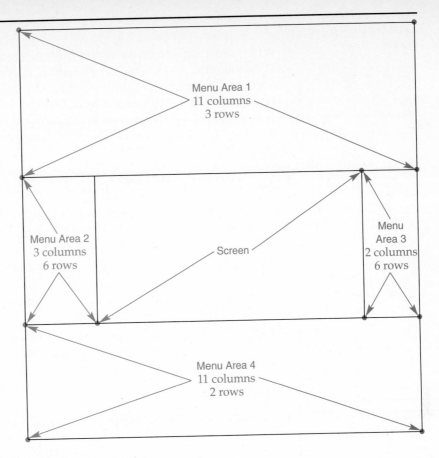

Figure 23-12.
Digitize the corners of the MENU1 tablet menu areas as indicated here. Complete the configuration process by picking the lower-left and upper-right corners of the screen pointing area.

If you insert this entry between two existing items, do not press [Enter]. Otherwise, you will insert a blank line into the menu.

Automating the Menu Editing Process

Modifying screen or tablet menus requires loading the text editor on a regular basis. This can become tedious. The process can be automated if you create a menu macro that loads the text editor and MNU file. If you are using the Notepad text editor, add the following item to your menu:

[EDITMENU]^C^CNOTEPAD;menu1.mnu;

When picked, this item cancels the current command and executes the **NOTEPAD** command to access the text editor. The file name of the menu is entered automatically.

If you use a text editor other than Notepad, just substitute its name in place of Notepad. For example, suppose an application named TextPad is used. The following entry could be placed in the screen menu section of the menu file:

[EDITMENU]^C^CTEXTPAD;menu1.mnu;

The **TEXTPAD** command will not work when entered at the Command: prompt unless you have altered the acad.pgp file as discussed in Chapter 28 of *AutoCAD and its Applications—Basics, AutoCAD 2000*. In order for the menu item above to work properly, you must first add a line to the acad.pgp file to make **TEXTPAD** a valid command in AutoCAD. Edit your acad.pgp file by adding the following line:

Textpad, Start txtpad32, 0,*File to edit:,

Be sure the information in the second entry, shown above as txtpad32, is the proper name of your text editor's executable file. In this case, txtpad32.exe is the file name used for the TextPad program.

Chapter 23 Customizing Tablet Menus

TABLET MENU TIPS

Tablet menus can be as simple or as complex as you want, and can contain just about any function you need. As you experiment with helpful commands and options, think of the problems you face when drawing. Design AutoCAD macros to solve problems and eliminate tedious tasks. Add them to your menu. Keep in mind the following guidelines:

✓ Use tablet menu picks to call button, screen, and image tile menus.

✓ Use tablet menu picks to call other tablet menus.

✓ Use a tablet menu pick that inserts a group of blocks from a prototype drawing into the current drawing. If the prototype drawing name is elec001, the menu macro should look like this:

    ^C^C–insert;elec001;^C

This inserts only the blocks and other named objects in the file, not the actual drawing on screen.

✓ Use tablet menu picks to display help screens and frequently used slides.

✓ Plot menu templates on heavy polyester film for durability.

✓ Be sure your template does not extend beyond the active area of your tablet.

✓ When customizing Menu Area 1 of the AutoCAD tablet menu, change the number of selection boxes to any number you need. Draw a new overlay containing the revised boxes. When configuring the customized tablet menu, be sure to use the **Config** option (not **Reconfig**) from the **Tablet:** screen menu. Enter the revised number of columns and rows.

✓ Any portion of the AutoCAD tablet menu can be changed to suit your needs. Just alter the part of the acad.mnu file that you wish to change.

✓ When customizing the acad.mnu file, always work with a copy, not the original file.

✓ If you work at a computer that other people use, return the tablet and menu configuration to the way it was before you changed it.

✓ Build your tablet menu in small pieces as you work.

Chapter Test

Answer the following questions on a separate sheet of paper.

1. How many menu areas are on the standard AutoCAD tablet menu template?
2. Provide the command and option entries that allow you to initially set up the AutoCAD tablet menu template.
   A. Command: _____
   B. Enter an option [ON/OFF/CAL/CFG]: _____
3. List the number of columns and rows found in each of the four menu areas in the AutoCAD tablet menu.
4. If you are using the **Tablet:** screen menu, which option allows you to quickly set up the AutoCAD tablet menu without entering the number of rows and columns?

5. How many selection boxes are provided in Menu Area 1 of the AutoCAD tablet menu?
6. Identify the first step used to customize the AutoCAD tablet menu.
7. Describe how the Menu Area 1 selection boxes are numbered in the acad.mnu file.
8. What command is used to load a menu file?
9. List two advantages of using tablet menus rather than on-screen menus when choosing commands.
10. Which commands should you automate first when designing a screen or tablet menu?
11. What file extension does AutoCAD use for the compiled version of the menu file?
12. How can you automate the process of loading a text editor and a menu file for editing purposes?
13. Provide the tablet menu macro that would allow you to make a pick to insert the blocks in a prototype drawing named pipe1 without inserting the actual drawing on screen.

Drawing Problems

1. Add ten new commands to Menu Area 1 of the AutoCAD tablet menu template. Follow these guidelines:
   A. Place the commands along the bottom row (I) of the menu area. They should occupy selection boxes I-1 through I-10.
   B. Plot a copy of a drawing of the Menu Area 1 grid and sketch the commands in the selection boxes. Sketch graphic symbols to represent the commands.
   C. Draw the command symbols and save them as blocks in AutoCAD. Place the command text and symbols in the Menu Area 1 drawing.
   D. Plot a final copy of the overlay on vellum or polyester film.
   E. Make a copy of the acad.mnu file and write the macros for the new commands.

2. Create an overlay for Menu Area 1 of the AutoCAD tablet menu using graphic symbols for one of the following drafting disciplines:
   - Architectural
   - Structural
   - HVAC
   - Mechanical
   - Industrial piping
   - Electrical
   - Electronics
   A. Use existing blocks or symbols that you have on file, or create new ones.
   B. Provide a tablet menu pick that allows you to insert all symbols of a prototype drawing file into a drawing without inserting the actual drawing on screen.
   C. Provide a tablet menu pick that calls the AutoCAD menu file.

3. Redesign Menu Area 1 of the AutoCAD tablet menu so that it contains a complete selection of dimensioning commands, options, and settings. Follow these guidelines:
   A. Use the standard configuration of 225 selection boxes or change the configuration to suit your personal requirements.
   B. Draw graphic symbols representing the various dimensioning commands in the related selection boxes.
   C. Plot a menu overlay on vellum or polyester film that can be slipped under the AutoCAD tablet menu template.

4. Design a custom tablet menu that occupies only the lower half of your digitizer tablet. Follow these guidelines:
   A. Design the menu so that it contains a screen pointing area and two menu areas.
   B. Sketch graphic symbols that represent frequently used commands and design an area for special commands that you have created.
   C. Make a drawing of the new tablet menu and plot it on vellum or polyester film. Plot the overlay as a mirror image of the original as discussed in this chapter.

5. Design a new tablet menu that occupies the entire active area of your digitizer tablet. Follow these guidelines:
   A. Provide four menu areas and a screen pointing area.
   B. Provide access to the AutoCAD tablet menu.
   C. Include an area for custom commands you have created, plus an area for drawing symbols saved as blocks or separate files. Allow the user to change the symbols area of the menu to use a different set of drawing symbols.
   D. Draw an overlay for the new tablet menu. Draw two separate, smaller overlays for the two sets of drawing symbols.
   E. Draw graphic symbols to represent the commands and place them in the menu overlay.
   F. Insert scaled-down copies of the blocks into the symbol overlays of the menu.
   G. Plot test copies of the tablet menu and the two symbol overlays and use them for several days.
   H. Plot final copies of the template and symbol overlays on vellum or polyester film. Plot them as mirror images of the originals as discussed in this chapter.

6. Design a custom tablet menu for a specific drafting discipline, such as electronics, piping, or mapping. Follow these guidelines:
   A. Create as many menu areas as you need, up to four.
   B. Provide space for a complete selection of drawing symbols. The symbols should reflect the field of drafting for which you will be designing the menu.
   C. Include only the commands that you will use often for the selected discipline.
   D. Provide the ability to load a variety of prototype drawings from the tablet menu.
   E. Create menu selections that allow you to do the following:
      • Edit a file using your text editor or word processor.
      • Edit the menu file that you design for this problem.
   F. Plot the tablet menu template on vellum or film using the mirroring technique discussed in this chapter.

CHAPTER 24

Introduction to AutoLISP

Learning Objectives

After completing this chapter, you will be able to:
- Locate, load, and run existing AutoLISP programs.
- Use basic AutoLISP functions at the command line.
- Define new AutoCAD commands.
- Write AutoLISP program files using the **Visual LISP** editor.

AutoLISP is a derivative, or dialect, of the LISP programming language. *LISP* (List Processing) is a high-level computer programming language used in artificial intelligence (AI) systems. In this reference, the term *high-level* does not mean *complex*, rather it means *powerful*. As a matter of fact, many AutoCAD users refer to AutoLISP as the "non-programmer's language" because it is easy to understand.

The AutoLISP dialect is specially designed by Autodesk to work with AutoCAD. It is a flexible language that allows the programmer to create custom commands and functions that can greatly increase productivity and drawing efficiency.

AutoLISP can be used in several ways. It is a built-in feature of AutoCAD and is therefore available at the Command: prompt. When AutoLISP commands and functions are issued inside parentheses, the AutoLISP interpreter automatically evaluates the entry and carries out the specified tasks. AutoLISP functions can be incorporated into the AutoCAD menu as toolbar buttons, screen menu items, and tablet menu picks. AutoLISP command and function definitions can be saved in an AutoLISP program file and then loaded into AutoCAD when needed. Items that are used frequently can be placed in the acad2000.lsp file, which is automatically loaded for the first drawing when AutoCAD starts. The acad2000doc.lsp file should contain functions that are to be available in all concurrent drawings during a session. AutoCAD also provides a special editing program called *Visual LISP*. This program offers powerful features designed specifically for writing and editing AutoLISP program files.

The benefits of using AutoLISP are endless. Third-party applications (add-on software programs that enhance AutoCAD) use AutoLISP to perform specialized functions, such as the creation of special symbols.

A person with a basic understanding of AutoLISP can create new commands and functions to automate many routine tasks. Working through this chapter, you will be able to add greater capabilities to your screen, tablet, and toolbar menu macros. You can also enter simple AutoLISP expressions at the Command: prompt. More experienced programmers can create powerful programs that quickly complete very complex design requirements. Several powerful AutoLISP programs are found in AutoCAD's Express Tools. Examples of possible new functions that might be designed using AutoLISP include the following:

- Automatic line breaks when inserting schematic symbols.
- Automatic creation of shapes with associated text objects.
- Parametric design applications that create geometry based on numeric entry.

Knowing the basics of AutoLISP gives you a better understanding of how AutoCAD works. By learning just a few simple functions, you can create new commands that make a significant difference in your daily productivity levels. Read through this chapter slowly while you are at a computer. Type all of the examples and exercises as you read them. This is the best way to get a feel for AutoLISP. An excellent resource for learning to create useful AutoLISP applications is *AutoLISP Programming*, published by Goodheart-Willcox.

NOTE For additional information on using AutoLISP, refer to the **Visual LISP and AutoLISP** book provided by AutoCAD. This book and its help topics are located in the **Contents** tab of the **Help Topics: AutoCAD Help** dialog box, which is accessed by pressing the [F1] function key, selecting the question mark icon at the far right of the **Standard** toolbar, picking **AutoCAD Help** from the **Help** pull-down menu, or entering ? or HELP at the Command: prompt.

AUTOLISP BASICS

LISP stands for *list processing*, indicating that AutoLISP processes lists. In the LISP language, a list can be defined as any number of data items enclosed in parentheses. Each item in a list must be separated from other items by a space.

When any entry is made at the Command: prompt, it is first checked to see if the first character was a parenthesis. The opening parenthesis tells AutoCAD that an AutoLISP expression is being entered. AutoCAD then sends the expression to the AutoLISP Interpreter for evaluation. The initial input can be supplied as direct keyboard entry or even a menu macro. The format for an AutoLISP expression, called *syntax*, is as follows:

(FunctionName AnyRequiredData…)

The first item in the AutoLISP expression is a function name. Some functions require additional information. For example, the addition function requires numeric data:

Command: (+ 2 4).⌐
6
Command:

Any required data for a function is referred to as an *argument*. Some functions use no arguments; others may require one or more. When entering an AutoLISP expression, it is important to *close* it using a closing parenthesis prior to pressing [Enter]. When you press [Enter], the AutoLISP Interpreter checks to see that the number of opening and closing parentheses match. If they do not, you are prompted as follows:

Command: (+ 2 4.⌐
(_>

The (_> indicates that you are missing one closing parenthesis. In this example, all that is necessary is to enter the single missing parenthesis and the function is complete:

```
(_> )↵
6
Command:
```

When the AutoLISP Interpreter evaluates an AutoLISP expression, it *returns* a value. An expression entered at the Command: prompt instructs the system to return its value to the command line. If a different prompt is active, the returned value is used as input for that prompt. For example, this next sequence uses the result of adding two numbers as the input at the Specify radius of circle or [Diameter]: prompt. Checking the **CIRCLERAD** system variable verifies that the value returned by AutoLISP was in fact applied to the circle radius.

```
Command: C or CIRCLE↵
Specify center point for circle or [3P/2P/Ttr (tan tan radius)]: (pick a point)
Specify radius of circle or [Diameter]: (+ 14.25 3.0)↵
Command: CIRCLERAD↵
Enter new value for CIRCLERAD <17.2500>: ↵
```

Basic AutoLISP Functions

The best way to get started learning AutoLISP is to enter a few functions at the command line and see what they do. The following discussion includes basic AutoLISP functions that are part of the foundation for all AutoLISP programs. At first, these functions and expressions will be entered at the command line. Later in the chapter, you will learn about creating and using AutoLISP program files. Practice using the functions as you read. Then, begin using them in menus and macros.

AutoLISP math functions

AutoLISP provides many different mathematical operators for performing calculations. All real number calculations in AutoLISP are accurate to 15 decimal places. AutoLISP distinguishes between real numbers and integers, handling each data type differently. Real numbers are numbers with a decimal point, such as 1.25, 7.0, and −0.438. Integers are whole numbers without a decimal point, such as 3, 91, and −115. If a mathematical expression has only integer arguments, the result is returned as an integer. If at least one real number is used, the result is returned as a real number. The following symbols are used for the four basic math functions:

Symbol	Function
+	Returns the sum of all the supplied number arguments.
−	Subtracts the sum of the second through the last number from the first number and returns the result.
*	Returns the product of all the supplied number arguments.
/	Divides the first number by the product of the second through the last numbers.

NOTE *Real numbers* are technically defined as those that have no imaginary part. They include integers and fractions, as well as decimal numbers. In applications involving AutoLISP, and throughout this discussion, real numbers are classified as those that always have a decimal part.

The following examples illustrate AutoLISP math expressions entered at the Command: prompt. As you practice entering these expressions, use the following procedure:

1. Start with an open parenthesis.

2. Separate each item in the expression with a space.
3. Close the expression with a closing parenthesis.

Using these guidelines, enter the following expressions at the Command: prompt. If you get lost at any time or do not return to the Command: prompt when expected, press the [Esc] key to cancel the AutoLISP entry.

```
Command: (+ 6 2)↵
8
Command: (+ 6.0 2)↵
8.0
Command: (– 15 9)↵
6
Command: (* 4 6)↵
24
Command: (/ 12 3)↵
4
Command: (/ 12 3.2)↵
3.75
Command: (/ 19 10)↵
1
```

An "incorrect" answer is returned in the last example. The result of dividing 19 by 10 should yield 1.9. When only integers are supplied as arguments, the result is returned as an integer. If the result were rounded, it would round to 2. However, the result returned is simply the integer portion of the actual answer. The result is not rounded, it is truncated. To get the correct result in division expressions such as the one above, specify at least one of the arguments as a real number:

```
Command: (/ 19.0 10)↵
1.9
```

When entering real numbers between 1 and –1, you must include the leading zero. If the zero is not entered, you will get an error message:

```
Command: (+ .5 16)↵
; error: misplaced dot on input
Command:
```

The correct entry is as follows:

```
Command: (+ 0.5 16)↵
16.5
```

EXERCISE 24-1

❑ Solve the following equations by using AutoLISP functions at the Command: prompt. Write down the expression you use for each equation and your answers on a separate sheet of paper.
  ❑ 57 + 12
  ❑ 86.4 + 16
  ❑ 24 + 12 + 8 + 35
  ❑ 8 – 3
  ❑ 29 – 17
  ❑ 89.16 – 14.6
  ❑ 8 × 4
  ❑ 16 × 5 × 35
  ❑ 7.3 × 22
  ❑ 45 ÷ 9
  ❑ 60 ÷ 2
  ❑ 76 ÷ 27.3

AutoCAD and its Applications—Advanced

Nested expressions

The term *nested* refers to an expression that is used as part of another expression. For example, to add 15 to the product of 3.75 and 2.125, you can nest the multiplication expression in the following AutoLISP addition expression:

Command: **(+ 15 (* 3.75 2.125))**↵
22.9688

Nested expressions are evaluated from the deepest nested level outward. In the previous expression, the multiplication operation is evaluated first, and the result is applied to the addition operation. Here are some examples of nested expressions:

Command: **(+ 24 (* 5 4))**↵
44
Command: **(* 12 (/ 60 20))**↵
36
Command: **(/ 39 (* 1.6 11))**↵
2.21591

NOTE

AutoLISP performs all mathematical calculations to 15 decimal places, but only displays six significant digits. For example, take a close look at this expression:

Command: **(+ 15 (* 3.75 2.125))**↵
22.9688

The actual result is 22.96875, but AutoLISP displays only six significant digits at the command line and rounds the number for display only. This is true for large and small numbers alike. The next example shows how AutoLISP uses exponential notation to display larger numbers using only six digits:

Command: **(* 1000 1575.25)**↵
1.57525e+006

The final example uses a numeric printing function set to show eight decimal places in order to indicate that the number is not actually rounded, and that no precision is lost:

Command: **(RTOS (+ 15 (* 3.75 2.125)) 2 8)**↵
"14.96875000"

EXERCISE 24-2

❏ Use the proper AutoLISP expressions to solve the following problems. Write the expressions and answers on a separate sheet of paper.
   ❏ 56.3 + (12 ÷ 3)
   ❏ 23 − (17.65 ÷ 4)
   ❏ 14 ÷ (12 ÷ 3.6)
   ❏ 47 ÷ (31 − 16.4)
   ❏ 257 ÷ (34 − 3.6)
   ❏ 123.65 + (84 − 43.8)
   ❏ 16 ÷ (46 − 23)

Variables

All programming languages make use of variables to temporarily store information. The variable name can be used in another expression anywhere in the program. When AutoLISP encounters a variable in an expression, it uses the value of the variable to evaluate the expression. A variable name cannot be made up of only numeric characters, nor can it contain any of the following characters:

✓ Open parenthesis (()
✓ Close parenthesis ())
✓ Period (.)
✓ Apostrophe (')
✓ Quotation marks ("")
✓ Semicolon (;)

The **SETQ** AutoLISP function is used to set variable values. A **SETQ** expression requires a variable name and value as arguments. The following example shows an expression that creates a variable named A and assigns it a value of 5:

```
Command: (SETQ A 5).⌐
5
```

If you try to use an illegal variable name, an error message is returned. The following example tries to create a variable named 2 with an assigned value of 7. Since 2 is not a valid variable name, an error message is returned:

```
Command: (SETQ 2 7).⌐
; error: syntax error
```

Once a variable name has been assigned, it can be used in subsequent AutoLISP expressions or even accessed directly at the command line. To access a variable value at the command line, precede the variable name with an exclamation mark (!). For example:

```
Command: !A.⌐
5
```

```
Command: C or CIRCLE.⌐
Specify center point for circle or [3P/2P/Ttr (tan tan radius)]: (pick a point)
Specify radius of circle or [Diameter] <17.2500>: !A.⌐
5
```

To use the value of a variable in any expression, simply include the variable in the appropriate location. The following sequence sets and uses a series of variables:

```
Command: (SETQ B (– A 1)).⌐
4
Command: (SETQ C (– A B)).⌐
1
Command: (SETQ D (* (+ A B) 2)).⌐
18
```

Look closely at the example illustrated in Figure 24-1. Find the three separate expressions inside parentheses. AutoLISP evaluates Expression 3 first. The result is applied to Expression 2, which is then evaluated. The result of Expression 2 is applied to 1. The final evaluation determines the value of Variable D.

Figure 24-1.
Each AutoLISP expression must be enclosed with parentheses. In this evaluation of Variable D, Expression 3 is evaluated first, then Expression 2, and finally Expression 1.

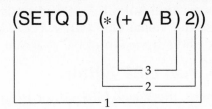

EXERCISE 24-3

❏ Using a separate sheet of paper, write AutoLISP expressions for the following variables in the proper format. After writing each expression, enter it into the computer to test your solution.
A. Assign the value of 4 to the variable ONE.
B. Assign the value of 3 + 2 to the variable TWO.
C. Assign the value of ONE + TWO to the variable THREE.
D. Assign the value of THREE + (TWO – ONE) to the variable FOUR.

PROFESSIONAL TIP   When working at the command line with AutoLISP, use AutoCAD's command line editing features to your best advantage. Remember that you can use the up and down arrow keys to display previously entered lines of code. Additionally, you can use the left and right arrow keys to position the cursor to delete or insert text within a line.

AutoLISP Program Files

Entering AutoLISP expressions at the command line is suitable for applications that are simple or unique. However, when more complex expressions are required or when the expressions you are using may be needed again, it is best to place them in an AutoLISP program file. This can be easily accomplished using the **Visual LISP** editor provided by AutoCAD. Even with the advantages provided by AutoCAD's command line editing features, AutoLISP programs can be more effectively developed using the **Visual LISP** editor. The creation of AutoLISP program files is discussed in the following sections.

A very common feature found in most AutoLISP files is a function definition. A *function definition* is a collection of AutoLISP language that performs any number of tasks. The function is assigned a name that is used to activate it. Some function definitions create new AutoCAD command names that can be entered at the command line.

Once written, an AutoLISP program file can be loaded and used whenever it is needed. AutoCAD automatically loads the acad2000.lsp file (if it is located in the Support File Search Path) when you first begin a drawing session. The acad2000doc.lsp file is loaded with each drawing that is opened. Any new AutoLISP commands or functions that you define in this file will be available in every drawing during a session.

The **Visual LISP** editor provides powerful editing features. The editor is an *interactive development environment* (IDE) that features AutoLISP development tools that are not available in standard text editing programs. If you have another text editor that you are experienced with, you may choose to use it instead of Visual LISP.

An AutoLISP file must be a text file, so if you choose to edit your AutoLISP files with a word processing program (such as Microsoft Word or WordPerfect), you must be sure to save the files as text only. Word processing files use special printing codes that control the font appearances, and AutoLISP cannot understand these codes. It is recommended that you use the **Visual LISP** editor, because it has tools specifically designed for use in writing and editing AutoLISP program files.

Introduction to the Visual LISP Editor

As previously mentioned, the **Visual LISP** editor is an interactive environment used to develop and edit AutoLISP functions. It is displayed by picking **Visual LISP Editor** from the **AutoLISP** cascading menu in the **Tools** pull-down menu, or by entering VLISP or VLIDE at the Command: prompt. When the **Visual LISP** editor is first displayed, it appears as shown in Figure 24-2. The windows within the editor can be minimized or maximized, and the editor itself can be temporarily closed to return to AutoCAD as necessary.

Figure 24-2.
The primary features of the **Visual LISP** editor.

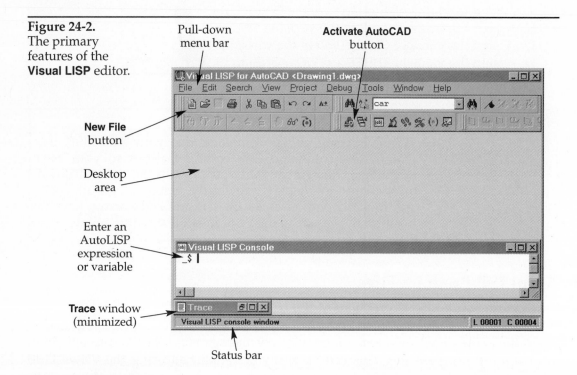

Visual LISP basics

The **Visual LISP** editor is a full-featured software application containing many powerful tools and features. This section provides only a brief introduction to Visual LISP. For a more detailed discussion of the features and applications of Visual LISP, refer to AutoCAD's *Visual LISP Developer's Guide* in the **Visual LISP and AutoLISP** help book.

To create a new AutoLISP program file, pick the **New file** button or select **New File** from the **File** pull-down menu. This opens a new text editor window for an untitled document on the desktop of the **Visual LISP** editor. See Figure 24-3. The different windows and features in the **Visual LISP** editor are described as follows:

- **Desktop.** This is the main area of the editor window. It is similar to the main program window in AutoCAD and can be used to relocate toolbars or windowed components, such as the **Visual LISP Console** or a text editor window.
- **Text editor window.** Text editor windows are used to write and edit AutoLISP programs. Different windows can be used to create new files, or view existing programs. The **Visual LISP** editor provides interactive feedback as you enter material to help you avoid errors.

Figure 24-3.
Picking the **New file** button or selecting **New File** from the **File** pull-down menu displays a text editor window in the **Visual LISP** editor program window.

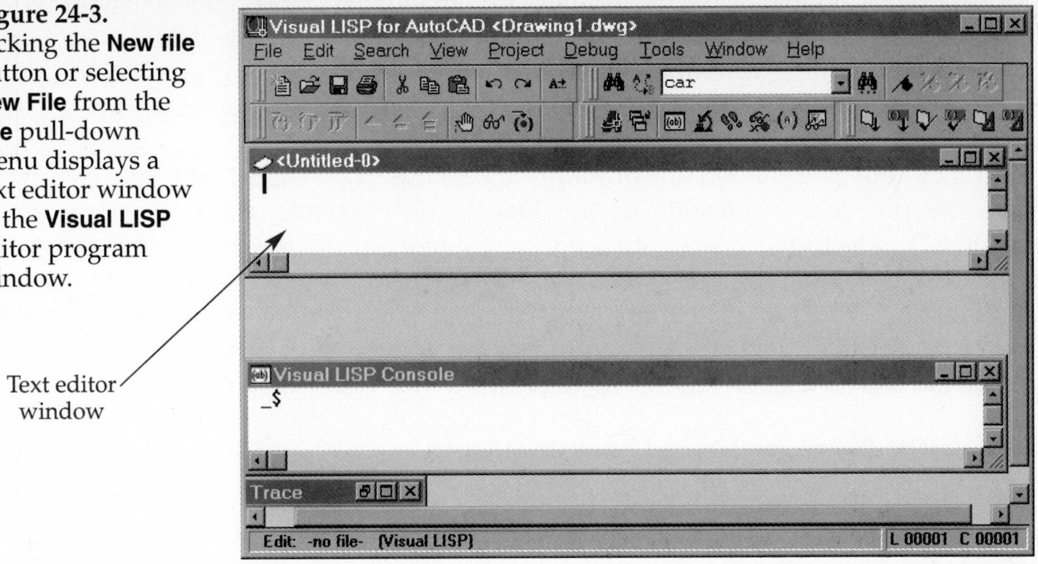

Text editor window

- **Visual LISP Console window.** This window provides several functions. You can use it to enter any AutoLISP expression to immediately see the results, or you can enter any AutoLISP variable to determine its value. You can also enter Visual LISP commands from this window, and copy text from the window to a text editor window.
- **Trace window.** This window is minimized when you first display the **Visual LISP** editor. It records a history of the execution of functions within your program and can be used to trace values when developing or debugging a program.
- **Status bar.** This area at the bottom of the **Visual LISP** editor is similar to the status bar in AutoCAD's main program window. It provides feedback regarding the status of the current window or application being used.

The interactive nature of the **Visual LISP** editor simplifies the task of creating AutoLISP program files. In addition to the tools previously discussed, several visual aids are provided to help identify functions as you enter text. For example, as you construct the expressions that make up your program, a color coding system provides immediate feedback in the form of colored text while you type. Text for any unrecognized items, such as a user variable or a portion of a function, is shown in black. For example, if you enter the **SETQ** function, the text is shown in black until you have entered the letters SET. Because AutoLISP recognizes the text entry SET as a valid function name, the color of the text is changed to blue. When you have entered the full **SETQ** function name, the text remains blue because AutoLISP also recognizes this function name. This can be very useful, because if you enter a function name and the text does not turn blue, you know that you have made an incorrect entry. The default color coding system used in the **Visual LISP** editor is illustrated below:

AutoLISP Text Elements	Associated Color
Built-in functions and protected symbols	Blue
Text strings	Magenta
Integers	Green
Real numbers	Teal
Comments	Magenta (with gray background)
Parentheses	Red
Unrecognized items	Black

Another valuable visual aid provided by the **Visual LISP** editor is instant parenthesis matching. When you enter a closing parenthesis in an expression, the cursor jumps to the opening parenthesis and then returns back to the current position. If the closing parenthesis does not have a match, the cursor does not jump. This helps indicate that a matching parenthesis is needed.

Once you have entered one or more expressions in the **Visual LISP** editor, you can save the file, test the results in the **Visual LISP Console** window, or return to AutoCAD to test your results. To load the contents of the file into AutoCAD, select **Load Text in Editor** from the **Tools** pull-down menu, or use the [Ctrl]+[Alt]+[E] key combination. You can then return to AutoCAD by picking the **Activate AutoCAD** button, or selecting **Activate AutoCAD** from the **Window** pull-down menu. The **VLISP** command can be used in AutoCAD to return to the **Visual LISP** editor.

Defining New AutoCAD Commands

In this section, you will use several of the built-in AutoLISP functions to create a new AutoCAD command. The **DEFUN** (define function) function is used to create new AutoCAD commands. The syntax for this function is as follows:

```
(DEFUN FunctionName (ArgumentList)
  (Expression)...
)
```

The function name can be any alphanumeric name, and is subject to the same conditions used for any variable name assigned with the **SETQ** function. If you prefix the *FunctionName* as shown above with C:, the name can be entered at the Command: prompt.

You must include an argument list in every function definition, even if it is empty. The argument list is used to declare local variables, and in more advanced applications, to indicate what arguments are required by a function. For many applications, the argument list is simply left empty.

Any number of expressions can be included in a function definition. All of the expressions contained in the definition are evaluated when the function name is called.

A very powerful, yet simple, application for a function definition is to create a shortcut command similar to one of the command aliases in the acad.pgp file. However, a shortcut command defined using AutoLISP can specify command options and even multiple commands to use. Remember that the command aliases defined in the acad.pgp file can only start a single command, and they cannot specify any command options.

This first example shows the definition for a new function named **ZX**. It issues the **ZOOM** command and performs the **Previous** option.

```
(DEFUN C:ZX ()
  (COMMAND "ZOOM" "PREVIOUS")
)
```

To see this function work, enter the definition at the command line:

```
Command: (DEFUN C:ZX () (COMMAND "ZOOM" "PREVIOUS"))↵
C:ZX
```

Notice that the new function name is returned by the **DEFUN** expression. The C: prefix indicates that it is accessible at the Command: prompt as follows:

```
Command: ZX↵
Command: nil
Command:
```

When activated, defined functions return the value of the last expression evaluated in the definition. Since the **COMMAND** function always returns a value of "nil," this is also returned when using the **ZX** function. The "nil" value has no effect. You can suppress it if you do not want it to appear each time you use a defined function. To suppress the value, add the **PRINC** function using no arguments to the end of the definition:

```
(DEFUN C:ZX ()
  (COMMAND "ZOOM" "PREVIOUS")
  (PRINC)
)
```

Entering a function definition at the Command: prompt is an inconvenient way to define custom functions. By storing such definitions in a text file, they can be loaded whenever needed.

PROFESSIONAL TIP

When defining new command names, keep in mind that most AutoCAD drafters are one-handed typists because the other hand is used for the pointing device. For example, when deciding on the name for a function that performs a **ZOOM Previous**, it may be easier for the user to type the ZX key combination rather than ZP. The [Z] and [P] keys are in opposite diagonal corners of the keyboard.

Creating Your First AutoLISP Program File

As discussed earlier, a typical use for an AutoLISP file is to hold function definitions. An AutoLISP program file can contain a single function, or it can contain several.

Many AutoLISP files are created to perform a single specific task. For example, the filter.lsp file creates and controls the **Object Selection Filters** dialog box. Other AutoLISP files hold a large number of function definitions, all of which become available when the file is loaded. One common application for the acad2000doc.lsp file is to create a series of function definitions for shortcut commands used to speed up routine drafting tasks.

To create your first AutoLISP file, begin by opening the **Visual LISP** editor, or another text editing application. In this first example, two function definitions are entered in the file. The first is the **ZX** function from the previous example. The second defines a command named **FC** (fillet corner) that sets the fillet radius to 0 and starts the **FILLET** command.

```
(DEFUN C:ZX ()
  (COMMAND "ZOOM" "PREVIOUS")
  (PRINC)
)

(DEFUN C:FC ()
  (COMMAND "FILLET" "R" 0 "FILLET")
  (PRINC)
)
```

Adding the appropriate documentation to your program files is recommended. When a semicolon (;) is encountered in a program file (except when it is part of a text string), any information to the right of the semicolon is ignored. This enables you to place comments and documentation in your AutoLISP files. The example below shows the appropriate documentation for this file, called myfirst.lsp:

```
; MyFirst.lsp
; by A. Novice

;C:ZX – To key ZOOM Previous command
(DEFUN C:ZX ()
  (COMMAND "ZOOM" "PREVIOUS")
  (PRINC)
)

;C:FC – Fillet Corner, Sets fillet radius to 0 and starts Fillet command.
(DEFUN C:FC ()
  (COMMAND "FILLET" "R" 0 "FILLET")
  (PRINC)
)
```

After entering these functions into the new text file, save the file as myfirst.lsp in the Acad2000\Support folder.

The **APPLOAD** command is used to load applications (such as AutoLISP files) into AutoCAD. To use this command, pick **Load...** from the **AutoLISP** cascading menu in the **Tools** pull-down menu, or enter AP or APPLOAD at the Command: prompt. The **Load/Unload Applications** dialog box appears, Figure 24-4.

APPLOAD
AP

Tools
↦ AutoLISP
   ↦ Load...

Figure 24-4.
The **Load/Unload Applications** dialog box is used to load AutoLISP program files into AutoCAD.

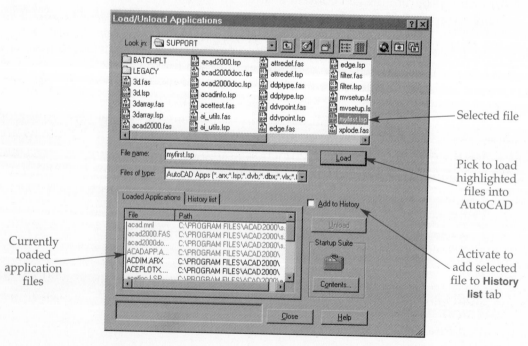

Selected file

Pick to load highlighted files into AutoCAD

Currently loaded application files

Activate to add selected file to **History list** tab

A list of currently loaded applications appears in the **Loaded Applications** tab. To locate an application file, use the file selection window near the top of the dialog box. Picking the **Load** button loads the currently selected application file. If the **Add to History** check box is activated, the loaded file will be added to the list in the **History list** tab. This tab provides convenient access to saved files during subsequent **APPLOAD** sessions and keeps you from having to search for frequently used files every time they are needed. You can highlight any number of files in the file list, and picking the **Load** button loads all of the highlighted file names. Picking the **Remove** button removes any highlighted files from the **History list** tab, but does not affect the actual AutoLISP files.

You can also load an AutoLISP file by highlighting the file in Windows Explorer and dragging and dropping it into the AutoCAD drawing area. This method is extremely convenient if Windows Explorer is active.

The **LOAD** function allows you to load an AutoLISP file at the command line. This function requires an AutoLISP file name as its argument and requires that the name be enclosed in quotation marks. To load the myfirst.lsp file using the **LOAD** function, the following sequence is used:

```
Command: (LOAD "MYFIRST")↵
C:FC
Command:
```

When the file has an LSP file extension, it is not necessary to include the extension in the **LOAD** expression. Therefore, you should use the standard LSP file extension for all AutoLISP files you create. If you are loading an AutoLISP file that does not use an LSP file extension, the actual extension must be included in the file name argument.

When an AutoLISP file is loaded and no errors are encountered, the result of evaluating the last expression in the file is returned to the screen. In the example above, the last expression in the file is the function definition for the **FC** function, so the function name is returned.

The **LOAD** function locates AutoLISP files located in the Support File Search Path. To load a file that exists elsewhere, the path name must also be specified. In the following example, the myfirst.lsp file is stored in the C:\My Documents\AutoLISP folder.

```
Command: (LOAD "C:/MY DOCUMENTS/AUTOLISP/MYFIRST")↵
C:FC
```

Notice that backslashes are not used in the path specification. In an AutoLISP text string, the backslash is used to specify special characters. For example, the string \n indicates a new line, or carriage return. When specifying file paths, you can use either forward slashes or double-backslashes (\\). Therefore, in the example above, the file to load could also have been specified as C:\\My Documents\\AutoLISP\\myfirst.

If you frequently load files that are in a folder not found in the Support File Search Path, it may be helpful to include the folder in the path. This is done using the **Options** dialog box. After displaying this dialog box, pick the **Files** tab and select Support File Search Path. Then, pick the **Add...** button and enter the desired folder.

As indicated previously, when you have defined one or more functions that you want to have available in all editing sessions, the definitions can be placed in the acad2000doc.lsp file.

NOTE	If the acad2000doc.lsp file already exists on your system, consult your system administrator or instructor prior to editing this file directly. The acad2000.lsp and acad2000doc.lsp files are often used by third-party applications, and changing them or accidentally redefining existing commands or functions may render certain features unusable.

PROFESSIONAL TIP	If you work frequently with AutoLISP files, you may wish to learn more about the more advanced features of the **Visual LISP** editor. Some of these advanced features include powerful formatting and debugging tools that make your programming time much more productive. For a complete discussion of these topics, refer to the *Visual LISP Developer's Guide*.

EXERCISE 24-4

❑ Use the **Visual LISP** editor to create an AutoLISP program file named EX24-4.LSP.
   ❑ Define at least 10 shortcut commands.
   ❑ Load EX24-4.LSP and test each of your functions.
❑ Make any necessary corrections and save the file again.

Creating Specialized Functions

Although shortcut commands represent a powerful AutoLISP implementation, AutoLISP can also be used to create highly specialized functions that perform unique tasks. Input can specify how the program should function in any given situation. This aspect of AutoLISP allows you to customize AutoCAD to meet the specific needs of your industry or department.

AutoLISP is a versatile tool, offering many different functions for working effectively with numeric data, text data, data files, and AutoCAD drawing objects. The following section introduces several basic AutoLISP functions, including some that are used for acquiring input from the user.

Providing for user input

There are many different data types for which AutoLISP can prompt. Depending on what it does, a program may need numeric input, text input, or specification of a point coordinate location. The **GETPOINT** function prompts for a point entry and pauses the program until the point is entered. For example:

   Command: **(SETQ PT1 (GETPOINT))**↵

After you press [Enter], AutoLISP waits for a value to be input for the PT1 variable. A prompt can be added to the original expression to clarify it as follows:

   Command: **(SETQ PT1 (GETPOINT "Enter a point: "))**↵
   Enter a point:

Whether you specify a prompt or not, AutoLISP now waits for you to enter a value to be assigned to the PT1 variable. Pick a point on screen. The coordinates for the selected point are assigned to PT1 and displayed at the command line. If you know the X,Y coordinates, enter them at the keyboard.

Command: **(SETQ PT1 (GETPOINT "Enter a point: "))**↵
Enter a point: **9.5,6.3.**↵

The following is an example of how closely AutoCAD and AutoLISP work together. First, define the two variables PT1 and PT2 as shown below. Then, enter the **LINE** command and use AutoLISP notation to return the values of PT1 and PT2 as the endpoints of the line.

Command: **(SETQ PT1 (GETPOINT "From point: "))**↵
From point: **2,2.**↵
Command: **(SETQ PT2 (GETPOINT "To point: "))**↵
To point: **6.25,2.**↵
Command: **LINE.**↵
Specify first point: **!PT1.**↵
(2.0 2.0 0.0)
Specify next point or [Undo]: **!PT2.**↵
(6.25 2.0 0.0)
Specify next point or [Undo]: ↵

AutoCAD uses the values you assigned to PT1 and PT2 for the points. The following is a sample function definition named **1LINE** that uses expressions similar to those given in the previous example. It draws a line object based on user input:

```
(DEFUN C:1LINE ()
   (SETQ PNT1 (GETPOINT "From point: "))
   (SETQ PNT2 (GETPOINT "To point: "))
   (COMMAND "LINE" PNT1 PNT2 "")
   (PRINC)
)
```

The pair of quotation marks near the end of the fourth line results in an [Enter] after the second point entry, ending the **LINE** command.

When developing AutoLISP routines, you may need to assign the length of a line or the distance between two points to a variable. The **GETDIST** function allows you to assign a distance to a variable. The optional prompt is not used in the following example:

Command: **(SETQ LGTH (GETDIST))**↵
(pick the first point)
Specify second point: *(pick the second point)*
distance

Use object snaps for accuracy if the points are on existing objects, or enter absolute coordinates if they are known. After the second point is picked or an exact distance is entered, the distance value is shown and assigned to the variable. In the example given, the distance is assigned to the variable LGTH. You can confirm the setting as follows:

Command: **!LGTH.**↵
distance

PROFESSIONAL TIP The sample AutoLISP expressions in this section are entered manually at the command line. AutoLISP expressions are more effective as part of a program file created using Visual LISP.

The **DISTANCE** function is similar to the **GETDIST** function. However, the **DISTANCE** function does not require picking two points. Instead, it measures the distance between two *existing* points. This function can be used to display a distance or to assign a distance to a variable.

Command: **(DISTANCE PT1 PT2).**↵
distance between PT1 and PT2

Command: **(SETQ D1 (DISTANCE PT1 PT2)).**↵
distance between PT1 and PT2

The first example returns the distance between the previously defined points PT1 and PT2. The second example applies that distance to the variable D1.

EXERCISE 24-5

❑ Use the proper AutoLISP language to write expressions for the functions given below. Write the expressions on a separate sheet of paper and test them by entering them into the computer.
A. Assign a point picked on screen to the variable PNT1.
B. Assign a point picked on screen to the variable PNT2.
C. Create the variable DIS and assign it the distance between PNT1 and PNT2.
D. Create a function named LINE1 that draws a line between PNT1 and PNT2.
E. Use the **DISTANCE** function to return the distance between PNT1 and PNT2.

Assigning text values to AutoLISP applications

Values assigned to AutoLISP variables do not have to be numeric values. In some applications, you may need to assign a word or line of text to a variable. To do so, use the **SETQ** function and enclose the word(s) in quotation marks as follows:

Command: **(SETQ W "What next?").**↵
"What next?"

You can also assign a word or line of text to a variable with the **GETSTRING** function. This function is similar to the **GETPOINT** function, because it prompts the user to enter a value. Look at the following example:

Command: **(SETQ E (GETSTRING)).**↵

Nothing is displayed on the command line because the optional prompt was not specified. AutoLISP is waiting for a "string" of characters. You can enter as many characters (numbers and letters) as needed. Once you press [Enter] or the space bar, the string is entered and displayed. To allow for spaces in the response, enter the letter T, without quotation marks, after the **GETSTRING** function:

Command: **(SETQ E (GETSTRING T)).**↵
HI THERE.↵
"HI THERE"
Command:

Confirm the value of the variable as follows:

Command: **!E.**↵
"HI THERE"

The **PROMPT** function can be used to simply display a message. The resulting message has no variable value. AutoLISP indicates this by printing nil after the prompt:

Command: **(PROMPT "Select an object:")**↲
Select an object: nil

You can use prompts in AutoLISP programs to provide information or to prompt the user.

EXERCISE 24-6

❑ Use the proper AutoLISP language to write expressions for the functions given below. Write out the expressions on a separate sheet of paper and then test them by entering them into the computer.
  A. Assign the word Void to the variable VO.
  B. Assign the text Enter text height to the variable TE.
  C. Create the variable JP as a point that is picked on the screen. Issue the prompt Pick a point:.
  D. Create the variable KP as a point that is picked on the screen, and issue the prompt Pick a point:.
  E. Set the distance between points JP and KP to the variable LP.
  F. Issue a prompt that says This is only an exercise.

Basic AutoLISP Review

Before applying the functions you have learned to an AutoLISP program, take a few minutes to review the following list. These functions are used in the next section.

- **(+, −, *, /).** These are the basic math functions used in AutoLISP. They must be entered as the first part of an expression. For example: (+ 6 8).
- **(SETQ).** The **SETQ** (set quote) function allows a value to be assigned to a variable. For example, the expression (SETQ CITY "San Francisco") sets the value San Francisco to the variable CITY.
- **(!).** An exclamation point entered before a variable returns the value of the variable. For example, the expression !CITY returns the value San Francisco.
- **(GETPOINT).** This function allows you to define a point location by entering coordinates at the keyboard or using the pointing device. The resulting value can be applied to a variable. For example, the expression (SETQ A (GETPOINT)) assigns a point to the variable A.
- **(GETDIST).** This function provides a distance between two points entered at the keyboard or picked on screen. The value can be applied to a variable, and a prompt can be used. For example, the expression (SETQ D2 (GETDIST "Pick two points:")) allows you to determine a distance and assign it to the variable D2.
- **(DISTANCE).** This function returns a distance between two existing points. For example, the expression (DISTANCE P1 P2) returns the distance between P1 and P2. The distance can also be assigned to a variable. For example: (SETQ D (DISTANCE P1 P2)).

- **(GETSTRING).** This function returns a word or string of characters entered by the user. No spaces are allowed. For example, the expression (GETSTRING) waits for a string of characters and displays the string when [Enter] or the space bar is pressed. The resulting text can be assigned to a variable. Spaces are allowed in the text string if a T follows the **GETSTRING** function. For example, the expression (SETQ TXT (GETSTRING T "Enter text:")) assigns the resulting text entered to the variable TXT.
- **(PROMPT).** Messages or prompts can be issued in a program using the **PROMPT** function. For example, the expression (PROMPT "Select an entity:") prints the Select an entity: prompt.

PROFESSIONAL TIP

Design your AutoLISP programs to closely resemble the way AutoCAD works. For example, it is easier for the user to read "back-to-back" prompts when the prompts appear on separate lines. Use the \n string to specify a new line for a prompt. For example: (SETQ PT2 (GETPOINT "\nTo point:"))

EXERCISE 24-7

❏ Write an AutoLISP program that places the text NOTES: at a location that you pick on screen. Name the file EX24-7.LSP.
❏ On a separate sheet of paper, write a description of the program in longhand. Then, write out each line of code.
❏ Create the program using the **Visual LISP** editor and then test it in AutoCAD.
❏ Use the following guidelines when writing the program:
  ❏ Provide a comment line giving the author, date, and name of the file.
  ❏ Define a function named NOTES with two variables, P1 and TXT.
  ❏ Specify the value for the variable P1 as the insertion location of the text. Include a prompt for the user to enter the text location.
  ❏ Give the variable TXT the text value NOTES:.
  ❏ Write an expression for the **TEXT** command that does the following: Uses P1 as the text location; enters a text height of 0.25"; enters a rotation angle of 0; and uses the value for the variable TXT as the text.

AUTOLISP—BEYOND THE BASICS

As you practice using AutoLISP, you will develop ideas for programs that require additional commands and functions. Some of these programs may require that the user pick two corners of a windowed selection set. Another program may use existing points to draw a shape. You may also need to locate a point using polar coordinate notation, or determine the angle of a line. All of these drawing tasks can be done with AutoLISP programs.

Providing for Additional User Input

The **GETREAL** function allows the user to define a variable value by entering a real number at the keyboard. Remember, as defined by AutoLISP, real numbers are classified separately from integers. A real number is considered to be more precise than an integer because it has a decimal value.

The **GETREAL** function works with numbers as units. You cannot respond with a value of feet and inches. Once issued, the function waits for user input. If input for a prompt is provided, a prompt is given and the real number is returned after a response. The **GETREAL** function can be used to set the value of a variable as follows:

Command: **(SETQ X (GETREAL "Enter number:"))**↲
Enter number: **34**↲
34.0

The **GETCORNER** function allows the user to pick the opposite corner of a rectangle and define it as a point value. This is similar to placing a window around objects to define a selection set in a drawing. An existing point serves as the first corner of the rectangle. When locating the opposite corner, the screen cursor appears as a "rubber band" box similar to the window used when defining a selection set.

The **GETCORNER** function can also be used to set the value of a variable. The second corner can be picked with the pointing device, or entered at the keyboard. The following is an example of using the **GETCORNER** function:

Command: **(SETQ PT1 (GETPOINT "\nPick a point:"))**↲
Pick a point: *(pick the point)*
Command: **(SETQ PT2 (GETCORNER PT1 "\nPick the second corner:"))**↲
Pick the second corner: *(pick the corner)*

Notice that the value of PT1 is set first. The point represented by PT1 becomes the base point for locating PT2. The two points (corners) located in this example can be used to construct an angled line, rectangle, or other shape. The points can also be applied to other functions.

Using the Values of System Variables

AutoCAD's system variables can be accessed for AutoLISP applications with the **GETVAR** and **SETVAR** functions. These functions can be useful if an application requires you to store the value of a system variable in an AutoLISP variable, change the system variable setting for your program, and then reset it to its original value.

The **GETVAR** function is used to return the value of a system variable. In the following example, two system variable settings are saved as variable values:

Command: **(SETQ V1 (GETVAR "TEXTSIZE"))**↲
current value of the **TEXTSIZE** *system variable*
Command: **(SETQ V2 (GETVAR "FILLETRAD"))**↲
current value of the **FILLETRAD** *system variable*

The **SETVAR** function is used to change an AutoCAD system variable setting. You can assign a new value to a variable as follows:

Command: **(SETVAR "TEXTSIZE" 0.25)**↲
0.25
Command: **(SETVAR "FILLETRAD" 0.25)**↲
0.25

Suppose you need to save a current system variable setting, change the variable, and then reset the variable to its original value after the command is executed. The **GETVAR** function can be used to supply a value to a variable, as shown in the first example on the **TEXTSIZE** system variable above. When the program is complete, the **SETVAR** function can be used to reset **TEXTSIZE** to its original value:

Command: **(SETVAR "TEXTSIZE" V1)**↲
0.125

This returns the value of **TEXTSIZE** to the value of the variable V1, which is 0.125 (the original system variable setting).

Working with Lists

In AutoLISP, a *list* is defined as a stored set of values that are enclosed in parentheses. Lists are commonly used to provide point locations and other data for use in functions. A list is created, for example, when you pick a point on screen in response to the **GETPOINT** function. The list is composed of three numbers—the X, Y, and Z coordinate values. You can tell it is a list because AutoLISP returns the numbers enclosed in parentheses. A number entered in response to the **GETREAL** function returns as a real number (it is not enclosed in parentheses). A single number is not a list. The following expression returns a list:

```
Command: (SETQ P1 (GETPOINT "Enter point:"))↵
Enter point: (pick a point)
(2.0 2.75 0.0)
```

The individual values in a list are called *atoms*, and can be used in an AutoLISP program to create new points to draw shapes. The **CAR** function retrieves the first atom in a list (for instance, the X coordinate in the previous example). The variable P1 in the example above is composed of the list (2.0 2.75 0.0). Thus, using the **CAR** function with this variable returns a value of 2.0. Enter the following:

```
Command: (CAR P1)↵
2.0
```

The second atom in a list (the Y coordinate) is retrieved with the **CADR** function. Find the second atom of the list related to the variable P1 by entering the following:

```
Command: (CADR P1)↵
2.75
```

You can create a new list of two coordinates by selecting values from existing points using the **CAR** and **CADR** functions. This is done with the **LIST** function. Values returned by this function are placed inside parentheses. The coordinates of the first variable, P1, can be combined with the coordinates of a second point variable named P2 to form a third point variable named P3. Study the following example, and the illustration in Figure 24-5. The coordinates of variable P1 are 2.0,2.75.

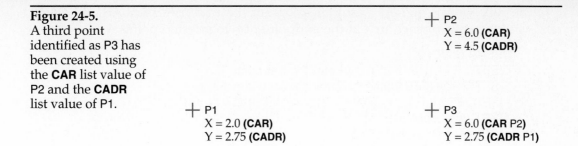

Figure 24-5.
A third point identified as P3 has been created using the **CAR** list value of P2 and the **CADR** list value of P1.

P2
X = 6.0 (**CAR**)
Y = 4.5 (**CADR**)

P1
X = 2.0 (**CAR**)
Y = 2.75 (**CADR**)

P3
X = 6.0 (**CAR** P2)
Y = 2.75 (**CADR** P1)

 Command: **(SETQ P2 (GETCORNER P1 "Enter second point:"))**↵
Enter second point: **6,4.5.**↵
(6.0 4.5 0.0)
Command: **(SETQ P3 (LIST (CAR P2) (CADR P1)))**↵
(6.0 2.75)

In AutoLISP, a function is followed by an argument. An argument consists of data that a function operates on or with. An expression must be composed of only one function and any required arguments. Therefore, the functions **CAR** and **CADR** must be separated because they are two different expressions combined to make a list. The **CAR** list value of P2 is to be the X value of P3, so it is given first. The **CADR** list value of P1 is placed second because it is to be the Y value of P3. Notice the number of closing parentheses at the end of the expression.

Now, with three points defined, there are many things you can do. For example, you can draw lines through the points to form a triangle, Figure 24-6. To do so, use the **COMMAND** function as follows:

 Command: **(COMMAND "LINE" P1 P2 P3 "C")**↵

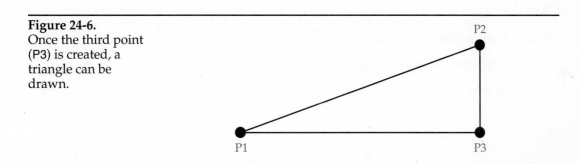

Figure 24-6.
Once the third point (P3) is created, a triangle can be drawn.

P2

P1

P3

The **CAR** and **CADR** functions allow you to work with 2D coordinates. The **CADDR** function allows you to use the Z value of a 3D coordinate (the third atom of a list). Enter the following at your keyboard:

 Command: **(SETQ B (LIST 3 4 6))**↵
 (3 4 6)

You have created a list of three atoms, or coordinate values. The third value is the Z coordinate. Retrieve that value with the **CADDR** function as follows:

 Command: **(CADDR B)**↵
 6

Since 6 is a single value as opposed to a list, it is not enclosed in parentheses. Now use the **CAR** and **CADR** functions to find the other two atoms of the list:

 Command: **(CAR B)**↵
 3
 Command: **(CADR B)**↵
 4

The following is a short AutoLISP program file that uses the **CAR** and **CADR** retrieval functions to place an X at the midpoint of two selected points.

```
(DEFUN C:MDPNT ()
   (SETQ PT1 (GETPOINT "\nEnter the first point:"))
   (SETQ PT2 (GETPOINT "\nEnter the second point:"))
   (SETQ PT3 (LIST (/ (+ (CAR PT1) (CAR PT2)) 2) (/ (+ (CADR PT1) (CADR PT2)) 2)))
   (SETVAR "PDMODE" 3)
   (COMMAND "POINT" PT3)
)
```

The **CDR** function allows you to retrieve the second and remaining values of a list. Earlier in this discussion, the list (3 4 6) was assigned to variable B. In the following example, the **CDR** function is used to return the list (4 6):

Command: **(CDR B).**⏎
(4 6)

This is now a separate list of two values, or coordinates, that can be manipulated with the **CAR** and **CADR** functions. Study Figure 24-7 and the following examples:

Command: **(CAR (CDR B)).**⏎
4
Command: **(CADR (CDR B)).**⏎
6

The first example is asking for the first atom (**CAR**) of the list (4 6). The values of this list were originally the last two atoms (**CDR**) of the list for variable B. In the second example, the second atom (**CADR**) of the list (4 6) is returned.

Figure 24-7.
The **CDR** function creates a list containing the second and remaining atoms of a list. The new list can be manipulated as necessary with the **CAR** and **CADR** functions.

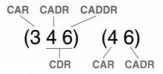

The four functions used to manipulate lists—**CAR, CADR, CADDR,** and **CDR**—may seem confusing at first. Practice using them and discover how they work. Practice with a list of numbers, coordinate values, or text strings. Remember, text strings must be enclosed in quotation marks. Try the following examples to see what happens. Enter the expressions at the Command: prompt exactly as shown and press [Enter] at the end of each line.

```
(SETQ NOTES (LIST "DO" "RE" "MI"))
(CAR NOTES)
(CADR NOTES)
(CADDR NOTES)
(CDR NOTES)
(SETQ LASTNOTES (CDR NOTES))
(CAR (CDR NOTES))
(CADR (CDR NOTES))
(CAR LASTNOTES)
(CADR LASTNOTES)
```

Review of list-retrieving and creating functions
- **(CAR).** Returns the first atom in a list.
- **(CADR).** Returns the second atom in a list.
- **(CADDR).** Returns the third atom in a list.
- **(CDR).** Returns the second and remaining atoms of a list. The returned values are placed in a list. If the original list contains two atoms, only the second atom is returned, and it is placed in a list.
- **(LIST).** Creates a list of all values entered after the function name.

EXERCISE 24-9

❑ Write an AutoLISP program that draws a right triangle using points provided by the user. The 90° angle can be on the left or right side.
❑ Write the program in proper AutoLISP format. Use the **Visual LISP** editor and save the file as EX24-9.LSP.
❑ Use the following guidelines to write the program:
  ❑ Define a function named TRIANGLE.
  ❑ Set the variable P1 as the first point of the triangle. Provide a user prompt.
  ❑ Set the variable P2 as the endpoint of the hypotenuse using the **GETCORNER** function. Place a user prompt on the next line.
  ❑ Set the variable P3 to the X coordinate of P2 and the Y coordinate of P1.
  ❑ Write an expression that draws a line through all three points and closes the triangle.
❑ Before saving the file, check for matching parentheses and quotation marks. Save the program and then test it.

USING POLAR COORDINATES AND ANGLES

The ability to work with angles is vital if you plan to do much AutoLISP programming. Four functions—**ANGLE, POLAR, GETANGLE,** and **GETORIENT**—allow you to use angles when writing program files. AutoLISP works with these functions using the radian system of angle measurement. This system of measurement is explained in the next section.

Measuring an Angle

The **ANGLE** function is used to calculate the angle between two given points. The value of the angle is given in radians. *Radian angle measurement* is a system in which 180° equals "pi" (π). Pi is approximately equal to 3.14159.

AutoLISP functions use radians for angular measurement, but AutoCAD commands use degrees. Therefore, to use a radian angle in an AutoCAD command, it must first be converted to degrees. Conversely, a degree angle to be used by AutoLISP must be converted to radians. The following formulas are used for those conversions.

- To convert degrees to radians, use the formula

  (* pi (/ *ad* 180.0))

  where *ad* = angle in degrees.
- To convert radians to degrees, use the formula

  (/ (* *ar* 180.0) pi)

  where *ar* = angle in radians.

The following example illustrates how the angle between two points can be set to a variable, then converted to degrees.

```
Command: (SETQ P1 (GETPOINT "Enter first point:"))↵
Enter first point: 1.75,5.25↵
(1.75 5.25 0.0)
Command: (SETQ P2 (GETPOINT "Enter second point:"))↵
Enter second point: 6.75,7.25↵
(6.75 7.25 0.0)
Command: (SETQ A1 (ANGLE P1 P2))↵
0.380506
```

The angle represented by the variable A1 is measured in radians (0.380506). To convert this value to degrees, use the following expression:

```
Command: (/ (* A1 180.0) PI)↵
21.8014
Command: !A1↵
0.380506
```

The value 21.8014 is the angle in degrees between P1 and P2. This conversion does not reset the variable A1 to the value in degrees. Make the value permanent by assigning it to the variable using the following expression:

```
Command: (SETQ A1 (/ (* A1 180.0) PI))↵
21.8014
Command: !A1↵
21.8014
```

The variable A1 now has a value of 21.8014°.

The following table gives common angles measured in degrees, the AutoLISP expressions used to convert the angular values to radian values, and the resulting values in radians.

Angle (degrees)	AutoLISP expression	Angle (radians)
0		0
30	(/ pi 6)	0.5236
45	(/ pi 4)	0.7854
60	(/ pi 3)	1.0472
90	(/ pi 2)	1.5708
135	(/ (* pi 3) 4)	2.3562
180	(+ pi)	3.1416
270	(/ (* pi 3) 2)	4.7124
360	(* pi 2)	6.2832

EXERCISE 24-10

❏ Using AutoLISP expressions, locate the endpoints of a line and store each endpoint as a variable.
❏ Use the **ANGLE** function to find the angle of the line. Set the value to the variable A.
❏ Use the proper formula to convert the radian value to degrees.
❏ Use the proper expression to assign the degree value to the variable A.

Providing for Angular Input by the User

The **GETANGLE** function allows the user to input an angular value for use in an application. This function is often used to set a variable that can be used by another function. The **GETANGLE** function automatically issues a Specify second point: prompt.

The following example illustrates how you can set a variable to an angular value input by the user:

Command: **(SETQ A (GETANGLE "Pick first point:"))**↵
Pick first point: *(pick the first point)*
Specify second point: *(pick the second point)*
angle (in radians)

The angular value is given in radians. To convert it to degrees, use the formula presented in the previous section.

The **GETANGLE** function uses the current **ANGBASE** (angle 0 direction) and **ANGDIR** (clockwise or counterclockwise) system variables. Therefore, if you have angles set to be measured from north (where **ANGBASE** = 90°), angles picked with the **GETANGLE** function will be measured from north. If the **ANGDIR** system variable is set to measure angles clockwise, the **GETANGLE** function will accept input of clockwise values, but returns counterclockwise values. A companion function to **GETANGLE** is **GETORIENT**. It is used in exactly the same manner as the **GETANGLE** function, but it always measures angles counterclockwise from east (0°), regardless of the current **ANGBASE** and **ANGDIR** system variable settings.

EXERCISE 24-11

❑ Use the **GETANGLE** function to assign an angular value to the variable ANG1.
  ❑ Convert the radian value to degrees using the proper AutoLISP expression. Assign the degree value to ANG1.
  ❑ Convert the degree value back to radians using the proper AutoLISP expression. Redefine the variable ANG1 with the radian value.
❑ Use the **GETORIENT** function to find the angle (in radians) of any two points.
❑ Using the proper AutoLISP expression, save the current setting of the **ANGBASE** system variable to the variable AB. Then, change the system variable setting to 90. To change the setting, use the **SETVAR** function and the proper AutoLISP expression for converting the degree value to radians (/ pi 2).
  ❑ Use the **GETORIENT** function again to find the angle of the two points.
  ❑ Use the **GETANGLE** function to find the angle of the two points.
  ❑ Reset the **ANGBASE** system variable to its default value.
  ❑ Compare the values obtained with the **GETORIENT** and **GETANGLE** functions. Explain the results.

Using Polar Coordinates

The **POLAR** function allows you to specify the angle and distance of a point relative to another point. Two variables must first be set for the **POLAR** function to work properly—the point that you are locating a new point from, and the distance between the two points. The syntax for the POLAR function is as follows:

(POLAR *base_point angle distance*)

For example, suppose you want to specify a point as P1, and then locate another point, P2, at a specific distance and angle from P1. Enter the following expressions:

Command: **(SETQ P1 (GETPOINT "Enter point:"))**↵
Enter point: **4.0,4.5**↵
Command: **(SETQ D (GETDIST P1 "Enter distance:"))**
Enter distance: **3.0**↵
Command: **(SETQ A (/ PI 3))**↵
1.0472

In this expression, the angle 60° is used. However, AutoLISP uses radians for angular values. Therefore, the degree value is converted to radians. The resulting angle of 1.0472 is saved as the variable A. Next, the **POLAR** function is used to locate the second point relative to P1 using the specified angle and distance. A line can then be drawn from P1 at 60° using the **COMMAND** function. The sequence is as follows:

Command: **(SETQ P2 (POLAR P1 A D))**↵
(5.5 7.09808)
Command: **(COMMAND "LINE" P1 P2)**↵

EXERCISE 24-12

❏ Write an AutoLISP program that draws a right triangle. If you need to, refer to EX24-9. However, use the **POLAR** function instead of the **LIST** functions.
❏ Write the program in proper AutoLISP format using the **Visual LISP** editor. Save the file as EX24-12.LSP and then enter the program into your computer to test it.
❏ Use the following guidelines for writing the program:
  ❏ Define a function named POLARTRI.
  ❏ Set the variable P1 as the first corner of the triangle. Provide a user prompt.
  ❏ Set the variable D as the length of one side.
  ❏ Set the variable P2 as the second corner located 0° from P1 at a distance of D.
  ❏ Set the variable P3 as the third corner located 90° from P2 at a distance of D.
  ❏ Write an expression that draws a line through all three points and closes the triangle.

LOCATING AUTOCAD'S AUTOLISP FILES

One of the best ways to become familiar with AutoLISP is to enter expressions and programs into your computer. Look for programs in books or magazines that you read. Get a feel for how the functions and arguments go together and how they work in AutoCAD. Make a habit of reading through one of the AutoCAD journals and experiment with the AutoLISP routines printed in them. Also, refer to the *Visual LISP Developer's Guide* for other samples.

A variety of AutoLISP programs are supplied with AutoCAD. AutoLISP files typically use the LSP file extension. There are four subfolders in your Acad2000 folder that contain various AutoLISP program files. The contents of three of these folders are shown in Figure 24-8.

The AutoLISP files found in the Support folder are standard files that support many of AutoCAD's built-in features. The files in the Sample\VisualLISP folder provide some sample AutoLISP programs, as well as some examples of AutoLISP working with external database applications. You will find many very powerful AutoLISP programs in the Express folder. The Tutorial folder provides a group of lesson files that are part of a tutorial program used to complete a drawing project with Visual LISP. You can use Windows Explorer to list the files in any of these folders. If you access the **View** pull-down menu in Explorer, you can then sort the files by selecting **by Type** from the **Arrange Icons** cascading menu. Sorting the files makes it easier to locate AutoLISP files.

Figure 24-8.
Many of the AutoLISP program files provided with AutoCAD can be found in several
subfolders located in the Acad2000 folder.

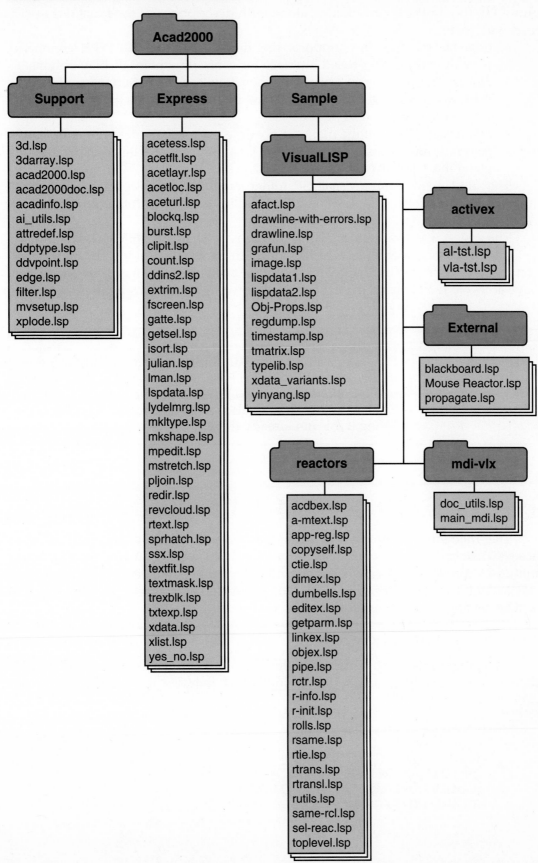

As previously mentioned, the Support folder contains standard files that support built-in AutoCAD functions. When the command that starts the function is entered, the associated program file is automatically loaded. The following is a short list of AutoLISP files in the Support folder, along with descriptions of the functions associated with each:

- **ddptype.lsp.** This file supports the function of the **DDPTYPE** command, providing the dialog-based interface for controlling point display options.
- **3d.lsp.** This routine is activated when you select <u>3</u>**D Surfaces...** from the **Surfaces** cascading menu in the **Dra<u>w</u>** pull-down menu. It activates the **3D Objects** dialog box.
- **3darray.lsp.** This routine makes it possible to create an arrangement of rows, columns, and levels of an object. See Chapter 2 for a detailed explanation of using the **3DARRAY** command.

The files in the Sample\VisualLISP folder provide examples for working with AutoLISP in a variety of applications. The files in the Express folder are part of the AutoCAD Express Tools.

The easiest way to access the Express Tools is by using the **MENULOAD** command to load the acetmain menu file, which is found in the Express folder. The **MENULOAD** command is discussed in Chapter 22. When the acetmain menu has been loaded, you have access to toolbars and the **E<u>x</u>press** pull-down menu for starting these functions.

PROFESSIONAL TIP

For easier access to any AutoLISP program file, add its folder in the Support File Search Path listing located in the **Files** tab of the **Options** dialog box. When using the Express Tools, the Express folder should also be added to the support path listing if it is not already there.

SAMPLE AUTOLISP PROGRAMS

The following programs are provided for you to copy and add to your acad2000doc.lsp file or to your custom menus. Practice using the routines for a few minutes a couple of times a week. This will help you begin to better understand and use AutoLISP. Train yourself to learn a new function every week. Before long, you will be writing your own useful programs.

Erasing the Entire Screen

This program sets two variables to the minimum and maximum screen limits. It then erases everything within those limits and redraws the screen. Name this program ZAP.LSP.

```
; ERASES ENTIRE LIMITS
(DEFUN C:ZAP ()
  (SETQ LMIN (GETVAR "LIMMIN"))
  (SETQ LMAX (GETVAR "LIMMAX"))
  (COMMAND "ERASE" "C" LMIN LMAX "")
  (COMMAND "REDRAW")
)
```

Setting the Current Layer

Similar to the built-in **Make Object's Layer Current** tool, this program asks for the user to point to an object on the layer to be set current. The program finds the layer of the object picked and sets the layer as current. Name this program LP.LSP.

```
; Author : Rod Rawls
(DEFUN C:LP (/ E)
    (WHILE (NOT (SETQ E (ENTSEL "\nSelect object on target layer...")))
        (ALERT "No object selected!")
    )
    (SETQ LN (CDR (ASSOC 8 (ENTGET (CAR E)))))
    (COMMAND "–LAYER" "S" LN "")
    (PRINC)
)
```

Cleaning Overlapping Corners

This program allows you to trim the overlapping ends of intersecting lines. You are requested to pick the two lines that intersect and overlap. The program does the rest. Name the program TRIMENDS.LSP.

```
; AUTHOR: GEORGE HEAD
; PRINTED IN THE JANUARY, 1988 ISSUE OF "CADENCE" MAGAZINE
(DEFUN C:CLEANC (/ O1 P1 P2)
    (SETQ O1 (GETVAR "OSMODE"))
    (SETVAR "OSMODE" 512)
    (COMMAND "FILLET" "R" 0)
    (SETQ P1 (GETPOINT "\nPick a line "))
    (SETQ P2 (GETPOINT "\nPick other line "))
    (COMMAND "FILLET" P1 P2)
    (SETVAR "OSMODE" O1)
)
```

Calculating the Length of Lines

This program calculates the length of all lines on a specified layer. It can be used for estimating and material takeoffs. This program works only with lines, not with polylines. Name the program LINEAR.LSP. After loading it into AutoCAD, respond to the first prompt by entering the name of the layer that contains the lines you wish to total. The calculation is given in current drawing units.

```
; AUTHOR       : JOE PUCILOWSKI
; COMPANY      : JOSEPH & ASSOCIATES
; ADDRESS      : 7809A RIVER RESORT LANE, TAMPA, FL
; NOTE         : THIS PROGRAM FIGURES THE TOTAL NUMBER OF LINEAR
;                  UNITS (FEET, INCHES, ETC.) OF LINES ON A SPECIFIC
    LAYER.
; REVISED      : BY ROD RAWLS
;
(DEFUN C:LINEAR     ()
    (SETQ       TOTAL  0
                E              (ENTNEXT)
                NUMLIN         0
                LAYPIK         (GETSTRING T "\nAdd up lines on layer: ")
    )
    (IF (TBLSEARCH "LAYER" LAYPIK)
        (PROGN
            (WHILE  E
```

```
        (SETQ ENTTYP (CDR (ASSOC 0 (SETQ EG (ENTGET E))))
              LAYNAM        (CDR (ASSOC 8 EG))
        )
        (IF
          (AND
                (EQUAL ENTTYP "LINE")
                (EQUAL LAYNAM LAYPIK)
          )
          (PROGN
                (SETQ LINLEN (DISTANCE (CDR (ASSOC 10 EG)) (CDR
                  (ASSOC 11 EG)))
                      TOTAL (+ TOTAL LINLEN)
                      NUMLIN (+ 1 NUMLIN)
                )
          )
        )
        (SETQ E (ENTNEXT E))
      )
      (PRINC
        (STRCAT        "\nFound "
          (ITOA NUMLIN)
          " lines on layer < "
          LAYPIK
          "> with a total of "
          (RTOS TOTAL)
          " linear units."
        )
      )
    )
    (PRINC "\nLayer does not exist.")
  )
  (PRINC)
)
```

Changing the Grid Rotation

This program, titled S.LSP, rotates the grid to the angle of any picked line. The second routine, SS.LSP, returns the grid to zero rotation.

```
; AUTHOR      : EBEN KUNZ
; COMPANY     : KUNZ ASSOCIATES ARCHITECTS
; Address     : 38 Greenwich Park, Boston, MA
;
(DEFUN C:S (/ PT1 PT2)
  (SETVAR "ORTHOMODE" 0)
  (SETQ PT1 (OSNAP (GETPOINT "\nPick line to match new Grid angle: \n")
  "NEA"))
  (SETQ PT2 (OSNAP PT1 "END"))
  (COMMAND "SNAP" "R" PT1 PT2)
  (SETVAR "SNAPMODE" 0)
)
(DEFUN C:SS ()
  (PROMPT "\nReturn Grid to zero.")
  (COMMAND "SNAP" "R" "" 0.0)
  (SETVAR "SNAPMODE" 0)
)
```

Moving Objects to the Current Layer

This simple program, titled CL.LSP, quickly changes selected objects to the current layer.

```
; AUTHOR      : BILL FANE
; COMPANY     : WEISER, INC.
; Address     : 6700 Beresford St., Burnaby, B.C.
;
(DEFUN C:CL (/ THINGS)
   (SETQ THINGS (SSGET))
   (COMMAND "CHANGE" THINGS "" "P" "LA"
        (GETVAR "CLAYER") "" )
)
```

Moving Objects to a Selected Layer

This routine, named LA.LSP, allows you to move objects to a layer by picking an object on the destination layer.

```
; AUTHOR      : SHELDON MCCARTHY
; COMPANY     : EPCM SERVICES LTD.
; Address     : 2404 Haines Road, Mississauga, Ontario
;
(DEFUN C:LA ()
   (SETQ 1A (CDR (ASSOC 8 (ENTGET (CAR (ENTSEL "Entity on destination
   layer: "))))))
   (PROMPT "Select objects to change:")
   (SSGET)
   (COMMAND "CHANGE" "P" "" "P" "LA" 1A "")
)
```

Chapter Test

Answer the following questions on a separate sheet of paper.

1. What is the standard extension used for AutoLISP files?
2. A comment is indicated in an AutoLISP file with a _____.
3. When in the drawing area, what are three ways to load the contents of the AutoLISP file named chgtext.lsp?
4. Define the terms *integer* and *real number* as related to applications in AutoLISP.
5. Write expressions in the proper AutoLISP format for the following arithmetic functions.

   A. 23 + 54
   B. 12.45 + 6.28
   C. 56 − 34
   D. 23.004 − 7.008
   E. 16 × 4.6
   F. 7.25 × 10.30
   G. 45 ÷ 23
   H. 147 ÷ 29.6
   I. 53 + (12 × 3.8)
   J. 567 ÷ (34 − 14)

6. Explain the purpose of the **SETQ** function.
7. Write the proper AutoLISP notation to assign the value of (67 − 34.5) to the variable NUM1.
8. What does the **GETPOINT** function allow you to do?
9. Write the proper AutoLISP notation that creates a list of the coordinate values X = 3.5 and Y = 5.25 and assigns it to the variable PT1.
10. Which AutoLISP function allows you to find the distance between two points?
11. Explain the purpose of the **GETSTRING** function.

12. Write the proper AutoLISP notation for assigning the string This is a test: to the variable TXT.
13. How do you allow spaces in a string of text when using the **GETSTRING** function?
14. Write the proper function notation for using the **PLINE** command in an AutoLISP expression.
15. What prefix must you enter before a function name in an expression to indicate it is accessible at the Command: prompt?
16. What is a *function definition*?
17. Define an *argument*.
18. What AutoLISP function is used to create new AutoCAD commands?
19. What is the purpose of the **Visual LISP** editor?
20. How is the **Visual LISP** editor accessed?
21. When entering text in the **Visual LISP** editor, which color indicates that you have entered a built-in function or a protected symbol?
22. Explain the purpose of the \n text string in AutoLISP.
23. Name the function that allows you to return a real number and use it as a variable value.
24. Which two functions allow you to work with system variables?
25. Define the following AutoLISP functions:
    A. **CAR**
    B. **CADR**
    C. **CDR**
    D. **CADDR**
    E. **LIST**
26. Write the proper AutoLISP notation to return the last two values of the list (4 7 3).
27. Write an expression to set a variable named A to the result of Question 26.
28. Write an expression to return the second value of the list created in Question 27.
29. Compare and contrast the **GETANGLE** and **GETORIENT** functions.
30. Write an expression to set the angle between points P3 and P4 to the variable A.
31. What system of angle measurement does AutoLISP use?
32. How do you express a 270° angle in the angular system AutoLISP uses?
33. Explain the purpose of the **POLAR** function.

Drawing Problems

*Write AutoLISP program files for the following problems. Use the **Visual LISP** editor. Save the files as P24-(problem number) with the LSP extension.*

1. Add the following capabilities to the right triangle function developed in Exercise 24-9.
   A. Use the **GETDIST** function instead of **GETCORNER**.
   B. Allow the angle of the hypotenuse to be picked.
   C. Allow the length of a side or the hypotenuse length to be picked.

2. Create an AutoLISP program similar to that in Problem 1, but write it so that it draws an equilateral triangle (with equal angles and equal sides). Use the **POLAR** function.

3. Write an AutoLISP program to draw a rectangle. Use only the **GETPOINT** function to set the opposite corners of the rectangle. Follow these guidelines:
   A. Set P1 as the first corner.
   B. Set P3 as the opposite corner.
   C. Set points P2 and P4 using the list functions of AutoLISP.
   D. Use the **LINE** command to draw the rectangle.

4. Revise the program in Problem 3 to draw a rectangle using the **GETCORNER** function to find the second corner.

5. Create an AutoLISP program to draw a square. Follow these guidelines:
   A. Set a variable for the length of one side.
   B. Set the variable P1 as the lower-left corner of the square.
   C. Use the **LINE** command to draw the square.

6. Revise the program in Problem 5 to draw a square using the **PLINE** command.

7. Use the program in Problem 6 to create a new command that draws a square and allows you to change the line thickness.
   A. Use the **PLINE** or **POLYGON** command to draw the square.
   B. Set a variable that enables the user to input the line thickness.

8. Add a **Fillet 0** command to your **Modify** pull-down menu. Use menu macros and AutoLISP expressions to create the command. Follow these guidelines:
   A. Retrieve the current fillet radius setting and assign it to an AutoLISP variable.
   B. Set the fillet radius to 0.
   C. Allow the user to select two lines and enter a 0 fillet.
   D. Reset the fillet radius to the original value.
   E. Assign an appropriate mnemonic shortcut key to the new command.

9. Write an AutoLISP program file that allows the user to measure the distance between two points using the **DIST** command. Use AutoLISP expressions to do the following:
   A. Assign the current unit precision for read-only linear units to an AutoLISP variable.
   B. Prompt for the desired unit precision from the user and store the value as a variable.
   C. Set the unit precision with the user-defined variable value.
   D. Allow the user to measure the distance between two selected points with the **DIST** command.
   E. Reset the unit precision to the original value.

10. Write an AutoLISP program that allows the user to draw parallel rectangles.
    A. Use the rectangle program from Problem 4, but replace the **LINE** command with the **PLINE** command.
    B. Provide a prompt that asks the user to enter an offset distance for a second rectangle to be placed inside the first rectangle.
    C. Use the **OFFSET** command to allow the user to draw the parallel rectangle inside the original.

11. Write an AutoLISP program to draw a rectangle and place a circle having a user-specified diameter in the center of the rectangle.
    A. Incorporate the rectangle program from Problem 4.
    B. Use the **ANGLE**, **POLAR**, and **DISTANCE** functions to find the center point of the rectangle.
    C. Prompt the user to enter the diameter of the circle.
    D. Use the **CIRCLE** command to draw the circle at the center point of the rectangle.

12. Write a program to draw a leader with a diameter dimension having plus and minus tolerances.
   A. Issue prompts that allow the user to set the **DIMTP** and **DIMTM** system variables and save the specified values to AutoLISP variables.
   B. Set the new values to the **DIMTP** and **DIMTM** system variables.
   C. Activate the **DIM** command and turn the **DIMTOL** system variable on.
   D. Activate the **DIAMETER** command. Using the **ENTSEL** function, issue a prompt that allows the user to select the circle being dimensioned. Set the selection specification to a variable as follows:

   (SETQ SC (ENTSEL "\nSelect arc or circle: "))

   E. Using the **GETPOINT** function, issue a prompt that allows the user to pick a location for the leader line and the default dimension text.
   F. Turn tolerancing off and exit the **DIM** command.

13. Write an AutoLISP program to draw a leader with a bubble attached to the end.
   A. Prompt the user for the start point of the leader and set it to the variable P1.
   B. Prompt the user for the endpoint of the leader and set it to the variable P2.
   C. Prompt the user for the text height and set it to a variable.
   D. Issue a prompt that asks for the text string (specify a maximum of two characters) and set the resulting text to a variable.
   E. Calculate the circle diameter at 2.5 or 3 times the text height and set it to a variable.
   F. Set the center point of the circle to a point relative to P2 using the **POLAR** function. Set the relative distance as the radius of the circle. Assign the center point to the variable P3.
   G. Use the **LEADER** command to draw a leader from P1 to P2.
   H. Draw the leader line with no shoulder and no annotation text.
   I. Draw a circle with the center point at P3.
   J. Draw text in the center of the circle using the appropriate justification option of the **TEXT** command.

14. Develop a program that writes a line of text and places a box around it.
   A. Prompt the user for the text height and set it to the variable TXHT.
   B. Prompt the user for a point representing the lower-left corner of the box and set it to a variable.
   C. Prompt for the text string from the user.
   D. Set the text string length to the variable LG1. Use the **STRLEN** function. The following is an example of using this function:

   (SETQ TEXT (GETSTRING T "Enter Text: "))
   (SETQ LG1 (STRLEN TEXT))

   E. Set the X length of the box to a variable using the following expression: (* LG1 TXHT).
   F. Set the Y length of the box to a variable using the following expression: (* 3 TXHT).
   G. Draw the box to lengths corresponding to the variables X and Y.
   H. Calculate the center point of the box, and set it to the variable CEN1.
   I. Draw the text string inside the box. Use the **MC** text justification option for point CEN1.

CHAPTER 25

Introduction to Dialog Control Language (DCL)

Learning Objectives

After completing this chapter, you will be able to:

■ Describe the types of files that control dialog boxes.
■ Define the components of a dialog box.
■ Write a DCL file for a basic dialog box.
■ Write an AutoLISP file to control a dialog box.
■ Associate an action with a dialog box tile.

Programmable dialog boxes can be used to completely customize the interface of AutoLISP programs. These dialog boxes allow LISP programs to work like many of AutoCAD's built-in functions. Using dialog boxes improves efficiency and reduces data entry errors.

Dialog boxes minimize the amount of typing required by the user. Rather than answering a series of text prompts on the command line, the user selects options from the dialog box. Dialog box fields can be filled in by the user in any order. While the dialog is still active, the user can revise values as necessary.

AutoLISP provides basic tools for controlling dialog boxes, but the dialog box itself must be defined using *Dialog Control Language* (*DCL*). The definition is written to an ASCII file with a .dcl file extension. When creating and editing DCL files, the **Visual LISP** editor provides many helpful tools including color coding.

DCL FILE FORMATS

A DCL file is formatted as an ASCII text file with a .dcl file extension. These files can have any valid file name, but a file name with 1 to 8 characters is recommended. Writing with DCL is easy. Many of the components of a DCL file are normal English words.

The components of a dialog box—such as edit boxes, images, and drop-down lists—are referred to as *tiles*. Tiles are defined by specifying various *attribute* values. Each attribute controls a specific property of the tile being defined, such as size, location, and default values.

When writing a DCL file, you do not use parentheses as you do with AutoLISP. When defining a dialog box or tile, all the required attributes are placed within {braces}. Indentation helps to separate individual elements, making the file more readable. Comments are preceded by two forward slashes (//). Semicolons are used at the end of an attribute definition line.

To view an example of DCL code, open the acad.dcl and base.dcl files with your text editor. These two files are found in the \ACAD2000\Support folder. A portion of the acad.dcl file is shown in Figure 25-1.

Figure 25-1.
A portion of the acad.dcl file.

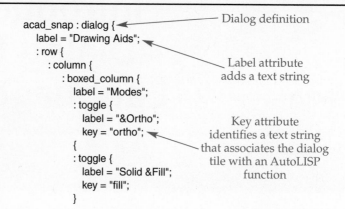

```
acad_snap : dialog {          ← Dialog definition
    label = "Drawing Aids";   ← Label attribute
    : row {                     adds a text string
        : column {
            : boxed_column {
                label = "Modes";
                : toggle {
                    label = "&Ortho";
                    key = "ortho";   ← Key attribute
                {                      identifies a text string
                : toggle {             that associates the dialog
                    label = "Solid &Fill";  tile with an AutoLISP
                    key = "fill";       function
                }
```

CAUTION

The base.dcl file contains standard prototype definitions. The acad.dcl file contains definitions for all the dialog boxes used by AutoCAD. *Do not edit either one of these files!* Altering them can cause AutoCAD's built-in dialog boxes to crash.

DCL Tiles

Your work in AutoCAD has provided you with a good background in how dialog boxes work. By now, you should be familiar with the use of buttons, edit boxes, radio buttons, and list boxes. This will be helpful as you design dialog interfaces for your AutoLISP programs.

DCL tiles are used individually or combined into structures called ***clusters***. For example, a series of button tiles can be placed in a column tile to control the arrangement of the buttons in the dialog box. The primary tile is the dialog box itself.

This chapter is only an introduction to DCL, and will cover basic DCL file construction and a few common tile types. For a full discussion of DCL and dialog creation and management techniques, refer to ***AutoLISP Programming*** published by Goodheart-Willcox Co., Inc.

The best way to begin understanding the format of a DCL file is to study a simple dialog box definition. The following DCL code defines the dialog box shown in Figure 25-2.

```
main : dialog {
    label  = "Dialog Box Example 1";
    : text_part {
            value    = "This is an example.";
    }
    ok_only;
}
```

Figure 25-2.
A sample custom dialog box.

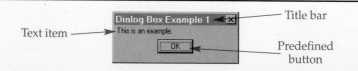

Text item — This is an example.
Title bar
Predefined button

Now, let's take a closer look at the definition of this dialog box.

```
main : dialog {
    label = "Dialog Box Example 1";
    : text_part {
          value   = "This is an example.";
    }
    ok_only;
}
```

The **dialog definition** is always the first tile definition. Everything within the braces defines the features of the dialog box. The word "main" indicates the name of the dialog box. This name is referenced by the controlling AutoLISP application. A colon (:) precedes all tile callouts. In the case of a dialog tile, the colon separates the name from the tile callout.

```
main : dialog {
    label = "Dialog Box Example 1";
    : text_part {
          value   = "This is an example.";
    }
    ok_only;
}
```

The **label** attribute of the dialog tile controls the text that appears in the title bar of the dialog box. The line is terminated with a semicolon. All attribute lines must be terminated with a semicolon.

```
main : dialog {
    label = "Dialog Box Example 1";
    : text_part {
          value   = "This is an example.";
    }
    ok_only;
}
```

The **text_part** tile allows placement of text items in a dialog box. The **value** attribute is used to specify the text that is displayed. Just as with the dialog tile, all of the attributes are defined between the braces.

```
main : dialog {
    label = "Dialog Box Example 1";
    : text_part {
          value   = "This is an example.";
    }
    ok_only;
}
```

This is a call to a **predefined tile** found in the base.dcl file. It is not preceded with a colon because it is not a specific definition. This line is terminated with a semicolon just like an attribute. No braces are required because this is not a tile definition, but a reference to a predefined tile.

There are many predefined tiles and subassemblies. A **subassembly** is a predefined tile cluster, such as OK_CANCEL and OK_CANCEL_HELP. The OK_ONLY tile places an **OK** button at the bottom of the dialog box, as shown in Figure 25-2.

Once you have defined a dialog box, the definition must then be saved in a DCL file. For this example, the dialog definition above is saved in the file EXAMPLE1.DCL. This is treated as any other support file, and should be saved in the AutoCAD support path.

For reference, look at the **Viewpoint Presets** dialog box shown in Figure 25-3. Various tiles of this dialog box are identified with the corresponding portion of the ddvpoint.dcl file.

Figure 25-3.
Some of the tile definitions and attributes associated with the **Viewpoint Presets** dialog box.

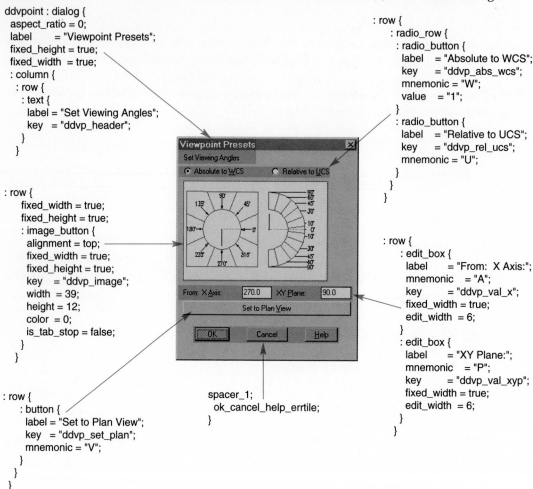

```
ddvpoint : dialog {
  aspect_ratio = 0;
  label     = "Viewpoint Presets";
  fixed_height = true;
  fixed_width  = true;
  : column {
    : row {
      : text {
        label = "Set Viewing Angles";
        key  = "ddvp_header";
      }
    }
  }

  : row {
    fixed_width = true;
    fixed_height = true;
    : image_button {
      alignment = top;
      fixed_width = true;
      fixed_height = true;
      key  = "ddvp_image";
      width = 39;
      height = 12;
      color = 0;
      is_tab_stop = false;
    }
  }

  : row {
    : button {
      label = "Set to Plan View";
      key  = "ddvp_set_plan";
      mnemonic = "V";
    }
  }
}
```

```
  : row {
    : radio_row {
      : radio_button {
        label    = "Absolute to WCS";
        key      = "ddvp_abs_wcs";
        mnemonic = "W";
        value    = "1";
      }
      : radio_button {
        label    = "Relative to UCS";
        key      = "ddvp_rel_ucs";
        mnemonic = "U";
      }
    }
  }

  : row {
    : edit_box {
      label     = "From:  X Axis:";
      mnemonic  = "A";
      key       = "ddvp_val_x";
      fixed_width = true;
      edit_width = 6;
    }
    : edit_box {
      label     = "XY Plane:";
      mnemonic  = "P";
      key       = "ddvp_val_xyp";
      fixed_width = true;
      edit_width  = 6;
    }
  }
```

```
  spacer_1;
  ok_cancel_help_errtile;
}
```

AUTOLISP AND DCL

A DCL file simply defines a dialog box. The dialog box cannot actually do anything without a controlling application. AutoLISP is frequently used to control dialog sessions. This section shows examples using the AutoLISP dialog handling functions.

In order to display a dialog box, the controlling application must first load the dialog definition. The **LOAD_DIALOG** function loads the specified dialog definition file:

(load_dialog "*filename*.dcl")

The file name is enclosed in quotation marks. The **LOAD_DIALOG** expression returns a positive integer that identifies the loaded DCL file. If the attempted load was unsuccessful, a negative integer is returned.

Once the descriptions within a specific DCL file are no longer needed, they can be removed from memory by using the **UNLOAD_DIALOG** function:

(unload_dialog dcl_id)

The next step is to activate a specific dialog box definition contained within the DCL file. The **NEW_DIALOG** function activates the dialog box specified, where *dlgname* is the name of the dialog box:

> (new_dialog *dlgname* dcl_id)

This function is case sensitive. The dialog definition used in the previous example is named main. Specifying Main or MAIN will not activate this dialog box, since the text string does not match exactly. The dcl_id argument represents the integer value returned by **LOAD_DIALOG**. **NEW_DIALOG** also supports additional, optional arguments, which are not discussed here.

To actually begin accepting input from the user, the **START_DIALOG** function must be used:

> (start_dialog)

This function has no arguments. It allows for input to be received from the dialog box initialized by the previous **NEW_DIALOG** expression.

With these basic AutoLISP functions, it is possible to display the dialog box shown in Figure 25-2. After the application file is written, it can be loaded into AutoCAD using the **LOAD** function or the **APPLOAD** command. The controlling AutoLISP application named EXAMPLE1.LSP appears as follows:

```
(setq DCL_ID (load_dialog "EXAMPLE1.DCL"))
(if (not (new_dialog "main" DCL_ID))
  (exit)
)
(start_dialog)
```

Now, let's take a closer look at the controlling code for this dialog box:

```
(setq DCL_ID (load_dialog "EXAMPLE1.DCL"))
(if (not (new_dialog "main" DCL_ID))
  (exit)
)
(start_dialog)
```

This expression loads the dialog definition found in example1.dcl and assigns the variable DCL_ID to the integer returned by **LOAD_DIALOG**.

```
(setq DCL_ID (load_dialog "EXAMPLE1.DCL"))
(if (not (new_dialog "main" DCL_ID))
  (exit)
)
(start_dialog)
```

If **NEW_DIALOG** is unable to activate the specified dialog box for any reason, this function exits (terminates) the application. This is an important safety feature. In many cases, loading an incorrect or incomplete definition can cause your system to lock up, often requiring that the system be rebooted.

```
(setq DCL_ID (load_dialog "EXAMPLE1.DCL"))
(if (not (new_dialog "main" DCL_ID))
  (exit)
)
(start_dialog)
```

This expression starts the dialog session using the dialog box indicated by the previous **NEW_DIALOG** expression.

EXERCISE 25-1

❏ Use the examples in the text to create EXAMPLE1.DCL and EXAMPLE1.LSP. Create each file in the **Visual LISP** editor.
❏ Load the AutoLISP program file and run the dialog box session to test the files.

Associating Functions with Tiles

Most tiles can be associated with actions. These actions vary from run-time error checking to performing tasks outside the dialog session. The **ACTION_TILE** function provides the basic means of associating tiles with actions.

> (action_tile *"key"* *"action-expression"*)

The *key* references the attribute assigned in the DCL file. The *action-expression* is the AutoLISP expression performed when the action is called. Both the key and action-expression arguments are supplied as text strings.

In order to access a specific tile from AutoLISP, the key of the tile must be referenced. The key is specified as an attribute in the DCL file. Tiles that are static (unchanging) do not require keys. Any tile that must be referenced in any way—such as setting or retrieving a value, associating an action, or enabling/disabling the tile—requires a key.

The next example changes the previous dialog box by adding a button that displays the current time when picked. The new or changed code is shown in color.

```
main : dialog {
    label = "Dialog Box Example 2";
    : text_part {
        value   = "";
        key     = "time";
    }
    : button {
        key     = "update";
        label   = "Display Current Time";
        mnemonic    = "C";
    }
    ok_only;
}
```

Save this file as EXAMPLE2.DCL.

Notice the addition of a key attribute to the text_part tile. This allows access by the AutoLISP application while the dialog session is running. Another addition is the button tile. A key is provided in the button tile so an association can be created with an action-expression. The label attribute provides the text displayed on the button. The mnemonic attribute underlines the specified letter within the label to allow keyboard access.

The AutoLISP application used to manage this dialog session is shown below.

```
(setq DCL_ID (load_dialog "EXAMPLE2.DCL"))
(if      (not (new_dialog "main" DCL_ID))
         (exit)
)
(defun  UPDTILE ()
    (setq CDVAR (rtos (getvar "CDATE") 2 16)
         CDTXT (strcat "Current Time: "
                     (substr CDVAR 10 2)
                   ":"
                     (substr CDVAR 12 2)
                   ":"
                     (substr CDVAR 14 2)
                 )
    )
    (set_tile "time" CDTXT)
)
(UPDTILE)
(action_tile "update" "(UPDTILE)")
(start_dialog)
```

Some AutoLISP functions that are not covered in this text are used in the above programming to retrieve and display the current date. The "update" button displays the current time when the button is picked. The dialog box displayed by this code is shown in Figure 25-4.

Figure 25-4.
The dialog box defined by example2.dcl and controlled by example2.lsp.

Mnemonic attribute is underlined

Label attribute from button tile

Commands that change the display or require user input (outside of the dialog interface) cannot be used while a dialog box is active. These AutoLISP functions are unavailable:

command	getangle	getpoint	grread	prompt
entdel	getcorner	getreal	grtext	redraw
entmake	getdist	getstring	grvecs	ssget (interactive)
entmod	getint	graphscr	menucmd	textpage
entsel	getkword	grclear	nentsel	textscr
entupd	getorient	grdraw	osnap	

When the desired action requires a large amount of AutoLISP code, it is best to define a function to perform the required tasks. This function is then called within the action-expression.

EXERCISE 25-2

❏ Use the examples in the text to create EXAMPLE2.DCL and EXAMPLE2.LSP. Load the AutoLISP program file and run the dialog session. What happens when the "time" button is picked?

There are many types of DCL tiles available. You can provide edit boxes for users to enter information directly, such as numeric or text information. You can create lists and drop-down lists to allow users to choose from preset selections. Buttons provide a simple means of initiating an action.

Images can be used to enhance dialog boxes. You can place company or personal logos on your dialog boxes. An interactive image, such as those that appear in the **New Distant Light** dialog box in Figure 25-5, can also be used. Tools such as text tiles, sliders, and clusters are used to control the layout of tiles in a dialog box.

A wide variety of attributes are available for controlling the appearance and function of a dialog session. In addition, several AutoLISP functions are provided to control your dialog session. You can disable or enable tiles and change the active tile. It is even possible to change the value or state of a tile based on an entry in another tile.

The following section provides some applications that use various dialog boxes. Study these examples for additional insight into the creation of dialog sessions. Be sure to have an appropriate reference handy, such as the *AutoCAD Customization Guide*, to look up DCL and AutoLISP terms. You can adapt or modify these files to produce dialog sessions of your own.

Figure 25-5.
The **New Distant Light** dialog box contains two interactive images.

Interactive images

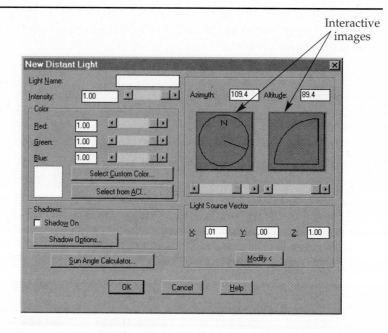

Dialog Example 3

Create the following DCL and AutoLISP files. Then, load the AutoLISP file. To initiate, type DRAW at the Command: prompt. See Figure 25-6.

Figure 25-6.
The dialog box displayed using the example3 DCL and LSP files.

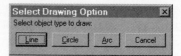

```
//EXAMPLE3.DCL
//Defines a dialog box that presents three drawing options to the user.
//
draw : dialog {
   label = "Select Drawing Option";
   :      text_part {
          label = "Select object type to draw: ";
   }
   : row {
        : button {
                key       = "line";
                label     = "Line";
                mnemonic       = "L";
                fixed_width    = true;
        }
        : button {
                key       = "circle";
                label     = "Circle";
                mnemonic       = "C";
                fixed_width    = true;
        }
        : button {
                key       = "arc";
                label     = "Arc";
                mnemonic       = "A";
                fixed_width    = true;
        }
        : button {
                key       = "cancel";
                label     = "Cancel";
                is_cancel      = true;
                fixed_width    = true;
        }
   }
}
```

```
;EXAMPLE3.LSP
;This file displays the dialog box defined in EXAMPLE3.DCL and begins the
; selected drawing command as specified by the user.
;
(defun C:DRAW (/ DCL_ID)
   (setq DCL_ID (load_dialog "EXAMPLE3.DCL"))
   (if   (not (new_dialog "draw" DCL_ID))
         (exit)
   )
   (action_tile "line" "(setq CMD $key) (done_dialog)")
   (action_tile "circle" "(setq CMD $key) (done_dialog)")
   (action_tile "arc" "(setq CMD $key) (done_dialog)")
   (action_tile "cancel" "(setq CMD nil) (done_dialog)")
   (start_dialog)
   (unload_dialog DCL_ID)
   (command CMD)
)
```

Dialog Example 4

This example allows you to select a new current layer from a drop-down list in a dialog box. To access the dialog box, type GOFOR at the Command: prompt. See Figure 25-7.

```
//EXAMPLE4.DCL
// Presents a list of layers to the user.
fourth : dialog {
    label = "Select Layer";
    : popup_list {
        label     = "New Current Layer:";
        mnemonic        = "N";
        key     = "lyr_pop";
        allow_accept    = true;
        width   = 32;
    }
    ok_cancel;
}
```

```
;;EXAMPLE4.LSP
;;
;;
(defun   CHECKOUT ()
    (setq LD (tblsearch "LAYER" (nth (atoi (get_tile "lyr_pop")) LL))
          LN (cdr (assoc 2 LD))
          LS (cdr (assoc 70 LD))
    )
    (if    (and
                    (/= 1 LS)
                    (/= 65 LS)
            )
            (progn
                    (setvar "CLAYER" (nth (atoi (get_tile "lyr_pop")) LL))
                    (done_dialog)
            )
            (alert "Selected layer is frozen!")
) )
(defun C:GOFOR ()
    (setq DCL_ID (load_dialog "EXAMPLE4.DCL"))
    (if (not (new_dialog "fourth" DCL_ID)) (exit))
    (start_list "lyr_pop")
    (setq LL '()
          NL (tblnext "LAYER" T)
          IDX 0
    )
    (while        NL
                    (if       (= (getvar "CLAYER") (cdr (assoc 2 NL)))
                            (setq CL IDX)
                            (setq IDX (1+ IDX))
                    )
                    (setq     LL (append LL (list (cdr (assoc 2 NL))))
                              NL (tblnext "LAYER")
    )             )
    (mapcar 'add_list LL)
    (end_list)
    (set_tile "lyr_pop" (itoa CL))
    (action_tile "lyr_pop" "(if (= $reason 4) (mode_tile \"accept\" 2))")
    (action_tile "accept" "(CHECKOUT)")
    (start_dialog)
    (unload_dialog DCL_ID)
    (princ)
)
```

Figure 25-7.
The dialog box
displayed using the
example4 DCL and
LSP files.

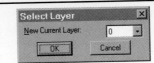

Chapter Test

Answer the following questions on a separate sheet of paper.

1. What are the two types of files that must be created to construct a *functioning* dialog box?
2. When referring to a dialog box, what is a tile?
3. When defining a dialog or tile, inside of what are all of the required attributes for a tile definition placed?
4. What symbol indicates a comment inside a DCL file?
5. Write the appropriate notation for the first line of a DCL file that defines a dialog box named **Test**.
6. Write the appropriate notation in a DCL file that defines the text in the title bar of a dialog box named **Select Application**.
7. Write the notation for defining a cluster of four buttons labeled **OK, NEXT, CANCEL,** and **HELP**.
8. What type of file is commonly used to control a DCL file?
9. Write the notation that would appear in the file in Question 8 that loads a dialog file named PICKFILE.
10. What is a *key* in a DCL file?
11. What is the function of a *mnemonic* attribute?
12. Write the proper DCL file notation for the first line that identifies a button.

Problems

1. Create a dialog box that contains the following items. Write the required DCL and AutoLISP files.
   A. Title bar—**Dialog Box Test**
   B. Label—**This is a test.**
   C. **OK** button

2. Create a dialog box that contains the following items. Write the required DCL and AutoLISP files.
   A. Title bar—**Date**
   B. Label—**Current date**
   C. Action button—**Display Current Date**
   D. **OK** button

3. Create a dialog box that performs the following tasks. Then, write the required DCL and AutoLISP files.
   A. Displays the current date.
   B. Displays the current time.
   C. Displays the current drawing name.
   D. Contains buttons to update current date and time.
   E. Contains an **OK** button.

Adding details to a model greatly improves the realism. Here, the flashlight model from Appendix A has several details added, including a lightbulb, batteries, and a reflector. Also notice that knurling has been added to the cap and handle.

AutoCAD and its Applications—Advanced

Solid Modeling Tutorial

A

INTRODUCTION

This tutorial is provided as a supplement to the solid modeling techniques presented in Chapter 10, Chapter 11, Chapter 12, and Chapter 13. It is a step-by-step process intended as a guide. Directions are given for each step of the process, but exact details regarding which commands to use, where to find them, and exact coordinate locations are not always given. This allows you to use your knowledge of AutoCAD, to consult the online help files, and to refer to the text for answers. The model for this tutorial is the injected plastic handle, cap, and lens for a flashlight shown in Figure A-1.

Figure A-1.

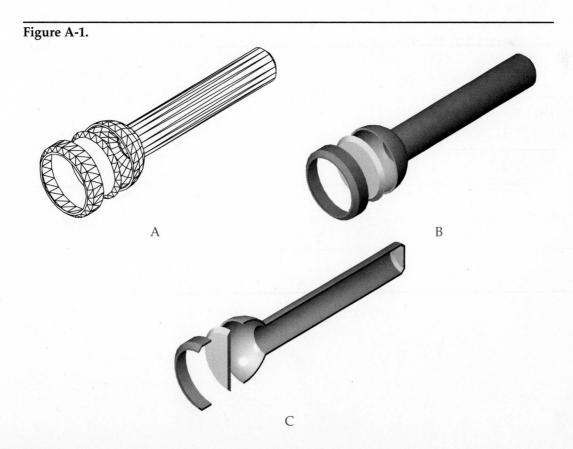

A

B

C

DRAWING SETUP

Start a new drawing using the acad.dwt template. Set **FACETRES** to 2.000. Set your preferred object snaps. The **Center** object snap may be especially useful for this tutorial. Finally, create the following four layers with the indicated colors.

Layer	Color
Handle	color 253
Cap	color 30
Lens	color 50
Construct	green (or your preference)

CONSTRUCTING THE HANDLE

The handle is the portion of the flashlight where the batteries are inserted. This is constructed from two simple "building blocks" that come with AutoCAD—a cylinder and a sphere.

1. Make the Handle layer current.
2. Change to the Southwest isometric viewpoint.
3. Rotate UCS to the LEFT UCS.
4. Draw a solid cylinder at 0,0,0 with a diameter of 2 units and height of 12 units.
5. Draw a solid sphere centered near end of the cylinder with a diameter of 4 units.
6. Make the Construct layer current.
7. Draw a 5 unit cube. Use the cube to remove front top half of the sphere. **Hint:** Use object snaps to align a corner of the cube in the center of the sphere. Then, change to different plan views to line up the cube.
8. Move the hemisphere .5 units along +Z axis of the LEFT UCS.
9. Union the sphere and cylinder.
10. Place a .25 unit, 45° chamfer on the small diameter end of the handle.
11. Create a **SOLIDEDIT** shell using an offset distance of .125 units. Remove the large-diameter surface when creating the shell. **Hint:** After removing the large-diameter surface, you may need to "add" the "cup" for this step to work correctly.

The handle is now a hollow shell .125 thick. This represents the plastic piece removed from the injection mold. See Figure A-2.

Figure A-2.

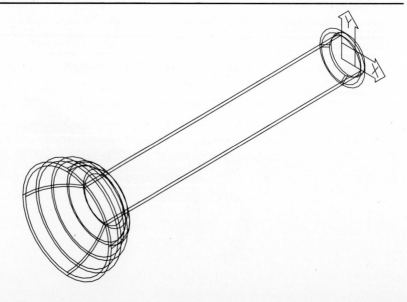

CONSTRUCTING THE CAP

Now, the cap for the flashlight is created. The cap is the portion that snaps onto the handle and contains the lens. The cap is created from a cylinder.

1. With the LEFT UCS current, move the UCS origin 15 units along the +Z axis. Save the new UCS as CAP.
2. Make the Cap layer current.
3. Draw a 4.25 unit diameter cylinder with a height of 1 unit centered at the CAP UCS origin.
4. Chamfer the near end of the cylinder with .25 unit, 45° chamfer.
5. Make the Construct layer current.
6. Draw 4 unit diameter circle centered at the CAP UCS origin.
7. Imprint the circle onto the cylinder body. Delete the source object.
8. Extrude the new face (imprint) into the cylinder .75 units with a 0° taper. **Hint:** Change to the Southeast isometric view.
9. Extrude the face an additional .25 units into the cylinder with a 45° inward taper. **Hint:** Switch back to the Southwest isometric view.

The cap is now a hollow shell with a thickness of .125 units. See Figure A-3. Like the handle, this represents the plastic piece removed from the injection mold.

Figure A-3.

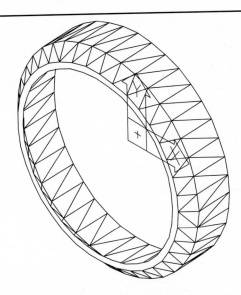

CONSTRUCTING THE LENS

The lens is the clear plastic piece inserted into the cap that light from the bulb passes through. This is simply a circle extruded with a taper.

1. With the CAP UCS current, move the UCS origin 4 units along +Z axis. Save the new UCS as LENS.
2. Make the Lens layer current.
3. Draw a 4 unit diameter circle centered at the origin of the LENS UCS.
4. Extrude the circle +.25 units with a 45° taper.
5. To place the lens between the cap and the handle, move it –5.5 on the Z axis of the LENS UCS.

The model now looks like an exploded assembly view. See Figure A-4.

A   B

CREATING THE CUTAWAY VIEW

The three objects represent the plastic pieces removed from the injection molds. Now, suppose you want to create a cutaway drawing to use in a presentation. First, save the current drawing as app-a.dwg. Then, save a copy as app-a-slice.dwg. This is the drawing used to create the cutaway.

1. Slice all three objects down the centerline. Pick in a manner that keeps the "back half" of the objects. **Hint:** The objects all share the same centerline, so you can pick centers and quadrants to define the slicing plane.
2. Change the face color of the cap's "cut face" to red.
3. Change the face color of the lens' "cut face" to cyan.
4. Change the face color of the handle's "cut face" to blue.

Now, the object can be rendered and printed in color. See Figure A-5. The color of the cut surfaces takes the place of hatching in a 2D cutaway drawing.

Figure A-5.

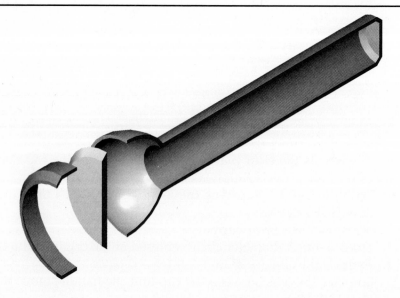

DISPLAYING THE MODEL

With the cutaway model complete, you may want to create a "dynamic display" of the model. This may be useful to have on screen in AutoCAD as you discuss the design with others.

1. Shade the model using Gouraud shading.
2. Using 3D orbit, set the display to a slow, continuous spin around the object.

OPTIONAL ADDITIONS

Once you have completed the model, you may want to add more detail. For example, you may want to create two batteries and insert them in the handle. You may also want to model a small lightbulb and design a metal reflector to hold it inside the cap. Add knurling around the circumference of the cap and handle to help grip the flashlight. Once you have modeled details, assign materials and place lights. Then, render the model. Make adjustments as necessary to achieve a realistic display.

B Common File Extensions

File Extension	Description
3DS	This is a native 3D Studio file, through R4.
AC$	A temporary work file.
ADS	An AutoCAD Development System application. Type (XLOAD *"filename"*) at the Command: prompt to load.
ADT	Audit report files created with the **AUDIT** command.
ARG	When you export a profile, you create a registry (.ARG) file.
ARX	An AutoCAD Runtime Extension application file.
BAK	Backup drawing files created by AutoCAD the second time a drawing is saved and all times thereafter.
BAT	An MS-DOS batch file that executes a series of commands.
BK*n*	Emergency backup files numbered sequentially (BK1, BK2, BK3, etc.) when AutoCAD unexpectedly terminates.
BMP	A Windows bitmap file.
C	An ADS source code file.
CC	An ADS source code file.
CDF	An attribute extract file in the comma delimited format.
CFG	A configuration file.
CUS	A custom dictionary file.
DCC	An ASCII text file that contains color settings for all dialog box elements.
DCE	A dialog box error report file created if errors are found when trying to load a DCL file.
DLL	A platform-specific, dynamic-linked library file.
DWF	Drawing Web format file for posting drawings on the Internet.
DWG	The native AutoCAD drawing file extension.
DWK	An AutoCAD drawing lock file.
DWL	A temporary lock file for an externally referenced drawing.
DXB	A drawing interchange file in binary format.
DXF	A drawing interchange file in ASCII format.
DXX	An attribute extract file in DXF format.
EPS	An encapsulated PostScript file.
ERR	An error file, created when AutoCAD "crashes," containing diagnostic information.
EXE	An executable program file.
GIF	A graphics interchange format raster file.
H	An ADS include file.
HLP	A Windows help file.

File Extension	Description
HTM	Hypertext Markup Language file for use with Internet applications.
INI	A program initialization file where basic settings for an application are stored.
LIN	A linetype library file.
LOG	This file is a history of all commands and variables used in a drawing session.
LSP	An AutoLISP file.
MID	An identification information file.
MLI	A materials library file.
MLN	A multiline library file.
MNC	A compiled menu file.
MND	A menu description file created for use with the **mc.exe** program.
MNL	A menu AutoLISP file.
MNR	A menu resource file.
MNS	A menu source file.
MNU	A menu template file in ASCII format.
MSG	An AutoCAD message file that contains information displayed when AutoCAD is opened or when the **ABOUT** command is used.
OLD	The original version of a converted drawing file.
PAT	A hatch pattern library file.
PC2	Complete plot configuration file for AutoCAD releases prior to AutoCAD 2000.
PC3	Complete information about a given plot device. Replaces **PC2** and **PCP** files.
PCP	A plot configuration parameters file for AutoCAD releases prior to AutoCAD 2000.
PCX	A bitmap raster image file that can be imported into AutoCAD.
PFA	A PostScript font file ASCII format.
PFB	A PostScript font file binary format.
PFM	A PostScript font metric file.
PLT	A plot output file. Also called a "plot file."
PS	A PostScript interpreter initialization file.
PSF	A PostScript font file.
RX	The acad.rx file contains a list of the ARX program files, which are loaded automatically when you start AutoCAD.
SAB	A binary file that stores solid model geometry.
SAT	An ASCII file that stores solid model geometry.
SCR	A command script file.
SDF	An attribute extract file in the space delimited format.
SHP	This file extension is used for both AutoCAD shape and font source files.
SHX	A compiled AutoCAD shape and font file.
SLB	A slide library file.
SLD	A slide file.
STL	A stereolithography file.
SV$	An automatically saved drawing file.
TGA	A Truevision rendered replay file.
TIF	A Tagged Image File format file.
TTF	A TrueType font file.
TXT	An ASCII text file.
UNT	A units conversion file.
WMF	A Windows Metafile format vector file.
XLG	An external references log file.
XMX	An external message file.

APPENDIX C

AutoCAD Command Aliases

The following aliases for AutoCAD commands are found in the acad.pgp file. This file is located in the Acad2000\Support folder. The examples given in this file are aliases for the most frequently used commands.

You can easily create your own aliases. The first part of the alias is the character(s) you type at the keyboard. The second part must begin with an asterisk followed by the name of the command the alias will execute. Do not put a space between the asterisk and the command. Always consult your instructor or supervisor before altering any file crucial to the operation of AutoCAD.

Command	Alias		Command	Alias
3DARRAY	3A		DDGRIPS	GR
3DFACE	3F		DDRMODES	RM
3DORBIT	3DO, ORBIT		DDUCS	UC
3DPOLY	3P		DDUCSP	UCP
ADCENTER	ADC		DDVPOINT	VP
ALIGN	AL		DIMALIGNED	DAL
APPLOAD	AP		DIMANGULAR	DAN
ARC	A		DIMBASELINE	DBA
AREA	AA		DIMCENTER	DCE
ARRAY	AR		DIMCONTINUE	DCO
ATTDEF	ATT		DIMDIAMETER	DDI
-ATTDEF	-ATT		DIMEDIT	DED
ATTEDIT	ATE		DIMLINEAR	DLI
-ATTEDIT	-ATE, ATTE		DIMORDINATE	DOR
BHATCH	BH, H		DIMOVERRIDE	DOV
BLOCK	B		DIMRADIUS	DRA
-BLOCK	-B		DIMSTYLE	D,DST
BOUNDARY	BO		DIST	DI
-BOUNDARY	-BO		DIVIDE	DIV
BREAK	BR		DONUT	DO
CHAMFER	CHA		DRAWORDER	DR
CHANGE	-CH		DSETTINGS	DS, SE
CIRCLE	C		DTEXT	DT
COLOR	COL		DVIEW	DV
COLOR	COLOUR		ELLIPSE	EL
COPY	CO		ERASE	E
DBCONNECT	DBC		EXPLODE	X
DDEDIT	ED		EXPORT	EXP

(Continued on next page)

(Continued from previous page)

Command	Alias
EXTEND	EX
EXTRUDE	EXT
FILLET	F
FILTER	FI
GROUP	G
-GROUP	-G
HATCH	-H
HATCHEDIT	HE
HIDE	HI
IMAGE	IM
-IMAGE	-IM
IMAGEADJUST	IAD
IMAGEATTACH	IAT
IMAGECLIP	ICL
IMPORT	IMP
INSERT	I
-INSERT	-I
INSERTOBJ	IO
INTERFERE	ING
INTERSECT	IN
LAYER	LA
-LAYER	-LA
-LAYOUT	LO
LENGTHEN	LEN
LINE	L
LINETYPE	LT, LTYPE
-LINETYPE	-LT, -LTYPE
LIST	LI, LS
LTSCALE	LTS
LWEIGHT	LINEWEIGHT, LW
MATCHPROP	MA
MEASURE	ME
MIRROR	MI
MLINE	ML
MOVE	M
MSPACE	MS
MTEXT	MT, T
-MTEXT	-T
MVIEW	MV
OFFSET	O
OPTIONS	OP, PR
OSNAP	OS
-OSNAP	-OS
PAN	P
-PAN	-P
-PARTIALOPEN	PARTIALOPEN
PASTESPEC	PA
PEDIT	PE
PLINE	PL
PLOT	PRINT
POINT	PO
POLYGON	POL
PREVIEW	PRE
PROPERTIES	CH, MO, PROPS
PROPERTIESCLOSE	PRCLOSE

Command	Alias
PSPACE	PS
PURGE	PU
QLEADER	LE
QUIT	EXIT
RECTANGLE	REC
REDRAW	R
REDRAWALL	RA
REGEN	RE
REGENALL	REA
REGION	REG
RENAME	REN
-RENAME	-REN
RENDER	RR
REVOLVE	REV
ROTATE	RO
RPREF	RPR
SCALE	SC
SCRIPT	SCR
SECTION	SEC
SETVAR	SET
SHADE	SHA
SLICE	SL
SNAP	SN
SOLID	SO
SPELL	SP
SPLINE	SPL
SPLINEDIT	SPE
STRETCH	S
STYLE	ST
SUBTRACT	SU
TABLET	TA
THICKNESS	TH
TILEMODE	TI
TOLERANCE	TOL
TOOLBAR	TO
TORUS	TOR
TRIM	TR
UNION	UNI
UNITS	UN
-UNITS	-UN
VIEW	V
-VIEW	-V
VPOINT	-VP
WBLOCK	W
-WBLOCK	-W
WEDGE	WE
XATTACH	XA
XBIND	XB
-XBIND	-XB
XCLIP	XC
XLINE	XL
XREF	XR
-XREF	-XR
ZOOM	Z

Advanced Application Commands

Command	Description
3D	This command allows you to create the following three-dimensional polygon mesh objects: box, cone, dish, dome, mesh, pyramid, sphere, torus, and wedge.
3DARRAY	This command allows you to create a three-dimensional polar or rectangular array of objects.
3DCLIP	This command enables the 3D orbit view and allows you to manipulate the view interactively using the **Adjust Clipping Planes** window.
3DCORBIT	This command enables the 3D orbit view functions and allows you to set the objects in continuous motion.
3DDISTANCE	This command establishes a closer or more distant view of the objects in the 3D orbit view.
3DFACE	This command creates a three-dimensional face. The face must have at least three and no more than four vertices.
3DMESH	This command creates a polygon mesh. You must give the coordinate location for each of the vertices in the mesh.
3DORBIT	This command enables the 3D orbit view and its interactive viewing functions.
3DPAN	This command permits the panning of objects in the 3D orbit view.
3DPOLY	This command creates a polyline in 3D space.
3DSIN	This command is used to import a 3D Studio file into AutoCAD.
3DSOUT	This command is used to save an AutoCAD drawing in the native 3D Studio file format. Only 3D objects are saved. Any 2D objects are lost.
3DSWIVEL	When using the 3D orbit view, this command allows you to adjust the target view of objects by creating the effect of turning a camera with the screen cursor.
3DZOOM	This command enables you to zoom in or out in the 3D orbit view.
ACISIN	This command allows you to import an ACIS solid model (SAT) file into AutoCAD.
ACISOUT	This command allows you to save solid objects created in AutoCAD to an ACIS solid model (SAT) file.
ALIGN	This command is used to move and rotate a selected object to align with other objects in 2D or 3D.
AMECONVERT	This command converts solid models created in an AME application to AutoCAD solids.
APPLOAD	This command is used to load and unload application files and define which applications are automatically loaded at startup.
AREA	This command calculates the area and perimeter of selected objects, or of defined areas.
ARX	This command loads and unloads ObjectARX applications and lists information about currently loaded applications.

Command	Description
BACKGROUND	This command sets up the background effects for your drawing.
BMPOUT	This command saves selected objects to a bitmap (BMP) format file.
BOX	This command creates a three-dimensional solid box.
BROWSER	This command launches the default Web browser defined in your system's registry.
CAMERA	This command is used to set the camera location and target point for viewing purposes.
CHAMFER	This command is used to bevel the edges of objects. A chamfer can be applied to a 2D or 3D object.
COMPILE	This command compiles shape and PostScript font files.
CONE	This command creates a three-dimensional solid cone.
COPYCLIP	This command is used to copy selected objects to the Windows Clipboard.
COPYLINK	This command copies the current view to the Windows Clipboard for linking to Object Linking and Embedding (OLE) applications.
CUTCLIP	This command removes selected objects from the drawing and places them on the Windows Clipboard.
CYLINDER	This command creates a three-dimensional solid cylinder.
DBCCLOSE	This command closes the **dbConnect Manager**.
DBCONNECT	This command opens the **dbConnect Manager** for access to database tables.
DBLIST	This command lists all data for every object in the current drawing in the **AutoCAD Text Window**.
DDUCS	See listing for the **UCSMAN** command.
DDUCSP	This command allows you to select from several preset User Coordinate Systems (UCS) using the **UCS** dialog box.
DDVPOINT	This command is used to set the 3D viewing direction.
DELAY	This command is used to specify a timed pause within a script file.
DSVIEWER	This command allows you to change your view of the drawing using the **Aerial View** window.
DVIEW	This command allows you to define a parallel projection or perspective view of selected objects.
DXBIN	This command is used to import binary format files.
EDGE	This command is used to make an edge of a 3D face visible or invisible.
EDGESURF	This command creates a three-dimensional polygon mesh using four objects to define the edges.
ELEV	This command is used to set the current elevation and thickness.
ETRANSMIT	This command creates a transmittal for sharing drawings using e-mail.
EXPORT	This command outputs objects using a specified file format.
EXTRUDE	This command is used to create 3D solid primitives by extruding existing 2D objects.
FILLET	This command is used to place fillets and rounds on the edges of 2D or 3D objects.
FOG	This command provides visual cues for the apparent distance of objects.
HIDE	This command is used to display 3D objects with hidden lines removed.
HYPERLINK	This command is used to attach a hyperlink to a graphical object or edit an existing hyperlink.
HYPERLINKOPTIONS	When working with hyperlinks, this command is used to control the display of the hyperlink cursor and related tooltips.
IMAGE	This command allows you to insert images using a variety of formats and manage the display of existing images.
IMAGEADJUST	This command controls the brightness, contrast, and fade values of the selected image.
IMAGEATTACH	This command is used to attach a new image object and definition.
IMAGECLIP	This command creates new clipping boundaries for individual image objects.
IMAGEFRAME	This command controls the visibility of the frame used for selecting an image.

Command	Description
IMAGEQUALITY	This command enables a setting that controls the display quality of images.
IMPORT	Various types of files can be imported into AutoCAD using this command.
INSERTOBJ	This command enables you to insert an object from an Object Linking and Embedding (OLE) application.
INTERFERE	This command creates a composite solid from the volume created by the interference of two or more solids.
INTERSECT	This command creates a composite solid or region from the intersection of two or more solids or regions and removes the nonintersecting areas.
LIGHT	This command is used to manage lights and lighting effects.
LOGFILEOFF	This command closes the file created by the **LOGFILEON** command.
LOGFILEON	When this command is enabled, the contents of the **AutoCAD Text Window** are recorded to a log file.
LSEDIT	This command is used to edit a landscape object.
LSLIB	This command is used to maintain landscape object libraries.
LSNEW	This command lets you add realistic landscape items, such as trees and bushes, to drawings.
MASSPROP	This command calculates and displays the mass properties of regions or solids.
MATLIB	This command opens the **Materials Library** dialog box, which is used to import and export materials to and from a library of materials.
MEETNOW	This command provides tools for using AutoCAD with Microsoft NetMeeting for online meetings.
MENU	This command is used to load a menu file.
MENULOAD	This command is used to load partial menu files.
MENUUNLOAD	This command is used to unload partial menu files.
MIRROR3D	This command is used to construct a mirror image of selected objects in 3D space using a mirror plane.
MODEL	When in a layout tab, this command allows you to switch to the **Model** tab and make it current.
MVIEW	This command is used to create floating viewports. It is also used to turn on existing floating viewports.
MVSETUP	This command allows you to set up the specifications of a drawing. It can be used in the **Model** tab or in a layout tab.
OLELINKS	This command is used to update, change, and cancel existing Object Linking and Embedding (OLE) links.
OLESCALE	The **OLE Properties** dialog box is opened with this command after an OLE object is selected. It is used to resize OLE objects, scale text, and control OLE plot quality.
OPTIONS	This command accesses the **Options** dialog box, which is used to customize the AutoCAD environment.
PASTECLIP	This command inserts the contents of the Windows Clipboard into the current drawing.
PASTEORIG	This command pastes an object containing AutoCAD data from the Windows Clipboard and uses the same coordinates from the original drawing for insertion.
PASTESPEC	This command inserts the contents of the Windows Clipboard and allows you to control the format of what is being inserted.
PEDIT	This command allows you to edit 2D or 3D polylines, and three-dimensional polygon meshes.
PFACE	This command allows you to create a three-dimensional polyface mesh. Each vertex must be individually specified.
PLAN	Entering this command displays a plan view of the current User Coordinate System (UCS), a saved UCS, or the World Coordinate System (WCS).
PSDRAG	When using the **PSIN** command, this command controls the appearance of the PostScript image as it is dragged into position.
PSFILL	This command is used to fill a two-dimensional polyline outline with a PostScript pattern.

Command	Description
PSIN	This command is used to import an encapsulated PostScript file into AutoCAD.
PSOUT	This command saves the drawing as an encapsulated PostScript file. You can save the entire drawing or a portion of the drawing.
PSPACE	This command switches the drawing from model space to paper space.
PUBLISHTOWEB	This command accesses a wizard that automatically creates Web pages for displaying drawings.
REGION	This command is used to create a region from selected objects.
REINIT	This command is used to reinitialize the digitizer, I/O port, and program parameters (acad.pgp) file.
RENDER	This command opens the **Render** dialog box and also initializes the AutoCAD **Render** window. The **Render** dialog box is used to create a realistically shaded image of a three-dimensional object.
RENDSCR	This command displays the last rendering created using the **RENDER** command.
REPLAY	This command is used to display a BMP, TGA, or TIF raster image file.
REVOLVE	This command is used to create a 3D solid by revolving a closed two-dimensional object about an axis.
REVSURF	This command creates a revolved surface by rotating a 2D object about a selected axis.
RMAT	The **Materials** dialog box is opened with this command. This dialog box allows you to manage materials used for rendering.
ROTATE3D	This command rotates selected objects about an axis in 3D space.
RPREF	This command allows you to set user preferences for rendering purposes.
RULESURF	This command creates a 3D ruled surface between two path curves. The curves can be points, arcs, lines, splines, circles, or polylines.
SAVEAS	This command allows you to save or rename a drawing using the desired file extension.
SAVEIMG	This command saves a rendered image to a BMP, TIF, or TGA file.
SCENE	This command is used to manage scenes in a drawing.
SECTION	This command creates a region from the intersection of a plane and a solid. The region can then be used to create a section view.
SETUV	This command is used to map materials onto objects.
SHADEMODE	This command displays a shaded image of the drawing in the current viewport. This command is faster than the **RENDER** command, but the image quality is not as good.
SHOWMAT	This command lists information about the material attached to a selected object and the attachment method used.
SLICE	This command is used to slice or "cut" a set of solids with a slicing plane.
SOLDRAW	This command is used to generate profiles and sections in floating viewports created with the **SOLVIEW** command.
SOLID	This command is used to draw polygons that are filled solid.
SOLIDEDIT	This command is used to edit 3D solid objects by modifying faces and edges.
SOLPROF	This command is used to create profile images of 3D solid objects in floating viewports.
SOLVIEW	Using orthographic projection, this command creates floating viewports for multiview and sectional view drawings of 3D solid and body objects.
SPHERE	This command creates a three-dimensional solid sphere.
STATS	This command displays information about rendering functions in the **Statistics** dialog box.
STLOUT	This command is used to save a solid object to a ASCII or binary format file.
SUBTRACT	This command creates a composite by subtracting the area or volume of one selection set from another selection set. It can be used for 2D regions and 3D solids.
TABLET	This command is used to calibrate and configure a digitizer tablet, and toggle its activation.

Command	Description
TABSURF	This command creates a 3D tabulated surface from a path curve and direction vector.
TORUS	This command creates a three-dimensional solid that resembles a donut.
TRANSPARENCY	The setting activated by this command controls whether the background pixels in a selected image are transparent or opaque.
TREESTAT	This command allows you to display information about the tree-structured spatial index of the current drawing.
UCS	This command is used to create and manage User Coordinate Systems (UCS) at the command line.
UCSICON	The setting activated by this command controls the visibility and placement of the UCS and WCS icons.
UCSMAN	This command activates the **UCS** dialog box and is used to manage defined User Coordinate Systems (UCS).
UNION	This command creates a composite by adding the area or volume of two selection sets. It can be used with 2D regions or 3D solids.
VBAIDE	This command opens the **Visual Basic** editor.
VBALOAD	The **Open VBA Project** dialog box is opened with this command. It allows you to load a global VBA project into the current drawing.
VBAMAN	This command opens the **VBA Manager** dialog box, which is used to load, unload, save, create, embed, and extract VBA projects.
VBARUN	This command is used to run a VBA macro.
VBASTMT	This command is used to enter a VBA statement, or expression, on the command line.
VBAUNLOAD	This command is used to unload a global VBA project.
VIEW	This command is used to create and restore saved views.
VIEWRES	The setting made with this command controls object resolution in the current viewport.
VLISP	This command opens the **Visual LISP** editor.
VPOINT	This command is used to set the viewing direction for a 3D display of the current drawing.
WEDGE	This command creates a three-dimensional solid wedge.
WMFIN	This command is used to import a Windows metafile (WMF file) into AutoCAD.
WMFOPTS	This command is used to set importing options for use with the **WMFIN** command.
WMFOUT	This command is used to save selected objects to a Windows metafile (WMF file).

New and Advanced Application System Variables

Variable names that appear in color are new to AutoCAD 2000.

Variable	Saved In	Default Value	Description
ACADLSPASDOC	Registry	0	Determines if acad.lsp is loaded in every drawing or just the first in a drawing session. 0 Loads in just the first drawing. 1 Loads in every drawing.
ACISOUTVER	Not saved	40	Determines the ACIS version of SAT files.
BINDTYPE	Not saved	0	Controls how xref names are handled when binding or editing in place. 0 Traditional binding behavior. 1 Insert-like behavior.
BACKZ	Drawing		Saves the back clipping plane offset from the target plane for the current viewport.
CELWEIGHT	Drawing	–1	Determines the line weight of new objects. –1 ByLayer. –2 ByBlock. –3 Default (controlled by **LWDEFAULT**). Other widths in millimeters can be entered.
CHAMFERA	Drawing	0.5000	First chamfer distance.
CHAMFERB	Drawing	0.5000	Second chamfer distance.
CHAMFERC	Drawing	1.0000	Chamfer length.
CHAMFERD	Drawing	0	Chamfer angle.
CHAMMODE	Not saved	0	Sets the method for creating chamfers. 0 Two chamfer distances are used. 1 One chamfer length and an angle are used.
CMDACTIVE	Not saved		Stores the bitcode that indicates whether an ordinary command, transparent command, script, or dialog box is active. The value is the sum of: 1 Ordinary command active. 2 Ordinary command and a transparent command active. 4 Script active. 8 Dialog box active 16 AutoLISP active.

Variable	Saved In	Default Value	Description
CMDECHO	Not saved	1	Determines if AutoCAD echoes prompts and input during AutoLISP. 0 Echo off. 1 Echo on.
COMPASS	Not saved	0	Determines if 3D compass is on or off in the current viewport. 0 Off. 1 On.
CPLOTSTYLE	Drawing	ByLayer	Plot style for new objects (read only).
CPROFILE	Registry	Unnamed	Name of current profile (read only).
CTAB	Drawing	*current*	Sets the current drawing tab (by name).
CVPORT	Drawing	2	Identification number of the current viewport. The identification number you specify must correspond to an active viewport. Also, the cursor must not be locked in that viewpoint. Tablet mode must be off.
DEFLPLSTYLE	Registry	*current*	The default plot style for new layers (read only).
DEFPLSTYLE	Registry	ByLayer	The default plot style for new objects (read only).
DELOBJ	Drawing	1	Determines if objects used to create other objects are kept in the drawing database. 0 Keep objects. 1 Delete objects.
DIASTAT	Not saved		Stores how the most recently used dialog box was exited. 0 Cancel. 1 OK.
DIMALTRND	Drawing	0.00	Determines the rounding of alternate dimensions.
DIMATFIT	Drawing	3	Determines arrangement of dimension text and arrows when both do not fit inside the extension lines. 0 Places both outside extension lines. 1 Relocates arrows before text. 2 Relocates text before arrows. 3 Relocates either for best fit.
DIMAZIN	Drawing	0	Suppresses leading and trailing zeros for angular dimensions. 0 Displays leading and trailing zeros. 1 Suppresses leading zeros. 2 Suppresses trailing zeros. 3 Suppresses leading and trailing zeros.
DIMDSEP	Drawing	. *(period)*	Sets a character to use as the decimal point for decimal dimensions.
DIMFRAC	Drawing	0	Sets the format for fractional dimensions. 0 Horizontal. 1 Diagonal. 2 Not stacked.
DIMLDRBLK	Drawing	0	Sets the type of arrowhead for leaders.

Variable	Saved In	Default Value	Description
DIMLUNIT	Drawing	2	Sets dimension units, except angular.
			1 Scientific.
			2 Decimal.
			3 Engineering.
			4 Architectural.
			5 Fractional.
			6 Windows desktop.
DIMLWD	Drawing	ByBlock	Sets the line weight for dimension lines.
			ByLayer.
			ByBlock.
			Number (100th of mm).
DIMLWE	Drawing	ByBlock	Sets the line weight for dimension lines.
			ByLayer.
			ByBlock.
			Number (100th of mm).
DIMTMOVE	Drawing	0	Specifies rules for moving dimension text.
			0 Moves dimension line with text.
			1 Adds a leader when dimension text is moved.
			2 Allows text to be moved freely (no leader).
DISPSILH	Drawing	0	Sets the displays of silhouette curves for solids when in hidden line mode.
			0 Off.
			1 On.
DWGCHECK	Registry	0	Sets the dialog box display when determining if the current drawing was last edited by a product other than AutoCAD.
			0 Suppresses the dialog box.
			1 Displays the dialog box.
EDGEMODE	Registry	0	Determines how cutting and boundary edges for the **TRIM** and **EXTEND** commands are calculated.
			0 Uses only the selected edge.
			1 Creates an imaginary extension from the selected object.
ELEVATION	Drawing	0.0000	Stores the current 3D elevation relative to the current UCS for the current space.
EXTNAMES	Drawing	1	Determines which parameter set is used for object names stored in symbol tables.
			0 Release 14 parameters.
			1 AutoCAD 2000 parameters.
FACETRATIO	Not saved	0	Sets the faceting aspect ratio (mesh density) for cylindrical and conic solids.
			0 Mesh is N by 1.
			1 Mesh is N by M.
FACETRES	Drawing	0.5	A relative measure of the number of tessellation lines used to display solids with **HIDE**. Value can range from 0.01 to 10.0.
FILLETRAD	Drawing	0.5000	The default radius used for fillets.
FRONTZ	Drawing		The front clipping plane offset from the target plane for the current viewport (read only).

Variable	Saved In	Default Value	Description
FULLOPEN	Not saved		Indicates if the current drawing is fully or partially open (read only).
			0 Partially open.
			1 Fully open.
HIDEPRECISION	Not saved	0	Sets the accuracy of hides and shades to either double or single precision.
			0 Single precision.
			1 Double precision.
HYPERLINKBASE	Drawing	*current*	Sets the path for all relative hyperlinks in the current drawing.
IMAGEHLT	Registry	0	Determines if a raster image frame or the entire image is highlighted when selected.
			0 Frame only.
			1 Entire image.
INETLOCATION	Registry	www.autodesk. com/acaduser	The location of the default URL.
INSUNITS	Drawing	0	Determines the drawing unit value when a block or image is "dragged" from the AutoCAD DesignCenter.
			0 No units.
			1 Inches.
			2 Feet.
			3 Miles.
			4 Millimeters.
			5 Centimeters.
			6 Meters.
			7 Kilometers.
			8 Microinches.
			9 Mils.
			10 Yards.
			11 Angstroms.
			12 Nanometers.
			13 Microns.
			14 Decimeters.
			15 Decameters.
			16 Hectometers.
			17 Gigameters.
			18 Astronomical Units.
			19 Light Years.
			20 Parsecs.
INSUNITDEFSOURCE	Registry	0	Specifies the source content units value. Can be from 0 to 20.
INSUNITDEFTARGET	Registry	0	Specifies the target drawing units value. Can be from 0 to 20.
ISOLINES	Drawing	4	Specifies the number of isolines per surface. Values can range from 0 to 2047.
LENSLENGTH	Drawing		Indicates the lens length (in millimeters) for perspective viewing (read only).
LOGFILEPATH	Registry	*ACAD path* acad.log	Sets the path for log files.

Variable	Saved In	Default Value	Description
LISPINIT	Registry	1	Determines if AutoLISP-defined functions and variables are preserved when a new drawing is opened or valid in the current drawing session only. 0 Preserved. 1 Valid in current drawing only.
LWDEFAULT	Registry	25	Sets the default line weight value (in mm).
LWDISPLAY	Drawing	0 (OFF)	Determines if line weights are displayed 0 (OFF) Not displayed. 1 (ON) Displayed.
LWUNITS	Registry	1	Determines if line weight units are shown as inches or millimeters. 0 Inches. 1 Millimeters.
MAXACTVP	Drawing	64	Determines the maximum number of viewports that can be displayed at one time.
MBUTTONPAN	Registry	1	Determines the action of the third mouse button or mouse wheel. 0 Action is defined in the AutoCAD menu file. 1 Allows panning by holding and dragging the button or wheel.
NOMUTT	Not saved	0	Suppresses the displaying of messages. 0 Displays messages. 1 Suppresses messages.
OFFSETGAPTYPE	Registry	0	Determines how polylines are offset when a gap is created by offsetting individual polyline segments. 0 Segments are extended to fill the gap. 1 Gaps are filleted. 2 Gaps are chamfered.
OLEHIDE	Registry	0	Sets display of OLE objects. 0 All OLE objects visible. 1 OLE objects visible in paper space only. 2 OLE objects visible in model space only. 3 No OLE objects visible.
OLEQUALITY	Registry	1	Sets the default quality of embedded OLE graphics. 0 Line art quality. 1 Text quality. 2 Graphics quality. 3 Photograph quality. 4 High-resolution photograph.
OLESTARTUP	Drawing	0	Determines if the source application of an embedded OLE object loads when plotting. 0 No load. 1 Load.
PAPERUPDATE	Registry	0	Determines if a warning dialog is displayed when trying to print a layout with a paper size different from the paper size specified by the plotter configuration file. 0 Displays a warning dialog box. 1 Sets paper size to the configured paper size of the plotter configuration file.

Variable	Saved In	Default Value	Description
PFACEVMAX	Not saved		Determines the maximum number of vertices per face (read only).
PLQUIET	Registry	0	Determines if optional dialog boxes and nonfatal errors for batch plotting and scripts are displayed.
			0 Displays plot dialog boxes and nonfatal errors.
			1 Logs nonfatal errors; suppresses the display of plot-related dialog boxes.
POLARADDANG	Registry	null	Stores up to 10 user-defined polar angles.
POLARANG	Registry	90	Determines the increment for polar angles.
POLARDIST	Registry	0.0000	Determines the snap increment for polar snap.
POLARMODE	Registry	1	Determines the setting for polar and object snap tracking. The value can be from 0 to 15 and is the sum of:
			Polar angle measurements
			0 Measure polar angles based on current UCS.
			1 Measure polar angles from selected objects.
			Object snap tracking
			0 Track orthogonally only.
			2 Use polar tracking settings in object snap tracking.
			Use additional polar tracking angles
			0 No.
			4 Yes.
			Acquire object snap tracking points
			0 Acquire automatically.
			8 Press [Shift] to acquire.
PROJMODE	Registry	1	Projection mode for **Trim** and **Extend**.
			0 No projection.
			1 Project to the XY plane of the current UCS.
			2 Project to the current view plane.
PROJECTNAME	Drawing	*current*	Assigns a project name for the drawing.
PSPROLOG	Registry	*current*	Assigns a name for a prolog section to be read from the acad.psf file when using **PSOUT**.
PSTYLEMODE	Drawing	0	Shows if the current drawing is in color-dependent or named plot style mode (read only).
			0 Named plot style.
			1 Color-dependent plot style.
PSTYLEPOLICY	Registry	1	Determines if an object's color property is associated with its plot style.
			0 No association.
			1 Associated.
PSVPSCALE	Not saved	0	Determines the view scale factor for all new viewports. A value of 0 means scaled to fit.
PSQUALITY	Registry	75	Controls the rendering quality of PostScript images.
			0 Disables PostScript image generation.
			< 0 Sets the number of pixels per drawing unit for the PostScript image.
			> 0 Sets the number of pixels per drawing unit and shows PostScript paths as unfilled outlines.

Variable	Saved In	Default Value	Description
PUCSBASE	Drawing	*current*	Sets the UCS that defines the origin and orientation of orthographic UCS settings in paper space.
RASTERPREVIEW	Registry	1	Determines if a BMP preview image is saved with the drawing.
			0 No preview.
			1 Preview.
REFEDITNAME	Not saved	*current*	Shows if the drawing is in reference-editing state (read only).
SAVEFILEPATH	Registry	C:\WINDOWS\ TEMP	Sets the location for temporary files.
SHADEDGE	Drawing	3	Controls shading of edges in shadings.
			0 Faces shaded, edges not highlighted.
			1 Faces shaded, edges drawn in background color.
			2 Faces not filled, edges in object color.
			3 Faces in object color, edges in background color.
SHADEDIF	Drawing	70	Ratio of diffuse reflective light relative to ambient light.
SDI	Registry	0	Determines if AutoCAD runs in single or multiple document interface.
			0 MDI on.
			1 MDI off.
			2 (Read only, not saved) MDI disabled because AutoCAD has loaded an application that does not support multiple drawings.
			3 (Read only, not saved) MDI is disabled because the user has set SDI to 1 and AutoCAD has loaded an application that does not support multiple drawings.
SHORTCUTMENU	Registry	11	Determines if Default, Edit, and Command mode shortcut menus are available in the drawing area. Value is a sum of:
			0 Disables shortcut menus (restores R14 legacy behavior).
			1 Enables Default mode shortcut menus.
			2 Enables Edit mode shortcut menus.
			4 Enables Command mode shortcut menus.
			8 Enables Command mode shortcut menus only when command options are currently available from the command line.
SNAPTYPE	Registry	0	Sets the snap style for the current viewport.
			0 Grid or standard snap.
			1 Polar snap.
SOLIDCHECK	Not saved	1	Determines if solid validation is on or off for the current drawing session.
			0 Off.
			1 On.
SPLFRAME	Drawing	0	Controls display of spline and spline-fit polylines.
			0 Does not display the control polygon.
			1 Displays the control polygon.

Variable	Saved In	Default Value	Description
SPLINESEGS	Drawing	8	Number of line segments for each spline-fit polyline generated by **PEDIT Spline**.
SPLINETYPE	Drawing	6	Type of spline curve to be generated by **PEDIT Spline**.
			5 Quadratic B-spline.
			6 Cubic B-spline.
SURFTAB1	Drawing	6	Number of tabulations generated for **RULESURF** and **TABSURF**. Mesh density in the M direction for **REVSURF** and **EDGESURF**.
SURFTAB2	Drawing	6	Mesh density in the N direction for **REVSURF** and **EDGESURF**.
SURFTYPE	Drawing	6	Controls the surface-fitting done by **PEDIT Smooth**.
			5 Quadratic B-spline surface.
			6 Cubic B-spline surface.
			8 Bézier surface.
SURFU	Drawing	6	Surface density in the M direction.
SURFV	Drawing	6	Surface density in the N direction.
TARGET	Drawing		Location of the target point for the current viewpoint in UCS coordinates (read only).
TDUCREATE	Drawing		Stores the time and date a drawing is created (read only).
TDUUPDATE	Drawing		Stores the time and date of the last update (read only).
THICKNESS	Drawing	0.0000	Sets the current 3D thickness.
TILEMODE	Drawing	1	Sets the model tab or last layout tab current.
			0 Makes the last active layout tab (paper space) current.
			1 Makes the model tab current.
TRACKPATH	Registry	0	Controls the display of polar and object snap tracking alignment paths.
			0 Displays full screen object snap tracking path.
			1 Displays object snap tracking path only between the alignment point and From point to the cursor location.
			2 Polar tracking path is not displayed.
			3 Polar and object snap tracking paths are not displayed.
TRIMMODE	Registry	1	Controls edge trimming for chamfers and fillets.
			0 Leaves edges intact.
			1 Trims edges.
TSPACEFAC	Not saved	1	Sets multiline text line spacing as a factor of text height. Can be from 0.25 to 4.0.
TSPACETYPE	Not saved	1	Controls the type of line spacing used in multiline text.
			1 At least.
			2 Exactly.
TSTACKALIGN	Drawing	1	Determines vertical alignment of stacked text.
			0 Bottom aligned.
			1 Center aligned.
			2 Top aligned.

Variable	Saved In	Default Value	Description
	Drawing	70	Percentage of stacked text fraction height relative to the height of the selected text. Can be from 1 to 127.
	Registry	90	Default angle when rotating the UCS around one of its axes.
	Drawing	World	The UCS that defines the origin and orientation of orthographic UCS settings.
UCSFOLLOW	Drawing	0	Generates a plan view in a viewport whenever the UCS is changed. 0 UCS does not affect the view. 1 Any UCS change causes a change to plan view of the new UCS in the current viewport.
UCSICON	Drawing	3	Controls the displays of the user coordinate system icon. 0 No display. 1 Icon is displayed. 2 If icon is displayed, it is shown at the UCS origin, if possible 3 Icon is displayed at the UCS origin.
UCSNAME	Drawing		Indicates the name of the current coordinate system (read only).
UCSORG	Drawing		Indicates the origin point in World coordinates of the current UCS (read only).
	Registry	1	Sets if an orthographic UCS is automatically set current when an orthographic view is restored. 0 Current UCS is retained. 1 Orthographic UCS is set current.
	Registry	1	Controls if the current UCS is saved when a view is named. 0 UCS is not saved. 1 UCS is saved.
	Drawing	1	Controls if the UCS in all viewports change to reflect the UCS of the active viewport. 0 Changes. 1 Does not change.
UCSXDIR	Drawing		The X direction of the current UCS for the current space (read only).
UCSYDIR	Drawing		The Y direction of the current UCS for the current space (read only).
VIEWCTR	Drawing		The center of view in the current viewport, in UCS coordinates (read only).
VIEWDIR	Drawing		The viewing direction in the current viewport, in UCS coordinates (read only).
VIEWMODE	Drawing		Determines the viewing mode for the current viewport using bit-code (read only). 0 Disabled. 1 Perspective view active. 2 Front clipping on. 4 Back clipping on. 8 UCS follow mode on. 16 Front clip not at eye.
VIEWSIZE	Drawing		Height of view in current viewport (read only).

Variable	Saved In	Default Value	Description
VIEWTWIST	Drawing		View twist angle for the current viewport (read only).
VSMAX	Drawing		Upper-right corner of the current viewport virtual screen, in UCS coordinates (read only).
VSMIN	Drawing		Lower-left corner of the current viewport virtual screen, in UCS coordinates (read only).
WHIPARC	Registry	0	Sets the display smoothness of circles and arcs. 0 Circles and arcs are shown as a series of vectors. 1 Circles and arcs are shown as true circles and arcs.
WMFBKGND	Not saved	1	Determines if the background of AutoCAD objects is transparent in other applications. 0 Transparent background. 1 Background is the AutoCAD drawing area color.
WORLDUCS	Not saved		Shows if the UCS coincides with the WCS (read only). 0 UCS and WCS are different. 1 UCS and WCS coincide.
WORLDVIEW	Drawing	1	Controls whether UCS changes to WCS during **DVIEW, 3DORBIT,** or **VPOINT**. 0 UCS does not change. 1 UCS changes to the WCS until the command is terminated. 2 UCS changes relative to the UCS specified by the **UCSBASE** system variable.
WRITESTAT	Not saved	1	Shows if a drawing can be written to (read only). 0 Read only. 1 Can be written to.
XEDIT	Drawing	1	Determines if the current drawing can be edited in place when referenced by another drawing. 0 Cannot be edited in place. 1 Can be edited in place.
XFADECTL	Registry	50	Sets fading intensity for references being edited in place. 0 0% fading (min). 90 90% fading (max).
ZOOMFACTOR	Registry	10	Sets zoom increments for the mouse wheel. Can be between 3 and 100.

Basic AutoLISP Commands

The following is a list of basic AutoLISP commands with a brief definition of each command. These commands are covered in Chapter 24 and Chapter 25 of this text. Detailed definitions of these and all other AutoLISP commands are found in the *AutoCAD Customization Guide*.

Command	Description
+ *(addition)*	Adds all numbers.
− *(subtraction)*	Subtracts the second and following numbers from the first and returns the difference.
* *(multiplication)*	Multiplies all numbers.
/ *(division)*	Divides the first number by the product of the remaining numbers and returns the quotient.
= *(equal to)*	Returns a total if all arguments are equal. Returns *nil* otherwise.
ANGLE	Returns the angle from the X axis of the current UCS to a line defined by two endpoints, as measured counterclockwise. The value is given in radians.
ARXLOAD	Loads an AutoCAD Runtime Extension application.
ARXUNLOAD	Unloads an AutoCAD Runtime Extension application.
CAR	Returns the first element of a list.
CADR	Returns the second element of a list.
CADDR	Returns the third element of a list.
CDR	Returns the second and remaining elements of a list. If the list contains more than two elements, the returned values are placed in a list.
DEFUN	Defines a function.
DISTANCE	Returns the distance between two points. The distance is measured in 3D space.
GETANGLE	Waits for a user-input angle and returns the angle in radians. The user can input the angle at the keyboard or use the pointing device to pick points on screen.
GETCORNER	Waits for the user to input the second corner of a rectangle using the pointing device.
GETDIST	Waits for a user to input distance. The distance can be entered at the keyboard or using the pointing device to pick points on screen.
GETORIENT	Waits for a user-input and returns the angle in radians. This is similar to the **GETANGLE** function, but the **ANGBASE** and **ANGDIR** system variables do not affect it.
GETPOINT	Waits for a user-input point and returns the point.
GETREAL	Waits for a user-input real number and returns the real number.
GETSTRING	Waits for a user-input string and returns the string.
GETVAR	Returns the value assigned to a specified AutoCAD system variable.

Command	Description
GRAPHSCR	If the text screen is currently displayed, switches to the AutoCAD graphics screen.
LOAD_DIALOG	Loads a Dialog Control Language file.
NEW_DIALOG	Opens a specified dialog box. This function can also specify a default action of the dialog box.
POLAR	Returns the coordinates of a 3D point a specified angle and distance from a specified point.
PRINC	Prints a specified expression on the command line. This function can also be used to write a specified expression to a file.
PROMPT	Displays a specified string on the command line.
START_DIALOG	Opens a specified dialog box and makes AutoCAD ready to accept user input.
STRLEN	Reports the number of characters in a string.
TERPRI	Prints a new line on the command line.
TEXTSCR	If the graphics screen is currently displayed, switches to the AutoCAD text screen.
UNLOAD_DIALOG	Unloads a Dialog Control Language file.

AutoCAD 2000i Features

The following sections provide additional discussion on some of the new features introduced in AutoCAD 2000i. Most new features are discussed within the text chapters. However, the following topics require additional coverage.

MODIFYING THE UCS ICON

The appearance of the UCS icon can be changed in AutoCAD 2000i using the settings in the **UCS Icon** dialog box. See Figure G-1. This dialog box is accessed by selecting **UCS Icon** and then **Properties...** from the **Display** cascading menu in the **View** pull-down menu or by entering UCSICON followed by P (for the **Properties** option) at the Command: prompt.

The **UCS Icon** dialog box allows you to modify three characteristics of the UCS icon:

- **Style.** Select either a 2D or 3D icon in the **UCS icon style** area. You can also specify the line width as 1, 2, or 3 pixels. If the **3D** style is selected, the **Cone** option is available.
- **Size.** The **UCS icon size** area contains a text box and a slider. The value in the text box is the size of the UCS icon expressed as a percentage of the viewport size. Modify this value by entering a new value in the text box or by adjusting the slider.

Figure G-1.
The **UCS Icon** dialog box allows you to change the appearance of the UCS icon.

Set size as percentage of viewport

Set line thickness

Preview of settings

Set style for icon

Set icon color

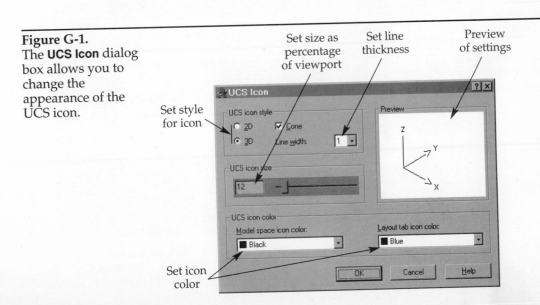

- **Color.** Use the drop-down lists in the **UCS icon color** area to set the color of the UCS icon. Notice that different colors can be set for the **Model** tab and **Layout** tab.

INTERNET FEATURES

AutoCAD 2000i has updated and expanded the Internet features provided with AutoCAD 2000. The next sections detail the following topics:

- **Insert Hyperlink dialog box.** By attaching hyperlinks to drawing objects, someone viewing the drawing can access other views, drawings, Web pages, or e-mail addresses with a single mouse pick.
- **Publishing to the Web.** AutoCAD 2000i includes a **Publish to Web** wizard, which automates the process of creating a Web page to display AutoCAD drawings.
- **Preparing e-mail transmittals.** When you want to transfer a drawing using e-mail, the **eTransmit** feature automatically creates a transmittal file for the drawing, including all associated files.
- **Internet meetings.** When used in conjunction with Microsoft NetMeeting, the **Meet Now** tools allow AutoCAD drawings to be viewed and edited by all participants in an online meeting.

Insert Hyperlink Dialog Box

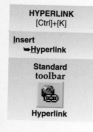

HYPERLINK
[Ctrl]+[K]

Insert
➥Hyperlink

Standard
toolbar

Hyperlink

The procedure for inserting a hyperlink into a drawing is discussed on page 390. Simply stated, a hyperlink can be attached to any object(s) in the drawing. The hyperlink can link the object to a drawing file, a Web page, or an e-mail address. The **Insert Hyperlink** dialog box is used to define the hyperlink.

To access the **Insert Hyperlink** dialog box, pick the **Insert Hyperlink** button from the **Standard** toolbar, select **Hyperlink...** from the **Insert** pull-down menu, type HYPERLINK at the Command: prompt, or use the [Ctrl]+[K] key combination. After selecting the object to which the hyperlink is to be attached, the **Insert Hyperlink** dialog box appears.

There are three groups of settings available in the **Insert Hyperlink** dialog box, each related to one of the three options in the **Link to:** list. See Figure G-2.

Figure G-2.
Define hyperlinks using the **Insert Hyperlink** dialog box. Each button in the **Link to:** list provides a different set of options. Here, the **Existing File or Web Page** options are displayed.

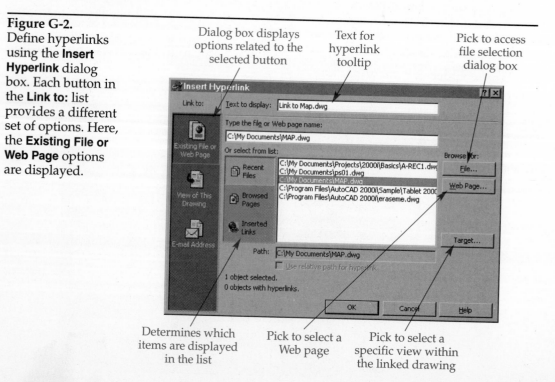

Dialog box displays options related to the selected button

Text for hyperlink tooltip

Pick to access file selection dialog box

Determines which items are displayed in the list

Pick to select a Web page

Pick to select a specific view within the linked drawing

To create a link to an existing file or Web page, select the **Existing File or Web Page** button. When this button is selected, the settings shown in Figure G-2 are available. Use one of the following methods to select the linked file or Web page:

- Use the **Recent Files, Browsed Pages**, and **Inserted Links** buttons to display the desired content in the list, and then pick the file from the list.
- Enter the file path and name in the **Type the file or Web page name:** text box.
- Pick the **File...** button to select the file using a standard file selection dialog box.
- Pick the **Web Page...** button to select a Web page using the **Browse the Web** dialog box.

If you create a link to a drawing, you can specify a named view or tab to be displayed when the link is picked. Pick the **Target...** button to access the **Select Place in Document** dialog box. This dialog box lists the named views, model tab, and layout tabs contained in the linked drawing. Pick the view or tab you want initially displayed and then pick the **OK** button.

By default, the file path and name are displayed in a tooltip when the cursor is held over the hyperlink for a moment. However, you can specify the text that appears in the tooltip in the **Text to display:** text box.

In addition to linking to other drawing files or Web pages, you can also create a hyperlink to another view within the same drawing. Pick the **View of This Drawing** button in the **Insert Hyperlink** dialog box and the **Select a view of this** list is displayed. See Figure G-3. The list includes named views and layout tabs. Pick the item to be accessed by the link and then pick the **OK** button.

You can also create hyperlinks that access e-mail addresses. To do so, pick the **E-mail Address** button in the **Link to:** list of the **Insert Hyperlink** dialog box. The options shown in Figure G-4 are displayed. Type the e-mail address in the **E-mail address:** text box or select an e-mail address from the **Recently used e-mail addresses:** list. When the hyperlink is selected, the default e-mail program opens with a message addressed to the linked e-mail address.

Figure G-3.
To create a link to another view within the current drawing, pick the **View of This Drawing** button in the **Insert Hyperlink** dialog box. Pick the view or tab from the list.

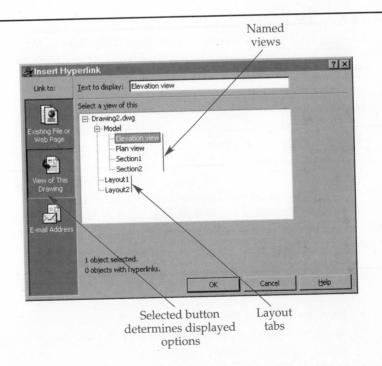

Named views

Selected button determines displayed options

Layout tabs

Figure G-4.
Pick the **E-mail Address** button in the **Insert Hyperlink** dialog box to automatically access the default e-mail program and specify an e-mail address.

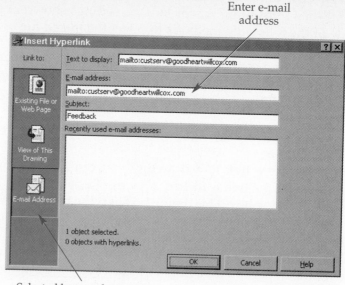

Enter e-mail address

Selected button determines displayed options

PUBLISHTOWEB

File
→ Publish to Web...
Tools
→ Wizards
→ Publish to Web...

Standard toolbar

Publish to Web

Publishing to the Web

The **Publish to Web** wizard automatically creates a formatted HTML file using standard templates and DWF or JPEG versions of a drawing. To access the **Publish to Web** wizard, pick the **Publish to Web** button in the **Standard** toolbar, select **Publish to Web...** from the **File** pull-down menu, select **Publish to Web...** from the **Wizards** cascading menu in the **Tools** pull-down menu, or type PUBLISHTOWEB at the Command: prompt.

Creating a Web page

The **Begin** page is displayed when you access the **Publish to Web** wizard. See Figure G-5. On this page, you have the option of creating a new Web page or editing an existing Web page. Pick the **Create New Web Page** radio button to access the **Create Web Page** page. Editing an existing Web page is discussed in the next section.

Figure G-6 shows the **Create Web Page** page. Three items are defined on this page:
- **Web page name.** The Web page name appears at the top of the Web page.
- **Web page folder location.** Select the folder in which the Web page folder is to be located.
- **Web page description.** The text entered in this box appears on the Web page below the title.

After specifying the Web page title, description, and location, pick the **Next** button to access the **Select Template** page. See Figure G-7.

The **Select Template** page includes a list of three Web page templates. When you pick one of the templates, a preview image and template description are displayed. The following templates, which are illustrated in Figure G-8, are available:
- **Name and DWF image.** This Web page provides a list of drawings. Only the selected drawing is displayed, and only a single display size is available. This template uses DWF format for the images.
- **Medium JPEG & Thumbnails.** This template creates a Web page displaying thumbnails of the drawings. Pick on a thumbnail to display a medium-sized image of the drawing.
- **Large JPEG & Thumbnails.** This option is nearly identical to the **Medium JPEG & Thumbnails** option. However, this template provides a larger image when a thumbnail is picked.

AutoCAD and its Applications—Advanced

Figure G-5.
The **Begin** page of the **Publish to Web** wizard gives you the option of creating a new Web page or editing an existing Web page.

These pages are not available when creating a Web page

Pick to create a Web page

Pick to edit a Web page

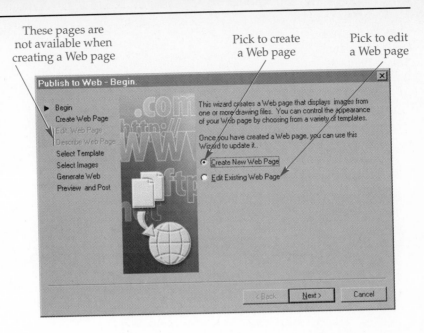

Figure G-6.
Specify the Web page title, description, and folder location in the **Create New Web Page** page. The example illustrated in this and following figures creates a Web page displaying some of the sample drawings supplied with AutoCAD 2000i.

Enter a Web page title

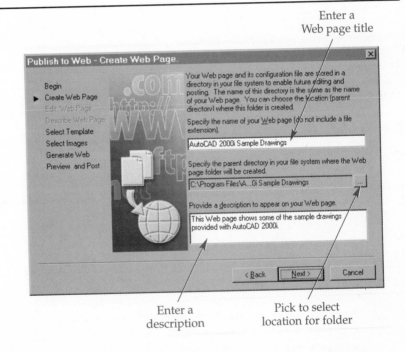

Enter a description

Pick to select location for folder

| **NOTE** | The Web page templates allow you to choose between DWF and JPEG images. JPEG images do not display as well as DWF images, but they are normally smaller files and do not require a DWF plug-in viewer. |

After picking the Web page template, pick the **Next** button to access the **Select Images** page. See Figure G-9. Use the **Drawing** and **Layout** text boxes to select a drawing and view to be displayed on the Web page. Enter a title to appear under the image in the **Label** text box and enter a description in the **Description** text box. Pick the **Add** button to add the selected drawing to the **Image list**. If you wish to delete an image from the Web page, highlight the label in the **Image list** and pick the **Remove** button. The **Move Up** and **Move Down** buttons are used to change the position of the

Figure G-7.
Choose the Web page template in the **Select Template** page.

List of available templates

Preview of template

Template description

Figure G-8.
Select the Web page template most appropriate for your Web page.

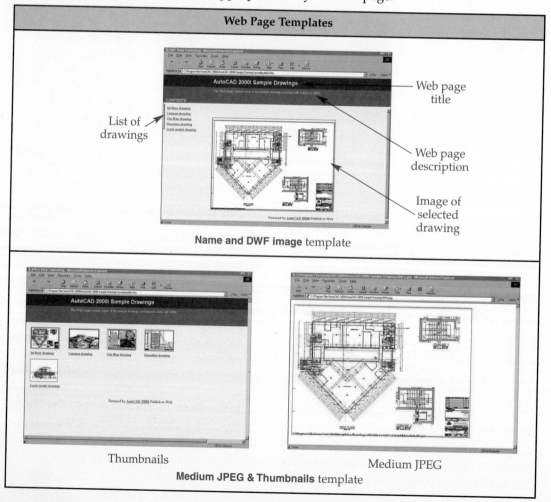

Web Page Templates

Web page title

List of drawings

Web page description

Image of selected drawing

Name and DWF image template

Thumbnails

Medium JPEG

Medium JPEG & Thumbnails template

AutoCAD and its Applications—Advanced

Figure G-8 *(continued).*

Web Page Templates *(continued)*

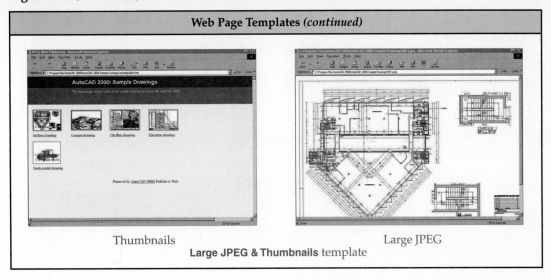

Thumbnails   Large JPEG

Large JPEG & Thumbnails template

Figure G-9.
The **Select Images** page provides options for choosing the specific drawings and views to be displayed in the Web page.

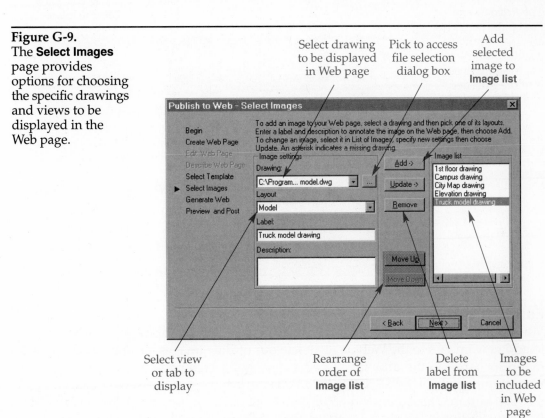

labels in the **Image list**. The **Update** button recreates the image based on the current drawing file.

Once the images are selected, pick the **Next** button to access the **Generate Web Page** page. See Figure G-10. When creating a new Web page, all images are generated, regardless of which radio button option is selected. These options are only effective when editing a Web page.

After AutoCAD has generated the Web page, the **Preview and Post** page appears. See Figure G-11. Pick the **Preview** button to view the Web page. Pick the **Post Now...** button to access the **Posting Web** dialog box, in which the Web page can be posted.

Figure G-10.
AutoCAD creates the Web page when you pick the **Next** button in the **Generate Web Page** page.

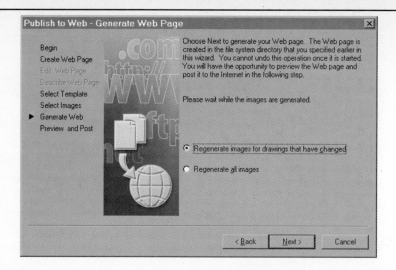

Figure G-11.
The **Preview and Post** page provides an opportunity to preview the Web page before posting it to the Internet.

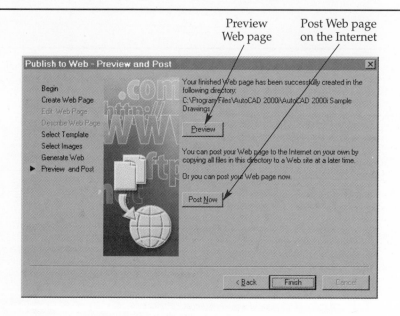

Preview Web page

Post Web page on the Internet

Editing a Web page

There are many instances in which a Web page requires updating. You may want to add new images to the Web page, delete out-of-date images, or update an image to reflect a change in the drawing. To edit an existing Web page, access the **Publish to Web** wizard, pick the **Edit Existing Web Page** radio button in the **Begin** page, and pick the **Next** button. This accesses the **Edit Web Page** page, shown in Figure G-12. Pick the **Browse...** button to access a standard file selection dialog box. Select the **Preview...** button to view the selected Web page.

When editing a Web page, the pages displayed by the **Publish to Web** wizard are nearly identical to those displayed while creating a Web page. The following are items specific to editing Web pages:

- **Describe Web Page.** This page provides an opportunity to modify the Web page title and description.
- **Select Template.** Use this page if you wish to change the Web page template.
- **Select Images.** This page allows you to add new images, delete existing images, or update existing images.
- **Generate Web.** Select the **Regenerate images for drawings that have changed** radio buttons to prevent unchanged images from being regenerated. This saves time when creating the Web page.

Figure G-12.
Pick the Web page to be edited from the list in the **Edit Web Page** page.

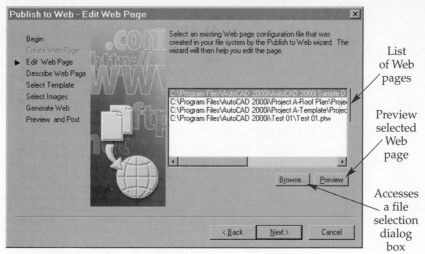

PROFESSIONAL TIP

The images contained in a Web page are not automatically updated when the drawing from which the image was created is changed. Be sure to update Web pages often to make sure the images are current.

EXERCISE G-1

❏ Select six drawings to be included in a Web page. You can use completed drawing problems or sample drawings provided with AutoCAD.
❏ Create a Web page containing the six drawings. Name the Web page Named DWF, and use the **Name and DWF image** template.
❏ Create a second Web page named Medium JPEG. Use the same six drawings (and the same views and layouts), but select the **Medium JPEG & Thumbnails** template.
❏ Create a third Web page named Large JPEG using the identical drawings and views. Select the **Large JPEG & Thumbnails** template.
❏ Access Windows Explorer and compare the amount of memory used by the folders containing the three Web pages.

Preparing E-Mail Transmittals

There are many instances when drawing files are transmitted using e-mail. However, the recipient of the drawing may not have the font files, plot style table files, and xref files associated with the transmitted drawing. When this occurs, at best the drawing features will be displayed differently on the recipient's computer. At worst, critical components can be absent from the drawing.

The **eTransmit** feature simplifies the process of sending a drawing file by e-mail by creating a transmittal file. The transmittal file contains the DWG file and all font files, plot style table files, and xrefs associated with the drawing.

To use the **eTransmit** feature, pick the **eTransmit** button from the **Standard** toolbar, select **eTransmit** from the **File** pull-down menu, or type ETRANSMIT at the Command: prompt. This accesses the **Create Transmittal** dialog box, which is shown in Figure G-13.

ETRANSMIT

File
➥ Transmit...

Standard toolbar

eTransmit

Figure G-13.
The **General** tab of the **Create Transmittal** dialog box provides options for transmittal features and format.

Select type of transmittal

Location of transmittal

Add notes to be included in the transmittal report

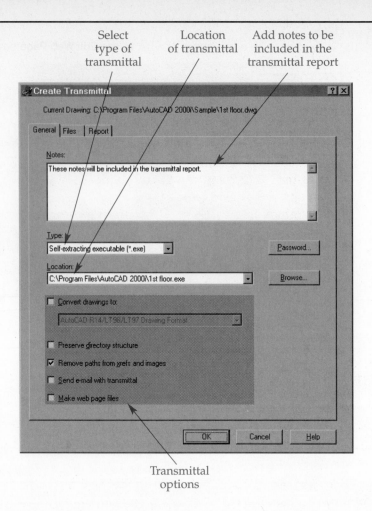

Transmittal options

Use the **General** tab of the **Create Transmittal** dialog box to specify the settings for the transmittal file. The following options are available:

- **Notes: text box.** Text entered in this text box is included in the transmittal report, which is a text file included in the transmittal.
- **Type: drop-down list.** The transmittal can be created in one of three formats. The files can be compressed into a self-extracting zip (EXE) file. The recipient can then simply double-click on the file and the individual files are automatically extracted. Another option is compressing the files into a single zip (ZIP) file. With this option, the user must have a utility program designed to work with ZIP files. The third option is to create a folder containing all files to be transmitted.
- **Location: drop-down list.** Pick the **Browse...** button to select a location for the transmittal to be placed.

PROFESSIONAL TIP

When transmitting files through e-mail, the smaller the size of the files being transferred, the quicker they are sent and received. Therefore, it is generally best to minimize the size of the files being transferred. If the recipient has a ZIP utility, sending a ZIP file is the best option because a ZIP file is smaller than a corresponding self-extracting zip file. The folder option results in the slowest transmittal.

AutoCAD and its Applications—Advanced

- **Convert drawings to.** Pick this check box if you want to convert the drawing files to an older version of AutoCAD. This option is useful when the recipient is using an older version of AutoCAD. Select the version from the drop-down list.
- **Preserve directory structure.** This option maintains the folder locations of the transmitted files. That is, every folder containing a transmitted file, plus every folder containing a folder containing a transmitted file is included in the transmittal.
- **Remove paths from xrefs and images.** Pick this option to remove the paths of these associated files. This allows the recipient to relocate the xrefs and image files.
- **Send e-mail with transmittal.** Automatically starts the default e-mail program when a transmittal is created.
- **Make Web page files.** Select this option to produce a Web page with a link to the transmittal.

The **Files** tab of the **Create Transmittal** dialog box displays the files to be included in the transmittal. See Figure G-14. These are four categories of associated files that can be included in the transmittal:

- Font maps
- Shape files
- Plot style table files
- Xrefs

The **Include fonts** check box determines if font map files and shape files are included in the transmittal. If the drawings being transmitted use standard AutoCAD fonts, it is likely that the recipient already has these files, so there is no need to send them.

Pick the **Add File...** button to access the **Add file to transmittal** dialog box. Select any other files to be included in the transmittal.

Figure G-14.
The **Files** tab of the **Create Transmittal** dialog box shows the files to be transmitted.

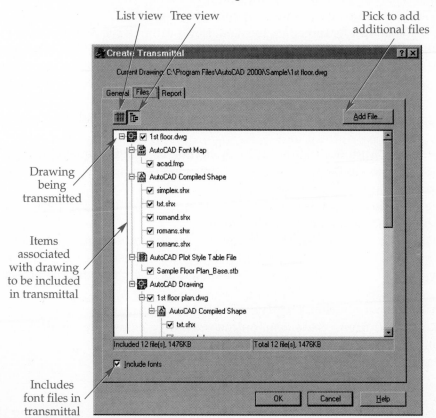

A transmittal report is included in the transmittal. The report records the time and date when the transmittal is created, lists the files included in the transmittal, and includes some general notes regarding the file types included in the transmittal. The report is saved as a TXT file with the same name as the transmittal. The **Report** tab in the **Create Transmittal** dialog box displays the text to be included in the transmittal report.

EXERCISE G-2

❑ Open the City map.dwg drawing provided in the AutoCAD 2000i\Sample folder.
❑ Use **eTransmit** to create a ZIP file containing the drawing and all related files.
❑ Create a second transmittal file using the self-extracting zip file format.
❑ Create a third transmittal using the Folder (set of files) option.
❑ Using Windows Explorer, compare the file size of the ZIP file, the self-extracting zip (EXE) file, and the transmittal folder.

Internet Meetings

AutoCAD 2000i includes the **Meet Now** feature, which works with Microsoft NetMeeting to allow online meetings between users at different locations. Using the **Meet Now** feature, up to eight AutoCAD users can meet online and collaborate on drawing files.

Online meeting participants can share an AutoCAD session. Thus, all participants can view a drawing while changes are being made. In addition, control of the drawing can be transferred between participants, so any participant can edit the drawing. However, only one participant can edit the drawing at a time.

Additional NetMeeting features are also available during the online meeting. A chat window allows participants to share comments instantaneously. A virtual whiteboard allows participants to record information throughout the meeting. Audio and video capabilities can be used with the proper hardware.

To access the **Meet Now** feature, pick the **Meet Now** button in the **Standard** toolbar, select **Meet Now...** from the **Tools** pull-down menu, or type MEETNOW at the Command: prompt. This activates the NetMeeting program and displays the **Online Meeting** toolbar, shown in Figure G-15. The **Online Meeting** toolbar includes the following tools:

MEETNOW

Tools
➥ Meet Now...

Standard
toolbar

Meet Now

- **Participant List drop-down list.** This lists the names of the meeting participants.
- **Call Participant button.** Pick this button to access the **Find Someone** dialog box or the **Call Someone Direct** dialog box, from which you can contact potential participants to invite them to the meeting.
- **Remove Participants button.** Pick this button to disconnect the participant listed in the **Participant List** from the meeting.
- **Allow Others to Edit button.** This button toggles the guest editing privileges, which allow you to give other participants control of the drawing.
- **Display Chat Window button.** Displays the NetMeeting chat window on each participant's screen.
- **Display Whiteboard button.** Displays the NetMeeting whiteboard.
- **End Meeting button.** Ends the online meeting, closes the NetMeeting program, and hides the **Online Meeting** toolbar.
- **Help button.** Accesses the AutoCAD help system.

Figure G-15.
The **Online Meeting** toolbar provides specific tools for using AutoCAD during an online meeting.

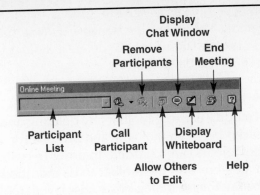

Display
Chat Window

Remove
Participants

End
Meeting

Participant
List

Call
Participant

Display
Whiteboard

Allow Others
to Edit

Help

NOTE

In order to use the **Meet Now** feature efficiently, you must be familiar with online meetings and Microsoft NetMeeting software. Complete coverage of these topics is beyond the scope of this text, which simply provides a general introduction to the capabilities of the **Meet Now** feature.

CUSTOMIZING TOOLBARS

The tools provided for customizing toolbars, creating custom toolbar buttons, and specifying customized keyboard shortcuts have been slightly modified for AutoCAD 2000i. The **Toolbars** dialog box from AutoCAD 2000 has been incorporated into the **Toolbars** tab of the **Customize** dialog box for AutoCAD 2000i. See Figure G-16.

The names of the toolbars contained in the menu selected in the **Menu Group** list are displayed in **Toolbars** list. A check in the box next to the toolbar name indicates that the toolbar is currently displayed. Pick the check box or the toolbar name to toggle the toolbar's visibility.

Figure G-16.
The **Toolbars** tab of the **Customize** dialog box is used to control toolbar display, create new toolbars, and rename and delete existing toolbars.

Toolbar
display
options

Delete
selected
toolbar

Rename an
existing
toolbar

Create a
new toolbar

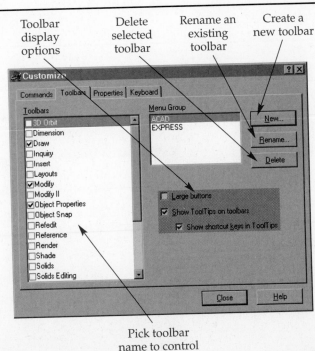

Pick toolbar
name to control
visibility

To rename a toolbar, select the toolbar in the **Toolbars** list and then pick the **Rename...** button. This opens the **Rename Toolbar** dialog box. Type a new name in the text box and pick the **OK** button. To delete a toolbar, select the toolbar in the **Toolbars** list and then pick the **Delete** button.

Customizing Existing Toolbars

You can modify existing toolbars by deleting and adding buttons. Buttons can be copied or moved between toolbars, and buttons for commands that are not available in the default toolbars can be added. In order to customize existing toolbars, both the **Customize** dialog box and the toolbar to be modified must be displayed.

While the **Customize** dialog box is displayed, toolbar buttons can be deleted from toolbars and added to toolbars. To delete a button from a toolbar, simply pick the toolbar button, hold down the left mouse button, and then drag the cursor into the drawing area (away from the toolbar). Release the pick button, and a warning box asks if you want to delete the button. Pick the **OK** button to delete the button.

When adding buttons to a toolbar, you can select the button to be added from an existing toolbar or from the **Commands** tab of the **Customize** dialog box. See Figure G-17. The **Commands** tab includes buttons for many commands that are not included in one of the default toolbars.

To select a button from the **Commands** tab, first select the category in which the button is classified, and then locate the command and button in the **Commands:** list. Pick on the button image or command name, hold the left mouse button, and drag the cursor to the toolbar to which the button is being added. Position the cursor in the location where you want the new button inserted, and a cursor icon appears in the toolbar. When the cursor icon is located where you want the button, release the left mouse button and the toolbar button is added.

You can move and copy toolbar buttons between existing toolbars using a similar process. To move a button, pick on the button, hold the left mouse button, and drag the cursor to the other toolbar. Position the cursor and release the left mouse button, and the button is moved. Use this same process to copy a button between toolbars, but hold the [Ctrl] key when you release the left mouse button to place the button in the new toolbar. Keep in mind that the **Customize** dialog box must be displayed in order to transfer buttons between existing toolbars.

Figure G-17.
Select toolbar buttons from the **Commands** tab of the **Customize** dialog box

Select general category

Commands within the selected category

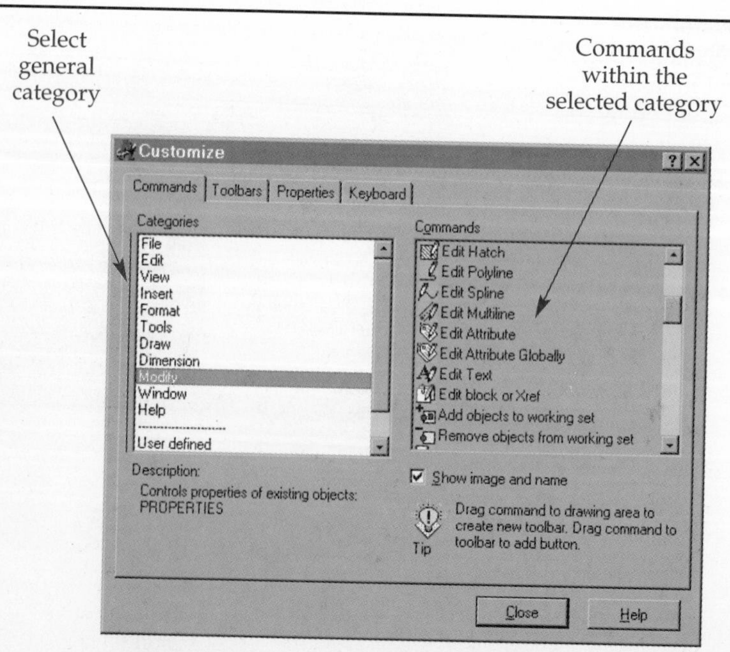

Creating New Toolbars

AutoCAD has many predefined toolbars. However, you can create additional toolbars containing buttons related to specific projects or tasks. To create a new toolbar, pick the **New...** button in the **Toolbars** tab of the **Customize** dialog box. This accesses the **New Toolbar** dialog box. Enter a name for the toolbar and select the menu group in which the toolbar is to be saved. Pick the **OK** button and the new toolbar appears. Add buttons to the new toolbar using the methods discussed in the previous section.

Creating New Buttons

The procedure for creating new buttons in AutoCAD 2000 is discussed beginning on page 487. The procedure is identical in AutoCAD 2000i, with the following minor exceptions:

- The new custom button and new custom flyout are located in the User Defined category of the **Commands** tab in the **Customize** dialog box. See Figure G-18.
- You must right-click on a custom button and then pick **Properties...** from the shortcut menu to define a new button.
- The **Button Properties** dialog box of AutoCAD 2000 is replaced with the **Button Properties** tab of the **Customize** dialog box in AutoCAD 2000i. See Figure G-19. However, the features within the tab remain unchanged.

NOTE You can view the properties of a existing button by picking the button while the **Customize** dialog box is displayed.

Figure G-18.
Custom buttons are located in the User Defined category of the **Commands** tab in the **Customize** dialog box.

Drag to toolbar to create custom buttons

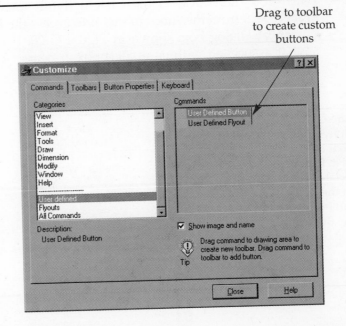

Figure G-19.
The **Button Properties** tab of the **Customize** dialog box contains settings for the button name, image, and macro.

Enter button name

Enter a help string

Preview of button image

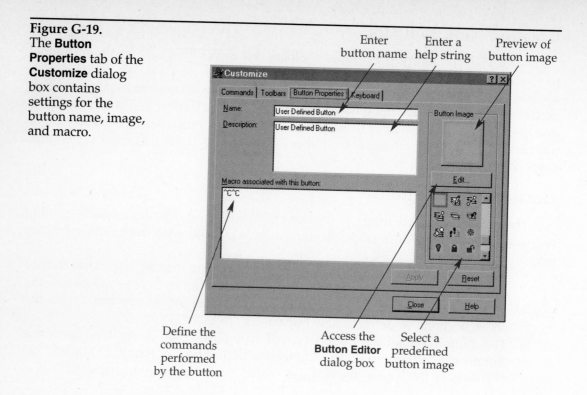

Define the commands performed by the button

Access the **Button Editor** dialog box

Select a predefined button image

Creating Flyouts

The procedure for creating a custom flyout in AutoCAD 2000 is explained beginning on page 492. The procedure is identical in AutoCAD 2000i, except for the following:

- The new flyout button is copied from the User Defined category in the **Commands** tab of the **Customize** dialog box.
- When you right-click on the custom flyout to display its properties, pick **Properties...** from the shortcut menu to access the **Flyout Properties** tab of the **Customize** dialog box, shown in Figure G-20. If the flyout does not have a toolbar associated with it, an alert box appears. Select the associated toolbar from the list and pick the **Apply** button.

Figure G-20.
Each flyout has a toolbar associated with it. Pick the associated toolbar from the list in the **Flyout Properties** tab of the **Customize** dialog box.

Select toolbar to be associated with flyout

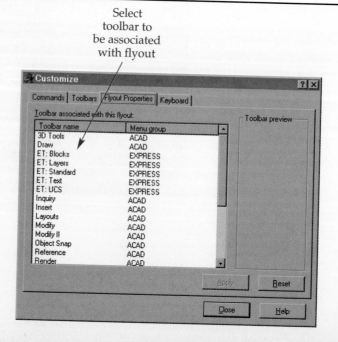

A

T

U